Janus and Minerva

About the Book and Author

In these essays, one of the most eminent political scientists of our time examines international relations from a variety of perspectives connected by timeless and common themes: the conflict between the ever-present risk of violence and the quest for international order, the tensions between the imperatives of power and those of morality, the ties that bind domestic and foreign policy, the ambiguities of the nuclear revolution, the break between prenuclear and post-1945 politics, and the dangers created by the competition between the nuclear superpowers. Assessing the development of the discipline of international relations, the author presents both a summary of the field's significant findings and a critical discussion of its most representative traditions of realism and liberalism. Written between 1960 and 1985, many of these essays have not been previously published in English. They reflect the author's own intellectual evolution and represent a complete picture of his approach to the study of world politics.

Stanley Hoffmann is Douglas Dillon Professor of the Civilization of France at Harvard University and chairman of the Center for European Studies. His numerous publications include *Duties Beyond Borders* and *Primacy or World Order: American Foreign Policy Since the Cold War.*

Janus and Minerva

Essays in the Theory and Practice of International Politics

Stanley Hoffmann

Westview Press / Boulder and London

To the memory of
Raymond Aron (1905–1983)
and Hedley Bull (1933–1985)
and to the future of Michael Smith

All rights reserved. No part of this publication may be reproduced or transmitted in any form or by any means, electronic or mechanical, including photocopy, recording, or any information storage and retrieval system, without permission in writing from the publisher.

Copyright © 1987 by Westview Press, Inc.

Published in 1987 in the United States of America by Westview Press, Inc.; Frederick A. Praeger, Publisher; 5500 Central Avenue, Boulder, Colorado 80301

Library of Congress Cataloging-in-Publication Data
Hoffmann, Stanley.
  Janus and Minerva: essays in the theory and practice of international politics.
  Includes bibliographical references.
  1. World politics—1945-   . 2. International relations. I. Title.
D1058.H54 1987   327.1'01   86-13263
ISBN 0-8133-0390-7 (alk. paper)

Printed and bound in the United States of America

∞ The paper used in this publication meets the requirements of the American National Standard for Permanence of Paper for Printed Library Materials Z39.48-1984.

10   9   8   7   6   5   4   3

Contents

Preface..ix
Acknowledgments..xiii

Part One
Theories and Theorists

1 An American Social Science: International Relations.............3
2 Rousseau on War and Peace....................................25
3 Raymond Aron and the Theory of International Relations........52
4 Hans Morgenthau: The Limits and Influence of "Realism".......70

Part Two
Order and Violence

5 Is There an International Order?.............................85
6 The Future of the International Political System: A Sketch..122
7 International Systems and International Law.................149
8 The Problem of Intervention.................................178
9 Nuclear Worries: France and the United States...............194

Part Three
Actors and Interactions

10 On the Origins of the Cold War.............................207
11 Grasping the Bear: Patterns and Puzzles of Soviet
   International Behavior.....................................224
12 Cries and Whimpers: Thoughts on West European–
   American Relations in the 1980s............................243
13 Domestic Politics and Interdependence......................268

Part Four
Sermons and Suggestions

14 International Organization and the International System....293
15 Taming the Eagle: U.S. Foreign Policy and National Security....316
16 Beyond Terror?...349
17 Reaching for the Most Difficult: Human Rights
   as a Foreign Policy Goal...................................370

18	Liberalism and International Affairs	394
19	On the Political Psychology of Peace and War: A Critique and an Agenda	418

Part Five
Conclusion

20	The Sound and the Fury: The Social Scientist Versus War in History	439

Preface

The essays that make up this book were written during the past twenty-five years. Three were part of *The State of War* (Praeger Publishers, 1965), now out of print. Others have been published between 1970 and 1985. Five were not previously published in English, including two that I have translated from the French. Almost all have been revised for this volume.

In the foreword to *The State of War*, I wrote that

> my basic concern, throughout these essays, is to elaborate a certain kind of theoretical approach to international relations. For the reasons summed up in the first chapter, I want this approach to be closely tied first to history and second to the teachings and insights of political philosophy.
>
> To move from method to substance: the central conception in these essays is one that Hobbes and Rousseau developed and that the whole record of history suggests. International politics is "a state of war"—a competition of units in the kind of state of nature that knows no restraints other than those which the changing necessities of the game and the shallow conveniences of the players impose. Obviously, there are oases of real peace and periods in which the competition is less fierce, but, as I have tried to suggest, the "state of war" is the aspect of international relations that dominates.
>
> The central concept of the "state of war" stresses the fundamental difference between domestic politics and foreign policy. I am aware of the criticisms hurled by scholars against this distinction, which is a distinction of "ideal-types"; but their objections strike me as based on either (a) marginal cases, in which the distinction breaks down—cases whose existence I would not at all deny but which I continue to see as exceptions to the rule; (b) the fact that in a revolutionary era of world politics, the boundary between the two realms is generally violated—which often contributes to making domestic politics like the ideal-type of international relations, but not at all to turning international relations into the ideal-type of domestic politics; or (c) wishful thinking.

Twenty years later, I find that I have been persistent, but not obstinate. The emphasis in these essays is still on the stark realities of a contest whose rules—empirical, legal, or moral—are fragile because they are subjected to the whims of the very states they are supposed to restrain, and whose survival nuclear weapons puts in question. But I have moved in two directions that were not so visible in the book of twenty years ago. Indeed, one was missing altogether. Since the late 1960s, I have focused on those arenas of world politics in which one finds the confrontation and, often, cooperation of domestic policies, rather than on the clash of national security interests or of designs for territorial expansion and diplomatic advantages—the arenas of what some of my colleagues have called "complex interdependence" in the world political economy. In this domain, states are not the only actors; moreover, the relevant "model" for understanding the logic of behavior is neither that of the ideal-type of domestic politics nor that of the state of war. During the past fifteen years, many scholars of international affairs have specialized in the research and theory of this enormous field. I owe much of my interest in it to the incisive intelligence of Miriam Camps and to my friendship with Joseph Nye and Robert Keohane.

The essays of the early 1960s were relentlessly analytic and critical—but not exclusively so. One, which appeared in *The State of War* but is not reproduced here, described contemporary international politics as a roulette game played with a nuclear ball and asked that nations (1) choose cooperation over unilateral action, (2) inject a long-term concern for preserving the game into their policies, and (3) launch a "cumulative movement" toward world order. Many of the more recent essays make these notions more explicit and thus express an increasingly normative bent, which is reflected, here, in the title and chapters of Part Four. This evolution also corresponds to a general shift in scholarship: the revival of prescriptive approaches, ranging from what might be called normative futurology (the production of what, in the late 1950s, I had called relevant utopias) to moral philosophy about world affairs. The shocks inflicted even on "realist" scholars by the Vietnam War and, above all, by the endless dilemmas of our nuclear predicament have been the two principal goads prompting this shift. But the inevitable salience of human rights issues in a world of often horrible political systems, and of distributive justice in a world of inequity, has also pushed students of international affairs in the direction of moral philosophy.

These growing concerns have led me to make some changes in several of the older essays—either actual revisions or, in the case of Chapter 7, an addendum. They have also incited me to stress two points that explain the title. The first point, made obvious by the reference to Janus, concerns the multiple ambiguity of international politics:

1. There is, of course, the customary alternation of war and peace. And, in the nuclear age, there is the still unanswered question as to whether the determination to wage nuclear war if need be, entailed by the institution on which our future rests—namely, deterrence—can and will preserve global peace forever; plus the other (fortunately) still unanswered question as to whether nuclear war, if it breaks out between the superpowers, will be controllable and quickly ended.

2. Then there is the ambiguity of contemporary international politics, which reveals both a very traditional face and a very new one. The traditional predominance of conflict and violence is still visible in much of the diplomatic-strategic behavior of states and in many of the maneuvers, shocks, and breakdowns over economic issues (whether between the so-called North and South, or among industrial nations). But there is also the considerable

limitation both of ends and of means imposed by nuclear prudence, through deterrence and self-deterrence (no nuclear power, after Nagasaki, has used its "absolute" weapons against a non-nuclear state); and there are all the restraints and all the pooled efforts characteristic of "complex interdependence." Hence the paradox of an international system that is both revolutionary and moderate, and the question about its remarkable but not assured stability.

3. There is, indeed, the ambiguity of international security today. Is security sufficiently ensured by the fact that neither superpower can hope to wipe out the nuclear means of retaliation of its rival, and that each one knows—whatever the rival's intentions and plans may be, and whatever technological folly and doctrinal hubris may concoct—that nuclear war could lead to total destruction? Or are things increasingly out of control, as the qualitative arms race becomes ever more sophisticated, the abundance of nuclear weapons entices planners to treat them ever more like ordinary weapons, and the weaknesses of national systems of command and control appear more glaring?

4. There is, as a result, an ambiguity about the future. Will it be the kind of painful but gradual pacification of the human landscape anticipated by Kant—the progressive prevalence of restraints over violence, of cooperation over hostility, of a common humanity over the innumerable divisions of the human race? Or will a "scenario" that is often mentioned here, and that, rightly, fascinates students of contemporary world affairs—that of the summer of 1914—be not just a warning but a tragic model for our future?

There is finally another kind of ambiguity, one that affects the community of students of international relations. Even among the most prudent, the most aware of the obstacles that national prejudices, the emotions of the public, the stodginess of the elites, and the concerns of the decisionmakers everywhere erect against innovation and radical moves beyond "politics as usual," the normative prescriptions seem to go farther than what the interstate traffic can bear (in the case of the more utopian writers, the gap between what is politically customary and what they advocate is an abyss). Yet the perils, the shortsightedness, of the usual are such—and the needs for survival and welfare are so vast—that an atrophy of the normative function would be a disaster. It is certainly too much to hope that this function could operate as a counterpressure on citizens and public figures otherwise absorbed by domestic priorities, national preferences, and daily routines. But that normative function is a vital mission, both because one can never be sure that it remains totally without influence, and because it also plays another important role: that of Cassandra, a combination of conscience and protest. It is what Raymond Aron called the part of wisdom—hence the reference to Minerva.

This book, like *The State of War*, is dedicated to Aron; as I wrote then, his imprint on the ideas expressed here is not difficult to discern—even, I must now add, when I go a bit farther than he was willing to go (for his acute sense of reality always reined in the part of Minerva in him). It is also dedicated to my friend Hedley Bull, whose early death was a tragedy for the field to which he brought so much scholarship, style, humor, and wisdom, and who knew so well how to combine history, political philosophy, and the analysis of "anarchical society." Finally, it is dedicated to Michael Smith, who, first as a student and later as a colleague, has accompanied me for fifteen years in exploring the lanes and dead ends of "realism," in visiting the temple of Janus, and in finding a place for Minerva in the ethical mazes of foreign policy.

Stanley Hoffmann

Acknowledgments

Chapters 1, 12, and 17 first appeared in *Daedalus*: Summer 1977, pp. 41-59; Summer 1984, pp. 19-49; and Fall 1983, pp. 221-252, respectively. Reprinted by permission.

Chapters 2, 7, and 20 first appeared in Stanley Hoffmann, *The State of War: Essays in the Theory and Practice of International Politics* (New York: Praeger Publishers, 1965).

Chapter 3 first appeared in *International Studies Quarterly* 29 (1985), pp. 13-27. Reprinted by permission.

Chapter 4 is adapted from two essays, one published in *Social Research* 48, no. 4, (Winter 1981), pp. 653-659; and the other in *The Atlantic* (November 1985). Reprinted by permission.

Chapter 6 first appeared in Samuel P. Huntington and Joseph S. Nye (eds.), *Global Dilemmas* (Washington, D.C.: Center for International Affairs and University Press of America, 1985), pp. 280-307. Reprinted by permission.

Chapter 8 first appeared in Hedley Bull (ed.), *Intervention in World Politics* (Oxford: Oxford University Press, 1984). Reprinted by permission.

Chapter 10 first appeared in Lynn H. Miller and Ronald W. Pruessen, *Reflections on the Cold War* (Philadelphia: Temple University Press, 1974). Reprinted by permission.

Chapter 13 first appeared in Organization for Economic Cooperation and Development, *From Marshall Plan to Global Interdependence* (Paris: OECD, 1978). Reprinted by permission.

Chapter 14 first appeared in *International Organization* 24, no. 3 (1970), pp. 389-413. Reprinted by permission.

Parts of Chapter 16 first appeared in SIPRI, *Policies for Common Security* (London and Philadelphia: Taylor and Francis, 1985). Reprinted by permission.

Chapter 19, the presidential address delivered at the convention of the International Society of Political Psychology in June 1985, was published in *Political Psychology* 7, no. 1 (March 1986), pp. 1–21. Reprinted by permission.

Chapters 5, 9, 11, 15, and 18 have not previously been published in English:

> Chapter 5 was published in French in Madeleine Grawitz and Jean Leca (eds.), *Traité de science politique*, Vol. 1, Ch. 9 (Paris: Presses Universitaires, 1985), pp. 665–698.

> Chapter 9 was published in French in *Le Débat*, no. 36 (September 1985).

> Chapter 11 was written for a conference on the psychology of U.S.-Soviet relations at the Rockefeller Center in Bellagio (May 1985).

> Chapter 15 was a report to the Field Foundation (1983).

> Chapter 18 was presented as a lecture in the Trilling Seminar series at Columbia University in November 1984.

PART ONE
Theories and Theorists

1

An American Social Science: International Relations

In the past forty years, international relations has developed as a largely autonomous part of political science. Even though it has shared many of political science's vicissitudes—battles among various orientations, theories, and methods—it also has a story of its own. What follows is an attempt at neither a complete balance sheet nor a capsule history—merely a set of reflections on the specific accomplishments and frustrations of a particular field of scholarship.[1]

Only in America

Political science has a much longer history than international relations. The attempt at studying systematically the patterns of conflict and cooperation among mutually alien actors—a shorthand definition of the subject matter—is recent. To be sure, we can all trace our ancestry back to Thucydides, just as political scientists can trace theirs to Aristotle. But Thucydides was a historian. He was, to be sure, a historian of genius, rightly convinced that he was writing for all times because he was using one particular incident to describe a permanent logic of behavior. Yet he was careful to avoid explicit generalizations, "if . . . then" propositions, and analytic categories or classificatory terms. Modern sociology and political science emancipated themselves from political and social history, political philosophy, and public law in the nineteenth century. International relations did not, even though the kind of social (or asocial) action described by Thucydides never disappeared from a fragmented world, and flourished particularly in the period of the European balance of power. One can wonder why this was so. After all, here was a realm in which political philosophy had much less to offer than it did to those who wondered about the common good in the domestic order. Except for the vast body of Roman Catholic literature preoccupied with just war, and not very relevant to a world of sovereign states, there were only the recipes of Machiavelli; the marginal comments on the international state of nature in Hobbes', Locke's, and Rousseau's writings; some pages of Hume; two short and tantalizing essays of Kant; compressed considerations by Hegel; and oversimplified fragments by Marx. Even so, the little political philosophy that was available should have been sufficiently provocative to make students want to look into the realities. For the philosophers disagreed about the nature of the international milieu and the ways of making it more bearable; and they wrote about the difference between a domestic order stable enough to afford a search for the ideal state, and an international contest in which order has to be established first, and which often clashes with any aspiration to justice. Similarly, the contrast between the precepts of law and the realities of politics was sufficiently greater in the international realm than in the domestic realm, to make one want to shift from the normative to the empirical, if only in order to understand better the plight of the normative. Without a study of political relations, how could one understand the fumblings and failures of international law, or the tormented debates on the foundation of obligation among sovereigns unconstrained by common values or superior power? And the chaos of data provided by diplomatic history did not require any less ordering than the masses of facts turned up by the history of states and societies.

Why did a social science of international relations nevertheless fail to appear? The answer to the discrepancy may well be found in that sweeping phenomenon which Tocqueville identified as the distinctive feature of the modern age: democratization. As domestic societies moved from their Old Regimes to their modern conditions—parties and interests competing for the allegiance of large classes of citizens; the social mobilization of previously dispersed subjects; the politics of large agglomerations and unified markets; an increasingly universal suffrage; the rise of parliamentary institutions or plebiscitarian techniques; the fall of fixed barriers, whether geographic or social, within nations—the study of flux began in earnest, if only in order to provide concerned observers and insecure officials with some clues about regularities and predictions of somewhat less mythical, if also less sweeping nature than those grandiosely strewn around by philosophers of history. With democratization, as Comte had predicted, came the age of positivism (his only mistake was to confuse his own brand of metaphysics, or his grand speculations, with positive science). But international politics remained the sport of kings, or the preserve of cabinets—the last refuge of secrecy, the last domain of largely hereditary castes of diplomats.

Raymond Aron has characterized international relations as the specialized activity of diplomats and soldiers. However, soldiers, to paraphrase Clausewitz, have their own grammar but not their own logic. It is not an accident if armies, having been democratized by the ordeals of the French Revolution and Napoleonic era, found their empirical grammarian in Clausewitz, whereas the still restricted club of statesmen and ambassadors playing with the fate of nations found no logician to account for its activities. Indeed, the historians who dealt with these succeeded only in keeping them beyond the pale of the kind of modern science that was beginning to look at societies, by perpetuating the myth of foreign policy's "primacy," isolated from domestic politics. There was, to be sure, one country in which foreign policy was put under domestic checks and balances, knew no career caste, and paid little respect to the rules and rituals of the initiated European happy few: the United States of America. But this country happened to be remarkably uninvolved in the kinds of contests that were the daily fare of other actors. Either it remained aloof, eager merely for continental consolidation and economic growth; or else it expanded, not by conflicts and deals with equals, but by short spurts of solipsistic exuberance at the expense of much weaker neighbors. International relations is the science of the tests and trials of several intertwined actors. Where they were intertwined, no science grew. In the United States before the 1930s, there was no reason for it to grow.

It was only the twentieth century that brought democratization to foreign policy. Diplomatic issues moved from the calculations of the few to the passions of the many, both because more states joined in the game that had been the preserve of a small number of (mainly European) actors and (mainly extra-European) stakes, and above all because within many states parties and interests established links or pushed claims across national borders. And yet, a World War that saw the mobilization and slaughter of millions, marked the demise of the old diplomatic order, and ended as a kind of debate between Wilson and Lenin for the allegiance of mankind, brought forth little "scientific analysis" of international relations. Indeed, the rude intrusion of grand ideology into this realm gave a new lease of life to utopian thinking, and delayed the advent of social science. Not "how it is, and why," but "how things should be improved, reformed, overhauled," was the order of the day. Old Liberal normative dreams were being licensed by the League of Nations covenant, while at the same time the young Soviet Union was calling for the abolition of diplomacy itself.

It is against this reassertion of utopia, and particularly against the kind of "as if" thinking that mistook the savage world of the 1930s for a community, the League for a modern Church, and collective security for a common duty, that E. H. Carr wrote the book which can be treated as the first "scientific" treatment of modern world politics: *Twenty Years Crisis*[2]—the work of a historian intent on deflating the pretenses of Liberalism, and driven thereby to laying the foundations both of a discipline and of a normative approach, "realism," that was to have quite a future. Two paradoxes are worth noting. This historian who was founding a social science, did it in reaction against another historian, whose normative approach Carr deemed illusory—Toynbee, not the philosopher of the *Study of History*, but the idealistic commentator of the *Royal Yearbook of International Affairs*. And Carr, in his eagerness to knock out the illusions of the idealists, not only swallowed some of the "tough" arguments which the revisionist powers such as Mussolini's Italy, Hitler's Germany, and the militaristic Japan had been using against the order of Versailles—arguments aimed at showing that idealism served the interests of the status quo powers—but also "objectively," as *Pravda* would say, served the cause of appeasement. There was a triple lesson here: about the springs of empirical analysis (less a desire to understand for its own sweet sake, than an itch to refute); about the impossibility, even for opponents of a normative orientation, to separate the empirical and the normative in their own work; and about the pitfalls of any normative dogmatism in a realm which is both a field for objective investigation and a battlefield between predatory beasts and their prey.

But it was not in England that Carr's pioneering effort bore fruit. It was in the United States that international relations became a discipline. Both the circumstances and the causes deserve some scrutiny. The circumstances were, obviously, the rise of the United States to world power, a rise accompanied by two contradictory impulses: renewed utopianism, as exemplified by the plans for postwar international organization; and a mix of revulsion against, and guilt about, the peculiar prewar brew of impotent American idealism (as symbolized by the "nonrecognition" doctrine), escapist isolationism (the neutrality laws), and participation in appeasement. Two books brought to America the kind of realism Carr had developed in England. One was Nicholas Spykman's *America's Strategy in World Politics*,[3] which was more a treatise in the geopolitical tradition of Admiral Mahan or Mackinder than a book about the principal characteristics of interstate politics; but it told Americans that foreign policy is about power, not merely or even primarily about ideals, and it taught that the struggle for power was the real name for world politics. The other book was Hans Morgenthau's *Politics Among Nations*.[4] If our discipline has any founding father, it is Morgenthau. He was not a historian by training; he had been a teacher of international law. Like Carr, he was revolting against utopian thinking, past and present. But where Carr had been an ironic and polemical Englishman sparring with other Englishmen about the nature of diplomacy in the thirties—a discussion which assumed that readers knew enough diplomatic history to make pedantic allusions unnecessary—Morgenthau was a refugee from suicidal Europe, with a missionary impulse to teach the new world power all the lessons it had been able to ignore until then but could no longer afford to reject. He was but one participant in the "sea change," one of the many social scientists whom Hitler had driven to the New World, and who brought to a country whose social science suffered from "hyperfactualism" and conformity the leaven of critical perspectives and philosophical concerns.[5] But he was, among his colleagues, the only one whose interests made him the founder of a discipline.

Eager to educate the heathen, not merely to joust with fellow literati, Morgenthau quite deliberately couched his work in the terms of general propositions and grounded them in history. Steeped in a scholarly tradition that stressed the difference between social sciences and natural sciences, he was determined both to erect an empirical science opposed to the utopias of the international lawyers and the political ideologues, and to affirm the unity of empirical research and of philosophical inquiry into the right kind of social order. He wanted to be normative, but to root his norms in the realities of politics, not in the aspirations of politicians or in the constructs of lawyers. The model of interstate relations which Morgenthau proposed, and the precepts of "realism" which he presented as the only valid recipes for foreign policy success as well as for international moderation, were derived from the views of nineteenth-century and early twentieth-century historians of statecraft (such as Treitschke, and also Weber). Hence the paradox of introducing to the America of the cold war, and of making analytically and dogmatically explicit, notions and a "wisdom" about statecraft that had remained largely implicit in the age to which they best applied, and whose validity for the age of nuclear weapons, ideological confrontations, mass politics, and economic interdependence was at least open to question.

Be that as it may, Morgenthau's work played a doubly useful role—one that it may be hard to appreciate fully if one looks at the scene either from the outside (as does Aron), or thirty years later, as does the new generation of American scholars. On the one hand, his very determination to lay down the law made Morgenthau search for the laws, or regularities, of state behavior, the types of policies, the chief configurations of power; by tying his sweeping analyses to two masts, the concept of power and the notion of the national interest, he was boldly positing the existence of a field of scientific endeavor, separate from history or law. On the other hand, the very breadth of his brushstrokes, the ambiguities hidden by his peremptory pronouncements about power, the subjective uncertainties denied by his assertion of an objective national interest, and even more the sleights of hand entailed by his pretense that the best analytic scheme necessarily yields the only sound normative advice—all of this incited readers to react and, by reacting, criticizing, correcting, refuting, to build on Morgenthau's foundations. Those who rejected his blueprint were led to try other designs. He was both a goad and a foil. (Indeed, the more one agreed with his approach, the more one was irritated by his flaws, and eager to differentiate one's own product). A less arrogantly dogmatic scholar, a writer more modest both in his empirical scope and in his normative assertions, would never have had such an impact on scholarship. Less sweeping, he would not have imposed the idea that here was a realm with properties of its own. Less trenchant, he would not have made scholars burn with the itch to bring him down a peg or two. One of the many reasons why Raymond Aron's monumental *Peace and War*[6]—a book far more ambitious in its scope and far more sophisticated in its analyses than *Politics Among Nations*—incited no comparable reaction from scholarly readers may well have been the greater judiciousness and modesty of Aron's normative conclusions. Humane skeptics invite nods and sighs, not sound and fury; and sound and fury are good for creative scholarship. Moreover, Aron's own scholarship was overwhelming enough to be discouraging; Morgenthau's was just shaky enough to inspire improvements.

Still, *Politics Among Nations* would not have played such a seminal role, if the ground in which the seeds were planted had not been so receptive. The development of international relations as a discipline in the United States results from the convergence of three factors: intellectual predispositions, political circumstances, and institutional opportunities. The intellectual predispositions are those which account for the formidable explosion of the social sciences in general in this country, since the end of the Second World War. There is, first, the profound conviction, in a nation which Ralf Dahrendorf has called the Applied Enlightenment,[7] that all problems can be resolved, that the way to resolve them is to apply the scientific method—assumed to be value free, and to combine empirical investigation, hypothesis formation, and testing—and that the resort to science will yield practical applications that will bring progress. What is specifically American is the scope of these beliefs, or the depth of this faith: they encompass the social world as well as the natural world, and they go beyond the concern for problem-solving (after all, there are trial-and-error, piecemeal ways of solving problems): they entail a conviction that there is, in each area, a kind of masterkey—not merely an intellectual, but an operational paradigm. Without this paradigm, there can be muddling through, but no continuous progress; once one has it, the practical recipes will follow. We are in the presence of a fascinating sort of national ideology: it magnifies and expands eighteenth-century postulates. What has ensured their triumph and their growth is the absence of any counterideology, on the Right or the Left, that challenges this faith either radically (as conservative thought did, in Europe) or by subordinating its validity to a change in the social system. Moreover, on the whole, the national experience of economic development, social integration, and external success has kept reinforcing this set of beliefs.

Second, and as a kind of practical consequence, the very prestige and sophistication of the "exact sciences" were bound to benefit the social ones as well. The voices of gloom or skepticism that lament the differences between the natural world and the social world have never been very potent in America. Precisely because the social world is one of conflict, precisely because national history had entailed civil and foreign wars, the quest for certainty, the desire to find a sure way of avoiding fiascoes and traumas, was even more burning in the realm of the social sciences. The very contrast between an ideology of progress through the deliberate application of reason to human concerns—an ideology which fuses faith in instrumental reason and faith in moral reason—and a social reality in which the irrational often prevails both in the realm of values and in the choice of means, breeds a kind of inflation of social science establishments and pretensions. At the end of the war, a new dogma appeared. One of the social sciences, economics, was deemed to have met the expectations of the national ideology, and to have become a science on the model of the exact ones; it was celebrated for its contribution to the solution of the age-old problems of scarcity and inequality. This triumph goaded the other social sciences. Political science, the mother or stepmother of international relations, was particularly spurred. It was here that the temptation to emulate economics was greatest. Like economics, political science deals with a universal yet specialized realm of human activity. Its emphasis is not on the origins and effects of culture, nor on the structures of community or of voluntary association, but on the creative and coercive role of a certain kind of power, and on its interplay with social conflict. This also drew it closer to that other science of scarcity, competition, and power, economics, than to disciplines like anthropology or sociology, which deal with more diffuse phenomena and which are less obsessed by the solution of pressing problems by means of enlightened central action.

Nations in which this grandiose and activist ideology of science is less overwhelming have also known, after the Second World War, a considerable expansion of the social sciences. But the United States often served as model and as lever.[8] And political science abroad has usually been more reflective than reformist, more descriptive than therapeutic; although, here and in sociology, foreign social scientists reacted against the traditional intelligentsia of moralists, philosophers, and aesthetes by stressing that knowledge (not old-fashioned wisdom) *was* power (or at least influence), they were not driven by the dream of knowledge *for* power. Moreover, when (inevitably) disillusionment set in, it took often far more drastic forms—identity crises within the professions, violent indictments outside—than in the United States. An ideology on probation cannot afford a fall. An ideology serenely hegemonial reacts to failure in the manner of the work horse in Orwell's *Animal Farm*, or of Avis: "I will try harder."

A third predisposition was provided by a transplanted element: the scholars who had immigrated from abroad. They played a huge role in the development of American science in general. This role was particularly important in the social sciences. Here, they provided not merely an additional injection of talent, but talent of a different sort. No social science is more interesting than the questions it asks, and these were scholars whose philosophical training and personal experience moved them to ask far bigger questions than those much of American social science had asked so far, questions about ends, not just about means; about choices, not just about techniques; about social wholes, not just about small towns or units of government. So they often served as conceptualizers, and blended their analytic skills with the research talents of the "natives." Moreover, they brought with them a sense of history, an awareness of the diversity of social experiences, that could only stir comparative research and make something more universal of the frequently parochial American social science. In the field of international relations, in addition to Morgenthau, there was a galaxy of foreign-born scholars, all concerned with transcending empiricism: the wise and learned Arnold Wolfers, Klaus Knorr, Karl Deutsch, Ernst Haas, George Liska, and the young Kissinger and Brzezinski, to name only a few. They (and quite especially those among them who had crossed the Atlantic in their childhood or adolescence) wanted to find out the meaning and the causes of the catastrophe that had uprooted them, and perhaps the keys to a better world.

The last two names bring us to politics. And politics mattered. Hans Morgenthau has often written as if truth and power were bound to be enemies (Hannah Arendt has been even more categorical). And yet he shaped his truths so as to guide those in power. The growth of the discipline cannot be separated from the American role in world affairs after 1945. First, by definition (or tautology), political scientists are fascinated with power—either because they want it, at least vicariously, or because they fear it and want to understand the monster, as Judith Shklar has suggested with her usual devastating lucidity.[9] And in the postwar years, what part of power was more interesting than the imperial bit? America the sudden leader of a coalition, the sole economic superpower, the nuclear monopolist, later the nuclear superior, was far more interesting to many students than local politics, or the politics of Congress, or the politics of group pluralism. Almost inevitably, a concern for America's conduct in the world blended with a study of international relations, for the whole world seemed to be the stake of the American-Soviet confrontation. Here was a domain which was both a virgin field for study and the arena of a titanic contest. To study United States foreign policy was to study the international system. To study the international system could not fail to bring one back to the role of the United States. Moreover, the temptation to give advice, to offer courses of action, or to criticize the official ones was made even more irresistible by the spotty character and the *gaffes* of past American behavior in world affairs, by the thinness of the veneer of professionalism in American diplomacy, by the eagerness of officialdom for guidance—America was the one-eyed leading the cripples. Thus, two drives merged, for the benefit of the discipline and to its detriment also, in some ways: the desire to concentrate on what is the most relevant, and the tendency (implicit or explicit) to want to be useful, not only as a scientist, but as an expert citizen whose science can help promote intelligently the embattled values of his country (a motive that was not negligible, among newcomers to America especially). For it was all too easy to assume that the values that underlie scientific research—the respect for truth, freedom of investigation, of discussion, and of publication—were also those for which Washington stood in world affairs.

Second, as I have just said, what the scholars offered, the policy-makers wanted. Indeed, there is a remarkable chronological convergence between their needs and the scholars' performances. Let us oversimplify greatly. What the leaders looked for, once the cold war started, was some intellectual compass which would serve multiple functions: exorcise isolationism, and justify a permanent and global involvement in world affairs; rationalize the accumulation of power, the techniques of intervention, and the methods of containment apparently required by the cold war; explain to a public of idealists why international politics does not leave much leeway for pure good will, and indeed besmirches purity; appease the frustrations of the bellicose by showing why unlimited force or extremism on behalf of liberty was no virtue; and reassure a nation eager for ultimate accommodation, about the possibility of both avoiding war and achieving its ideals. "Realism," however critical of specific policies, however (and thus self-contradictorily) diverse in its recommendations, precisely provided what was necessary. Indeed, there was always a sufficient margin of disagreement between its suggestions and actual policies, and also between its many champions, to prevent it from being nothing but a rationalization of cold war policies. And yet the first wave of writings—those of Morgenthau, Wolfers, ur-Kissinger, Kennan, Osgood, Walt Rostow, or McGeorge Bundy—gave both the new intellectual enterprise and the new diplomacy the general foundations they needed. The second wave—roughly, from 1957 to the mid-1960s—turned strategy in the nuclear age into a dominant field within the discipline. This coincided with the preoccupation of officialdom to replace the reassuring but implausible simplicities of massive retaliation with a doctrine that would be more sophisticated; but it also reflected the conviction that force, in a mixture of nuclear deterrence and conventional (or subconventional) limited uses, remained both the most important aspect of power and a major American asset. Here again, in the literature, the attempt at finding principles for any "strategy of conflict" in a nuclear world is inseparable from the tendency to devise a strategy for America, at a time when both sides had weapons of mass destruction, and when there were serious problems of alliance management, guerrilla wars, or "wars of national liberation." A third wave is quite recent: I refer to the growing literature on the politics of international economic relations. It coincides with what could be called the post-Viet Nam aversion for force, and with the surge of economic issues to the top of the diplomatic agenda, caused by a combination of factors: the degradation of the Bretton Woods system, the increasing importance of economic growth and social welfare in the domestic politics of advanced societies, the resurgence of aggressive or protectionist impulses in order to limit the bad effects or to maximize the gains from interdependence, the revolt of the Third World. Once more, the priorities of research and those of policy-making blend.

The political preeminence of the United States is the factor I would stress most in explaining why the discipline has fared so badly, by comparison, in the rest of the world (I leave aside countries like the Soviet Union and China, in which it would be hard to speak of free social science scholarship!). Insofar as it deals primarily with the contemporary world, it seems to require the convergence of a scholarly community capable of looking, so to speak, at global phenomena (i.e., of going beyond the study of the nation's foreign policy, or of the interstate politics of an area) and of a political establishment concerned with world affairs; each one then strengthens the other. When the political elites are obsessed only with what is happening to their country, because it lacks the power to shape what is happening elsewhere, or because this lack of power has bred habits of dependence on another state (such as the United States), or because (as in the case of Japan and West Germany) there are severe constraints on the global use of the nation's power, the chances are that the scholars will not have the motivation or receive the impulse necessary to turn individual efforts into a genuine scientific enterprise, and will either turn to other fields with more solid traditions and outlets (such as, say, electoral behavior in France and Britain) or merely reflect, more or less slavishly, and with some delays, American fashions; or else there will be often brilliant individual contributions, but unconnected and unsupported: a Hedley Bull in Australia and England, a Pierre Hassner in

France, to name just these two, do not make a discipline. Even in England and France, which have become nuclear powers, strategic studies have been to a very large extent the preserve of a few intellectual military men, concerned either with reconciling national policy with the predominant doctrines of deterrence, or with challenging these. But the predominant doctrines have remained American, as if even in the more abstract efforts at theorizing about a weapon that has transformed world politics, it mattered if one was the citizen or host of a country with a worldwide writ. Scholars do not like to think about their intellectual dependence on the status of their country, and on the ambitions of its political elite; it disturbs their sense of belonging to a cosmopolitan, free-floating community of science. Even the sociology of knowledge, which has often looked at the debts of scholars to their countries, has been singularly coy about this particular kind of bond. And yet, the link exists. And it is sometimes reinforced by institutional arrangements.

In the case of the United States, there have been three institutional factors that have acted as multipliers of political connection—factors which have not existed, and certainly not simultaneously, elsewhere. One is the most direct and visible tie between the scholarly world and the world of power: the "in-and-outer" system of government, which puts academics and researchers not merely in the corridors but also in the kitchens of power. Actually, it may be wise to distinguish two phases. In the late forties and fifties, those kitchens remained the preserves of the old establishment: a mix of career civil servants, businessmen, and lawyers. They had to cope with the whole world, with a persistent enemy, with the travails of economic reconstruction and the turmoil of nuclear deterrence. They needed both data and ideas, and they turned to the universities. This was the age of the academic as consultant (officially or not), and this was the period in which much research got funded by those departments that had the biggest resources (Defense more than State). The year 1960 was a turning point. Academics became proconsuls and joined the old boys; often they tried to prove that they could cook spicier dishes and stir pots more vigorously than their colleagues. If one had some doubts about "policy scientists," these could only be doubled by the spectacle of scientific policy-makers. Be that as it may, the Washington connection turned an intellectual interchange into a professional one. In countries with a tight separation between the career of bureaucracy or politics and the academic *métier*, such exchanges are limited to occasional formal occasions—seminars or colloquia— and frequent *diners en ville*; but the former tend to be sterile, and the latter hover between witty debates on current affairs, and small talk.

A second institutional factor of great importance is the role of what I have elsewhere called the relays between the kitchens of power and the academic salons. The most important of these dumbwaiters is the network of foundations that fed international relations research after the war, and whose role is essential if one wants to understand exactly why the three waves of scholarship coincided so aptly with the consecutive concerns of the statesmen. A combination of intellectual encouragement to "frontiers of knowledge" and civic desire to be of service, the sociological peculiarities of boards of directors composed, to a large extent, of former academics and former officials, the happy accident of vast financial resources that kept growing until the end of the sixties, all this made of the foundations a golden half-way house between Washington and academia. Wasps served in the CIA—pardon, the institution—as well as State; ex-State officials served in the foundations; and even those professors who had some reservations about serving in the government, had no objection to applying to the foundations. It was a seamless pluralism. These precious relays exist virtually nowhere else.

The third institutional opportunity was provided by the universities themselves. They had two immense virtues. They were flexible; because of their own variety, which ensured both competition and specialization, and also because of the almost complete absence of the straitjackets of public regulations, quasi-feudal traditions, financial dependence, and intellectual routine which have so often paralyzed the universities of postwar Europe. The latter got caught in the contradiction between their own past—a combination of vocational training and general education for the elites—and the sudden demands of mass higher education; they could vacillate from confusion to collapse, but the one thing they could rarely do was to innovate. The other virtue of American universities resulted in part from the fact that mass higher education was already a *fait accompli*: they had large departments of political science, which could serve as the matrices of the discipline of International Relations. In France until the late sixties, in Britain until the spread of the new universities, international relations remained the handmaid of law, or the laughingstock of historians; and when political science departments began to mushroom, the other reasons for the development of the discipline in America were still missing. Only in America could a creative sociologist write about the university as the most characteristic institution of the postindustrial age, the laboratory of its discoveries.[10] In other countries, universities are rarely the arenas of research; and when they are, the research funded by public institutions concentrates on issues of public policy which are rarely international—partly for the political reason I have mentioned above, partly because the existence of a career foreign service with its own training programs perpetuates the tendency to look at international relations as if it were still traditional diplomacy. Civil servants obliged to deal with radically new tasks such as urbanization, the management of banks and industries, or housing sometimes think they can learn from the social sciences. Civil servants who deal with so "traditional" a task as national security and diplomacy do not always realize that the same old labels are stuck on bottles whose shapes as well as their content are new. And when diplomats discover that they too have to cope with the new, technical issues of technology, science, and economics, it is to "domestic" specialists of these subjects that they turn—if they turn at all.

Even in America

If one looks at the field thirty years after the beginning of the "realist" revolution, can one point to any great breakthroughs? The remarks which follow are, of course, thoroughly subjective, and undoubtedly jaundiced. I am more struck by the dead ends than by the breakthroughs; by the particular, often brilliant, occasionally elegant, but generally nonadditive contributions to specific parts of the field, than by its overall development; by the contradictions that have rent its community of scholars, than by its harmony. The specific contributions have been well analyzed in a recent volume of the *Handbook of Political Science*,[11] and I shall not repeat what is said there. If I had to single out three significant "advances," I would list the concept of the international system, an attempt to do for international relations what the concept of a political regime does for "domestic" political science: it is a way of ordering data, a construct for describing both the way in which the parts relate, and the way in which patterns of interaction change. It emerged from the first period I have described above, and continues to be of importance. Next, I would mention the way in which the literature on deterrence has analyzed and codified "rules of the game" which have been accepted as such by American statesmen, and which have served as the intellectual foundation of the search for tacit as well as explicit interstate restraints: MAD ("Mutual Assured Destruction") and arms control are the two controversial but influential offsprings of the doomsday science. Third, there is the current attempt to study the political roots, the originality, and the effects of economic interdependence, particularly in order to establish whether it shatters the "realist" paradigm, which sees international relations as marked by the predominance of conflict among state actors. And yet, if I were asked to assign three books from the discipline to a recluse on a desert island, I would have to confess a double embarrassment: for I would select one that is more than two thousand years old—Thucydides' *Peloponnesian War*, and as for the two contemporary ones, Kenneth Waltz' *Man, the State and War*[12] is a work in the tradition of political philosophy, and Aron's *Peace and War* is a work in the grand tradition of historical sociology, which dismisses many of the scientific pretenses of the postwar American scholars, and emanates from the genius of a French disciple of Montesquieu, Clausewitz, and Weber. All three works avoid jargon; the two contemporary ones carry their erudition lightly: the sweat of toil is missing. How more unscientific can you get?

Let us return to the ideology I alluded to earlier. There was the hope of turning a field of inquiry into a science, and the hope that this science would be useful. Both quests have turned out to be frustrating. The desire to proceed scientifically, which has been manifest in all the social sciences, has run into three particular snags here. First, there was (and there remains) the problem of theory. I have discussed elsewhere at some length the difficulties scholars have encountered when they tried to formulate laws accounting for the behavior of states, and theories that would explain those laws and allow for prediction. A more recent analysis, by Kenneth Waltz, comes to an interesting conclusion: if theory is to mean here what it does in physics, then the only "theory" of international relations is that of the balance of power, and it is unfortunately insufficient to help us understand the field! The other so-called general theories are not more than grand conceptualizations, using "confused, vague and fluctuating definitions of variables."[13] This may well be the case; Waltz seems to blame the theorists, rather than asking whether the fiasco does not result from the very nature of the field. Can there *be* a theory of undetermined behavior, which is what "diplomatic-strategic action," to use Aron's terms, amounts to?

Aron has, in my opinion, demonstrated why a theory of undetermined behavior cannot consist of a set of propositions explaining general laws that make prediction possible, and can do little more than define basic concepts, analyze basic configurations, sketch out the permanent features of a constant logic of behavior, in other words make the field intelligible.[14] It is therefore not surprising if many of the theories dissected, or vivisected, by Waltz, are, as he puts it, reductionist, such as the theories of imperialism, which are what he had called in his earlier book "second image" theories (they find the causes of interstate relations in what happens *within* the units); or else, the theories he dismisses were all produced during the first phase—the neophytish (or fetish) stage—of postwar research: the search for the scientific equivalent of the philosopher's stone has been far less ardent in the past twenty years. Waltz' own attempt at laying the groundwork for theory is conceptually so rigorous as to leave out much of the reality he wants to account for. I agree with him that a theory explaining reality must be removed from it and cannot be arrived at by mere induction; but if it is so removed that what it "explains" has little relation to what occurs, what is the use? One finds some of the same problems in all political science; but Waltz is right in stating that international relations suffers from a peculiar "absence of common sense clues": the key variables are far clearer in domestic political systems, whereas here "the subject is created, and recreated, by those who work on it."[15] Still, here as in the rest of political science, it is the fascination with economics that has led scholars to pursue the chimera of the masterkey. They have believed that the study of a purposive activity aimed at a bewildering variety of ends, political action, could be treated like the study of instrumental action, economic behavior. They have tried in vain to make the concept of power play the same role as money in economics. And they have acted as if the mere production of partial theories unrelated to a grand theory was tantamount to failure.

A "science" without a theory may still be a science with a paradigm; and, until recently, the paradigm has been that of permanent conflict among state actors—the realist paradigm. However, in the absence of a theory, a second question has been hard to answer: what is it that should be explained? The field has both suffered and benefited from a triple fragmentation—benefited, insofar as much ingenious research has been brought to each fragment, yet suffered because the pieces of the puzzle do not fit. First, there has been (and still is) the so-called level of analysis problem. Should we be primarily concerned with the international system, that is, the interactions among the units? Or should we concentrate our efforts on the units themselves? There are two conflicting hypotheses behind these strategies. One postulates that the system has, so to speak, some sort of life of its own, even if some of the actors obviously have a greater role than others in shaping and changing the rules of interaction. The other approach postulates that the actors themselves are the strategic level for understanding what goes on among them. One says, in effect: Grasp the patterns of interaction, and you will understand why the actors behave as they do; the other one says: Look at the actors' moves, and you will comprehend the outcomes. Students of the international system and students of foreign-policy making have never really blended their research. My own conclusion is that of a writer who has worked both sides of the street: I am dissatisfied with each, but I admit that it is hard to be on both at once. The study of the international system provides one with a fine framework, but no more—precisely because the system may well put constraints on and provide opportunities for the actors, but does not "dictate" their behavior; and the study of the actors tells you, inevitably, more about the actors than about the interactions. But what used to be called linkage theory (before linkage became a Kissinger-inspired technique), that is, propositions about the bonds between foreign policy and international politics, has remained in the frozen stage of static taxonomies.

Second, there has also been fragmentation at each level of analysis. One could say, not so flippantly, that each student of international systems has hugged his own version of what that abstract scheme "is." Aron's is not Richard Rosecrance's, which is not Morton Kaplan's. Moreover, each one has tended to look at the postwar international system in a different way (once again, in the absence of a single theory, it is not easy to determine authoritatively the dynamics of a particular system that still unfolds under one's eyes). A dozen years ago, scholars acted as if they were competing for a prize to the best discourse on the subject: are we in a bipolar system? Waltz, Liska, Kissinger, and many others (including me) took part, but since there was no Academy, there was no prize. In recent years, the new contest is about "Persistence or Demise of the Realist paradigm?": Is the state-centered concept of international politics, with its focus on the diplomatic-strategic chessboard and its obsession with the use of force, still relevant to the age of interdependence? Aron, Joseph Nye and Robert Keohane, Edward Morse, Bull, and many others (including myself) are busy evaluating. As before, I suspect that the verdict will be history's, and that like the long-awaited Orator in Ionesco's *Chairs*, it will speak in incomprehensible gibberish. At the other level of analysis, we have accumulated masses of studies of concrete foreign policies, and moved from the period of Chinese boxes—the decision-making theories of the 1950s—to the age of the "bureaucratic politics" model. The former provided endless items for laundry lists; the other one draws attention to the kitchen where the meal is being cooked, but forgets to tell us that what matters is whether the chefs cook what they want or what they are ordered to prepare, and assumes all too readily that what they do is determined by their particular assignment in the kitchen, rather than by what they have learned outside, or their personal quirks.

Third, there has been functional fragmentation as well. If there is, or can be, no satisfactory general theory, if the "overarching concepts" are excessively loose-fitting clothes, why not try greater rigor on a smaller scale? At the systemic level, we have thus witnessed such clusters of research as work on regional integration (where, for once, the theoretical ingenuity of scholars has far outreached the practical, "real-life" accomplishments of statesmen), modern theories of imperialism, arms race models and measurements of wars, recent studies of transnational relations and international economics. At the foreign policy level (although it tries to straddle both) the main cluster has been that of strategic literature; and there is now a growing literature on decision-making in the United States. Unfortunately, each cluster has tended to foster its own jargon; and this kind of fragmentation has had other effects, which will be discussed below.

Finally, the quest for science has led to a heated and largely futile battle of methodologies, in answer to a third question: Whatever it is we want to study, how should we do it? Actually, it is a double battle. On the one hand, there is the debate between those "traditionalists" who, precisely because of the resistance the field itself opposes to rigorous theoretical formulations, extol the virtues of an approach that would remain as close to historical scholarship and to the concerns of political philosophy as possible (this is the position taken by Hedley Bull), and all those who, whatever their own brand of theorizing, believe that there can be a political science of international relations—if not in the form of a single theory, at least in that of systematic conceptualizations, classifications, hypotheses, etc.—a science which can be guided in its questions by the interrogations of past philosophers, yet finds reliance on philosophical discourse and diplomatic intuition both insufficient and somewhat alien to the enterprise of empirical analysis. There is little likelihood that this debate will ever come to a conclusion—especially because neither side is totally consistent, and each one tends to oversimplify what it actually does. On the other hand, here as in other branches of political science, there is the battle of the literates versus the numerates; or, if you prefer, the debate about the proper place and contributions of quantitative methods and mathematical models. The fact that the practitioners of the latter tend to hug the word science, and to put beyond the pale of science all those who, while equally concerned with moving "from the unique to the general" and with considering "classes of events and types of entities," believe that these cannot be reduced to numbers or that science does not consist in "accumulating coefficients of correlation" . . . "without asking which theories lead one to expect what kind of a connection among which variables"[16]—this fact has made for rather strained relations among scholars of different methodological persuasions. In domestic political science, behaviorists and old-fashioned scholars have found coexistence easier, because their respective approaches fit separate parts of the field—electoral behavior or the behavior of legislative bodies lends itself to mathematical treatment. In international affairs, such a functional division of labor is much harder to apply. As a result, the prophets of quantitative methodologies dismiss as mere hunches based on "insight" (a word they often use as if it were an insult) the elaborate ruminations of their opponents, and these in turn ridicule the costly calculations that tell one nothing about causes or lump together different types of the same phenomenon (say, wars), and the endless correlations among variables lifted from their context, that all too often conclude that . . . no conclusive evidence can be derived from them: endless nonanswers to trivial questions.

If there is little agreement as to what constitutes a science, and little enthusiasm for the state of the science of international relations, what about the other great expectation, that of usefulness? I am struck by one apparent contradiction. The champions of a science of international affairs have, on the whole, declared their independence from philosophy and their allegiance to objective empiricism. And yet, most of them have wanted to draw consequences for the real world from their research: the greater the drive to predict (or the tendency to equate science, not just with intelligibility but with control and prediction), the greater the inclination to play the role of the wise adviser—or of the engineer. It is in the nature of human affairs, and of the social sciences.

But in this specific realm, there are some very peculiar problems. The first could be called: advice to whom? Many scholars, especially those whose level of analysis is systemic, implicitly write as if they were addressing themselves to a world government, or as if they aimed at reaching those who wish to transcend the traditional logic of national self-righteousness and state calculations (the same can be said, even more strongly, of theorists of regional or functional integration; they tend to distribute recipes for going beyond the nation-state). Unfortunately, the chair of World Statecraft is empty, and change comes (if at all) through the operations of state agents. And so, scholars of this kind oscillate from condemnation of state practices that make for conflict, or retard integration, or promote injustice, to advice to state agents on how to transcend the limits of the game which it is however these agents' role and duty to perpetuate, or advice to international secretariats and subnational bureaux on the best strategy for undercutting and turning the resistance of national statecraft. These are all perfect guarantees of unhappy consciousness for the scholars.

Other scholars, especially among those whose level of analysis is national decision-making, see themselves as efficient Machiavellians—they are advising the Prince on how best to manage his power and on how best to promote the national interest. This is particularly the case of the strategists, the group which contains the highest proportion of researchers turned consultants and policymakers. "Systemic" writers who are fully aware of the differences between an international system and a community of mankind, that is, the "realists," do their best to make advice to the only Prince who still matters—the national statesman, bound to enhance the interests of his state—coincide with their views of the interests of the whole. They advocate "enlightened" concepts of the national interest, or "world order" policies that would somewhat reconcile the needs of the part and of the whole. But this is a difficult exercise. The logical thrust of "realism" is the promotion of the national interest, that is, not unhappy global consciousness but happy national celebration. "Realists" who become aware of the perils of realism in a world of nuclear interconnection and economic interdependence—writers like Morgenthau, or myself—suffer from the addition of two causes of unhappiness: that which afflicts all "systemic" writers in search of a radically new order, and that which comes from knowing only too well that utopianism does not work.

Thus, basically, in their relations which the real world, the scholars are torn between irrelevance and absorption. Many do not like irrelevance, and want even the most esoteric or abstract research to be of use. The oscillation I have described above is what they want to escape from, and yet they do not want to be absorbed by that machine for self-righteousness, the service of the Prince. But their only excuse is the populist dream—the romantic hope that "the people" can be aroused and led to force the elites that control the levers of action, either out of power altogether or to change their ways. Much of peace research, once it got tired of advocating for the solution of world conflicts the discrete techniques used for accommodation in domestic affairs, has been traveling down that route. It is one on which scholarship risks finding both irrelevance and absorption, for the policies advocated here do inspire both those intelligentsias that want to displace certain elites in developing countries, and those established elites that are eager to boost national power against foreign dominance. Yet if the former come to power, and if the latter follow the advice of "dependencia" theorists, the result is not likely to be a world of peace and justice, but a world of revolutions, and new conflicts, and new inequities.

As for the scholars who want to avoid esoterica or romanticism and who set their sights on Washington, they, in turn, run into problems. There are two reasons why the Washingtonian temptation is so strong. There is the simple fact that international politics remains the politics of states: whether or not, in the abstract, the actor is the shaper of or is shaped by the system, in reality there is no doubt that the United States remains the most potent player. And there is the fact that a science of contemporary politics needs data, and that in this realm, whereas much is public—in the records of international organizations, speeches, published state documents—a great deal remains either classified or accessible only to insiders: the specific reasons for a decision, the way in which it was reached, the bargains that led to a common stand, the meanderings of a negotiation, the circumstances of a breakdown. Far more than domestic political science, international relations is an insider's game, even for scholars concerned with the systemic level.

But a first problem lies in the fact that gathering information from and about the most potent actor, creates an irresistible urge to nudge the player:

the closer the Washingtonian connection, the greater the temptation of letting oneself be absorbed. Second, outsider advice always suffers from oversimplification. When it comes to tactical suggestions, the insiders, who control not only all the facts but also the links connecting separate realms of policy, have the advantage. This increases the scholar's urge to get in closer. Third, once one starts rolling down the slope from research-with-practical-effects, to practical-advocacy-derived-from-research, the tendency to slight the research and to slant the advocacy for reasons either of personal career or of political or bureaucratic opportunity, will become insidious. Which means that the author may still be highly useful as an intelligent and skilled decision-maker—but not as a scholar. Either his science will be of little use, or else, in his attempt to apply a particular pet theory or dogma, he may well become a public danger. This does not mean that the experience of policy-making is fateful to the scholar, that the greatest hope for the science would lie in blowing up the bridge that leads across the moat into the citadel of power. A scholar-turned-statesman can, if his science is wise and his tactics flexible, find ways of applying it soundly; and he can later draw on his experience for improving his scholarly analytical work. But it is a delicate exercise which few have performed well.

Because of America

The problems I have examined have arisen mainly in America, because the profession of international relations specialists happens to be so preponderantly American. Insofar as it flourishes elsewhere, the same difficulties appear: they result from the nature of the field. But because of the American predominance, the discipline has also taken some additional traits which are essentially American, and less in evidence in those other countries where the field is now becoming an object of serious study.

The most striking is the quest for certainty.[17] It explains the rage for premature theoretical formulation, the desire to calculate the incalculable (not merely power but status), the crusade to replace discussions of motives with such more objective data as word counts and vote counts, the crowding of strategic research (here, the ends are given, and it becomes a quest for the means). International relations should be the science of uncertainty, of the limits of action, of the ways in which states try to manage but never quite succeed in eliminating their own insecurity. There has, instead, been a drive to eliminate from the discipline all that exists in the field itself—hence a quest for precision that turns out false or misleading. Hence also two important and related gaps. One is the study of statecraft as an art. With very few exceptions (such as *A World Restored*) it has been left to historians. (One could say much of the same about domestic political science). The other is the study of perceptions and misperceptions, the subjective yet essential side of international politics. Robert Jervis' work is beginning to fill that gap, but it is not certain that his example will be widely followed.[18] Almost by essence, the study of diplomatic statecraft and of perceptions refuses to lend itself to mathematical formulations, or to a small number of significant generalizations (one may generalize, but the result is likely to be trivial). Taxonomies and case studies do not quench the thirst to predict and to advocate.

A second feature, intimately tied to the discipline's principal residence rather than to its nature, is the preponderance of studies dealing with the present. Historians continue to examine past diplomatic history in their way. Political scientists concerned with international affairs have concentrated on the politics of the postwar era; and when they have turned to the past, it has all too often been either in highly summary, I would say almost "college outline" fashion, or in the way long ago denounced by Barrington Moore, Jr., which consists in feeding data detached from their context into computers. This is a very serious weakness. It leads not only to the neglect of a wealth of past experiences—those of earlier imperial systems, of systems of interstate relations outside Europe, of foreign policy-making in domestic polities far different from the contemporary ones—but also to a real deficiency in our understanding of the international system of the present. Because we have an inadequate basis for comparison, we are tempted to exaggerate either continuity with a past that we know badly, or the radical originality of the present, depending on whether we are more struck by the features we deem permanent, or with those we do not believe existed before. And yet a more rigorous examination of the past might reveal that what we sense as new really is not, and that some of the "traditional" features are far more complex than we think.

There are many reasons for this flaw. One is the fear of "falling back into history"—the fear that if we study the past in depth, we may indeed find generalizations difficult and categorization either endless or pointless; and we may lose the thread of "science." A related reason is the fact that American political scientists do not receive sufficient training either in history or in foreign languages, indispensable for work on past relations among states. A third reason is to be found in the very circumstances of the discipline's birth and development. In a way, the key question has not been, "What should we know?" It has been, "What should we do?"—about the Russians, the Chinese, the bomb, the oil producers. We have tried to know as much as we needed in order to know how to act—and rarely more: a motivation that we find in other parts of political science (the study of political development, for instance), where some disillusionment has set in. But we can say to ourselves that there are no shortcuts to political development, that the United States cannot build nations for others, and that we should go back to the foundation, that is, to an understanding of the others' past. We are unable to say to ourselves that we must stop having a diplomacy, and impose a moratorium on our advising drive until we have found out more about the past of diplomatic-strategic behavior. And the interest which, quite naturally, the government and, less wisely but understandably, the foundations have shown in supporting research that deals with the present (or extrapolates it into the future, or scrutinizes the near future so as to discern what would be sound action in the present) has kept the scholars' attention riveted on the contemporary scene.

The stress on the present and the heavily American orientation have combined to leave in the dark, at least relatively, several important issues—issues whose study is essential to a determination of the dynamics of international politics. One is the relation of domestic politics (and not merely bureaucratic politics) to international affairs—we need to examine in far greater detail the way in which the goals of states have originated, not (or not only) from the geopolitical position of the actors, but from the play of domestic political forces and economic interests; or the way in which statesmen, even when they seemed to act primarily for the world stage, nevertheless also wanted their moves abroad to reach certain objectives within; or the way in which external issues have shaped domestic alignments and affected internal battles. The desire to distinguish the discipline of international relations from the rest of political science is partly responsible for this gap; scholars who study a given political system do not usually pay all that much attention to foreign policy, and the specialists of international politics simply do not know enough about foreign political systems. The only country for which the bond between domestic and external behavior has been examined in some depth is, not so surprisingly, the United States. Here again, an assessment of the originality of the present—with its visible merging of domestic and foreign policy concerns, especially in the realm of international economic affairs—requires a much deeper understanding of the past relations between domestic politics and foreign policy. We may dis-cover that the realist paradigm, which stresses the primacy of foreign policy, has to be seriously amended, not only for the present but for the past.

Another zone of relative darkness is the functioning of the international hierarchy, or, if you prefer, the nature of the relations between the weak and the strong. There has been (especially in the strategic literature) a glaring focus on bipolarity, accompanied by the presumption that moves to undermine it (such as nuclear proliferation) would be calamitous (it may not be a coincidence if the French have, on the whole, taken a very different line). Much of the study of power in international affairs has been remarkably Athenian, if one may refer to the famous Melian dialogue in Thucydides (the strong do what they can, the weak what they must). How the strong have often dealt with the weak in ways far more oblique, or less successful than the simple notion of a high correlation between might and achievements would suggest; how and under what conditions the weak have been able to offset their inferiority—these are issues which, until OPEC came along, had not been at the center of research and for which, again, far more historical work ought to be undertaken.

What was supposed to be a celebration of creativity seems to have degenerated into a series of complaints. We have found here an acute form of a general problem that afflicts social science—the tension between the need for so-called basic research, which asks the more general and penetrating questions that derive from the nature of the activity under study, and the desire of those who, in the real world, support, demand, or orient the research, for quick answers to pressing issues. And if the desire often seems more compelling than the need, it is because of the scholars' own tendency to succumb to the Comtian temptation of social engineering. This temptation is enhanced by the opportunities the United States provides to scholar-kings (or advisers to the Prince), or else by the anxiety which scholars, however "objective" they try to be, cannot help but feel about a world threatened with destruction and chaos by the very logic of traditional interstate behavior.

Born and raised in America, the discipline of international relations is, so to speak, too close to the fire. It needs triple distance: it should move away from the contemporary, toward the past; from the perspective of a superpower (and a highly conservative one), toward that of the weak and the revolutionary—away from the impossible quest for stability; from the glide into policy science, back to the steep ascent toward the peaks which the questions raised by traditional political philosophy represent. This would also be a way of putting the fragments into which the discipline explodes, if not together, at least in perspective. But where, in the social sciences, are the scientific priorities the decisive ones? Without the possibilities that exist in this country, the discipline might well have avoided being stunted, only by avoiding being born. The French say that if one does not have what one would like, one must be content with what one has got. Resigned, perhaps. But content? A state of dissatisfaction is a goad to research. Scholars in international relations have two good reasons to be dissatisfied: the state of the world, the state of their discipline. If only those two reasons always converged!

References

1. For an earlier discussion, see my *Contemporary Theory in International Relations* (Englewood Cliffs, N.J.: Prentice-Hall, 1960).
2. E. H. Carr, *Twenty Years Crisis* (London: Macmillan, 1939).
3. Nicholas Spykman, *America's Strategy in World Politics* (New York: Harcourt, Brace, 1942).
4. Hans Morgenthau, *Politics Among Nations* (New York: Knopf, 1948).
5. Cf. H. Stuart Hughes, *The Sea Change* (New York: Knopf, 1975).
6. Raymond Aron, *Peace and War* (Paris: Calmann-Lévy 1962; New York: Doubleday, 1966).
7. Ralf Dahrendorf, *Die angewandte Aufklärung* (Munich: Piper, 1963).
8. See the Ph.D. thesis (Harvard University, Department of History) of Diana Pinto, who deals with postwar sociology in Italy and France.
9. Judith Shklar, in an introduction to the field of political science written for Harvard freshmen.
10. Cf. Daniel Bell, *The Coming of Post-Industrial Society* (New York: Basic Books, 1973).
11. *Handbook of Political Science*, Vol. 8, *International Politics*, Fred I. Greenstein and Nelson W. Polsby, eds. (Reading, Mass.: Addison-Wesley, 1975).

12. Kenneth Waltz, *Man, the State and War* (New York: Columbia University Press, 1959).
13. *Handbook of Political Science*, Vol. 8, *International Politics*, ch. 1, p. 14.
14. See my *The State of War*, ch. 2.
15. *Handbook of Political Science*, Vol. 8, *International Politics*, p. 8.
16. Ibid., p. 12.
17. On this point, see also Albert O. Hirschman, "The Search for Paradigms as a Hindrance to Understanding," *World Politics*, April 1970, pp. 329-343.
18. See Robert Jervis, *Perception and Misperception in International Politics* (Princeton: Princeton University Press, 1976).

2

Rousseau on War and Peace

For many reasons, Rousseau's writings on international relations should interest students of Rousseau and, more generally, of international relations. The former have recently celebrated the two-hundredth anniversary of *Emile* and *The Social Contract*. Those works, and the *Discourse on the Origin and Bases of Inequality Among Men*, have been analyzed *ad infinitum* and well. But Rousseau's ideas on war and peace, dispersed in various books and fragments, some of which are lost,[1] have had only occasional attention and then often of the hit-and-miss variety.[2] Incomplete as his own treatment of relations among states was, the frequency and intensity of his references indicate the depth of his concern.

Students in search of theories of international politics will also find Rousseau's views useful in the interconnected areas of empirical or causal theory and of normative theory. In the quest for models of state behavior or in the analysis of the nature and cause of war, social scientists could do (and often have done) worse than take and test Rousseau's formulations: in Arnold Wolfers' words, they were "far removed from amateurish guesswork" and "cannot fail to be valuable to anyone seeking to understand what makes the clock tick in international relations."[3] Significantly, Rousseau's remarks point to the same conclusions as those in Raymond Aron's exhaustive and systematic study *Peace and War*. For today's revolutionary system of international politics confirms the sharp and gloomy analysis of Rousseau, whose pessimism was all too easily discounted in the moderate system that died at Sarajevo.

More specifically, the normative aspect of Rousseau's writings is relevant today because of his awareness of a dilemma that also dominated Kant's thought and that has become vital in any consideration of world politics in the nuclear age. We can no longer afford to be preoccupied only with the issue to which political philosophers used to give most of their attention—the "conditions of a just peace" in domestic society, the search for the good state, for the legitimate political regime. We are also (perhaps primarily) concerned with conditions of peace in international society, because the very institution of the state—celebrated as the source of order, liberty, and morality for citizens—has also turned out to be a source of international chaos and consequently of physical danger and moral agony. How to be both a good citizen of a nation and a good citizen of the world; how to prevent the state from oppressing its subjects or from obliging them to behave immorally toward outsiders, under the pressure of international competition, without meanwhile destroying the bond of loyalty and sense of identity that link each citizen to his compatriots—these have become the major issues for political thinkers today. Rousseau considered those issues at some length and thought he could resolve the dilemma: the formula he devised, in *The Social Contract*, to rescue man from the fall into which the passing of the state of nature had plunged him, was also supposed to put an end to international disorder. However, the philosopher who was the sharpest critic of man's plight in society (both domestic and international) provides only an escape from the international jungle he had so brilliantly described, not a solution.

I

Kenneth Waltz's admirable book *Man, The State and War* has helped the understanding of world politics by distinguishing three "images" of international competition. But I am not so sure he has similarly served some of the authors with whom he deals—Hobbes, Rousseau, and Kant in particular. With each, any sharp separation between conceptions of human nature, of the state, and of the international milieu destroys the unity of his philosophy. At the risk of covering very familiar ground, therefore, it needs to be shown first how Rousseau's trenchant critique of world politics and his "model" or image of states in conflict derive from his most fundamental notions about man and society.

For that purpose, compare Rousseau's picture with that of Hobbes, whom he constantly invokes and attacks. Rousseau's point of departure is just as individualistic or atomistic as Hobbes's: they begin neither with God or society, nor with man as a social and moral being; Rousseau made it clear that there was at the outset no such thing as a general society of mankind.[4] Both begin with man, an atom in the state of nature—neither moral nor immoral, neither good nor bad. But Rousseau's concept of the state of nature is not like Hobbes's; his owes much to Montesquieu's happier version.[5] Hobbes's men in a state of nature led miserable lives: they were strong enough to kill each other, too weak to be safe, and driven into deadly competition for scarce goods by an infinity of desires and an unlimited passion for getting what they wanted—an unlimited quest for power. Quite the opposite, Rousseau's state of nature was characterized by men who were graced by a generous nature that provided them with more goods than they needed; there was enough space between and among them to prevent their desires exceeding their needs.[6] Consequently, if, by accident, two men should happen to clash over the same food, the most likely result would be flight, not fight; if they fought at all, it would be a minor brawl.[7] Independence, indifference, abundance, *amour de soi* (a healthy concern with self-preservation, limited to the fulfillment of basic needs), compassion—

such are the key features of the idyll.[8] Man's life on earth may be solitary and brutish, but it is pleasant precisely because of these qualities.

Rousseau shares Montesquieu's concept of a state of nature that is peaceful and unperturbed by inequality, Montesquieu's belief that trouble began when the state of nature faded, and Montesquieu's distinction of three stages in man's development—an original state of nature, a state of *de facto* society that is a "fallen" state of nature, and a state of civil society—and he charges Hobbes with having mistakenly confused the first two stages. Nevertheless, Rousseau's idea of the genesis of civil society is very different from Montesquieu's. The latter, quite traditionally, saw man as a social animal, society as the outcome of a natural human drives[9]: even though its first effects are inequality, competition, and war, these are only temporary nuisances that the establishment of political communities endowed with laws is intended to eliminate. (In this respect, Montesquieu's analysis does not differ from Locke's.) Rousseau, however, believes that *de facto* society resulted not from man's sociability[10] (in itself a notion he discards), but from a combination of accidents and physical necessities. It is the human "situation," not human nature, that is responsible; nature's tricks and the growing needs of a growing population, not man's natural desires, bring men together.[11] And he sees *de facto* society not as a mere nuisance but as a genuine fall that affects mankind after settlements have appeared, as communications and contacts develop, property spreads, and inequality sets in.[12] Thus, his analysis of man in *de facto* society comes close to Hobbes' image of man in the state of nature—a picture of fear, waste, want, and war; in both instances, the springs of conflict are defined as competition, diffidence, and glory. Thus, a close, if superficial, resemblance marks Hobbes' and Rousseau's accounts of the establishment of civil society: the former sees in it a necessary escape from general war, a liberation from fear and want; the latter concedes that this was indeed the purpose of the enterprise.[13]

Here, however, the resemblance ends. Rousseau's judgment of the effects of civil society differs from Hobbes'; their similar descriptions of man's predicament before the appearance of the state conceal conflicting notions on the origins of this predicament and totally different emphases on what is evil about it. Hobbes finds the causes of conflict in man's nature; those causes will remain, latent and repressed, in man-under-laws; the only thing that can be ruled out (at least, within the state) is violence. Hobbes's concern and supreme value is safety; consequently, civil society, which makes safety possible, is a blessing. His obsession is with the use of force, which can be managed, whereas its causes cannot. Thus, civil society does not change man's nature but merely transforms his possibilities of action: it suppresses some and, as a result, increases and protects others.

Rousseau's analysis is very different. He is concerned more with the roots of violence than with its manifestations, not because he does not care for peace, but because he denies that these roots are in man's nature and because his supreme concern is man's freedom, conscience, and virtue, which require that the roots of violence be torn out. To him, *de facto* society is evil not just because it is a state of war but because it is a state of moral contradiction and disgrace which corrupts man's peaceful nature and of which violence is merely the outcome. Entry into society effects a mutation in Rousseau's man. On the one hand, through contacts with other human beings, he gains a moral sense and becomes able dimly to conceive the ideal of force at the service of a law that would be his own—the idea of a positively defined freedom, consisting not merely in the absence of hindrances to action (as in Hobbes' and also in Rousseau's state of nature) but in the capacity to be one's own master. On the other hand, man has lost his original independence and innocence; his condition is the worst of all possible worlds, for he enjoys neither the old, negative freedom which is lost forever, nor the new, positive one to which he can aspire. He is capable of moral understanding but not of moral fulfillment. The old "natural law," based on the instincts of self-preservation and compassion, is dying; but the very forces that killed it prevent the new natural law, understood as the moral dictates of reason, from acquiring sufficient strength.[14] The passions bred by inequality, the inflation of desires fostered by society, gradually starve out compassion and submerge *l'amour de soi* in *l'amour propre*—a concern for oneself that comes not from the natural desire for self-preservation, but from an artificial reaction to other people's judgments, opinions, attitudes, and actions toward oneself. Thus, what makes of man in *de facto* society so miserable a being is not merely the violence to which he is exposed: it is what triggers the violence, an insecurity that did not exist in the state of nature, which stems not from man's real nature but from his cupidity[15]—not so much a physical as a psychological need to compare oneself to others, a fall from *être* to *paraître* and from original indolence to social restlessness—and that is evil even if it does not lead to the actual use of force.

Thus, Rousseau and Hobbes agree here on one point only: civil society rules out violence among citizens. However, whereas Hobbes' ideal state is the Leviathan in which man submits to the force that protects his life, removes external hindrances to his action, and leaves him free to indulge in all the drives and desires that motivate and move him (as long as he does so peaceably), a civil society based exclusively on self-preservation is an absurd one for Rousseau. For, in it, all the vices that marred *de facto* society would be perpetuated—except one, violence among the citizens—with the addition of two new, and huge, evils: international wars, and tyranny. If civil society, which replaces man's natural independence with its network of conventions, makes man the permanent pawn of others, it is a curse. Only the society that makes man autonomous is good. In other words, the philosopher's quest cannot stop with the elimination of violence, it must be pursued until the origins of conflict themselves have been eliminated. The absence of violence is not the supreme good: violence is a symptom; its causes must be cured—and they can be, since, in Rousseau's view, they do not lie in human nature. *The Social Contract* provides the formula through which a civil society can be established, in which not only violence but the "evil propensities" of man-in-society will be purged, in which his inevitable passions will be turned to the common good, and "rational natural law" can flourish, thanks to the civil laws decreed by the general will.

The differences between Hobbes and Rousseau on the subject of world politics are as serious, and rather paradoxical. Hobbes has little to say on the subject, but what he does say is that the international state of nature is less intolerable than the "individual" state of nature. To be sure, both are marked by the same quest for power, and for the same reasons.[16] Both show insecurity and conflict; states, consequently, have to be armed and prepared. Both show the same deficiency of law: in the absence of superior power, the "laws of nature" are mere precepts of self-interest whose application depends on their perpetually uncertain observance by others. However, while Hobbes explains how insecurity incites men to crawl out of their state of nature to set up the Leviathan, he does not invite the Leviathans to follow suit. Here is the key of the paradox: in the international competition, it is the state itself that serves as a cushion. Even though international politics, in the absence of constraining power, is not a state of peace, even though it is a condition in which the nasty features of human nature (repressed, within civil society, by the setting up of the Leviathan) can, so to speak, re-emerge at their worst, nevertheless the international state of war is *bearable*. It is the *intolerable* aspect of the "individual" state of war that drives men to sacrifice their "right of nature" so as to preserve their existence.

There are two reasons why the international state of nature is less atrocious. First, states are stronger than men in the state of nature: their "security dilemma," their fear of annihilation, is less pressing.[17] Secondly, the very existence of the state is a guarantee for the security of the citizens: no man is safe in the state of nature, whereas inter-state war does not affect the daily lives of all men. Consequently, "laws of nature" *à la* Hobbes have a greater chance of being observed in the international state of nature: since there is greater force behind the partners to an inter-state compact than there is behind individual signatories of a contract, the risk of violation will be less; the idea of reciprocity of interests, on which the solidity of international law depends, emerges here. Moreover, each state has an essentially domestic interest in self-restraint, since, should it implicate its population in all-out wars of extermination, the subjects' duty of obedience to it would disappear.

Thus, surprisingly enough, Hobbes ends by differing not too much from Montesquieu, who thought that just as the establishment of the state restored peace among men, the development of international law among states would allow them to live under conditions of merely troubled peace, not permanent war.[18] We can see in Hobbes the father of utilitarian theories of international law and relations, and we can extrapolate from his theories, for policy guidance, the notion of the balance of power: by definition, it is fragile, but it is a relatively efficient technique for enforcing the "laws of nature," since it corresponds to the interests all participants have in keeping the competition moderate. Should the "security dilemma" worsen, should the competition become more intense, should the risk of total destruction, affecting all citizens, become intolerable, we could also surmise that Hobbes's relative complacency would lose its justification; the same arguments he used to justify the Leviathan would have to be applied to the establishment of a world-wide one.

Rousseau's views are far less reassuring. With Hobbes, he recognizes that the criterion that distinguishes world politics from politics of a civil society is the ever-present possibility of violence which he, like Hobbes, terms a "state of war" (whether war is actually in progress or not)[19]; it is also clear that, for both, the fragmentation of power in the international system is the immediate cause of the state of war. To use Waltz's useful classification, both Rousseau and Hobbes are "third-image" writers to this extent. However, their agreement stops here. On four main points, they are in conflict.

First, they differ in their judgments on the nature of international violence. For Hobbes, violence is an expression of human nature, whenever it is not repressed by a Leviathan; international war remains inevitable because man is an asocial animal, even after the establishment of civil societies. For Rousseau, war is *not* a human necessity or drive, because man is not social by nature. "One kills in order to win; no man is so ferocious that he tries to win in order to kill."[20] War is a social institution: hence Rousseau's famous insistence on the idea that wars are, by nature, contests between states (i.e., artificial bodies) but not between individuals and consequently ought to be waged as such. This idea was directly inspired by Montesquieu's writings,[21] but Rousseau formulated it more categorically, so as to make clear that man, *dénaturé* by bad social institutions, is alienated, his acts springing not from his true self but from a distorted self which society has manufactured and for which society alone is responsible. Since nothing in human nature forces one man to kill another, the aims of wars are always far removed from citizens' lives: the stakes of war are not man's needs, but the frills and fancies grafted on those needs by society.[22]

Second, Rousseau does not share Hobbes' belief that the state is a mitigating force in international conflict. The same reasons that made man miserable in *de facto* society (or make him so in inadequate civil societies) are at work among nations. He singles out two factors of insecurity especially. One is mutual dependence: insecurity among men grows because each one is at the mercy of others' services or opinions; relations among states are also plagued by such entanglements. In both cases, he denounces economic dependence most acidly, as if it were the serpent's apple. It is one of Rousseau's deepest insights, one that shatters a large part of the liberal vision of world affairs—that interdependence breeds not accommodation and harmony but suspicion and incompatibility.[23] Another cause of insecurity is inequality, that *inégalité de combinaison* which results from division of labor and multiplies the effects of natural inequality[24]; similarly, the unevenness of states is the fuel of world conflict.[25] Hobbes had stressed natural equality as the main incentive to competition, and assumed that all men (and all states) were equally driven by their nature toward power and conflict. Rousseau remarks instead that (just as it is enough that one man say, "this is mine," for property claims to mushroom) the emergence of one state is enough to force all other human settlements to choose between annihilation or resistance—which means other states are established in a kind of chain reaction. Once again, very rightly, the blame must be put on the dynamics of the situation: even if most states wanted to live in peace, they could not do so as long as a few major delinquents made trouble.

Moreover, international quarrels are in many respects far worse than the competition among men before the establishment of civil society. States, far from dampening violence, amplify it.

(a) There is a difference in the scope of violence. Rousseau makes a fundamental distinction between kinds of violent conflicts: only organized violence among consolidated groups deserves to be called war. War is "a permanent condition that requires constant relations." Throughout most of the period that precedes civil society, relations among men were too unsettled for genuine wars to develop: insecurity resulted merely in "fights" and "murders."[26] Only after the appearance of states, in which laws are made that delimit the rights and duties of the nation, and that often promote close relations with other nations, can real wars break out—not, of course, among the citizens, but among states. One may object that, just before the emergence of civil society, according to Rousseau himself, human settlement had become sufficiently stable (and the growth of human greed, dependence, and inequality sufficiently disastrous) for a real "state of war" to break out among men.[27] Also, Rousseau himself defines war as arising from "links between things rather than between men."[28] Specifically, contests over "things" (such as possessions) had already developed in *de facto* societies. This is true, but violence within and among these societies remained less devastating than wars among states. The roots of the older kind of war were individual greed—the rapacity of the rich, the envy of the poor—in other words, inequality among men (even if those men were beginning to be organized, for instance, in "gangs of bandits"); the root of inter-state war is inequality among nations; and the inequality of men has sharper limits than the inequality of states. The size of a state is always relative: "it is forced to compare itself in order to know itself"; its "absolute size" is meaningless, for its rank depends on what other states are, plan, and do. Thus, by definition, each state is always totally dependent on all the others.[29] Its security dilemma affords no escape: if it is strong, its power makes it a danger to peace; if it is weak, it becomes a tempting pawn. Restlessness is at its worst on the world scene.

(b) A difference in the stakes also makes war among states far worse than war among men. In *de facto* society, the stakes of fighting remained essentially individualistic and therefore limited. As against hit-and-run raids to steal land or goods, inter-state war offers clashes over territory, resources, and manpower on a grand scale.

(c) Another difference is in the intensity of war. The Leviathan, in accordance with Hobbes' mechanistic conception of society, was made of the sum total of the citizens. This Rousseau denies; he points out that the state is always weaker than the sum total of the citizens' "particular forces."[30] Paradoxically, whereas Hobbes nevertheless believed that the impact of war on the citizens would be limited, Rousseau came to the opposite conclusion. For he saw that the state must try to compensate for its deficiency in collective force with passion—the one element Hobbes had left out. Prophetically, Rousseau warned that the body politic was moved not by cold *raison d'état* but by passions: hence the ferocity of wars. The passions that had pitted man against man before the appearance of civil society remained somehow dampened by what was left of human compassion, while the passions that states mobilized against one another ignored such restraint. Here we find another deep insight: what makes of states, in Nietzsche's terms, the coldest of cold monsters, is not reason of state, but the horrible fact that their passions are untouched (or unrelieved) by commiseration.

(d) Consequently, the effects of international conflict are far more nefarious than those of conflicts among men. States being more powerful than individual men (even though each state's strength may be less than the cumulative total strength of its citizens), their antagonisms produce greater upheavals than the clashes of individuals. There are more murders in one day of battle than there had been for centuries in the state of nature.[31]

A third major area of difference between Hobbes' and Rousseau's approaches to world politics concerns ethics in international relations. In Hobbes, the problem of ethical action in politics can hardly be called important; it is a pure matter of definition, since human nature does not change after man's entry into society. Moral action in the Leviathan consists simply of obeying the sovereign's law. In international politics, there is no such law, and consequently one is left with the clash or occasional convergence of different national moralities. Rousseau could not be satisfied with such simple amorality. In all his work, he treated ethics and politics as one and the same thing. To him, the "state of war" is a moral scandal because it is the mark, and to a considerable extent, indeed, the cause, of man's failure to fulfill his moral development in civil society. As he described it in the second *Discourse*, men entered civil society in order to live under laws, so as not only to escape from the murders and fights of *de facto* society, but also to be able to follow the dictates of "rational natural law"—which cannot have any force unless men are protected by the civil laws of society. But instead of the reconciliation of ethics and politics, the citizen is faced with a new and worse moral dilemma.

To begin with, man's very effort to assure domestic order, peace, and justice (by setting up the state) has provoked chaos and conflict on the international level; the nations remain vis-à-vis in a "state of nature" similar to the fallen state that had been man's tragic lot just before civil society was founded. "We have prevented particular wars only so as to start general ones which are a thousand times worse"; "all the horrors of war stem from men's efforts to prevent it."[32] Consequently, the citizen is caught in what Rousseau calls a *système mixte*[33]—torn between the laws of the domestic social order and the violence that results from sovereign states in a world state of nature. Now, to be morally torn is the greatest misery; to be "dragged by nature and by men into opposite directions" obliges man to "end his life without having been able to come to terms with himself."[34] Rousseau implies that the chance for autonomy in the domestic order—where the citizen can hope for the fusion of force and a law that would be his own—does not exist in the international (dis)order because of the fragmentation of sovereignties. Thus, as long as the world competition lasts, even the citizen of the ideal state may find no opportunity for moral action beyond the limits of the state; the human conscience may remain unhappy.

On the other hand, this global competition does more than thwart moral action beyond the state: its very existence gives political leaders a good pretext for putting or keeping man "in chains." Even the establishment of the first civil societies is described as a sort of trick by which the rich ensnare the poor and consolidate inequality under the pretext of mutual protection against outsiders.[35] Later, princes are able to stunt domestic efforts toward self-government and to perpetuate tyranny because of the "necessities" that war entails.[36] Thus, international insecurity and tyranny reinforce each other. Man is not merely caught between domestic order and external chaos, but torn by yet another contradiction: within civil society—whose order, being corrupt, preserves the evils of *de facto* society, *minus* internal wars but *plus* tyranny—the contradiction between nostalgia for the independence he has lost and a yearning for moral and political autonomy.

War, therefore, does more than curtail the scope of such autonomy: it threatens to make its achievement *within* the state impossible. Precisely because of this peril, Kant put the imperative of peace at the center of his philosophy. But Kant noted that the increasing costs of war would oblige rulers "not to hinder the weak and slow independent efforts of their people" to move toward constitutional government.[37] The experience of this century has confirmed Rousseau's gloom rather than Kant's hopes.

Rousseau's study of international relations raised the question whether it would not be better to have no civil society at all than to have many, for the *système mixte* is the worst evil. Not only is the present state far bloodier than the fallen state of nature; it is also one in which—although the causes of war are ever more remote from the citizens' lives—killing has become a duty taught by the state.[38] The moral tragedy is that, "by uniting with some men, we become the enemies of mankind"—which we had never been before.[39]

In a summary of the Abbé de Saint Pierre's peace plan, Rousseau analyzed the special bonds that history, legal institutions, and religion had forged among European nations. Precisely because of these bonds, he remarked, the condition of those nations was worse than if no European society existed at all.[40] It is his same concern for moral oneness, his same insight that it is better to be isolated (and thus not experience the agonies of moral choice) than to be dependent on others (and thus be unable, because of competition or inequality, to practice the moral virtues that society both engenders and frustrates).

A fourth crucial difference between Hobbes and Rousseau relates to how they view techniques for mitigating international conflict. Hobbes assumed that different "reasons of state" could converge on common interests. Rousseau demolishes this major part of the liberal (or neo-liberal—I mean, "realist") ideology of international politics, with arguments of enormous importance for the theory of international politics.

1. Rousseau first deals with what might be called restraints through explicit or tacit agreements. Neither international law nor the balance of power can really restrain international competition. Though not instances of actual war, they are tactics in the strategy of the state of war.[41] The balance of power may block major conquests, but it perpetuates instability and preserves or aggravates each participant's dissatisfaction.[42] International law is both weak and dangerous: its fragility is inherent, and due to the very nature of international obligation. It is but the expression of the "law of nature," superseded within states by civil laws but still operative among states. It consists neither of the commands of self-preservation and compassion, which faded after the fall from the original state of nature, nor of the dictates of moral reason, which have force only within the ideal state. Instead, it is the law of corrupted nature, the law of *amour-propre* and competition, tempered merely by the attempt to replace compassion with conventions. These are weak substitutes indeed, for the basis of obligation is shaky: nothing guarantees the efficacy of international law but the particular interest of the state to which it applies.[43] Moreover, international law is often worse than fragile. Alliances and treaties (like the laws of imperfect states) merely perpetuate inequality.[44] States often use international law as an instrument against one another in the state of war: not only are peace treaties nothing but stratagems, but recognition and the regulation of foreign trade can also be diplomatic weapons.[45] Peaceful international politics, of which international law is one aspect, is but the continuation of war by other means.

The foundation of Rousseau's reasoning here is his conviction that in a competitive situation as fierce as that among nations, common interests are evanescent and hardly significant. Each player in the game is after his own interest. Consequently, one must distinguish the *real* from the apparent interest of the players. Rousseau calls the apparent interest what the scholar (who superimposes on the competitive situation a fictitious community independent of the players' moves) is normally tempted to call the real— i.e., the common interest in self-restraint. Something close to a miracle would be needed, Rousseau thought, to make the separate calculations of individual advantage converge on a solution favorable to all. Furthermore, advantages are appreciated only "by their differences": if they are common to all, *they will be real to none*.[46]

It is easy to see how so gloomy an analysis applies to contemporary schemes of arms control. These assume that the main powers have a common interest in peace, which could be strengthened by the adoption of measures that would preserve existing advantages (the possession of national armaments) and add new ones (guarantees against surprise attack). Efforts to agree on such schemes have foundered precisely because of the asymmetries in the position of the major powers: each tries to annihilate the enemy's advantages while keeping its own factors of superiority.[47] Each acknowledges a risk of war but remains unwilling to deprive itself of the freedom of action that an unfettered right to use (or threaten to use) its weapons gives it. Each is confident that it can handle the danger of war by unilateral measures of restraint.[48] Rousseau wrote that princes who make war do so not because they are unaware of the perils but because they are confident of their wisdom.[49]

Rousseau's refutation of the "common-interest" argument, and his conviction that commerce only exacerbates greed and the competition among nations and among men, thus led him also to reject a view that Kant and liberals of the eighteenth and nineteenth centuries found too attractive to resist—that commerce breeds peace.[50]

2. If restraints based on common interests are fictitious, what about the possibility of self-restraint, resulting from each state's own effort to define a rational line of conduct, as one can define a rational strategy for a commercial firm? Rousseau's analysis shows why it is futile to try to reduce risk and uncertainty in international affairs by defining *a* rational foreign policy.[51] Economic competition has the simplifying feature of a currency in which all gains and losses can be calculated—money, but Rousseau realized that stakes in international competition cannot all be converted into monetary units or into any true measure[52]: land, men, spoils, prestige, or "degrees of power." (He had no clear idea of an ideological competition, although his remark about the passions of states can easily be extended to it. Such competition is even less "quantifiable.") On the other hand, the "rules of the game" are too fluid, its purely psychological elements too important, to allow for a meaningful definition of rationality: in the absence of a law subordinating the separate interests, or of legal procedures to channel them, states are condemned by their very independence to the hazards of *fortuna*.

3. Any analyst of international relations who sees world politics as a state of permanent war is tempted to propose radical remedies—to suggest that men and nations spontaneously move into a broad daylight of reconciliation. Rousseau's writings contain more or less explicit criticisms of many schemes that the imagination of men of good will had invented. So far as St. Pierre's peace plan was a forerunner of modern international organization, Rousseau's critique of it goes to the very foundation of that halfway house between state sovereignty and world government which flourishes today and which Kant presented both as a moral imperative and as the object of a hidden plan of nature. Rousseau suggests, in terms close to those Walter Schiffer applied to the League of Nations,[53] that as long as states behave as they have customarily behaved, they are unlikely to be willing to achieve lasting peace through international organizations; and, if their behavior were sufficiently reformed to make their adoption possible, the need for such a league would become much less pressing.[54] On the

other hand, anticipating Kant's philosophy of history, Rousseau argues that "what is useful to the public" can be introduced only by force, because of the resistance put up by selfish interests. But he adds that if wars and revolutions are necessary to impose federative leagues on men, they are fearful means indeed and may do more harm than the leagues could ever prevent.[55] This is an admirable, though depressing, comment on the dialectic of history in our own century, which required two world wars to establish two rather weak world organizations. It places a major reservation on Kant's hope that the hidden plan of nature would bring states together through a process of ever more damaging wars.

Rousseau did not deal with disarmament plans, which did not proliferate until the nineteenth century. But his analysis of unevenness and international insecurity, and his refutation of the "common-interest" argument, cuts through hundreds of pages of peace plans.[56]

We are left with a frightening picture of world politics. Nations are apparently condemned to a "state of war." The only restraints are unilateral and temporary; islands of peace are always threatened. Rousseau does not deny that these islands may exist: he assumes not a war of all against all, but a struggle in which the existence of even one "relationship of major tension" may make amity impossible and neutrality difficult.[57] Here, precisely as in his analysis of society in the *Discourse on Inequality*, Rousseau's vision is not historical, but of an ideal-type: it is "the essence of things, not events," that he wants to account for.[58] Consequently, one cannot refute him by pointing out that a few permanent neutrals (like his own Switzerland) have succeeded in staying out of the competition; or that some international systems are more moderate or some restraints more lasting than others—not so much because they are based on common interests as because they operate in times when the range of stakes (the scope of the competition) is narrower than at other moments. Rousseau's answer is obviously that nothing guarantees the preservation of oases of peace or the perpetuation of moments of grace: whenever the system becomes revolutionary again, his analysis is valid.

Yet Rousseau proposed a way out of the *système mixte* of the domestic order—a way of making *être* and *paraître*, *amour propre* and *amour de soi*, less incompatible. What about the international conditions of physical violence, moral division, and psychological bad faith? For his answers here, we must turn from his empirical theory to his normative theory—or to whatever we can find in its stead.

II

The loss of Rousseau's manuscript on confederations makes it difficult to know in full detail his solution to the problem of international "anarchy." But it is possible to put together pieces of the puzzle and to assess the relevance of the result to present-day world politics.

More than once Rousseau has been victimized by his interpreters. Recently, it has been fashionable to make him the father of "totalitarian democracy."

This is not the place to deal with such a distortion, but two points need to be made. One is to establish Rousseau's intentions without projecting into his work the intentions of disciples or others. The second is to deal with his views on their merits. This may entail showing that his ideal is incapable of execution and of any enforcement that would not thwart his intentions.[59] There may be, therefore, serious difficulties in making his work relevant to the world in which we live, but one should absolve him of responsibility for the perversions of his thought that have been produced by attempts to apply his vision.

Let us start with what Rousseau's intentions were not. He did *not* suggest that the way out of the international jungle was the establishment of a world state, nor was he the father of modern nationalism. It is true that his analysis of the international milieu provides what Waltz has called the third image, in which the absence of any common superior over the states is seen as the "permissive" cause of war.[60] But Rousseau does not therefore propose a European or a world federation to put an end to war. The passage Waltz quotes[61] in order to show that Rousseau endorsed such a formula appears in Rousseau's digest of St. Pierre's peace plan, which he thereupon mercilessly destroys in a subsequent critique.

But it is not enough to note the absence of any "world federalist" or "world government" solution in Rousseau's argument; the important question is why Rousseau brushed it aside. For we have an apparently puzzling contrast. He had shown that the "state of war" in *de facto* society convinced men to become citizens, i.e., to establish states so as to put an end to violence at least within civil society. And he had described this movement as having spread because some men (the rich) were able to convince others of their common interest in security under laws[62]—even though he had also said that men in the fallen state of nature were as incapable of making common interests triumph over antagonistic ones as sovereign states were in the international jungle.[63] If, then, men were driven by insecurity to heed the common interest after all, in Hobbesian fashion, why should not nations reach the same conclusion? Their "state of war" Rousseau himself described as worse than the state of violence among men in *de facto* society. If the social contract would set up an ideal state endowed not only with a monopoly of force but also with the capacity to make men morally free and virtuous, why should not a similar compact establishing a world state be the basis of universal peace and the guarantee of "republican government" in each component unit?

The answers to these questions are only implicit in Rousseau's work. They can be summed up as follows: in the world as it is, such a universal state is impossible; in a world composed of ideal states, it would be neither desirable nor necessary.

Let us first take the world as it is. The prospects of peace and unity are dim precisely because fights among nations are worse than feuds among men before states appeared. Men finally became aware and convinced of their common interest in establishing civil societies, but their purpose was to protect the "ins" against the "outs." It was not an end to competition, merely a *displacement* of it. There is, then, a difference not merely of degree but of essence between the creation of a state and the building of the world state: the former merely *orders* conflict (in the sense of abolishing domestic violence, but allowing and indeed fostering external turmoil); the latter would *eliminate* the competitive use of force.[64] Moreover, this ordering of conflict, to the extent that it makes international war so much more formidable than the state of war in *de facto* society, further weakens the influence "common-interest" arguments can exert upon states. The earlier violence was still anarchic and mild enough to be overcome by such reasoning, but wars among states have become institutionalized; the more intense the fighting, the higher the stakes (in the sense of being greater and being more distant from the citizens' lives, with such elements as national pride and prestige involved), and the more devastating the effects, the less likely are rational arguments of common interest to be heard. Indeed, Rousseau suggests that one component of the original "law of nature," the remnants of which may have played a role in convincing men to abolish war among themselves, has left even fewer traces (and thus kept far less vigor) among states—compassion.[65] So we are faced with units—the states—whose *amour-propre* (hence insecurity) is far more inflated than finite man's could ever be and whose compassion is practically nil. Finally, we must not forget that international conflict is a safeguard for tyrants: world insecurity assures domestic security; for them, would not world peace entail domestic insecurity?

Thus one comes to a triple and dismal conclusion. The only combinations of states likely to emerge in the world are competitive ones, alliances and leagues whose members temporarily agree to suspend the competition among themselves in order better to resist or to attack other contenders. The "general society of mankind," which existed neither in the original state of nature nor in the corrupt state of *de facto* society, is not likely to result from the international world either. Lastly, should the domination of one state be imposed on all others through conquest, the resulting world empire could not be the carrier of world peace, for the rule of force can never become legitimate: the compact between conqueror and conquered, "far from liquidating the state of war, assumes its continuance."[66]

But what about the ideal world—that of *The Social Contract?* Here again, a world federation or a world state is ruled out. A federation with a legislative body and coercive powers would conflict with the character of sovereignty as defined in *The Social Contract*: sovereignty is indivisible. The essence of the general will—indestructible, inalienable, incapable of being represented—is such that any formula of shared legislative powers, which federation requires, would destroy that identity of freedom and authority which *The Social Contract* purports to achieve, and would restore heteronomy.[67] Moreover, such a federation would rule over far too vast a territory; Rousseau believed that chances for autonomy exist only in small states; like Montesquieu and like the Greek philosophers, he saw large states as major threats to freedom.⁶⁸ A world-wide "city of the Social Contract" was inconceivable, since the legislative general will could not assemble in any given place. The bigger the state, the weightier the bureaucracy; the greater the need for a strong (i.e., dangerous) executive, the greater the need for intransigent virtue among the citizens; the smaller the likely "ratio in which the wills of individual citizens stand to the general will or, in other words, customs [*moeurs*] to laws," the greater the need for repressive force.⁶⁹

All those arguments convinced Kant, too, of the impossibility of a world government. If we start with Rousseau's conception of the ideal state—small, ruled by an indivisible general will—then the only links among states that do not conflict with it are confederations, which may have common executive organs appointed or instructed by the legislators, but in which the legislators (i.e., the general wills) would remain separate national entities. Associations of governments are possible, but not of peoples, just as Rousseau's idea of sovereignty rules out genuine local self-government except in the form of regional delegations from the executive.⁷⁰

Thus the road to a "general society of mankind" does not pass through a world government. Rousseau's constant sarcasms about "cosmopolitans" should be kept in mind.⁷¹ The arguments of a number of Frenchmen opposing European supranational institutions have a clearly Rousseauistic ring: there is, at present, no European nation, only a variety of European nations that wish to cooperate; *legitimate* decisions among them can be taken only by the agents of the separate popular wills; otherwise, the decisions would only represent either the will of one of those communities imposed on the others, or the will of "technocrats"—executive agents operating in a political vacuum. And not all Frenchmen who object to European supranationality (or to the spread of majority rule in the U.N.) are conservatives. In this respect (as well as in some of his constitutional ideas), General de Gaulle appeals to a certain Jacobin tradition that justifiably claims Rousseau as one of its prophets.

However, Jacobinism (not to mention General de Gaulle) brings to mind modern nationalism and particularly the militant nation-state that has often turned a war into a crusade. On this score, Rousseau has been accused of being the father of a form of social organization that has been a worse enemy of peace than the princes he so bitterly denounced. Who can deny that he did indeed constantly celebrate patriotism, identify the good citizen with the good patriot,⁷² lecture the Corsicans on the need for a national character,⁷³ and give the Poles a formidable list of recipes for the deliberate creation of a Polish national spirit that could defy the invaders and the ages?⁷⁴ In particular, the pages on national education in Rousseau's essay on Poland foreshadow the missionary zeal of the French First and Third Republics in this essential area of public life.

Here again, however, we must be careful. National pride: yes, Rousseau thought it essential, for it would lend its dynamism, indeed its substance, to the general will; but nationalism as we know it now, definitely not; not because Rousseau was unaware of its consequences—having noted that every patriot is harsh to foreigners, he added that this explained why the wars waged by republics are often worse than those waged by kings.[75] But, as we have observed, to Rousseau war was a source of tyranny and the perpetuation of all those evils of society which the "good society"—that of *The Social Contract*—aimed at eliminating. Indeed, he rejected *la religion du citoyen* as doubly evil: it made the citizens "bloodthirsty and intolerant" and it threatened the nation's security by impelling it into wars with all other nations.[76] Because he thought princes had a vested interest in war, he attacked them vigorously in his critique of St. Pierre's project—where republics are never mentioned.[77] Whoever wants to be free must refrain from becoming a conqueror, he told the Poles. Yet in order to be free, to obey only one's own (higher) will, one must keep invaders out—or if (like the Poles) one is too weak to do so, one must at least be able to prevent them from forcing the inner sanctum of the citizens' conscience into submission. This makes Rousseau's enthusiasm for a citizens' army understandable: to him, it is essentially a defensive army, incapable of undertaking aggression (to which a professional army is more suited), but more capable of making an aggressor's life untenable.[78]

Aggressive nationalism would have destroyed Rousseau's ideal. For he wanted a *polis* in which the irreversible consequences of man's entry into civil society—the development of passions and desires, the urge to look at one's reflection in other people's eyes, the mirror game of social vanity—could be channeled to good, i.e., moral, uses. Patriotism is such a good use, for it combines *amour-propre* and virtue.[79] The building of national character is an attempt to dissociate the two elements of *amour-propre*, vanity and pride, so as to smother the former under the latter. Vanity is the result of comparisons with others and of "the fruit of opinion"; pride is born of one's own achievements.[80] The competitions that he advocates for schools and public games, the medals and distinctions he recommends, the national (but not nationalist) celebrations he describes, are all efforts to make the seeds of human vanity sprout into flowers of legitimate collective pride.[81] Rousseau favors a kind of Stakhanovism among citizens, but one that aims at civic virtue, not at national power: the citizens are invited to compete with one another to such a purpose, not to compete with or compare themselves to foreigners.[82] And if he wants them to celebrate work, it is not in order to promote the state's grandeur, but because work is the condition and guarantee of civic virtue; whereas leisure and luxury, credit and speculation are the surest roads to corruption.[83] The Switzerland of his days or the United States of Tocqueville's would be much better examples than any of the new nations of the postwar world—precisely because events have made Rousseau's ideal impossible, as we shall see.

For the community of peaceful but proud nations Rousseau had in mind was a very special sort. Interdependence, the result of our proliferating needs and wants, is evil whenever it engenders dependence. (Rousseau's most eminent quality is one his critics have often denied him—consistency.) Independence, once society appears, is possible for man only in the modern form—not as isolation but as autonomy.

Autonomy can be sought in one of two ways. If man lives in an already corrupted society, he ought to be educated so as to be preserved from corruption and to fulfill himself apart from the polity: autonomy here means following the universal precepts of individual moral behavior, i.e., enjoying the benefits of civil society (a moral sense) without participating in its evils. This is the way of Émile. If man lives in a society that is still pure, autonomy means behaving as a citizen, following the imperatives of the general will —i.e., of man's higher self defined as the self that participates in and wants the common good of his community. This is the way of *The Social Contract*. But this latter kind of autonomy (the only one that really protects man from the disastrous effects of political decisions made without his consent and participation) can be achieved only in small communities. So, if they are to avoid becoming the stakes or the tools of others, these communities must be as self-sufficient as possible. They must aim at an autarky as different, as Iring Fetscher has shown, from the pre-belligerent autarky of Nazism as patriotism is from aggressive nationalism.[84] In the original state of nature, man, enjoying the "absolute existence" of an "absolute whole,"[85] was both independent and self-sufficient; in the ideal society, his independence is transmuted into autonomy, and independence and autarky become the attributes of the state. Indeed, only if the state is an "absolute whole" can the citizen be autonomous. Otherwise, the tyranny of world competition will rule the state, and the citizen can be neither free nor virtuous. "The nation will not be famous, but it will be happy. Others will not mention it. It will have little prestige outside. But it will have abundance, peace and freedom within."[86]

Rousseau's philosophy remains consistent also in its discontinuities. There is a break between man in the state of nature and man in society. There is a break between man-in-society brought up for himself and man brought up exclusively as a citizen. A third break lies between the ideal society, in which, so to speak, man is reconciled with himself, and the international milieu: so as not to live any longer in any sort of mixed system, the citizen of the good state will do his best not to be an actor on the world stage. Were the whole planet covered with small, essentially self-sufficient republics, endowed with civic pride but no national vanity and equipped with purely defensive militias, then the world *ipso facto* be at peace. A general society of mankind would emerge, composed not of "cosmopolitans" or "world citizens" but of good citizens—men who would have arrived at the modern, or social, equivalent of natural man's *amour de soi* and compassion, by curbing *amour-propre*, overcoming those passions which "speak louder than [their] conscience,"[87] and practicing patriotism without belligerency. However, this general society would not entail a "real union," with formal links between its member nations, just as there was no real union between men in the original state of nature.

The state of nature was a state of independent men who followed, in their rare encounters, the dictates of the (non-rational) natural law of self-preservation and compassion; the ideal international society would be like pearls juxtaposed but not on a string: independent states that would observe, in their infrequent and relaxed contacts, the commands of "rational natural law," the rules of the original natural law re-established, by reason, on new foundations.[88] Thanks to the self-sufficiency of each nation, our natural reluctance to inflict harm (i.e., our compassion) would no longer be stifled by fear of being harmed.[89] Whereas only through the social contract can man both escape his fallen state of nature and fulfill his moral development, it is now clear why there is no need to envisage a similar compact among states founded on the contract's formula.

Thus, the solution to the problem of war and peace, in Rousseau's mind, is really a "second-image" solution: establish ideal states all over the world, and peace will follow—without the need for a world league *à la* Kant. It is also a "first-image" solution: in the ideal state, man's nature is rescued from the despondency of mixed systems, and he is again at peace with himself. Here, we are very far from contemporary schemes for world peace and very close to the Greek ideal of the primacy of domestic politics: the road to peace passes through the ethical (small) state.

However, there is no guarantee that all states will ever be ideal or ever be capable of practicing the austere virtues of the frugal, self-sufficient nation. Some may continue to depend on others for food or other supplies and thereby risk becoming objects in the international competition; others may be so naturally wealthy as to excite the envy of the "have-nots." All the causes of conflict, that is, may still be with us. Moreover, even if the princes disappear, we have no assurance that in some state the general will could not be corrupted, and superseded by a mere will of all, expressing nothing but human passions, or by a particular will. So, purely domestic reasons may also bring a return to international competition. Finally, when republics occasionally clash, the patriot's tendency to be "harsh toward foreigners" may once again overcome the "reluctance to inflict harm."

For such eventualities, and *not* for a world of peaceful, "general-will" states, Rousseau advocates confederations.[90] Those leagues are not the crowning of his theory, as Kant's league of states is for Kant the summit of mankind's grubby ascent. As in Montesquieu, confederations mark not the *end* of conflict but a way for a number of small states to get together, without sacrificing sovereignty, for defensive purposes in the world conflict. They do not signal international sunshine; they provide a shelter against the storm. This is the logic of peace-via-deterrence, rather than of peace-through-law.

Thus, Rousseau's answers to the problem of peace are two. On the one hand, a world *not* composed of ideal states admits of only two ways of mitigating conflict: the observance of those "true principles of the law of war," which he opposes to Grotius' precepts, and which are based on the postulate that war is a contest among states but not men[91]; the other way is the confederation. But the former is obviously too fragile to be effective: Rousseau himself tells us that nations obey legal rules only as long as they believe they have an interest in obeying them.[92] And the latter formula does not end folly: it merely provides small states with a way of being wise among fools[93]; it tells them to be hedgehogs in the midst of insecurity. We can only speculate for how long Rousseau thought such associations could be made to last; his analysis of international competition leads to skepticism about the solidity of the leagues he had in mind.

On the other hand, his principal answer—the ideal world of small, self-sufficient, self-centered states governed by the general will—is a "solution" to the problem of war only because it is an evasion of politics. Here, we find the most serious of the difficulties of realization to which I alluded earlier. Rousseau's ideal is utopian, in the first place, because it can hardly be achieved so long as the whole world is not covered with such communities; in the second place, because even if they had spread over the whole planet, they would remain what he wants them to be only under conditions that are hard to imagine. In order not to be dragged into the competition again—in order not to be diverted from the closed-circuit practice of patriotism into the open contest of ambition and vanity—the small community ought to be not just self-sufficient but *insulated*. Should its citizens have more than accidental or occasional contacts with foreigners, then they may be tempted to revert to the evil practice of "comparing oneself in order to know oneself." Presumably, the general will—which is always right—will remain unaffected by those contacts and comparisons. However, the judgment that discloses the general will is not always enlightened.[94] The broader the range of relations among communities, the greater is the peril of a resurgent collective *amour-propre* at the expense of the common good, and the risk of a rising tide of envy, fear, aggressiveness, or greed to corrode the general will. If the outside world is *not* to become the crack in the domestic synthesis of freedom and authority, then the world must remain a distant and very lightly pressing reality. Otherwise, the citizen's autonomy will be threatened.

These conditions are met only exceptionally, and never on a sufficient scale to abolish the state of war. Not every community can be an island, and even Corsica got into trouble. America in the nineteenth century would be a partial example, but, even then, she found herself in contact with others to the north and south.

Lessons may be learned from her experience. When a nation puts into practice Rousseau's teachings about patriotism and national character in a context not of isolation but of intercourse with other nations, the thin line between patriotism and nationalism tends to vanish, despite Rousseau's intent. The general will itself becomes corrupted, and the national institutions, however closely patterned after those Rousseau wanted, may be diverted toward the quest for all those stakes that princes traditionally pursue. Competition among citizens for patriotic distinctions can all too easily turn into competition in xenophobia. Whenever this happens, Rousseau's ideal is perverted in a particularly ugly way. When the state is the expression of the general will, and not just the secular arm of a tyrant or prince, then Rousseau's formula about wars being waged among *states* and not among *peoples*, affecting individuals neither as men nor even as citizens but only as soldiers, loses its point.[95] When the states *are* the peoples, when all the citizens are soldiers, wars come close to that evil from which Hobbes hoped the state would shelter the people—shocks in which whole populations are thrown against each other. Total war instead of complete peace; a general will that is right because it is national, rather than rational: Rousseau would have been aghast at such a perversion. He wanted the ideal of the general will realized in a context of isolation, but events have decreed otherwise. Self-government and self-determination spread in a context of international conflict.

In addition, not only has the historical context thwarted the ideal, but the evolution of the world economy and of communications has made nations even more interdependent and increasingly eager to join the race for wealth. The modern world has repudiated Rousseau's ideal of a community pleased with its frugality, proud of its austerity, hostile to machines and to division of labor, opposed to big cities or feverish social mobility. If nations want to be self-sufficient, it is only in the sense of having an economy balanced enough to withstand external shocks, but this implies a domestic expansion of production and wealth. Today's new nations behave as if there were an international obligation to furnish aid for their development—an obligation that increases mutual dependence and leads to a more frantic pace in the growth of the induced desires that industrial society engenders.

Paradoxically, Rousseau, who recognized that man could never revert to the state of nature, advocated for nations a return to an isolation that the march of history had proved impossible long before he wrote. But the paradox is more apparent than real, for he recognized also that most of the states of his day were too corrupt ever to be capable of applying the principles of *The Social Contract*: only a few small nations could still be saved—obviously not enough to make universal peace possible.[96] It follows that if that peace is obtainable only on Rousseau's conditions, we are condemned to the competition he so searchingly described. The question arising from this depressing conclusion is whether, despite Rousseau, peace cannot be reached in our world instead of in utopia. Here we must turn to Kant.

III

Both Rousseau and Kant identify peace and morality; both consider that the man who listens to the imperative of morality within him must want peace, and that the good community shuns war.[97] However, a sharp difference in their conceptions of man's nature and of society's role explains the different outcomes of their quests for peace. The battle between man's selfish desires and his moral imperative Rousseau describes as a consequence of *society*, which was responsible for the former and in which the latter emerges. But Kant sees this battle as a permanent feature of *man*: the moral imperative is already at work in the state of nature; it is that very imperative which creates a duty to get out of the state of nature; for, like Hobbes and in opposition to Rousseau, Kant argues that precisely because of those selfish desires, the state of nature is a state of war.

Consequently, society, which is the *cause* of a fall for Rousseau's man, since it frustrates and perverts the very moral sense it brings forth in him, Kant sees on the contrary as a *condition* of moral progress, since it is the prerequisite to the establishment of law and to moral action (obstacles to which it is the function of law to remove). But if society causes no fall, reform of society cannot bring redemption, either. In the ideal society of *The Social Contract*, man succeeds in subordinating his particular interests to the general will; thus, authority and freedom are reconciled, and the drama of man's moral division, the battle between the lower and the higher self, comes to an end; political and moral problems are solved together. For Kant, the best society is not the one that *makes* man behave morally, it is the one in which man is most free to behave morally if he wants to. If world peace presupposes republican states, it is because they are least likely to be bellicose. Kant's conception of constitutional government is less demanding than Rousseau's: it is almost the opposition between the open and the closed society. On the other hand, the establishment of republics all over the world does not eliminate the problem of war, as a world of "general will" communities would: man's evil propensities may still prevail. Hence there is a need for *additional* legal guarantees to make eternal peace less shaky, in the absence of the world republic that Kant rejects.

So, whereas Rousseau's solution to the problem of war is in the establishment of the good society, Kant, who found the root of war in man's nature, not in society's "denaturation" of man, could not fulfill the imperative of peace with the setting up of ideal states—hence the league for eternal peace. Yet, because man remains free either to heed the categorical imperative or to follow his selfish drives, Kant's peace plan would have set up merely a desirable goal, had it not been accompanied by a philosophy of history that turned this moral end into an historical terminus. Kant's paradoxical conception was of world peace achieved not because of man's moral progress but despite man's moral failings, and brought about not by man's deliberate efforts but by a hidden plan of nature that relies on two highly non-moral factors—catastrophes and the convergence of selfish interests. Both are supposed to lead nations to harmony through interdependence—the very opposite of Rousseau's ideal.

Rousseau's empirical theory contradicts in advance the main assumptions of Kant's system. Concerning the league of republican states, Rousseau pointed out that there were major differences between law within each of those states—law backed by the force of the citizens—and the law among them—law whose strength depends on the plausibility of ending conflict and competition, rather than the other way around. Rousseau's argument is that such an end to conflict is possible only as long as contacts between states are limited—in which case no such international law would be necessary. Should these contacts be intense—and intensity is precisely what

Kant's philosophy of history counts upon—then the league itself would become an arena and a stake for conflicting ambitions.

One international development of the past twelve years may serve as a test of these respective doctrines. Is not the West European community that has grown since 1950 an example of a league of states with similar constitutional regimes, having established among them what a modern writer has called a "security community,"[98] because of the lessons of two disastrous world wars and because of the convergence of particular interests, especially in trade and production? Ernst Haas' fine analysis of the uniting of Europe[99] has shown that it is precisely through this convergence of interests, interests that now focus on the common institutions Europeans have erected, that the European communities have expanded. Does Kant's philosophy of politics and history provide a better guide to peace than Rousseau's rejection of a philosophy of progress and his apparent conviction that nations have only a choice between abolishing foreign politics or doing their best to survive in the competition?

I doubt that the West European experiment would have dispelled Rousseau's gloom. He would have thought the nature of the enterprise much closer to his idea of a confederation against "unjust aggressors,"[100] than to the federal ideal advanced by many present-day optimists. On most matters that affect the vital interests of the participants, supranationality fades away, and decisions must be made in a very traditional manner. (See, for instance, what happened during the European coal crisis of 1959, in the negotiations on a common agricultural policy, and those on the admission of Great Britain to the European Economic Community.) The legislative powers of the Common Assembly are few, and the enforcing powers of the European civil servants remain sharply limited. To be sure, such a confederation suspends the use of force among its members. However, the reason why such an oasis of peace can bloom is not that world peace is getting nearer, but that an external danger has brought threatened nations together. There is a shift of alignments within a continuing state of war: no less, but no more. In relations among the confederates (due to the very persistence of the state of war), considerations of prestige and calculations of power count as much as cooperation for peace. The politics of the participants display enough jockeying for leadership, enough disagreements on purposes, functions, and institutions, and enough divergent estimates of the "common interest" to make Rousseau's pessimistic analysis relevant.[101] A defensive *external* common purpose does not eliminate the *internal* rivalries that international competition and the clash of *amours-propres* in close contact perpetuate.

In addition, the forces that have brought about the confederation are not unmixed blessings. Rousseau was dubious about the value of harmony forged out of catastrophes. He might say now that all the gains Europeans have made do not quite erase Europe's political collapse through world wars, or eliminate Europe's dependence on the United States for military security. He was dubious, too, of the contributions that selfish and commercial interests make to peace. He would have noticed that the very prospects of wealth and power—which attract members and applicants to the European community—also turn so successful an enterprise into an added cause of tension and fear in world politics as a whole. Those who are left out resent their exclusion. Those who want to enter produce divisions among those who are there already. Outsiders protest about discrimination. Insiders warn against dilution. After all, military conflict was only one aspect of the state of war as Rousseau defined it. He saw greed as a major source of trouble, quite capable of causing states to want to weaken one another—an intention that is the essence of the state of war.

IV

Whoever studies contemporary international relations cannot but hear, behind the clash of interests and ideologies, a kind of permanent dialogue between Rousseau and Kant. Kant put forward an ideal of international organization for peace that does indeed correspond to the categorical imperative of autonomy which survives in man's heart; this imperative will be frustrated as long as war prevents man from being his own master. Far from displaying the easy optimism and the underestimation of conflict into which later liberals fell, Kant draws the picture of a world dragged into peace by conflict and by greed; if the hope of progress is a duty that the imperative of autonomy imposes on us, the expectation of linear progress is a major fallacy. Rousseau tells us, however, that the very intercourse of nations breeds conflict; that if it is not possible to end such intercourse, the only remedies are fragile mitigating devices; that it is not enough to try to suppress violence, which is the mere expression of drives that are the essence of international politics—a point that contemporary writers and international organizations tend to forget, in their fascination with the nuclear monster. He reminds us that there can be no assurance that each nation will be able to remain its own master, for the competition itself may always become the overriding tyrant. Just as there is no real middle ground between the general will's austere democracy and *"le Hobbisme le plus parfait,"*[102] so there is no lasting shelter between the state of war and the utopia of isolated communities: there are merely differences of degree in the intensity of the struggle. Citizens are thus condemned to remain in a *système mixte* that permanently threatens the reconciliation of law and force which *The Social Contract* tries to accomplish.

The statesman's difficulty is that he *must* play the game of international competition, from which he can escape only exceptionally, and at the same time he *ought* not to lose sight of Kant's ideal. He ought not to give up the hope of a future world community, but he cannot act as if it already existed. Thus, his task comes at least as close to squaring a circle as the job Rousseau had set for himself in *The Social Contract*: how to fight for the particular interest of the nation so as not to jeopardize the eventual reconciliation of national interests, without which no "international community" could ever emerge. Only when the statesman succeeds in this is the tyranny of world conflict alleviated for the citizen. Rousseau's contribution is in the nature not of a solution but of a warning. Total success cannot take the form of a world Leviathan, which would be either artificial or arbitrary. Although total success requires, in Rousseau's vision, a world that the evolution of history has ruled out, nothing short of total success can be more than a temporary relief from that plague which, as in Camus' Oran, may at any time wake up its rats and send them to die in a happy city.

Notes

1. See the strange story of Rousseau's manuscript on federations, in J. L. Windenberger, *La République confédérative des petits États* (Paris, 1899), chap. 2.

2. One discussion, however, although incidental to a general analysis of Rousseau's politics, is admirable: Iring Fetscher, *Rousseaus politische Philosophie* (Neuwied, 1960), chap. 4.

3. Arnold Wolfers and Laurence W. Martin, eds., *The Anglo-American Tradition in Foreign Affairs* (New Haven, 1956), p. xiii.

4. First draft of *The Social Contract*, in C. E. Vaughan, *The Political Writings of J. J. Rousseau* (Cambridge, Eng., 1915), I, 447 ff. Vaughan's edition is the most useful to date of Rousseau's many, often fragmentary, political writings. Many of my references are to untitled fragments that are assembled in this book, in which case I have simply cited the pages on which they appear in the Vaughan edition, since this is how they can be most easily identified.

5. See *L'Esprit des Lois*, Book I. For a searching analysis of Montesquieu's concept of the state of nature and of laws of reason prior to positive laws, see Raymond Aron, *Les Grandes Doctrines de sociologie politique* (mimeo.; Paris, 1960), pp. 42–55. Two important differences distinguish Rousseau's and Montesquieu's state of nature: (1) in Montesquieu's state of nature, laws of reason, which he calls "relations of justice prior to positive laws" and which are moral standards and goals for men, already exist—in addition to the "natural law" derived from man's nature in the state of nature (self-preservation, sociability, etc.). In Rousseau's state of nature, only the latter exist (self-preservation and compassion). In this respect, Montesquieu is closer to Locke, Rousseau to Hobbes. (2) For Montesquieu, the state of nature is just an early stage of man's development; for Rousseau, it represents a state of liberty and happiness that makes society appear as the cause of man's fall and that can only be recaptured under the thoroughly new guise of moral autonomy and good citizenship. (Hobbes's state of nature, in contrast, expresses an analysis of human nature that remains valid in civil society, the latter entailing neither moral progress nor moral disgrace, but merely physical safety.)

6. *Discourse on Inequality*, Vaughan, I, 159 ff., 203 ff.

7. *Ibid.*, p. 203; and *Economie Politique*, Vaughan, I, 293–94.

8. *Ibid.*, pp. 305–6.

9. *L'Esprit des Lois*, Book I, end of chap. 2. Consequently, and paradoxically, the establishment of civil society is treated as beneficial both by Montesquieu and by Hobbes: the former sees it as the outcome of man's social inclinations and the remedy of early society's defects (*cf.* Locke); the latter sees it as man's chance for salvation from violent death. Rousseau, on the other hand, sees in most civil societies a perpetuation of man's fall.

10. Vaughan, I, 138.
11. *Discourse on Inequality*, Vaughan, I, 173 ff. See also Rousseau's *Essai sur l'origine des langues* (*Oeuvres Complètes*, Paris, 1905, Vol. I).
12. This, again, is very close to Montesquieu. See *L'Esprit des Lois*, Book I, chap. 3.
13. *Discourse on Inequality*, Vaughan, I, 179 ff.
14. First draft of *The Social Contract*, Vaughan, I, 448–49.
15. *Ibid.*, p. 447. Property, which Rousseau singles out in the second *Discourse* as a crucial factor in inequality and consequently in violence, should not be seen as a *cause* of war but as a *consequence* of the "cupidity" and insecurity that dominate men once their original isolation comes to an end.
16. Hobbes, *Leviathan*, chaps. 13, 17.
17. *Ibid.*, chap. 13.
18. Montesquieu, *op. cit.*, chap. 3.
19. See Vaughan, I, 300; *Leviathan*, chap. 13.
20. Vaughan, I, 313.
21. Montesquieu, *op. cit.*, chap. 3, and Book X, chaps. 2, 3.
22. Vaughan, I, 312–13.
23. *Discourse on Inequality*, Vaughan, I, 203 ff.; first draft of *The Social Contract*, Vaughan, I, 447 ff., and *Project for Corsica*, Vaughan, II, 308 ff.
24. *Discourse on Inequality*, Vaughan, I, 178.
25. *Ibid.*, and Vaughan, I, 297. Strangely enough, Proudhon, who spent so much time attacking Rousseau, follows Rousseau very closely in Volume II of his book *La Guerre et La Paix*: it is the same attack on greed, property, and inequality as in Rousseau's second *Discourse*; war is seen as the result of disputes over wealth, due to the end of primeval abundance and to the "somber rapacity" that grips societies when man's original temperance fades away.
26. *Discourse on Inequality*, Vaughan, I, 180, and Vaughan, I, 294; II, 29.
27. *Discourse on Inequality*, Vaughan, I, 180.
28. Vaughan, II, 29.
29. *L'État de Guerre*, Vaughan, I, 297–98.
30. *Ibid.*, pp. 298–99.
31. *Discourse on Inequality*, Vaughan, I, 182. It can be seen from what precedes that Rousseau finds the causes of war not only in the structure of a milieu of clashing sovereignties, but also in the corrupt nature of existing states, and in the "evil propensities" of man, the last due not to his original nature but to the "fall" that society entailed and almost all states have perpetuated.
32. Vaughan, I, 295, 365.
33. Vaughan, I, 304–6; *Emile*, Vaughan, II, 158.
34. Vaughan, II, 147.
35. *Discourse on Inequality*, Vaughan, I, 179–81.
36. *Critique of St. Pierre's Project*, Vaughan, I, 389 ff.
37. Kant, "Idea for a Universal History," in *The Philosophy of Kant*, C. J. Friedrich, ed. (New York, 1959), p. 128.
38. *Discourse on Inequality*, Vaughan, I, 182.
39. Vaughan, I, 365. Man was not the "enemy of mankind" either in the original state of nature, when he was a peaceful being, or even in *de facto* society, when his contacts with others may have been bloody but were limited in scope; see Vaughan, I, 453.
40. Vaughan, I, 374.
41. Vaughan, I, 300.

42. Vaughan, I, 371 ff.
43. Vaughan, I, 304-5. Compare Aron, *Peace and War*, chap. 23.
44. Vaughan, II, 308.
45. Vaughan, I, 299.
46. Vaughan, I, pp. 389, 391, 392.
47. E.g., the U-2 affair in 1960, the United States' insistence on piercing the Soviet wall of secrecy; the Soviet Union's inclusion of proposals aiming at the dismantling of America's foreign bases in all its disarmament plans.
48. See Hoffmann, "Les règles du jeu," *Les Cahiers de la République*, March, 1962.
49. Vaughan, I, 390-91.
50. Vaughan, I, 391.
51. The most brilliant contemporary analysis is in Aron's *Peace and War*, "Introduction" and "Final Note." Rousseau's and Aron's arguments contradict the faith in moderation advocates of the "national interest" as the norm of foreign policy have so often proclaimed in recent years.
52. Vaughan, I, 391.
53. *The Legal Community of Mankind* (New York, 1954), esp. p. 199.
54. Vaughan, I, 388.
55. Vaughan, I, p. 396.
56. One study has aptly pointed out the three main reasons why all disarmament negotiations have failed: the desire of states to catch up when they are behind in the race, security fears, and difficulties of enforcement. Evan Luard, *Peace and Opinion* (Oxford, 1962), chap. 2.
57. Compare Arnold Wolfers, "The Pole of Power and the Pole of Indifference," *World Politics*, IV (October, 1951), 39-63.
58. Vaughan, I, 297.
59. This is what I attempted to do in: "Du Contrat Social, ou le mirage de la volonté générale," *Revue Internationale d'Histoire Politique et Constitutionnelle*, October, 1954, pp. 288-315.
60. Waltz, *op. cit.*, p. 232.
61. *Ibid.*, pp. 185-86.
62. *Discourse on Inequality*, Vaughan, I, 180-81.
63. Vaughan, I, 450-51.
64. Or, more accurately, it would reserve to the world-state the monopoly of the legitimate use of force.
65. *Discourse on Inequality*, Vaughan, I, 182.
66. Vaughan, II, 31 (and in general, Book I, chap. 4 of *The Social Contract*).
67. See the reasoning in Windenberger, *op. cit.*, chap. 6.
68. See Vaughan, I, 484 ff.; II, 56 ff., 64 ff., 154, 442-43.
69. Vaughan, II, 66.
70. See Hoffmann, "Areal Division of Powers in the Writings of French Political Thinkers," in A. Maass, ed., *Area and Power* (Chicago, 1959), pp. 120-24.
71. Vaughan, I, 182; II, 144-45. See also the passage on Socrates and Cato in *Economie Politique*, Vaughan, I, 251-52.
72. Iring Fetscher, *op. cit.*, pp. 194 ff.
73. Vaughan, II, 319.
74. Vaughan, II, 319, 348 ff., 431 ff.
75. Vaughan, II, 144.
76. Vaughan, II, 129.
77. Vaughan, I, 389-92.

78. Vaughan, II, 486–92.
79. Vaughan, I, 251. See Fetscher, *op. cit.*, pp. 62 ff.
80. Vaughan, I, 217; II, 319, 344–45, 441.
81. Vaughan, II, 434 ff.; Fetscher, *op cit.*, pp. 194 ff.
82. See esp. Vaughan, II, 437 ff.
83. Vaughan, II, 346–47. See also the remarkable passage: "In all that depends on human labor, one must carefully rule out machines and inventions capable of making work shorter, of reducing the amount of manpower needed, and of producing the same results with less effort." Vaughan, I, 320.
84. *Op. cit.*, pp. 241 ff.
85. Vaughan, II, 145.
86. Vaughan, II, 353. Abundance here means the welfare that accrues from the citizens' work, not from private wealth: "everybody must live and nobody must get rich. . . . Poverty became noticeable in Switzerland only after money had begun to circulate." Rousseau's distrust of commerce and finance runs through *The Social Contract*, the second *Discourse*, and the *Project for Corsica*: the Corsicans are invited to be a pastoral nation, for in agricultural self-sufficiency lies independence; in commerce lies wealth, but wealth brings dependence. Vaughan, II, 311, 322, 330.
87. Vaughan, I, 452.
88. Vaughan, I, 138.
89. Vaughan, I, 494.
90. Here, again, Rousseau learned much from Montesquieu. See *L'Esprit des Lois*, Book IX, chaps. 1–3. On Rousseau's confederations, see Vaughan's discussion, I, 95 ff.
91. Vaughan, II, 159.
92. See Windenberger, *op. cit.*, pp. 143–44.
93. Vaughan, I, 387; II, 158.
94. Vaughan, II, 50.
95. Vaughan, I, 300 ff.
96. *Oeuvres*, IX, 287; Vaughan, II, 146.
97. On Kant's philosophy of peace, see C. J. Friedrich, *Inevitable Peace* (Cambridge, Mass., 1948), and Pierre Hassner's admirable study, "Les Concepts de guerre et de paix chez Kant," *Revue française de science politique*, Vol. 11 (September, 1961). I have followed Hassner's demonstration.
98. See Karl Deutsch *et al.*, *Political Community and the North Atlantic Area* (Princeton, N.J., 1957).
99. *The Uniting of Europe* (Stanford, Calif., 1958); "The Challenge of Regionalism," *International Organization*, Vol. 12 (Autumn, 1958).
100. Vaughan, II, 158.
101. Compare Aron, *Peace and War*, pp. 729 ff.
102. Vaughan, II, 161.

# 3

Raymond Aron and the Theory of International Relations

I

The scope of Raymond Aron's work has always caused his commentators and his disciples to despair. Many unpublished works will probably be released in the near future. However, Aron's death makes it possible to study in depth, at last, his scientific contribution and to separate the two activities which he led jointly and never fully distinguished: journalism, or commentaries of current events which he thought he had the duty to clarify and to interpret, and theoretical writings, the works of a philosopher of history who was also a sociologist of contemporary societies and a critic of the social and political thought of most great writers in history.

The only purpose of this essay is to sum up Raymond Aron's scientific contribution to the theory of International Relations. I will therefore leave aside books, or parts of books, that deal primarily with current affairs, nor will I examine that part of his work which takes the form of historical narrative, for instance the major parts of *The Imperial Republic*. Nor will I discuss the first volume of *Clausewitz*, which belongs in the realm of the criticism of ideas, nor repeat what I wrote 30 years ago in my detailed account of *Peace and War*, shortly after the publication of this master work in France (Hoffmann, 1965). However, at the end of this essay, I discuss a posthumous publication in which he re-examines his own main concepts and contributions.

Nobody who reads again Raymond Aron's enormous work can fail to be struck by its originality. He was original by comparison with earlier French writers. Until the early 1950s foreign policy and the relations among states had been the bailiwick of historians, of lawyers and to a lesser extent of economists. Raymond Aron is the man who, in France, almost single-handedly created an autonomous discipline of international relations at the crossroads of history, law, and economics, but also of political science and sociology. This discipline, as he conceived it, consisted in a coherent and rigorous system of questions aimed at making intelligible the constant rules and the changing forms of a specific and original type of social action: the behavior on the world scene of the agents of the units in contest, i.e.

diplomats and soldiers. This is what he called diplomatico-strategic behavior. The laws and forms of this behavior were already being studied during those same years by important colleagues of Aron in the United States. In all his books and articles he never ceased dialoguing with his American counterparts, and particularly with Hans Morgenthau, the German *émigré* thinker whose influence both on academics and on practitioners has been so enormous in the United States. He also exchanged ideas with Henry Kissinger, who was both an academic and a practitioner. But even if one compares him with American specialists of international relations, Aron seems strikingly original. As we shall see, his mind had a broader scope, his constructions were much more flexible (hence many criticisms by American authors in desperate need of certainty), and his analyses sometimes preceded those which appeared on this side of the Atlantic.

II

Raymond Aron's ambition was doubly paradoxical—but he was a master at paradoxes—his thought was both bold and modest. What could have been more bold than his determination to offer a general theory, starting from the specific features of international relations: the 'multiplicity of autonomous centers of decision and therefore the risk of war' (Aron, 1962: 28) or, another way of putting it, 'the legitimacy and legality of the actors' resort to armed force' (Aron, 1972: 363). A number of important features follow from this. First, all actors must observe an imperative rule of behavior: 'the need to calculate means' (Aron, 1962: 28). Second, he derived from his starting point six fundamental questions for the study of diplomatic contellations. Three of these were objective questions: the scope of the field, the constellation of power relations in this field, and the techniques and technology of war. There were also three subjective, or 'ideologico-political' questions: mutual recognition or nonrecognition among the actors, the relations between domestic and foreign policy, the meaning and goals of foreign policy. Third, he formulated his substantive answers to these questions through the study of international systems and the typology of these systems. He defined systems as milieus organized for and through the competition among the units, and his key distinction is between multipolar and bipolar systems.

Systems analysis had become quite fashionable and developed in the United States towards the end of the 1950s. But Raymond Aron's approach was original in two ways. On the one hand, since he starts from the *distinctiveness* of international relations, from the fundamental difference between foreign policy and domestic politics, between the ideal type of strategic-diplomatic behavior (no power above the units, no or few common values) and the ideal type of domestic or, so to speak, civic behavior, he takes great care to use only concepts characteristic of international relations. In contrast, his American colleagues often resorted to 'concepts which also can be used in realms other than international affairs' (Aron, 1972: 362), such as power and conflict. Raymond Aron always carefully indicates the difference between 'power politics' as it unfolds in a milieu which is dominated by the risk of force among competing units, and the use of coercive power within a domestic community by a state which has (to use Weber's definition) the legitimate monopoly of this power. He also distinguishes tensions and conflicts—the raw material of any society—from wars, which are violent conflicts among political units. On the other hand, the conception of systems that Raymond Aron developed, and his opinion about their constraining or determining power over the units which are the system's constitutive elements, are much more modest, for instance, than the claims of Morton Kaplan for system dominance.

This is the other, and perhaps most interesting side of his theoretical undertaking. Nobody has shown more convincingly how impossible it is, in the field of international relations, to succeed in establishing a 'hypothetico-deductive system in which the relations among the terms or variables would take a mathematical form' (Aron, 1972: 358). This is so because unlike other kinds of social actions, the behavior of the diplomat and of the soldier has no 'rational end' (Aron, 1962: 28) comparable to the goal of the football player (winning) or to the ends of economic actors (maximization of satisfactions). Several conclusions follow from this. First, theory cannot go much beyond a 'conceptual analysis', whose objective is 'the definition of a subsystem's specificity, the listing of the main variables, and the formulation of some hypotheses about the system's functioning' (Aron, 1972: 366-367). Second, it is much more difficult than in the case of economic theory to separate such abstract theory or conceptualization from the concrete sociological and historical study, the logic of behavior from the specific characteristics of the actors. Only the concrete study can help make the behavior of the actors, their calculations of forces, and the stakes they give to their conflicts intelligible. In order to understand an international system one cannot simply grasp the rules of the game among abstract entities or variables called x, y, or z; one must know what the distinctive features of well-differentiated national states are. This is why systems are 'in the epistemological meaning of this term, indefinite'; 'from no theory could one deduce as an inevitable consequence the industrial assassination of millions of Jews by the Nazis' (Aron, 1972: 368); nor can one deduce those transnational relations among individuals or those interstate transactions which constitute peaceful trade among communities. In other words, Raymond Aron's conceptualization leads to the theory of what Jean-Jacques Rousseau had called the 'state of war', but not to the theory of transnational society or of the world economic system, which follow other rules and another logic. Even within its more limited and legitimate domain the theory of the state of war, by itself, does not allow one to grasp the behavior of the actors.

When Aron deals with this behavior his analysis seems to belong within the realist school, the most illustrious and venerable school of international relations. Its members include the very founding father of the study of interstate affairs, Thucydides, as well as Machiavelli, Hobbes, Max Weber (whom Raymond Aron admired so much) and among contemporaries E. H. Carr, Hans Morgenthau, Reinhold Niebuhr, and George Kennan. All 'realists' agree on the following points: the need for the units to calculate forces, the decisive role of force among the ingredients of power, the permanence of national ambitions and of threats to survival, the imperative of a balance of power, the impossibility of an 'ethics of law' and of peace through law, the wisdom of an ethics of responsibility instead of an ethics of conviction, the importance of geopolitical factors in the definition of states' goals, the preponderant role of states among all the actors on the world stage, and the possibility of conceptualizing politics as 'the intelligence of a personified state' (a concept Aron borrowed from Clausewitz) rather than as the intelligence of a class, ideology, or complex and indeterminate bureaucratic process.

However, if one compares Raymond Aron to the other realists one discovers four series of differences. The most important is conceptual. On the one hand, as I have already indicated, Aron parts company with Machiavelli, Hobbes, and Morgenthau. He refuses to see in the quest for power the essence of all politics; he carefully distinguishes foreign from domestic policy and between power as a means and power as an end. On the other hand, within the specific domain of international relations Aron distrusts catch-all concepts which at first sight appear to grasp the specificity of diplomatico-strategic behavior, but, when used, turn out to be equivocal or dangerous. This is why he acidly criticized the notion of the national interest which was the keystone of Morgenthau's theory. He saw in it a formula derived from 'the practice and the theory of happy eras', during which there existed 'an unwritten code of what was legitimate and illegitimate', whereas during revolutionary eras 'no state limits its objective to the national interest defined in the way Mazarin or Bismarck did' (Aron, 1972: 475); in these periods, the national interest is essentially defined in ideological terms.

Second, Aron's critique of excessively abstract or simplistic concepts is tied to a crucial feature of his unique understanding of realism. He links up with Thucydides, and so to speak, plunges theory into history in order to prevent theory from ever going beyond the teachings of history and from becoming more rigid and more prescriptive than history allows. In this respect, the contrast between Aron and American theorists is striking. He shares neither their normative ambitions nor their faith in the possibility to predict events. He also wants to submit general concepts to the touchstone and criticism of history. For Aron, theory's mission is both to complete, and to be inserted into, the 'historical sociology' of international relations. For it is history which shows the indeterminate nature of systems. Aron has always rejected determinism and monistic theses which try to explain complex phenomena through a single factor (Aron, 1983: 293). He has always sought to distinguish the deeper causes of events from accidents, and to show how the conjunction of different historical series proceeds. 'The course of international relations remains supremely historical in all the meanings of this term: there are unceasing changes, the systems, which are multiple and fragile, suffer the effects of all the transformations, decisions taken by one man or a few set into motion millions of people and provoke irreversible mutations' (Aron, 1972: 379-380). It is in *The Century of Total War* (Aron, 1951), the book in which he analyzes the origins and dynamics of the First World War, that he has most incisively shown how a 'diplomatic failure' and a 'technical surprise' converged in producing a catastrophe nobody had wanted, a 'hyperbolic war' nobody had foreseen. Many years later, in his book on American diplomacy, he showed once again both the inevitable nature of the Cold War and the much more accidental character of many of its developments.

A third important difference concerns the idea of the primacy of foreign policy which one finds among so many 'realists'. Kenneth Waltz, who can be identified with the realist school and who has tried to build as rigorously as possible the foundations of a theory of international relations (Waltz, 1979), has attempted to reduce theory to the study of the relations between a system's 'structure' (defined as the distribution of power among the units) and the relations among these units. This approach excludes taking into account all of the subsystems constituted by political and economic regimes, by social relations and by ideologies within societies. Even if, as in *The Imperial Republic*, Aron sometimes dealt too briefly or superficially with the domestic determinants of foreign policy, he asserted that 'the theory of international relations does not entail, even in the abstract, a discrimination between endogenous and exogenous variables' (Aron, 1972: 371). It is 'the similarity or, on the contrary, the hostility of the regimes that exist within states' (Aron, 1983: 452) which dictates the crucial distinction between homogeneous and heterogeneous systems which Aron had borrowed from the Greek author P. Papaligouras. This distinction follows from the idea that 'the external behavior of states is not determined by the ratio of forces alone' (Aron, 1962: 108); objectives are at least partly set by the nature of the regime and by its ideology. The outcome of the limited conflicts of the nuclear era is no longer dictated by the ratio of forces alone. Witness the results of the war in Vietnam; in Vietnam, it was the impossibility of reaching the political aim, a South Vietnamese government capable of defending itself alone, which led to the military defeat of the stronger power (Aron, 1972: 548). Aron, when he analyzes the weight of domestic conditions in international relations, mainly underlines two points. One is the importance of the nature of the regime. Contrary to what some pseudo-realists have said, the foreign policy of the Soviet Union, according to Aron, differs profoundly from that of Czarist Russia (Aron, 1972: 433). Ever since *Le grand schisme* (Aron, 1948) Aron has carefully studied the peculiarities of Soviet foreign policy and the different interpretations which have been formulated about it. The other point concerns the knot that ties together civil wars and interstate wars—an idea which again links Aron with Thucydides: 'one cannot imagine a nonviolent diplomacy as long as one has not eliminated violence from intrastate politics' (Aron, 1962: 717). This is why he has shown so much interest in the theory and practice of revolutionary wars (particularly in the chapters on Lenin and Mao in the second volume of *Clausewitz*) and in the factors of domestic conflict in the Middle East, the most dangerous zone of troubles.

The last difference between Aron and contemporary 'realists' is about the relations between the interstate system and the world economic system. Concerning the latter, realists have, on the whole, tended either to neglect it or to deny it its autonomy within international relations. Insofar as the world economy, as in the 19th century, seemed to belong primarily in the realm of transnational society, i.e., of exchange relations between private individuals and groups, rather than in the realm of interstate relations, realists have ignored it. And realists have assimilated the world economic system to diplomatico-strategic conduct, insofar as relations among states formed the main part of this system, as during the mercantilist era: their analysis of the world economy thus proceeded in terms of power rather than wealth, zero-sum gains rather than growth, and conflict for resources rather than cooperation and trade. What mattered were the rules of the game imposed by the mightiest state in its own interest.

Aron has never written a systematic study of the world economic order comparable to *Peace and War*. But he has dealt with it here and there, and reached much more subtle conclusions than the realists. On the one hand, he too understood that even during the liberal era it was the dominant economic power, Great Britain, which set the rules of the monetary and commercial game; but, on the other hand, he recognized that insofar as the world economy is part of interstate relations it is nevertheless partly independent from the diplomatico-strategic system. The logic of behavior of the dominant power—England in the 19th century, the United States since 1945—is not a simple extension of the logic of military power. Rules of the world economy cannot be reduced to the quasi-warlike rules of mercantilism; the system of the gold exchange standard and later the Bretton Woods system have allowed the rivals, first of England and then of the United States, to prosper and to grow.

Nor do these remarks of Aron coincide with the theories of the 'interdependence school', i.e. the American neorealists who also show the difference between strategic action linked to the use of force and economic action undertaken (not only by states but also by other actors such as multinational enterprises and international organizations) in areas where the resort to force makes no sense. The difference between the pioneers of interdependence theory and Aron owes less to a disagreement over that theory than to Aron's skepticism concerning what might be called the underlying ideology behind the theory, the ideology of a 'fading away of sovereignties' (Aron, 1976: 284), of a sort of gradual pacification of international relations through the extension to the realm of 'complex interdependence', of a gradual loss of importance of the diplomatico-strategic system, and of a growing regulation of world order thanks to 'international regimes'. According to Aron, the constraints which limit the sovereignty of some actors are either voluntarily (i.e. not irreversibly) accepted by these states (for instance the open world market) or else they are imposed by the more mighty states; and it is always the interstate system based on calculations of force which dominates international society, even if, in daily affairs, a major war has become less likely and the restraints imposed by economic interdependence are more visible.

Thus Aron's relation to the pure realists and to the neorealists is complex, but his opposition to the Marxist-Leninist conception and to the kind of diluted Marxism represented by the 'dependencia school' is sharply marked. Just as he criticized the concept of the national interest, he many times dismantled the Leninist theory of imperialism. He showed the weaknesses in Lenin's reasoning (a concatenation of postulates each one of which was in contradiction with the facts and not necessarily linked with the other postulates). He also noted that the phenomena which this theory claimed to explain—colonial conquests or wars among imperial powers—could be explained by other factors, such as the strategic-diplomatic contest. This same rejection of an 'inexorable dialectic which passes over the heads of men' instead of studying 'the action of some men and some interests' (Aron, 1972: 499), is evident in Aron's critique of the theory of exploitation of the periphery by the center. The theory seems to him doubly debatable, insofar as economic exploitation is not demonstrated everywhere (in certain cases the periphery has benefited from the investments of capital by the center much more than it has suffered from them) and insofar as economic exploitation is a phenomenon different from political domination. In this area as in all the others Aron remained tied to the conception he had laid out in his *Introduction to the Philosophy of History* (Aron, 1938): history cannot be grasped in its totality, one can only study fragments of reality, and try to understand the relations among those fragments. Nevertheless, even if one has to resist the temptation of trying to grasp and account for wholes, one has to try to understand the logic and the causes of different types of behavior and to make them intelligible—even if the cost of thus lowering one's sight is a certain dispersion of analyses, or conclusions that seem like forests of question marks.

III

Nobody has more persistently tried to understand the nuclear era of international relations, to measure the extent to which the invention of weapons of total destruction revolutionized world politics, than Raymond Aron. Bernard Brodie and he were the first to define the meaning of that revolution: the possibility which a state that possesses a serious nuclear arsenal now has of *destroying* the state and society of an enemy, instead of having first to *defeat* its enemy's armed forces, as in the past.

The main contribution of Raymond Aron to our understanding of the new era consists of three series of analyses: the ambiguities of deterrence, the persistence of Clausewitz (i.e. of war and of the need for strategic calculations), the necessity and originality of the Cold War. Aron ceaselessly commented on and criticized American authors and actors who were trying to formulate and to apply the strategy of deterrence. He always knew that one of the consequences of the appearance of weapons of mutual assured destruction, one of the effects of what McGeorge Bundy has recently called 'existential deterrence' (Bundy, 1983), by contrast with the strategic *doctrines* of deterrence, was this: in the realm of strategic thermonuclear weapons, the notion of balanced forces cannot be reduced to a simple calculation of the number of warheads or missiles at the disposal of the rival states. 'There exists a balanced state of deterrence when each of the nuclear powers has the same capacity as its rival to deter a direct aggression or an extreme provocation.' This means, in the first place, that the nature of the weapons, the capacity to survive an enemy first strike and to penetrate the defenses of the enemy, is more important than numerical equality. Second, it means that since deterrence is 'a relation between two wills, the balance of deterrence is a psychotechnical equilibrium' (Aron, 1962: 669). Will or determination matters more than technological credibility. Third, 'resorting to allies in order to restore a fractured equilibrium is a thing of the past' (Aron, 1962: 670): if one of the two superpowers could either disarm or destroy the other without being destroyed or seriously damaged in return, the fact that the victim has a network of allies would not matter. Fourth, 'the credibility of deterrence presupposes a reference to the *whole* situation and can never be reduced to a simple military calculation.' What matters is knowing 'who can deter whom from what, through what kinds of threats, in what kind of circumstances' (Aron, 1976: 247). We are here in the domain of political art. The fifth consequence of the nuclear revolution is that arms which are so devastating but whose use perhaps exposes whoever resorts to them to total retaliation, do not constitute very useful means of political intimidation: 'nuclear blackmail, or the use of the nuclear threat toward positive ends, does not belong to the mental universe of statesmen. . . . These weapons' purpose is to destroy the positive intention—real or assumed—of the aggressor' (Aron, 1976: 242).

Thus, deterrence is not an exact science, and not only because of the decisive role played by will (in conformity with the Clausewitzian notion of war). In matters of deterrence 'it is impossible, by definition, to avoid one danger without increasing another' (Aron, 1963: 96). The more terrifying the menace, the more one threatens one's adversary with total destruction, the less the threat appears credible since each of the antagonists has the means of mutual assured destruction, even after having been hit by a first strike. On the other hand, the more one tries to make the threat credible by giving oneself the means of waging limited nuclear attacks, and particularly by giving oneself the means to strike the enemy's forces first, as in traditional war, the more one risks making war itself more conceivable. (This is true, I would add, especially since the enemy, whose strategic forces are to some extent vulnerable to the other side's first strike, will fear losing his weapons if he does not use them first.) The supreme threat—the threat of total destruction—is highly deterrent in the abstract, but not very credible since it is suicidal; and a counterforce threat is extremely credible, especially because of the recent revolution of accuracy, but it deters less. If one tries to reinforce its deterrent power, by increasing the risk of escalation (the nuclear version of what Clausewitz had called climbing to the extremes), by adding for instance tactical nuclear weapons to strategic ones, 'here again an antinomy appears,' according to Aron (1976: 162–163). 'Everything that increases the likelihood of escalation in advance contributes to deterrence but also makes it, by definition, more difficult to limit war if it breaks out after all.' Moreover, escalation is both 'a danger that one wants to avoid' (by trying to preserve thresholds, stages, distinctions between conventional war, tactical atomic war, limited strategic nuclear war, and mutual assured destruction) and 'a threat that one neither wants nor is able to give up' (Aron, 1963: 227).

There is a second antinomy which is no less important: the more deterrence works at the global level (i.e. the more stability exists on top), the less stability exists at the lower levels. Aron defines stability as 'a situation in which the duellists have an absolute incentive not to use their weapons because both have the ability to destroy one another, and neither has the ability to disarm the other' (Aron, 1976: 149). The less the superpowers will be tempted to use the absolute weapon, the freer they will feel to use conventional weapons unless, again, they deliberately multiply risks of escalation; but insofar as the threat of escalation becomes less credible and seems more like a bluff, the less it guarantees stability at those lower levels.

This connection between global stability and local turbulence explains precisely why one can write about the persistence of Clausewitz. Aron always asserted that nuclear weapons did not abolish but merely decentralized violence in two ways. First of all, they fragment the global system into subsystems each one with its own configuration, rules, and factors of interstate violence. This fragmentation is made even more remarkable by the fact that the other great contemporary revolution which Aron stressed so often is the extension of the diplomatic field to the whole world; because of the nuclear revolution, this single international system is divided up into pieces which are, so-to-speak, less dangerous for the whole but also more warlike than it; the 'total diplomacy' characteristic of a heterogeneous world system thus lends itself, despite everything else, to a certain limitation of stakes and means. Second, this decentralization of armed violence takes the form of intrastate violence, which the superpowers' competition sometimes creates and often exploits. In this complex world where, as Aron put it, one has had to save war (or rather wars: limited wars among states and often unlimited civil wars) in order to save mankind (from a nuclear war that might become total), the notion of a global balance of forces still matters, that of a regional balance matters even more. But one must understand that the outcome of armed conflicts is not determined by the ratio of thermonuclear forces. On this point Aron sharply distinguishes himself from American writers such as Paul Nitze who appear to believe that that ratio determines the outcome of regional confrontations; Aron's clear analysis of the Korean War, which 'was not influenced by the nuclear weapons of the United States' (Aron, 1976: 245), and his very subtle analysis of the Cuban missile crisis of 1962 (Aron, 1976: 144–151) reveal his doubts on this point. Moreover, the calculation of forces must include many factors other than the purely military ones, as Clausewitz had well understood (Aron, 1976: 235).

The nuclear revolution still preserves peace at the global level, despite everything which tends to weaken or to minimize it (such as the new possibility of counterforce strategies), and despite everything that tends to undermine the stability of global deterrence (such as the new vulnerability of several components of the strategic forces). The nuclear revolution also preserves peace in Europe, where the risk of escalation in the event of a conventional war remains enormous. At the same time violence is so-to-speak safeguarded and even multiplied at lower levels and in other parts of the world. One conclusion thus becomes unavoidable: the necessity of the Cold War or, to go back to the formula Aron had used as early as in *Le grand schisme*, 'peace is impossible, war is unlikely.' There will still be wars like those of Korea, Vietnam and the Middle East. But, on one hand, they remain limited: the Korean War appeared like 'a turning point' because it did not become hyperbolic; 'for the first time in its history the United States gave up the idea of total victory' (Aron, 1983: 302–303); a negotiated peace therefore becomes possible again. On the other hand, at the global level, crises among the superpowers become the substitutes for war. All the armed confrontations have taken place between third parties, or between a superpower and an ally or client of the other superpower. In the crisis one finds 'the casuistry of cooperation' and the 'casuistry of deterrence' (Aron, 1976: 164) intertwined; it is the idea of the common interest to avoid mutual destruction which prevails. This is why the Cold War, an inevitable consequence of heterogeneity and bipolarity, must be analyzed as profoundly different from war: 'I am trying to assert, against the dominant opinion, that the Cold War is not a war in Clausewitz's sense', since the characteristic feature of war is 'the predominant resort to physical violence' (Aron, 1983: 656). Even if 'the blurring of the line that separates peace and war' is obvious, peace has not become the continuation of war by other means. Even though thermonuclear weapons are not 'a diplomatic instrument that can be used at any time and in any place' in order to deter aggression, 'for the foreseeable future it is likely that general and total war will not occur' (Aron, 1983: 505).

IV

Aron has always believed that the theoretical and sociological analysis of international relations inevitably led to 'more or less uncertain recommendations, or prescriptions based on regularities or on obvious notions' (Aron, 1962: 563). The very indeterminacy of diplomatico-strategic behavior makes it possible to raise 'the Machiavellian problem', i.e. the problem of legitimate means, and 'the Kantian problem', the problem 'of universal peace' (Aron, 1962: 565). The normative implications of Aron's theory are contained within the contradiction between violent history and peaceful ideals, the contradiction between the constraints which weigh on the statesman, responsible for his country's interests in a world in which the use of force remains possible and legitimate, and moral conscience, which protests against the bloody anarchy of the international milieu and demands universal peace.

Raymond Aron has never systematically examined what possibilities remain for reconciling this imperative and those constraints. He was irritated by the kind of idealism whose recipes for escaping anarchy presuppose that the problem has already been resolved, and superbly push aside the enormous weight of constraints. He was eager to point out the debilitating weakness of international law and the unlikelihood of world federalism. He was even skeptical about the contribution that arms control negotiations between the superpowers could bring to the pacification of mankind. He distrusted 'beautiful souls' who were deceived by their own illusions. He disdained authors who recommend changing the behavior of a nation by acting on a single domestic factor, but who do not understand the multiple links between domestic and external factors and the perverse effects of dealing with a single one (Aron, 1972: 393-394). Overall he had decided early on to limit his own 'liberty of criticism' towards statesmen 'by asking the question: in his stead, what would I do?' (Aron, 1983: 644) (an attitude which risks depriving the commentator or critic of any perspective or distance, and courts, in other words, exactly the opposite danger from the one run by idealists who place themselves far above this contentious earth).

For all these reasons Aron had curbed his own Kantian inclinations—too much, for my own taste. He was a passionate liberal, but he was convinced that a pacified world, in which relations among human groups would at long last be governed by the categorical imperative, was impossible. As a good Kantian he knew that there is no moral duty to accomplish the impossible. He reminded his readers that, in the world as it is, it is often violence alone that allows liberal values to survive, or makes possible the survival or liberation of those few countries in which liberal values have been able to blossom, or provides a defense against totalitarianism (Aron, 1976: 285-286). Warning his readers against illusions was more important to him than attempting to discover how, the world being what it is, citizens and statesmen could nevertheless, more radically than in the past, try to cope with the deepest causes of collective violence and consolidate the chances for a lasting peace. Aron rarely hesitated to condemn domestic practices which were repugnant to his values. He was one of the first to create, in the 1930s, the category of 'totalitarian' regimes. But he was always much more reluctant to judge the foreign behavior of states, and for instance to condemn American behavior in Vietnam or even some episodes of American conduct there.

This rejection of moralism resulted partly from his contempt for those whom Kant called political moralists, i.e. ideologues at the service of the prince, and partly from his skepticism about the possibility of a moral politics following Kantian prescriptions. But he never went all the way, to the endorsement of immorality, nor did he ever accept what he called the ethics of struggle, 'which orders individuals to be brave and disciplined and to sacrifice themselves and which orders collectivities to keep their commitments and to care for their honor', but 'easily debases itself into becoming the ethics of criminals' and 'will never provide any perspective of lasting peace or universality' (Aron, 1962: 595). Aron had an ethics to propose. This disciple of Weber believed in an 'ethics of wisdom' which takes into account both the necessity to calculate forces, i.e. the duty of selfishness which states must obey, *and* the aspiration to universality, i.e. to a victory of that part of human nature which is not 'a beast of prey' (Aron, 1962: 596). He criticized Weber's own tragic realism because Weber believed that international relations were the closed arena of inexpiable conflicts of values, and that the statesman's duty was therefore only to promote national values by looking after the nation's might.

What gives a chance to such an ethics, what makes it possible not to find in the ethics of struggle the only possible one, is Aron's familiar distinction between the rational and the reasonable. Diplomatico-strategic conduct does not lend itself to mathematical treatment, there are no games with 'a mathematical solution defining rational behavior' (Aron, 1962: 756); this is even more true in the atomic era, since for all players 'thermonuclear war means an infinite loss' and one cannot 'calculate the rational decision when the loss risks being infinite'. The game is 'essentially historical and psychological' and therefore does not 'rule out reasonable behavior' (Aron, 1962: 763). On the contrary, what makes reasonable behavior even more desirable is the fact that the stakes are nothing less than mankind's survival, and what makes reasonable behavior even more possible is the fact that 'strategy in the thermonuclear age is more distant from the model of rational strategy than the strategy followed through the thousands of years of prenuclear armaments' (Aron, 1962: 763; 1976: 181).

The ethics of wisdom is that of moderation. It had already been advocated by Thucydides, through the speeches of his characters, and by Clausewitz as Aron analyzes him. (Aron, wrongly in my opinion, deemed Thucydides amoral.) Aron showed Clausewitz to be both the theorist of hyperbolic war, as an ideal type and as one of history's realities, *and* the philosopher who wanted to subordinate violence to political calculations and recommended a limitation of objectives, as in the other, more desirable, kind of wars. Like Thucydides, Aron knew that it is during civil wars that moderation is most impossible to preserve, and that it is when collective passions, class ideologies, or racial hostilities displace 'the intelligence of the personified state' that chances for moderation disappear: 'nothing guarantees the moderation of states, but the politics of a personified ideology or of a messianic class excludes moderation and entails a struggle to the death' (Aron, 1976: 263).

This is why Aron retrospectively condemned America's subordination, during the Second World War, of political objectives to military considerations, and why he criticized the allied objective of unconditional surrender (Aron, 1972: 452). This is why, for the future, he demanded that such a goal be ruled out even in the case of a general war (Aron, 1972: 490) and that communications be maintained among adversaries 'in order to avoid errors by excess or default' (Aron, 1976: 183). Now that 'decapitation weapons' have arrived, Aron's warning is of the greatest importance. What Aron calls for is 'political understanding', necessary in order to limit wars if they happen, in order to 'slow down escalation and bring the enemies back toward armed mutual observation' (Aron, 1976: 237-238), and in order to overcome and manage inevitable crises.

Thus, in the atomic era, it is the limitation of violence which wisdom requires. We must 'aim consciously at the geographical localization and toward reachable objectives, without total victory' (Aron, 1972: 491). Concerning strategic weapons, wisdom according to Aron is on the side of flexible response rather than massive retaliation. The latter risks being incapable of deterring the adversary from partial attacks; in this case, the attacked statesman would be forced, disastrously, to choose only between capitulation and total, suicidal war. Flexible response is a way of avoiding the all-or-nothing choice; it 'aims effectively at reducing to a minimum the risks of escalation and total war' (Aron, 1963: 139); the threat entailed by flexible response is, furthermore, less incredible; an important point, since deterrence cannot be based on a gigantic but incredible threat. Aron therefore always believed in the usefulness of increasing conventional forces, for such a course would make the threat of a limited or flexible resort to nuclear weapons more believable. According to him, escalation is not inevitable after a first use of nuclear weapons, especially as technological evolution brings forth more accurate and less devastating weapons; even after such a first use, opportunities for wisdom remain. This is one of the reasons why Aron saw no contradiction between a strategy of gradual resort to force (including if necessary a passage from conventional to nuclear weapons), and the preservation of the threat of a first use of nuclear weapons in case of a conventional war in Europe. Robert McNamara and the other fathers of flexible response today want the United States to abandon such a threat, because they believe that a first use in Europe would lead to total war and that the threat has therefore stopped being believable (McNamara, 1983: 59-80; Ball, 1983). Henry Kissinger has recently tended to move in the same direction. For several reasons Aron, however, did not want to give up this threat. Unlike the American Catholic bishops, he did not believe escalation to be fatal, especially if the nuclear weapons used were tactical ones. He thought that the threat, even if it is not totally credible, has the advantage of preserving uncertainty on the potential aggressor's side ('an element of bluff seems to be inevitable in diplomatic crises' [Aron, 1983: 462]). He feared that giving up the threat would in no way eliminate the risk of actual nuclear war breaking out. Finally, he believed that giving it up would signal that NATO would accept defeat rather than resort to nuclear weapons, something which he deemed neither entirely credible nor desirable.

This defense of a flexible strategy (of threat and of use) led Raymond Aron toward a rather critical attitude toward the French nuclear force, toward the theory of the equalizing power of the atom that General Gallois had developed 20 years before, and toward the French theory of deterrence of the strong by the weak. He saw in the French force a 'beginning of an insurance policy against the unpredictability of the diplomatic future' (Aron, 1963: 137) but nevertheless he deemed it devoid of credibility as a countercity force, except against a nuclear attack aimed at France alone, a scenario he thought quite implausible (Aron, 1976: 179). Furthermore, 'the political destiny of France cannot be separated from that of the rest of Western Europe, and the French force alone could not prevent the Sovietization of Europe' (Aron, 1983: 467). Therefore, in Aron's opinion, the usefulness of the French force lies less in its contribution to national independence than in the supplementary reinforcement it brings to the 'efficiency of the American force as a deterrent' (Aron, 1976: 179). The French force has some value only in the Atlantic Alliance; out of the alliance, it can only give France 'a reprieve' in order to adjust to Sovietization.

According to many people on the other side of the argument, flexible response and the development of means to wage limited wars—even limited nuclear wars—in the hope of avoiding escalation and the destruction of cities, risk making war conceivable and 'banal' again and making a resort to nuclear weapons more likely because it would appear less terrifying. Aron was aware of these objections. But he replied with three arguments of his own. First, it is impossible to enjoy a 'farewell to arms' at all levels, the world being what it is. Moreover, thanks to the 'paradox of our era: it is the possibility of unlimited violence which restrains effective violence even without any actual threat of resorting to it' (Aron, 1976: 183). (This is very close to Bundy's more recent speculations on the effects of existential deterrence.) Finally, since 'the principle of annihilation' no longer applies 'to armed forces alone, war, even absolute war, aimed at disarming the enemy' can no longer 'serve as an instrument of policy' (Aron, 1976: 283). Now that illusions about peace through law have also been blown away, there exists a chance for moderation. When the stakes are very high, it is now possible to commit the state's credit without necessarily ending in the 'cash payment' of a major war, and one should now be able to substitute limited stakes for stakes that are too dangerous because they are 'intangible and unlimited' (Aron, 1976: 182).

This is precisely why Aron, the archtypical vigilant anti-totalitarian liberal, asserted—against those in the United States who had proposed, in the past, a 'Cato-like strategy' against the Soviet Union, or who now proclaim that only a change of regime in Moscow could make coexistence possible in the long-term—that 'to survive is to win' (Aron, 1962: 654) and that the West needs to pursue a 'moderate strategy' (Aron, 1962: 687). It should have no illusions about transforming the Soviet regime from the outside. The West's triple goal ought to be 'physical survival through the avoidance of (global) thermonuclear war', 'moral survival by safeguarding liberal civilization', and peace 'through the mutual acceptance by both blocs of their right to exist' (Aron, 1962: 666). This is also why the very real risk of a 'suicidal explosion' (Aron, 1983: 304) coming out of limited wars appeared to him, toward the end of his life, less serious than the internal disarray of the West, the unpredictability of the United States, the serious malaise of West Germany, the gradual suicide of Europe. And thus Raymond Aron, always on the lookout for chances for wisdom, and although he reasserted the primary importance of the interstate system within international society, nevertheless acknowledged that the future of that system, now that the nuclear weapons of the superpowers neutralize one another to some extent, depends above all on domestic politics, the transnational movement of ideas and ideologies, and the evolution of the world economic system.

V

The problems besetting the international system preoccupied Aron throughout the last years of his life. A few months after his death, a book was published under his name. It consists of studies about present-day international relations. The bulk of this book is formed by an essay on which he was still working when he died, and whose title, 'The Last Years of the Century' ('Les dernières années du siècle'), was given to the whole book. This essay had a double purpose. The first one was to provide a new presentation of *Peace and War* in order both to reply to certain theoretical objections made against the very conception which Aron had used as the framework of his analyses, as well as to evaluate the changes that had occurred in the world since 1961 (the date of the completion of *Peace and War*). The other purpose was to think about threats and prospects in the future, from 1983 to the year 2000; Aron asked himself, as Oswald Spengler had done before concerning the end of the last century, whether these next years would be 'decisive'. When he died in October 1983, Aron had left two versions of his essay; a first draft was almost finished, a second version was incomplete. The published text is a kind of synthesis of the two drafts (Aron, 1984).

Thus, the book addresses itself to theorists, historians, and futurologists of international relations. As I indicated above, the theory developed in *Peace and War* had not satisfied lovers of general laws and determinists of all sorts. Aron had obstinately shown the indeterminacy of diplomatico-strategic behavior, the complexity of correlations, and the uncertainties of national might and of international systems. But this eclectic and synthetic work was based on a rigorous conception. Aron had borrowed from Jean-Jacques Rousseau the idea of a radical difference between the relatively well ordered condition of civil society and the warlike state of nature in which states find themselves. Moreover, within the multiple relationships which form a world society, he had only studied interstate relations in the diplomatico-strategic realm, thus neglecting the world economy and transnational phenomena (such as the movement of ideas) or supranational ones. Finally, he assimilated the state to a single actor making decisions.

In the last 20 years criticisms had multiplied against those postulates and choices. Some critics, impressed by the moderation which atomic weapons imposed on the superpowers, as well as by the moderation which the economic interdependence of states entails, have rejected the model of the state of nature altogether. Other critics, of a Marxist or para-Marxist orientation, believe that the study of world order must begin not with the relations among states, but with the world economic system, i.e. the relations between the capitalist center and the exploited periphery. Others still emphasize the complexity and incoherence of decisionmaking in modern states, where leaders, bureaucrats, and pressure groups fight it out. On all three points Aron in this essay maintained his original stand. According to him, the concept of the state as rational actor does not ignore the complexity of decisionmaking processes. Also, there is no 'causal predominance' of the world economic system: it is the interstate system, i.e. the competition of states, which determines the alternation of peace and war. Finally, the model of the state of nature is still relevant; or rather, insofar as the contrast between civil society and the state of war appears exaggerated, it is because, today, in many countries civil society itself is in trouble, either because of the heterogeneity of society or because of the internal effects of the competition which dominates interstate relations: the conflict between the United States and the Soviet Union. On these three points, Aron seems to me to be essentially right.

Those who are interested in the theory of world order will find in the second chapter of the posthumous essay a new analysis which goes beyond *Peace and War*: the analysis of the world economy. Aron discusses two notions which he criticizes for their excesses, without rejecting them *in toto*. The first is the notion of American imperialism. Aron recognizes the unique situation of the United States, because of its military power and because of the transnational role of the dollar. He denies that America exhibited a systematic will to exploit ('the Europeans owe their thirty glorious years of growth to the Americans'), and he concludes that American economic policy and diplomacy are neither independent of one another nor inseparable. He examines in less detail the theory of the exploitation of the periphery by the rich center, which he deems not proven.

The analysis of current issues provides the substance of chapters 3 to 6. Aron concludes that the main changes that have occurred in the last 20 years concern the relation of forces between the superpowers and the evolution of minds in West Germany. He continues to say that the ratio of nuclear strategic forces of Washington and Moscow has not determined, so far, the outcome of conflicts between the two rivals in any part of the world. But he fears that strategic parity will make the situation of Western Europe more dangerous. His concern about the 'coupling' between West European and American security explains not only his opposition to any American renunciation of the threat of a first use of nuclear weapons in case of a Soviet conventional attack, but also his strong stand in favor of the deployment of American middle-range missiles on West European soil.

The fragility of the relations among states and of the situation within states in the Middle East worries him even more. He mentions the contradiction between the Zionist dream and the reality of the state of Israel, based on force.

A longer chapter devoted to the Soviet Union rejects various theories or hypotheses—that of a possible collapse of the regime; that of Alain Besançon, according to whom there is no such thing as a Soviet economy (Aron compares it with a war economy in which two sectors exist, 'one to which everything good and everything possible goes and one to which one sends what is indispensable or what is left'), the theory of Castoriad about the rule of the military in Moscow, and the theory of some Reagan followers about the impossibility for the Soviet Union to sustain an accelerated arms race. For Aron the Soviet Union remains totalitarian: it still has a state ideology, and the civil society and the state are still indistinguishable. But he reaches complex conclusions about the Soviet Union's diplomatico-strategic action: the Soviet Union's successes are not primarily caused by military might, and the Soviet military buildup can be explained more by the will to meet the challenge of American power, and by the hope that an increase in Russian power will cause the disintegration of the adversary's coalition, than by a will to aggression.

As always, almost all of Aron's analyses are extraordinarily subtle and show his desire to be fair. This does not mean that one must agree on all points. I think that he overestimated the progression of the Soviet military machine and also, probably, the possibility of controlling a limited nuclear war, especially in Europe. In many places, he wrote that the American strategy of the 1970s was that of mutual assured destruction, which was dangerous for extended deterrence covering Europe. In reality, American strategic plans have always targeted military objectives first, not cities; it was in 1974 that the Secretary of Defense, James Schlesinger, proclaimed a doctrine of limited nuclear options, i.e., a limited counter-force doctrine. Mutual assured destruction, from the doctrinal viewpoint, was never more than an attempt at imposing a ceiling on the expenditures the military requested; on the other hand, it corresponds to a reality: the existence on both sides of means of destroying the whole world, the risk of escalation that exists even if the war begins only with attacks against military objectives.

These disagreements on concrete issues do not concern the forward look, Aron's answer to the question concerning the future. He gives it in the last two chapters of the essay. It is the same as in 1947: peace is impossible, war is unlikely. Between the Soviet Union, which is certainly neither saturated nor satisfied but cautious, which counts on a favorable evolution in various parts of the world, and which has no 'motive for urgent and dangerous action', and an insular America, the danger of an apocalyptic confrontation is small. According to Aron the Atlantic Alliance will last; instability in Central America should not lead to a world war. The most dangerous part of the world is the Gulf area; Aron is pessimistic about the future of the regimes in the Gulf states. He says that he is not among 'those who believe in a major war, waged with nuclear weapons, during the years to come.' In 1914, statesmen 'could not imagine what war would cost the winners and the vanquished alike'; in 1939 war had been wanted by 'a man who was following his demon'. Let us hope that in the relations of the superpowers, the only states capable of waging a general war, no demon-like or obtuse statesman will come and put an end to the mix of inevitable hostility and complicity which has preserved peace until now. Let us also hope that the race to new weapons (and new domains for weapons) as well as the importance of many stakes will lead statesmen neither to think again that they could wage war while avoiding the worst nor to calculate that a defeat might be worse than a war that could perhaps be controlled.

Aron himself, ever since his *Introduction to the Philosophy of History* which determined his conception and his method, has taught us the futility of prophecy, the impossibility of grasping the whole of reality, the role of events and accidents. May the serenity of this glance at the future turn out to be as justified as the conceptions that he has developed throughout his life about the society and the world of his time. In any case, it is symbolic that this last essay is, once again, an attempt at making intelligible the history that we are in the middle of living, and also that it has remained incomplete. For one is never finished, and the future remains undetermined.

References

Aron, R. (1938) *Introduction à la philosophie de l'histoire.* Paris, France: Gallimard.
Aron, R. (1948) *Le grand schisme* Paris, France: Gallimard.
Aron, R. (1951) *Les guerres en chaîne.* Paris, France: Gallimard.
Aron, R. (1962) *Paix et guerre.* Paris, France: Calmann-Lévy.
Aron, R. (1963) *Le grand débat.* Paris, France: Calmann-Lévy.
Aron, R. (1972) *Etudes politiques.* Paris, France: Gallimard.
Aron, R. (1976) *Penser la guerre, Clausewitz.* Vol. 2, *L'âge planétaire.* Paris, France: Gallimard.
Aron, R. (1983) *Mémoires.* Paris, Julliard.
Aron, R. (1984) *Les dernières années du siècle.* Paris, France: Commentaire/Julliard.
Ball, G. (1983) The Cosmic Bluff. *New York Review of Books,* 21 July.
Bundy, M. (1983) The Catholic Bishops and the Bomb, *New York Review of Books,* 16 June.
Hoffmann, S. (1965) *The State of War.* New York, NY: Praeger.
McNamara, R. (1983) The Military Role of Nuclear Weapons, *Foreign Affairs* 62(1): 59–80.
Waltz, K. (1979) *Theory of International Politics.* Reading, MA: Addison-Wesley.

4

Hans Morgenthau: The Limits and Influence of "Realism"

I

Hans Morgenthau has been considered, by students of international relations, the most forceful and incisive spokesman of the "realist" school. He was not the only one: E. H. Carr in England, Arnold Wolfers and George Kennan in this country, and Raymond Aron in France wrote in the same spirit. But Morgenthau was both a theorist and a fighter. It was he who, on the very first page of *Politics Among Nations*, proclaimed that the history of modern political thought was "the story of a contest between two schools that differ fundamentally in their conceptions of the nature of man, society and politics"—idealists and realists. Already here, we find both what was remarkable and what was exasperating about Morgenthau. Remarkable and admirable were his determination to drive out illusions, wishful thinking, fuzzy analysis and pious hopes—as a refugee from the continent of appeasement, he knew what he was saying—as well as his pugnacious instinct for sharpening intellectual arguments. The appeal to history as against abstract principles—echoes of Burke—the conviction that in human affairs "the realization of the lesser evil" is both more likely and less costly than that of "absolute good," the bracing emphasis on conflict as the daily reality of politics were particularly necessary in this country, at that time—not only because of the flings of idealism in which Americans had indulged during the two world wars, but also because the inevitable frustration of excessive hopes could only lead either to the equally unrealistic abdication of isolationism or to the equally excessive flings of "crusadism," whose perils Morgenthau knew well.

But there was something exasperating about elevating a somewhat parochial debate between cheerful liberals devoid of any sense of tragedy and cool conservatives devoid of grand designs into "the history of modern political thought." There was no room in this neat division for any of the varieties of totalitarian thinking that had emerged in this century and ravaged the world. Nor did Morgenthau face the central dilemma of "realism." If political realism means no more than the six principles he listed in that same first chapter, it provides no adequate guidelines either for analysis or for evaluation. But if political realism means something more precise and constraining, it becomes inaccurate as a theory of international relations, and ethically unacceptable.

In its broadest form, the only service it performs is to protect us from varieties of un-realism—such as the moralistic or legalistic approaches Morgenthau scorned. But to tell us that "theory consists in ascertaining facts and giving them meaning through reason" begs one of the most difficult questions any student of the field must confront: What, indeed, are the most important facts, and what is their significance? Two recent debates illustrate the quandary. For more than ten years now, some scholars (such as Robert W. Tucker) have asserted that the traditional rules of behavior of states have not been abolished by nuclear weapons, by economic interdependence, by the emergence of states whose power is above all economic but not military; other scholars have written about the "modernization" of international relations, the growing dis-utility of force, the irrelevance of past models, the birth of global politics. The facts are not in dispute, but clearly each group emphasizes some and dismisses others. For the past several years, scholars and policymakers have argued about the meaning of the Soviet arms buildup, of Soviet statements on nuclear war, and more recently of the Soviet invasion of Afghanistan. Robert Osgood has distinguished two schools—hawks and doves, if you like. Are the realists those who, like Kennan, stress the conservative and defensive motivations of Moscow, or those who discern a scheme for world domination by installments?

Morgenthau recognized that reality could be given a meaning only if we had "a rational outline, a map." But the map he gave us was of little help. It is true that "statesmen think and act in terms of interest defined as power," but only at a level of generality that is fatuous. Morgenthau himself told us that interest is both of the essence of politics and forever changing. A map that tells us that the main road can go in any direction is of little use. It may well be that there can be no general theory of the ways in which statesmen define the national interests—only descriptions and classifications. But Morgenthau's dogmatic insistence on the "objective laws" of politics tended to make him look for the determinants of the national interest in the external environment—the nation's position in the world and in history, so to speak—more than in the domestic milieu. The latter does more than shape the elements of national power; it also shapes the perceptions and conceptions of interest. As for power, insofar as it is presented as the currency of politics, it is a notion that leaves unanswered two of the most important questions any student of international politics must ask: First, how profound are the differences between politics within a community endowed with central power, and politics in a milieu of separate entities competing over resources, territories, and peoples, without any superior power? Do the same rules apply in both cases, and if they do not—if politics in the international state of nature and politics in civil society are fundamentally different—of what use is the concept of power? Second, is power a means, an objective, or the necessary goal for the actors? Is the maximization of power a rational objective? If the answer is no, is it only because of considerations of prudence—because of the physics of the balance of power—or would it still be unadvisable if the balancing mechanisms broke down?

Morgenthau's conviction that a realistic policy was also a moral one—that his map served as a normative as well as empirical theory—was particularly troublesome. If the question asked by political realists is: "How does this policy affect the power of the nation?" they can be moved only by considerations of prudence. What, then, happens to morality? An ethics of self-restraint is one that recommends moderation even when it would not be imprudent for a state to keep expanding. It is one whose goals are not simply derived from the game itself. If the political realist asks no question other than the one Morgenthau assigned to him, his only criterion would be success—a criterion as elusive politically as it is faulty ethically. Moreover, there is no guaranteed harmony—far from it—between the actor and the system, in international affairs; what may be good—that is, advantageous—for the state may be disastrous for the system. Both the statesman concerned exclusively with ethical goals for his nation and the statesman who worries about the achievement of certain moral goals throughout the world have to go beyond "interest defined as power" in their quest. Some goals are certainly assigned by the contest; but there are always objectives beyond survival and security (and there are many choices to be made even concerning those); the nature of these objectives depends in part on implicit or explicit ethical concerns that lie beyond the sphere of politics as defined by Morgenthau.

Ultimately, the notion, dear to Morgenthau, of the autonomy of the political sphere is misleading. In one sense, it is quite obvious: There is a political domain that cannot be reduced to economics, law, or ethics. But politics divorced from economics, law, or ethics becomes a kind of "pure game" that is played by nobody, for the simple reason that it would be a game without either cards or stakes. Morgenthau adds that a man who would be nothing but "political man" would be a beast, lacking in moral restraints. But this interesting statement testifies to a quite inaccurate conception of politics—or rather to a Hobbesian conception which Hobbes himself deemed so disastrous for human survival that it had to be abandoned and replaced by the very different politics of the Leviathan. Moreover, while there is *a* political domain, there are, in the world, multiple, competing conceptions of politics—of the proper goals and means of political action. For a theorist, the temptation of reducing them to a common alphabet and grammar is great, but it must be resisted; for while we do need a map, it is essential that it bear some resemblance to the world it aims at outlining for us.

There was, in Morgenthau's work, a constant tension between his awareness of the diversity of politics—he was at his best as a subtle analyst of concrete situations—and his desire to reduce politics to a single type he deemed politically prudent and ethically wise; but this desire made of him an idealist in disguise, a somewhat conservative liberal in revolt against other, imprudent liberals. And there was also a tension between the fundamentally Hobbesian conception of politics that informed his analysis and his awareness of the fact that, in the nuclear age, the contest for power unrestrained by superior authority was likely to lead, not to the modest utopia of harmony among moderate national interests, but to the destruction of the world. Between the need to debunk grandiose utopias (which grew out of his skepticism, his sense of history and his life experiences) and the need for a radical leap beyond politics-as-usual (which derived from his sense of logic, his awareness of the significance of the absolute weapon, and his deep concern for peace), there was a gap which he never filled.

Insofar as the Hobbesian model always remained present, beneath the sharp accounts and classifications of the varieties of foreign-policy behavior, it is legitimate to equate "realism," not just with the debatable and elastic principles of Morgenthau's first chapter, but also with a more rigorous theory of international politics that defines the states as the only actors on the world scene, makes of military power the decisive currency, and sees the hierarchy of military might as *the* hierarchy in the international system. It is against this conception that those I once called the *modernes* have been arguing throughout the 1970s, stressing the importance of nonstate actors, of transnational and transgovernmental coalitions, of nonmilitary forms of power, and of multiple hierarchies depending on the "issue-area" or on the international regime. Critics of the *modernes* have replied that these findings are perfectly compatible with "realism"; but this is so only if realism is defined as little more than a systematic attempt at analyzing reality and at understanding power relations in the world. Even if one grants, as the champions of the narrower version of realism keep saying, that military power remains the ultima ratio, that the distribution of might remains the latent structure of the international system, and that the concern for survival and security remains the essence of foreign policy, even if, in other words, one believes that international relations today is closer to the Thucydidean model than to the model of the global political community, there are just too many phenomena which the narrow version cannot quite account for: precisely all those effects of nuclear weapons and economic interdependence which induce new restraints on and introduce new complications into the traditional game of power.

Moreover, the narrower version both rests on and leads to an ethical assumption: the impossibility of moving beyond that game or, rather, of going beyond the traditional techniques of moderation, of which the balance of power is the most successful example. This is not only a morally objectionable postulate or conclusion, given the fate of such techniques in the past and the formidable inequities and violations of human rights that the game has usually tolerated or even encouraged. It is also unnecessary to accept it, since "realism," in any version, only demonstrates that there can be no leap into Erewhon, no escape from "the workmanlike manipulation of the perennial forces" of the political universe. It does not, and cannot, prove that one is doomed to repeat the past and that there is no middle ground, however narrow, between the limited and fragile moderation of the past and the impossible abolition of the game.

Morgenthau's great contribution lies, on the one hand, in his perceptive "anatomy lessons," in his skill in detecting the essence of specific situations, in his wisdom as a critic and adviser; on the other hand, in his insistence on the possibility of a science of international politics, which could only be established apart from history, law, or ethics. But if science is the reduction of uncertainty, that particular science has oscillated between the trivialities obtained through the (frequently mindless) application of the scientific—that is, largely quantitative—method and the complexities accumulated in the attempt to explain and account for the uncertainties of the real world. Moreover, in the social sciences, the intention of separating facts and values can never be fully carried out, and empirical theory can never be kept entirely separate from normative concerns. As a result, we are all realists now, but there are not two realists who agree either in their analysis of what is, or on what ought to be, or on how to get from here to there. Thirty-seven years after the first appearance of *Politics Among Nations*, it looks as if Morgenthau has won his battle but lost an unwinnable war.

II

A new, posthumous edition of Hans J. Morgenthau's famous and influential textbook, *Politics Among Nations*, has just been published.[1] Morgenthau died in the summer of 1980, at the age of 76; the new edition of his book was prepared by his former student, friend, and disciple, Kenneth W. Thompson, who teaches at the University of Virginia.

Morgenthau was a refugee from Nazi Germany. The fact that he had studied, practiced, and taught law in Europe made his book even more remarkable, for it was a declaration of war against the legalistic and moralistic tradition that had prevailed in the U.S. approach to foreign policy. What Morgenthau offered in its stead was "realism"—a highly ambitious effort directed both at theory and at policy advice, summed up in the first few pages of the book, where he had listed "six principles of political realism."

The tradition Morgenthau attacked was that of Woodrow Wilson—in a sense, the culmination of the liberal approach to foreign affairs. This tradition brought together two main historical strands: Kant, with his plan for perpetual peace through a confederation of states endowed with representative governments; and the British nineteenth-century liberals, with their notion of a world of nations linked through trade and ruled by the enlightened power of public opinion. It was a visionary conception, insofar as it looked forward to, and indeed predicted, the end of war as a means for resolving conflicts, the subordination of conflict to the common interests of mankind, and the decline of naked power as a result of domestic restraints and international agreements for reducing armaments and submitting disputes to impartial third parties. It is out of that tradition that modern international organization emerged—first in the form of the League of Nations, later in that of the United Nations—with its ambitious attempt to outlaw aggression and to provide for collective security against it. The goal was nothing less than the drastic curbing of state sovereignty—the legal notion of the state as the only source of law within its territory and, by extension, the political notion of the state's power to act abroad as it pleases, subject only to those legal restraints it has freely accepted. Instead, there would be a strong, comprehensive system of international legal rules, enforced by international agencies—indeed, ideally or ultimately, by a world state.

This conception was not only visionary; it was also radical, insofar as it presupposed a drastic change in the behavior of states. It was moralistic as well, insofar as the legal rules that would become supreme embodied either the Kantian ethics of unconditional and universal categorical imperatives (e.g., avoidance of aggression, and of violations of treaties) or the utilitarian ethics of the greatest good of the greatest number. It was based on an optimistic reading of human nature—or at least on a belief, both in its own perfectibility and in the power of the "right" institutions to bring out the best in human beings. It was also based on a distrust not only of unilateral uses of state power but, to some extent, of power altogether; for although it approved common exercises of power (such as collective security), it reserved them for exceptionally grave cases or submitted them to strict conditions. In other words, it clearly preferred persuasion and prevention to sanctions and coercion.

Hans Morgenthau's "principles of political realism" dismissed this approach, reverting instead to a conception represented by the very writers whom liberals had tried to refute: those writers who, like Morgenthau, argued that human nature does not change, that international politics is a struggle for power, and that the restraints—of law, morality, or opinion—are fragile and limited. Where the liberals hailed a march to community, the realists saw only a kind of barely tempered anarchy, a contest of sovereign actors with no allegiance to any power higher than their own. The realists followed the tradition of Thucydides, who analyzed the Peloponnesian War between Athens and Sparta; of Machiavelli, who listed the rules of survival for the princes of Italian city-states; of Hobbes, who starkly described the state of nature (or war, for that matter) in which states live, unlike individuals secure under the power of a state. In such a world, international agencies can perform only modest services; they certainly cannot enforce peace. The only morality is one of prudence—in Morgenthau's terms, one involving "the weighing of the consequences of alternative political actions" rather than "conformity with the moral law." And change can come only through "the workmanlike manipulation of the perennial forces that have shaped the past as they will the future." In short, there is no room in world affairs for grand solutions, such as the end of war.

The enormous influence of a doctrine that was anything but original is easy to explain in terms of the place and the moment. The United States, insulated from world politics (except for the very unhappy experience of 1917–1919), and, indeed, founded in repudiation of European politics, had been the champion *par excellence* of the liberal, internationalist, radical approach. Even after refusing to join Wilson's brainchild, the League of Nations, the isolationist United States had continued to deprecate power, as in its toothless policy of "nonrecognition" of Japanese conquests in the 1930s as well as in its neutrality legislation (the United States' own contribution to the appeasement of the dictators). Even though Franklin D. Roosevelt soon proved to be an enthusiastic player of power politics, the national tradition was so strong that much attention was focused, in 1943–1945, on the birth of the United Nations, rather than on the ominous power conflicts among the "Big Three"—namely, the United States, Britain, and the USSR. FDR himself, after Yalta, told Congress that the agreements reached in Crimea meant the end of traditional power games! By 1948, however, the liberal approach was bankrupt: the UN was paralyzed by the cold war; no collective security machinery could be set up; and the world, instead of being ruled by law, was split into two camps. An observer of the behavior of the two superpowers could not fail to be struck by the similarities with Athens and Sparta and *their* conflict, twenty-four centuries earlier.

In short, Morgenthau's text provided both an explanation and a road map. The liberal dream had gone wrong because it was based on a misreading of the nature of world politics. Understanding this nature required one to think in terms of power. And thinking about power led one to conclude that policy ought to seek a balance of power, not a utopia of peace—or, rather, that peace had a chance of being preserved by such a balance, but no chance of emerging from legalistic schemes and wishful thinking about world public opinion or disarmament. This was a tough message. But it was just what the elites of a disconcerted yet most powerful nation needed to hear. Morgenthau's ambition was to be the teacher of realism in the New World, bringing Old World wisdom to the continent of Utopia. Thirty years later, Henry Kissinger, who had (briefly) studied with Morgenthau and had become his friend, described his own ambition as a statesman in almost the same terms: as a matter of teaching "unsentimental" power politics to a nation without a "geopolitical" tradition but with an idealistic one, a legalistic one, and a merely pragmatic one (i.e., a "problem-solving" tradition). Obviously, if, in the 1970s, another German refugee had to teach "realism" all over again, and if he too did not fully succeed—as the attempted return to idealism under Carter showed—Morgenthau's message must have fallen on deaf ears, despite its early popularity. What had, in fact, happened?

It is a story full of paradoxes. To begin with, we must separate the two universes that Morgenthau had wanted to unite—namely, the realms of theory and of policy. Scholars working on the theory of world politics remain divided into two groups—realists and utopians. The latter continue to seek a drastic transformation of the world, out of anarchy, toward peace. But in the United States, at least, these scholars are not in the mainstream of political science. In the mainstream, we are all "realists" now, even though it is a realism that Morgenthau would not have approved of or recognized. Morgenthau wrote extensively and vehemently against the way in which so-called scientific approaches to the study of politics—the use of quantitative methods, or the development of formal models, or the search for abstract general laws—squeeze the political out of politics. And yet, one vast body of theory is now concerned with strategic questions—the study of nuclear deterrence and strategy, in which technological considerations often prevail over political ones, and the quest for certainty and precision often brushes aside all the psychological or bureaucratic irrationalities that make the idea of a "science" of war absurd.

It must also be noted that Morgenthau paid rather little attention to international economics: he looked at the economy mainly as an ingredient of state power. Today, some of the most innovative theoretical work in international politics deals with the ways in which states pool their power and collaborate in order to achieve, jointly, economic goals that they could not meet through unilateral or hostile action. This research thus rehabilitates those international agencies whose significance Morgenthau deemed dubious. Moreover, "security" realists, who focus on conflict, and "political economy" realists, intrigued by cooperation, rarely communicate.

In the world of policy, we find another paradox. Generations of students were taught by Morgenthau himself—at the University of Chicago, later at City College in New York—or by disciples of Morgenthau. Many foreign-service officers acknowledge his intellectual influence. The main message—no foreign policy without power—has been absorbed by every policymaker, by every member of the "informed public." But Morgenthau, on the whole, has been misunderstood (just as another "realist," George Kennan, complains of having been misconstrued). Why? In looking at the sum of Morgenthau's (very abundant) writings on foreign affairs, we find three main themes. One was clearly understood—although it was the most misleading. The other two were not.

What most readers of *Politics Among Nations* remember is "the main signpost" of political realism: "the concept of interest defined in terms of power." States pursue (and ought to pursue) their national interests; in politics, interest is analyzed in terms of power, just as in economics, interest is defined in terms of wealth. Now, this notion was, of course, tremendously appealing to the leaders of a country that had emerged from the biggest war in history, with more power than any nation had ever had—in both economic and military affairs (i.e., with respect to the nuclear monopoly). The postwar United States was both disturbed about the insecurity vast power brings—especially in a global contest against an empire seen as mysterious and deeply alien—and exhilarated about the possibilities of power, which its political leaders explored and applied exuberantly: alliances, economic and military aid, bases abroad, weapons development, covert action, interventions, propaganda, and so on. Morgenthau's celebration of power as the yardstick of foreign policy was thus perceived as an intellectual blessing. It put the seal of legitimacy on the United States' global activism. For if power is the substance of the national interest, huge power justifies a very extensive definition both of that interest and of the vast commitments entailed by it.

But there were two enormous problems with this view. One resulted from the flaws in Morgenthau's own theory. Power ought to be seen, above all, as a (complex) means toward ends. The implication is that one ought to start with a definition of those ends and then devise the amount of power needed to reach them, distinguish among the very different sorts of power appropriate to different ends, decide, if necessary, how to increase the kinds of power required for the absolutely indispensable ends, and delete those ends for which power is missing, or those ends that simply cannot be reached either with the kinds of power that one is able to produce or with the kinds of power at one's disposal that is actually usable—for, in the nuclear age especially, not all power is rationally usable. Morgenthau put the cart (power) before the horse (the selection of goals). And, as many critics pointed out at once, defining "interest" in terms of power did not succeed in giving to the concept of the national interest the clarity, objectivity, and durability that Morgenthau claimed and sought. Especially in a democracy, the definition of the national interest is likely to be a matter of debate, and to result at least as much from a clash of partisan views as from the permanent necessities of geopolitical position or from the unavoidable requirements of external conflicts.

The second problem was the failure of so many policymakers to catch Morgenthau's second theme: the need for moderation and prudence. Morgenthau was no apostle of conflict; indeed, his textbook ends with chapters on "peace through accommodation," and with a plea for the revival of diplomacy. Readers marked by the searing experience of democratic weakness in the 1930s saw in his book only the condemnation of appeasement as a method for coping with imperialistic powers. They failed to realize that Morgenthau's thought, unlike that of Dean Acheson or Harry Truman, was not obsessed by the "Munich analogy." Something strange happened to Morgenthau's realism on the way to Washington: there, the celebration of power blended with, instead of replacing, the old U.S. idealism and crusading spirit. Those who read Morgenthau in Washington used his concept of the national interest as a way of justifying a definition of the United States' interests that was practically limitless and made compromise difficult—namely, resistance against the expansion of Communism in all its forms (as Norman Podhoretz often still advocates) or at least the expansion, direct or indirect, of Soviet power, anywhere in the world. This is a definition not so much shaped by U.S. priorities as driven by fears about Soviet behavior. Like Kennan, Morgenthau pointed to the Soviet challenge, but he never embraced the sort of realism that is found so often on the Right—the one according to which we are locked in a struggle to the finish with the Soviet Union, are justified in using, on behalf of our interests, every weapon or trick that the Soviets use on behalf of theirs, and must prevail because there is no room in this world for both philosophies of power and sets of values.

Morgenthau, like another great realist, Charles de Gaulle, analyzed the Soviet Union as an expansionist power rather than as an ideology on the march. He was critical of the sufferings to which any "nationalistic universalism" (i.e., any crusading nationalism that claims a universal mandate) dooms humanity: the U.S. as well as the Soviet version, the democratic as well as the Communist version. Nevertheless, Morgenthau's plea for power was put at the service of the old ideals of collective security, international law, and resistance to aggression, now interpreted as the cause of the free world against the Soviet Union. As the United States was meant to provide the secular arm for this vision, its national interest was described as identical with the interest of the world community (one finds this ideology in the speeches of Dean Rusk as well as those of Eugene Rostow)—a form of "nationalistic universalism" if ever there was one.

Just as Kennan protested against the "militarization of containment," Morgenthau vigorously objected to the policy excesses that resulted from the blend of the old and the new approaches. Indeed, he particularly objected to the Vietnam War. He deplored the inflexibility and high risks of the new, bipolar balance of power to which U.S. "pactomania" contributed, all the while covering the world with alliances centered in Washington; surely the restraining effects of the old eighteenth- and nineteenth-century balance had come from the flexible alignments among a half-dozen major players. In the first national teach-in about the Vietnam War, in Washington in May 1965, the father of "political realism" was the chief prosecutor against Lyndon Johnson's policy, defended by men who had blended realism and universalism or, like Zbigniew Brzezinski and Walt Rostow, had turned realism into an anti-Communism ram. Today, Vietnam revisionism is popular, and it focuses on the undeniable horrors of the Communist regimes in Vietnam and Cambodia. But it conveniently forgets that the United States lost that war because its goals were simply unreachable at a price tolerable either to the world at large or to the U.S. conscience and political system. Morgenthau, who never had any illusions about Communism, never lost sight of the essentials: the limits on the effectiveness and usability of the United States' huge power, and the distortion of its national interest imposed for so many years by its obsession with Vietnam.

Morgenthau's preoccupation with the United States' most disastrous war sprang not only from his concern for restraint and accommodation but also from the third theme of his work (one that, unlike the second, he never fully succeeded in integrating with the first)—namely, that national power in a world of competing states was compatible with a quest for moderation or détente. But the realist view of the world as a system of sovereign actors, the states, was being undermined by two forces that Morgenthau was perceptive and incisive enough to recognize fully. On the one hand, there was the force of revolutionary movements: those that recently destroyed the colonial empires, and those that currently challenge an often unjust and repressive *status quo* in many countries, especially the developing nations. Attempts to deal with these movements by such traditional methods of statecraft as military interventions, or to forcibly preserve the *status quo* out of fear of Communism or in order to support local leaders allied with the United States, he deemed futile and dangerous. In other words, states were no longer the only actors on the stage, and the national interest could not be defined without taking into account either the sweeping movements operating across borders or the domestic realities within many shaky states. In short, this kind of realism was, in fact, far more fluid, less dogmatic, than his state-centered principles suggested, and one that led him to be very critical of Kissinger's statecraft in Vietnam, Chile, or Bangladesh.

On the other hand, there was the nuclear revolution. Along with Bernard Brodie and Raymond Aron, Morgenthau grasped almost at once the radical potential of the new weapons. Nuclear war could not be an instrument of politics. And no power would ever again be capable of ensuring its security—for there is no adequate defense against nuclear weapons, and deterrence rests on a suicidal threat. Sovereignty no longer meant invulnerability. Dying for one's country had lost its meaning, if it also meant the end of mankind.

Morgenthau was at his best when he analyzed the many dilemmas of deterrence with which policymakers have been struggling for forty years. He was among the first to denounce the meaninglessness of nuclear superiority (once each side has the means to devastate the other even after being attacked), and to criticize those strategists who tried to negate the nuclear revolution by thinking of ways to use the atomic weapons as if they were conventional ones—that is, for warfighting or winning purposes. Thus, he saw clearly the contradiction between the organization of humanity into states claiming sovereignty and the imperative of preventing nuclear weapons from destroying the world. In coping with such a peril, ordinary diplomatic processes risked being too slow, arms control too limited, international agencies too ineffectual, prudence too fragile in crises requiring instant decisions about military moves that could all too easily get out of control. And yet the very structure of the world, its division into states, the superpowers' contest, continued to relegate to the realm of utopia disarmament and world government the idealists' fantasies he had so scathingly denounced, yet whose intellectual appeal rested on their case against state sovereignty, a case whose strength he himself recognized.

It is this contradiction that has kept utopianism alive, not only among a fraction of the academic writers on world affairs (the pioneers of "peace research," for instance) but also in parts of the public (particularly the members of peace movements, here and abroad). For these men and women, even Morgenthau's moderate brand of realism may seem far too complacent: If the game of states is to be saved from its own bent toward self-destruction, it will have to be, not merely played wisely, but superseded altogether. Instead, U.S. statesmen have usually opted for the kind of cold war "realism" that Morgenthau deplored (both in its idealistic disguises, as in the 1950s and 1960s, or in some of the rhetoric of the Reagan administration, and in its cool but manipulative and conservative variety, under Kissinger). Occasionally (as under Carter), these policymakers have reverted to the kinds of utopianism Morgenthau had written against. The golden mean—a limited definition of interests, a sophisticated approach to power—has eluded them.

Today, utopianism remains the twin of wishful thinking. But realism, even of the kind Morgenthau had advocated, remains unsatisfactory in a world where, in Churchill's unforgettable words, safety is the sturdy child of terror, and survival the twin brother of annihilation. What is needed, both among intellectuals and in statecraft, is a quest for a new realism, one that acknowledges and starts with the stark realities of a divided world, yet tries—through cooperation and collective action in a variety of fields—to change the game sufficiently to prevent revolutionary hurricanes and nuclear explosions from destroying it, and us, altogether. A realism of "the struggle for power" is not enough. And a realism of struggle *and* world order has not yet emerged.

Notes

1. Hans J. Morgenthau, *Politics Among Nations* (New York: Knopf, 1985).

PART TWO

Order and Violence

5

Is There an International Order?

Conceptions of Order

Social Order Defined

There are many ways of defining "social order." The most general definition is as follows: the norms, practices, and processes that ensure the satisfaction of the fundamental needs of the social group in question. This definition is uncomfortably vague, but it has the advantage of cleansing the word order of all the normative or ideological biases that often burden its uses. Another advantage is that it allows us to compare different types of social groups, or different social groups belonging to the same type.

The group that will be discussed in this essay is the international milieu. It is not humankind considered as a single society precisely because, as was pointed out by Rousseau (1964), there is no general society of mankind. Humanity has constantly been and remains divided into units whose nature has changed with the centuries. But these units have always been sufficiently numerous and complicated to ensure the failure of all attempts at establishing a universal empire, all dreams of world federation. When one talks about the international milieu, one therefore refers not to one but to two realities. The first is the *interstate milieu*—that is, the relations that exist among various units that act on the world scene as the holders of public power and as the expression of the wishes and aspirations of the individuals and groups that make them up. The second reality is *transnational society*—the relations that are formed across the borders of those units, among the individuals and the groups.

The study of international order calls for three preliminary remarks. First, the problem of world order is quite different from that of domestic political order or from that of order within the social groups that exist within the political unit. What characterizes international order is anarchy (i.e., the absence of central power above the units); it is also the absence or weakness of common norms. Thus, one immediately sees where the

---

I am grateful to my friend and colleague Robert O. Keohane for his comments on this essay.

problem lies. It is both analytical and normative: can there be both anarchy and order?

Second, the problem of order is a variable one, depending on the nature of the units. To simplify, let us say that there are mainly three types of structures. That which seems farthest away from pure anarchy is obviously empire, imposed by one people upon others. The resulting structure is vertical, a power of command that tries to reproduce those relations between the rulers and the ruled that existed within the initial imperial entity. For both internal and external reasons, however, empire cannot be dealt with as though it were a mere variety of domestic order. On the one hand, the relations between the imperial and the dominated countries are rarely the same as the relations between central power and the subjects in the dominant unit. On the other hand, there have always been "horizontal" relations among empires, or between the empire and other units, insofar as there has never been a universal empire, and as each empire has therefore been forced to protect itself against threats at its borders.

The second type of structure is that of feudalism—a fragmentation of public power, a puzzle of public and private powers with overlapping jurisdictions, a maze of hierarchical links without clearly delimited territorial borders, a mix of different rights and obligations concerning the same lands. Thus, feudalism was an anarchical structure, but one in which anarchy was softened by the very absence of any concept of absolute property and exclusive sovereignty, as well as tempered by the importance of common customary and, above all, religious norms. To simplify again, let us say that empire offers a kind of central (but not universal) power and very few common values, whereas the feudal system offers shared and dispersed power as well as a common faith.

The third structure has neither central power nor common values. It is the milieu constituted by "sovereign" units—that is, units whose central power claims the monopoly of violence within (to quote Max Weber's definition of the state) and claims abroad the exclusive right of making decisions in behalf of its subjects. Thus, it is a milieu based on a clear territorial differentiation among units, and on the idea that each territory can, in principle, have only one central power. Historically, this can be the power of sovereign cities, as in ancient Greece or in Renaissance Italy; or it can be the power of states—what has sometimes been called the system of the Westphalia treaties, although these treaties merely ratified an older state of affairs. Precisely because the problem of order *and* anarchy exists above all in this third type of structure, it is the one that is usually the subject of study in the theory of international relations. This is why, when we shall deal with the interstate milieu, we will discuss only this kind of structure. And since it is not obvious that one can really talk about order when one deals with an anarchical structure, I have preferred the word *milieu* to the word *society*, which presupposes a positive answer to the problem of order.

Third, whereas the literature about the interstate milieu and its problems is very rich, the same cannot be said about the literature on transnational society. This is so mainly for three reasons. The scope of the transnational society depends on the scope of the means of communication, on the material facility with which exchanges can be organized across borders. Such means have always existed, but only since the great discoveries and, above all, the industrial revolution have such exchanges developed on a grand scale. Moreover, the establishment and intensity of transnational relations are linked to the type of economic system that exists within the main units: the precondition for transnational society is the willingness of the governments to let a part of economic, scientific, and intellectual life escape from their grip and organize itself, inside and outside, in relatively autonomous ways. Finally, even while this is the case, as during the "liberal" era in the nineteenth century, transnational society operates in a framework and according to rules determined by the preponderant state or states: it is a limited and conditional autonomy.

Specificity

Most students of the interstate milieu emphasize the specificity of the problem of order in this realm. At the outset, we find two question marks.

First, if one calls order the satisfaction of the elementary or fundamental needs of the group, which group are we talking about? Hedley Bull (1977) makes a distinction between *international* order (he meant interstate) and *world* order. World order would allow the basic needs of humankind to be met—such needs as the survival, and the provision of the minimum necessary for the existence, of men and women. Interstate order concerns only the essential needs of states: (1) preservation of their own existence and (2) security. One sees at once that international order can exist even if world order does not. One only has to imagine states that respect each other but remain perfectly indifferent to those domestic practices that would allow, here or there, governments to commit genocide against people or to exploit economically important parts of their populations. In legal terms, it is the problem of the difference between the rights of states (and mutual respect of their sovereignty) and human rights. Conversely, one also sees that world order necessarily presupposes, at a minimum, a very special kind of interstate order, endowed with effective procedures of cooperation among states and even with means of coercing states in order to ensure the minimal satisfaction of human needs. Thus there is tension rather than complementarity between those two notions of order; they correspond, respectively, to a partly fictitious global society and to a group that is altogether real (the states), yet abstract (what is the state independent of the individuals and the groups?) and extraordinarily limited.

Second, if one concerns oneself only with interstate order (as writings about politics usually do) one sees immediately why and to what extent the satisfaction of the states' basic needs—survival and security—is always threatened. The two key problems of political life—who commands and who benefits—receive completely different answers depending on whether or not there exists a consensus on the organization and regulation of the group, effective procedures for the selection of the leaders and the distribution of resources, and rules for the solution of conflicts. The trouble is that in the interstate milieu, contrary to what happens within the social group that constitutes the nation, social relations do not constitute a mix of society (relations of reciprocity, corresponding to an elaborate division of labor) and community (unconditional cooperation, corresponding to a collective will to live together); they offer instead a mix of limited society (relations of coexistence among units that are not highly differentiated—because the division of labor among them is weak—but, on the contrary, resemble one another because they fulfill the same functions) and anarchy, which results from the absence of a central monopoly of the legitimate use of violence at the disposal of a public power whose mission would be to define and carry out the collective functions and whose authority would be applied directly on individuals. On the contrary, we are in the domain of self-help, in a milieu that is dominated by the ever-present possibility of a resort to force, and whose common institutions depend entirely on the consent of the sovereign units that make them up.

Three problems arise therefore: Concerning *politics*, there is obviously a fundamental difference between the way in which power is used within a political unit close to the ideal-type of a nation whose political system rests on popular consensus, and power politics in the interstate milieu. To be sure, as some theorists have pointed out, following Hobbes (1971), all politics is about power (Morgenthau, 1948). But Raymond Aron (1962) has been right to emphasize the difference between the two ideal-types (even though, in the real world, the contrast is often less sharp). In one case, power serves common values, coercion can be exerted only if it follows certain rules and in well-defined areas, the conflicts among groups can entail the use of only limited kinds of power (not force), and social hierarchy is not constantly threatened. In the other instance, the contest among the units risks becoming violent at any time and could therefore infect all of the interstate relationships (not to mention even the intrastate ones); and a hierarchy among the units is always challenged. Therefore, insofar as power is concerned, there is a difference both in the scope of the area in which it can be deployed in its naked or brute aspects, and in its intensity or forms. Aron's conclusion was that although foreign policy, like domestic politics, has no single and necessary end, comparable to victory for the football player or to gain for "homo economicus," "strategic-diplomatic behavior" nevertheless has a meaning (the risk of war) and an imperative (the calculation of means). The "plurality of centers of decision" that makes this calculation indispensable at the same time makes it hazardous, inasmuch as the interstate milieu is one in which suspicion, distrust, misunderstanding and hostility prevail, whereas in the ideal-type of national society conflicts do not prevent transparency and take place in a context of cooperation. The relations between conflict and cooperation are so to speak reversed, as soon as one finds oneself in a milieu in which each player is free to resort to force.

Concerning *law*, there are fundamental differences between domestic public law and international law. The school of jurisprudence that tends to minimize the importance of rules, command, and sanctions in law, and to emphasize instead its functional aspects and its role as a social process, tries to erase those differences. But this school is blind about one essential matter—the contrast between the social groups that create, and are regulated by, the two types of law. The national group is made up of individuals and associations to whom the legal norms worked out by central power apply; social integration is such (and partly results from the fact) that the legal network covers the whole of society. The sanction of law is ensured by the state (through the justice system and the police) and imposed directly on the individuals and groups. In the interstate milieu, the group consists mainly of the states; law is of a contractual rather than hierarchical nature; it is not applied directly to individuals and groups within the states; and the scope of regulation does not cover the whole of transnational relations. Sanction is both weak, given the limited weight of common institutions, and at the mercy of self-help. Thus, between public law and international law there is a triple difference concerning the degree of institutionalization (there are no world executive, legislative, and judicial powers comparable to those which exist within states), the substance itself (one is a law of uniformity, the other very often a law of differentiation), and authority or efficiency (international law can self-destruct). This is not to say that law plays no role in world order; indeed, it provides a minimum of order by making many interstate or transnational activities predictable, by removing them from the domain of conflicts or from perpetual challenges. But it is precisely in the vital realm of power relations that it is at its weakest.

Concerning *ethics*, one finds the same contrast. In domestic affairs the conflict of conceptions or ideologies is rarely totally destructive; the political and constitutional framework and the common values provide individuals and groups with important opportunities or chances for moral action: since order is ensured, they can search for justice. In the interstate realm, as Aron (1962) and Arnold Wolfers (1971) have observed, the conflict of values served by secular arms endowed with weapons often covers the whole field of relations among the units; threats against their survival and security in a world of self-help limit and sometimes destroy the opportunities for moral action; the first imperative is survival; justice comes only later.

All these distinctive features of the international milieu show how precarious interstate order is. It is both an order that is constantly threatened—as war regularly puts at stake the survival and security of some of the units at least, sometimes even the most important ones—and an order based on force, on the balances and calculations of shifting and uncertain forces. But the interstate milieu is nevertheless not a realm of chaos and anarchy at all times: there is such a thing as peace. For the regime of "each one for himself" often succeeds in preventing self-help from becoming a war of all against all. While peace prevails, the scope and intensity of cooperative interstate relations can increase. How order can appear and last against all obstacles; what peculiar forms it takes in a decentralized milieu where conflicts, the stuff of any social order, always risk destroying the conventions of nonviolence and blowing up the bridges of cooperation; how these forms change and how order gets reshaped after having been demolished: these are the questions that have interested writers—past political philosophers as well as contemporary social scientists. We shall briefly examine their respective contributions. Against chronology, we will start with the "science" of international relations, which wants above all to be analytical (and sometimes predictive), whereas the great writers of the past were both analytical and prescriptive (an admittedly imperfect distinction, insofar as scientific analysis inevitably leads, as Aron used to write, to prudent or wise advice, or even serves above all to highlight and justify certain prescriptions, as in the contemporary "realist" school).

Levels of Analysis

In contemporary social science, one can distinguish three levels of analysis in the study of international order. The most elementary or descriptive is the chart of practices and institutions that have ensured or still ensure a minimum of order, the analysis of their respective advantages and weaknesses, and the criticism of failed attempts to do more. Thus, Hedley Bull reviews the role of law and international organizations, the classical balance of power system, and the failure of efforts to go beyond the nation state. I. L. Claude (1962) has also tried to show why the balancing system has been more successful than collective security and why the idea of world government has not caught on.

More interesting is the second level, that of a general theory of interstate relations. Currently, the paradigm remains that of the "realist" school, which emphasizes the dominant role of states on the world scene, the imperative of calculating forces in a realm dominated by power politics, and the crucial importance of the military ingredients of power and of geopolitical considerations in the setting of the states' goals. The realist school also criticizes idealistic illusions: the very nature of the game explains the weakness of international law, the failure of efforts to transfer the monopoly of legitimate violence to international organization, and the instability of the diplomacy of balance. However, at the same time, that school tries to show that the game does not rule out the preservation of order and that the intelligent self-interest of the actors requires them not to push self-help too far. Thus, in the works of Hans Morgenthau and George Kennan (1951), the critique of legalism and moralism is wedded to praise for moderate diplomacy, to an argument for a restrained definition of the national interest. An order that rests on a balance of forces, on a limitation of ambitions, on resistance to demagogic pressures at home, and on the absence of ideological crusades, is both a recurrent reality (as in the eighteenth and nineteenth centuries) and a sensible idea. This had already been the message of E. H. Carr's (1980) work before the Second World War: against Toynbee, the champion of collective security, Carr showed that force operates in all the realms of international relations (including the so-called liberal world economy), and he recommended that the states on top of the hierarchy make peaceful concessions to rising states. Bull's book describes the techniques of order within the framework of a "Grotian" theory, according to which there exists an interstate society—an imperfect society, of course, given the absence of central power, but it is real and reflects the acceptance of common norms, the mutual recognition of common needs by the states.

The third level is that of the theories of interstate systems. The realist school's point of departure is foreign policy: the state is the privileged actor. Systemic theories start from the network or milieu made up of competing units. These theories try to identify the main variables and the rules of the game despite the absence in the interstate milieu of those constitutional norms which provide an often very constraining framework for the activities of parties, bureaucracies, and interests within a national society. The basic idea is that even in a milieu without any sovereign at the top, the freedom of maneuver enjoyed by the centers of decision is limited by the configuration of the whole system. This constellation also determines the distinctive features of the order that exists at any given moment or else allows one to understand why there is no order.

This is not the place for a synthesis of systemic theories, which raise problems that go far beyond the study of interstate order. But it is necessary to mention the main characteristics of these theories:

1. They all make a distinction, expressly or not, between the *structure* of the system (i.e., on the whole, the distribution of power in the diplomatic field) and the *processes* (i.e., the relations among the units). (Morton Kaplan [1957] codified this distinction.) But they do not agree on two essential points. On the one hand, they disagree about the definition of the variables indispensable to a study of systems. Kenneth Waltz (1979) believes that this study can be concerned only with an analysis of the relations between the structure and the processes; it must deal only with what is *inter*state. At the other end we find Aron, who believes that one must take into account variables that Waltz deems exogenous: the nature of the political regimes within the units, transnational forces (ideologies or technologies), the world economic system. Obviously, the narrow and rigorous conception of Waltz results in a rather mechanistic conception of order (equilibrium of forces); the very open conception of Aron (criticized as too loose by Waltz) includes all kinds of factors on which equilibrium actually depends, or which threaten its existence. On the other hand, the theorists disagree about the constraining or determining character of the system. Morton Kaplan tends to make of it a society endowed with rules that are necessary and sufficient to preserve the game, rules that the players must observe or else violate only at their own risk. Aron, once more, is very skeptical on this point: the actors are the ones who set and can change the rules, and each configuration allows them a certain margin of choice—a margin that is particularly large for the most powerful players.

2. All of the aforementioned systemic theories result in typologies. Most of them (those of Kaplan, Waltz, Aron, etc.) distinguish bipolar from

multipolar systems, depending on the number of major powers. For these theories, and contrary to the theory of the world capitalist system developed by Wallerstein (1979), it is the "horizontal" structure of power that matters for a typology of systems, not the "vertical" method of organization of economic exchange relationships. But whereas Waltz believes that the fewer "poles" there are, the more likely the system is to be stable, Kaplan and Aron think that in bipolar systems the dialectic of hostility is more likely to prevail and the diplomacy of flexibility and moderation is more likely to fail (especially because a bipolar system is usually heterogeneous, according to the definition provided by Aron, who distinguishes homogeneous and heterogeneous systems depending on whether the states belong to the same type and share the same values or not). Robert Gilpin's theory (1981) differs from the preceding ones insofar as he describes the international system as a pattern dominated by a hegemonic power, whose authority decreases as the costs of domination begin to be higher than its advantages, as the law of diminishing returns begins to apply and as rivals begin to challenge it: at this moment a war breaks out, which puts a new hegemonic power on top. Here, order depends, for its shape and duration, on the existence and specific features of each dominant state.

3. Strangely, none of the systemic theories offers a satisfactory conception of change. The very definition of the system by Kenneth Waltz allows him to take into account only changes in the distribution of power. As John Ruggie (1983) has noted, Waltz ignores the difference between a system of units of the feudal type and a system in which the actors are sovereign territorial units; it also ignores what Ruggie, following Durkheim, calls the "dynamic density" of relations among the actors—an important factor of change insofar as such density, when it increases, can transform or empty of its content the sovereignty of states and change the very nature of power or the conditions of its use. In Aron's very open theory, general wars provoke a change of system, and the causes of such wars can be and usually are very numerous. Gilpin's theory, according to Robert Keohane (1983), does not explain why certain powers become dominant rather than others.

4. All the theories of international systems postulate that order, insofar as it exists, depends both on the configuration of the power of *states* (despite the disagreement about what the most desirable one may be) and on the practices of *states* (coalitions, alliances, unilateral measures of armament and expansion). These theories are in conflict with Wallerstein's rather sketchy one. In Wallerstein's view, order results from the uneven exchanges imposed by the world capitalist system; he denies the autonomy of states, which are merely the instruments of this system. The theories of interstate systems do not ignore the various manifestations of domination, but they emphasize domination by a state or the regulation of the world market by states.

Models of Order

The scientific study of international relations cannot be said to have led to very clear conclusions about interstate order: the precariousness of the techniques of order and of the calculations of forces is compounded by the cacophony of analyses. What do we find if we turn to the great writers of the past?

We find first of all that the idea of order is much more central. Modern theorists usually reach this idea through the study of the essence of foreign policy or of types of systems (Aron, Morgenthau, Waltz). Political philosophy discusses the problem of order directly and in two ways: it asks whether there is such an order and of what sort it is; and it indicates what ought to be done so as to create or to consolidate order. Let us use the first question as our thread. We find two models.

The first is the model of precarious peace or troubled order. It unfolds as soon as the catholic conception of the Christian community—in which God is the only real sovereign, the princes are considered to be the servants of divine and natural law, and force is subject to the very strict conditions of the just war theory, which regulates its causes, procedures, and means—begins to yield to the pressure of facts: the appearance of the modern territorial state of absolute sovereignty, the loss of authority by the Pope and the church, the secularization of natural law (Johnson, 1975). The new model is both a retreat from the old one and a conceptualization of the new interstate system. This sytem is analyzed as a milieu in which there are forces capable of ensuring a minimum of order. They result from common sociability or common interests, and they lead to common norms—those of international law. Thus world politics is not a state of war: Locke (1967) carefully distinguishes between the state of nature (in which states find themselves) and the state of war. The former is characterized not by violence but by the absence of a common judge and a common sovereign—hence all the weaknesses and excesses of self-help. Nevertheless, states acknowledge the obligations of mutual respect and aid that result from natural law, whereas the state of war is one of generalized mischief. This is why the state of nature is preferable to a world tyranny.

The second model is quite different; it is that of the "state of war." One finds reference to it between the lines of Thucydides' work (1964) and, of course, in Machiavelli's prescriptions (1940), even though the latter does not find domestic politics any less war-like. One finds it in its purest state in Hobbes, later repeated and corrected by Rousseau and Kant (1949) and by Hegel (1953). In the relations among states, everything is war or the preparation of war; the so-called common norms are fragile, temporary, proportional to the quantity of power that supports them, dependent on a momentary convergence of interests. No common Reason moderates the ambitions and calculations of each actor; there is only an instrumental rationality: the quest of the best means toward a particular aim, the calculation of forces, resulting not in harmony but in conflict. War is inherent in the structure of the interstate order and even in the practices (such as the balance) that try to prevent war, according to Rousseau. What the champions of this model disagree about is the origin of this sad state of affairs: is it human nature (Hobbes), the impossibility for man to act according to his moral conscience in the state of nature (Kant), the corruption of innocent human nature by civil society (Rousseau), the alienation imposed by relations of production in capitalist societies (Marx) or the division of the world into states (Hegel)?

In each camp, disagreement concerning prescriptions is just as vast. Those who defend the first model all believe that there are means to strengthen the precarious interstate order, but their choice of prescriptions depends on their analysis of the deeper causes of this precariousness. On the whole, one can distinguish two schools. In his first book, Waltz (1959) distinguished three images of the causes of war: human nature, the domestic regime of the units, and the anarchical structure of the interstate milieu. The first image does not take us very far by itself. Some philosophers believe that the common order could become much stronger if one acted on the domestic, political, and economic regime: this is the doctrine of the liberals, whether they advocate a political regime based on popular consent, the separation of powers, the rule of enlightened opinion, or the limitation of the scope of the state, or else preach for a liberal economy—that is, the replacement of command by the market, the giving-up of conquests, the triumph of the theory of comparative advantage, trade as a source of wealth for individuals and no longer as a source of might for the state (Adam Smith, Cobden, J. B. Say, etc.) (Silberner, 1957). Other writers offer recipes to make the structure of the interstate milieu less anarchical; in the case of Hume (1817) it is the doctrine of the balance of power.

Those who uphold the second model are divided into two categories. Some consider that the "state of war" is bearable after all: Hobbes distinguishes the war of all against all among individuals (each one of whose survival is threatened, and who must therefore abandon their original freedom and set up a Leviathan) from war among states, which does not necessarily impinge on all individuals, especially those of strong states; hence contracts among states, bolstered by their weapons, are more solid than contracts among the puny individuals, naked in the state of nature. Hegel, who believed that war was necessary and beneficient—a kind of rough remedy against the decay of civil society—thought that conflicts between civilized states would become ritualized. But such optimism has not been shared by those who believe that the state of war is unbearable or morally unacceptable. Kant, who joined the liberal thinkers, proclaimed both the duty of establishing constitutional regimes—the only ones capable of resisting the call of war and of establishing among themselves a confederation that would abolish the resort to force—and the existence of a "plan of nature" that would oblige men to give up war by making it unbearably atrocious. Marx expected that the proletarian revolution would put an end to the war among states. Rousseau, who, contrary to Kant, believed that the contest of states would either prevent the replacement of tyrants or princes by "republicans" or else would drag even these into the usual wars, saw no other solution than national insulation (see Chapter 2).

Let us return to the clash of the two models, each of which corresponds to one aspect of reality: the first, to what Aron has called "a practice and theory of happy periods when, within a stabilized civilization, the contests among states about both means and stakes remained within the limits set by an unwritten code of legitimacy and illegitimacy" (Aron, 1972). These are the characteristics of the periods of homogeneous multipolar systems. The second model describes accurately the periods of total war and of descent into total war. It also has the somber virtue of underlining the fragility of common norms and of the remedies advocated by the champions of the first model. The logic of behavior illuminated by the second model—for instance, in Rousseau's famous metaphor of the stag hunt: what the hunter wants is not a common gain but an advantage for himself—is indeed the logic of state behavior. But those who believe in the first model are correct in noting that the determination of all players to maximize their might or their respective gains risks bringing about disaster for all, and that even the search for a particular advantage sometimes requires prudence and moderation so as not to provoke a formidable coalition of all those who feel threatened. Even if the rule of self-help leaves very little authority to common norms and organizations, the simple interplay of individual calculations can, under certain conditions, result in fragile order rather than in permanent war.

Prenuclear Order

The Order of the Great Powers

Let us move from theories to empirical data and sum up the conclusions of research on the methods used for the establishment or maintenance of interstate order. We can start from the notion of three dimensions of the international system which I have presented elsewhere (Hoffmann, 1978): the horizontal dimension concerns the relations between the main actors; the vertical dimension pertains to the relations between the strong and the weak; and the functional dimension relates to the areas covered by interstate relations. For each dimension, one can ask questions about the mechanisms for order, the techniques or instruments, and the conditions of success.

The horizontal dimension is the one that has been most thoroughly studied. The reason for this, obviously, is that in a system of competing units, order or disorder, peace or chaos, depend above all on the relations that exist among those actors whose power is big enough to provoke armed conflicts of considerable scope. The problem for each unit is how to move ahead on the chessboard and how to slow down the advance of the others. The mechanism that has functioned in multipolar systems is that of the balance of power. As is well known, this term has been used in many ways, which Ernst Haas (1953) among others has clarified. Sometimes the term describes any *distribution* of power. Sometimes it applies to a *policy*: the active determination of a state to curtail the ambitions of another and to save the system for any one power's hegemony, through the concerted opposition of those who might be its victims. This had been England's policy in the eighteenth and nineteenth centuries. Sometimes the term designates a *system*, and describes a multipolar pattern in which great powers systematically coalesce in order to limit the ambitions of one of them. All the states in the coalition need not deliberately wage a policy of balance; indeed, most may have no wider concern than their immediate interest, but the system obviously functions best when one or several states aim at the preservation of equilibrium in the system (England, as mentioned above, or Bismarck between 1871 and 1890, even though Germany's disproportionate industrial and military power on the continent, and the wounds opened by the settlement of the Franco-Prussian War, threatened in the long run the very balance Bismarck was trying to maintain).

The balance-of-power system is a kind of compromise between the principle of sovereignty or self-help and the principle of the common interest. When it functions perfectly or close to perfection, it incites each of the major actors to observe self-restraint, in order not to allow others to impose restraints upon it. The mechanism of the balance is one of coalition: either the coalition of "all against one" or else, when the troublemaker has been wise enough to recruit allies, the stalemating coalition set up by those who want to preserve the status quo. It is a mechanism that obviously requires a great deal of flexibility. In other words, there ought to be no permanent alliances or hostilities that would make the system too rigid, thus supposing a certain indifference toward the domestic political regime of the state with whom one allies oneself. Moreover, it is a mechanism that tries sometimes to deter the troublemaker, and sometimes to defeat him if one has not succeeded in deterring him. Hence the diversity of the techniques used by the balance of power. Deterrence can take not only the form of a threat of war but also the more enticing form of territorial compensations or formulas for neutralizing or internationalizing a territory the troublemaker may want to acquire partly in order to prevent other countries from dominating it. If deterrence fails, a war for limited objectives—the goal being to oblige the troublemaker to back down—becomes an indispensable instrument. In such a system, then, the unilateral resort to force is a factor of trouble, but the collective resort of force is a technique of order. Insofar as the states have only limited objectives and fight each other only with moderation, the periods of the balance are those in which diplomacy and international law prosper. But international law—while it tries to delimit the domain within which the state can, in full sovereignty, exert its power, and while it regulates the means of war, seeks to limit its effects (for instance, by safeguarding neutral states) and attempts to protect victims—nevertheless does not question the freedom each state has to resort to force if it wants to.

The works of authors such as Edward Gulick (1955) and Henry Kissinger (1957) have also examined the conditions necessary for the good functioning of the balance of power system. The power of the major actors should not be too uneven; it is useful for their competition to take place mainly in areas far from those in which their vital interests are at stake; above all, it is essential that they be both vigilant and flexible. Without vigilance, changes can be very threatening for the balance (as in Prussia's progress between 1862 and 1871, or Hitler's moves in the 1930s) and could occur without either deterrence or repression. Flexibility, in its turn, disappears when the "unwritten code of legitimacy and illegitimacy" fades away, when the sense of belonging to a (contentious) community of the great powers is submerged by national egotism. This tends to happen when the rise of nationalism subjects the delicate diplomacy of balance to irresistible domestic pressures. Moreover, the mechanism of coalitions for limited ends deteriorated in the beginning of the twentieth century because each of the two alliances that confronted one another aimed no longer at limited, concrete objectives, but at the worldwide preservation of each camp's credibility; and also because nationalism threatened the very survival of one of the actors, the multinational state of Austria-Hungary, while making any further frustrations unbearable for two of the chief rivals: Germany and Russia (Lebow, 1981).

The other source of possible failure of the mechanism is, as in 1789, the revolutionary transformation of the domestic regime of one of the main actors; in such a case, even a coalition of all the others, carried out according to the earlier methods, becomes incapable of stopping the dynamism and proselytizing thrust of the enemy (Kim, 1970).

Are there comparable mechanisms of order between the rivals of bipolar systems? Waltz, who thinks that they are stable—because they do not, he believes, lead to a general war—rests his case only on the very special example of the contemporary interstate system (see below). One must note, on the one hand, that the multipolar balance of power systems entailed general wars (i.e., wars with the participation of all the major powers); but such wars were limited in intensity and objectives, and the systems allowed for considerable transformations in the distribution of power (the emergence of new major actors, the widening of the diplomatic field) without any general war in the sense of a war that puts an end to the system itself. On the other hand, Thucydides' analysis of the bipolar system of Greek city-states shows how unstable it was, and how it lacked any "horizontal" mechanism of order: the uneven alliance between each rival and its clients or vassals may have been set up by it as an instrument for balance and deterrence, but the adversary saw in it a threatening springboard, and war came out of it. For each of the two rivals, there soon was no choice other than that between appeasement and total war.

Thus the conclusions that one reaches concerning the horizontal dimension of systems are mixed. Even if one looks only at interstate patterns (i.e., a few centuries of history), one sees that the mechanism that best ensures moderation (i.e., the mechanism of the balance) has functioned well only during limited periods; that this good functioning depended on temporary conditions of homogeneity and was particularly susceptible to the vicissitudes of domestic transformations in the major actors; that among the transnational forces which affect the behavior of states, centrifugal ones like nationalism prevailed over integrative ones: the failure of the Workers' Internationale in 1914 demonstrated this. Nevertheless, there have been zones and periods of order, even if it was based on the rotating possibility of a resort to force.

The Strong and the Weak

In moving to the vertical dimension, one finds that the spectacle is even darker in some respects. Here one often discovers the pure and simple triumph of force. This is the realm in which, according to the famous statement of the Athenian generals quoted by Thucydides, the mighty do what they can, the weak do what they must. Conversely, however, this triumph of force has often made order possible, albeit a hierarchical order. The only formula that has sometimes protected weak states and saved them from the grip of a great power (often in exchange for a kind of collective supervision exerted by the European Concert) has precisely been the mechanism of the balance of power. Even that did not always work, as the successive partitions of Poland in the eighteenth and nineteenth centuries have shown. But, as we have seen, the game of balance has not always been played well; during its fiascoes, the big powers have regularly tried to acquire the territories they desired. Moreover, the balancing system applied only to Europe. The quest for resources and territory was free in the rest of the world—except in the United States, protected by the Monroe Doctrine; however, Central America could not escape from the interventions of the United States.

The constitution of an empire is one of the most frequent phenomena in the history of international relations. But it is not the best known, despite the very abundant literature on imperialism since the beginning of this century. Hobson, Hilferding, Rosa Luxemburg, and Lenin (Brewer, 1980) have all studied imperialism as an economic phenomenon, tied to the operations of the capitalist system, even though their interpretations were very different. Schumpeter (1955) was alone in analyzing it as a political phenomenon—as a tendency toward "objectless" expansion by the elites in power. But he too put his finger only on one sort of imperialism—that of the military and feudal castes that were still in power in certain European countries; according to him, a political regime that would follow the pure logic of capitalism would not be imperialist: here, we are in the orbit of liberal thought.

As Benjamin Cohen (1973) has recognized, imperialism is a political phenomenon that has to be distinguished from economic exploitation and domination: the formation of an empire is all of this, plus political control. A simple survey of history shows two things: first, that one finds this phenomenon whatever the prevailing economic system may be. Some empires have been built on slavery, some were mercantile colonial empires (Venice, Portugal, the Low Countries, the first British empire), some have been colonial empires in the age of modern industrial capitalism. Moreover, although the quest for economic profit has rarely been absent, it has not been the only or even always the main motive: Napoleon's thirst for conquests, Hitler's rage for racial domination, the ambition of absolute security that propels the empire created by the Soviet Union, Mohammed's religious proselytizing, and often—even in Rome's expansion—a notion of civilizing mission, all these political factors have played a crucial role.

Techniques have varied; but in every instance force has been the centerpiece, both in the conquest of territories and in the protection of empires against external threats and internal revolts. Such protection often seemed to require constant expansion (expansion was of course also caused by many other factors: the desire for economic domination or for control of the main routes of trade, the ambitions of rulers, etc.). For the maintenance of empires, force has taken various forms: occupation and annexation, or else a mobile army kept at the center but quickly deployed in case of threats to the areas that needed to be protected; Edward Luttwak's (1976) analysis of the strategy of the Roman empire is exemplary in this respect. But force alone was never enough. Empires rested on five pillars: (1) force, (2) diplomacy—a vertical diplomacy that manipulated the domestic politics of the vassals, and thus resembles the diplomacy aimed at maintaining order in the "camps" or uneven alliances created by the competing great powers of bipolar systems: Athens and Sparta yesterday, Washington and Moscow today; these alliances are networks that allow Big Brother to rely on the loyalty of its allies, by making sure that the rulers of these allied countries are "friends" and by bringing them often to the headquarters of the empire both for information and for favors; (3) bureaucracy, well analyzed by Eisenstadt (1963), and effective above all when it allows local customs and a certain amount of local administration to remain in place; (4) the guarantee of peace constituted by what the British called "law and order" (Romans had already understood it): a system of law (such as the *jus gentium*, the private contractual law of the Roman Empire), of good justice, and of vigilant police; and finally, of course, (5) economic rewards for reliable vassals.

It is when force becomes the single pillar that empire is threatened; or else when the costs of maintaining the empire begin to exceed the resources at the center, either because war and political domination absorb a growing part of those resources; or because private consumption increases at the expense of the share raised by the government; or else, as pointed out by Gilpin, because imperial power is weakened by the competition of other states, whose rise it has not been able to prevent and whose behavior has often been inspired by its own example; or else—and this is a transnational factor—when there develops at the center of the empire an ideology of decolonization, i.e., when the sense of superiority and mission or the conviction of the legitimacy of conquest weakens, something that is most likely to happen when the political regime at the center is based on democratic principles which the empire violates or contradicts, and which the enslaved peoples, after protracted docility, begin to claim in turn.

As for the conditions for setting up empires, they too are multiple. In the modern era there are, of course, all the factors listed by theorists of (economic) imperialism: underconsumption (Hobson), monopoly or finance capitalism (Hilferding, Lenin)—the big financial and industrial groups that need the cloak of the state in order to dominate markets. But in every era two other factors have to be taken into account: the technological advantage of the conquerors (some empires set up by Europeans in nineteenth-century Africa were established by a handful of men with modern weapons) and the often very weak condition of the conquered political groupings: peoples without states, or else old states in decay, incapable of organizing resistance. The latter factor is a "peripheral" one that has been neglected by those theories which examine only the thrust from the "center," those that Tony Smith (1981) has rightly criticized.

Empire is not the only kind of vertical order in the history of international relations. One should also look at the very special case of the overlapping hierarchical relations in feudal Europe, where the idea of Empire survived and where the personal links of fiefdom combined with the considerable influence of the Church to ensure a complex and troubled order. Even when looking only at interstate systems, one should also note the existence of hierarchical relations that were less coercive than empires, even outside the core areas in which the game of the balance was providing some moderation: some countries were able to preserve their independence in the heart of regions that were being colonized, because of their political skill (Siam) or their military capacity for self-defense (Abyssinia before 1935). Also, the states of Latin America preserved their formal independence despite the enormous preponderance of the United States, for complicated reasons such as the opposition of many Americans to direct political domination (even though recurrent interventions and the establishment of protectorates seemed all right). One notes also the mix of economic dependence and formal independence of countries such as Canada and Mexico. Pre-1914 China, too, is an interesting case: the main European countries and Japan all helped themselves and somehow neutralized one another; the United States, by insisting on an "open door" policy, contributed to preserving the formal independence of the country. Once the balancing system disappeared, Japan undertook the colonization of its huge and weak neighbor.

The war of 1914 did not result from the confrontation of the colonial empires (such a confrontation had pitted England against France and Russia, and the clash between Germany and France over Morocco did not lead to war). But unlimited general wars have been the outcomes of certain imperial attempts: those which unfolded over the main diplomatic fields rather than at the periphery. Thus Napoleon's grandiose enterprise ran into the coalition that England tirelessly shaped. Hitler's awful undertaking dragged into total war the countries most threatened by his ambitions despite their desire to avoid that war, and it was Japan's dream of creating a vast "co-prosperity sphere" for itself in Eastern and Southeast Asia that provoked, belatedly, the diplomatic resistance of the United States, and then Japan's decision to attack the United States before it could be strangled by Washington's economic pressure.

The Economic Order

Let us move on to the functional dimension. The study of interstate relations has always mainly been that of strategic-diplomatic behavior: the stakes are the independence, subjugation, or even elimination of the units, the territorial expansion or the frustration of the mighty, the preservation or the breakdown of the balance. It was during the unlimited general wars (such as the Peloponnesian War, the wars of the French revolution and Empire, and World Wars I and II) that the functions of the system proliferated; they included the birth and death not only of states but of political regimes, the speeding up of the diffusion of new technologies and ideas. During the periods in which horizontal order reigned, ideas and economic techniques also circulated, of course, but primarily because of transnational exchanges. This fact raises the problem of the relations between the interstate system and transnational society, and particularly the problem of economic exchanges. It is a double problem: to what extent have these exchanges belonged to transnational society rather than to the system of states? To what extent has the organization of economic exchanges contributed to international order?

The answer to the first question can only be historical. A relatively intense transnational society has existed only during limited periods, and it was never fully autonomous. Most often the flag has followed trade; commercial exchanges opened the way first for economic and later for political settlers (as observed in the constitution of nineteenth-century colonial empires according to Staley [1935] and to Robinson and Gallagher [1961]). The transnational society of "depoliticized" exchanges was, in the nineteenth century, a liberal ideal and a partial reality; but one must emphasize the word *partial*. Indeed, many of those exchanges took place, in uneven fashion, within the borders of empires, where the colonial power preserved for itself if not an economic monopoly, at least considerable advantages in the exploitation of local resources and the export of its own capital and goals. Once more, we find the game of power, extended to the economic realm behind the colonial fences.

Furthermore, in the exchanges among formally sovereign states or among empires, the role of power remained considerable. First, the "rules of the game" were set by the country that was the most powerful in the world economy—that is, the most developed and the best endowed in means of expansion and economic control because of its fleet and of its vast network of bases (the matter was thus one of both economic and military might). This was England's role, as the whole young American school of international political economy has observed, following Kindleberger (1977). Its members refer not only to the famous imperialism of free trade described by British authors, but also to the nineteenth-century monetary system based on gold and on the pound sterling linked to gold. Next, precisely because those apparently liberal rules of trade and automatic rules of money seemed to benefit London at the expense of England's competitors, and also because England did not always enforce those rules, the challengers did not take a long time to fight back; they used as their inspiration Friedrich List's theory of national economy. This was a neo-mercantilism that was presented as temporary, and necessary for the protection of fledgling industries, but it led rather quickly to industrial protectionism (and to the gradual decrease of Britain's advance, once Germany and the United States began to develop) as well as to agricultural protectionism, which was deemed indispensable for the preservation either of the small peasantry that constituted the backbone of the French Third Republic, or of the Junkers, or of the United States' farmers. Thus, neither the attempts to demonstrate the absurdity of conquest (made one more time, on the eve of World War I, by Norman Angell in 1914) nor the attacks on state interventionism by the liberal school had succeeded.

To what extent has the organization of economic exchanges contributed to a peaceful world order? Liberals believed that it would so contribute, as long as it was left to individuals operating freely across borders and not to states. On the other hand, the theorists of imperialism, looking at the post-1870 world, mocked the idea of free trade as a dream and denounced a reality composed not of individual merchants and producers but of corporate capitalist groups manipulating their respective states in order to exploit raw materials, grab markets, and accumulate wealth, thus provoking dangerous interstate conflicts over the division of the spoils.

Let us turn from the theories to the facts. Did the long periods during which the "mercantilist" state considered wealth to be a form of power and sought relative advantages in the contest for resources and markets contribute to order or to chaos? The answer appears evident (and it is precisely because mercantilism seems to lead to war that the liberals equated economic freedom with peace). But is it really obvious? There were, of course, many wars of greed and loot, not only between "advanced" conquerors and "underdeveloped" victims of conquests (we have already mentioned the economic factor in imperial conquests, yet also stated that empires were, in a fashion, zones of order) but also between European rivals (England and the Low Countries). The rise of protectionism certainly contributed to the collapse of the common code of European diplomacy after the end of the nineteenth century. The economic and monetary policies followed by most of the states during the Great Depression of 1929—what the British have called "beggar thy neighbor policies," which pushed the costs of the crisis on the other countries—have certainly contributed to the general deterioration of the interstate system. Thus, the liberal critique is partly correct. Nevertheless, most of the important wars that have shaken up or destroyed the European balance have no economic explanation: the ambitions of Louis XIV or of Frederick the Great, the dreams of Napoleon, Bismarck's will to Prussian power, the malaise of being an "encircled" great nation that ran so deep in the Germany of Wilhelm II, the racial delirium of Hitler, have many other roots. Is the case of Japan in 1941 an exception? Even there, the will to achieve exclusive economic domination was inseparable from the geopolitical demand for a place in the sun. We can also observe that even if the interstate economic system has not been the main cause of disorder, the great hope of a kind of pacification of the world by economic progress—commerce and industry—so well described by Aron (1958) was not fulfilled before 1945. And we can finally observe that even the limited depoliticization of the nineteenth century, or the establishment before 1914 of a kind of transnational society of business people, scientists, and labor unions, prevented neither the "nationalization" of intellectuals and proletarians, nor the manipulation of finance by governments (see Kennan's studies [1979] on German-Russian and Franco-Russian relations). Moreover, this transnational society was able to exist only so long as the political regimes of the main actors relied, for economic development, on free enterprise and on the market.

To conclude: interstate order has always been, in many ways, the order of power and particularly of military might—hence its precariousness. If general wars did not always put in question the very existence of the actors, it was often because of the mechanism of the balance and also because the means of total destruction, the material possibility for the loser to annihilate the winner, did not exist. This is no longer the case.

Contemporary Order

The Study of Contemporary Order

Is there a contemporary interstate order? The manifold originality of the present situation has often been described. It is the first worldwide system: the diplomatic field now extends to the whole planet and even to a part of space. For the first time, the game is capable of killing not only some but all of the players and of putting an end to itself because of the invention of thermonuclear weapons. The system is both bipolar—only two states have this capacity of "assured mutual destruction"—and furiously heterogeneous (the rivalry of the Big Two is both a conflict of power and an ideological war). But it has shown, until now, a remarkable flexibility (i.e., a capacity to absorb enormous changes in the distribution of power) and moderation (the absence of armed confrontation between the two chief rivals); in this respect, it is more like the balancing systems than like the bipolar systems of the past. What provides this (relative) order in a world in which each of the superpowers has given itself a network of allies or vassals, where the inequality between rich and poor increases, where the domestic fragility of so many states provokes innumerable interventions and armed conflicts, where the multiplication of units injects an additional complicating factor? (I refer to the contradiction between the principle of sovereignty, an equalitarian principle that remains the foundation of international law and order, and an extraordinarily heterogeneous reality, given that the sovereign "units" extend from huge empires to almost fictitious states, from nations with complex and differentiated political systems to countries governed in the most primitive and brutal fashion.)

This problem has been discussed by contemporary political science with a vigor and a heat that have sometimes been fueled by insufficient understanding of or interest in history—with, of course, some striking exceptions: Morgenthau, Deutsch (1968), Kissinger, (three Europeans) Rosecrance (1963) and Osgood (1957) in the United States, Aron in France, and Bull in England. It is a triple problem. Why is there a certain amount of order? What are its forms and limits? What are its chances of lasting? We shall try to answer these questions by looking again successively at the three dimensions of the system. Three preliminary remarks are necessary. First, the study of contemporary international order has become, for reasons discussed elsewhere (see Chapter 1), mainly an American specialty: the intellectual and organizational autonomy of political science in the United States is largely responsible for it, the resources of American universities have contributed to it, and so has the position of the United States in the world system (but this position does not explain everything: for instance, France's national will to independence has never been served by a systematic policy aimed at orienting research in the direction of international affairs despite the presence in France of scholars as impressive as Aron, Hassner, Grosser, and Duroselle). Second, those who have studied contemporary order, its conditions, and its prospects are on the whole astonishingly optimistic, even if they do not all agree with Kenneth Waltz's ideas (1981) on the stability of bipolar systems and on the advantages of nuclear proliferation. Aron had conluded as early as 1948 that peace was impossible but war unlikely, and he held to this view until death. Finally, research has moved in the direction of increasing specialization, with a few exceptions (sometimes more apparent than real: the rigor of Waltz's general theory leaves out a good deal of reality). In particular, strategic experts and students of international economic relations have developed different concepts and jargons, and there are many difficult problems of connection and synthesis.

The horizontal dimension remains the most important one in the strategic-diplomatic system. The superpowers have, so far, despite all their disagreements and crises, successfully preserved world peace. Why? The most frequent explanation is the nuclear revolution, defined by Bernard Brodie (1959) and by Aron (1963) as the capacity of the state that owns the "absolute weapon" to *destroy* the enemy without first having to *defeat* the enemy's armies. When two rival great powers have this capacity, it becomes suicidal; then, according to Churchill's memorable formula, security is the sturdy child of terror and survival the twin brother of annihilation.

As usual, things are not quite as simple. On the one hand, the Americans enjoyed for a good dozen years first the monopoly of nuclear weapons and later a quasi-monopoly of the means to hit the rival's territory with them. The United States' moderation, during this phase, can be explained in part by two intellectual factors—horror at the thought of preventive war, and an apparent conviction that even though the Soviet Union, like Nazi Germany, was a totalitarian and expansionist power, its leaders, unlike Hitler, could be gradually constrained to change Soviet external behavior without a world war. There was also an external factor—the Soviet Union's conventional threat in Europe: thus, bipolar equilibrium has been a "balance of imbalances." On the other hand, as Kennan (1982) and the other critics of nuclear deterrence have asserted, can one prove that the Soviet Union and the United States would have fought a war if thermonuclear bombs had not been invented? Neither Soviet expansionism nor America's thirst for power are matched with a policy of large-scale armed aggression. But it is at least likely that the nuclear revolution has considerably strengthened incentives to preserve prudence. It is also plausible that peace has been maintained in part because of the Soviet conviction (already mentioned by Kennan, even at the time when he tried to force the United States to discover the existence of the Soviet threat) that the very course of history guarantees the ultimate triumph of "socialism"; and in part because of the United States' faith in the success of "containment" without major war, given the enormous global assets at the disposal of the United States.

How does an order no longer that of the balancing systems function? It is different from the balancing order for two reasons. Those earlier systems were multipolar, whereas today the distance that separates the two superpowers from all the others, in the strategic-diplomatic realm, is immense. Moreover, the balance of nuclear forces is not a matter of coalitions: "resorting to allies in order to restore a damaged balance is a thing of the past" (Aron, 1966), insofar as the central strategic forces are concerned, even if being able to resort to allies remains essential for the global balance (although such balance no longer occurs in the old form of a game of shifting alignments, on the contrary) and above all for regional blances. In fact, at the central strategic level, each of the superpowers detests the complications introduced by the nuclear forces of third parties—even their own allies: the break between the Soviet Union and China has been partly caused by the conflict between Russia's will to a nuclear monopoly in its camp and partly by China's blunt challenge. The lack of American enthusiasm for the French nuclear force is well known (as for the British force, Washington has largely succeeded in domesticating it).

The crucial mechanism of horizontal order today is nuclear deterrence— the threat of intolerable but assured retaliation in case of aggression. Strategists and statesmen have devised a kind of formula for stable deterrence—that is, for being able to manage crises without having either the fear that the rival would have an enormous advantage in striking first or the temptation of doing so oneself. This formula entails, on the one hand, the protection of the retaliatory force in such a way that even after an enemy first strike it would remain able to inflict unacceptable damage, and, on the other hand, the absence both of a network of civil defense capable of sheltering the bulk of one's population, and of a network of active defense (antimissile systems for the protection of cities) effective enough to inspire a hope of ravaging one's enemy without risking terrible losses of population in retaliation. The invulnerability of nuclear forces, the vulnerability of the population—such has been the very paradoxical equation of stable balance, the theory of which has been worked out by Glenn Snyder (1961), Thomas Schelling (1960), and Albert Wohlstetter in the United States, and by Aron (1965, 1966, 1985) in France.

Independent even of technological evolution (see below), uncertainty over two connected issues has nevertheless continued to exist. Against what kinds of aggressions does the nuclear threat protect one, and what makes this threat credible? As the nuclear arsenal of the Soviet Union caught up with that of the United States, and as one reached what McGeorge Bundy (1983) has called "existential deterrence" (a condition in which each side has the capacity to destroy the other), the policy of threatening total destruction in case of aggression became less plausible (in that it was now suicidal), except as a means of deterring the enemy from a direct and massive nuclear attack. But as a deterrent against a limited atomic or conventional aggression against a third party whose protection is deemed vital (such as Western Europe for the United States), the terrifying threat of "massive retaliation" has ceased being entirely credible. This is why, in the 1960s, the Americans shifted to the new doctrine of "flexible response"; it was less terrifying but more credible, and—despite the fears expressed by many commentators, and by European statesmen, at the time—not any the less deterring, insofar as the risk of escalation in case of a conventional war, or in case of a resort to tactical nuclear weapons, remained extremely high. At the other end of the spectrum, it has always been obvious that one could not prevent either limited enemy operations or wars of national liberations waged by allies of Moscow, by threatening nuclear war in areas of secondary interest. If in vital areas the credibility of a "flexible" nuclear threat against conventional aggression is reinforced by the presence of conventional forces capable of slowing down the enemy's advance by themselves, the enemy is obliged to be equally cautious, when the stake he seeks is one his rival considers very important but impossible to defend by conventional means alone; for, in this instance, the risk of rapid escalation to the nuclear level is very high (as in Berlin and the Middle East).

The effects of mutual nuclear deterrence have been extremely important.

1. There has been, not a decrease of violence (there are far too many factors of conflict in this world), but a decentralization of violence; stability at the central and global levels has not prevented instability at the lower levels (conventional wars, guerrilla wars, subversion). However, all of these wars have pitted against each other either third countries or a superpower and a third country—whether allied or not to the other superpower.

2. There has been, at the same time, a fragmentation of the strategic-diplomatic system into regional subsystems. In that connection, the outcome of conflicts has depended much more on the balance of forces in the area and on purely domestic factors (for instance, the internal weakness of South Vietnam) than on the strategic nuclear balance. The effects listed under this paragraph and the one above have forced attention back to the problem of limited wars; they can continue to be, according to Clausewitz's famous formula, a continuation of policy by other means (Kissinger, 1957; Osgood, 1957).

3. Direct military confrontations between the superpowers have been replaced by crises. These have broken out either because of the moves of one power in a zone considered vital by the other (Berlin blockade, 1948; Soviet pressure on Berlin, 1958–1961; Cuban missile crisis, 1962) or as the by-product of a war between third parties (Middle East, 1973). These crises have been managed without violence, and their outcome has resulted sometimes from the regional balance of forces (Cuba) and sometimes from the fact that the very importance of the stake for the superpower on the defensive obliged the other side to behave with considerable prudence (Berlin). There has been a notable absence of major crises between the superpowers since the Cuban missile crisis (the brief U.S.-Soviet confrontation of October 1973 was already far more limited in its stakes and duration). Is this because each side has become more aware of the need for prudence, and of the unpredictability of major crises, in an age of nuclear parity and abundance? Is it because earlier Soviet probes in areas of vital interest for the United States had been attempts at compensating for a nuclear inferiority that has now been amply remedied? Were the crises in the 1970s and 1980s avoided at first because post-Vietnam America refused to treat Soviet moves in Africa as a major challenge (and had only very limited ways of responding to the Soviet invasion of Afghanistan), and later because three paralyzing crises of political succession occurred in Moscow—factors that have now run their course?

4. Stability at the strategic level, the common interest in avoiding general destruction through accident or escalation, and the concern to slow down military expenditures have made possible various negotiations for the control of strategic arms. But these factors have had only limited results—namely, the ban on atmospheric tests agreed upon by the two superpowers (1963), the ban on antiballistic missile defense systems (1972), quantitative limits imposed on offensive arms by the interim agreement of 1972 and by the unratified but generally observed SALT II agreement since 1979. One could argue that the main advantage of these long and complicated discussions has been communication between the superpowers.

5. Past bipolar systems have always been unstable: at every moment the precarious balance risked being upset by the defection of an ally or the decision of a neutral to join one or the other camp. The paradox of the bipolar nuclear system is this: as major maneuvers in vital areas have become too dangerous, the quest for marginal advantages in secondary areas (Africa, Southeast Asia) or the exploitation of internal factors in the countries of those areas have often become more frantic; but at the same time, such gains have not proved capable of affecting the global balance dramatically. Moreover, each of the superpowers has observed certain rules that have contributed to stability. Thus, each one of them has implicitly recognized, in one instance the other power's zone of imperial domination (Eastern Europe), in the other case a less well-defined "right" of the United States to preserve a preponderant influence in Central America even at the expense of forces allied to Moscow. Also, each superpower has in fact, if not always

in strategic doctrine, treated nuclear weapons as fundamentally different from conventional ones (despite a variety of sometimes ambiguous threats, the United States has never used nuclear weapons against its non-nuclear enemies: North Korea, China during the Korean war, or North Vietnam). Finally, each superpower has, *de facto* and later *de jure*, treated as inviolable by force the line that separates Western from Eastern Europe, even though it keeps Germany divided.

Will this complex order, which has lasted forty years, be able to last forever? Will the dialectic that has been fatal in past bipolar conflicts—the dialectic of credibility and commitment—prevail in the end over the rules of the game that have preserved order so far? There are two reasons to worry, and these reasons may become compounded.

The first of these reasons pertains to the political relations between the superpowers. The study of balance of power systems shows that moderation can end by blowing up the fuses. The more compromises one has made earlier, the more, next time, one may be tempted to refuse to yield again, especially if one has reasons to believe that the position of the rival will be stronger in the future if one retreats once more now, and that the rival has better incentives to back down because the stakes are less serious from him (as in 1914). The very scope of the conflict of interests and power between the Big Two—not to mention their ideological conflict—makes future crises almost certain; so is the risk that each one will be manipulated by important allies or clients. Can one be sure that crisis management will always succeed, and that there will never be a direct military confrontation? Will prudence prevail, if one or the other superpower begins to believe that it is on the decline and that it must take strong measures to stop or to reverse the trend?

The second reason is technological in nature. The United States and the Soviet Union have moved from inaccurate countercity nuclear weapons (complemented by short-range tactical nuclear weapons) to accurate strategic arms capable of hitting the enemy's command systems and forces, including a part of its strategic forces (land-based missiles especially). Thus, a major part of the decisive arsenals has become vulnerable again, and one has gotten closer to the universe of "normal" or traditional war—that is, to the possibility of first defeating the other side's military capabilities in the hope of thus avoiding total destruction (i.e., limiting damage). Each side now tries to deter the other by providing itself with credible means of waging a counterforce nuclear war or a limited war against military targets, rather than by threatening the other, less credibly, with total destruction. Whereas in "assured mutual destruction" nobody can win, the idea of a classical-type victory becomes conceivable again. To be sure, the risk of escalation has not disappeared: neither side can destroy the other's retaliation forces in a first strike. Since total destruction remains a possibility (this is the very meaning of existential deterrence) and since the chances of controlling a nuclear conflict remain uncertain, the restraint of existential deterrence still operates. However, there now exist three (contradictory) possibilities, all of which pose a danger to the order we now experience.

The apocalyptic possibility is the temptation each side may have, in a major crisis, of striking first at the systems of command and control (including the satellites) and at the vulnerable strategic forces of the other side out of fear of losing its own vulnerable nuclear forces and its own system of command and control, or other important military elements, if the enemy should strike first. The race to defensive systems in space risks the same effect: recreating the hope or fear of an advantage to the side that strikes first. The country that is ahead in the construction of such systems might believe that, in a major crisis, it could initiate the use of atomic weapons without risking intolerable retaliation because of its network of protection; or else, the country that is falling behind may come to believe that it has an interest in striking the enemy's vulnerable systems and forces before they become beyond reach; or else, each side will have an interest in multiplying accurate offensive forces capable of destroying the enemy's defensive systems. Thus it is crisis stability that technological evolution undermines. Such stability could be restored if each side gave up the competition in space, or if it replaced its land-based missiles with multiple warheads, which constitute most attractive targets, with single warhead or mobile missiles or even submarines.

Yet, even then, two perils would still remain. One or the other side may be tempted to resort to a limited use of nuclear weapons in order to protect or to gain a major stake, in the hope of being able to prevent escalation and to limit damage thanks to the new precision of the weapons; but it might not succeed in doing so, because of what Clausewitz used to call "friction." Or else the very risk of escalation, and the likely difficulty of limiting war after a first resort to nuclear weapons in highly populated zones stuffed with such arms, might lead the rival powers to abandon—in fact or in their doctrines—the very thought of such a resort; this would make it possible to go back to conventional wars (preferably limited ones), even between the superpowers. This is precisely what concerns many West Europeans: they believe that such a war would become more likely if NATO abandoned the threat of a first use of nuclear weapons because it feared the catastrophic effects of a failure of nuclear deterrence and of an execution of the threat. The Europeans' anxiety may well be excessive, so long as conventional and nuclear weapons remain packed together; but it constitutes the present-day form of the dilemma: "either a threat of nuclear war that is total, terrifying but not very credible, or a risk of limited war that is less terrifying but more likely." In the future, the deterrent effect of the risk could be much smaller than in the days of "flexible response."

The Superpowers and Other States

For the time being, the duelists, while accumulating weapons, keep their powder dry. Many commentators have written about the effects of this kind of paralysis on the interstate hierarchy—that is, the vertical dimension of the system. The indefinite postponement of the "payment in cash" or the "minute of truth" between the superpowers is said to have made for a kind of emancipation of the smaller powers, to which what General Gallois (1963) has called the equalizing power of the atom is assumed to have contributed.

Hierarchy is obviously not what it used to be, but one must, in the first place, understand why. Five causes come to mind.

1. The first cause involves the possibility for a weak client to blackmail a big power—for instance, by threatening it either with collapse or with a change of camp unless it receives some help from Big Brother. There is nothing original in this: in any bipolar system the big powers' contest for the allegiance of the small ones puts cards into the hands of the latter. (The other causes, which are connected, are much more original.)

2. The second cause concerns the emancipation of the former colonies, the destruction of overseas empires that has led to the creation of many new states, endowed with the rights entailed by sovereignty and above all with the possibilities of collective maneuver and protection that result from belonging to the UN and to various regional organizations (many of these—the Organization of African Unity, the Association of South-East Asian Nations, the Arab League despite its constant splits, the Organization of American States despite the heavy presence of the United States, the European Community—help reinforce small and middle-sized states through the technique of association; the General Assembly of the UN has the same function).

3. The next cause lies in the realm of values: in Western countries resistance to the use of force against the weak has developed; it is a kind of postimperial sense of guilt (the famous Vietnam syndrome plays a comparable role in the United States), but it is also the expression of liberal values.

4. Moreover, it is certain that each of the superpowers often has good reasons to fear that too brutal an intervention in a third country would provoke a counterintervention by its rival, leading to risks and costs exceeding the stakes. As for less-great powers eager to restore a hierarchy upset by even weaker ones, the example of Great Britain and France at Suez (1956) has shown that there can be an objective collusion of the superpowers in order to call the lesser ones back to order; in addition, the example of the rather weak "lesson" administered by China to Vietnam in 1980 has shown the moderating influence exerted by China's need not to expose itself too much to Soviet reprisals and American discontent.

5. Finally, the fragmentation of the system—the relative autonomy of the regional subsystems because of the relative mutual neutralization of the superpowers—gives to the actors on those more limited stages an equally relative liberty of maneuver and the opportunity (or the illusion—if we think of the Shah of Iran, of Nasser, of Soekarno or Nkrumah) of splashing around "like the Big Boys" and of seeking—often aggressively—regional preponderance (hence, in 1983-1985, the case of Libya or Syria).

The relative emancipation of the small and less-great powers has manifested itself in two particularly impressive ways. There has been, though more slowly than some feared, a proliferation of nuclear weapons and of the means to obtain them, despite the pressures of the nuclear "haves" (in particular, the 1968 nonproliferation treaty). For the moment, this process has had no disastrous effect; but would that always be the case, once these weapons were introduced in areas where hatreds are inexpiable, the stakes are nothing less than the life and death of states, and the conditions of stable deterrence that exist among the superpowers are utterly missing?

Above all, small and middle-sized powers have resorted to force with much more zest and sometimes far fewer limits than the superpowers: there have been wars in the Middle-East (Israel and the Arab states, Iraq against Iran), in Korea, in Vietnam, between India and Pakistan, Turkish interventions in Cyprus, Vietnam's invasion of Cambodia, the Argentine invasion of the Falkland Islands, the large-scale terrorism sponsored by Libya, Syria, and Khomeini's Iran, and so on. At times these operations took place in the interstices of the U.S.-Soviet contest, so to speak; at times each belligerent had taken the precaution of receiving aid or protection from one of the superpowers. But even in those instances it is almost impossible to attribute these conflicts to the competition between the two great rivals: the complexity, the heterogeneity of the system, prevents them from reducing all international affairs to their confrontation (this is indeed one of the more original factors of moderation in the postwar bipolar system).

Must one therefore agree with Robert W. Tucker (1977), who believes that the subversion of traditional hierarchy breeds chaos? One should realize, however, in the second place, that the dialogue between the Athenians and the unfortunate leaders of Melos has not become entirely irrelevant. The big powers do not allow the lesser ones to undermine the fragile order of the system very much more than they allowed it yesterday. And they still have many means at their disposal.

First, the most intensive use of force remains—obviously—the privilege of the most powerful, even if it has not been able to prevent decolonization (partly because force is badly equipped to crush a people well organized for guerrilla warfare, partly because the metropolitan countries had neither the means nor the will to raise all the forces that would have been needed to defeat and keep down those who dared claim the right to self-determination). The Soviet Union has preserved its empire in Eastern Europe by force; despite all the costs, it has invaded Afghanistan; it has exploited favorable circumstances (the predictable absence of U.S. reactions) in order to set up, by means of airlifted Cubans, client regimes in Angola and Ethiopia. The United States has used force more discreetly but with success in Guatemala (1954), Santo Domingo (1965), and Grenada (1983), and it is trying to do so in Nicaragua. Israel has expanded through conquest in an area where its military might makes of it a kind of local superpower. And Vietnam is still in Cambodia, despite the guerrilla forces that China supports there.

Second, while alliances provide clients with means of blackmail, they also provide the superpowers with important instruments for influence or pressure, particularly through the use of military assistance and economic aid.

Third, the frequent prudence that characterizes the direct armed interventions of the superpowers is offset by the formidable expansion of what could be called the weapon of subversion. Conquest may not always be possible or desirable, but the manipulation of the domestic politics of small powers is made particularly tempting and frequent by the weakness and artificiality of so many of those states.

Fourth, the emancipation or the maneuvers of states that seek to become "regional hegemonic powers" find their limits in their domestic, economic, social, and political weaknesses, which dispel illusions and force reality back sooner or later. Often, such states lack effective instruments for action abroad; they are racked by domestic conflicts that make ambitious foreign policies impossible; they do not have the military means even if their economic resources are great; they are deep in debt; and so on.

Such is the picture. Until now both the partial subversion of traditional hierarchy and its partial persistence have contributed to give to interstate order a Hobbesian aspect. Except in the East, it is no longer the rough peace of empires, but it often resembles a kind of war of all against all, made bearable by its very fragmentation. The main risk for world order comes from the unpredictable combination of what is new (the contentious emancipation of the small) with what is old (the forced subordination of the small). In a bipolar system this emancipation, even though it multiplies partial violence, defuses somewhat the central confrontation or removes certain areas from its reach, but the chief rivals either try to reinsert themselves or are themselves called in. When this intervention happens, the partial subordination of the small, the classical game of manipulating (and being manipulated by) weak regimes, the hazards of uneven alliances, of clients bought or rented in order to checkmate the rival great power, risk (as in the cases of Corcyra and Potidea, or in the Balkans of 1914) bringing about a huge confrontation in those corners of the earth where the vital interests of the superpowers, the partial autonomy of their clients, regional antagonisms and domestic troubles are combined. Certainly this is the case in the Middle East, and perhaps also in the Far East, where the game is even more complicated as it is played by both superpowers, two middle powers, and several small ones.

The World Economic Order

What about the functional dimension? It has been the subject of a considerable number of studies, especially since the end of the 1960s, when the crisis of the world monetary system (the fixed exchange rates regime of Bretton Woods), followed by the oil crisis, put the spotlight back on the economic dimensions of international politics, especially since detente allowed temporary relief from strategic headaches.

Here is the first surprise: everybody now agrees that transnational society is strongly politicized *and* that the world political economy is not exclusively interstate. The collective book edited by Robert Keohane and Joseph Nye (1972) is very clear on this point. On the one hand, the state's agenda is at least as economic as it is strategic-diplomatic. This is so both because global strategy, thanks to those ominous absolute weapons, has become viscous if not frozen and, above all, because growth, development, and welfare have become the essential goals in every country: they constitute the aspirations of the people and the responsibility of the states themselves. (Whatever the relative importance of commercial exchanges now as compared to the period before 1914, Waltz, always enamored of paradoxes, has argued that they were higher then; however, their political meaning has completely changed, given the huge increase in the economic functions of governments.) The satisfaction of such needs cannot be obtained by autarchy. This is so especially because the rules of the game, set, as in the past, by the dominant economic and military power (the United States), are those of the "open" international economy, with the lowering of tariff barriers and the convertibility of currencies. (It is so also, paradoxically, because the state's economic goals can sometimes be reached best neither through autarchy nor through following the rules, but through cheating.) There are, of course, closed command economies—those of the "socialist" countries—but insofar as they do not insulate themselves and want the benefit of international trade and credit, they contribute in their own way to the politicization of economic relations.

On the other hand, everybody also recognizes that world economic relations are handled not only by the states but by a whole series of other, transnational actors. Some of those are private and dispose of a considerable margin of autonomy both from their state of origin and from their host states; I refer to multinational corporations, which act according to a world logic of profit that often takes very little account of borders (see the works of Raymond Vernon [1971]). Others are public actors, of two sorts: fragments of governments that also have some autonomy and often ally with the corresponding fragments of foreign bureaucracies against other sections of the national bureaucracy: governors of central banks, officials in charge of energy, the military, and so forth. The other kind is composed of regional or international organizations whose functions are economic and whose secretariats are often very influential.

What remains, obviously, is the other question previously raised about the economic dimension before 1945. Has this system, which is both interstate and transnational, contributed to order? Here comes the second surprise: we find two main conflicting theories—one is cheerful, one is somber—but both answer yes.

The dark theory is the *dependencia* school, or the school of center-periphery relations (André Gunder Frank [1977], Samir Amin [1980], Galtung [1980], and many others). It is dark, because it describes the exploitation of the underdeveloped countries of the periphery and of the peripheral social classes in the advanced countries, by the elites (bourgeoisies) of the latter. In particular, the exploited countries are doomed either to remain exporters of primary products or to create only those industries that are built for the satisfaction of multinational corporations and controlled by them. The surplusses and the technicians, the resources and the brains, are confiscated, as it were, by the exploiters. Thus ruled out is an autonomous economic development that would be guided by the interests of the impoverished masses: an agriculture capable of feeding the people instead of being geared to export, an industry meeting the basic needs of the people rather than introducing highly sophisticated and capital-intensive technologies. This theory has often been criticized (see Tony Smith [1981] and Raymond Vernon [1971])—in particular, because it underestimates the capacity of the "peripheries" to resist and the benefits that they can derive from foreign investments for their own development. But this debate about reality should not make one forget that the theory recognizes, and protests against, the existence in the realm of economic relations of an order that is, once more, the order of the strong: the capitalist "centers." For what we find here is a modernized theory of economic imperialism, presented as a capitalist necessity.

The rosy theory, on the other hand, is that of interdependence. It is an essentially American theory (Richard Cooper [1968], Edward Morse [1976], the book written jointly by Keohane and Nye [1977], Vernon, etc.). The most accomplished presentation is Keohane and Nye's concept of "complex interdependence." It describes not only geographic fragmentation but also functional fragmentation and specialization in an international system that has exploded into "vertical" subsystems, of which the strategic-diplomatic variety is just one example. To each form of power (monetary, commercial, energy, etc.) corresponds a subsystem that has its own configuration. The subsystems other than the strategic-diplomatic one constitute games that do not entail a resort of force, which is of no use in the realm of exchanges and development. Unlike many of the strategic ones, these are not, at least in the long run, zero-sum games; the interdependence of economic variables provides each player with an interest in fostering the growth of the other players, so we are in a realm where each side seeks an absolute gain, not a relative advantage. The idea that comes out of this model is that of games whose outcome is determined, not by the ratio of the players' military forces, but by the distinctive structure of each of the games (the distribution of the type of power which is involved in it: power is not "fungible," it is heterogeneous) as well as by more random factors (the relative importance of the game for each player and his skill in the art of forming coalitions and of controlling the agenda). It is not an idealist fantasy, since it starts with power and acknowledges inequality (as when the power of a main player pushes onto others the costs of adjustments to change). But it is an attractive picture, since it suggests both a sort of taming of the power of the mighty (insofar as the hierarchy is not the same in all subsystems, and also insofar as the game rules out the use of the one form of power most characteristic of the mighty: military force) and a kind of "fading away of sovereignties" (Aron, 1985)—both the small and the large ones—in favor of collective solutions. The order that is thus described as spreading is quite original, for it requires no common values other than a vague notion of long-term compatibility of economic interests, nor any hegemonial power setting the rules of the games (Keohane, 1984), nor any central common power—only what these writers call "international regimes," the role of which is to facilitate and manage the bargains. Unlike traditional utopias of world government, or of world or regional federalism (or functional "supranationality"), such regimes entail not a transfer of sovereignty to a new set of central institutions above the existing states but the *pooling* of sovereignties—that is, a preference for joint rather than often fruitless or counterproductive unilateral action. Nevertheless, one gets the picture of an incipient and partial, fragmentary and fragmented, world society whose processes can be compared to those of a domestic political one: a new, less narrow, and above all less short-term definition of the national interest, the usefulness of compromise, the preference for collective solutions as the best way toward individual gains, the interest in setting up and safeguarding agencies that facilitate, carry out, and perpetrate such compromises. This, in short, is what ensures order.

It is clear that the two theories emphasize absolutely different techniques: the predatory economic and political logic of capitalism in one case (a factor that comes from within the dominant economies) and, in the other instance, bargaining and those international institutions that both result from it and embody it, as in the conception of Jean Monnet, turned into a theory by Ernst Haas (1953), the mentor of many of the "interdependence" theorists. The collective work edited by Stephen Krasner (1982) on "international regimes" is both edifying and troubling (because of a mix of conceptual uncertainties and tautologies). One of the theories produces a kind of unity of the strategic-diplomatic and the economic, to the advantage of the latter, which is considered to be the motor of all world politics (it is a boneless Marxism); the other clearly separates, and fragments, the economic from what might be called the Clausewitzian (whose importance, even for the preservation of the world economic system, it recognizes).

Unfortunately, one can reach a far less firm conclusion (whether it is firm and depressed, or firm and complacent) concerning the existence and solidity of world economic order if one starts from a different approach. This approach is one that also recognizes the diversity of games or subsystems but is less sure of the victory of the cumulative logic of interdependence. Here are the reasons.

1. We remain, even here, in the realm of self-help. The oil crisis of 1973 demonstrated that certain states, when they coalesce around a quasi-monopoly or an oligopoly, can obtain a formidable redistribution of resources through shock tactics very different from "bargaining." In each game, the dominant power can seek either to obtain a relative gain or to rid itself of burdens that have become unbearable (i.e., to reduce its vulnerability to interdependence) by abruptly and unilaterally changing the rules of that game (see what the United States did to the world monetary system in 1971, then in 1973, and ever since. Washington has been determined to

let the dollar be shaped by priorities of domestic economic policy while keeping its role as the world's currency).

2. Despite, or perhaps because of, their relative autonomy as actors on the world stage, private banks and technical international organizations can be led by the very logic of interdependence or of mutual interests to follow policies that turn out to be disastrous in the event of an international recession: this is the threat that the debts of underdeveloped countries, including some oil-producing ones, have held over all world economic relations.

3. Because of the weakness of "international regimes," which are far from covering all the realms of interdependence (cf. the difficulties concerning the law of the seas), and from being endowed with extensive and constraining powers (even the most advanced such regime, that of the European community, is recurrently paralyzed), the economic subsystems are submitted not to a kind of common rationality but to the hazards of coalition, to the very frequent determination of the players to put their immediate national interest ahead of the interests of the group, and to the efforts of some to increase their independence even at the price of tearing up the cloth of interdependence.

4. The economy is both a field and a weapon. Although the politicization of the economic subsystems does not mean that they are dominated by the ratio of military forces, it is nevertheless true that in the strategic-diplomatic game the economic weapon is very frequently used (see the work of Klaus Knorr, 1975): embargoes, sanctions, and rewards abound. This use drives a few more holes into that cloth, and shows that the relations between the subsystems are more complex and less reassuring than the theory of order through interdependence suggests.

5. Economic contests are about both wealth and power. Many of the demands presented by developing countries in the UN and in a variety of international regimes are aimed at increasing the power of these countries to shape the rules of the various games, at setting the agendas, at extracting resources and better terms of trade from the richer states. They also aim, often, at replacing the allocation of goods by a market they deem skewed at their expense, with allocation by political decisions and deals in which they would play a larger part. Many industrial nations reject such demands (cf. the U.S. and West German refusal to accept the law of the seas convention). As Stephen D. Krasner (1985) has pointed out, this conflict, which does not rule out specific bargains and, one might add, leaves room for many variations among the contenders on both sides, is likely to be enduring. It shows that the common condition of interdependence does not abolish the possibility of struggles over who commands and who benefits most from it—any more than domestic solidarity abolishes contests over the levers and stakes of politics among parties and interest groups.

Normative Scholarship

This is what we have: an order which, on top, preserves global peace by preparing for atomic war in all its forms and by multiplying weapons that one hopes never to have to use because they are so horrible, but which one is not at all sure to be able to control, should they be used. It is an order whose most visible daily aspects—both the by-products of this strange equilibrium of deterrence, and the results of domestic and regional circumstances—are the frenzied acquisition of weapons and the proliferation of armed conflicts on a small scale (but small only by comparison to collective Apocalypse). It is an economic order marked by the blinding contrast between the old principle of sovereignty and the obvious impossibility of resolving by oneself almost any of the problems posed by the imperative of welfare and development, as well as by the crisis of economic science, which deprives even the champions of any given method for national or collective progress of their certainties. One can easily understand why researchers deal only with different parts of the monster, or else reduce it to a reassuring skeleton.

The risk that we might some day see general war made less unlikely by "impossible peace" (local wars or economic chaos) nevertheless goads many scholars and thinkers into "praxeology"—that is, the attempt to draw political prescriptions from their analyses, or even to define a kind of moral policy that would allow a less fragile and less unfair order to prevail. What is striking in these analyses is the discredit of institutions that were once the focus of so many hopes. Peace-through-law appears only in the form of "international regimes," but these are more concerned with bargains than with legal rules, and one is generally agreed (see Robert Jervis [1982]) that such regimes have only meager chances in the realm of security. Nobody seems to believe anymore in the chances of collective security; because of its constraining character, it is too contrary to the freedom of judgment and action implied by sovereignty; and, because of the way in which it would oblige the international "community" to punish any aggressor, it is in conflict with the imperatives of prudence in the nuclear age, in which the localization or insulation of conflicts appears far preferable to their generalization. The failure of the United Nations in the peaceful settlement of disputes and the retreat of the UN in peacekeeping (i.e., its attempt to preserve or restore peace not through collective security but by sending forces of interposition) result both from the impossibility for the world organization to transcend the cold war and from the increase in the number of serious conflicts among those nonaligned states on which Dag Hammarskjöld had wanted to rely in order to impress and curb the superpowers.

Peace-by-federation, in its turn, has lost its champions: those who had put their hopes in this admirable formula or in the contagion of functional regional federalism have had to take into account the failures of attempts at regional integration, noted by Erns Haas (1953). There are still popular movements, often vehement ones, for partial or total disarmament. But most scholars do not aim so high; they would be satisfied even with a nuclear freeze or a somewhat vigorous resumption of arms control, or with agreements to limit the sales of arms and to preserve regional military balances at a reasonable level.

Symptomatic of such political disillusionment is the fact that the two most ambitious attempts at praxeology— that of the Council on Foreign Relations, the "1980s Project," and the more radical and utopian undertaking by Richard Falk (1975), the "World Order Models Project"—are much less explicit about order in the realm of security than about the desirable forms of cooperative order and transfers of sovereignty in the economic realm (forms inspired by the theorists of interdependence in the first case, and in the latter one by the doctrinaires of *dependencia* who, like Galtung, advocate a mix of individual or collective self-sufficiency of the poor countries and of central management of humanity's common goods under the direction of those countries, as against the two imperial superpowers). About the strategic-diplomatic realm, the "1980s Project" says very little (except that the "regime of nuclear deterrence" should be preserved and nuclear proliferation slowed down), and the radical project counts on the will of the people for disarmament; here, at any rate, ecology comes before strategy.

The renewal, in the United States and to a lesser degree in England, of works of applied ethics dealing with political issues reflects altogether the increasing interest of philosophers for problems of social ethics, the new interest of political scientists for the ethical dimensions of their field, and the idea that it is, after all, more important to help citizens and statesmen clarify their goals and choices than to prescribe to them more or less peremptorily desirable processes and institutions. This renewal also reflects the thought that even though the quest for order in international affairs comes before that of justice, each order has its own features—features that express an underlying conception of justice. In the past, it was a conception of justice based on the right of the mighty, in all the dimensions of the system. Today, this right is no longer recognized by the weaker ones, who now have some effective means of resistance. Above all, in the atomic age the dangers of force as a means of settling conflicts and as the foundation of empires have become enormous. Hence the idea that an agreement on what is just has become a prerequisite for order. But is such an agreement conceivable in so unharmonious a world? Here we are far beyond the realist school, which, at best, dealt with ethics by describing the enlightened national interest as moral, out of fear of falling into the pitfalls and hypocrisies of moralism in the furious world of states.

Current ethical reflection takes many forms. Some theorists call for an order rather modestly based on what Michael Walzer (1977) has called the "legalist paradigm": mutual recognition by the states of their right to independence (nonintervention, but also duty to resist aggression). This right is based on and derived from the principle of the right of peoples to self-determination. Others, such as Charles Beitz (1979), want to apply to the whole world the principles that John Rawls (1971), in his *Theory of Justice*, wanted to apply only to the citizens of a political community. These authors try to define norms of justice not for the states but for humankind. Others adopt an intermediary position (Hoffmann, 1981). All of these works examine the conditions in which, in the nuclear era, war could still be considered just (see the statement of the National Conference of Bishops, 1983); like the Bishops, these writers condemn any resort—or almost any resort—to atomic weapons, but many hesitate to condemn the deterrent threat; they also ask themselves what the chances for and the desirable substance of an international policy of human rights would be. They examine what forms a policy of distributive justice should take, if it wanted to overcome both the selfishness of the rich states and the corruption and defensiveness of the political regimes in the poor countries.

Do such efforts show a will to think more deeply about world order, at a time when the imperatives of survival and development seem to dictate some counsels of moderation and mutual help to statesmen despite the clash of interests, ideologies, and values? Or is it merely a "hope of the hopeless," a last perspective open to scholars scared by what their analyses unveil, but thoroughly devoid of political illusions?

References

Amin, Samir, *L'accumulation à l'échelle mondiale* (Paris, 1980).
Angell, Norman, *The Great Illusion* (London, 1914).
Aron, Raymond, *Le grand schisme* (Paris, 1948).
———, *La société industrielle et la guerre* (Paris, 1958).
———, *Paix et guerre* (Paris, 1962). [In English: *Peace and War*, New York, 1966.]
———, *Le grand débat* (Paris, 1963). [In English: *The Great Debate*, Garden City, 1965.]
———, *Ecrits politiques* (Paris, 1972), p. 475.
———, *Penser la guerre: Clausewitz*, 2 vols. (Paris, 1976). [In English: *Clausewitz*, New York, 1985.]
Beitz, Charles, *Political Theory and International Relations* (Princeton, 1979).
Brewer, Anthony, *Marxist Theories of Development* (London, 1980).
Brodie, Bernard, *Strategy and the Missile Age* (Princeton, 1959).
Bull, Hedley, *The Anarchical Society* (New York, 1977).
Bundy, McGeorge, "The Bishops and the Bomb," *New York Review of Books* (June 16, 1983).
Carr, E. H., *The Twenty Years' Crisis* (London, 1980).
Claude, I. L., *Power and International Relations* (New York, 1962).
Cohen, Benjamin, *The Question of Imperialism* (New York, 1973).
Cooper, Richard, *The Economics of Interdependence* (New York, 1968).
Deutsch, Karl, *The Analysis of International Relations* (Englewood Cliffs, 1968).
Eisenstadt, Schmuel, *The Political Systems of Bureaucratic Empire* (New York, 1963).
Falk, Richard, *A Study of Future Worlds* (New York, 1975).
Gallois, Pierre, *Pour ou contre la force de frappe* (Paris, 1963).
Galtung, Johan, *The True Worlds* (New York, 1980).
Gilpin, Robert, *War and Change in World Politics* (New York, 1981).
Gulick, Edward, *Europe's Classical Balance of Power* (New York, 1955).
Gunder Frank, André, *L'accumulation mondiale* (Paris, 1977).
Haas, Ernst, *American Political Science Review*, 1953.
———, *The Uniting of Europe* (Stanford, 1958).
———, *The Obsolescence of Regional Integration Theory* (Berkeley, 1975).

Hegel, Georg, "Philosophy of Right and Law," in C. J. Friedrich (ed.), *The Philosophy of Hegel* (New York, 1953).
Henkin, Louis, *How Nations Behave* (New York, 1979).
Hobbes, Thomas, *Leviathan* (Paris, 1971).
Hoffmann, Stanley, *The State of War* (New York, 1965).
———, *Primacy of World Order* (New York, 1978).
———, *Duties Beyond Borders* (Syracuse, 1981).
Hume, David, *Philosophical Essays on Morals, Literature and Politics* (Georgetown, 1817).
Jervis, Robert, in S. Krasner (ed.), "International Regimes," *International Organization* 36 (Spring 1982).
Johnson, James, *Ideology, Reason, and the Limitation of War* (Princeton, 1975).
Kant, Emmanuel, "Idea for a Universal History" and "Eternal Peace," in C. J. Friedrich (ed.), *The Philosophy of Kant* (New York, 1949).
Kaplan, Morton, *System and Process in International Relations* (New York, 1957).
Kaplan, Morton, and Katzenbach, Nicholas, *The Political Foundations of International Law* (New York, 1961).
Kennan, George, *American Diplomacy 1900–1950* (Chicago, 1951).
———, *The Decline of Bismarck's European Order* (Princeton, 1979).
———, *The Fateful Alliance* (Pantheon, 1984).
———, *The Nuclear Delusion* (New York, 1982).
Keohane, Robert, "Theory of World Politics," in Ada Finifter, *Political Science: the State of the Discipline* (Washington, 1983).
———, *After Hegemony* (Princeton, 1984).
Keohane, Robert, and Nye, Joseph (eds.), *Transnational Relations and World Politics* (Cambridge, 1972).
———, *Power and Interdependence* (Bonston, 1977).
Kim, Kyung Won, *Revolution and International System* (New York, 1970).
Kindleberger, Charles, *America in the World Economy* (New York, 1977).
Kissinger, Henry, *A World Restored* (New York, 1957).
———, *Nuclear Weapons and Foreign Policy* (New York, 1957).
Knorr, Klaus, *The Power of Nations* (New York, 1975).
Krassner, Stephen (ed.), "International Regimes," *International Organization* 36 (Spring 1982).
———, *Structural Conflict* (Berkeley, 1985).
Lebow, Richard Ned, *Between Peace and War: The Nature of International Crisis* (Baltimore, 1981).
Locke, *Deuxième traité du gouvernement civil* (Paris, 1967).
Luttwak, Edward, *The Grand Strategy of the Roman Empire* (Baltimore, 1976).
Machiavelli, Niccolo, *The Prince and Discourses* (New York, 1940).
Marx, Karl, *Communist Manifesto*.
Morgenthau, Hans, *Politics Among Nations* (New York, 1948).
Morse, Edward, *Modernization and the Transformation of International Relations* (New York, 1976).
National Conference of Catholic Bishops, *The Challenge of Peace* (Washington, 1983).
Osgood, Robert, *Limited War* (Chicago, 1957).
Rawls, John, *A Theory of Justice* (Cambridge, 1971).
Robinson, Ronald, and Gallagher, John, *Africa and the Victorians* (London, 1961).
Rosecrance, *Action and Reaction in World Politics* (Boston, 1963).
Rousseau, Jean-Jacques, *Du contrat social: écrits politiques* (Paris, 1964).

Ruggie, John, "Continuity and Transformation in the World Polity," *World Politics* 35 (January 1983).
Schelling, Thomas, *The Strategy of Conflict* (Cambridge, 1960).
Schumpeter, Joseph, *Imperialism and Social Classes* (New York, 1955).
Silberner, Edmund, *La guerre et la paix dans l'histoire des doctrines économiques* (Paris, 1957).
Smith, Tony, *The Pattern of Imperialism* (Cambridge, 1981).
Snyder, Glenn, *Deterrence and Defense* (Princeton, 1961).
Staley, Eugene, *War and the Private Investor* (New York, 1935).
Thucydides, *The Peloponnesian War* (New York, 1964).
Tucker, Robert W., *The Inequality of Nations* (New York, 1977).
Vernon, Raymond, *Sovereignty at Bay* (New York, 1971).
Wallerstein, Immanuel, *The Capitalist World Economy* (New York, 1979).
Waltz, Kenneth, *Man, the State and War* (New York, 1959).
———, "The Myth of National Interdependence," in Charles Kindleberger (ed.), *The International Corporation* (Cambridge, 1970).
———, *Theory of International Politics* (Reading 1979).
———, "The Spread of Nuclear Weapons," *Adelphi Paper* no. 171 (London, 1981).
Walzer, Michael, *Just and Unjust Wars* (New York, 1977).
Wohlstetter, Albert, "The Delicate Balance of Terror," *Foreign Affairs* (January 1959).
Wolfers, Arnold, *Discord and Collaboration* (Baltimore, 1962).

6

The Future of the International Political System: A Sketch

Thoughts on Change

This essay will examine, sketchily, the coming evolution of the international political system. This is a risky exercise, for several reasons.

1. In the first place, any effort at discovering the future in a given field is made easier when there exists, for that field, a theory of change: a set of hypotheses and propositions, derived from or confirmed by empirical research, that identify the main factors of continuity and causes of transformation. It so happens that we have no satisfactory theory of change in international relations at all. To be sure, we have several theories of the international system. This is not the occasion to review them in detail, but it is necessary to point out their weaknesses as theories of change.

Let us set aside Immanuel Wallerstein's theory of the world capitalist system,[1] derived from Fernand Braudel's work on the world economy. Here, clearly, change results from the transformation of capitalism, and particularly of the market. But how these changes are reflected in or translated into changes in the relations *among states*, how the evolution of the capitalist system dictates or shapes that of the international polity (whose form—the coexistence and competition of multiple political systems—Wallerstein declares necessary to the world economy) is nowhere made clear. Indeed, in his second volume, the simplicity of his scheme (the core-periphery distinction) dissolves into an unwieldy mass of specific analyses.

Robert Gilpin's theory of change[2] focuses on the rise, decline, and fall of "hegemons," but it suffers from two weaknesses. It provides a better account of the international economic system than of the international political one; for instance, Britain may well have been the economic hegemon in the nineteenth century, and thus was able to dictate the terms of the international monetary system and (often) of international trade. But the international political system was quite obviously multipolar; the image of Britain as the "holder" of the balance of power is only partly accurate (and it reflects geography—Britain's distance from the continent—rather than superiority); the so-called holder was not able to prevent the rise of formidable challengers. Moreover, as Robert Keohane has pointed out, Gilpin's theory "does not account well for the rise of the hegemon in the first place, or for the fact that certain contenders emerge rather than others."[3]

Turning to theories of the international political system itself, we find the ambitious attempt by Kenneth Waltz.[4] I have only little to add to what I have written about it earlier and, above all, to recent criticisms by John Ruggie and Keohane.[5] Waltz's general conception, as Ruggie has shown, puts the problem of change into a "structural" straitjacket: change can come only from a revolution in the ordering principle of the system (such as a switch from anarchy to central rule), or from a transformation in the distribution of capabilities among the actors. But, on the one hand, Waltz seems to consider as a significant change in the latter only a passage from a bipolar to a multipolar structure (or vice versa); and he leaves out as factors of change both what Ruggie calls a missing dimension, the prevailing type of domestic relations between state and society, and what he calls a determinant, the "dynamic density" of relations among states.[6] On the other hand, Waltz's conception of power, which underlines his view of the distribution of capabilities, does not fully take into account either the non-fungibility of power (i.e., the fact that in a given international system there may be different hierarchies and structures, corresponding to different kinds of power) or the essential difference between the availability, the uses, and the effectiveness of power, which makes the mere distribution of capabilities an insufficient indicator of power. As for Waltz's more specific theory of the balance of power, it is "so general that it hardly meets the difficult tests that he himself establishes for theory," and it fails to "state precisely the conditions under which coalitions will change."[7]

All this means that we have neither a complete nor an integrated theory of change. What we have is a number of conclusions derived from history. One is the idea of turbulence in periods of hegemonic decline—turbulence not only in the world economy but also in the international political system, when the loss of economic predominance corresponds to an overall decline in relative power. Another concerns the existence of two ways in which multipolar systems lead to a general war (and balance-of-power systems are destroyed): through gradual erosion of the restraints observed by the major actors (an erosion that can result from domestic changes, or from a change in the relations among these actors, or from the interaction between these two levels) or through deliberate destruction of these restraints following a revolutionary change in the polity of one of the major players. Still another conclusion concerns, literally, the explosiveness of bipolar systems, given each "pole's" dialectic of commitment and credibility and its fear of decisive loss resulting either from a client's defection or from a neutral's alignment with one's adversary (i.e., the dilemma of appearing either provocative or "appeasing").

2. A second difficulty, however, lies in the fact that these "lessons from the past" may not be valid for the present international system, whose original features will be sketched below. Do these features amount to a difference in kind, or merely a difference in degree? Is the simple distinction

between bipolarity and multipolarity still significant? What is the relationship today between systemic constraints and domestic determinants?

Let us linger a moment on the last of these questions. It is of course true that "under different systemic conditions states will define their self-interests differently."[8] The system's main features—the distribution of power, the rules of the various games of world politics—constrain and shape the behavior of the players and penalize transgressions. On the other hand, however, there is little agreement on just what constitutes the current "systemic conditions" (to give one example, most observers believe that bipolarity is inherently unstable, and that economic interdependence today is high—although Waltz thinks the opposite). On the other hand, while systemic conditions are obviously an important constraint or a determinant of state behavior, they also provide an opportunity for state action, and indeed a target for efforts at change. Nothing is more pernicious than a view of international relations that exaggerates the power of the system. A simple reflection here is useful. All "realists," pure or modified, tell us that we live in a global order of anarchy (the absence of central power and, I would add, of any consensus on goals and procedures). If this is the case, then attention should be put primarily on the *actors*, not on the system: on the way in which they interpret the latter, define their own interests, constitute their power, and set their goals. When one wants to understand an actor's behavior, there is no *a priori* reason to attach greater importance either to systemic imperatives or to geopolitical necessities than to purely domestic factors. Moreover, in a bipolar system, dominated by two contending "hegemons," it is even more obvious that the decision-making process, the political regime, its relations with society, the belief systems of the leaders, and the specific resources and power positions of these two actors must be given decisive importance, since any bipolar contest is a struggle about the shape and leadership of the international system.

However, putting questions about change where they largely belong (i.e., at the level of the units) does not simplify the task of futurologists. We now have to cope not only with a question to which we need an answer in order to begin to know what the future will be (one only the future will settle)—whether we can apply to the present system notions derived from bygone ones but also with the multiple possibilities of evolution or revolution in the major actors, and with the uncertain effects of the contest in the international system on the actors' own polities. To look for the roots of systemic change solely at the level of the system, as does Waltz, has the virtue of simplifying one's task (at the cost of providing irrelevant or skimpy answers). To look for those roots wherever they may be has the defect of making the task almost impossible. At a minimum, it suggests that we shall talk not about the future of the international political system, but of possible *futures*.

3. Talking about futures is necessary for still another reason. Past international systems have succeeded one another through the dark intercession of general wars. But those wars, occurring when they did, were not always

inevitable. Like most historical events, they usually resulted from the interplay of the necessary and the contingent, of fundamental trends (in the system or in the main units) and accidents; they were "over-determined." Except when they were deliberately provoked by a revolutionary power, or when they came out of a crisis in which such a power consciously accepted the risk of the general war that it deemed inevitable sooner or later (barring the capitulation of its foes), they were produced at least as much by the particular circumstances of a given crisis as by the deeper reasons for hostility or clashes of interests characteristic of the system—by the momentary configuration at least as much as by the more permanent structure. This point has been intelligently shown, in the case of 1914, by Richard Ned Lebow.[9] To be sure, it is not always easy to know in advance whether one is in the universe of revolutionary thrusts or in the more ordinary world of clashes between conservative and revisionist powers (moreover, when does a revisionist state cross the great divide and become a revolutionary challenge—a question raised by the Japanese case of 1931-1941?). But the role of accidents cannot be neglected: at one moment, a crisis may be "managed" intelligently; whereas the same kind of crisis at a later moment, or a different kind of crisis at almost the same one, could lead to disaster for reasons that have far more to do with the circumstances than with the deeper trends. This consideration is relevant to our present condition—unless one has already decided that this bipolar system is exactly like past ones and that, as before, the current struggle between one revolutionary power and one *status quo* actor is doomed to end in global conflict.

4. A last reason for which this exercise is risky is that it will be limited, primarily, to the international political system: a study of the future of the world economy is beyond my reach and competence, and yet it is clear that certain trends and crises in the world economy could have extraordinarily serious effects on the international political order. It is therefore not possible to leave this matter out altogether; but my primary emphasis will be on what Raymond Aron used to call the strategic-diplomatic game.

The Present International Political System

The main characteristic is its *originality*: it does not approximate any of our models of the past.

1. The future of the international political system can be discussed only if one begins with a clear picture of the nature of the present one.

In particular, it differs from classical bipolar systems. To be sure, in the strategic-diplomatic arena, there are still only two major powers. But nuclear prudence inhibits the actual use of the atomic arsenals of these powers, and it has also, so far, led them to great restraint in their use of conventional forces against one another. This condition does not amount to an "equalization" of power between more and less mighty states, but it somehow reduces the distance separating them and, above all, makes a violent outcome of the great powers' contest less certain. Moreover, classical bipolarity described a system in which the strategic-diplomatic arena was, if not the only one, at least by far the most important one for the states' interactions. Today, there are other important games, and they are not bipolar. In the nineteenth century, economic interdependence developed in the transnational *society* that coexisted with the interstate *political* system. It now characterizes several of the arenas of *interstate* relations, because of the decisive *political* importance of economic issues in the agendas of most states—that is, because of the profound changes in state-society relations in an era of managed economies. In these arenas, one of the two superpowers is not a major actor, given the nature of its own polity and ideology (an anticapitalist command economy); and, as I have tried to describe it elsewhere, economic interdependence as a political factor brings as many handicaps as it provides benefits and opportunities to the other superpower.[10]

Thus, what might be called the structural heterogeneity of the system (if one refers to the existence of different international structures corresponding to the different kinds of power: military, monetary, industrial, etc.) is one of the differences between the present system and past bipolar ones. Another kind of heterogeneity is original: that which results from geopolitical diversity. Past bipolar contests were waged on reasonably homogeneous fields (in the sense that in the system described by Thucydides, say, both the Greek city-states and the neighboring "barbarians" took part in a single interstate contest). In the present system, the first global one, we find both one worldwide contest: the superpowers' rivalry *and* tenacious local rivalries or configurations, which can be used by the superpowers for their competition (and whose actors can call in the superpowers for their own purposes) but which also have a life of their own, as well as their own rules. Thus, the ability of the superpowers to absorb and to blend all other important conflicts into their own is not unlimited.

Nor does the present system resemble past balance-of-power ones. Today, there are only two dominant military powers, capable of projecting their might all over the world; and these powers are locked in a formidable ideological conflict, of the sort that has ruled out so far the kinds of fluid alignments and ideologically neutral mechanisms characteristic of balance-of-power systems. The balance of power and the balance of (nuclear) terror are profoundly different: the former required flexible coalitions and allowed for (indeed, demanded) a willingness to use force in behalf of equilibrium if deterrence failed (as it was often bound to fail, in a world of anarchy— i.e., separate calculations and uncertain commitments). The balance of terror is not a matter of coalitions (the British, French, and Chinese nuclear forces may complicate Soviet calculations, but they do not enter much into the plans of U.S. strategists); its preservation actually requires abstention from nuclear war (since nobody knows whether and how a resort to nuclear weapons could be kept limited and controlled) as well as great prudence in the use of conventional force.

All past "anarchic" systems, whether bipolar or multipolar (i.e., all truly *international* systems, by contrast with imperial ones) were based on a structure in which military might was the main currency, the distribution of power among actors was fairly clear and easy to evaluate, and the "dynamic density" of relations was relatively limited. This is no longer the case.

2. The present system is marked by a peculiar mix of *resiliency* and *fragility*. In this respect, it resembles balance-of-power systems. But the resemblance is only superficial. In the latter, resiliency was provided by the balancing mechanism's ability to moderate ambitions and conflicts; fragility resulted primarily from the very existence of sovereignty: a jungle of ambitions uncoerced by higher power. The current scene is different in several ways. First, diversity characterizes the structure of power. The non-fungibility of power produces a "vertical" fragmentation of the system into partly separate arenas, each one with its hierarchy of players: a factor of resiliency, on the whole—except to the extent that several of these arenas can be profoundly affected by moves occurring in one of them (cf. the ripples created by the OPEC decisions of 1973 and 1979) or by internal conditions in the polity of a major actor (cf. the effects of a recession in the United States), and, of course, except to the extent that major crises in the strategic-diplomatic arena can have disastrous repercussions in others (cf. the oil embargo of 1973). A thorough study of the relations and exchanges between the different "games" of world affairs remains to be made.

Second, another original aspect is the nature and multiplicity of *restraints* affecting each kind of power. Some restraints result from the risks of rash action (in the nuclear realm as well as because of the "boomerang" effects of economic power in an interdependent world economy); and other restraints result from common norms and procedures (international regimes). At first, these are—again—factors of resiliency. But they also provide irresistible temptations for manipulation and blackmail: of the weak by the powerful, of course, but also of the strong by the weak (cf. client-superpower relations in the Middle East, or the threat of default of debtor countries) and of the mighty by the mighty (cf. threats of first use of nuclear weapons, or war-fighting scenarios).

The very density of relations increases the ambiguity of the system. The dependence of all actors on the system—either, quite starkly, for survival, insofar as a nuclear war destroying the system could also, this time, annihilate all the actors, or for economic development and welfare—is a factor of resiliency. But density also means ideological alignments based on a certain solidarity of domestic regimes and political forces; disruptive technologcal revolutions and demographic explosions; uncertainty about the future of essential resources (such as oil); and increasing vulnerability to events and decisions of external origin. One therefore witnesses countless attempts at harming others (for instance, by forcing on them burdens imported from abroad); attempts at re-exporting vulnerability and at reducing the costs of interdependence for oneself; and attempts at developing in the strategic-diplomatic domain mutually hostile—hence highly dangerous—alignments.

One more original feature of the system: the "horizontal" fragmentation of power into a variety of subsystems also contributes to the mix of resiliency and fragility. The relative autonomy of regional concerns dampens the superpowers' contest, or divides it into reasonably separate compartments. But the inevitable connection between each subsystem and the global cold war can also serve as escalatory factors, either if a confrontation in one arena should lead to a worsening of the superpowers' contest in other areas, or if the superpowers' conflict in one of them should affect their vital interests.

3. Let us move away from comparisons and focus on the chief characteristics of the present world political system. It is both "revolutionary" and "moderate": revolutionary because of the bipolar military contest, and because of the continuing ideological confrontation (which persists even though several Communist powers have defected from the Soviet camp, even though the power of attraction of the Leninist model has receded—especially among industrial societies—and despite the presence of highly undemocratic regimes in the "free world" alliances). It is also revolutionary to the extent that the collapse of the (previously porous but visible) barriers between domestic politics and international politics has led to generalized intervention.[11] The system is moderate insofar as it has shown enough flexibility to absorb enormous changes in the distribution of capabilities since 1945, as well as in the number of actors and in the make-up of alignments; and also to the extent that, until now, major crises have been managed or contained (for instance, except for civil violence, wars in the Middle East have remained limited.) Like past international systems, the present one can be described as consisting of a core and a periphery—the (crucial) difference with the past residing in the fact that this periphery is not dominated by the imperial presence of the major powers but, rather, is occupied by at least legally independent actors. The *core* is constituted by the superpowers' camps. Its two main features are the nuclear "game" and the alliance systems. Until now, despite profound technological changes, the nuclear game has remained one of mutual deterrence, resting ultimately on the possibility of "mutual assured destruction," whatever strategic doctrine one may concoct in order to avoid it. And, so far, mutual deterrence has in fact extended to the protection of major allies against conventional attack by the other superpower (to be distinguished from protection against conventional retaliation aimed at an ally that had itself initiated a war, as in the cases of North Korea and North Vietnam). This is one of the reasons for which the alliance systems—the Warsaw Pact and NATO, and also the US-Japanese alliance—have survived a number of tests and storms. (There are of course other reasons: the shared sense of threat, Soviet willingness to use force in order to prevent defections in Eastern Europe, etc.)

As for the *periphery*, it is not possible here to describe the specific features and "rules of the game" of each subsystem. Some have been deeply marked by the active role or interference of both superpowers (Middle East); others have shown a relatively greater autonomy from them (Africa); still others have been functioning either under the (often unwelcome) protection or in the more distant shadow of the United States (OAS, ASEAN). The frequency and intensity of U.S.-Soviet confrontations in these subsystems have varied a great deal: in Africa, the two periods of tension were those in the early 1960s and the middle and late 1970s, and in Central America, those in the early 1960s and the present.

There was always a risk that the "core contest" would spill over into all the peripheries and become truly global—i.e., that in each subsystem there would be a struggle for dominance, so to speak, between the truly local (internal and interstate) factors of conflict and the U.S.-Soviet "relation of major tension," which the latter would win. But is is only in the last few years that this potential danger has become a reality: because of the increase in the military capabilities of the USSR, especially its power to project military might at great distances, and because of the strong U.S. reaction to it. This new Soviet ability does not, however, eliminate one constant difference in the strategic maps of the two chief adversaries. The principal concern of the USSR remains the security of its camp (i.e., real or potential threats on its immediate periphery); hence its main thrusts and moves concern Europe, the Middle East, and the Far East. The United States, of course, is concerned about its famous back- (or is it front-) yard in Central America and the Caribbean. But its main resources in the contest are devoted to areas separated from its own territory by huge distances: Western Europe, the Far East, and the Middle East.

Of the various subsystems, two deserve closer attention: the Middle Eastern one, which, because of its strategic and economic importance to the Western allies, constitutes a sort of second core for the United States; and the Far Eastern one, which constitutes the same for the USSR. It is in the Middle Eastern subsystem that the struggle between indigenous factors of conflict and "imported" ones is most intense, complex, and fluctuating, given both the extraordinary diversity of local hostilities (communal, as in Lebanon or among Palestinians; religious versus secular; inter-Arab; Arab-Israeli; Arab-Iranian; etc.) and the importance of the superpowers' interests and commitments. The Far Eastern area is a subsystem in the process of formation (two criteria being a specific configuration of forces and a certain density of relations that form distinctive patterns). It is composed of the two superpowers, Japan, China, and the two Koreas. The centrality of this area to both superpowers now (here, part of the territory of the USSR is included, and part of the U.S. one may be threatened by Soviet weapons deployed there), the increasing importance of the U.S.-Japanese alliance and of China, the fact that some of the major factors of conflict involve at least one of the superpowers (China-USSR, Japan-USSR, and, because of the alliance of the United States with Seoul, North Korea-United States), the rising role of the Pacific nations in the world economy—all of these factors suggest that this particular subsystem may well deserve to be treated in the future as part of the core. But it is a subsystem with four major actors, not two, and, as a result, its "rules of the game" are quire different from those of the NATO–Warsaw Pact "core."

Until now, nuclear proliferation has proceeded in such a way as to remain under the umbrella of the superpowers' own nuclear forces: the

British and French deterrents, whatever their independence in theory, are clearly within the core, and China's own strategy and diplomacy are delicately linked to the U.S.-Soviet contest. The next "proliferators" (including the two quasi-nuclear powers, Israel and India) have their own priorities and regional concerns; we shall examine later whether the further spread of nuclear weapons is likely to increase either the fragility or the fragmentation of the system.

The dominant theme of this analysis—the ambiguity of the system—is reinforced if one examines how the international economic system interacts with the international political one. The world economy can be envisaged in two ways. It is, first of all, the air in which the actors breathe. When the quality of the air deteriorates, as it did in the 1970s and early 1980s the capabilities of these actors are obviously affected, as is the general climate of international relations. In the second place, the world economy is also a separate field, a set of arenas, in which the players act. As a field, it has made a contribution both to the moderation of the international system *and* to conflict. The latter is obvious: economic power has been widely used as a tool of the "state of war," either against political adversaries (through boycotts, embargoes, and sanctions) or even against allies or partners, in order to gain temporary advantages or to change the rules of the game (cf. Nixon on August 15, 1971; or OPEC in 1973). Indeed, the very scope of the state's attempt to control the national economy—through fiscal and monetary policy, trade legislation, the manipulation of interest rates, a host of non-tariff barriers, subsidies, and directives for industrial policy, and so on—has opened up vast new fronts for interstate competition. On the other hand, in the non-Communist world, the existence of a reasonably open international economy has contributed to moderation in two ways: (1) through the operations of "complex interdependence,"[12] which, in the phase of U.S. hegemony, led the United States to define its interest in a way that furthered the development of a partly autonomous transnational society, away from the interstate contests, and also entailed enlightened assistance to other countries, in order to promote absolute increases in prosperity rather than relative national gains. Later, interdependence put definite limits on the mutual manipulations of state, or on coalitions of states eager to improve their relative positions at the expense of others. And (2) this open world economy, partly transnational (and capitalist), partly interstate (and managed) has required a whole network of international regimes, with their own restraints on state actions, their procedures for the settlement of disputes, and the ability, resulting from their very existence, to create a stake in their own survival among the member states (and thus to change the way in which these states define their interests).

4. Obviously, until now the ambiguity of the postwar international system has been benevolent: resiliency has prevailed over fragility, moderation over revolution, economic interdependence and nuclear prudence over all the factors of conflict. The central question is whether this will still be the case in the future. What is likely to happen to all the moderating factors?

Is it possible for a system of "anarchy," in which states preserve the means to inflict harm on others (one of the possible definitions of sovereignty) and, indeed, dispose of unprecedented capabilities for doing so, is it possible, especially for a system in which so many causes of conflict ferment, to maintain itself without either self-destruction or what might be called self-transcendence—that is, the passage to a very different sort of system, no longer based on state sovereignty?

Approaches to the Future

1. In order to make educated guesses about the future, it is not very useful to begin with a prognosis of the future of the system's structure, defined as the distribution of capabilities. In the first place, it is unlikely that the coming changes will be such as to challenge the preeminence of the superpowers in the strategic-diplomatic arena. The potential rivals—Western Europe, Japan, China—are not likely to narrow the gap greatly: China's industrial base remains weak and small; the various inhibitions that have reduced Japan's role in that arena may weaken, but even if they should disappear altogether there are physical limits to Japan's potential might; and there is no sign of a West European ability to overcome the divisions and hang-ups that have prevented its emergence as an entity (other than in the skinny form of the Economic Community).

To be sure, there may be considerable shifts in the distribution of economic capabilities: the phenomenon of the Asian "new industrialized countries" may not remain exceptional. Thus, regional and functional hierarchies could change a great deal. However, the non-fungibility of power prevents one from drawing any definite conclusions about the effect of these changes in the strategic-diplomatic realm. This effect will depend on what the actors will *want* to do with them. We are thus driven back to a consideration of the system as a whole, or of the various subsystems (insofar as they limit or shape the specific uses that states assign to their power), and to guesses about the domestic evolution of the actors—that is, regarding the nature of their regimes and of state-society relations, which largely determine their decisions about the kinds of capabilities they want, and about what to do with them.

2. If the structure of power is of little help for prediction, there remain three different modes of analysis, or ways of speculating about the future, which, I believe, need to be combined. The first requires that we look at *long-term trends* in the international political system and in the polities. I have elsewhere[13] mentioned three main trends. The most obvious concerns the persistence of the U.S.-Soviet competition on a global scale, with approximate strategic parity (since neither power will allow the other to pull ahead dangerously). The competition would end or lose its saliency only if the USSR gave up its colossal challenge and turned inward as a result of, or in order to cope with, its domestic problems—if, being forced by U.S. pressure to choose between butter and guns, it settled for butter.

The long-term inability of the Soviet system either to improve its economic performance or else to reform drastically enough to remove economic bottlenecks and waste has been stressed by many. Not clear, however, is just how decisive this flaw will be—that is, whether partial adjustments will be successful in preventing paralysis or decline, and to what extent the pressure of the external contest will in fact continue to legitimize the regime, preserve the unchallenged priority of the military sector, and inspire creative efforts at reconciling the political system and the need for economic efficiency.

Unless one indulges in a kind of "catastrophic optimism" about the Soviet Union's future, one can still discern only too well all the factors that will keep driving the contest. Throughout history, two major powers have always found reasons to clash, and attempts to cooperate or to carve up spheres have been impossible either to negotiate or to maintain. Ideological opposition, in these instances, has exacerbated the clashes of power. In the military realm, technology—whether pursued "for its own sake" or so as not to let one's opponent get ahead—will contribute to the rivalry. There are, of course, conflicting interests as well: the Soviet insistence on a very high degree of security is incompatible with the U.S. interest in preventing the vassalization of all of the Soviet Union's neighbors; the Soviet interest in preserving the East European *glacis* is incompatible with the Western interest in helping traditional Western-oriented nations regain some autonomy; and nowhere is the struggle of interests more visible than that over Germany. Interests create perceptions of threats; but perceptions of threats also create interests: each superpower is likely to continue to act as if every move by the other, even in an area of relatively low priority to itself, *ipso facto* creates a need to thwart the move or to prevent a further extension or exploitation of it, in order to protect its own reputation for strength and credibility. Finally, domestic needs feed the contest: the existence of external perils is an important source of legitimacy for the Soviet regime, and while the same is certainly not true of the United States, powerful military and economic lobbies there have a stake either in preserving a certain level of hostility or in safeguarding various parts of the world from the threats that emanate directly or indirectly from Moscow or its allies. Moreover, the failure or perceived failure of an administration to "meet the Soviet challenge" guarantees its demise.

A second long-term trend is *nationalism*, which will undoubtedly remain a major force in a world whose units base their legitimacy on the principle of self-determination, and where most actors are and will continue to be engaged in "nation-building." The desire for national independence and self-assertion will be fed by the very diversity and strength of factors that actually negate sovereignty: modern imperialism, such as that of the USSR; continuing attempts by various actors to extend or to protect spheres of control (such as the United States in Central America, Vietnam in Cambodia, Khadafi's Libya in parts of Africa, etc.); the presence in many countries of temporary or traditional foreign minorities who provoke resentments and stir prejudices; the frustration of modernization (a process seen as imposed from abroad); the absence of control of many developing countries over their economic future because of the grip of multinational corporations or of international organizations (such as the IMF); indeed, the frustrating sense many governments have of pushing, in the realm of economics, a multitude of levers that do not respond, because they are either held by someone else or are capable of being moved only by combined (hence partly unsatisfactory) action. Thus, there is a kind of symbiosis between nationalism and universal intervention or manipulation.

A third trend is *revolution*, which occurs in a great variety of forms: political and social, left wing or right wing. The shakiness of the political structures of so many states, the communal conflicts, ideological antagonisms, religious hatreds, and social cleavages in so many countries, the lack of fit between political regimes imposed by past masters (foreign or domestic) and societies undergoing an almost unmanageable process of transformation, guarantee endless cycles of revolution, external interventions, and counterrevolutions.

On the whole, however, these long-term trends tell us very little about the future of the international political system—except that there will be a great deal of turbulence. The central question is, of course, how much, how intense, how dangerous—and the trends, by themselves, don't answer it. The fate of the system depends on whether the U.S.-Soviet contest will be managed or not (i.e., on the rivals' capacity to handle crises): Will the superpowers be able to accommodate nationalist demands, and will these demands take forms destructive of the world economic order, embroil the rival superpowers, and be accompanied by nuclear proliferation? Will revolutions occur essentially because of domestic conditions or as a result of subversion, will they be accepted by the superpowers or resisted by one or the other of them, and will they take place in areas of such importance to the superpowers as to provoke major confrontations between them? The effects of nationalism and revolution will also depend a great deal on the kinds of leaders countries will produce: in this age of "structural" analysis, personalities matter perhaps more than ever.

3. We should therefore turn to another kind of analysis: a prediction of *crises*: Around which flash points could these trends lead to dangerous explosions? As past experiences have shown, crises (bloody or not) provide moments of truth and reveal the dynamics, strengths, and weaknesses of a system. They produce either occasions for the great powers to crank up the various regulatory mechanisms of the balance of power (as during much of the nineteenth century) or circumstances in which one discovers that these mechanisms do not work (as in the period of the 1860s and early 1870s), or points of crystallization for the tightening of alliances (as in the years before 1914), or instants of triumph for unchecked troublemakers (like the Rhineland and Munich crises).

Many long-expected crises never happen (remember the death-of-Tito crisis scenario?). What follows is clearly debatable; nevertheless, one can try to locate those possible crises that could have system-wide repercussions.

The most dangerous would be a military confrontation in the present core of the system, which could result either from a particular form of weapons deployment deemed physically (and not just politically) intolerable by the other superpower or from a serious clash in the European theater. Under what conditions could the latter occur? One can imagine major unrest in Eastern Europe, including East Berlin, resulting in Western attempts to help rebels beyond the wall or the iron curtain, or Warsaw Pact attempts to pursue in the West groups fleeing from the East. One can also develop a scenario of dangerous instability arising from a drift of the Federal Republic toward neutralism, encouraged by one side and resisted by the other. The very likelihood of general nuclear war coming out of a major crisis in Europe argues against these scenarios; on the other hand, the importance of the superpowers' stakes and arsenals make any crisis there particularly dangerous, as neither side can afford to see its key alliance system disintegrate. More believable perhaps would be a Soviet decision to move preventively—with or without nuclear weapons—on what remains the USSR's main front, if the general atmosphere, or a crisis elsewhere, had deteriorated so badly as to convince the Kremlin of the high probability of a U.S. attack.

One can also—all too easily—speculate about typical crises in the Far Eastern and Middle Eastern subsystems. In both cases, it is the infernal machine of ambiguous commitments by the superpowers to third parties (with whom they have no formal and effective military alliance) that could result in a conflagration. We have had several rehearsals of conflagrations in the past. Moreover, in the Far Eastern system (as in Europe) there are also tight alliances on the U.S. side; but the situation in the Far East is more fluid, hence more dangerous, than in Europe. Another, but less restrained, effort by China to "punish" Vietnam, leading to Soviet intervention (i.e., to a Soviet decision to cut down a deeply feared and distrusted rival before it becomes too powerful) and to a U.S. counterintervention; another Korean war, with Soviet support for North Korea and Soviet threats aimed at Japan; Soviet attempts to prevent by threats a Japanese rearmament, leading to menacing new deployments by both superpowers; a Soviet decision to punish Israel, should the latter attack a Soviet client (such as Syria), or a U.S. decision to seek a showdown with Syria and the USSR over Lebanon, or to punish Syria, Libya, or Iran for acts of terrorism, leading to a Soviet move to protect the United States' "victim"; more Islamic revolutions leading to attacks on Americans, to U.S. intervention and Soviet counterintervention; a Soviet move into Iran, at the request of a pro-Soviet Iranian government, followed by a U.S. intervention there; a U.S. decision to shore up Iraq, followed by (or following) a Soviet one to back Iran militarily: these are the all-too-plausible crises that could get out of hand, because of the difficulty of limiting the scope of superpower collisions in these areas, and because of the dangerous ability of weaker states and loose, violent forces to manipulate the superpower contest, to blackmail their big brothers or cousins.

There are other crises with a potential for escalation. It is unlikely that "proxy wars" comparable to what happened in Angola, and could occur again in Southern Africa, would result in a violent clash between the superpowers' forces themselves, and it is equally unlikely that U.S. moves in Central America would lead to a heavy Soviet commitment (going beyond the provision of military assistance to local clients). But a U.S. military move against Cuba, caused by Cuban support to anti-U.S. forces or regimes in Central America, might force the Soviets to react there or elsewhere, because of their own need for "credibility." And, in the more distant future, a regional nuclear war between countries other than the current nuclear "Big Five" might trigger a superpower confrontation, if the "Big Two" chose sides, or if the war affected important clients of one of the other superpowers. Whether a "third party" nuclear war leads to the superpowers' entanglement or disconnection depends both on the importance of the stakes for them in a given case and on the state of their relations (when they deteriorate, the importance of local stakes increase).

Could a world economic crisis have a disastrous efect on the international political system? Yes, in one or the other of two hypotheses. One might be called the 1973 scenario, plus: an act of economic warfare accompanying a regional explosion but leading, this time, to a military intervention by the threatened Western powers and to a Soviet counterintervention. The other hypothesis is that of a major crisis in the network of international economic and financial institutions (such as a chain of bank collapses, following the default of several debtor countries), leading to political turbulence in important developing nations and, thereafter, to new alignments, or to violent external diversions sought by these countries' leaders.

"Crisis analysis" has the merit of concentrating the mind on perfectly real perils. But there are two flaws in this method. One is the impossibility of predicting which of these shocks is most likely to happen, or when, and of assigning a meaningful degree of probability to any of them. The other is the impossibility, by definition, of predicting surprises—say, the accidental shooting down by the Soviets of a U.S. civilian airliner with hundreds of passengers abroad, followed by a perfectly imaginable process of emotional as well as political and military escalation.

4. Surprises cannot be forecast (one can only predict that some will happen), but one can try to deal with the other flaw: one can define those *political choices* made by the key actors, which could either make the kinds of dangerous crises described above more likely or, on the contrary, help avert them. Thinking about these choices obliges one to conclude (not very hopefully) that the curent phase of international politics is particularly important—that a series of decisions to be made in the near future will either switch the train of international affairs on reasonably smooth tracks or else direct it toward disaster.

Three series of choices are of crucial importance. The first, and most important, are those presently being made by the superpowers concerning their contest. They are of two kinds. The first relates to the future of the nuclear competition. The trend of the arms race is dismal: both sides are providing themselves with a new arsenal that undermines crisis stability—

that is, one likely to heighten tension in case of a political crisis (and to add, as I suggested above, an autonomous source of conflicts to all the political issues that divide them already, over the location—on earth and in space—of counterforce weapons). The protracted crisis provoked by the SS-20 aimed at the United States and Europe, and by the NATO decision of December 1979 to put Pershing II and cruise missiles in Western Europe, at a time when there was no sharp political conflict there between East and West—other than Western dismay over Poland—is a first example. The often documented evolution of nuclear strategy from primary reliance on countercity weapons to the development of accurate counterforce ballistic and cruise missiles, the resulting vulnerability of a sizable fraction of each side's nuclear force (hence the emergence of an incentive to strike first, before one is hit), the recent U.S. drive to build a defensive system that entails the risk of extending the arms race into outer space and to heighten insecurity, the forthcoming proliferation of cheap, slower but powerful, and hard-to-verify cruise missiles—all these decisions have drastically changed the nature of the "nuclear question." An arms race with increasing numbers of vulnerable and unverifiable weapons that threaten each other's key forces and command systems would be extremely dangerous. Much, therefore, depends on whether the superpowers decide to reduce their vulnerabilities by either replacing their MIRV-ed land-based missiles with single warhead ones or (better still) with small, mobile ones that will not be targetable by the other side; and also on whether, in their arms control negotiations, they make a serious effort to stop, while there is still time, the trend toward nuclear war fighting (of which the ability to hit land-based missiles is only one aspect): by banning antisatellite systems and the development of defensive antiballistic systems, by trying to curb or even to eliminate land- and sea-based cruise missiles and to limit the number of bombers carrying long-range ones, and by agreeing not to deploy submarines with a counterforce capability.[14] Agreements that leave each side with a considerable amount of freedom to modernize their forces, toward more counterforce, are of very little use; proposals aimed at obliging the other side to restructure its forces, or to end its modernization efforts, while protecting one's own plans, are political warfare tactics.

A second kind of choice concerns the future of the political relations between Moscow and Washington. No single decision or set of decisions is likely to prevent all collisions: many of these, as we have seen, will tend to result from local moves made by secondary players capable of enlisting often hesitant superpowers. But how episodic crises will be resolved depends largely on the overall context or flavor of U.S.-Soviet relations, and on what might be called the basic stance chosen by the two rivals. At present, we are still on a collision course. The United States seems determined to make Moscow responsible for every challenge to a U.S. position anywhere, or to an ally or client of the United States. It often appears to believe that no worthwhile agreement can be signed with the Soviets, not only because of their behavior abroad but because of their regime. The other side may reach the conclusion that it is faced with an adversary whose hostility is implacable. The effects of these mutually reinforcing decisions to wage a new cold war, the impact of such a set of self- and mutually fulfilling prophecies regarding the "core" as well as the triangular relationship of Washington, Moscow, and Beijing, will increase tension and insecurity. A period of rhetorical and actual confrontations between the superpowers always adds to the strains that already weaken the polities in several Western European countries and the hesitation of even firmly anti-Soviet Europeans to support U.S. policies outside the NATO sphere; and the Soviets will be tempted to exploit such fissures. As for the Chinese, while they worry that any U.S.-Soviet détente might lead to a kind of euphoric "lowering of the guard" in either the United States or in NATO, thus allowing the Soviets to put more pressure, directly or indirectly, on China, high tension between Moscow and Washington in addition to a U.S. policy that almost automatically supports any force in the Third World that declares itself anti-Soviet or anti-Communist are likely to push Beijing away from Washington, into a subtle, complex, and somewhat unsettling game of balancing. Staying on this collision course will make many of the crises listed above both more probable and more difficult to manage; an erosion of restraints is the most predictable outcome. The alternative track is that of a return to a mixed strategy on both sides—a mix of competition (which is unavoidable) and cooperation, devoid of the illusions harbored by each side in the early 1970s, and allowing for better crisis management and prevention.[15]

A second series of choices capable of affecting the possibility and seriousness of crises will be made by other important actors. In Western Europe, the choice remains what it has been for almost thirty years: between "more of the same" and greater political and military unity. "More of the same," as predicted by several observers,[16] in fact means increasing fragmentation, both within and among the nations of Western Europe, and more tensions between the United States (impatient with its allies' reluctance to support the United States everywhere and to make a greater effort toward conventional defense) and those allies, dubious about the strategic evolution of the United States (in terms of both nuclear war-fighting *and* the emphasis on a conventional defense of Europe) as well as about Washington's overall world policy. Greater political and military unity would introduce, on the world stage, a new actor interested in helping moderate the U.S.-Soviet competition, capable both of stilling recurrent U.S. fears of a Western European drift toward finlandization or neutralization and of closing down one of the Soviets' main avenues of diplomatic intrigue and baiting. But such unity remains unlikely, partly because of the difficulty of squaring the nuclear circle (i.e., the problem of a German finger on a European trigger, and that of collective decision-making in nuclear matters) and partly because of the continuing prevalence of national concerns.

Another important choice is one Japan must make concerning the scope and speed of its rearmament. A decision to increase both considerably would probably heighten tension in East Asia; it would worry Japan's former victims (including China) as well as the Soviet Union. Moscow feels threatened by a more militarized U.S.-Japanese alliance no longer aimed at China and seems determined to retaliate by increasing its own conventional and nuclear forces around Japan.

A third important choice is that which will have to be made by Israel. The divisions among its Arab neighbors, the savage wars among its own enemies, the current hard-line consensus in its public opinion, may encourage a kind of tough immobilism, a belief that its opponents are neither capable nor really willing to challenge the gradual absorption into a greater Israel of the territories occupied in 1967. Successful in the short run, such a strategy is likely to backfire in the long run: Syria will not resign itself to the loss of the Golan Heights, the Palestinians will not resign themselves to dispersion and annexation, the Arab world in general—especially with the sting and threat of Islamic fundamentalism—will not accept the loss of all of Jerusalem, the USSR will continue to seek ways of challenging the U.S.-Israeli axis. An Israeli decision to exchange territory for peace, entailing both solid guarantees of security for Israel and a divestment of the occupied territories, is both unlikely now and necessary in order to prevent the Middle East from becoming the powder keg of the next world war.

The third series of important choices affecting the likelihood, intensity, and manageability of crises will be made in the world economic system. I will list them only briefly. The most important decision-maker here remains the United States, because of its weight in the world economy and its financial system, and because of the role of the dollar as the world's main currency for reserves and transactions. Whether the world economy will help fuel or dampen crises will depend on the kinds of decisions taken by the United States (and also by the other major industrial powers of the non-Communist world) in four vital areas. These areas are as follows: energy (reliance on a market that could once more be the victim of political decisions and disruptions in the Middle East, versus the pursuit of policies of conservation, storage, and diversification); money (a continuation of the present float, with its frequent and wide fluctuations because of divergent domestic policies and performances, versus an attempt to limit the range of these oscillations by coordination among the major economies and currencies); the international financial system (attempts to solve the debt problem by a combination of short-term rescue operations and stringent, socially and politically explosive conditions imposed by the IMF and other lenders, versus an effort at defining a long-term policy aimed both at avoiding imprudent loans and at preventing the recurrence of emergencies) and the international trade system (a continuing drift toward protectionism as the way of preventing the traumatic decline of major industries, versus a firmer commitment to liberalism—essential for the access of goods from the developing countries to the markets of the industrial nations—accompanied by domestic adjustment measures on a far greater scale than in the past).

All these choices obviously depend to a very large extent on the internal variables operating in the countries I have mentioned; and the outcome of internal struggles—among voters, parties, interest groups, or oligarchs—is only slightly, or occasionally, determined by foreign affairs: this is the major predicament of "futurology" in this area.

Through the Crystal Ball, Darkly

1. Let us nevertheless try to put the elements together. They allow us to see what the international political system is most likely *not* to be. First, it is clear that there is no atrophy of military power. It will continue to be sought by states, both as a means of action on the world stage (at a minimum, as a protection against external meddlers) and as a vital internal instrument for the support or maintenance of (often shaky) regimes in power. Other forms of power will continue to be very important, but they will not replace military might. This does not mean that the history of the international political system will be only that of the distribution of military capabilities and of the interactions of armies and arsenals. On the one hand, the purposes for which military might can be used *effectively* will continue to be the traditional goals, not the whole range of economic pursuits that contemporary states are interested in; and even among the traditional ones, the conquest and subjugation of alien populations are likely to run into formidable obstacles, because of the force of nationalism and of the multiple possibilities—ranging from passive resistance to guerrilla warfare and terrorism—which raise the cost of domination. As for the use of nuclear weapons for purposes of political intimidation, there is no reason why it should be successful when the target country has either nuclear weapons of its own or a nuclear protector, given the risk of an uncontrollable nuclear war, should the attempt at political coercion backfire: the effective political use of weapons whose military use is likely to be suicidal appears most difficult. On the other hand, the very *usability* of military power will continue to be constricted by two kinds of restraints: the very uneven ones that result, in certain polities but not in others, from domestic obstacles, institutional or moral, and those that result from the nature of weapons. In peacetime, nuclear weapons will increasingly be useful only as deterrents against a nuclear attack (the credibility of extended deterrence against a conventional attack on allies will diminish) or, in the case of secondary nuclear powers, against a conventional attack by a non-nuclear power unprotected by a nuclear big brother.

Second, the system will become neither multipolar in the global strategic arena (see the first section under "Approaches to the Future") nor bipolar in every structure. Even if, miraculously, the superpowers decided to reduce their nuclear arsenals drastically, the gap between them and the other nuclear powers would remain huge (moreover, they would probably try to apply curbs to the secondary nuclear forces before agreeing to their partial disarmament); and their unique capacity to raise vast armies and fleets equipped with the most advanced weapons and endowed with enormous mobility will persist. At the same time, the other structures of power, the other arenas of the international system, will not fold back into the strategic one; and this being the case, there will remain considerable opportunities for action—and mischief—for powers other than the big two. Even in the strategic arena, the fragmentation into regional subsystems, in each of which statesmen have to take into account not only the global balance of terror but also the regional balance of power (i.e., of conventional forces), offers a major role to local hegemons and to middle or even smaller powers. These are obviously less mighty than the superpowers; nevertheless, they are able either to bring more resources to bear on one particular front than the global powers, or to manipulate them, or both. Thus, one of the key questions will be that of the relations between the regional strategic arenas, or subsystems, and the global one. (The reader may ask: What about the regional balance of terror—for instance, the West Europeans' reference to the "Eurostrategic" balance? It may have a meaning with respect to short-range tactical weapons. But so-called intermediate-range missiles such as the SS-20s and Pershing IIs are "fungible" with long-range ones such as sea-based ICBMs; the notion of a regional nuclear balance between the camps is entirely artificial; and the targets are regional, not the weapons that can hit them.)

Third, the separation between domestic and international politics, between the internal operations of governments and their external behavior, will not return. Even in past systems, conduct abroad was always largely determined by factors within: a certain kind of realist theory (though certainly not rooted in Thucydides' writings) has been entirely misleading, in suggesting a purely "geopolitical" model of decision-making. But conduct abroad was not always, or even usually, aimed at affecting conditions within other countries; and it is in this respect that I foresee a continuation of present practices, both in the various economic arenas of interdependence and in the strategic and diplomatic games, given the persistence of ideological rivalries and transnational movements (manipulated by states), the exceedingly tempting pretexts for intervention in domestic affairs, and even the demands for new, non-exploitative or manipulative interventions, such as for the protection of human rights. A change would require an enormous internal strengthening of, and improved human conditions in, the various units; but it is difficult to imagine even massive external economic assistance capable of reaching such a goal.

2. If these are the parameters, or if this is the range within which the possible futures are to be found, then the major questions we face are those that follow (and the answers to them will determine which of these possible futures will be realized). They can all be summed up in one set of alternatives: *continuity versus* (a considerable amount of) *discontinuity* in world politics. It is discontinuity that is, in my opinion, desirable. I am convinced that continuity, in the sense of politics as usual, will lead to undesirable, perhaps catastrophic, results—even though the experience of the postwar system so far has not been catastrophic. But the reasons that have kept it manageable, the reasons for which its ambiguity has been more benevolent than dark, are not guaranteed to last.

The first question is, precisely, whether the current bases of moderation of the system will turn out to be more resilient than fragile, or vice versa. These bases have taken two forms: the nuclear revolution and economic interdependence, or, if you prefer, the will to survive and the will to prosper. But has the nuclear revolution really transformed the nature of world politics radically? Will there be no more global "moment of truth"? Has Clausewitz's relevance been relegated to limited wars? In one sense, as many writers have asserted, the nuclear revolution cannot be undone, and we will continue to live with what McGeorge Bundy has called "existential deterrence": "As long as each side retains survivable strength so that no leaders can ever suppose that he could 'disarm' his nuclear opponent completely, nuclear war remains an overwhelmingly unattractive proposition for both sides."[17] But there are those, on both sides, who believe that this revolution can be undone, or that the best way of reinforcing deterrence is to provide oneself with the ability to destroy part (or, through defense, even all) of one's opponents' forces, rather than by merely safeguarding one's ability to devastate his cities. And while Bundy is right in saying that "most 'scenarios' for nuclear warfare between the Soviet Union and the United States reflect nothing more than the state of mind of their authors,"[18] there is no reason to be reassured if these "authors" happen to be the top decision-makers. Bundy's fine essay was a plea for leaving existential deterrence alone. But the rival governments have, for many years now, done exactly the opposite. As a result, there is a clash between the logic of existential deterrence and that of nuclear warfighting scenarios; and no guarantee that the former will always prevail.

As for economic interdependence, the same kind of question can be asked: Has it effected, in the behavior of states, a revolution comparable to the nuclear one? I am relatively more optimistic about this second base of moderation than about the first. The capacity of the developing countries to hurt and disrupt the economies of the advanced ones without grievously hurting themselves is very limited, for many reasons. OPEC, a dubious model, has remained exceptional. The economic solidarity of the industrial countries in the open world economy, on the other hand, is reinforced by strategic considerations: they are, on the whole, members of an alliance system that is an essential structure of power in the "state of war." However, once more, the success achieved so far in managing crises does not guarantee comparable success in the future. There are other sources of trouble than deliberate acts of economic warfare. Another major world recession could lead to an economic and political collapse of key developing countries that could raise far more havoc than any OPEC. And if the more advanced countries, flooded by immigrant workers coming from developing countries in which they cannot find decent employment, react brutally against this flood, the delicate tissue of interdependence might be torn in ways dangerous for both the world economy and the international political system.

A second question immediately follows from this. Will the logic of sovereignty (or anarchy) prevail over that of international regimes (or collective management), or vice versa? Another way of formulating this question would be: Will states define and calculate their interests, on the whole, in the traditional way, which emphasizes the short run, domestic pressures or priorities, and relative gains; or will they realize that short-run advantages are increasingly elusive and transitory, and that the goals they seek—at home and abroad—can be obtained only through collective solutions?

Until now, the areas in which states have understood that, as Ernst Haas has put it, "hunting hares separately may not be as good as hunting a stag through collective effort"[19] have been limited in number and have not included conflict management. There, traditional attitudes have prevailed partly because the superpowers have so far managed their cold war, and because the tolerance of a certain amount of violence has seemed preferable to the constraints on national freedom of action which a set of effective security regimes would entail. The modicum of insecurity inherent in a world of anarchy (cooled by nuclear caution and partly diffused by fragmentation) has been preferred by every major actor to the collective insecurity that might be inherent in a regime controlled by others or permanently subjected to a struggle for control. The alternatives have not been a collective stag hunt, or "starving to death."[20] The conditions under which international regimes have spread or survived[21] have been (1) the existence of a dominant power whose norms and procedures for the regime may not have seemed the best solution to all other states, but were accepted because the advantages these states could nevertheless derive from the regime exceeded those of refusing to join it (a notion that suggests that the dominant power itself had to define its interest in a sharable, i.e., enlightened, way); or (2) the existence of a common good, in an area where individual efforts were clearly ineffective or counterproductive, and little was lost by giving up the appearance of sovereignty; or (3) the possibility of a bargain in which the benefits across the board outweigh the losses, and the gain in predictability outweighs the burden of restraints on state action (if one analyzes the European Community as an international regime, one sees that these last two conditions have been met).[22] It is therefore rather obvious why such regimes have not spread to the realm of security, why the collapse of the international monetary regime of Bretton Woods has not been followed by the construction of a new one, and why the United States has resisted signing the Law-of-the-Seas agreement reached after many years of complicated bargaining.

A proliferation of international regimes would not change the "ordering principle" of the international system, nor even "the principles on the basis of which the constituent units are separable from one another."[23] Anarchy and sovereignty would not be abolished, but the significance of both would be profoundly transformed. Indeed, in each "sovereign" domain, there would be two rules, in effect: that of the state and that of the regimes (in which the state takes part). The utopia of a world state would continue to elude our grasp, not only because of the possibility of regimes breaking up (or down), when the balance of gains and losses, opportunities and restraints, shifts too drastically at the expense of some key members, but also because the insoluble problem of "steering" a world without a single hegemon would not be resolved. There would still be a formidable problem of coordination—both across issues and among states, with much maneuvering aimed either at making it possible for a state that is powerful in one arena to translate some of this power into gains in areas when it is weak, or at blocking such transfers by trying to insulate each regime from the others. Nevertheless, we would be much closer to the world of politics described by the theorists of "complex interdependence" than to that of the "state of war." Steering would become less troublesome if it occurred within the framework and through the procedures and bargains of regimes.

A third question brings us back to the level of the key actors. Will they undergo the kind of domestic transformations that would make a taming of the logic of sovereignty possible, a strengthening of "existential deterrence," economic interdependence and international regimes less problematic? In the case of the United States, two kinds of changes would be needed. One concerns the political system: the capacity both for greater continuity and for more long-range strategic thinking would be indispensable. Is this capacity achievable, given the four-year presidential term, the weakness of the career civil servants and the priorities of the "in-and-outers," the fragmentation of agencies, the effects of the separation of powers, the flimsy tone and heavy weight of the media? The other changes concern political style, which these institutional features partly shape and help preserve. One would need to break away decisively from the two archetypes of American exceptionalism: the missionary impulse, internationalist though it tends to be, insofar as it does not facilitate the necessary compromises with other peoples' or governments' blemishes, entails a combination of naiveté and excessive expectations, and breeds disappointments and disruptive backlashes. Even more, the impulse to be the world's sheriff needs to be discarded, not only because of the macho stance that it introduces into U.S. diplomacy, not only because of the excessive emphasis on will rather than skill, on resolve and credibility rather than influence and maneuver, but also because of the kind of insecurity it injects into the American public mind—the fear of "loss of nerve," the need to prove one's stamina or toughness by doing silly things (or doing something) even if they aren't worth doing, even if they divert resources, even if the purposes, other than demonstrating strength, are unclear.

The USSR, for its part, would have to go even farther: beyond the point that many of Reagan's advisers have wanted to reach (a turn of the regime inward, toward domestic reform). The USSR would have to transform the very essence of its regime and to overcome some of the most ancient traits of Russian political culture. The regime is a formidable machinery for central and total control, still oiled by an ideology that provides legitimacy, carries an assumption of external hostility, and dictates an imperative of expansion abroad. The least one can say is that it does not make the participation in a host of international regimes easy, nor does it leave much room for providing these with strong, unfettered powers of enforcement (although, in my opinion, it would be wrong to believe that it rules all of this out *ab initio*); in short, in the Soviet calculation of gains and costs, fears of loss of control and of creeping ideological erosion will be weighted very heavily. The Russian political culture, with its often almost paranoid fear of external invasion, penetration, defilement, and encirclement, its passionate concern for the absolute security of the fatherland's borders, and its chauvinistic feelings toward many other—lesser—breeds, obviously remains a formidable obstacle. We are very close to a vicious circle here. The political regime and public mind of the USSR could be moved away from their profound suspiciousness and attachment to all the trappings of traditional sovereignty if, in a moderate international system, the advantages of moderation, greater openness, and broader cooperation with non-Communist states became visible; but the regime and culture are precisely the reasons that reduce the chances for the existence of such a system and the flow of such benefits.

3. Let us, then, at last put the pieces together. There are so many pieces, it is true, that the number of possibilities appears unlimited. But there is a way of reducing this chaos: by presenting three plausible models of the future. The "real world" is likely to resemble one of them, more or less—depending on the way in which the variables combine.

The first model is that of an "ideal" world (ideal, that is, within the range of possible worlds, thus excluding either a world government or an end of the international political system). It would have two chief characteristics. One is a general reduction of violence. In the relations between the superpowers, this would entail reaching an arms control agreement based on these principles: the elimination of unverifiable, non-survivable, and counterforce weapons, and the primacy of crisis stability. It would also mean a political context of fairly broad cooperation, allowing not only for the prevention or defusing of East-West crises but also for joint action to prevent the inevitable regional conflicts or domestic turbulence in third countries from reaching dangerous levels—that is, action aimed at insulating the areas of violence and at reducing the intensity, length, and scope of armed conflict. In this context, another subject for joint action would be a strategy aimed at slowing down nuclear proliferation, by providing guarantees to states tempted by nuclear weapons for security reasons and effective sanctions against proliferators through agreements with other suppliers.

Obviously, the other feature of such a system would be the spread of international regimes—particularly to the area in which such regimes have had the least success so far: security. A global nuclear arms control regime would have to include all the nuclear powers; and it should be designed in such a way as to not reward cheating or breaking out. It would also have to entail mutual information about weapons developments. A global conventional regime might at first be limited to a series of confidence-building measures, but it would be reinforced by a network of regional security regimes that would include agreements of outside arms suppliers to curtail their sales of weapons as well as assurances by countries within

The Future of the International Political System

the region to keep their own armaments to certain levels and types of weapons. In order to be effective, these regimes would need to possess regional or international peace forces whose presence could not be ended at the whim of one of the parties, and which would have fairly extensive powers of self-defense, given the prevalence of conflict in most parts of the world. The establishment of regional regimes should, in this model, not wait for and depend on the consent of all the countries of the area: some potential troublemakers may have to be isolated; but at least the tacit consent of both superpowers would be necessary. The solidity of such regional regimes would be buttressed by efforts, undertaken at the global (UN) or regional level, to resolve the disputes from which violence springs, with the active participation of the superpowers serving, in a sense, as diplomacy's secular arms.

A second model corresponds to a gloomier vision: that of a world in which the superpowers' relationship remains troubled, and in which they as well as other actors are reluctant to give up the advantages of sovereignty in the realm of security—except on a temporary, ad hoc basis that leaves little room for institutionalization. In this model, the United States and the USSR would continue to sign arms-control agreements in order to regulate, and to reduce the costs of, the arms race, but a great deal of qualitative "modernization" would be allowed, including the development of some defensive systems, of weapons that are unverifiable (because of their size and/or mobility), and of survivable counterforce systems. Some nuclear proliferation would also take place, in the absence of a stringent international antiproliferation regime.

In such a world, the main peril for global peace would reside, not in the nuclear arms race, or even in the core, but in the various regional subsystems, in the continuing involvement of the superpowers, enthusiastic or reluctant but driven by their contest, and in the periodic testing of the limits of their commitments. In other words, it would resemble the current international political system, or rather the system as it was before the new cold war: troubled global peace, leaving room for occasionally large, but fragmented, regional explosions. It suggests that an increase will occur in the tendency of smaller states to resort to force, in their capacity to build quite vulnerable and provocative nuclear forces, and in their ability to exploit the superpowers' rivalry and to trigger the intervention of their respective superpower protector; at a minimum, regional violence will get much worse. One difference might be the greater possibility (avoided so far) of limited direct conventional clashes between the superpowers (or also between the USSR and China) through the dynamics of these subsystems.

The third model is a doomsday one. It predicts that the constant juggling, the recurrent tense, unsettling improvisation of temporary halts and lasting nonsolutions is unlikely to work in the long run: one can't succeed everywhere, always. It assumes either the failure of further superpower efforts at arms control, or the failure of those agreements that might still be reached to reverse the trend toward counterforce and vulnerability. It expects the international political system, despite all of its original features, to end in the same way as past systems, dominated either by two powers or by two armed camps: sooner or later (just as Pleikus were said to be like streetcars), there comes an Epidamnus or a Potideia, or an accident such as the Sarajevo assassination, and each superpower or camp decides that there is no room for compromise, that it cannot yield without disastrous effects, that waiting until the next crisis will only benefit the adversary, and that it is easier in any case for the other side to pull back. The vulnerability of an important part of one's nuclear arsenal, or the hope of gaining a significant advantage by striking first, or the fear that the adversary would gain the advantage unless one preempts would help make the peaceful settlement of such a crisis impossible. Finally, the model postulates that either a major conventional confrontation in the core area or in one of the other vital subsystems (Middle and Far East) where the USSR has important geographical advantages, or the superpowers' recourse to limited nuclear warfare, is bound to remain uncontrollable and will lead to mutual assured destruction.

4. Which model *shall* it be? "Realists" will tend to believe that it must be some form of the second, because the first is too utopian, and the perils of the third are too obvious not to be somehow conjured. But I see no room for complacency. First, the history of past systems tells us something that remains valid despite all the original features of the present one: psychologically, after a series of more or less successfully managed crises that have left frayed nerves and generalized discontent, the willingness to compromise, to restrain, tends to erode, and repressed resentments and regrets take their revenge. The dark side of protracted troubled peace is a kind of gradual, almost imperceptible resignation to submit to the fire next time.

Second, past pluses are rapidly turning into minuses: the changes in the nature of the nuclear arsenal may have the effect that "deterrence," which used to be a form of reassurance, is turning into a kind of provocation; the institutions of international economic interdependence have all been battered by the crises of the past dozen years, and national economic power as an instrument of coercion plays a prominent role alongside the "pooled" economic power or the bargaining kind of economic power found in international regimes. The heterogeneity of the system, its fragmentation into separate compartments because of both the nuclear revolution and the autonomy of local causes of conflicts, seems to inject in the superpowers a desire to overcome these obstacles, to impose the artificial unity of their contest on the world, and to offset local disadvantages in one subsystem with "horizontal escalation" in a more favorable one.

Third, the increase in radical hostility and the halting nature of the U.S.-Soviet dialogue at a time of nuclear parity (which did not exist in the late 1940s) and of incomparably more sophisticated arsenals are ominous new features. Another such feature is the increasing military might of a number of countries in the regional subsystems. With the stakes of regional conflicts rising and the superpowers' rivalry heating up, their willingness and ability to stay out or to keep their involvements limited are likely to be very sorely tested.

The question we face, therefore, changes from What is most likely to happen to What *should* we do to prevent the doomsday model from becoming a reality—since, in the past, the reasons for which the international political system resembled the second model are disappearing or cannot be expected to last forever. Obviously, we face a convergence of political and moral imperatives. Both political scientists and professional moralists (so to speak) such as the American bishops have been driven to the conclusion that the political commands of survival, development, and moderation are also ethical demands, and that the moral imperatives of peace and justice cannot be separated from a close political and military analysis and strategy. What we should do is work toward the first model and adopt it as a goal, however difficult and distant. As students of political affairs, we must therefore try to describe as rigorously as we can the kinds of mechanisms required by this model to function, and to specify as sharply as we can the conditions needed to bring it about and to keep it going (a quarter of a century ago, I had called for the formulation of "relevant utopias"; this is the same concern).

But what can we do, as citizens? Even the thumbnail sketch I have provided here shows the abyss between where we are and where we ought to go. What is required is nothing less than a bet on the transformation of the superpowers and on a change in the logic of foreign policy. Can one, this time, count on what has never worked before—the power of arguments (remember Norman Angell?), the ability of statesmen to recoil before a "mad momentum" and to reverse it? This time, there may not be the leeway in which to pour belated regrets into rueful memoirs, and to say: "if only I had listened"; but statesmen caught by the iron logic of their roles still act as if they did not have to listen or to innovate—as long as their opponents did not do it first. And so, one comes reluctantly to the conclusion that the only path toward the least somber of the three models may be one that passes through a crisis disastrous enough to scare and convert everyone, but not so disastrous as to be fatal to all; and since one cannot wish for such a risk, one's best hope remains the persistence of the second model, despite all the reasons I have given to suggest that one can no longer count on it.

Notes

1. Immanuel Wallerstein, *The Modern World System* (New York: Academic Press, 1974 and 1980).

2. Robert Gilpin, *War and Change in World Politics* (New York: Cambridge University Press, 1981).

3. Robert Keohane, "Theory of World Politics: Structural Realism and Beyond," in Ada W. Finifter, *Political Science: the State of the Discipline* (Washington, D.C.: American Political Science Association, 1983), p. 519.

4. Kenneth Waltz, *Theory of International Politics* (Reading, Mass.: Addison-Wesley, 1979).

5. For Keohane, see "Theory of World Politics"; Ruggie's critique appears in "Continuity and Transformation in the World Polity: Toward a Neorealist Synthesis," *World Politics* (January 1983), pp. 261–285.

6. A quarter of a century ago, I had listed state-society relations, transnational forces, and the scope of relations among the crucial elements of an international system whose transformations determined the passage from one system to another. See Hoffmann, *Contemporary Theory in International Relations* (Englewood Cliffs, N.J.: Prentice-Hall, 1960).

7. Keohane, "Theory of World Politics," p. 513.

8. Ibid., p. 529.

9. Richard Ned Lebow, *Between Peace and War* (Baltimore: Johns Hopkins University Press, 1981.

10. See Hoffmann, *Primacy or World Order*, Part 2 (New York: McGraw-Hill, 1978).

11. This point is developed further in Hoffmann, *Dead Ends* (Cambridge, Mass.: Ballinger, 1983), Chapters 1 and 12, and Chapter 8 of this volume.

12. The now classic description is in Robert Keohane and Joseph Nye, *Power and Interdependence* (Boston: Little, Brown, 1977).

13. Hoffmann, *Dead Ends*, Chapter 1.

14. See Chapter 16 of this volume.

15. For a more detailed elaboration, see my, and other, contributions to Joseph Nye (ed.), *The Making of America's Soviet Policy* (New Haven, Conn.: Yale University Press, 1984).

16. See especially A. W. de Porte, *Europe Between the Superpowers* (New Haven, Yale University Press, 1979).

17. McGeorge Bundy, "The Bishops and the Bomb," *New York Review* (June 16, 1983), p. 6.

18. Ibid., p. 4.

19. Ernst Haas, "Postwar Conflict Management," *International Organization* (Fall 1983), p. 235.

20. Ibid., p. 235.

21. See the issue of *International Organization* on international regimes (Spring 1962).

22. See "Reflections on the Nation-State in Europe Today," *Journal of Common Market Studies* (September–December 1982), pp. 21–37.

23. Ruggie, "Continuity and Transformation," p. 274.

7

International Systems and International Law

My purposes in this essay are two: to undertake, in introductory form, one of the many tasks a historical sociology of international relations could perform—the comparative study of a type of international relations that appears in almost any international system, i.e., international law; secondly, to present the rudimentary outlines of a theory of international law that might be called sociological or functional.[1]

International law is one of the aspects of international politics that reflect most sharply the essential differences between domestic and world affairs. Many traditional distinctions tend to disappear, owing to an "international civil war" that projects primarily domestic institutions (such as parliaments and pressure groups) into world politics and injects world-wide ideological clashes into domestic affairs. But international law, like its Siamese twin and enemy, war, remains a crystallization of all that keeps world politics *sui generis*. If theory is concerned primarily with the distinctive features of systems rather than with the search for general laws that are valid for all systems, international law becomes a most useful approach to international politics.

I propose here to examine the relations between international law and international systems, first in general terms and subsequently in more concrete form with evidence derived from history. Finally, in the light of such a historical presentation, I will examine briefly two of the main politico-legal problems raised by international law.

I

Most theories of domestic politics start with an ideal-type of (1) a community—an unconditional consensus on cooperation, a belief in a common good (however vague) and in the precedence of this common good over particular interests; and (2) an organization, the State, which has created this community or was established by it, and which is endowed with the monopoly of the legitimate use of force. The theory of international politics must start from the ideal-type of milieu in which (1) the behavior of the members ranges from, at best, that of partners in a society—who cooperate on a limited number of issues, rarely unconditionally, and give primary allegiance to themselves, not the society—to that of accomplices in chaos (the social group made up of the states is always on the verge of becoming a fiction); and (2) there is no monopoly of power, over and above that possessed by the members. Thus, whereas procedures for cooperation, for the creation and expression of consent, exist in both domestic and world politics, the permanent possibility of free and legitimate recourse to violence remains the mark of international relations.

This simple point of departure is of decisive importance both for the understanding of international law and for the delimitation of international systems.

Law is a body of rules for human conduct established for the ordering of a social group and enforceable by external power. Domestic law orders the national group by acting directly on the individual citizens and by regulating all the problems that are deemed to be of social importance; it is enforced by the power of the state, exerted directly on individuals. By contrast, international law suffers from three forms of precariousness. The first is its low degree of institutionalization. The second is its unique substance: in the domestic order, which regulates a great mass of individuals, law is an instrument of homogeneity; the international order regulates a small number of subjects and consequently, its law is a law of differentiation, caught between the Charybdis of universality at the cost of vagueness and the Scylla of precision at the cost of heterogeneity. The scope of the subject matter is limited by the reluctance of the subjects to submit themselves to extensive regulations and by the inefficiency of premature regulations: hence, numerous gaps in the body of rules. The third is the limited amount of solidity or authority in international law. I do not refer here to efficiency in Kelsen's meaning of the term, for it is true that most forms of international law are obeyed, but to the obscurities or ambiguities that mar existing rules, since they are established by the subjects themselves; to the fact, analyzed by de Visscher, that the greatest solidarities exist in matters that least affect the power and policies of the subjects, and vice versa; and to the fact that, in Julius Stone's words, international law is the one legal order that provides for its own destruction by the mere force of its own subjects.[2]

An international system is a pattern of relations among the basic units of world politics, characterized by the scope of the objectives pursued by those units and of the tasks performed among them, as well as by the means used to achieve those goals and perform those tasks. This pattern is largely determined by the structure of the world, the nature of the forces that operate across or within the major units, and the capabilities, patterns of power, and political cultures of those units. Such a definition corresponds to accepted definitions of domestic political systems, which are also characterized by the scope of political objectives (the limited state versus the totalitarian state, the welfare state versus the free-enterprise state) and the methods of organizing power (constitutional relations among the branches of government, types of party systems).

The international system is both an analytic scheme and a postulate. It is a way in which the scholar tries to give structure and meaning to a complex and confusing mass of data. It is also the expression of an assumption that is indispensable to the scholar—that history can be ordered, that there are distinguishable patterns of relations and key variables that can be discerned without artificiality or arbitrariness. A historical sociology of international politics must try to study the international systems that have emerged in history just as political scientists study real (by contrast with imagined) domestic political systems.

Yet here the difficulty begins. The domestic political system is easy to delimit. Its existence is certain: it manifests itself through the combination of positive legal norms and laws of political behavior that result from the social structure, economic regime, traditions, formal institutions of the country, etc. Its limits in time are indicated by easily recognizable changes in the key variables: a revolution that substitutes a new constitutional order for the old one, a radical transformation of the electoral system or of the party system, etc. The international system is much less easy to delimit.

To begin with, its existence is more hypothetical. The analytic scheme corresponds to a historical reality only if three conditions are met. Relations among the units must be regular; they must reach a certain amount of intensity. Secondly, for the system to be more than a hypothesis, of which reality is merely a vague approximation, the units must have a modicum of awareness of their interdependence. In a domestic political system, given the underlying consensus and the overriding central power, the actors (parties, interest groups, etc.) are aware of the existence and structure of the whole. They are system-conscious even if they are competitive or antagonistic. But the international system is more open and more problematic. Such system-consciousness (much in evidence after 1648, much less so in the sixteenth century) is even less synonymous with solidarity than in a domestic system: the lack of consensus and of central power makes it clear why awareness of the interdependence and hostility are perfectly compatible, since the former entails only that the moves and calculations resulting from the latter take into account the existence and possible reactions of the other parts of the system, not that the maintenance of the system be the unit's goal. The third component is specificity. In a domestic system, differentiation between the social system as a whole and the political system is always difficult, but there is always a visible (if partly dependent) subsystem of political institutions. In international affairs, the difference between what is "within" and "without," between domestic affairs and trans-unit relations is not always clear. I am not referring to periods when domestic affairs become stakes in the international competition (when the boundaries between domestic and foreign affairs, although transgressed, are still recognizable), but to periods when the boundaries that separate "within" from "without" fade away. It is hard to discuss an empire's international relations as if it were itself an international system; it is equally difficult to apply the concept to feudal periods during which territoriality is scrambled.

Secondly, the limits of an international system in space are also often problematic. At times, different systems coexist on the map but ignore each other. It is also possible for a single system (say, the European one in the seventeenth and eighteenth centuries) to be composed of different subsystems, within each one of which relations were far more intense than in the overall system.

The problem of the limits in time is the most serious of all. As Raymond Aron has observed, periodization is both necessary and dangerous: the historian is free in his choice of criteria, but he should refrain from attributing to the periods he establishes consequences that only empirical evidence can prove.[3] The choice of criteria is obviously dictated by one's concerns as a scholar: one will say that there has been a change *of* system (rather than change merely *in* the system) when the key variables one has selected have undergone a decisive change; the choice of the key variables and of the amount of change deemed decisive depends on the purpose of the study. Given my own conception of international politics and the resulting emphasis on conflict, the criteria I would propose are what I would call the *stakes of conflict*. A new system emerges—

1. When there is a new answer to the question: what *are* the units in potential conflict?—i.e., when the basic structure of the world has changed (as in the passage from the city-state system to the Roman Empire; from the Empire to the medieval system; from the medieval hierarchy to the modern "horizontal" system of multiple sovereignties).

2. When there is a new answer to the question: what *can* the units do to one another in a conflict?—i.e., when there is a basic change in the technology of conflict. (Such a change may also transform the basic structure of the world: as John Herz has reminded us, the gunpowder revolution ushered in the era of the "impermeable" territorial state.[4]) Even within the same type of basic structure, a fundamental innovation in the technology of conflict changes the nature of the international system: the atomic revolution rendered obsolete previous multiple-sovereignty systems because it meant the passage from a relative to an absolute power of destruction and consequently the end of great-power "impermeability." An effective diffusion of nuclear power could mean still another system.

3. When there is a new answer to the question: what do the units *want* to do to one another? Here, we try to distinguish systems according to the scope of the units' purposes and to the techniques they use to meet their objectives or to prevent rivals from achieving theirs.

If we combine the criteria, we come to the fundamental distinction between stable systems and revolutionary ones. A stable system is one in which the stakes of conflict are limited; relations among the actors are marked by moderation in scope and means. Whatever the system's basic structure and the state of the technology of conflict, the units act so as to limit the amount of harm they could inflict upon one another. In a revolutionary system, this moderation disappears. When one major actor's decision to discard it coincides with or brings about a revolution in the technology of conflict or a change in the basic structure of the world (or both), the system is particularly unstable.[5] In other words, in a stable system, the life or essential values of the basic units are not constantly in question, and the main actors agree on the rules according to which competition among them will take place; in a revolutionary system, the incompatibility of purposes rules out such agreement.

For each kind of basic structure in the world and each kind of technology of conflict, we may arrive at the ideal-type of a stable system by asking: what are the conditions from which moderation in scope and means is most likely to follow? At times, actual historical systems meet these conditions, but often they do not; and they are, of course, marked by constant change in all their elements. The changes (1) do not affect the system at all, when they do not hurt or remove the essential conditions of stability; (2) merely weaken the system, when they cripple some of those conditions but do not wholly destroy the moderation in scope and means; (3) ruin the system altogether if such deterioration, instead of leading to temporary disturbances, brings about a breakdown in moderation, a revolution in the technology of conflict or in the basic structure of the world.

Whether a change affecting the essential conditions of stability damages the system decisively depends on the circumstances. A breakdown requires the collapse of a large number of such conditions. This can happen either when one of the main actors decides to overthrow the system and succeeds in removing so many of the conditions of stability that the system does indeed collapse—i.e., when the actor's move leads not simply to any kind of conflict, but to a revolutionary one; or when previous deterioration leads to a conflict that may not begin as revolutionary but becomes so because it develops into a decisive additional factor of disruption. In both cases, the end of the stable system is marked by general war.[6]

In the world of multiple sovereignties before the appearance of absolute weapons, it was the balance-of-power system that brought stability to international politics, a pattern of relations among states which, through shifting alliances and the use of various diplomatic techniques, tends to limit the ambitions of the main units, to preserve a relative equilibrium among them, and to reduce the amount of violence among them. The ideal conditions for such a system are the following:

1. In the structure of the world: a greater number of major states than two; relative equilibrium of power among them; the existence of a frontier zone where the major states can expand without fatally colliding, which is a prerequisite of the kind of flexibility that a balancing system needs.

2. Related to transnational forces: technological stability; a common outlook among the leaders of the major states, provided by either similar regimes or a common attitude to religion or similar beliefs about the purpose of the state. A common outlook allows for horizontal ties as strong as or stronger than the political ties that attach those leaders to their domestic communities; a common conception of legitimacy can thus develop.

3. Related to domestic affairs within the major units: the existence of political systems in which the state exercises only limited control over its citizens' international loyalties and activities.

The outcome of these conditions is a system in which the major units' objectives are limited to only moderate increases in power or prestige, and in which many of the tasks that could be performed through the processes of world politics remain beyond their pale. The means used by the major units in their mutual relations are coalitions, designed to prevent any single unit from disrupting stability, either by rewarding him for his cooperation or by punishing him for misbehavior (but not, however, making it impossible for him to cooperate again).

The ideal conditions for international stability can be defined as *evenness* in the situation of the major units—just as a large degree of identity among the members of a state is necessary for the emergence of the general will. Conversely, the process of deterioration that leads to disturbances within the system and might provoke its breakdown can be summed up as the re-introduction of unevenness or heterogeneity.[7] This process includes the appearance of the following conditions:

1. In the structure of the world: irrepressible ambitions of individual rulers;[8] ambitions kindled by disparity in power between one major actor and its neighbors or other major units; the end of the frontier zones, which increases the likelihood of and stakes in direct clashes between the major units.

2. In the forces that cut across these units: a technological revolution, which leads to instability when it produces competition; the destruction of transnational ties either under the impact of national integration, which inevitably submits diplomacy to greater internal pressures, or because of an ideological explosion set off by a disparity of regimes or beliefs.

3. In the domestic affairs of the major units: strong integrative trends leading to nationalism; the expansion of state control over the foreign activities of the citizens for either economic or ideological purposes.

Let us turn now to the relation of international law to various international systems. International law can be studied as a product of international systems and as a repertory of normative theory about each one of them. On the one hand, it is shaped by all the elements that compose an international system:

1. It reflects the structure of the world. The nature of the actors determine whether the law of the system is the "law of coordination" made by territorial states or the external public law of an empire, or whether it will disappear altogether, as it did during much of the medieval period. The size of the diplomatic field determines the degree of universality of the legal order. The degree of unity of international law and the efficiency of a good deal of its provisions depends on the existence, duration, and seriousness of a relationship of major tension.

2. It reflects transnational forces. Technology is of considerable importance: the intensity or density of legal relations among the actors depends largely

on the state of the arts. The unity and authority of the legal order depend on the presence and number of transnational ideologies and conceptions of legitimacy.

3. The domestic situation of the major units is also relevant to international law, which has always reflected the patterns of power and the political cultures of the main actors.[9] The development of law by treaties and the reception of rules of international law within the national units depend on provisions of constitutions and decisions of domestic courts.

4. Finally, international law reflects relations among the units. It is shaped by their scope: the breadth and nature of the subject matter regulated by law vary according to the range and character of the goals the units try to reach and of the tasks they try to perform. In particular, rules of law often express the policies of the major units. Moreover, customs and treaties reflect the methods by which units try to meet their objectives, and they regulate at least some of the techniques used.

On the other hand, if we turn from empirical systems to normative theories of international law, we find a critical assessment of international systems from the viewpoint of world order. In any political system, order is achieved if the following three requirements are met: security—i.e., dealing with the problem of conflict by assuring the survival and safety of the members of the system; satisfaction—i.e., dealing with the problem of assent, and obtaining it through constraint or consent; flexibility—i.e., dealing with the problem of change (which is crucial, since assent is never definitive or total), by establishing procedures capable of absorbing shocks and channeling grievances. In a world divided into many nations, order is always threatened. Legal theorists ask whether order is possible at all; if so, whether the system is capable of ensuring it; and if not, what kind of measures are necessary to obtain it. On the whole, in each period of history, there have been those who deny either the possibility or the desirability of a stable legal order; the utopians, who also question the effectiveness of the existing system but propose to substitute a radically different one; and the adjusters, who try to show how and to what extent order can be established or preserved within the existing system. We learn a great deal about the nature and operation of a given international system if we study the range of disagreements among these three groups; the more stable the system, the narrower this range.

Since international law constitutes the formal part of the reigning order and expresses the more lasting interests of the actors—their long- or middle-range strategy, rather than their daily tactics—the link between the solidity or authority of international law and the stability of the international system is strong. The basic function of international law is to organize the coexistence of various nations: this presupposes that their existence is assured. In stable international systems, it is possible to distinguish three kinds of international law:[10]

1. The law of the political framework—the network of agreements that define the conditions and some of the rules of the political game among

states. By "conditions," I mean such provisions as the settlement of borders after wars, the main alignments as expressed in treaties of alliance, periodic conferences among major powers; by "rules," I mean provisions that determine the mutual commitments of states or procedures for the settlement of major disputes.

2. The law of reciprocity, which defines the conditions and rules of inter-state relations in areas that less vitally affect the power and politics of the states. This is a large zone in which states can be assumed to have a mutual and lasting interest in common rules—a zone of predictability, on which the competition in politically more sensitive areas rests and depends. We can distinguish two kinds of laws of reciprocity: the law of delimitation, which defines the rights and privileges of states—in peacetime over such matters as diplomatic relations, territory, and people, in wartime over weapons, military objectives, noncombatants, etc.; and the law of cooperation, which regulates joint interests, particularly in commerce.

3. The law of community, which deals with problems that can best be handled, not on the basis of a reciprocity of interests among states understood as separate and competing units, but on the basis of a community of action independent of politics—problems of a technical or scientific nature to which national borders are irrelevant.

These distinctions are sound and legitimate in a stable period, for when the survival of the nations involved is insured, a hierarchy of interests becomes possible. The law of the political framework deals the cards with which the players try to reach such objectives as greater power, or prestige, or the triumph of ideals; the law of reciprocity provides the underpinning of national security and defines those functions and attributes of the state that are not at stake in political contests. But in a revolutionary system, the distinction between these two kinds of law becomes extremely fuzzy; when survival is not assured, the limits that the law of reciprocity sets to states' privileges or jurisdictions become obstacles in the quest for greater security and power, while cooperation over joint interests is replaced by conflict or competition which challenges previous rules. In such a system, the power and policies of states are directly involved in almost every aspect of international activity.[11] Thus, in a revolutionary system, the great bulk of international law partakes of the somewhat shaky authority of the law of the political framework.

The difference in the solidity of law in revolutionary and stable systems is reflected in the contrasting impacts of political change on law. Changes that do not destroy a stable system do not lethally affect the legal order, precisely because customs and agreements express strategic rather than tactical interests. To be sure, the body of rules reflects such changes if they are of sufficient magnitude: in particular, the disappearance of some of the essential conditions for an ideal stable system has repercussions on the law of the political framework, which is the most sensitive to such tremors; it may also leave its mark on the law of reciprocity, because certain kinds of agreements become increasingly rare, or codification becomes more troublesome, or difficulties appear in the discharge of treaties. However, the law of reciprocity may continue to develop even when the ideal conditions for stability are no longer present (as was shown in the flowering of such law just before World War I) precisely because it reflects mutual interests that the fluctuations of politics do not impair so long as the stable system lasts. Also, while the essential moderation in the scope and means of international relations continues, the gaps and uncertainties of law are not disruptive factors: in the areas which are not regulated or in which the rules are ambiguous, a purely political decision or interpretation by the states concerned will be needed, but, given the system, no destructive effects are likely to follow.

In a revolutionary system, however, gaps and ambiguities become wedges for destruction or subversion of the international order in the interest of any of the actors. The absence of agreement on the rules of the game, the increase in the stakes of conflict, and the reign of insecurity mean that political changes will have the following effects on international law: (1) just as theories and concepts outlive the system that justified them, regulations that have become obsolete nevertheless continue to be considered valid (although they are less and less respected) because of the increasing difficulty in agreeing on new rules, or because they serve the interests of some of the contending units; (2) new problems thrown up by political or technological change remain unregulated, for the same reasons; (3) new regulations appear which attempt to deal with some of the changes but turn out to be incompatible with the new system; and (4) since international systems change essentially through general wars, the collapse of previous laws of war is usually the first effect of the change on the legal order.

This conglomeration of ruin, gaps, and "dysfunctional" old or new rules denotes the major areas of friction and tensions in world politics during the lifetime of revolutionary systems and particularly in periods of passage from one system to another.

Thus, it is in balance-of-power systems that the authority of international law has been greatest: as Oppenheim stated, the existence of the balance is a condition of the flourishing of authoritative international law.[12] However, this condition is at the same time a limitation:

1. Even when the balance functions under optimum conditions, the political framework may remain largely unregulated. We must distinguish between systems in which the balance is more or less automatic or mechanical and systems in which it is institutionalized to a greater degree—a distinction among stable systems based in particular on the law of the political framework.

2. Even under optimum conditions, the balance sometimes operates at the expense of law. In a system of "sovereign" states, the principles of equality and consent are essential to the legal order. But daily practices may conflict with these norms: a preponderance of power often forces small, or isolated large, states to assent to measures that go against their objectives or detract from the formal equality of all the units.

3. Among the many power configurations that characterize the relations of units in a balance-of-power system, there is one that threatens the solidity

of international law (especially the law of the political framework) more permanently: when optimum conditions are met, the most likely result is the "mechanism of imbalance"—a coalition of a majority of the main actors against an isolated would-be disrupter; but when those conditions are not all present, there may develop an opposition of blocs of comparable strength, so that alignments stiffen instead of remaining flexible. The authority and unity of international law may then be imperiled.

II

Three concrete examples of relations between international systems and international law will support the preceding generalizations.

The first example is that of international law during the balance-of-power system that lasted from the Peace of Westphalia until the French Revolution.

The balance operated effectively because the treaties of Westphalia had redistributed territory so as to create a number of major states capable of neutralizing each other and had also removed the poisonous element of religious conflict. Within the main units, mercantilism and absolutism gradually weakened. New transnational ties developed; the "corporate identity" of monarchs, diplomats, and officers across national boundaries led to a consensus on the legitimacy of the balance, just as the community of European intellectuals produced a consensus on the values of the Enlightenment. The political result was a mechanical balance, frequently disturbed however, either because a state could never be sure in advance whether or when others would try to curb it, or because of individual ambitions. Hence, numerous limited wars occurred: stylized wars of position that only rarely affected the civilian population.

Although there was little international law of the political framework, the law of reciprocity developed in a way that reflected both the moderation and the volatility of a balancing system. In the area of trade, statesmen came to realize that law was the best technique for obtaining an increase in national wealth and power (as in past mercantilist practice), but safely; the idea of harmony of interests replaced the earlier expectation of conflict—hence, numerous measures to protect commerce at sea, especially in wartime. Neutrality for the first time became possible, a good bargain, and a subject of legal regulation. Yet, the balance of power imposed limits to the development of law. To preserve the system, it was required at the end of wars to restore equilibrium among the major powers at the expense of small states; these compensations proved that the norm of territorial integrity was effective only as long as it was backed by force and that it was subordinated to the preservation of the balance. Also, there were gaps wherever rules would have restricted state power too sharply: maritime warfare remained anarchical; there was no adequate procedure for the settlement of disputes developed except in rare instances of delicate arbitration.

The response of theory to these developments was most interesting. In the previous revolutionary system, a large gap had separated destroyers of the medieval dream of unity—like Machiavelli, creators of new dreams—like Crucé or Sully, and the numerous would-be rescuers of the medieval theory—who reasserted the supremacy of natural law and the doctrine of just war, but who secularized the former, hedged in the latter with qualifications, and came to recognize the existence of an international law created by the will of states. Now, in a system of increasing moderation, the gap narrowed. Even those who denied the efficiency of "covenants without the sword" showed that self-restraint might prevent all-out war. At the other pole, the Kantian utopia also reflected the new optimism: to establish order among the states was going to require an essential change in the regimes but not the end of the division of the world into separate units, and it would be effected by the invisible hand of history. The theorists on the middle ground, still trying to save the idea of a legal community of mankind, gradually abandoned the idea of natural law as the bonding cement of this community—a retreat that would have been taken as an invitation to and confession of chaos in the preceding period, but that could now be accepted without anguish; a positivistic emphasis on the fundamental rights of states as the foundation of order no longer seemed necessarily self-defeating. The expectation of a harmony of interests had been fed by the system.

The collapse of that system was a sudden, swift chain reaction. The decisive factor was the change in France's regime—which shows that the study of international systems must extend to the analysis of the political ones they include. The French Revolution, in turn, destroyed transnational links: the heterogeneity of regimes introduced an explosive element into Europe; after a brief period of idealistic pacifism—a revulsion against maintaining the balance of power, that sport of kings—the revolutionaries, turning to messianism, lit the fuse. This attempt to destroy old regimes everywhere removed another essential condition of the balance: nationalism in France led to the imposition of full government control on its citizens' acts and thoughts. Next, equilibrium among the major powers was destroyed by the French victories—an incentive to exploit unevenness even further. Then, Napoleon's ambitions produced the first modern instance of total power politics, based on an ideological inspiration and waged by total domestic and international means. A further series of changes in the conditions of stability resulted: constant shifts in the map of Europe; a transformation of the domestic order of many of the units involved, who moved away from feudal absolutism to defeat France's nationalism with its own weapons; the creation of two opposed ideological camps. Consequently, international law was thoroughly disrupted: the law of neutrality collapsed; wars of total mobilization, movement, and extermination of civilians replaced the ballet of limited wars. We have here the example of a system breaking down because of the deliberate attempt by one of its major component units to destroy it and because of this unit's capacity temporarily to succeed by exploiting the dynamism of revolution.

Let us now examine the international system of the nineteenth century. The defeat of the force that had destroyed the previous system—France—

and the apparent collapse of French-inspired ideals seemed to make a return to stability possible. The victors of 1815 decided to restore a balancing system, which they saw as the pattern that could best ensure stability, by giving security to the main powers, providing the greatest amount of flexibility, and obtaining the assent of all participating units, including France (on which only a far tighter organization than the victors were capable of maintaining could have imposed a punitive peace with any chance of success).

Some of the victors wanted a new kind of balancing system, however; what is interesting here is the discrepancy between their intention and performance. Although England was willing to return to a mechanical balance of power, Austria and Russia wanted to extend the scope and means of world politics. Whereas the eighteenth-century balance had excluded intervention in domestic affairs, Metternich and Alexander now wanted an organized balancing system that would include a formula for domestic order in its concept of legitimacy and dispose of means of enforcement against the rise of liberal and nationalist forces. The international law of the political framework would have become an explicit and powerful instrument of the great powers' common policy of preserving the Vienna order in both its international and its internal aspects. But this was not to happen, for it soon appeared that a voluntary system of cooperation was too weak to control developments within nations that a previous balancing system had already been powerless to prevent. In other words, so extensive a community could not be created by superstructural means alone. The failure of the Holy Alliance proved that an effective new balancing system could be obtained only through a return to moderation, not through an ambitious extension, in scope and means.

In the beginning, almost all the conditions for a successful balance were present. The structure of the world was marked by a double hierarchy: the distinction between a civilized core and a frontier, and, within the core, between small and large states. No permanent relation of major tension emerged until after 1870. In the core area, technology expanded but never to a degree that gave one major actor power of life and death over another. Despite the clash of political ideologies, supranational ties persisted: the dominant ideologies were themselves either supranational or favorable to the maintenance of bonds between national elites; the *Internationale* of diplomats allowed for a consensus on the rules of the game. Although regimes were far from identical, the limited state developed everywhere. The conduct of foreign affairs could be divorced from domestic passions. Constitutionalism, marked by the legalization of public affairs and the growth of the judicial apparatus, made notable advances. Liberalism led to a separation between state and society.

Consequently, relations among states were once again characterized by moderation in scope and means. First, the number of tasks performed by the processes of world politics was limited to conflict and political accommodation. The failure of Metternich's hope meant that, within the core area, domestic developments were not a legitimate object of international politics: the "neutrality of alignment"[13] necessary to the effectiveness of the balance required neutrality toward regimes as well, which was possible so long as internal revolutions made no attempt to disrupt the international system. The separation of state and society removed another vast zone from world politics—the field of private transnational activities, especially economic ones. Secondly, the objectives of the major units also remained moderate in scope: they sought limited increments of power and influence within the core area and, on the whole, avoided the destruction of value systems or national existences in this area. As for moderation in means, it was shown by the return to limited wars, the practice of nonintervention within the core area, and the multiplication of international conferences of all kinds.

In this system, international law—the law of the European core area—appeared in all three of the aspects described above, within the limits defined. The law of the political framework was the law of the Concert: as the instrument of the society of the major powers whereby they could supervise small states and control the individual ambitions of each member, it consecrated the power relations that developed for this purpose—hence the prevalence of legal techniques of neutralization and internationalization. These techniques implied agreement on common abstention from or common action in a given area or problem; they resulted from the consensus on moderation and cooperation.[14] But since this law was a balancing technique, not a way of overcoming the balance, its development was hampered by the usual limitations. Many rules merely expressed the independence of states: for instance, the principle of unanimity in Concert meetings. Law was violated whenever the maintenance of the system required it—e.g., at both ends of Concert activities: the composition of the meetings violated the principle of equality, and the process of enforcement often twisted the independence, integrity, or free consent of small powers. Lastly, there were major gaps in the law of the framework, as exemplified by the purely voluntary character of Concert meetings and by the total freedom to resort to war. These limitations and violations became increasingly dangerous for world order during the 1860's, when the balance was too fluid—i.e., when the mechanism of imbalance did not function, owing to the divisions or passivity of a majority of the big powers—and during the last years before World War I, when the hardening of the blocs produced arteriosclerosis in the Concert.[15]

The law of reciprocity was a projection of the constitutional state into world affairs, a reflection of mutual interests, and a product of the balancing system, which curtailed states' objectives. The law of delimitation became firmly established. The law of cooperation progressed considerably in commerce, where the retreat from mercantilism opened a "depoliticized" zone for free trade and for the free establishment of aliens, and in the settlement of disputes, as states became willing to resort to judicial procedures in a variety of cases involving either private citizens in the "depoliticized" area or state interests directly, but which the actors found convenient to arbitrate since the balance of power had made resort to force less profitable, or because the development of domestic legal institutions had given greater prestige to legal than to diplomatic mechanisms. But, in all its branches, the law of reciprocity suffered from the same weakness as the law of the political framework. Different standards for the treatment of foreigners applied by the major states to "civilized" nations and to backward areas showed the limit of the norm of equality. The treatment of debtors by creditor nations proved that the law often identified right with might. "Depoliticization" came to an end either when citizens ran into trouble abroad and appealed to their country of origin, or when a dispute fell within one of the numerous areas excluded by reservations in arbitration treaties. Spectacular failures at the Hague Conferences left many gaps in the laws of war and for the settlement of disputes. Again, these weaknesses became more severe when the Concert did not function well; at the end of the period, a return to protectionism, tariff wars, and the failure of the London Conference on maritime warfare were signs of deterioration.

The law that best reflected all the elements of the system was the law of war and neutrality. Since war was a legitimate method of settling disputes, and since law attempted not to curtail the ends sovereignty served but to regulate the means it used, war was entitled to a *status*: it received a legal framework, which distinguished sharply between peace and war (hence the need for a formal declaration at one end, a treaty at the other) and between international and civil strife. Within this framework, the means of war and the various categories of war victims were regulated.

Secondly, since total war practices were banned by the balance of power, and war had once again become a method of settlement of disputes but not a way of eliminating one's antagonist, war was considered to be merely a *moment*; it was a dispute between states, not between individuals—hence the customs and court decisions on the effects of war on treaties and, more importantly, the crucial distinction between combatants and noncombatants in war, between the duties of the neutral state and those of neutral citizens. Furthermore, it was a political dispute, not an interruption of economic processes—hence the protection of the neutral trader, who was maintaining the continuity of these processes, and the inviolability of as much of the belligerents' private property as was possible, both at sea and in occupied territory.

The law of community also expanded, through countless conferences, conventions, and even institutions; it regulated an increasing number of administrative and technical functions.

Consequently, the law of the nineteenth-century balance-of-power system, in matters that directly affected the power and the policies of the major states, was the transcription of the balancing process in normative terms, the expression of a system in which each state submitted to law insofar as the rules were supported by the pressure of stronger force. In other matters, law grew out of the restrictions to which power consented, in a liberal century, for the development of nonpolitical forces of reciprocity and for the devaluation of borders.

One result of this double role of law was a fairly effective system of world order. Security was achieved in the core area, especially for the major national units; lesser ones bought survival at the cost of supervision and, often, partial sacrifices of sovereignty. The Concert tried to preserve flexibility by acting to legalize and harness revolutionary changes. Assent was never complete, but as long as the major powers preferred, or had no choice but to prefer, the maintenance of the system to the gains they might hope to reap by destroying it, this was enough.

Another result was a new *rapprochement* among the three groups of theorists, who now agreed on a number of crucial points: the possibility of avoiding chaos; the basic character of the state as the foundation of world order (and the definition of the state in terms of will); and, paradoxically, the weaknesses of international law in the world as it was (an admission that, as in the previous stable period, could be made because of the general moderation of world politics). Even "deniers" such as Hegel believed in a European family, or a "higher praetor," which would prevent the warring states from turning inevitable war into inexpiable hate. Even the visionaries no longer dreamed of supranational utopias: they thought the world was moving toward a community of harmonious nation-states, thanks to free trade and public opinion. The positivists dealing with the previously avoided problem of the basis of legal obligation, could come up with auto-limitation, *Vereinbarung,* or an indivisible community of interests, without feeling that these were circular answers. At an earlier period, stressing the differences between international and municipal law, and the individual rights of the state, they had sounded almost like the cynics. Now, on the contrary, the positivists and the visionaries were close.[16] Both saw a new world almost without power, but they failed to realize that the retreat of power from certain spheres had been the result of a highly political balancing process—which was in its death throes just when the theorists believed the millennium was coming.

The deterioration of the system had, once again, started with a change in the domestic order, but this time it was a change that occurred in most of the major units, and it was gradual, not deliberate. The emergence of the modern nation-state weakened some of the essential conditions for an ideal balance of power; for in a nation-state, the population is mobilized around national symbols, and the development of the machinery of the state reinforces international integration at the expense of transnational ties. After 1870, the army's weight in domestic affairs increased everywhere, pushing the nations toward imperialism. Consequently, a change occurred in the structure of the world that almost obliterated the difference between disturbances within and destruction of the system: the end of the frontier. In addition, horizontal links between major powers were progressively weakened by the rise of mass nationalism, the success of philosophies of conflict and of national or racial superiority, and nationalities' movements that sought allies among the major powers. The legitimacy of states that were not based on the national principle was challenged; thus, international legitimacy was concerned again with domestic affairs; heterogeneity returned to the system. As a result, relations among states took on new and threatening aspects. The very frequency of disturbances, due to the uncertainty of the balance, created a climate of dissatisfaction in which small powers tried to escape the control of bigger ones. The big states, also looking for a way out, could agree only on temporary adjustments, which would not tie their hands for the future but which infuriated the small powers. In such a climate, the freezing of the balance of power after Bismarck's departure meant the end of "neutrality of alignment"; the replacement of the hierarchical system of the Concert with a vertical one, in which blocs composed of large *and* small states faced each other; hence a change in means (the decline of the Concert, the return to arms races) and an increase in scope (economic affairs became vital again in international politics). Another change in means—the resort to general war—dealt the death blow to the system; the "technical surprise" of World War I, to use Aron's expression, made the objectives of states once again incompatible and increasingly more universal.

Lastly, I would like to discuss the relation of international law to world politics in the present revolutionary system.

The structure of the world today is characterized by one consolidation and two deep transformations. On the one hand, the diplomatic field, which the previous system had gradually extended and unified, embraces the whole world for the first time. On the other hand, bipolarity has replaced the multiplicity of major actors (and put an end to the mechanism of imbalance); and the splintering of the frontier into a large number of new units has obliterated the distinction between a core area and the rest.

Secondly, a gigantic technological revolution has led to a competition to be foremost in industrial power, and it has not been accompanied by the restoration of universal transnational links. The diversity of regimes, "isolationist" reactions in many nations (especially new ones) to the intrusion of foreign affairs into all spheres of life, the tendency of the dominant forms of political regime to project and promote themselves throughout the world—these conditions have resulted in the absence of any clear and extensive conception of international legitimacy, and in huge ideological rivalries. New transnational links have emerged as a consequence of the latter, but they are divisive, competitive, and often negative solidarities.

The spiritual and temporal control of the state over its citizens has increased everywhere. Just as the old territorial essence of sovereignty was becoming obsolete, the spreading ethics of nationalism and the universal practices of public welfare have given to sovereignty an incandescent "personal" core.

The outcome is a series of revolutionary changes in the scope and means of world politics. There is no longer a "depoliticized" zone of major importance. The collapse of empires has made economic development, once dealt with by private investment or behind the walls of empires, one of the largest issues of world politics. Nor has the separation of domestic and international affairs been sustained: the logic of intervention, either to enforce a degree of conformity within one's own camp or to subvert the adversary's, has made the diffusion of political "ways of life" one of the tasks performed by world politics.[17] Consequently, the objectives of states have expanded so that the full realization of the goals of one unit or bloc would often involve the physical or moral death of another unit or camp, and such goals include blueprints for domestic as well as for international order. As for means, they have never been so varied: "total diplomacy" ranges from highly institutionalized military alliances to economic warfare, from propaganda to a host of international organizations; quasi-Doomsday machines and traditional limited wars coexist with revolutionary guerrilla wars. There is one moderating force that makes this revolutionary system an original one: the possibility for one power alone to inflict unacceptable damage on its enemies, however numerous. This makes a return to the principle of imbalance unlikely in case of a new multipolar system, but it also makes the actors hesitate far more to resort to violence than the dynamism of a revolutionary system would otherwise allow—hence the appearance of an extremely delicate and uncertain restraint.

In comparison with the pre-1914 system, the present one is marked by extraordinary and continuing changes and by great complexity.[18] Such changes and complexity have had an enormous impact on international law; the European legal order of the past could not be stretched to the dimensions of the new system without major changes.

Let us look first at the impact of these changes. In the first place, huge chunks of the traditional body of rules have been destroyed.

Basic distinctions which established in the legal order the restraints of the balance-of-power system have lost their meaning or justification. The distinction between matters of domestic jurisdiction and matters regulated by international law has practically vanished, in a period when the choice of a regime largely determines the international conduct of a state. The distinction between civilized nations and the others is challenged by the new states' objections to many traditional rules (e.g., in regard to territorial waters or even diplomatic representation). The distinction between private acts for which the state is not responsible and public acts has been destroyed through the intervention or subversion of "private" groups manipulated by their governments, and through the growing importance of transactions between large foreign or international "private" companies and the state. The distinction between war and peace has been replaced by what Philip Jessup has called situations of intermediacy: a period of irreconcilable oppositions, ideological clashes, *and* fear of total war could not but engender wars without declaration, armistices without peace, nonbelligerency without war, and aid to insurgents without recognition of belligerency.

Consequently, many traditional rules have been destroyed by massive violations. Many provisions of war and neutrality could not outlive the technological and political conditions of the nineteenth century, nor could the law forbidding states to help foreign insurgents or subversives. Similarly, many rules that governed territorial jurisdiction have vanished: instead of a fairly clear distinction among a number of separate zones and the sharp definition of the conditions in which state power could be exercised in each of them, there are now blurred, overlapping, and multiplying zones. The size of those on which states claim rights has grown; the claims themselves have steadily expanded, even over the open seas and often through unilateral moves. Traditional rules on the treatment of foreign property have been generally disregarded. These changes have reflected all the transformations in the international system: the increase in the number of nations often leading the least viable or secure ones to demand the fullest amount of control over the greatest amount of space; the technological revolution provoking a rush into air space; the decline of the old transnational consensus affecting the freedom of the seas; the modern welfare state and the totalitarian regimes attempting to grab resources wherever possible and to remove previously accepted restrictions on territorial sovereignty; the cold war leading to U-2 flights and to weapons tests in the ocean, and adding military overtones to the struggle over the extent of the territorial seas; the anticolonial revolution becoming a basic force in this struggle and in the spread of expropriation; the Arab-Israeli conflict having repercussions on canals and straits.

Many of the gaps in the body of rules have created opportunities for chaos. The silence of international law on the upper limits of air space may lead to dangerous and conflicting claims. International law has little to say about most modern methods of propaganda, subversion, and intervention short of the actual use of force. Nor did it foresee that traditional privileges of domestic jurisdiction—such as the right to grant nationality, regulate the conduct of aliens, treat citizens as the state sees fit, and recognize new states or governments—would be used as weapons in the struggle among states. Here we find what is probably the best example of the different meanings for world order of gaps in stable and revolutionary systems. In the nineteenth century, recognition was deemed a political privilege, not a legal duty, but no arbitrary consequences followed because, on the whole, very simple tests were applied: a check on whether the state existed, whether the government was in control, and whether the state accepted the existing framework of international law and politics. Since international law was flexible and contained no requirements about regimes or alignments, there was little trouble. Today, the same privilege has become a nightmare because of the collapse of the old consensus on international legitimacy (states now use criteria for recognition that are nothing more than tests of conformity to their own concept of legitimacy) and also because of a new aspect of legitimacy: the nature of the regime or the way it came to power. This is as true in the case of anticolonial conflict as it is in the cold war. Finally, international law has nothing to say about most of the weapons that have appeared since 1914.

Other traditional rules have become simply more uncertain in their operation because of changes in the international system. Those dealing with state immunities were established at a time when the state did not engage its "majesty" in trading or manufacturing activities; court reactions to the development of these activities have been conflicting and shifting. The validity of interventions in the domestic life of another state at the request of its government becomes dubious when there is a domestic contest about the legitimacy or legality of that government. Treaties also reflect the forces of disintegration that have appeared: the increase in the number of nations has led to the "individualization of rules" through reservations, or to the use of vague expressions (as, say, "genuine link," used in the recent Geneva provision dealing with flags of convenience) or to conflicts between obligations accepted by one nation in agreements on similar matters but binding different groups of states. Domestic hostility to the increasing scope of international treaties has brought about difficulties in their ratification and has led to moves such as the Bricker offensive. The intensity of inter-state conflicts has made resort to the *rebus sic stantibus* argument more frequent than ever.

Thus, much of present international law is obsolete, precisely because it reflects a dead system. But the new international system has had a second kind of effect on international law: some rules that are supposed to be valid today, which express attempts to impose a new scheme of world order that has drawn the lesson of the balance of power's ultimate failure, are premature; the scheme from which they derive has proved to be unfit for the present revolutionary world.

On the one hand, there was an attempt to give to the law of the political framework a greater scope than it had in the past, by curbing state sovereignty in matters as vital as the settlement of political disputes and the resort to war, by subordinating the conduct of states to rules administered by international organization. The success of this effort presupposed a stable world that was not to be deeply divided by ideological conflict, in which existed a basic homogeneity of regimes and beliefs, and in which the transnational forces of public opinion and "world parliamentarism" would keep disputes at a reasonably low level.

The fundamental flaw of the formula is in the ambiguous nature of international organization: it is an "as if" international community, which leaves the basic character of the world system unchanged and in which decisions are still made by states. Consequently, its success depends entirely on whether there is a system of basically satisfied, democratic units tied together by a common concept of legitimacy; if there is not, the organization itself has no power to bring such a world about. If this indispensable happy world does not exist at the start, the major powers must bring it to life—and their ability to do so is totally absent. As a result, a new and dangerous discrepancy has come to plague world order—between the United Nation's Charter provisions and practices on disputes (the power of the U.N. organs is limited to frequently ineffective recommendations), and the Charter's sweeping ban on the use of force—which encourages states to refine their techniques of offensive action short of force, and which drives victims of such tactics to disregard the ban.[19] The attempt to revert to a "just-war" concept has proved to be impossible or absurd in a world of conflicting legitimacies.

The other effort was a direct projection into the international sphere of the legal relationships that exist between groups or individuals in a constitutional state. International jurisdiction for the settlement of many disputes, international protection of human rights, the establishment of a criminal code thanks to which the punishment of warmongers would be the judicial side of a coin whose political side was the outlawing of war—all these measures reflected a utopian legal community of mankind. They have suffered a fate even worse than the fictitious political community. International adjudication can be effective only when international relations are not fundamentally at variance with the conditions of a liberal state—when a large zone of private activities is not controlled by governments, when state objectives are not so incompatible as to rule out a joint resort to the judge. The predominance of the desire to change the law over mere disagreements on interpretation of it, and the opposition in the values of the major ideological camps, have led to a decline in the importance of the World Court and a full-scale revolt against international adjudication. Human rights are unlikely to receive adequate international protection at a time when the core of sovereignty lies in the bonds between the state and its subjects.

Out of the dialectic of the obsolete and the premature, contemporary international law has managed to show a third effect of the changes in the international system. There is some evidence of a "third way" that is neither a return to the old system nor a realization of the Wilsonian utopia, but the elaboration of rules that do correspond to the few elements of stability in the present system. Although U.N. Charter provisions are used by all nations to enhance their own interests, procedures and institutions that correspond to the general desire to avoid total war have been developed by the U.N. If the competition of East and West for the allegiance of the "Third World" tends to become constantly more intense, it nevertheless remains peaceful on the whole; consequently, an international law and numerous international organs devoted to technical assistance and economic development have appeared, which correspond to the convergent interests of all three groups in channeling some measures through the procedures of a "universal actor." On the ruins of the nineteenth-century law of reciprocity, a few new conventions of delimitation and cooperation have been signed, dealing with the "humanitarian" side of war, or the continental shelf, or the joint exploitation of sea resources or the Antarctic.

This is not much. Some of those developments (e.g., concerning the continental shelf) reflect a very traditional kind of agreement to increase, not curtail, states' powers. The U.N. apparatus designed to prevent extension of conflict is an improvised one; the contemporary internationalization of trouble spots remains an *ad hoc* practice despite efforts to turn it into a general rule, and mutual East-West interests in preventing nuclear war have expressed themselves in parallel unilateral measures more often than in firm agreements. Only in the area of community—scientific research, health, communications—have there been few obstacles. Nevertheless, such developments suffice to give contemporary international law a Janus-like aspect: it has one face that announces chaos, and one that promises order.[20]

Contemporary law also reflects the heterogeneity of the present system—indeed, of every element in the system; hence, there is a permanent contradiction between such heterogeneity and the formal homogeneity of a legal system whose members are supposedly equal.

Contemporary law reflects the heterogeneity of a structure in which, although the nation-state is the basic unit and also a common aspiration, more than ever before there is a major disparity between states that meet the traditional criteria of statehood—a population, a territory, a government—and those that are governments still in search of their nation, governments that operate within explosively artificial borders.[21]

Present-day law also reflects the asymmetry of domestic regimes: the difficulties met by various attempts at codification, or at regulating international trade, air communications, and commerce in raw materials, or at establishing common standards of inspection for arms control, have shown how much the attitudes of a welfare state and a free-enterprise state, and, even more, of an industrialized state and an underdeveloped state, differ in international economic matters, or how radically the conceptions of secrecy in a democracy and a totalitarian state diverge.

Contemporary law also reflects the heterogeneity of the system with respect to transnational forces. Technological unevenness has left its mark: pressure has come mainly from the underprivileged states for legal regulation of space; the opposition of the nuclear "haves" and "have-nots" has limited the effectiveness of international cooperation for the peaceful uses of nuclear energy. As for ideological asymmetry, anti-imperialism, backed by a majority in the U.N., has put its mark on the new protocols to the law of war dealing with combatants, which give combatant status to "national liberation" guerrillas, over the opposition of several Western countries. Also, even though Soviet international law appears to differ little in its *rules* from Western law, there are significant variations in the interpretation of and general attitude toward law, which correspond to the differences in the nature of the regimes;[22] in particular, there is a considerable difference in the attitude toward the use of force within each camp's sphere. Efforts to negotiate various agreements on human rights have shown the incompatibility of competing concepts of world order on crucial issues.

Present-day law also reflects many contradictions in the relations between national units. In the first place, it shows traces of a basic contradiction that affects the policy of every state: between determination to increase national power, security, welfare, and prestige as much as possible by one's own means, and dependence on others for those very purposes. If we look at the principal source of law—treaties—we see that at the same time as such agreements suffer from the weaknesses I have mentioned above, they extend to objects never before regulated by world law (labor, human rights) and never before subjects of law (international organizations). If we look at the military function of the state—the state as fortress—we see that every state tries to ensure its security by expanding its sovereignty as far as it can (especially in the air) or developing its own weapons systems or armies, and also by participating in military alliances, which often involve a radical transformation of its traditional territorial sovereignty. If we look at the economic function of the states—the state as provider of welfare— we see that each tries to develop its own resources and acquire additional ones wherever it can (for instance, under the sea), but also that each has to join with others in order to promote the welfare of its own citizens or to receive indispensable aid.

In the second place, international law reflects the complexity of international legal situations in the face of the main issues of contemporary world politics. On the one hand, some of the provisions of the Geneva Conventions on the law of the sea, most expropriation practices, and votes in the U.N. on the question of self-determination all reflect an alignment over one main political issue, a coalition of nations interested in overthrowing the norms of the nineteenth-century system against the *status quo* Western states that are the heirs of this system. On the other hand, on cold-war issues, there are layers of states belonging to different ages of politics. On the top, the two super-powers enjoy a large amount of independence (except from one another) and extensive advantages within their respective alliances (military bases, status-of-forces agreements). Under them, there are allies who are developing their own deterrents; they continue to depend on one or the other super-power for their ultimate protection, but they are capable of bargaining hard before conceding privileges to it. Next, we find other allies who are more or less reluctant, more or less gilt-edged satellites (depending on the ideological camp to which they belong): hence, outbreaks of neutralism and of fear of war. Fourth and last, we find the states that have joined no military camp and live in a kind of fictitious nineteenth-century world of territorial sovereignty.

Lastly, law reflects the bizarre coexistence of revolutionary international relations and elements of stability introduced by the "mutual dependence" of the balance of terror, just at the time when the role of the military establishment in national decisionmaking has become greater than ever and weapons have begun to live a life of their own almost apart from events in the political universe.

The reactions of theorists to these developments reflect both the heterogeneity of the international legal order, and the impact of changes in the international system on this order. On the one hand, there is little in common between totalitarian theories of law and non-totalitarian theories: we have here both conflict and asymmetry. The former are non-scholarly analyses of the international system from the viewpoint of a desired world order: they are instruments at the service of a state strategy. They are not normative examinations of the ideal order and of the discrepancy between the actual and the ideal: they are policy sciences showing how the actual should be used or abused in order to reach the ideal determined by official doctrine. On the other hand, within the non-totalitarian theories, changes in the international system have shattered the fragile *rapprochement* that had once united the main tendencies. Both nineteenth-century extremes have disappeared. It has become impossible to believe in a dialectic of clashing units with a happy ending and in a vision of a world that moves inevitably toward law, order, and harmony. Even the middle group—positivism—has suffered severely from the marks that the free wills of states have left on world order. Gone is the common faith in the avoidance of chaos, or agreement on the indispensability of the state as the basis of the international system: theories today range from ones that nevertheless maintain this claim to those that make anguished pleas for world government. Vanished, also, is the agreement on differences between international and domestic law: some still stress these differences and some offer subtle, if unconvincing, demonstrations of the similarities.

It is characteristic of revolutionary systems that doctrines not only multiply but often pose as what they are not. Thus, today, "deniers" or cynics are either sorrowful (rather than gloating), or else are disguised as "policy-oriented" theorists who dissolve rules and principles into a maze of processes, messages, and alternatives. Today's utopians are either straightforward adepts of world government, outright natural-law revivalists, natural-law thinkers in pseudo-sociological disguise, or "pure theorists of law" who derive normative order from empirical chaos by what I would call a parthenogenesis of law. In the middle, there are persistent, but troubled, positivists and sociologists of law who seem more adept at examining the weaknesses of law than at finding formulas which would disguise them, as positivism used to do, more adept at maintaining that it is absurd to separate the legal order from its political roots than at attempting to close the gap between the aspiration for order and the practice of chaos.

III

The basis of obligation is the same in every legal order: a consciousness among the subjects that this order is needed if one is to reach a common end. Law is not obtained by deduction from a preexisting natural law or objective law *à la* Duguit; it is a creation toward an end. Thus, the purpose and the legal order cannot be separated, Kelsen's theory notwithstanding. The solidity or authority of a legal order depends on the nature and substance of the common end—which, finally, depends on the group: if the group shows a high degree of community of purpose and is organized by central power, the binding force of the legal order will be great, not otherwise.

The feeble consciousness of a common end among multiple units that allow no central power to impose its vision or to promote theirs, permanently weakens the binding force of international law by comparison with domestic law. But there are variations in the degree to which such a common end exists in international politics and, consequently, in the binding force of international law. There are variations in *level:* as we have seen, there are, in stable periods, three superimposed groups with different common ends and therefore with an international law of varying force. The law of community is strongest because it rests on a common positive purpose. The law of reciprocity is only relatively strong, because it is the law of a limited partnership whose members' common end is a set of mutual interests. The law of the political framework is weakest, for it is the law of a collection of units engaged in a struggle whose common end is limited to a narrow sphere—the rules of the game—and subordinated to the fluctuations of the balance of power.

Secondly, there are variations in *time:* it is not the same in stable and in revolutionary systems. The legal order of the nineteenth-century system was modest, because of the moderation in the scope and means of international relations and because national freedom of action was curtailed by the balance of power rather than by law, and it was efficient, because it was able within these limits to serve as a restraint on the states and also to consolidate their interdependence. Legal theories reflected both this modesty and efficiency. Contemporary law, on the contrary, must serve a system in which the extension of international relations seems to require a far wider range of common purposes but in which heterogeneity has drastically reduced this range. There is consequently a divorce between the difficulties of practice and the delirium of theory; the practices of international law are both highly ambitious and relatively inefficient. The increase in the scope of law's subject matter demonstrates the ambition, but, on vital issues, "society" is limited to a few identical or convergent interests that are sometimes even too narrow or too flimsy to provide a firm basis for developing any law. There is today no strong enough consciousness of or representation of a common legal order of mankind.[23]

Finally, there are variations in *space*. Given the narrow range of common ends and the absence of central global power, regional solidarities, institutions, and legal orders have appeared. They differ in their political foundations: the Soviet bloc remains a "Roman" system in which the common ends are largely imposed by central power; the Atlantic "community" is really a modern limited partnership, whose sharing of ends is far from total and where cooperation is far from unconditional. The European Community attempts to progress beyond inter-state cooperation and to build a transnational community. They also differ in degree of institutionalization, and in the subject matter they cover. The binding force of law depends on all the factors.

Another problem to be treated in the light of a theory of the relations between international systems and international law is that of sovereignty.[24]

Let us start with the classical definition given by the World Court in the Wimbledon case. Sovereignty means that the state "is subject to no other state and has full and exclusive powers within its jurisdiction without prejudice to the limits set by applicable law."²⁵ Thus, sovereignty is the situation of the state that has no political superior but is nevertheless bound by international law. First, the exercise of its sovereignty—for instance, signing agreements that may restrict its legal freedom of action—does not exhaust, indeed is a demonstration of, its sovereignty. Secondly, the relations between sovereignty and international law are characterized by the principle of domestic jurisdiction: matters not regulated by the former fall within the latter. Thirdly, relations among states are marked by the principle of equality (whatever their size, all states are in the same situation: their only superior is international law), by the duty of nonintervention, and by the right of self-preservation.

The trouble with this set of definitions is that their neatness is illusory. If we look at relations among states, we see a broad gamut of situations—from the mythic state-in-isolation, which exercises all the privileges of sovereignty without any other limit than that of general international law, to the member state of a federation. There is, in fact, a hierarchy of legal status determined according to the amount of sovereignty whose exercise has been given away to, or restricted in favor of, other states or international agencies. The nature and range of this hierarchy vary with each international system. Sovereignty, rather than being a reservoir that is either full or empty, is a divisible nexus of powers of which some may be kept, some limited, some lost. The point at which sovereignty can be assumed to have vanished is a matter of definition. Given such a hierarchy of situations, the equality of states is mythical.

If we look next at the relations between states and international law, we find that the definitions are illusory because the term "international law" is fuzzy: the "limit" or "restraint" it imposes is ambiguous and shifting—ambiguous because of the conditions of elaboration and enforcement of international law, which are the product of the states, shifting because the norms of international law vary from system to system.²⁶

Thus, the actual substance of sovereignty depends on the international system and, in each system, on the position of a state on the ladder I have mentioned. In a stable system, such as the nineteenth century's, sovereignty is a fairly clear nexus of sharply defined powers: the world appears as a juxtaposition of well-defined units whose respective rights are neatly delimited, which allow few exceptions to the principle of full territorial jurisdiction, and which have few institutional links among them; cooperation is organized by diplomacy and the market; limits on sovereignty are set by general international law (customs and general treaties). In today's revolutionary system, on the other hand, sovereignty is infinitely more complex. The diversity of legal status is great, owing to multiple patterns of military, economic, and political cooperation, which introduce various forms of inequality—hence the predominance of treaties over customs and the prevalence of less-than-universal treaties. Secondly, the sum of powers of which sovereignty is composed, and the limitations imposed by law, are in constant flux and are increasing, because of the intensity of international relations. (The same paradox had marked the revolutionary system in the early seventeenth century.) Thus, the edges of sovereignty have become blurred. Although the basic legal unit remains the state, powers of action in the world are widely scattered among states, blocs, and international organizations, yet concentrated among the major industrial centers or (in matters of life and death for the planet) full nuclear powers.[27]

After the dust has settled, a new stable system will probably be one in which many state powers will be permanently redistributed among global and regional actors. Despite the general aspiration (especially among new nations) to return to a world of non-intervening sovereign states, the traditional substance of sovereignty is barely compatible with the political and technological conditions of the present world. However, we are bound to remain with the present system for quite a while; a decline of military blocs in the missile age would not make the competition of East and West any less fierce; the emergence of new nations does not make their resentment of their former masters, their demands on the well-endowed states, and their own political uncertainties any less dangerous; the spread of nuclear power does not make the international system any less explosive. We are in the midst of a succession of revolutionary systems—not on the verge of a stable one, and the solidity of international law will continue to remain in doubt.

Addendum

Twenty years after I wrote this essay, I find that in discussing international law in the post-1945 international system, although I recognized law's "Janus-like aspect," I did not sufficiently analyze the "face that promises order."

The latter resulted not merely, as indicated above, from nuclear prudence—the imperative of survival—but also from economic interdependence—the imperative of welfare. The former has made possible, in addition to the legal agreements already mentioned, what could be called a minimal law of the political framework: the various arms control agreements signed by the superpowers, the non-proliferation treaty of 1968, the Helsinki agreements of 1975. Economic interdependence has led to many developments in the law of cooperation, particularly in such domains as world trade and regional assistance to developing countries (e.g., the Lomé agreements). Here, reciprocity has sometimes gone beyond what Robert Keohane calls "strategic reciprocity" (exchanges of items of equivalent value); it has become what he calls "diffuse reciprocity," based on norms of obligations and encased in international regimes.[28]

The lines that separated the three kinds of law distinguished in Chapter 7 have become fuzzy. Nuclear prudence has blurred the distinction between the political framework and the provisions that define the rights and duties of states with respect to weapons (test bans, non-nuclear zones). Economic interdependence has made of the law of cooperation that regulates the joint interests of states something often as vital to them as the law of the political framework. The role played in world economic affairs both by transnational groupings (including alliances of fragments of national bureaucracies) and by international or regional organizations, in addition to states, has helped blur the distinction between the law of reciprocity and the law of community—a distinction already weakened by the phenomenon of diffuse reciprocity, which results from a less conflictual or selfish definition of state self-interest.

To be sure, such progress is neither irreversible (witness what happened to the Bretton Woods monetary regime, or what may be happening to the ABM treaty of 1972 and to the demilitarization of outer space) nor irresistible (as was shown by the failure of the long attempt at obtaining a world-wide agreement on the law of the seas). Nevertheless, the post-war system, contrary to the statement made in the last sentence of the chapter, is both revolutionary *and* stable. What is true is that this system is revolutionary enough to provide, so to speak, for its stability in ways less solemn than international law, which creates rights and duties, and thereby, as I wrote in another essay, that it "is a form of policy that changes the stakes and often 'escalates' the intensity of political contests."[29] This is why states have preferred either informal restraints (which are more easily avoidable or reversible) or procedural restraints (those set up by international regimes)—that is, frameworks of cooperation within which bargains can be made and unmade by ordinary political processes.

Notes

1. These adjectives are borrowed from Julius Stone, "Problems Confronting Sociological Enquiries Concerning International Law," *Recueil des Cours de l'Académie de Droit International*, 89 (1956), I, and Hans J. Morgenthau, *Dilemmas of Politics* (Chicago, 1958), chap. 11, respectively. The only additional works that try to establish a political sociology of international law are Charles de Visscher, *Theory and Reality in Public International Law*, tr. by Percy E. Corbett (Princeton, N.J., 1957); Percy E. Corbett, *Law in Diplomacy* (Princeton, N.J., 1959); B. Landheer, "Contemporary Sociological Theories and International Law," *Recueil des Cours* . . . , 91 (1957), I; and, to some extent, John Herz, *International Politics in the Atomic Age* (New York, 1959), and Morton A. Kaplan and Nicholas Katzenbach, "The Patterns of International Politics and of International Law," *American Political Science Review*, LIII (September, 1959), 693–712—the last two pieces being concerned more with politics than with law. See also Hoffmann, "Quelques aspects du rôle du Droit International dans la politique étrangère des Etats," in Association Française de Science Politique, *La Politique étrangère et ses fondements* (Paris, 1954), pp. 239–77.
2. *Legal Controls of International Conflict* (New York, 1954), p. 1.
3. "Evidence and Inference in History," *Daedalus*, 87 (Fall, 1958), 11–39.
4. *International Politics in the Atomic Age* (New York, 1959).
5. The number of violent conflicts is not involved in these definitions. A stable period may be marked by frequent wars as long as they remain limited in objectives and methods. A revolutionary period may not necessarily be marked by all-out general war, if the technology of conflict introduces a mutual interest in avoiding the total destruction such a war would entail. But as long as this restraint does not bring back moderation in the purposes and means of conflicts other than all-out

war, the system remains largely revolutionary, although it disposes of an element of stability—a fragile element, given all the other circumstances.

6. Besides making the fundamental distinction between stable and revolutionary systems, we have to distinguish among stable and among revolutionary ones. Here, our criteria should be, in addition to the basic structure of the world and the state of the technology of conflict: in the case of stable systems, the *kind* of means used by the actors in their competition and cooperation (see below, Part Two, for the distinction between the stable system which preceded the French Revolution and the stable system which followed the Congress of Vienna; both were "balance of power" systems, but the latter was more institutionalized than the former); in the case of revolutionary systems, the type of *objectives* for which the conflict takes place (religious allegiance, form of government).

7. Panayis Papaligouras, *Théorie de la société internationale* (Geneva, 1941).

8. They do not, by themselves, destroy the balancing system, but they make its operation uncertain and increase the likelihood of "in-system" wars, which may in turn destroy the system if other essential conditions for an ideal balance have also disappeared, or if the logic of war destroys previous limitations on the instruments of conflict.

9. See Corbett, *op. cit.*, especially chaps. 1-3.

10. See Georg Schwarzenberger, *Power Politics* (New York, 1951), chap. 13, and Morgenthau, *op. cit.*, pp. 228-29.

11. Scholars may argue that important mutual interests still exist and that states have little to gain by turning the zone of predictability into a battlefield. But what seems irrational to the scholar from the viewpoint of international society seems rational to the statesman from the viewpoint of his own national calculation, given the peculiar logic of such calculations in fiercely competitive situations. An "objectively" common interest might not be perceived by the antagonists, and, even if it were, there remains an abyss between such perception and a formal legal agreement that might still sanction it. On these points, see Kenneth Waltz, *Man, the State, and War*, pp. 192 ff.

12. See the first editions of his *International Law: A Treatise*, Vol. I (London, 1905 and 1912).

13. See Kaplan and Katzenbach, *op. cit.*

14. For a more detailed analysis, see Hoffmann, *Organisations internationales et pouvoirs politiques des Etats* (Paris, 1954), Part 1.

15. It was in 1871 that Russia denounced the Black Sea provisions of the Paris Treaty, in 1908 that Austria annexed Bosnia-Herzegovina.

16. See Walter Schiffer, *The Legal Community of Mankind* (New York, 1954).

17. Many of the difficulties of the U.N. operation in the Congo stemmed from the attempt to distinguish between domestic and international aspects of the crisis—an exercise in fiction.

18. We speak of a "loose bipolar system" in which "bloc actors" tend to become more important than unit actors—but, at the same time, the rate of obsolescence of strategies and the diffusion of nuclear power challenge such a view. Inversely, we refer to the fragmentation of the old frontier into multiple new sovereignties, but, at the same time, the necessities of the struggle against colonialism and for development might lead to the gradual emergence of "bloc actors" there. We discuss the atomic age, but, as Herz observes, many interstate relations are still in a pre-atomic phase. We have both a revolutionary system and a tacit agreement on one rule of the game—to avoid total war.

19. See, for instance, the arguments of D. W. Bowett, *Self-defense in International Law* (New York, 1958), pp. 145 ff., and Julius Stone, *Aggression and World Order* (Berkeley, Calif., 1958), chap. 5. Contra, Joseph Kunz, "Sanctions in International Law," *American Journal of International Law,* LIV (April, 1960), 324–47.

20. Similarly, during the period of the Thirty Years' War, legal developments were ambiguous, for the war destroyed the previous unity of the Civitas Christiana and the secular authority of the Church but, at the same time, brought into shape the modern territorial state through a succession of wars.

21. See Rupert Emerson, *From Empire to Nation* (Cambridge, Mass., 1960), chap. 6.

22. For a recent discussion of those points, see the *Proceedings of the American Society of International Law,* 1959, pp. 21–45.

23. Statesmen have mutually exclusive images of world order, in which the highest power remains the state; individual citizens have no way of breaking the statesmen's monopoly: the citizens' efforts at promoting their transnational common ends through law rarely succeed in transcending the borders of the state, which continues to fulfill most of their needs and to be seen as the best protection against outside tempests. Indeed, the development of contemporary law has occurred especially in those areas where individuals raised demands which the state could not satisfy alone: hence the law of international functions and economic integration, whose binding force seems quite strong.

24. For a sharp analysis, see W. J. Rees, "The Theory of Sovereignty Restated," in Peter Laslett, ed., *Philosophy, Politics and Society* (New York, 1956).

25. Permanent Court of International Justice, Series A, No. 1 (1923).

26. The best combination of ambiguity and change is provided with the concept of domestic jurisdiction. On the one hand, the area regulated by international law has been drastically expanded; on the other hand, this increasing "legalization" of inter-state relations could become an effective restraint only if there were institutions able to prevent states from extending the plea of domestic jurisdiction to issues where it does not apply—and from rejecting the plea when it is still justified. Instead, we find that states successfully invoke the argument even in areas clearly regulated by law (cf. the Interhandel dispute) and refuse to listen to it whenever a problem is of international concern, although it may not be regulated by law (cf. the attitude of the General Assembly of the U.N.).

27. On the impact of such concentration, see François Perroux, *La coexistence pacifique* (3 vols.; Paris, 1958).

28. Keohane, "Reciprocity in International Relations," unpublished paper, 1984.

29. Hoffmann, *The State of War,* chap. 5, p. 132.

8

The Problem of Intervention

A general presentation on the subject of intervention is likely to contain little that is original, and to consist only of an endless series of classifications. The reason for this is very simple. The subject is practically the same as that of international politics in general from the beginning of time to the present. This makes it, of course, both important and very topical. If one looks only at the events of 1981-3, one finds the following: perhaps not a resurgence of American military interventionism (neither the American administration nor the American people are ready for new Vietnams and a distinction must be made between the administration's rhetoric and reality), but some new American military activities in El Salvador, together with threats concerning Nicaragua and the landing in Grenada; Cuban support for resistance movements in El Salvador and in Guatemala; the Soviet Union's continuing operations and difficulties in Afghanistan; a military coup in Poland, with which the Soviet Union clearly had something to do (the imposition of martial law followed a whole series of Soviet threats over several months); French military activities in Chad, as well as Libyan ones in Chad and in Sudan; a continuing contest on the battlefield and in the United Nations over who constitutes the legitimate government of Cambodia; an attempt by the United States government to revoke the Clark amendment prohibiting American intervention in the civil strife in Angola; continuing negotiations by the group of five on the future of Namibia; an Israeli invasion of Lebanon aimed at changing the political structure as well as the military balance there. All these events clearly come under the heading of intervention: they occur on every continent, involving every kind of act and every kind of actor.

I shall start with a discussion of intervention as a set of facts, so as to present a broad picture of intervention in international relations. Then I shall look at it as an issue, as a problem to be solved, before coming to the obvious conclusion that it is insoluble.

Intervention as a Set of Facts

Let us begin with a definition. Nothing can be more static or less rewarding. Nevertheless, when one talks about concepts such as aggression, or imperialism, or intervention, a definition is necessary. We do have to distinguish intervention from other forms of international politics. In the widest sense, to be sure, every act of a state constitutes intervention. When the Israelis, in 1981, bombed the nuclear reactor near Baghdad, it clearly was a rather brutal form of intervention. In India, where perceptions of the outside world sometimes almost reduce it to one single country, Pakistan, a recent American decision to sell F-16 aeroplanes to Pakistan is being seen as an intervention in Indian affairs, just as in Algeria the American decision to sell arms to Morocco is seen as an intervention in North African affairs. Many Americans thought that the French-Mexican communiqué of 1981 about El Salvador constituted an intervention; they certainly believe that the French decision to sell arms to Nicaragua was an intervention, and if one listens to Radio Moscow, which competes for the domination of the short waves with the BBC World Service, one hears day after day that the NATO powers are blatantly intervening in the internal affairs of Poland and blocking its process of renewal. So clearly anything can constitute an intervention; indeed, even non-acts can constitute interventions: remember the effects of British and French non-intervention in the Spanish Civil War. It was Talleyrand, the great cynic and wise man, who said that intervention and non-intervention are the same thing. The West German decision not to take sanctions against the Soviet Union over Poland does, in a sense, constitute an intervention on the side of General Jaruzelski, if not of Mr. Brezhnev, and if one talks to Palestinians, one will certainly hear that America's indifference toward the autonomy talks and the Camp David process, and America's failure to protest against the use of American-made weapons in the invasion of Lebanon by Israel amount to intervention on the side of the Israelis.

For clarity's sake, however, ways must be found of delimiting the subject. The literature provides three ways of doing it. One is by reference to the type of activity involved: a classic definition by Oppenheim restricts interventions to those acts which constitute 'dictatorial interference.' My own preference is not to define intervention by reference to the type of activity. To say that only acts of dictatorial interference constitute interventions narrows the subject too much. After all, the purpose of intervention is the same as that of all other forms of foreign policy; it is to make you do what I want you to do, whether or not you wish to do it. But how I try to achieve this can take an enormous variety of forms. Some are explicitly coercive interventions, through the use or threat of force—from sending an army into your country if you don't behave to unleashing terrorists such as the assassination squads of President Qaddafi. Another kind of explicitly coercive intervention takes the form of economic coercion—trade and credit sanctions, boycotts, embargoes. Explicit coercion can also be achieved through subsidies, aid to revolutionary groups or to opponents of a regime that one wants to unseat. Other kinds of intervention I call implicitly coercive. These do not constitute obvious dictatorial interference, and yet they are still interventions aimed at forcing you to do something which you might otherwise not particularly want to do. One form this takes—a very old one in international politics—is bribery: rewards to friends, encouraging them to do things which they may have some misgivings about, but for which they can then be recompensed. One modern form of bribery is aid to shaky governments designed to make them both less shaky and more favorable to one's own side. If a state is very wealthy, it can resort to bribery on a large scale; the United States has practiced this, sometimes with virtuosity, sometimes with mixed results (I am thinking of American support of the Shah of Iran, and of present American policies in Pakistan). But aiding shaky governments so that they do what one wants is also what the Soviet Union and the Cubans have been attempting in places like Angola and Ethiopia. In the protracted Lebanese civil war, Israeli support of the late Major Haddad in Southern Lebanon has been one way for Israel to exert influence. Another form of intervention which is implicitly coercive but not obviously dictatorial, is propaganda bombardment, so to speak. This bewildering variety of techniques explains why, in my opinion, one cannot delimit intervention by reference to the type of activity; the choice of the latter depends on the specific objective, on the circumstances, on the intervening state's resources, and on the kinds of policy instruments at its disposal.

A second means of delimitation is by reference to the type of actor. The word has been used so loosely that one sometimes talks about intervention by private groups. I prefer to limit consideration of it to acts of states, of groups fighting for statehood, and of collections of states, such as international organizations. In other words, I include as examples of intervention the activities of private organizations, like multinational corporations, for instance, only if they are backed by a state, or act on behalf of a state (multinational corporations, incidentally, are not the only such actors; there was a period in the beginning of the cold war when American labor unions exerted considerable influence in various other parts of the world, in Western Europe and in Africa, for instance, setting up friendly labor unions; this was not totally independent of the policies of the US government).

The most important delimitation is the third: by type of target. Here, I propose to restrict the concept of intervention to *acts which try to affect not the external activities, but the domestic affairs of a state*. In other words, I would not consider as an intervention, for the present purposes, acts such as the quasi-annexation of the Golan Heights by Israel or, to take a very different example, the German declaration of unlimited submarine warfare in the First World War. I will not, in other words, look at intervention as an act, or a series of acts, aimed at the foreign relations or the external behavior of a state. I restrict it to acts aimed at affecting the domestic affairs of the state, either because the state itself is the target of attempts at control from the outside (this is particularly the case when the nature of authority in that state is in question, when it is not clear who should be or who is the legitimate authority in civil wars for instance), or because an attempt at affecting domestic affairs is deemed the best way of influencing the

The Problem of Intervention

external behavior of a state (if one wants an actor to behave in a certain way on the world stage, what better method is there than to see to it that it has the 'right' kind of government?).

Even when one has restricted the subject to acts aimed at affecting the domestic affairs of others, one still finds that it is ubiquitous. It is therefore necessary to introduce some more dynamic considerations.

There are, in international affairs, some fundamental contradictions which underlie the whole subject of intervention. The most fundamental is this. International society, for some centuries now, has been founded on the principle of sovereignty; in other words, the state is supposed to be the master of what goes on inside its territory, and international relations are relations between sovereign states, each one of which has certain rights and obligations derived from the very fact of statehood. If one accepts the principle of sovereignty as the corner-stone of international society, this means (and it has been recognized by international lawyers ever since the time of Wolff and Vattel in the eighteenth century) that intervention, defined as an act aimed at influencing the domestic affairs of a state, is quite clearly illegitimate. On the other hand, the principle of sovereignty also entails the rule of self-help, and there is an innate contradiction between the illegitimacy of intervention and the legitimacy of self-help. In fact, the choice in international affairs has never been between intervening and observing the sacred principle of non-intervention. The choice has always been between individual intervention and collective intervention, or else between the establishment of conditions in which intervention will become less likely, and living in conditions in which intervention is more likely. In other words, the key variable is the nature of the international system. This first, most basic contradiction results from the very nature of an international milieu of decentralized units with no common superior.

There is a second contradiction which issues from the particular nature of international society in the twentieth century. The principle of sovereignty is not the only corner-stone of contemporary international relations; the constitutive principle of international order in this century is not the respect of *any* sovereignty, but the principle of self-determination—a principle of both domestic and external legitimacy. We profess to believe, rightly or wrongly, that precisely because the notion of sovereignty, which leads to self-help, can become a source of chaos, chaos would be best avoided if all the states were based on the principle of self-determination or of nationality. This adds an entirely new element to the study of intervention, because it seems to legitimize intervention on behalf of self-determination and raises the whole issue of national liberation movements and of their status in the world.

There is a third contradiction. One finds recurring in international affairs a belief that the best way of ensuring some kind of order or moderation, the best way of preventing state sovereignty and even the principle of national self-determination from leading to chaos, the best way of starving out opportunities for intervention, is to insist on a principle of governmental legitimacy. This is the familiar idea, according to which the best possible conditions for order in international affairs will exist if all the governments are of a certain type. Such a notion lay behind the Holy Alliance of 1815, with its commitment to dynastic legitimacy. To take another example, many liberals in the nineteenth century believed that (as Kant maintained) the best kind of international order would be one in which all governments were constitutional governments. Such notions introduce another paradox, because they seem to legitimize intervention to promote a principle of governmental legitimacy.

If one looks at the historical evolution of intervention, there are two questions, the answers to which determine its shape and its scope. First, is there at any given moment a prevailing principle of domestic legitimacy or not? Those familiar with Raymond Aron's book on *Peace and War* will remember that he sees in this particular question the criterion that determines whether an international system is 'homogeneous' or 'heterogeneous.'[1] An international system is homogeneous when all the units have the same principle of domestic legitimacy. In such a situation this does not mean that there will be no interventions; in the seventeenth and eighteenth centuries, when there was a dominant principle of domestic legitimacy, and most of the units were monarchies, many wars nevertheless took place because of contending claims to the same throne. Much international politics consisted of seeing to it that state A, or rather king A, placed (or was forcibly prevented from placing) a brother-in-law, a cousin, the wife of a cousin, or the wife of a brother-in-law, on a foreign throne. In other words, manipulation of the dynastic principle was a way of ensuring alliances and of expanding influence; this persisted even into the nineteenth century. It was the cause or the pretext for the Franco-Prussian War of 1870-1, when the French Emperor thought it highly insulting and dangerous to have a Hohenzollern as a potential King of Spain. What produces interventions even when there exists a single principle of domestic legitimacy is the perennial dialectic of relations between the weak and the strong.

When there are several principles of domestic legitimacy in competition— that is to say when, to use Aron's definition, the international system is heterogeneous—the gravest danger exists for international order. The best example here is that of the French Revolution, where a violent clash occurred between the old dynastic principle, upheld by the main courts in Europe, and the new French principle, enshrined in the Declaration of 15 December 1792, which essentially proclaimed French support for what we would now call movements of national liberation in various countries. The result was a kind of war of religion between the two principles, a war which was confusing when the principle of national liberation came to be upheld by Napoleon. As is usual in international affairs, the clash of principles became a clash of power, and French expansionism took precedence over French revolutionary Messianism; what had been supposed to be a support for national liberation became a pretext for territorial annexation.

If one moves on a little in time, one comes to the classical scene of 1815, discussed in Henry Kissinger's *A World Restored*.[2] At the Congress of Vienna and in the world outside, the conflict was between three different principles: the monarchic or dynastic principle upheld by the Austrians and by the Russians, representative government favored by the British and the French, and a more democratic and national principle supported by the liberal and nationalist forces operating in several countries. In Vienna, as is well known, there was a solemn debate between Metternich and the Tsar, who were advocating intervention on behalf of the dynastic principle, and the British, Castlereagh and later Canning, who essentially rejected the idea of intervention.

Another era in which interventions proliferated because there was no agreement on the principle of domestic legitimacy, is the period between the two World Wars, when three conflicting principles were again battling with each other: the democratic one, which seemed to have been enshrined in the Versailles Treaty and in the League of Nations Covenant, what could be called the Fascist principle, and the Communist one. The best example of the resulting chaos, the crucible really, was the Spanish Civil War, in which all three forces were at work, two in the form of outright intervention and one in the form of a shabby non-intervention.

Still, nothing may ever have been quite as complex as the situation which prevails now, in the period since the end of the Second World War. The following elements of the international system make for universal intervention. First, there are all the battles over the application of the principle of self-determination. Everybody pays lip-service to it as the constitutive principle of international order, and yet it is fraught with so many uncertainties that it is a major source of strife and a major invitation to external intrusions. In much of the world, a conflict rages between the principle of self-determination, which assumes that the state should be the expression of a nation, and the existence of borders which have very often been artificially carved up by the colonial powers. Is the principle of self-determination an essentially theoretical notion, under whose influence independence is given to states within those artificial borders, and a kind of license granted to these states to try to make a nation out of the people within them, or must it be taken so seriously that one has to concede to every group which considers itself a nation the right to set itself up as a state, even at the expense of the traditional borders and of pre-existing states? The longest list of interventions is of those that have occurred over and around the uncertainties of the principle of self-determination. In no particular order, either geographic or chronological, one can mention the international debate over Taiwan, and over the independence of South Vietnam, the wars between Somalia and Ethiopia, and between Ethiopia and Eritrea, the attempted secession of Biafra from Nigeria, the secession of Bangladesh from Pakistan, the Chinese claim to Tibet, the Indonesian claim to West Irian and East Timor, the recent battles over Western Sahara, Syrian and Israeli interventions in Lebanon, resulting from the clash of two nationalities—Israeli and Palestinian—over the same area, the Turkish interventions in Cyprus, Black African support for independence movements in Zimbabwe and Namibia: there has been a maelstrom of interventions around the mists of self-determination.

A second contemporary factor is the conflict between two versions of what constitutes democratic self-government. Everybody, again, pays lip-service to one principle of governmental legitimacy, which is the democratic principle; but we have in fact two different principles in competition, the Western notion of democracy—which, to simplify, I shall call democracy—and the Communist version of democracy—which, to simplify, I shall call totalitarianism. What happened in late 1981 and early 1982 in Poland is a very good example of that particular contest. To the West, the fact that the Polish workers had their own idea about domestic legitimacy was a triumph for democracy; for the Soviet Union, it was a challenge to their particular version of party control. Soviet intervention in Afghanistan must also be mentioned in this context—as well as the attempted American invasion of Cuba in 1961, or the successful American interventions in Guatemala in 1954 and in Grenada in 1983.

But these are not the only focal points for intervention. The world would be too simple if only these existed. We find, in addition, a number of other factors, which are very hard to fit into any neat theoretical scheme. There are, for instance, some interventions which could be described as belatedly colonial, such as Argentina's attempt at seizing control of the Falkland Islands on the basis of dubious and distant historical claims, and others which could be called colonial left-overs. When General de Gaulle, in his inimitable way, decolonized, he did it by signing treaties with a number of African states, which allowed France to intervene in the domestic affairs of those states whenever their government felt sufficiently threatened to call on France to come to its help; and those treaties were acted upon quite a number of times. We have witnessed a new fuel of interventions in recent years: the force of Islamic fundamentalism, which President Qaddafi and Ayatollah Khomeini claim to incarnate. Libya has tried to overthrow or to control several governments, and the war between Iraq and Iran is concerned not only with territorial claims but with each side's attempt to overthrow the other's ruler. Finally, there are splits in the communist world, rival versions of the totalitarian orthodoxy, and the conflict over Cambodia—whether the legitimate government of Cambodia is either a government of murderers who happen to be real Cambodians, or a government of puppets who happen to be put in by the Vietnamese—is largely a consequence of that split. In other words, a generalization of intervention is of the essence of the highly heterogeneous post-war international system, and it is aggravated by a second question.

The first question referred to the presence or absence, at any given moment, of a principle of domestic legitimacy. It dealt, so to speak, with the frame and foundations of the house of international relations. The second question deals with what goes on within the house: is there a mechanism of international order and moderation at a given moment or not? The only mechanism of moderation known in the past, alas, has been the balance-of-power system, and we must briefly examine the relations between intervention and the balance of power. It is a very complicated relationship, because, on the one hand, when the balance-of-power system functions well, it deters, or coerces, trouble-makers, and therefore either limits the opportunities for interventions which trouble-makers may want to exploit, or at least deprives these of some of the results they expect from their intervention. In other words, when the system works it has the effect of protecting the independence of the weakest states from the designs of a particular troublemaker; and if one looks at the history of recurrent Russian meddling in the affairs of the decomposing Ottoman Empire, in the eighteenth and nineteenth centuries, one sees that very often Russian advances were stopped or limited by the operation of the balance of power, as in the Crimean War of 1854-6 or in the big Eastern crisis of 1875-8. Also, the fact that the balance-of-power system is a mechanism of shifting alliances means that in order to operate well it has to be quite indifferent to domestic regimes: against a trouble-maker, you ought to be able to align yourself with any other sort of state, whether its government is of the left or right, whether it is monarchical or representative; this requirement for flexibility, which entails a certain indifference to the domestic order, explains why, for instance, British Foreign Ministers were opposed to Austrian intervention in Spain in the 1820s.

However, this is only part of the story. When the balance of power operates, it dampens interventions, but it certainly does not stop them, for a whole variety of reasons. The first one is that the balancing mechanism itself, when it functions, opens up possibilities of collective intervention. The best way of my preventing you from intervening and reaping benefits for yourself alone, is by our intervening all together, so that we can each gain a little bit. And that, of course, is not good for the target of the intervention. But this was very often what happened in the age of the European Concert; this is the way in which the Greek crisis of the 1820s and the independence of Belgium in 1830 were handled; this is the way in which the French were prevented from being the only beneficiaries of the big crisis in Lebanon in 1860-1. Again, in order to prevent the Russians from gaining inch after inch at the expense of the Ottoman Empire, the European powers resorted recurrently to collective interventions: in the finances of the Ottoman Empire, which were being put under collective supervision, over the establishment of an autonomous Crete, over the independence of Albania, and so on. In other words, for a small state the balance of power could be a mixed blessing because instead of being eaten by one great power, one could be gnawed by all five or six.

Secondly, the balancing mechanism opened up not merely the possibility of collective intervention, but also the possibility of the great powers simply getting together, quite cynically, to carve up the target. The most extreme case is that of unfortunate Poland, which nature put in a position where no people should be: between the Germans and the Russians. But in fact Poland, which one always gives as an example, is only one instance among many, for there were several successive partitions of the Ottoman Empire, decided collectively by the European powers, giving rise to the emergence of feuding Balkan successor states.

Thirdly, interventions continued quite simply because from time to time the balance of power did not work; the mechanism of alignments against the trouble-maker did not always operate. This is how the Austrians annexed Bosnia in 1908; this is how the British came to occupy Egypt, and then spent sixty years explaining that they wanted to give up; this is how Napoleon III got involved in Italy in the 1850s, at a time when no power was willing to stop him; this is how Bismarck began his march to the unification of Germany.

A fourth reason why intervention was perfectly compatible with the balance of power was that the very indifference of the balance toward domestic regimes made it perfectly possible at times for one particular country to intervene in the domestic affairs of a state without being stopped by others. The indifference of the system as such cut both ways. It meant, on the one hand, that there would be no collective interventions to impose, let us say, the monarchic or the constitutional principle, but it also meant that when the Russians came in to help the Austrians crush revolutions in Austria or in Hungary, and when Russians again intervened to crush revolutions in Poland, nobody did anything about it.

And finally interventions flourished because the balance-of-power system was never applied overseas—to affairs outside the European system; if one looks at the way in which most colonial empires were established in the nineteenth century, it was through intervention and the manipulation of local forces.

So, the balance-of-power system was unsatisfactory for purposes of controlling intervention. Of course, when there is no balance-of-power system and the world lives under a bipolar one, things are more unsatisfactory still, and this has been the experience, not only at the time of Thucydides, who gives an account of interventions in a system dominated by Sparta and Athens, but again in the international system that followed the Second World War. In the periods of acute cold war—in other words, the late forties, fifties, and early sixties, and again in the late seventies and the eighties—the forms of intervention caused by the rivalry between the United States and the Soviet Union become countless. There are interventions for self-protection, for protecting one's stakes, for protecting one's clients: in mild form, for instance, the American intervention in the 1948 election campaign in Italy; or the American landing of marines on the sunny beaches of Lebanon in the midst of all the swimmers in 1958; the American intervention in South Vietnam, much less mild; the recurrent Soviet interventions in Eastern Europe. These self-protecting interventions are best summarized by the so-called Brezhnev Doctrine of 1968—fraternal assistance to socialism—and by what some authors have called the Johnson doctrine of the 1960s, the declaration that the United States would not tolerate the threat of communism in the Latin American or Central American sphere (although actually it antedates Johnson and can be traced back to the Rio treaty). Self-protection is also the motive of the recurrent American policy of throwing a mantle of protection over regimes, to safeguard them against internal upheaval when they happen to sit on very large amounts of natural resources to which the West wants access—as in the Middle East. But self-protection is only one form. Some interventions are sanctions— several American measures after the Soviet invasion of Afghanistan and the proclamation of martial law in Poland for instance. There are also counter-offensive interventions—the US interventions in Guatemala, Grenada, and Nicaragua; the attempt at the Bay of Pigs. There are interventions for the expansion of influence—the Soviet Union in Afghanistan, the Soviet Union and Cuba in Angola and Ethiopia, Vietnam in Cambodia.

Why do we find this generalization of intervention in the current bipolar international system? It is partly because there is an ideological contest— two ways of life, two conceptions of both domestic and international order in conflict. Another reason is the abundance of targets of opportunity: the world now consists of many artificial states which are states only by general tolerance, but which are wracked by enormous internal difficulties—weak regimes, ethnic conflicts, religious or communal tensions, economic turmoil— and therefore constitute easy prey for the superpowers. A further reason is the phenomenon of compensation, what some authors have called the internalization of conflict; since the major stakes in international affairs are somewhat unreachable because of the fear of nuclear war (the major stakes are still in Europe and in the Far East, but neither side can do much about them without risk of blowing up the world), by compensation it is easier to fight over what government will be in control of what territory in areas which are less explosive. The moderation of means induced by the peril of nuclear war, and the superpowers' need to limit their goals for the same reason, leave ample room for interventions aimed at changing the international milieu by affecting the domestic political make-up of other countries.

Such is the scope of the phenomenon, and the reasons for it. One last word about its prevalence in the bipolar competition. The best example here is provided by Kissinger's foreign policy. His own ideal was a return to moderation, to a world in which there would be a clear distinction between domestic and external affairs, in which foreign policy would concern itself only with the external activities of states, whatever their domestic regimes; that explains why, as a good *Realpolitiker*, he was perfectly willing to deal with a communist state like China or even with a radical one like Assad's Syria. On the other hand, the very logic of the bipolar conflict obliged him to behave much more like Metternich than like Castlereagh. Since he was in effect obsessed with the Soviet-American conflict, one of his constant concerns was to see to it that countries in what he considered to be the preserve of the West did not acquire regimes hostile to it. This fear was carried to its most extreme length in his policy towards Allende's Chile. The very logic of the system—of the bipolar conflict—led him to a series of interventions in domestic affairs, beyond the pale of inter-state relations.

Intervention as an Issue

If such is the scope of the problem, the question may be asked: what can one do about it? I now come to the treatment of intervention as a problem to be solved.

There have been two kinds of attempts at controlling intervention. Both have failed. The first is that of international law and the United Nations Charter. The Charter, interestingly enough, is not a very satisfactory instrument when it comes to the problem of intervention, because it deals with it in a very limited way. It concerns itself first of all only with certain types of actions. What it bans is the use of force and the threat of force. As I noted earlier, there are many other ways of intervening, in which force or even the threat of force remain implicit, below the visible surface. Furthermore, the Charter only aims at protecting the territorial integrity and the political independence of a state; it does not deal with other ways of undermining a state, such as trying to change the nature of its government. One could argue for instance that what has been happening in Warsaw does not affect the territorial integrity of Poland. As for its political independence, that in a sense has been given away since 1945, and is not at stake. What is at stake is something quite different: the autonomy of the government itself. And indeed, the United Nations Charter is very silent on what has been the most frequent type of intervention, intervention to determine the outcome of a civil war—whether we think about South Vietnam, or Lebanon, or Chad, or Angola, or Afghanistan. The Charter is based on a model which draws a sharp distinction between external and domestic affairs; the evil against which it is supposed to operate is that of the massive crossing of established borders by armies; and that has not been the main problem of post-war international relations. It does not really deal with such cases as Poland in 1981 or, say, a state buying friends with arms, when those friends are fairly shaky regimes.

The second attempt at controlling intervention has been the attempt by international or regional organizations, or by what some of my colleagues would call international regimes, at introducing a modicum of order, by collectivizing intervention in the way in which the European Concert sometimes collectivized it. If one looks at the record, one can reach three conclusions about it. The first one is that in the political domain—in political conflicts—collectivization has been of very limited effectiveness. The most extensive attempt, horridly complicated, was the intervention by the United Nations in the Congo crisis of 1960; it led to an endless series of knots into which the members of the UN tied themselves, over who the legitimate government in the Congo was and what the new nation's proper borders were. The most recent attempts at collectivizing have been through the Organization of African Unity. They have not worked very well in Chad, nor in relation to Amin's Uganda. Nor has the UN been able to save Lebanon from further, brutal outside interventions. The most persistent attempt has been collective pressure on South Africa through the UN, including the use of sanctions; results have been very meagre. The only successful attempt at an intervention on behalf of the international community that one can readily summon to mind, was not really a collective attempt at all—it was the skilful diplomacy of Lord Soames in the case of Zimbabwe, the exception which does not quite confirm the rule.

Secondly, interestingly enough, collective intervention has become routine in economic affairs. While most states resent attempts by other states to intervene through the use of economic instruments, the resort to such tools of intervention by bodies like the International Monetary Fund, the World Bank, or the OECD has become perfectly normal. All IMF loans come with conditions relating to the balance of payments policies, or the monetary and budgetary policies of the recipients; these are forms of intervention; they are collective and they are not only accepted, they are sometimes even welcomed.

The third conclusion concerns a failure, again; the attempt by the Carter administration at establishing a collective regime of intervention in order to stop or slow down nuclear proliferation, and to go beyond the strictures of the 1968 non-proliferation treaty and the rather weak safeguards of the International Atomic Energy Agency. Here, we were back in the political sphere. This effort failed because of disagreements about what would constitute the most effective form of intervention—the debate between those who thought that denial was best and those who thought that controls were best; and it failed above all because of the conflict between the logic of world order, which tried to impose a collective and restrictive regime impartially on all possible proliferators, and the logic of the cold war, which suggested that one be kind to those potential proliferators who are one's friends in the cold war. The issue over which this came to a boil is that of Pakistan's nuclear program. The record of control of interventions in international law and organization is bleak; what still prevails is self-help, as was demonstrated by the Israeli raid against Iraq's reactor—called by some, grimly or jokingly, the most effective anti-proliferation measure so far.

I now turn to the theory or philosophy of the subject. If one cannot control intervention, one can at least speculate; indeed, there is at present a very big debate on the legitimacy of intervention. If interventions, like wars, are here to stay, perhaps all one can do is pontificate. This allows one, if not to stop them, at least to judge them. Thus, I shall now examine attempts by theorists to write guidelines distinguishing between what is legitimate intervention and what is not.

Here, liberals find themselves with a special problem. For a Marxist-Leninist, there is no problem in making a double-edged use of international law; the principle of sovereignty is there to defend one's conquests, and one is justified in intervening to protect them. On the other hand, one can provide legitimate aid to liberation movements, aimed at changing the correlation of forces, at exploiting and pushing forward those deep forces of history which justify carrying the revolution further. For a liberal, however, there is a dilemma. On the one hand, liberalism is a universalistic conception: it assumes that there are values which transcend the mere fact of sovereignty, or the mere legal rights entailed by sovereignty; it holds that we have the moral right to judge what goes on inside the sovereign unit, and that there are some ethical principles and human rights which transcend borders. So, from this viewpoint, liberalism contains a logic of rightful intervention. On the other hand, liberals also recognize that violence and war are the greatest enemies of liberty, and would be the inevitable result of generalized intervention; that is a pragmatic argument against it. And there is also a moral argument against intervention, which was made particularly strongly by John Stuart Mill: liberty can really only come from oneself. You cannot receive it from the outside. This explains why Kant is so silent on the issue of intervention. For Kant, the pre-conditions of world peace were essentially what we call today self-determination and self-government. Nowhere does he advocate a crusade to establish self-determination and self-government; indeed, he condemns "interference by force in the constitution and government" of another state. This also accounts for the contradictions of Woodrow Wilson, who had a splendid vision of a harmonious world reshaped according to the Fourteen Points, yet did not want to accept too tough a series of principles and obligations of enforcement in the Covenant of the League of Nations. He wanted (and in a sense fell over) article 10, but was dubious about actual collective security.

What one finds at present in the literature is agreement on two issues and disagreement on three. The two issues on which there seems to be agreement are the following. First, humanitarian intervention is deemed legitimate: intervention by force against a state which practices genocide on a large scale or which would, for instance, starve its inhabitants. This is the argument that was used by some to justify the removal of such monsters as Idi Amin and Bokassa, to explain Indian intervention for the independence of Bangladesh, and to defend the elimination of Pol Pot by invasion. The problem with this argument is that in the real world things are more ambiguous; it is hard to know whether an intervention which starts as a humanitarian move does not later become self-serving. The case of Cambodia is pertinent: Vietnam's attack started as a successful attempt at removing Pol Pot, but ended as the imposition of Vietnamese rule. Since international mechanisms have been paralysed—since there are really no cases in which international organization has given a collective sanction to this sort of humanitarian intervention—it has always been done by self-help. It was Tanzania that went into Uganda, not the Organization of African Unity, which was divided over the issue. So that even in this one instance in which all the theorists agree, there is a need to inject a loud note of practical caution.

I would say the same about the second issue on which theorists, for the most part, agree: that interventions to promote the principle of self-determination are legitimate. (An exception is Charles Beitz, who denies moral validity to the principle.) Michael Walzer, in his admirable book on

Just and Unjust Wars, and in a subsequent article in which he replies to his critics, states that interventions to support the Hungarian insurrection aimed at secession from Austria in 1848, or to help the Blacks obtain a state of their own in contemporary South Africa, would have been or would be legitimate.[3] But, here again, there are great practical difficulties. First, there is no agreement on the nature and size of the unit that can legitimately claim self-determination: a major issue, as the Biafran civil war showed. Secondly, what happens when two nations fight over the same ground, as in Palestine? Thirdly, even if one firmly believes in the moral importance of securing the principle of self-determination and even when the borders are fairly clear, there may often be several contenders to be the rightful beneficiaries of the principle: in the case of Zimbabwe, for example, Bishop Muzorewa, Nkomo, and Mugabe. In other words, even here, in practice, the need for prudence overwhelms, in my opinion at least, the moral argument for intervention.

Now come the cases of disagreement among theorists. The first is the case of counter-intervention. Walzer argues that if state A has intervened in a civil war on one side, state B is entitled to intervene on the other side in order to restore a certain kind of balance. It is a neutral rule, like most rules of international law. There has been a debate over this, some people saying that intervention is only legitimate on the side of the 'good guys,' so that if the first side that intervenes is on the good side, no counter-intervention aimed merely at restoring an artificial balance ought to be allowed. My own position is that, in the abstract, counter-intervention is indeed legitimate only when intervention occurred on the side of anti-democratic forces; but in reality, the attempt to apply sharp distinctions between good and bad sides, and between intervention and counter-intervention, is likely to be immensely frustrating and endlessly controversial. The tragic case of the war in Vietnam is a case in point; present-day El Salvador offers the same difficulties.

The second major disagreement is over whether interventions to promote democracy or self-government are legitimate or not. Walzer, in his book, adopts J. S. Mill's argument, namely that it is legitimate to intervene for self-determination, but not in order to establish democracy. Mill's argument is that freedom from tyranny is something which one has to fight for oneself; one cannot receive it from the outside. In addition, self-determination is the only agreed principle of international order: democracy, at this point, is really not agreed. Walzer's position has been attacked by critics who have pointed out that modern governments have formidable means of repression, so that one cannot always wrest freedom for oneself without external aid; moreover, the right of a state to be protected from outside intervention is ultimately based on the domestic nature of that state—on the presumed fit between the government and the governed: when a state has a tyrannical government, it ought not to be so protected. To this Walzer has replied by distinguishing between the right of revolution, which citizens have, and external intervention, which foreigners have no right to perpetrate.

One must, however, weigh the consequences even of legitimate interventions for democracy: in a world of self-help they will tend to be both self-serving and triggers of chaos.

The last disagreement is on the subject of intervention (by means other than force) for the promotion of human rights—basic political and economic human rights. It is a different issue from the previous ones. What is at issue here is not intervention for establishing the right kind of state sovereignty, sovereignty based on self-determination and self-government. It is intervention on behalf of human rights transcending sovereignty, i.e., interventions to limit the internal scope of the sovereign's power. There are strong arguments for legitimizing collective intervention for the promotion of human rights. After all, states behave externally in a way which is very largely shaped by the manner in which they treat their citizens at home. Also, the legal rights which states enjoy do indeed derive from the nature of domestic relations within the state. The rights of states are not absolute: if a state has various rights in international affairs, it is because there is a certain assumption of a fit between the government and the citizens. There are thus very strong arguments, both prudential and moral, for collective intervention on behalf of human rights. However, there is one formidable argument on the other side. It has to do not with the diversity of cultural practices (real enough, but the question is precisely whether tolerance of diversity must entail the tolerance of violations of basic rights), but with the problem of effectiveness and consequences. In the world as it is, what starts as a policy to promote human rights is likely to degenerate into a political instrument of interstate battle; indeed, if one looks at the evolution of American policy on human rights, one sees that it tends to become one more cold-war tool and one more justification of interventions not so much for the promotion of human rights everywhere, as for the protection of one's allies, even when those allies—to put it gently—stink. This is why the theoretical debate on legitimacy is at the same time a vigorous one, since there is a deep division of views, and also ultimately quite misleading if one moves back from the world of abstractions to the real world, in which moral arguments tend to become used as instruments of battle in a decentralized system of self-help.

Ultimately, the only remedies to the problem of intervention are of two kinds. One is to be a good Utopian; then, the problem becomes very easy to solve. All one has to do is transcend world politics by establishing some form of world government (it is now fashionable to call it 'non-territorial, central guidance' just as it became fashionable not to talk about the state but instead to refer to 'authoritative allocations of values'). If one can abolish the units of world politics and give oneself, in imagination, some collective decision-maker, then the problem is solved because there is no longer intervention—by definition, just as when the British government decides to transfer aid from one region of Britain to another, this is not intervention but economic policy. The other remedy, which will always be partial, is quite simply to try to establish the kind of international system which will provide few opportunities for intervention. At the present time, this requires two conditions. One is the internal strengthening of the various units, most of which are, today, very weak indeed, so that these will have a greater power of autonomous resistance to external penetration and manipulation, and fewer temptations to resort to external intervention in order to compensate for or escape from their weakness. One can try to achieve this through massive economic aid, for instance; still, even if economists knew what the necessary effects of economic aid are, which they do not, strengthening the units is probably beyond anybody's reach, given the nature of most of them, which are either formidably artificial or, as in the case of India, face such enormous problems, like population control, that it is very hard to see how the outside world can cope with the task. The second condition for having an improved international system is a relative ideological disarmament of the main competitors, and that seems to be very far away. Given that conditions in the world are likely to endure for a very long time, intervention has only too bright a future.

Notes

1. Raymond Aron: *Peace and War. A Theory of International Relations*, Weidenfell and Nicolson, London, 1966.
2. Henry A. Kissinger: *A World Restored*, Houghton Mifflin, Boston, 1957.
3. Michael Walzer: *Just and Unjust Wars*, Basic Books, New York, 1977; 'The Moral Standing of States,' *Philosophy and Public Affairs*, Spring 1980, vol. 9, No. 3.

9

Nuclear Worries: France and the United States

I

In France, a public debate on defense and national security has been going on for a couple of years. It is now in its tenth year in the United States. There had been a vigorous American debate between 1957 and 1963, the period during which official strategy switched from the doctrine of massive retaliation to that of flexible response and most of the important works on nuclear strategy were published. This debate had abated until 1976, the year in which a committee of experts from the private sector had contradicted the CIA's evaluation of Soviet military power and pointed with alarm to the increasing Soviet nuclear threat. Since then, a new and highly complicated quarrel has developed, with the participation, as usual, of politicians, high civil servants, academic or think-tank strategists, and theologians.

An observer of both the French and the American debates on defense cannot fail to be struck by the fact that they do not deal with the same worries. The French debate goes around in circles (caress a circle and it will become vicious, says Ionesco). The American one shows officials and scholars caught in a maelstrom, dragged toward an increasingly less predictable and increasingly more disturbing future.

What are the issues, as seen from Paris? Deep down they are always the same: What defense policy in Europe is it in France's national interest to pursue, given the superiority of the Warsaw Pact's conventional forces and the uncertainty that affects the credibility of the United States' nuclear guarantee—i.e., of the United States' threat of a first resort to nuclear weapons in case of a Soviet conventional attack? Like the other European countries, France thinks above all about deterrence: Any failure of deterrence, whether it leads to a conventional or to a nuclear war, would probably mean the destruction of Western Europe. This is precisely why the French government so strongly supported the United States in the battle over the Pershing II and land-based cruise missiles in 1983. From the viewpoint of the would-be aggressor, the physical presence of these missiles on West-European soil, which increases the danger of nuclear war in case of an attack, can only strengthen the arguments for prudence. Unless, of course, Moscow sees in these deployments nothing but a bluff—i.e., deems unlikely a U.S. decision, should war come, to launch those missiles against the territory of the Soviet Union. It so happens that the Americans themselves, for many years, have shown increasing reluctance, either toward any strategy that would require them to use nuclear weapons *first*, or against a strategy that because of the absence of adequate conventional forces would require them to resort to such weapons *quickly*. Thus, two problems are raised for France: What can France do to contribute to deterrence? And, should deterrence fail, what part should France take in the war in Europe? The answers given by official French policy in the 1960s—when General de Gaulle was already expressing doubts about the U.S. nuclear guarantee—were quite clear. The French nuclear force, based on a concept of the deterrence "of the strong by the weak," was conceived as a crucial element for deterrence: both as the means of deterring a direct attack against France and as an addition to the U.S. nuclear guarantee to the whole of Western Europe. However, should deterrence fail, France was deemed to have no interest in taking part in the "forward battle." Its interest was to wait until its vital interests were threatened—by the arrival of Soviet troops near France's borders—before trying to prevent an invasion by the threat of resorting to its atomic weapons.

Ever since the middle of the 1970s, serious doubts have been expressed about this conception. The credibility of the French nuclear threat—a threat whose execution could lead to the total destruction of a country—seems particularly weak if it is aimed at a non-nuclear attack against the French territory. Hence France's interest in preventing the Soviet Union from reaching the Rhine, as was recognized by President Giscard d'Estaing in 1976. Hence also, however, a double headache. On the one hand, the idea of French participation in the forward battle entails a reduced priority for the nuclear force, which many French people believed aimed at preserving France from any new conventional war in Europe. On the other hand, how can such French participation be reconciled with French military autonomy—a vital policy objective, reached in the 1960s only, thanks to the French nuclear force and France's exit from NATO? Moreover, would such a French commitment toward its allies have a real deterrent effect on the enemy, or must one continue to think that the deterrence of a conventional attack against West Germany can be provided only by the threat of a first use of nuclear weapons? In such a case, given the uncertainty that hangs over the American threat, must France extend its nuclear guarantee to West Germany? But then again, what happens to French autonomy—i.e., to the right of France's president to decide when the moment comes whether it is necessary to commit France's nuclear force and thus to put in question the country's very existence? Moreover, would a French nuclear guarantee to the Federal Republic be any more credible than the United States' guarantee, despite the considerable planned increase in France's nuclear potential in the 1980s and 1990s?

As is well known, some French people have suggested that these contradictions could be overcome by building a European defense system. The obstacles to such a system remain as overwhelming as they were twenty or thirty years ago.[1] If such a solution is ruled out, only three possibilities remain. One is the *status quo*, which is not very satisfactory. One can be called the Lellouche solution.[2] One is an intermediary approach. The Lellouche solution would mean both a return of French conventional forces to NATO, in order to take part in the "watch on the Elbe," and—something that would please the Americans much less—the adoption by France, whose forward divisions would be endowed with tactical nuclear weapons, of a nuclear initiative, even if the U.S. high command does not wish it. Hence the negative reactions of a number of French officials.[3] Hence also the adoption by the French government of a much less daring solution—one that certainly does not go as far as either Lellouche's plea or former Chancellor Helmut Schmidt's call of June 1984: essentially, it consists of coordinating the new French Rapid Deployment Force with NATO's armies, of putting that force at NATO's disposal in case of war—but without nuclear weapons and without a French nuclear guarantee for West Germany (i.e., it does not go beyond granting the possibility of such a guarantee in case of need, as determined by the French president). This solution has the advantage of preserving the principle of French military independence and of strengthening Franco-German solidarity in security matters. But it does not put an end to the contradiction between NATO's priority to conventional forces and France's nuclear priority; and, above all, it does not fill the hole in the American nuclear umbrella deployed over Western Europe.

What is most remarkable is not the evolution of French official doctrine, nor the obvious impossibility, for France, to provide by its own means a satisfactory answer to the alliance's military dilemmas and difficulties, or, for Europe, to give itself a defense organization that would not be dominated by the United States. Despite the evolution in French thinking, these two deficiencies are permanent and structural. What is most remarkable is the United States' indifference to this debate. To be sure, Americans recognize that the French and British nuclear forces, whose might will increase in coming years, contribute to the deterrence of Soviet aggression. But insofar as they wonder whether the credibility of the United States' guarantee is waning, they ask themselves the same question about that of secondary forces, which are above all countercity forces, in case of a Soviet conventional attack. Moreover, they deplore the complication created by these secondary nuclear arsenals for arms control negotiations. The prospect of the French Rapid Deployment Force's participation in an eventual battle is welcome, but it would make only a small contribution to the strengthening of NATO's conventional potential, which most American experts demand.

True, on one point the French and American worries seem to coincide. I am referring to President Reagan's Strategic Defense Initiative (S.D.I.). But even in this realm the concerns are not identical. The French, along with many other Europeans, fear that the arms race for defensive systems will drive one more nail in the coffin of a Western strategy that entails, in case of need, a first resort to nuclear weapons. These weapons, which are aimed at vital Soviet military targets, may no longer be able to penetrate into the Soviet Union. The French and many other Europeans ask themselves whether an America safely sheltered by its antinuclear Maginot Line would still feel like taking risks of war—even conventional war—for the defense of Europe. The French and the British fear that a successful superpower race to defenses would reduce dramatically the threat still represented by the two smaller nations' nuclear forces. S.D.I. thus seems to bring closer the European nightmare of a Europe devastated either by a conventional war or by a "limited nuclear war"—one that would spare only the "sanctuary" of the two superpowers, but not Western Europe, since the Soviet airplanes, cruise missiles, and shorter-range nuclear systems aimed at Europe would still be beyond the reach of the United States' defensive system. But, as we shall see, this is not all that is at stake in the noisy debate that S.D.I. has provoked in the United States.

II

What do we find on the American side of the Atlantic? We find four kinds of fears, in which technological concerns and political worries mix. They can be summed up in one phrase: fear of nuclear deterrence's self-destabilization. The world appears to be moving away at great speed from the notion that has dominated U.S. strategic thinking for thirty years—the idea of stable deterrence. This is a condition in which neither of the two rivals has any incentive to strike first because it knows that the other side would still be able to destroy it in retaliation (deterrence by the threat of mutual assured destruction, or MAD), and in which the Soviet Union has no incentive for a conventional attack against vital U.S. interests (Europe, Middle East) because of the risk of nuclear escalation (extended deterrence, which, unlike MAD, rests on uncertainty). What is happening, on the one hand, is a crisis of the crisis stability obtained through MAD. On the other hand, as we observed before, the credibility of extended deterrence is diminishing precisely because it is the United States that in this instance would have to take the fatal initiative of a nuclear war, in which strategic parity seems to guarantee mutual destruction. Behind all of this there stands the 1914 analogy: the drama of a sudden crisis in which vital interests are at stake on both sides, and in which each side might take measures—of preparation and alert—that the other would pretty much consider to be acts of war, to which it would react by initiating the use of force out of fear of the disastrous consequences that would result from leaving that initiative to the enemy; thus, both sides would in fact lose control over events. The book recently published by my Harvard colleagues, *Hawks, Doves and Owls*,[4] suggests a whole series of measures designed to prevent a new "summer 1914."

The first fear is that of mismanagement of crises resulting from the very nature of the decision-making systems. In an acute crisis, the military might recommend to their civilian leaders measures (for instance, nuclear alerts) to which the enemy would be obliged to reply very quickly and which could be irreversible. Uncertainty about the ways in which two huge, hostile military machines (each one of which is opaque to the other) might interact would be compounded by the deficiencies of effective civilian control over the military. The military enjoys a vast autonomy in the Soviet Union; U.S. civilian leaders have illusions about the degree of genuine control they have over the military command and, in particular, over the margin of freedom available to them for deciding when to resort to nuclear weapons. Some American experts believe that the integration of nuclear weapons in the United States' military forces, and the insufficient understanding that U.S. presidents (except Jimmy Carter) have had of the intricacies of the United States' famous S.I.O.P. (the plan of strategic operations in case of war) are such that, without the president being aware of it, any serious conflict would risk degenerating very rapidly into a nuclear war. Clearly, one finds here again the mad momentum of mobilization schedules and war plans characteristic of July 1914.

The second fear is that of the temptation of preemptive war in case of a serious crisis—precisely what the MAD doctrine was supposed to rule out. The fact is that each of the superpowers now has the means to destroy in a first strike an important part of the other side's nuclear forces—not enough to disarm the foe, but enough to reduce considerably the damage it could inflict in retaliation. It is also a fact that S.D.I. could make matters worse despite Reagan's optimistic vision. For what the Soviets are afraid of is the following scenario: a U.S. first strike—with land-based missiles (Minutemen with powerful and accurate nuclear warheads, MX's with ten such warheads), Trident II submarines with comparable capabilities, bombers, cruise missiles, and Pershing IIs—against the Soviet Union's land-based missiles (still three-fourths of the Soviet nuclear arsenal) and against other vital Soviet military targets. Soviet retaliation would be both limited by the very scope of the losses thus inflicted on the USSR's forces and eroded by the defensive systems deployed by the United States. What the Americans fear is a symmetrical scenario: especially if the United States succeeds in putting in place a defensive network more advanced and more effective than the Soviet Union's defensive capabilities, the Soviet Union, in a serious crisis, could gain an advantage by attacking U.S. land-based missiles, airports, and seaports before the U.S. defensive network became impenetrable. Such an attack would be carried out by the huge land-based missiles the Soviet Union has been building for more than ten years, as well as by cruise missiles on Soviet submarines or surface ships near the United States' coasts. In each of those two scenarios, we also find the advantage each side would have in destroying at the start the other side's political and military command system (including the very important enemy satellites). The weaknesses experts claim to find in these systems are such that each side would have an incentive, by attacking the enemy's system first, to prevent the enemy from hitting and crippling its own system.

Of course, one may complacently believe that the two superpowers will continue to hesitate before proceeding to the cosmic roll of the dice that a preemptive attack would constitute. Should such an attack succeed only in part—and even if it succeeds fully—retaliation would remain formidable. But a third fear has appeared, one that is also provoked by technological evolution. The new weapons squeeze, so to speak, the concept of stable deterrence between the anvil of the temptation to strike first massively and the hammer of "limited nuclear war." The development of accurate nuclear weapons, with limited range and fallout, has given increasingly more substance to the lure of replacing the doctrine of MAD with a doctrine of restrained and discriminatory counterforce war, as advocated by the champion of this notion, Albert Wohlstetter.[5] He starts from a very convincing critique of MAD. The threat of destroying cities in retaliation against an enemy nuclear attack has lost much of its credibility in an era of nuclear parity—i.e., collective suicide. If a nation's strategic doctrine leaves it with no other recourse than that one, its leaders will have only an abominable choice between suicide (mutual genocide, or nuclear winter) and capitulation. The "solution" is provided by a new revolution in the nuclear revolution: weapons capable of being less destructive and more accurate than those that existed twenty or thirty years ago. Hence the idea of a menu of "limited" options at the disposal of the leaders; it would have the merit of reinforcing extended deterrence—i.e., of making the threat of a first resort to nuclear weapons more credible for the defense of Europe against a conventional attack. But this idea, which wants to be reassuring insofar as it treats nuclear weapons as if they were conventional, is nevertheless most disturbing for a number of reasons.[6]

First, is it certain that the existence of such a menu would have greater deterring power than the threat of total destruction, even if there is an undeniable element of bluff in the latter threat? Is there no risk of lulling leaders into believing that there can be tolerable nuclear wars? Moreover, if deterrence failed, could one really limit the wreckage and control the game? If the Americans were the first to resort to nuclear weapons in order to stop an invasion of Germany or Iran, would the Soviets interpret this crossing of the nuclear threshold as a sort of warning shot aimed at making them think twice, or as proof that Washington has indeed chosen nuclear war—in which case, as the Soviets have so often announced, they would reply not with an equally limited strike but with a general attack against the enemy's nuclear potential? The idea of limited counterforce war presupposes both a sort of tacit agreement between the enemies for the rational conduct of warfare (something that is highly unlikely, for if both sides had been rational one would not have come to such a pass) and, on each side as well as in the interaction between the two forces, the absence of this uncontrollable factor in which passions (including the passion to win) and accidents combine—the factor called "friction" by Clausewitz.

Obviously such prospects are unpleasant. This is where the dream or mirage of S.D.I. comes in. It is a mirage, according to most scientists, if the purpose, as President Reagan seems to hope, is to replace deterrence with defense and to make both preventive attack and limited nuclear war impossible (except on the territory of third parties) thanks to the strategic defense of cities and of the country as a whole. If, as most experts believe, the main purpose of the defense network is to protect the now vulnerable land-based missiles—i.e., not to replace but to strengthen deterrence—the difficulty lies in the likelihood of offensive countermeasures capable of destroying or overwhelming these defenses (hence the reluctance even of a hawk like Paul Nitze, who has set to the deployment of such a network very strict preconditions concerning the comparative cost of defense versus offensive countermeasures and the ability of the defenses to survive a direct attack on them).

Thus, what many Americans fear in the huge effort toward S.D.I. is not the effect of its deployment on the defense of Europe. It is, on the one hand, the possible contribution it could make to the temptation of preventive war—i.e., a new weakening of crisis stability, which is exactly the opposite from S.D.I.'s goal—and, on the other hand, the flagrant contradiction, mentioned even by someone as unenthusiastic about arms control agreements as former Defense Secretary James Schlesinger,[7] between the negotiation of treaties for the reduction of offensive weapons and the development of S.D.I. For if the United States tries to build defensive networks, the Soviets—even if they did not have, in the realm of antiballistic missile defense, the technological difficulties they seem to fear—would retaliate at least in part by increasing their offensive capabilities (this is exactly what the Americans themselves did in the past against Soviet efforts in defense matters: remember the development of MIRV to counter the apparent Soviet ABM effort).

This is where the fourth fear appears: the fear of a failure of the Geneva arms control negotiations. Only a success in Geneva would allow, if not the elimination, at least the reduction of the risk represented by what I earlier termed the anvil and the hammer. An agreement that would deal above all with nuclear weapons capable of destroying the foe's strategic weapons, command systems, and satellites, as well as with the unverifiable weapons, would allow governments to make less dangerous war plans. It would give them more time to strengthen their command and control systems. But the emphatic demand made until now by the U.S. government of a drastic reduction of those Soviet strategic weapons that threaten the U.S. arsenal, without any hint of a willingness to give up S.D.I. in exchange, risks making these negotiations fail and thus provoking a formidable double acceleration of the arms race: both in space (S.D.I. and antisatellite weapons) and in the realm of offensive forces.

Obviously there is an abyss between American and French concerns. Many French people continue to cling to the idea that since the nuclear bomb has preserved peace, more bombs make for more peace—thus completely ignoring the qualitative evolution that undermines stable deterrence.

And while Europeans ask themselves what effects U.S. and Soviet defensive systems would have on Europe, and what technological fallout Europe could reap in Washington's defense programs, Americans see in this huge "research" undertaking (which in fact goes way beyond research) at the minimum a threat to the 1972 ABM treaty—the most important of the treaties concerning nuclear weapons signed and ratified by the superpowers—and at worst a contribution to instability and to the arms race, one that is particularly lamentable given the distant and limited chances of technical success on the part of S.D.I.

III

What about Europe in all of this? The perspectives described above can only provoke new tensions between Americans and Europeans. The latter (even the French, who have been indifferent to or distrustful of arms control in the past) have a major interest in a success in Geneva, not only because it would mean a rapprochement between the superpowers—and what Europe needs above all is peace—but also because failure would worsen the military competition between the superpowers, and the risks entailed by this competition would only sharpen the United States' tendencies toward an "agonizing reappraisal" of NATO's strategy as it has been set and frozen for twenty years.

This strategy continues to rest on the threat of a first resort to nuclear weapons. Now, (1) this possibility increases the first of the four fears I have mentioned: in a serious crisis the military might ask the U.S. president for a release—i.e., for the right to use nuclear weapons when the military deems it necessary. And it would be difficult for the president to refuse. (2) The threat of a first nuclear strike by NATO risks aggravating the Soviet temptation of a preemptive nuclear attack, especially against the vulnerable atomic weapons deployed in Western Europe. (3) It is obviously in Europe that the temptation of "limited" atomic war, played as a game of chess, is both greatest and most dangerous, given the abundance of nuclear explosives accumulated in that powderkeg (hence the risk of uncontrollable escalation).

This is why many Americans, even among fervent Atlanticists, recommend either giving up the threat and the strategy of a first strike or, at a minimum, moving away from the front or even altogether eliminating short-range atomic weapons whose presence near the Iron Curtain would force NATO's command in case of war to choose between an almost immediate use, which could make nuclear war irreversible, and the destruction of this arsenal by an enemy atomic or conventional attack. The most "optimistic" believe that limited nuclear "exchanges" that would hit only Western Europe and the Soviet Union's East European satellites are conceivable, since the Soviet Union has an interest in respecting the American sanctuary as long as the Soviet territory has not been hit. But they recognize that the Pershing II and cruise missiles deployed in Western Europe complicate matters singularly, since their range extends to important parts of European Russia; above all, such "limited" prospects are not only shaky but particularly repugnant to the Europeans.

Other Americans would prefer a purely conventional strategy, based on the new precision-guided conventional arms. But, on the one hand, many Europeans and Americans remain skeptical about a technological *deus ex machina* in this realm: these weapons can be as useful to the aggressor as to the defender, and therefore they may not help NATO offset the Soviet superiority in men and tanks—not to mention European skepticism about the deterring power of *any* conventional defense. On the other hand, some Americans fear that even a strategy of conventional defense would end in nuclear escalation as long as U.S. nuclear weapons are deployed in Western Europe. The combination of these fears leads to a peremptory conclusion that, while logical, is one expressed only rarely so far: the need for a complete withdrawal of U.S. forces from Europe, thereby leaving the Europeans with the choice between different ways of fending for themselves.[8]

Obviously we have not yet reached this point. But there is a serious potential for discord between the two sides of the Atlantic, for two reasons at least. A major part of the American public seems to believe that the United States' official strategic doctrine is no first use—that is, the deployment of nuclear weapons only in case of an enemy nuclear attack (against the United States or its main allies). The thesis according to which a first *resort* to nuclear weapons against a conventional attack would be suicidal, and that *therefore* the *threat* of such a resort is a bluff that is both incredible and dangerous, has become increasingly popular. (It may not be irrelevant to note that the American Catholic Bishops have been criticized above all for having, on the one hand, condemned almost every conceivable *use* of nuclear weapons but, on the other hand, having deemed nuclear deterrence—i.e., the *threat* of using nuclear weapons—acceptable under certain conditions; it is the same kind of ambiguity which the champions of no first use reject.) Moreover, the American pendulum, after having for seven or eight years swung toward an increase in the military budget, is moving back in the opposite direction. The yearly cost of Europe's defense, according to American calculations, is somewhere between $130 and 177 billion. For the time being the determination to reduce military expenditures is concentrated on the unfortunate MX and on the elimination of waste. Will it stop there if the Europeans are increasingly perceived as refusing to make the necessary contributions to conventional war, and as preferring to let Big Brother take the risks of atomic war?

The worst is obviously not inevitable. There could be a bargain in Geneva: the reduction of offensive weapons would be accompanied by the erection of a solid barrier between research (obviously difficult to stop) and development in matters of defense. Under such conditions, NATO could perhaps both proceed with conventional modernization and improvements, and adopt, more or less officially and without drama, the doctrine of no early first use. This would allow the French debate to stay where it is. But if things should get worse between the superpowers, the French dilemma—

preserving nuclear autonomy and priority, but at the cost of increasing nuclear ineffectiveness in the face of non-nuclear threats and defensive systems, or else reinforcing the conventional potential of the NATO Alliance at the cost of military autonomy and despite the insufficiency of conventional forces both for deterrence and for defense—would become more and more acute, the incapacity of the Europeans to establish a security system of their own both in the conventional and in the nuclear realms would become more and more tragic, transatlantic discord would become more and more acrimonious, and humankind's predicament would become more and more gloomy.

Notes

1. Stanley Hoffmann, "L'avenir de la défense européenne," *Intervention*, no. 8 (February–April 1984), pp. 80–84.
2. Pierre Lellouche, *L'avenir de la guerre* (Paris: Fayard, 1985).
3. *Le Monde* (June 5, 1985), p. 2.
4. Graham Allison, Albert Carnesale, and Joseph Nye, *Hawks, Doves and Owls* (New York: Norton, 1985).
5. Albert Wohlstetter, "Critique de la dissuasion pure," *Commentaire* 7, no. 25 (Spring 1984), pp. 23–42; Wohlstetter, "Between an Unfree World and None," *Foreign Affairs* (Summer 1985), pp. 962–994.
6. See my "Réponse à Wohlstetter," *Commentaire* (Spring 1984), pp. 48–50.
7. James Schlesinger, "The Eagle and the Bear," *Foreign Affairs* (Summer 1985), pp. 937–961.
8. See Earl Ravenal, "Europe Without America," *Foreign Affairs* (Summer 1985), pp. 1020–1035.

PART THREE

Actors and Interactions

10

On the Origins of the Cold War

We are intensely aware today, particularly in the United States, of the challenge to the orthodox view of the origins of the Cold War. I would like to begin by discussing these competing interpretations and, in particular, the revisionist view. After a brief critique of these two contrasting conceptions, I shall present some views of my own about the process which led us into forty years of Cold War. It is a complicated and interesting process.

It is not surprising that we should now be faced with two conflicting interpretations—one which is a kind of official justificatory conception, and one which is iconoclastically revisionist. The growth of this challenge to the "official" view of history has happened in America after practically every war. That it has developed with regard to the Cold War is interesting in itself because the Cold War is, after all, still with us. The debate between the two explanations is interesting also because it is important to know how we got into it—and not only to understand why the Cold War led to the Vietnam war. Moreover, this debate tells us something about how history is written, and perhaps something about how history should not be written. Finally, an examination of these competing views also tells us something about how United States foreign policy is made.

The official view of the origins of the Cold War—which was best presented, implicitly at least, in Dean Acheson's modestly titled book *Present at the Creation*—is that, on the whole, the Cold War began because of bad Soviet behavior. This particular view generally starts with the wartime alliance. It emphasizes how the United States trusted and helped the Soviet Union during the war, and it assumes that the Soviets themselves were, in fact, largely responsible for the war itself, which might not have started if Stalin had not made his deal with Hitler in 1939. Throughout the period of the wartime alliance, the United States expected that the Soviet Union would join us after the war in the creation of a new world order which would be based upon the cooperation of the great powers, in which democratic regimes would prevail and be safe from outside intervention, and in which spheres of influence—even disguised as "regionalism"—would be scrapped. Such a view was reflected in the United Nations charter. Parenthetically, it is interesting to note that in working out schemes for this postwar world order in the years 1943 through 1945, the most serious conflicts were not between the United States and the Soviet Union but between the United States and Great Britain. These conflicts centered on such matters as the international monetary and trade systems, the emancipation of colonial territories, and so on.[1] Finally, the orthodox thesis states that the United States had no intention of becoming a world policeman after the war—certainly not *the* world policeman. In fact, it shows that throughout the war the United States overestimated the power which Great Britain would still have afterward, and expected a large measure of American disengagement.

All this, according to the official thesis, was destroyed by the aggressive behavior of the Soviet Union, which gradually increased its domination over Eastern Europe. As early as 1942 and 1943, the Soviet Union tightened its control of numerous Communist parties in the Balkans and in Western Europe, even beyond the line which the Red Army would reach at the end of the war. As examples of Soviet maneuvers which made cooperation difficult, this thesis points to: the Soviets' manipulation of Polish Communists in order to eliminate non-Communist forces from Poland; the establishment of bilateral links between Moscow and its neighbors, and Moscow's opposition to any linkages between these states which it might not control; Moscow's violation of the Yalta understanding on free elections in Poland; the Soviets' behavior in occupied Germany, in various interallied commissions, and in peace treaty conferences.

According to this view, the United States was then obliged, as the result of Soviet behavior, to face a choice it had not wanted. It was a choice between: on the one hand, tolerating a vacuum which could have been filled only by the Soviet Union, given the decline of England, the collapse of Western Europe, the decrepitude of China, and the fall of Japan; and on the other, taking leadership in a world in which there were now no major powers other than the Soviet Union and the United States. In other words, according to this first view, the United States had no imperial designs, but found itself forced to assume the leadership of a coalition. Nor was it the United States' fault that this was a coalition of unequals. The coalition it found itself leading was defensive, not offensive; leadership of that coalition was imposed, not planned.

This is the official line. If one looks at the facts—which is sometimes useful—one finds that this line goes much too far. Although it is certain that the Soviet Union deliberately extended its influence, these were limited moves and, certainly in the case of Germany, moves that seemed to be more preventive than anything else. On the whole, the Soviet Union did stick to and respect the divisions into national spheres of influence that it had arrived at with Churchill (it had been difficult to get the United States to agree). If one looks at the situations in Greece and in China, one finds that the behavior of the Communist parties in these two important countries was not at all dictated from Moscow. As for Germany, where the Soviets used their occupation zone as a major bargaining tool, the Soviets obviously had security fears and enormous economic needs which they wanted to satisfy, given the destruction they had suffered.

To be more specific, there was a fundamental ambiguity in Soviet policy in Germany, where they did not have one basic approach. But if any consistent thread did appear in Soviet policy there immediately after the end of the war, it was the need to take certain strong positions which could be exploited later for bargaining purposes and as leverage (for instance, in order to weaken any United States resolve to remain in Europe) rather than anything more precise. Most important, if one looks at the behavior of Communist parties in Western Europe in the period 1945 through 1947, one finds that they were far from being huge, disruptive, subversive organisms. In fact, they were still in their patriotic nationalist phase, willing to participate in coalition governments and to play the game of electoral democracy, telling their supporters, particularly the workers, to work and produce and rebuild these countries.

Clearly, then, the standard thesis goes beyond the facts. It does so, in part, because of something which the revisionists point out and to which I will return—the old tradition of anti-Communism and anti-Soviet suspiciousness in this country.[2] It may also have gone too far because of excessive Western—and especially American—expectations during World War II: the dream of harmony and cooperation after the war was bound to be disappointed, and disappointed Americans tend to overreact.

There was also a large amount of confusion in American thinking. It was not always clear whether what was lamented about Soviet behavior after 1945 was the division of Europe into spheres of influence—that is, the Soviet domination of one sphere—or the tendency which we thought the Communists had of going *beyond* their sphere of influence. The best example of this confusion we find in Kennan's own writings, in his memoirs. On the one hand, he indicated, in his own messages from that period, his conviction that Soviet control in Eastern Europe was shaky. He wrote that the Soviet threat was not military, that Soviet behavior was not adventurous, that the Soviets were interested primarily in a security zone. Yet there are other passages in his memoirs in which he talks about his fear of communization of the whole of Europe, and his description of the means of Soviet diplomacy suggests, at least implicitly, that he felt they had universal ends. So there was a confusion, based on uncertainty and fear, in America's image of Soviet behavior.

Eventually the revisionists entered the field and offered their own images. First, all of them go back for their interpretations much farther in time than the end, or even the beginning, of the wartime alliance. They generally start with 1917, not with the 1939 Hitler-Stalin pact or with 1941. One of the most representative spokesmen for the revisionists, Arno Mayer, presents the theory of an international civil war that has been going on at least since the Russian Revolution of 1917.[3] He describes the constant Western hostility to, and horrified fascination with, Communism, which resulted in recurrent attempts to intervene against Russia after 1917, as well as occasional strong sympathies for, or at least nonantipathy toward, Fascism in its anti-Communist implications. Revisionists also often concentrate on the immediate prewar years—in particular, on the impact Munich had on the Soviet Union, which felt itself rejected by the powers of Western Europe despite its offers to join in anti-Nazi collective security.

Insofar as they examine the wartime behavior of the Soviet Union, revisionists view it as essentially defensive and nationalist. They insist that the main objective of the Soviet Union was security in areas which had been traditional zones of Russian interest: in Eastern Europe and in the Balkans, in Turkey and all along the borders of the Soviet Union. They stress that the Soviets avoided major provocations and behaved with great prudence in Western Europe, precisely by encouraging the Communist parties to work in national coalitions—even at the cost of sacrificing chances of social revolution. They show that Stalin was eager to avoid provoking the British there and in the eastern Mediterranean, and that the whole emphasis within the Communist parties was on nationalism, not on Communism. They show that Stalin expected agreements with the Western powers along sphere-of-influence lines and accepted Russia's exclusion from any significant role in Italy or Japan.

So what went wrong, according to the revisionists, is largely the result of American imperialism, whose existence they attempt to prove as follows: first of all, there was the rejection, in at least three forms, of economic aid to the Soviet Union as soon as Roosevelt was dead. The United States immediately ended Lend-Lease, refused a loan to the Soviet Union, and decided to put an end to reparations from West Germany to the Soviet Union. These were moves against which Henry Wallace protested when he was still in the cabinet.

The second fact was what the revisionists call the American attempt to intimidate the Soviet Union in areas of legitimate Soviet concern, such as Eastern Europe, with an American demonstration of strength through the use of the atomic bomb. Alperovitz, in his well-known book,[4] presents the American decision to use the bomb on Japanese cities as being intended largely to impress the Soviet Union with America's monopoly. Similarly, as Kolko shows throughout his enormous volume on the American politics of war, the United States' constant wartime support to the London Poles—the most anti-Communist Poles—must have appeared to the Soviets as an attempt at intimidating them and at ensuring the future of an anti-Russian regime in Warsaw.

Finally, according to the revisionists, came the postwar attempt to universalize the Open Door, as symbolized by the Baruch Plan; it would have provided an international monopoly for the production of nuclear energy which would have been able to function without any veto by the Soviet Union. It was, in other words, a scheme that would have resulted in the sending of inspection teams into the Soviet Union, and it was based upon the notion that the United States would keep its nuclear weapons and not destroy them until and unless this Open Door international organization had been established. Incidentally, while the United States proposed this scheme, it excluded the Soviet Union from any part in the control of Italy, Japan, and West Germany. Concern for the Open Door—that is, preserving polities and markets for American influence and business—also manifested itself in Greece and Iran, as well as in America's opposition to British schemes for world trade and monetary arrangements (with the United States using now, against Britain, the ideology of free competition which the British had used against the Continent a century earlier).

These are the facts—accurate in themselves—which the revisionists mention. What about the value of the theory?[5] I think that the revisionists are far more nearly right than the official thesis in their treatment of the Soviet Union, in pointing out that the Soviet Union had limited territorial ambitions and that these ambitions were of a traditional nature (there was, after all, massive demobilization on the Soviet side). They are right too in pointing out that the leaders of the Soviet Union acted not as the brains behind a worldwide, Communist, ideological Frankenstein monster but as if they had read Hans Morgenthau's theory of power politics—which, incidentally, had not yet been propounded. The Kremlin leaders were much more concerned with the Russian national interest than with worldwide Communism. And the revisionists are right also in pointing out the complex nature of the Soviet Union's relations with outside Communist parties. This is a fact rightly stressed by Kolko—that the Soviets had little or no control over the Yugoslav, Greek, or Chinese Communist parties. The revisionists are right in pointing out that there were no instructions from Moscow to the Western European Communist parties to seize power or even to keep the arms they had accumulated during the resistance. They are right in pointing out the ambivalence of the Soviet Union toward Germany and the constant oscillation of Soviet policy between two possible lines: joint control of the whole of Germany with the Western powers, if at all possible, and—only if this was not to be possible—partition. Neither line entailed exclusive Soviet domination of all Germany. The revisionists are right in stating that the Soviets were concerned essentially with preventing Germany from becoming a Western, and potentially anti-Russian, preserve, and did not set up the East German regime until after the United States and Britain had begun to organize a West German entity. Thus the tragedy of partition grew out of Anglo-American hostility to the idea of a neutralized Germany under four-power control. (Whether this idea would have been workable at all is another story; my own opinion is profoundly skeptical.)

I think the revisionists are right also in showing that the notion of a worldwide Communist conspiracy was essentially a projection of America's own universalism. They are right in emphasizing that the United States in 1945 looked at the Soviet Union from a long tradition of distrust, which made us expect the worst. Americans felt a kind of disbelief about the Soviet Union, which was suspended only when it had to be—during the days of the Grand Alliance; this disbelief started all over again as soon as the Soviets proved to be difficult partners. And the revisionists are right in stressing that the United States faced world affairs with its own set of principles. As de Gaulle would say in his memoirs, "The United States looks at the world with complicated methods and simple ideas." In other words, American leaders did have some notion of designing a world which would look very much like the United States.

So the revisionists point to a paradox that, I think, has some validity. Whereas it was the Soviet Union that behaved according to a classical theory of power politics, it was the United States that behaved not at all like a classical great power playing a balance of power game but like an ideological power with a global vision. The United States behaved, then, in the way we thought the Soviets were behaving. In this respect, incidentally, the real father of revisionism, the one who first criticized this tendency of the United States to face the world with a set of principles of its own, was Walter Lippmann, in his writings about the Cold War in 1946 and 1947.

However, having said where the revisionists are right, I should also add that they have tended to develop a new mythology of their own. Here I would like to stress where their realism goes off into a fantasy world.

It does so, I think, because the revisionists all look at American foreign policy with an a priori ideological conception; they announce what United States policy is, which often makes it unnecessary for them to look at the data or at least to interpret them correctly. This isn't true of all the revisionists. Some of them make a valiant effort to look at the data—certainly this is true of Alperovitz. As for Kolko's large book, I suggest that none of the chapters is better than the bibliograpy he lists for each of them; and in the bibliographies, some of the listed books are of questionable value. There is in his book a kind of grand overview to which all details are subordinated. At its most extreme, the revisionist approach gives a kind of systematic, quasi-conspiratorial view of American foreign policy as an East Coast establishment plot. At the core of that plot is the economic interpretation, which assumes the need for ever-expanding markets. (Some emphasize the business drive; others stress agricultural expansionism.) This is an adaptation of the traditional socialist theory of imperialism; it sees United States foreign policy being led by men who, as Kolko puts it in his second and shorter book,[6] are all under the direct or indirect influence of the business interests. They are corporation lawyers, business executives, and the like. Everything is fitted into this design, and many quotations are strewn about to buttress the economic interpretation and present the search for new markets as the master key. Each time somebody talks about markets, you can be sure that even if the speech is made for purely Rotarian purposes, it is going to be picked out as damning and decisive by the revisionists.

Now this raises the essential problem of how one builds up an interpretation of a foreign policy. There is a serious danger in any a priori or ex ante method, be it Marxist or other. First of all, any approach in which you know the answer before you have asked the question effectively eliminates contradictions. The difficulty is that contradictions exist in every aspect of life. Second, it blows up small parts, or partial aspects, of the whole picture. And finally, it raises an interesting psychological problem: how is one to interpret the dynamics of foreign policy? If, in case after case, you find that what people thought they were doing is different from what the theory says that they were actually, really, "objectively" doing, then you have a problem. You must assume that people are in fact either mere puppets manipulated without their awareness—puppets who are now being told there was, for their motivations and actions, a purpose of which they were not aware—or else purposeful puppets conniving for, but carefully disguising, their real goals. But are policy makers either programmed automatons or cunning conspirators?

It isn't that what the revisionists say is necessarily false, but that they do iron out the kinks in history. It is a fact that through most of its history the United States was more concerned with raising the barrier at its gate—protectionism—than with enforcing open doors elsewhere—free trade. It is a fact that throughout this period the United States, at the same time that it was getting into trouble with the Soviet Union, did make effort after effort at accommodation. Truman might have been highly annoyed at the Russians—telling Molotov, quite literally, to go to hell—but he also sent messages to Stalin trying to patch things up. It is a fact that there were disagreements between the architects of United States policy—between Roosevelt and Hull, Hull and Welles, Truman and Byrnes, Acheson and Kennan. It is a fact that policy in the Third World was neither high-priority nor consistent (cf. Indonesia versus Indochina).

A different kind of contradiction, as I see it, is provided by the experience with the Marshall Plan. If the Soviets had accepted the Marshall Plan, which was offered to all of Europe, including the Soviet Union, they would have submitted themselves to receiving American aid and opened themselves to American industry, so that the outcome of the Marshall Plan would be evidence of American imperialism.[7] Yet the revisionists are also inclined to say that if Marshall aid had not been offered, this would have been a worse sign of American imperialism, because it would have proved that the United States wanted to cut the Soviet Union out. In other words, whatever the devil does is devilish. There is another of these contradictions in the fact that American economic investment was particularly high in areas that were not contested by the Soviet Union; areas in which the United States was supposedly in contest with the Soviet Union, such as Eastern Europe, were of practically no importance for American economic interests.

Now we come to the matter of blowing up parts of the picture. Alperovitz, in his book *Atomic Diplomacy*, discards or minimizes literally all the evidence that one could use to show that the Soviet Union was perhaps not the main target of the bomb dropped on Japan. Isn't it possible that the main target was Japan? Truman said that the atomic bomb was a weapon, that weapons were meant to be used, and that the decision to use it never cost him five minutes' sleep. Sometimes simplicity is its own answer. Perhaps things were not as complicated and men not as cunning as the revisionists believe. At least this alternative explanation should have been fully considered. Similarly, on the cancellation of Lend-Lease, the revisionists have made too much of the matter. Cancellation was largely a routine act by a new president who was inclined to the belief that when the war stops aid does too. Incidentally, this decision hit England at least as hard as it hit the Soviet Union.

Finally, on the problem of interpreting the dynamics of foreign policy, one must ask oneself why, if the moving force was economic expansiveness (or expansionism), it is so hard to find evidence of its impact on actual decisions (by contrast with its presence in speeches). One must ask oneself whether American officialdom really intended ever to go back on the concessions made at Yalta and to force the Soviet Union out of Eastern Europe or East Germany, as Christopher Lasch has charged, or whether it was merely expressing indignation at what we thought they were doing beyond what we thought had been agreed at Yalta. Had we intended to "roll back" the Russians, we would have behaved as the world's most clumsy imperialists, since we began by letting the Soviets take Berlin, Prague, and Vienna when we could have prevented them from at least seizing all three, and continued with a colossal demobilization—a point neglected by the revisionists. How did American officials actually see their objectives? If they did not see them the way the revisionists say they saw them, this does not mean that American objectives could not have appeared to the Soviets the way they now look to the revisionists, or that the results of American policy do not look the way the revisionists see them; but it does mean that there may perhaps be a gap between American intentions, as Americans understood them, and the eventual outcome. So the key problem is not to look for a master explanation but, as Max Weber and Raymond Aron have pointed out, to try to understand the contrasts—the permanent, ironical contrasts—between what people think they are doing and what they are actually achieving. In other words, the key is to be found in the realm of perceptions.

When we're dealing with theoretical work on international systems, we may not have to go into the problem of perceptions. At that level of abstraction, people don't even matter; only systems—that is, patterns of relationships—matter (although I've never met a system in the street). But if one is going to explain foreign policy, one must take perceptions into account. At the heart of this debate is the question: what shall social science look for? Should it, à la Marx, look for a grand philosophy of history and a grand explanation which provides the key to everything, in which case one can relax—and act—or should it follow Thucydides, and focus on people's perceptions and intentions, and on the frustrations and contradictions people get into when what they achieve is different from what they intended? I lean toward Thucydides, in this respect at least. And this leads me to conclude that while the revisionists are more nearly right when they deal with Soviet behavior than in their account of United States motivations, the official thesis, which distorts Soviet conduct, correctly reflects American perceptions (or misperceptions) and the self-image of American leaders. If American actions formed patterns that invite the revisionists' wrath, the explanation must be sought in the nature of America's style and institutions rather than in the realm of counterrevolutionary motives and economic drives.[8]

Let me now present my own view of what the Cold War really was about and what the process became. I think, first of all, that one has to look at objective realities. The existence of a huge power vacuum in Europe and of another one in Asia, following the collapse of the Axis powers, is such a reality. Next, one must look at intentions. Here, the revisionists' view of Soviet intentions is closer to the truth than their analysis of American intentions. When one looks at the latter, one should avoid projecting the 1960s backward. One has to keep in mind that much of American foreign policy at the time was extraordinarily improvised. Franklin Roosevelt's foreign office was still small, and his foreign policy machinery was extraordinarily primitive. He was a president who didn't listen to his secretary of state, but who had his own sources of information and advice. By 1945, American foreign policy machinery was not far from what it had been in 1940-41, when it was practically nonexistent. The American conceptions of the world, largely abstract and disembodied, both reflected and reacted against the absence of America from world affairs before that period. Quite naturally they expressed a certain American style, which Wilsonianism had already displayed, and which could be described as representing the hubris of worldwide do-goodism.

Then, after intentions, we have to look at perceptions, and here what is most important is how each side saw the other one. For how each side saw the other determined how each side acted. This is where the stuff of tragedy, I think, can be found. The Soviet Union saw the United States as being far more deliberate and far more vigilant than the United States actually was. And the United States saw the Soviet Union as being far more ambitious and more in control of everything than the Soviet Union actually was. This can be confirmed by anybody who works in the field of perceptions:[9] each side always tends to see his antagonist as being infinitely more cunning, centralized, controlling, and competent than he is or than he himself is. Now the origins of this battle of misperceptions have only little to do with objective reality, for each side was doubtlessly inclined to perceive the present in terms of extreme past experiences, domestic or external. The United States had a kind of fixation about—this time—not allowing another Hitler and not succumbing to another Munich; after all, United States officialdom felt slightly guilty for not having been vigilant in the 1930s, for not having paid much attention to the European scene, for having practiced until 1940 the policy of the ostrich. They didn't want this to happen again and had a strong tendency to interpret what was happening now in the light of what had happened then. The Soviet Union, for its part, had its own theories about Western capitalist behavior, based on its own experiences of the early 1920s and the 1930s.

The final element we should examine is the opportunities for action. Here, we need to move from generalities to something more precise. First of all, there were asymmetries in the two Policies.[10] The Soviet Union was probably uncertain as to whether the wartime collaboration would continue or not. Stalin showed some willingness at Yalta and at Potsdam to make at least some concessions in order to assure the permanency of the collaboration, perhaps in the hope of economic rewards, and it was largely because of those concessions that the UN was finally established. There is no doubt that the Soviet Union was determined to pursue a sphere-of-influence policy in Eastern Europe and to have a decisive say in the settlement of the German problem. While this may have been a strictly defensive conception, it does raise some traditional questions about great-power defensive conceptions. What specific policies were implied? Would it be defensive in cooperation with others or in conflict with them? Nor was it clear as to what was their ultimate vision of world affairs to be served by this conception. Was it a conservative or a revolutionary vision? This is a question, incidentally, which Kolko never reaches. Now, the shape and features of a Policy depend on the long-range vision and on the tactical policies.

As for American Policy, it was clearer about economic schemes than about political issues. There was obviously a great desire on the part of Roosevelt for peaceful collaboration with the Soviet Union. The president had an understanding of Soviet security concerns, which often made him extremely annoyed with Churchill throughout the war. But we also hesitated to pay for such collaboration the price the Soviets requested—to endorse their political control over their neighbors, especially Poland. Moreover, the American long-term vision of world affairs was essentially neither conservative nor revolutionary. It might better be called a reformist vision, a kind of Wilsonian view, accompanied and sharpened by FDR's sense of the need for great powers to play a leading role. The United States, by way of contrast with Marxism or Communism, did not think of a world revolution. Yet its long-range vision was not conservative, because United States leaders distrusted such conservative techniques of conflict management as the balance of power; the United States preferred a kind of Wilsonian concerted cooperation on the part of the great powers. Whereas this was not incompatible with some sphere of influence policy—after all, the United States itself insisted on its sphere of influence in Latin America, and enshrined it in the charter of the United Nations—it was not compatible with two different factors. It was incompatible with what appeared to us to be the revolutionary vision of the other side. What was required by the American vision was at least a harmony of ends on the part of the great powers. Second, it was not compatible with any tendency of the other side to confuse a sphere of preponderant influence with a sphere of exclusive property and domestic control. The distinction—between hegemony for security or economic reasons and controlling domination—was clearly made in Washington.

There is yet another paradox, which explains the momentum of the Cold War. The Soviet Union's policy was to a large extent defensive and cautious, but was pursued so vigorously that to many Americans and West Europeans, it looked like the policy of Genghis Khan reincarnate. On the other side, the United States had a policy which it viewed as defensive, but in some ways its own vision of the future was highly universal and implicitly imperialistic, in the sense that it wanted to see a world which would look much like the United States. And of course the United States, undevastated and indeed strengthened by the war, had the biggest weapons available to any nation in history.

Let us look at these ambiguities a bit more closely. What the Soviet Union started by doing was in itself ambiguous. Thus (leaving aside Finland, a nation that had fiercely resisted and was nevertheless willing to accommodate its giant neighbor, and Czechoslovakia, where the *coup de Prague* did not come until early 1948) the communization of Eastern Europe could be seen—as Louis Halle puts it in his book on the Cold War[11]—as a situational necessity for the leaders of the Kremlin. The Soviet Union found itself in countries essential for Soviet security—traditional invasion routes—yet where all the non-Communist forces were anti-Communist and anti-Soviet, and so what could they do? Obviously, the concern for external security led to measures of internal safety: they moved to eliminate the anti-Communist forces. But Soviet policy there could also be seen as a step toward ultimate world revolution. This ambiguity was present from the very start.

What was it that the United States perceived? What it saw was a shock to its own expectations. First, the United States, as a good, "liberal" power, was inclined to draw a clear boundary—its own Iron Curtain—between international politics and domestic affairs. The Soviets were viewed in Washington as entitled to a predominant foreign policy influence in Poland or Bulgaria or Hungary, just as they had in Finland, but they should not control the domestic affairs of those countries. Washington always made this perfectly artificial distinction without realizing that for the Soviets, at least in Eastern Europe, it was a hard one to apply, not only because in Marxist doctrine the distinction itself is absurd but also because of the political situation of those countries, where there was little middle ground between Communism and anti-Communism. Second, the United States, as a good, "liberal" power, saw international relations as a domain of give and take, and found itself facing Mr. Molotov's "nyet, nyet, nyet" intransigence instead. It therefore saw itself on the defensive. This is what the United States perceived by the end of 1945.

How the United States reacted to its own perceptions was in itself ambiguous. On the one hand, the United States discovered power; in fact, it did so with some glee, as manifested in Kennan's writings. The United States thus discovered what in a country like England had been known for many centuries: that in the absence of any world community, power means hard bargaining, not gestures; power means applying one's might locally to master local circumstances; power means having to discriminate between essential areas and the others. So, in 1945, the United States discovered what Morgenthau was to codify in 1948. But on the other hand, the United States also projected its own universalism, which was incompatible with traditional power politics, and in doing so, the United States reacted by supposing that if the Soviet Union misbehaved, it must be because of Soviet universalism. Therefore we translated from their acts—which, as we saw, were ambiguous—to their intentions; and the American response, based on this interpretation, was dictated by the American style. It was a response in universalist fashion, according to American values and practices. When something goes wrong outside, we offer economic aid and military assistance, because that is what we know how to do. Typical of American principles is the Truman Doctrine, which wasn't just an offer of aid to Turkey and Greece; it was a proclamation of the duty to protect free peoples everywhere against Communism. Then there was the "open society" element enshrined in the Baruch Plan, also typical of how this country reacts. Important changes in American foreign policy personnel—the departure of many of the Rooseveltian in-and-outers who had made the wartime alliance work, and their replacement by foreign service officers and military and civilian leaders deeply suspicious of the USSR—contributed to this response.[12]

How did the Soviets interpret an American reaction which was itself ambiguous? The Soviets obviously interpreted it as a challenge. The American scheme for an open international society, with majority rule and no veto, was seen as a grand design to suppress revolution and to subvert the Soviet Union. The Soviets naturally saw it as a challenge to their interests. What the Baruch Plan meant to them was that the United States would keep its bomb until such time as the Soviet Union knuckled under a majority scheme obviously controlled by the West. This was also the time when the Americans began to consolidate the western parts of Germany, when Communists were ousted from the governments of France and Italy. How did the Soviets react, following their interpretation of our ambiguous reaction to the ambiguous acts of the Soviet Union? The Soviets reacted with a considerable tightening of the screws. They mobilized the Communist parties in Western Europe in 1947-48 to go on strikes; they provoked a huge antibomb "peace" agitation in 1948; they established the Cominform. Inside the Soviet Union, they performed a similar tightening of screws, symbolized by the fall of Zhdanov; they staged—or helped—the coup in Prague, in February, 1948; and they established the Berlin blockade, which was essentially a reaction to American moves in Western Europe.

Now, whatever the implications of all these Soviet moves, they were probably not meant to be offensive. They were probably more, as Adam Ulam says in his book on Soviet foreign policy, an attempt to make the United States lose patience and heart, to drive a frustrated and exasperated United States back into isolationism.[13] We had practically promised Stalin that after the war was over we would go home. The United States, after all, had already demobilized, from about eight million persons under arms during World War II to less than half a million. Rather than moves toward promoting the Communist world revolution, Stalin's moves were attempts to show the Americans that staying in world affairs was going to be painful.

Ironically, only after Vietnam and the beginning of a detente did a long-expected and much-delayed isolationist swing in the United States reemerge.

How did the United States interpret these Soviet moves? Naturally, they were thought to be the justification of America's own vision and of America's old misgivings about Soviet universalism. The United States inferred from Soviet acts and capabilities to Soviet intentions, and reacted with an increase of pressure on the Soviets. Through a combination of power and universalism, the United States moved rapidly from Kennan's limited notion of containment, which was based on an assessment of the limits of Soviet power, and which would have been pluralistic, essentially nonmilitary, and transitional, to a wholly different policy—one symbolized, for example, by that famous document, NSC68, or by the Japanese peace treaty. United States policy was not pluralistic but hegemonic, in the sense that everything was to be under United States predominance; it put primary reliance on military pacts, presence, and support; and it became self-perpetuating, largely because the United States stuck to its universal vision—later christened "pragmatic" by Walt Rostow.

And yet, even when the United States reacted in this way, it kept trying to avoid a total militarization and division of the world. In the one place in which the United States did not react in military fashion—in fact, took its troops out—in South Korea, it thus provoked a power vacuum into which the North Koreans moved. The United States response to that action is well known. So even where the United States had not been consistent with its fears, there was a forced confirmation of its vision.

So much for the momentum. What lessons can one derive from this? Halle, in his book, talks about the interaction between the scorpion and the tarantula. The scorpion shows its aggressiveness toward the tarantula, but it merely reflects its defensiveness—its conviction that the tarantula secretly wants to kill the scorpion. And the tarantula naturally reacts by trying to kill the scorpion, thus confirming the scorpion's conviction that the tarantula is out to kill it. The story is instructive with regard to both the origins and the development of the Cold War. I think that it was a mistake then to attribute to the Soviet Union an aggressive, worldwide universalism, for one good reason—they didn't have the means for it. Whatever their dreams may have been, they had to adjust their ends to their means. Similarly, it is a mistake on the part of the revisionists to attribute to the United States of 1945 an aggressive economic and military universalism. To be sure, the United States had the means for it, but many of these means were not converted into power. The nuclear monopoly was not converted into political power, and never were the Soviets more active abroad than in the period when the United States had a nuclear monopoly. Nor did American actions really correspond to those alleged imperialistic intentions. The Baruch Plan, for instance, was not intent on depriving the Soviet Union of its enormous superiority in conventional weapons. It didn't even deal with this. The Marshall Plan, for all its self-interest aspects, was not an imperialistic design either, for it obviously aimed at the restoration of potential challengers or rivals.

Why, then, did each side so badly misperceive the other's intentions, and act on the basis of those misperceptions? The answer is to be found in a mix of specific features and general factors. Who were the two opponents? They were not just any two powers. The Peloponnesian War did not involve just any two powers; it involved Athens and Sparta. Similarly here, there was a revolutionary, if cautious, power pitted against a reformist, although confused, one. On one side was the Soviet Union, which had a long history of invasions, of disappointments and suspicions in the thirties, and which was fearful about its security. On the other was the United States, with a long history of oscillation between total noninvolvement in world affairs and involvement in order to save the world. Then, next to those specific features was the dialectic characteristic of any bipolar confrontation in history. It always seems to oppose two self-fulfilling prophecies. Here we find, as usual, the paradox of two largely defensive universalisms, with its three features. First, in this kind of dialectic, what is essential to each appears threatening to the other. Soviet security, interpreted in Communist fashion as entailing Communist regimes in Eastern Europe, seemed threatening to us. And the American vision of an open world, without vetoes or Iron Curtains, seemed threatening to the Soviets. Second, what each one may have regarded as admirably restrained on its part appeared ominous to the other. Soviet behavior in Greece and Western Europe appeared ominous to us; the Baruch Plan, which foresaw that the United States would ultimately give up its nuclear arsenal, appeared menacing to the Russians, because it was only ultimately that our weapons would be destroyed. Finally, in this kind of a confrontation, each one interprets the other's defensive moves as offensive. This is true partly because each expects them to be offensive (this points to the enormous importance of the images each had of the other). The Soviets saw the United States as a capitalist power, and therefore necessarily offensive toward a revolutionary power such as the USSR. We saw the Soviet Union not as a "normal" state but as the seat of a revolutionary movement whose purpose was to undermine the international system. Partly, each viewed the other's moves as offensive, because sometimes they were—sometimes, when fears are acute, defensive acts have definite offensive overtones, which only confirm the opponent's expectation. Thus, out of fear for Iran's independence, we pushed the Soviets out; and out of fear for their interests in West Germany, the Russians staged the blockade of Berlin.

There remains one last question—the question one always likes to ask. Was the Cold War inevitable? To a large extent, it appears to have been so. Some twenty years later, all kinds of people told us that it could have been avoided, if we had only had a somewhat more realistic diplomacy, if we had followed canons of moderation, such as not allowing power vacuums in important areas, and had not allowed ideological generalizations and escalations. Kennan, for instance, has generally taken this line, and has criticized the slant of the Truman Doctrine. This approach is, however, unworkable, partly because the givens had been provided by recent history and could not be undone—the power vacuums, for instance, and the presence of the Red Army in Central Europe, or the economic preponderance and nuclear advance of the United States—and partly because the precepts of Kennan are those of a moderate, multipolar system, in other words, a system in which powers are not ideologically in conflict and do speak the same language.

Given what the world was like, it seems to me, first of all, that intensification of the conflict was inevitable, if only because of the actual and potential might of the antagonists. De Gaulle's diplomatic techniques were often as brutal as the Soviets', but they created no comparable fears in Washington, precisely because his might was negligible.[14] Might creates opportunities—as we well know from Vietnam—even when intentions are limited. The presence of large Communist minorities in Western Europe was an opportunity for the Soviet Union. The possible power vacuum in South Korea was an opportunity. The facts that the United States alone defeated Japan and that the Western powers alone occupied Italy and half of Germany also provided opportunities for the West to exclude the Soviets. Even if one defines interests so narrowly that they are not necessarily in conflict, power creates interests in a broad sense. For a great power, security is a universal problem, which creates the temptation of camp building; and every great power has always believed that it had to increase its power to save the world. When one is strong, one's rival will always tend to jump from one's acts to one's capacities and to derive one's intentions from these.

Second, intensification also tends to increase without limit, because of ideology. Ideology is always partly a rationalization of great might. In modern history, many statesmen are elected—although sometimes it is the statesmen who elect the people—and normally these men are not cynical, but want to define their might in ideological terms. There is a human need to justify in one's own eyes, and in the eyes of others, what one does in terms of ultimate values beyond might. Moreover, each of these particular antagonists felt a need to offer its way of life to others, apart from any rationalization of its might. Hence, a dialectic developed, which was a combination of accurate perceptions—each party was aware of the hostility and of the long-range preferences of the other—and misperceptions as to what each side was up to in the short range.

The final contributing factor which made the whole process inevitable was the domestic styles of the two protagonists. Moderation was ruled out, not only by ideology and might but also by that style. The Soviet Union was led by a man who can be said to have had an absolute, cosmic distrust of everything that was not himself. We all know now, on the basis of more information than we care to have, what life under Stalin was like. Stalin needed the total subservience of everybody else around him, as was shown as much in domestic trials as in foreign purges. The war had deeply shaken the Soviet system. Domestic insecurity, the first concern, could not fail to have effects abroad (such as a tough policy of insulation). When Stalin disappeared, his successors had the problem of their own security. They did make some limited gestures of moderation, such as the Austrian peace treaty in 1955, but there were built-in limits to those gestures, because these men too had to succeed, if only to consolidate their weak domestic position. Success at home is never enough for a great power. In the United States, there was always an incompatibility between people like Kennan, who advocated moderate and non-public diplomacy, and the political process, institutions, and culture of the United States. What characterizes Kennan is his intense dislike of the whole American political system, essentially because he well understands that it does not make for the kind of cool cabinet diplomacy of which he is so fond. Moreover, the United States had to deal above all with insecurity abroad, for this nation, which found itself a world leader for the first time, did not know what kind of world it would be. This insecurity could not fail to have effects at home, where it expressed itself in extreme fashion, for instance, in the appearance of Joe McCarthy and in what his exploitation of collective paranoia did to various circles in American life, at home and abroad.

These are the reasons why it seems to me futile to look for one villain. If you like villains—and what American doesn't?—there are two to contend with. If you think, as Camus did, that in this world nobody is either entirely innocent or completely guilty, then the best explanation is that the Cold War developed between two nations which were partly villains and partly victims.

In the final analysis, perhaps the most significant shortcoming of the revisionists' counter-orthodoxy is that it is so much the mirror image of the orthodoxy. It merely reverses the black and the white, making the Americans the villains and the Soviets the moderates. The revisionists, like those holding the official view, look for grand explanations of a conspiratorial nature, although this time it is American economic imperialism rather than a worldwide Communist conspiracy that is the key. The revisionists, like their predecessors, oversimplify the history of others. (For example, the moment in Gabriel Kolko's book where I really had a sense of landing in a dreamland came when, at the end of the chapter on France, he explained that by October, 1944, the United States, which had long resisted the leadership of General de Gaulle, finally threw its support to him in order to suppress the French left. The French left, incidentally, got 67 percent of the vote in the election a year later, and so it had not been badly suppressed.) Finally, like the orthodox view, the revisionists' vision is somewhat abstract, vague, and too grandiose—it fails because it is too nearly perfect, because it refuses to take sufficiently into account all the little points about perceptions, intentions, misunderstandings, and just plain errors that I have tried to mention here. There has long existed this pattern of oscillation in American historiography; it has developed about World War I as well as about the Cold War. It is not up to me to decide whether this constant shift from one devil's view to another, without ever stopping in the middle, is the best way to political and scientific maturity.

Notes

1. See, on these points, Gabriel Kolko, *The Politics of War* (New York: Random House, 1968).
2. See Arno J. Mayer, *Politics and Diplomacy of Peacemaking* (New York: Knopf, 1967); and D. F. Fleming, *The Cold War and Its Origins*, 2 vols. (New York: Doubleday, 1961).
3. See also his essay, *Dynamics of Counterrevolution in Europe, 1890–1956* (New York: Harper Torchbook, 1971).
4. *Atomic Diplomacy: Hiroshima and Potsdam* (New York: Simon and Schuster, 1965).
5. Two excellent critiques of revisionism are: Charles S. Maier, "Revisionism and the Interpretation of Cold War Origins," in *Perspectives in American History* 4 (1970); and Robert W. Tucker, *The Radical Left and American Foreign Policy* (Baltimore: Johns Hopkins University Press, 1971).
6. *The Roots of American Foreign Policy* (Boston: Beacon Press, 1969).
7. See William Appleman Williams, *The Tragedy of American Diplomacy* (New York: Delta Books, 1962).
8. I have tried to describe the impact of America's style and institutions on foreign policy in *Gulliver's Troubles* (New York: McGraw-Hill, 1968).
9. See Robert Jervis, *Perception and Misperception in World Politics* (Princeton: Princeton University Press, 1976).
10. By Policy, I mean the sum total of vision, objectives, and policies (or tactics).
11. *The Cold War as History* (New York: Harper and Row, 1967).
12. See Martin Weil, *A Pretty Good Club* (New York: Norton, 1978).
13. *Expansion and Coexistence* (New York: Praeger, 1968).
14. Incidentally, even de Gaulle—normally more lucid about long-range trends—expected World War III to break out soon after the end of World War II.

11

Grasping the Bear:
Patterns and Puzzles of Soviet International Behavior

I

At a recent conference on current French affairs, the participants disagreed heatedly about the Socialist government's economic performance. Data and figures flew across the room like missiles. After a while, the chairman interrupted and said: "Ladies and gentlemen, this dispute is about facts: there can be no agreement."

This remark, paradoxical yet profound, comes to mind whenever one reflects on Soviet foreign policy, and on the way it is being interpreted in the West (I say the West, rather than the United States, because one finds the same diverging schools of thought in England, France, and West Germany as well). All we have are raw data—figures of weapons produced and deployed or of arms sold, the record of treaties signed, of troops sent into foreign countries, of diplomatic notes and of travels, of speeches at the UN or at Party Congresses, and so on. As in so many other cases, the data simply do not speak for themselves. Depending on how the observer connects them, on which ones are emphasized and which ones are played down, on the kind of relationship established between Soviet behavior and moves by the USSR's rivals, we get completely different stories (just as, when working recently on a chapter about the history of the nuclear arms race, five colleagues and I, while agreeing on the facts, clashed repeatedly about their meaning). In other words, it is the *interpretation* of the data that matters, and—even though it is supposed to be, and often actually is, "based on the facts"—it is the interpretation that determines the selection, hierarchy, and linkage of the data. Moreover, in the case of Soviet foreign policy, we possess fewer documents than those pertaining to, say, U.S. or British diplomacy: diplomatic archives are less accessible, memoirs are few, candid parliamentary debates are missing, investigative reporting is unknown, infighting (and its by-product, the news-leak) is suppressed. As a result, the role of interpretation has become even more important, and more *a priori*. And it explains why a sketch of Soviet foreign policy behavior is impossible to separate from a study of perceptions of Soviet conduct: the perceptions guide the sketch far more than the (supposedly objective) sketch breeds the perceptions.

It is therefore useful to begin by (1) distinguishing among the three principal schools of interpretation, and (2) listing the main issues of contention that appear in American discussions of Soviet international behavior.

None of the professional and sophisticated American experts falls entirely within the confines of any of the three schools; these categories are ideal-types, and respectable authors approximate, but do not entirely conform to, any one of them.

The first school sees in the Soviet Union a relentlessly expansionist power whose goal is world domination. At the service of this goal is a combination of massive, ever-increasing military might, and of modern methods of subversion ranging from support for revolutionary wars to the worldwide training and use of terrorists. Soviet policies of civil and active defense are interpreted, in connection with the Soviet build-up of offensive weapons, as showing a willingness to plan for, and to risk, general war, if the losses resulting from such a war can be kept limited and the gains expected from victory can be calculated as exceeding the damages suffered. This view could be called the model of implacable hostility and imperial designs.

The second school interprets Soviet conduct primarily in defensive and conservative terms. The USSR's dominant concern, here, is seen as the protection and consolidation of the Soviet Union and of its post–World War II conquests and gains, both against outside enemies and against internal revolts. The accumulation of military power is explained as a traditional Russian way of coping with insecurity: "If a little makes you more secure, a lot is better and best of all would be absolute superiority over all possible enemies"[1]—for nobody would dare attack you. Soviet actions outside of the Soviet *glacis* are seen as essentially preventive moves aimed at thwarting the designs or complicating the calculations of hostile countries. Whereas the first school finds in the contrast between Soviet military might and the weaknesses of the Soviet economic system a major danger for the West (since Moscow could be driven into ever more militant adventurism by these flaws), the second school believes that economic difficulties and rigidities, and the multiple obstacles to an effective *use* of military power abroad, account both for the substantially defensive nature of Soviet behavior and for the persistence of insecurity. The two schools also disagree completely about the nature of Soviet leadership: where one group sees a conservative, conformist gerontocracy, the other finds an elite whose legitimacy depends on the successful quest for successes abroad.

The third group—a broad "middle"—denies that the Soviets have a "masterplan" for world domination: preponderance may be a hope, but it is not the crucial objective that determines the setting of middle- or short-range goals. Nevertheless, the Soviet concern for security is given a far less benign interpretation than that offered by the second group. Even the "defensive" goal of security is, in fact, offensive to others, because the quest for absolute security must appear threatening to other countries and turn them into enemies; it thereby feeds and perpetuates at home a dangerous phobia of encirclement. This quest is also deemed responsible for a series of *offensive* moves abroad, aimed deliberately at weakening potential or actual rivals. Moreover, Soviet goals are not read as purely defensive, in any case. The USSR is not a *status quo* power; its objective is to change the "correlation of forces" to its advantage, to expand Soviet control and influence, and to reduce or eliminate the influence of its chief rivals in various parts of the world.

The main differences between the first school and the third lie in two areas. The third school views Soviet expansionism as essentially opportunistic—as the exploitation of opportunities often provided by local circumstances rather than created by Moscow. (Behind this difference one finds another one, in the reading of the international system: the first school's rendering of it is primarily "bipolar"—i.e., the U.S.-Soviet conflict is the dominant relationship, the key factor both in the global system and in the regional subsystems—whereas the third school sees greater autonomy in these subsystems and more of a tug-of-war between the push of the superpowers' contest and the pulls of local and regional circumstances.) There is also a disagreement about the domestic realities of the Soviet Union: internal difficulties are not denied by the third school, but they are also not interpreted as a potentially catastrophic spur to diversionary imperialism; rather, they are analyzed as creating serious dilemmas for Soviet military build-ups and external expansion. Nor are these internal problems viewed as so serious as to leave the Soviet leaders with no alternatives other than either the *fuite-en-avant* of foreign adventures or ignominious relegation to the "trash heap of history."

We are obviously at the level of very general interpretations, that do not concern themselves with every concrete event. Before offering my own sketchy analysis and puzzlements, however, I have found it useful to list the main points of contention, some of which cut across the frontiers of these three schools of thought.

1. The first one we have already touched upon: Is Soviet behavior offensive or defensive? As we have seen, there lies the great divide between the first two schools. The reply of the third school is full of nuances: Soviet conduct is seen as both: the USSR is trying not only to protect the post-1945 *status quo* in its imperial zone but also to upset it outside. Moreover, moves that are defensive according to the motives of the actors can all too easily be indistinguishable from offensive ones if the means used are threatening to others or if the results of the operation open up possibilities of further expansion (the invasion of Afghanistan comes immediately to mind).

2. A second question, also touched on earlier, concerns the degree of deliberateness of Soviet diplomacy. Here, it seems to me that the dividing line passes between the first school and the other two.

3. Is Soviet foreign policy primarily "regional" or actually "global"? Those who stress its regional focus believe that the Soviet Union considers its vital interests to lie in the areas close to the country's borders—Europe, the Middle East, and the Far East—whereas its activities in other parts of the world—Latin America and Africa, South and Southeast Asia—are seen as more episodic and less crucial. The globalists tend to discount this difference, either because of their belief in a sort of plan of global domination, or (if they belong to the third school) because they think that the combination of fruitful opportunities and growing military capabilities can create and develop important Soviet interests far indeed from the borders of the empire.

4. How cautious, or, on the contrary, how risky is Soviet behavior? Not surprisingly, the members of the first school tend to describe it certainly not as reckless (in this respect, but in this one only, they acknowledge a difference between Soviet conduct and that of Nazi Germany) but as quite audacious, with, at times, an addiction to brinkmanship (the comparison often made is with post-Bismarckian Imperial Germany). Both the development of Soviet strategic and intermediate land-based missiles and a number of episodes in Soviet foreign policy are cited as evidence. Members of the second school are more likely to stress Soviet caution—for example, in the Middle East or during the Vietnam War, or, currently, in Central America, or in dealing with Chinese hostility.

5. Is Soviet expansionism (whether deliberate or opportunistic) fueled by considerations of power or by ideological concerns? Both the first and the third schools are internally divided on this point. Some writers see Soviet conduct in terms of Russian "nationalism and great power urge,"[2] with ideology playing only a minor role (the Soviet Union's support for foreign Communists being strictly shaped by the power interests of Moscow)—certainly not a decisive one in the shaping of goals and the selection of opportunities. Others, who often point to Moscow's implacable demand for Communist party control in Eastern Europe, to the scale of Soviet activities in areas of little concern to the tsarist regime, and to the sophisticated use of methods of subversion, believe that the quasi-religious force and nature of Communist ideology remain distinctive and original features of Soviet behavior. One should remember that not only American historians but also statesmen were divided over this issue—with John Foster Dulles and Ronald Reagan stressing the ideology that guides and justifies the power, and Nixon and (post-1969) Kissinger bothered by the power but much less worried about the ideology.

6. How much continuity and how much discontinuity has there been in postwar Soviet foreign policy? I find little concern with this issue among authors of the second school, although it internally divides the first and the third. Some see a great constancy of objectives, a tendency to reenact almost mechanically the same moves, a very predictable stock of concerns and techniques. Others see distinct cycles and a more or less clear break between Soviet behavior in the era of U.S. nuclear monopoly and preponderance, and Soviet conduct in the era of nuclear parity.

II

I will now present my own views, without trying to write a history of Soviet postwar international behavior (an undertaking which I have neither the space nor the competence to complete). I will begin with what I consider to be the essential patterns, and then raise some questions that strike me as particularly intriguing.

1. Soviet behavior abroad is standard great-power behavior, with specific features that proceed from Russia's past and from Soviet ideology. It will come as a surprise to nobody if I state that the most obvious feature of Soviet conduct is indeed the quest for maximum security of the Soviet Union and of its gains from World War II—and (although not exclusively) the highly traditional, Russian, nature of that quest. What I mean by the latter is the belief that a preponderance of force is both the best deterrent of threats and the safest way of coping with foes if they fail to be deterred. This explains the very high level of conventional forces both in the Warsaw Pact and on the Chinese border; the creation of a powerful, modern navy capable of disrupting the other side's communication lines; the deliberate development of a nuclear arsenal capable not only of retaliation following an enemy surprise attack but also of destroying a sizable portion of the enemy's forces, military and industrial targets, and command and control installations in a preemptive strike aimed at limiting Soviet damage in case nuclear war appears inevitable or if limited nuclear strikes have already hit Soviet territory.[3] In the realm of nuclear weapons, the traditional approach to force has meant an unwillingness to settle for a strategy of pure deterrence (reliance on mutual assured destruction) and a preference for acquiring a capability for a war-fighting strategy, even though—contrary to what members of the first school sometimes say—the importance of the "nuclear revolution" has been duly recognized (to the extent of ruling out the "fatal inevitability" of war between opposing social systems). It has also meant an apparent conviction that the perception of strength required the eradication of any important numerical inferiority and, indeed, vindicated the search for superiority even in weapons that are hardly usable.[4]

The traditional nature of the quest for security has had three other effects. One is the important role played by the military in all decisions involving national security (for instance, arms control). Another has been the unwillingness to retreat from any of the territories conquered during World War II: the power to hold is obviously still seen as more "real" than the power to influence (others, or outcomes) at the cost of some territorial retreats. The third effect is more paradoxical and complex. The "communization" of countries such as Romania (in 1945), Poland, and East Germany appears to me to have resulted less from ideological proselytizing than from the quest for absolute certainty of control in countries where there seemed to be no middle ground between Communist power and anti-Soviet or anti-Communist forces (unlike the case in Finland, quite apart from the strategic difference in locations). However, ideology has played a "nontraditional" role here, not in the form of expanding Communism for the sake of the Revolution, but in the following way: the setting up, in the *glacis* of Eastern Europe, of Communist regimes tied to Moscow, not only by classical interstate links but also by links of subordination to Moscow's ruling party, has been an important way of consolidating the legitimacy of the Soviet regime *in the* USSR. As Seweryn Bialer has often pointed out,[5] that legitimacy was tested by the trials and established by the triumphs of World War II. The peculiar control of Eastern Europe—not only through superior force but also through the installation and preservation of regimes most of which, unlike that of the Soviet Union, are clearly not legitimate—is geared both to Russian security and to the Soviet regime's vindication.

The quest for security, fed by historical concerns about invasion and about the more subtle but corrosive infiltration of Western values, as well as by the ideological conviction of capitalist hostility and hatred of deviations, has also led to another constant feature of Soviet behavior: the fear of, and fight against, external penetration (except in the forms desired *and* controlled by the Soviet authorities, such as credits and trade). Hence, on the one hand, and in the most brutally vivid fashion, Soviet interventions to crush the possibility of new dissidence in Eastern Europe, following the defection of Tito's Yugoslavia. The repressions of 1953 (East Germany), 1956 (Hungary), 1968 (Czechoslovakia), 1981 (Poland) may well have been triggered in large part by a tight and nationalistic concern for the security of the Soviet *state*, but they contributed more than anything else since 1948 to U.S. hostility to the Soviet *regime*, seen as imposing its will and ideological structures on captive nations. On the other hand, that same fear of penetration explains the persistent Soviet hostility to schemes that would appear to legitimize foreign "spying" and prying into Soviet affairs: opposition to the Baruch Plan, the rejection of the Marshall Plan, and resistance to Eisenhower's open skies proposal—to any proposal for disarmament or arms control entailing large-scale and perhaps uncontrollable inspection, to any attempt to provide international agencies with essentially supranational powers—have been striking. If "national means of surveillance and inspection"—i.e., reconnaissance satellites—had not been invented, would arms control agreements have been possible? Soviet disarmament proposals have always specified a mere reduction or elimination of weapons in an otherwise unchanged world of sovereign states, whereas U.S. proposals have tended to subordinate the cuts in arms to the setting up of some central authority no Soviet veto could paralyze.

It is also, I believe, the peculiar Soviet quest for security that provides the main (if not the only) motive behind continuous efforts at keeping potential rivals weak, or at weakening hostile powers in the areas close to the Soviet Union—which happen to be the chief cauldrons of world politics. Preventing the recovery and, later, the rearmament of West Germany was the dominant concern of Soviet policy in Western Europe from 1948 to 1955. Fear that the deployment of U.S. intermediate-range missiles on West

German soil might some day allow the West Germans to have a finger on the nuclear trigger may well have been one component of Soviet violent opposition in 1981-1983—just as the desire to keep the Federal Republic away from nuclear weapons was one of the main reasons for the Soviet drive for a global nonproliferation treaty in the mid-1960s. Sometimes, it is the desire to preserve control in one's imperial zones that has led to the choice of what could not fail to seem an offensive move against the other side's own positions; it is clear now, after the erection of the Berlin Wall, that Krushchev's own Berlin crisis of 1958-1961 was aimed above all at consolidating East Germany, but the tactic—trying to force the Western powers to deal with the GDR over West Berlin—clearly threatened the Western position in Berlin.

The goal of weakening rivals, both in the quest for ever-greater security and as a normal great-power activity, explains a great deal about Soviet policies in Asia, the Middle East, and Africa as well. The bonds with Nasser were forged after Britain and the United States had begun to try to line up Arab states against the "Soviet threat." Later, the quest for allies in the Arab world (Syria and Iraq) remained a way of balancing the *de facto* United States-Israel alliance and of preventing Washington from becoming *the* indispensable outside power and broker in the Middle East, given Washington's links with both Israel and "moderate" Arab states. In Africa, Moscow has mainly tried to exploit retreats by Western powers: first in Guinea and the ex-Belgian Congo (with little success), later in Angola and the Horn of Africa. In the Far East, the fear of a repetition—on a far greater scale— of the Tito experience probably led the Soviets to try to hold back the development of Chinese nuclear power; the desire to weaken Washington's hold on the Western Pacific, obtained first through the occupation of and later through the U.S. alliance with Japan, must have been one of the factors in Soviet encouragement to North Korea in 1950 and in military support to Hanoi (the desire to have an ally on the southern flank of a hostile China being another reason). The U.S. alliance with Pakistan, and Pakistan's friendship with anti-Soviet China, led to the rapprochement and the 1971 treaty between Moscow and Delhi. It is no accident, to use *Pravda* language, that Soviet involvement in Afghanistan deepened following attempts by the shah of Iran, the United States' ally, to influence the policies of the Daud regime in Kabul. Again, it is impossible for the targets of such moves to see them as purely defensive, insofar as Soviet security seems in practice to entail insecurity, or weakened security, or submission for these targets as well as the extension of Soviet influence through the acquisition and support of local allies. Here, we are in a world shaped by the combination of two logics all too familiar to historians: the logic of a great power's definition of its security needs in quasi-absolute terms, and the logic of a bipolar contest, which always manages to impose on the main contestants moves that appear to result from such a definition, even when the domestic historical, political, and ideological reasons for it do not exist as powerfully as they do in the Soviet case.

2. A second constant feature of Soviet foreign policy is far less recognizable as a component of bipolar conflicts: the Soviet desire for a sort of condominium with the United States. To be sure, the members of the first school would see in this a mere first stage, a step toward world domination—indeed, recognition of the USSR as an equal by the United States would mark both a weakening of U.S. predominance and a legitimization of Soviet behavior. However, not all would-be hegemonic powers want to reach empire through the consent and acknowledgment of their main foe: usually, the road to triumph passes through its destruction—especially when the foe is not merely a rival power but a regime and social system condemned (indeed, doomed) by official ideology. Is it "nuclear prudence," then, that explains this feature? In part, certainly; but there is something about the Soviet drive for recognized equality that transcends the nuclear revolution, the (pardon me!) de-Clausewitzisation of total war: it has a cultural dimension as well as a historical one of long standing (like the mania of absolute security)—a profound desire to be treated as an equal by those who, traditionally, have been ahead in economic development, and who, in culture as well as foreign affairs, are still the legitimate granters of legitimacy.

There are two components in this Soviet drive. One is the determination to be recognized as an equal power by the still dominant nation, the United States. The problem, here, is the United States' double reluctance—in terms of power, since equality appears real only in the military realm (which it is therefore not in the U.S. interest to elevate further by treating armed might as synonymous with all power), and in ideological terms (given the repugnance of most Americans for the Soviet regime). Insofar as the Strategic Defense Initiative exploits U.S. technological advances and threatens the Soviets' position as a military superpower, Moscow's relentless hostility to its full development is not surprising: status is involved, as well as security. The other component is the desire to settle the world's problems—ranging from the fate of Germany to that of Israel or of South Africa—in partnership with the United States, and to deal with the chief rival at the expense of would-be challengers of both rivals' preeminence (China, West Germany, Japan, etc.). This desire has led to the Non-Proliferation Treaty and to the expansive statements adopted by the 1972 and 1973 summit meetings. The problem here, however, lies both in the unwillingness of successive U.S. administrations to put a formal seal of approval on Soviet interference in previously Western *chasses gardées*, and in the opposition of concerned third parties to leaving their fates to modern Metternichs and Alexanders.

Nevertheless, the Soviet drive strikes me as permanent, or rather as in eclipse only during the periods in which Washington seemed determined to blow up all bridges—the early years of the cold war, the early years of the Reagan era. Even Stalin, in his last year, dangled offers of cooperation in front of Truman and Eisenhower. Khrushchev (even if one remains unconvinced by Adam Ulam's thesis about his obsession with an agreement ruling out a nuclear West Germany and a nuclear China) clearly relished his visit to the United States and seemed to have aimed at dialogue and deals with Eisenhower and Kennedy. The détente policy that began, timidly, in 1963, and flourished in the early 1970s, entailed on the Soviet side—as Kissinger has documented it—a drive toward condominium, culminating in the statements of principles made at the 1972 and 1973 summits, and a quest for legitimization, culminating in the Helsinki agreements of 1975. It is not only in Mr. Shevchenko's recent memoirs that Mr. Gromyko appears as an enthusiast of a U.S.-Soviet partnership. Even in recent years, Soviet commentators have sometimes been heard to say that the United States is the only genuine interlocutor for the USSR. Talking to others is, thus, above all a way of creating disquiet in Washington, and of bringing the United States back to dialogue. Part of the problem has always been one of methods: given the American recalcitrance mentioned above, the Soviets have often acted as if shock tactics were needed to push the Americans toward duopoly (as in Khrushchev's Berlin and Cuban missile crises), or to pull Americans away from their own unilateralist predilections (weren't Soviet moves in Angola and in the Horn of Africa made, at least in part, in retaliation and warning against the exclusion of the Soviets from the Arab-Israeli peace process after the 1973 war?) But just as the German Kaiser's attempts at shocking the British into friendship and respect in the first years of this century had the opposite effect, the Soviets often missed their mark.

The two modes of Soviet diplomacy since the end of the wartime alliance have been either a return to duopoly or else, when Washington rejected it, a policy of partition and hostility often aimed, it seems, however clumsily, at pushing the United States back into the former. Obviously, a strategy of hostile expansion is costly, as well as often frustrating: one is at the mercy of one's clients (Soviet experiences in the Arab world have been bitter, and Soviet support of Cuba, Vietnam, Angola, and Mozambique has been expensive) and of occasions that may be few and far between. The ease with which the Soviet leadership appeared to have convinced itself that the détente policy of Nixon and Kissinger meant an American acceptance of a measure of condominium, the length of time it took Brezhnev to realize that détente was dead and the Politburo to understand that Reagan was very different from Nixon or Eisenhower indicate the Soviets' perfectly understandable preference for a policy of collaboration that would bring them economic blood transfusions, opportunities for influence abroad, lower vigilance, and greater diversity among their opponents, as well as some savings in military expenditures.

3. The second feature of Soviet behavior is clearly one that sharply distinguishes it from American behavior (even in the détente era, Washington envisaged no condominium). The first feature, the quest for absolute security, was partly unique (in its strong and multiple, traditional and "Soviet" internal roots), partly not (insofar as the bipolar contest itself has led the United States to a very broad, rather than selective, definition of its interests, and to recurrent fears of a universal Soviet threat). The third feature is one the two superpowers share. It is another characteristic of bipolar struggles:

insofar as each rival needs to marshal clients against the other, to deny clients to the other, and to prevent allies from switching sides, there occurs a subtle subversion of the hierarchy observable in the multipolar balance-of-power systems—the distinction between great and small powers. The weak now have ways of manipulating the strong, and the strong often find themselves at the mercy of the weak. This "systemic" feature is reinforced by other factors: occasional ideological solidarity, in the Soviet case; and a similarly ideological concern (but this time for democratic regimes) and occasional economic interests, in the American case. What this feature amounts to is, first, the ability of allies to extort support when they are endangered or in difficulty: Mao, in the early 1950s; Nasser, in the mid-1950s and again in 1969–1970, when he obtained advanced Soviet weaponry and Soviet advisers; Siad Barre's Somalia while it was allied to Moscow and Mengistu's Ethiopia after the reversal of alliances of 1977; North Vietnam during its war against the United States; Cuba in 1962; and Syria, in obtaining new Soviet-manned anti-aircraft missiles after losing its earlier ones in 1982—these are the best examples. Second, these allies are often able to initiate major operations of their own: sometimes with their "Big Brother's" consent (e.g., the North Koreans in June 1950; Somalia's pushes into Ogaden; the Communist coups in Prague in 1948 and in Afghanistan in 1978), sometimes despite Big Brother's ignorance (Nasser's nationalization of the Suez canal) or reluctance (Nasser's disastrous war in 1967, Sadat's crossing of the Suez canal in 1973, the North Vietnamese offensive of 1972, China's moves against Quemoy and Matsu); at other times, the small ally has been able to push Moscow into undertakings that had not been conceived of by the Soviets (as in Angola and Ethiopia; when Castro played a decisive role). Third, the Soviets have often been doubly at the mercy of their allies: when these were badly beaten or performed badly, thus obliging Moscow to choose between greater commitment and humiliating defeat (Nasser in 1967, Sadat at the end of October 1973, the Afghan muddle of 1979), and when these allies fully (Sadat, July 1972) or partly (Iraq in the 1980s, and Syria in 1974 and quite frequently in its handling of the PLO) emancipate themselves from Moscow's often tenuous hold.

III

1. At this point, we come to the first set of patterns that I have found intriguing and worth further discussion. I refer to the contradiction between the "vertical" pull of alliances (the call of "credibility") and the "horizontal" desire for co-management with the United States (or at least avoidance of major crises with the United States). Many of the Soviet Union's difficulties with its allies have resulted from the latter's sense of frustration, from their belief that Moscow did not provide them with enough support against Washington or a U.S. ally. This was certainly one of the many causes of tension between Russia and China in the 1950s. Castro was not pleased with the way in which Khrushchev negotiated his way out of Cuba after

the missile crisis, without any role for Castro, nor was Hanoi happy with the Soviets' advice in 1972. Moscow did nothing to rescue Nasser in June 1967. The attempts by Moscow at getting the United States to deal jointly with the Arab-Israeli dispute, and the Soviets' reluctance to provide advanced weapons to Egypt, led to Sadat's expulsion of Soviet advisers in the summer of 1972. In the summer and fall of 1973, Moscow tried both to warn the United States about the coming war in the Middle East and to supply Sadat with the means to fight it, and ended up distrusted both in Washington and in Cairo.

Can one detect a pattern in the handling of this tension, and argue that as the Soviets reached nuclear parity, they became more willing to put their alliances first? In support of such a thesis, one could point to Brezhnev's decision to resupply Egypt despite the humiliation of July 1972—both before and during the October 1973 war; to the Soviet moves in Angola, South Yemen, the Horn of Africa, and above all Afghanistan. On the other hand, even before full parity, Nasser had obtained Soviet support for his rejection of the Rogers Plan (a rejection that consolidated White House support for Israel's intransigence and thereby contributed in the long run to Egyptian dissatisfaction with the benefits from the link to Moscow). Nasser also prodded Brezhnev into sending missiles and Soviet personnel during the "war of attrition." Conversely, even in the era of parity, the Soviets showed remarkable prudence during the Israeli invasion of Lebanon and attack on Syrian and PLO forces, as well as in Central America. Clearly, although the contradiction arises again and again, the mode of resolution depends heavily on a calculation of comparative gains and risks that comes out differently in each case.

2. This brings us to a second issue: that of Soviet caution, particularly in handling the United States. The preponderance of American opinion—regarding Soviet tactics if not Soviet political and military strategy—stresses Moscow's prudence. Immediately after the end of the war, Stalin neither encouraged the Communist revolt in Greece nor favored a Communist takeover of Finland. He did not invade Yugoslavia following Tito's defection. He dealt with Chiang rather than with Mao about the future of China and advised Mao to do the same. He let the North Koreans invade the South but refrained from providing his allies with overt support. Nor did his successors come to the help of Arbenz in Guatemala. Despite the growth of Chinese nuclear might, the Soviets did not preempt in 1969. During the various Arab-Israeli wars of the 1950s, 1960s, 1970s, and 1980s, Moscow seemed more concerned with limiting Israeli gains than with helping its Arab allies win. The spectacular successes in Angola and the Horn were safe operations, insofar as no strong U.S. reaction was likely. From that viewpoint, even the invasion of Afghanistan was no breach of prudence. Moscow has been as cautious as Washington in the war between Iraq and Iran. Support for Allende, for the "progressive" regimes in Grenada and Nicaragua, for the rebels in El Salvador, has been verbal and vague. Finally, the pattern of Soviet military repression in Eastern Europe includes neither

Romania, following its assertion of diplomatic independence, nor Poland, where Soviet troops, both in 1956 and in 1980–1981, were used for blackmail, not for "restoring order."

All this is true. But it is not the whole picture. Some Soviet tests of strength were rather reckless, because they could easily have led to a military confrontation between the superpowers—the very thing both have clearly, and so far successfully, tried to prevent—or because the only way of avoiding a clash was a rather humiliating retreat. The two cases I have in mind are the Berlin blockade of 1948 and the Cuban missile crisis of 1962. In Berlin, as Vojtech Mastny puts it, "only the unlikely" (the air lift) "averted the possibility" of an open military clash.[6] In Cuba, whether one believes that Khrushchev was after a "quick fix" in order to close the gap between Moscow's limited nuclear capabilities and its rhetoric (the old Horelick explanation), or follows Ulam's hypothesis of a diplomatic gambit, or accepts Khrushchev's own doubly defensive apologia, one cannot help feeling that the world was put dangerously close to at least conventional war between the superpowers by a blatant disregard of the limits Kennedy himself had set with respect to Soviet protection of Cuba. One could also argue that, when the Soviets decided to build and then to MIRVe their heavy land-based missiles, and when they decided to build a separate arsenal of nuclear missiles aimed at Western Europe and at the Far East (the SS-20s), they deliberately chose to run the risk of a U.S. reaction that would ultimately leave a greater portion of their own nuclear forces exposed to counterforce strikes than of U.S. forces vulnerable to Soviet strikes.

3. This raises a third issue: a pattern of mistakes and miscalculations in the handling of several important powers. I am more impressed by the record of Soviet failures than by that of Soviet successes, which Americans, for complicated reasons, tend to exaggerate. Some of the failures derive from Moscow's inability to provide much more than arms to states that may have needed these weapons to emancipate themselves or to survive severe security crises but later find Soviet economic aid far inferior to Western help; this has been the Soviet predicament in Guinea, Ghana, and Mozambique, and part of the trouble in Egypt. But other failures have their origins in outright diplomatic mismanagement. Soviet objectives in Western Europe have been the prevention of West European recovery and consolidation, and the exacerbation of tensions among the countries of the half-continent and the United States. Again and again, Soviet tactics have had the opposite effect. The rejection of the Marshall Plan deprived Moscow of its best chance of influencing events in the West. The Prague coup of 1948, the Berlin blockade, and later the Korean War steeled the Western allies against the kinds of temptations Soviet diplomatic messages in 1950–1952 dangled in front of their eyes if they gave up the rearmament of West Germany.

The Soviets particularly mishandled their relations with the two biggest stakes of the postwar era—the defeated countries of World War II, with their biggest ally, China, and their chief rival, the United States. The Soviet transformation of East Germany into a satellite, the massive flow of German refugees from East Germany and Poland, the Berlin blockade, almost guaranteed the triumph of Konrad Adenauer's policy over that of Kurt Schumacher. Both the campaign against West German rearmament in the 1950s and the campaign against the Pershing and cruise missiles in the early 1980s backfired, because of too much pounding and threatening, and far too little finesse. The fact that each fiasco was followed by an elegant retreat does not mean that the lesson has been learned—only that the same bad tactics led to a failure that incites the Soviets to cut their losses. Japan has been antagonized by the Soviets' adamant position on the Kurile Islands and by heavy counterproductive threats about the effects of hypothetical Japanese rearmament.

The alienation of China was partly inevitable, given the divergence of interests of the two neighbors and the Chinese concern for autonomy and equality, and partly aggravated by a combination of Soviet paternalistic clumsiness *and* indulgence in the policy of direct dealings with the United States over issues (such as the nuclear one) in which China wanted to be a full partner. (The United States' refusal to help France become a nuclear power was less damaging than the Soviet *volte-face* of 1959!)

As for mistakes made in relations with the United States, three kinds appear prominent. The first, and probably most important, concerns the miscalculation of American reactions. If, as seems likely, many of Stalin's moves and probes in the period just following the end of World War II aimed at hastening the expected exit of Americans from Europe, they had the opposite effect. The Berlin blockade had a "devastating" impact "on the American assessment of the Soviet challenge" and led Truman to believe that Stalin's "goals, like Hitler's, were unlimited."[7] The U.S. failure to rescue Chiang made Stalin believe that the United States would let South Korea fall—another miscalculation, which led both to the activation of NSC 68 and to the U.S. campaign for West German rearmament. The renewed Soviet pressure on Berlin, under Khrushchev, strengthened Kennedy's determination to be tough (hence, in part, the huge U.S. nuclear rearmament) rather than weakening Western positions in Berlin. The deployment of missiles in Cuba was another colossal blunder. Brezhnev appears to have seriously miscalculated American reasons for détente, as I have argued elsewhere;[8] those reasons included neither resignation to a more unfavorable correlation of forces between the "free world" and the Soviet bloc nor acceptance of a condominium. Just as Dean Acheson's speech regarding the defense perimeter in the Pacific had not signified a decision to abandon South Korea, the U.S. failure to react to the Communist coup in Afghanistan in 1978 did not denote indifference to an actual Soviet invasion; the complete collapse of what was left of détente can hardly have been welcome to the Kremlin.

A second, related, kind of error has been the failure to understand the effects of discrete moves on the American mood toward the USSR (one finds symmetrical misjudgments in Washington). The invasion of Afghanistan ensured the triumph, in the Carter administration, of the hawks over those with more balanced views and prepared the coming to power of the Committee on the Present Danger. Earlier, Soviet moves in Africa, a brilliant exploitation of excellent opportunities that the United States was quite unwilling to match, nevertheless drew huge nails into the coffin of détente. Earlier still, the triumphant-spiteful launching of Sputnik propelled the United States into a space race it would ultimately win.

A third kind of mistake has been the frequent shortsightedness of Soviet positions. In arms control talks before 1985, the Soviet refusal ever to accept a trade between a weapon not yet built or deployed and a weapon already in place has led, on the one hand, to a far more uncompromising rejection of the Baruch Plan than would have served Soviet interests (in effect, it sealed the United States' nuclear predominance for almost twenty years) and, on the other hand, to the rejection of such U.S. offers as Carter's proposal in March 1977 of deep cuts (admittedly clumsy in its presentation) and the famous 1982 "walk in the woods" compromise. (As a result, Soviet offers of compromise on INF came too late.) It may have been equally shortsighted for Moscow to want so badly a formal recognition, by the West, of the inviolability of borders in Europe, at Helsinki: that principle had in fact been observed ever since 1945, and its consecration had to be paid for quite heavily—through the acceptance of formulas on exchanges and human rights that have plagued the USSR ever since.

4. A fourth interesting issue for discussion concerns Soviet goals in Western Europe. I tried to define the overall objective of the Soviet Union earlier. But there were several ways of preventing the consolidation both of Western Europe and of the Atlantic partnership. My own interpretation is as follows. First, in the period from 1945 to 1954, the Soviets showed considerable flexibility, or aptitude for ambivalence. While setting up a satellite in East Germany and contributing in many ways to the division of the continent, they nevertheless kept open the alternative of a sort of victors' condominium over Germany: it would have provided Moscow with at least a right of veto over developments in the Western part of the country and at most with the opportunity to prevent the rearmament of West Germany in alliance with the United States. In 1950-1952, it was the West that refused to be tempted by Soviet hints and notes about a reunited Germany; it wasn't until 1955 that the Warsaw Pact was established—six years after the North Atlantic Treaty, and following the London agreements on the Federal Republic's integration into NATO.

Second, regarding the subsequent period, I believe that Soviet policy has aimed at "maximum feasible misunderstanding" between the United States and its West European allies, not at the departure of U.S. forces from Europe: on balance, the USSR seems to prefer a (troubled) *status quo* in Western Europe over a change that could easily make the Federal Republic the dominant player there and could also strengthen anti-Soviet pressures in Eastern Europe (this is one of the many reasons for which I find the Brzezinski recipe for "transcending Yalta"[9]—a Western Europe with a lesser

U.S. presence and role—thoroughly unconvincing). Among the bits of evidence for this interpretation, I would mention the gradual disappearance of the ritual reference to a dissolution of the blocs in Soviet diplomatic rhetoric and Brezhnev's unexpected contribution to the defeat of the Mansfield amendment in 1971 (MBFR talks, so far, have done nothing for mutual force reductions, but they have done something to legitimize the predominant role of the superpowers in their respective halves of Europe).

5. A fifth issue pertains to cycles, or to continuity versus discontinuity. My view is that there is the same mix of continuity and discontinuity in Soviet policy as in that of the United States (American politics give a far greater impression of discontinuity, but the main goals and instruments have been remarkably stable). The constants I have suggested provide the continuity, but there are considerable variations as well. Note, for instance, the great difference in style between Stalin's policy of "anti-cosmopolitanism," forcible consolidation, and probes at the margin (Iran, Berlin, South Korea), and Khrushchev's policy of bluff, bluster, world pretenses, and ultimately unsuccessful attempts at combining activism far from the Soviet borders (Cuba, the ex-Belgian Congo, Laos) and superpower cooperation. The long Brezhnev era strikes me as an attempt both to replace cosmic bluff with the realities of military power that Khrushchev—a military budget slasher— had failed to provide, despite his boasts and threats about massive retaliation, *and* to pursue in a more disciplined way activism abroad (particularly in the Middle East, later in Africa) and dialogue with Washington (partly, at least, as a way of neutralizing China). The remarkable caution of the four years between 1981 and 1985 reflects, in my opinion, a certain disenchantment with the fruits and costs of activism, a belief that the United States, sooner or later, will discover that there is no safe or sane alternative to a dialogue, and the difficulties of Brezhnev's succession—rather than the success of Reagan's own strategy.

6. There is a related issue: initiative versus reaction. The Soviet Union, as a revolutionary power in the international system, is often seen as initiating challenges and crises. Indeed, many American commentators have criticized U.S. diplomacy for being too "reactive," inasmuch as containment entails a defensive strategy. And yet one could argue, first, that many Soviet initiatives were taken at the request of allies or clients—whom it seemed to Moscow, rightly or wrongly, more advantageous to help or unleash than to restrain and disappoint: Kim-il-Sung in 1950, later Nasser, Lumumba, Castro, Ho-chi-Minh, and so on. Second, some spectacular initiatives were reactions, blunt or brutal, to hemorrhages, such as the Berlin Wall and the invasion of Afghanistan (also a manifestation of that fear of unraveling at the borders, characteristic of the mix of Soviet security and ideological concerns in the *glacis*).

Thirdly, many moves were reactions to U.S. initiatives (have Americans ever sufficiently pondered the effect of *their* acts on Moscow?). The Prague coup came after the Truman Doctrine and the Marshall Plan; the Berlin blockade followed the decision on monetary reform in the Western parts of Germany; the Warsaw Pact was set up after Bonn's entry into NATO; the Soviet grand game in Africa, in the mid-1970s, followed the quasi-exclusion of the USSR from the Arab-Israeli settlements that Kissinger was negotiating. Above all, even if the United States, at times, underestimated the Soviet nuclear build-up, Washington often "taught" dangerous lessons to Moscow: McNamara's huge program of land-based missiles preceded that of Moscow; the Soviet heavy ICBMs seemed aimed at matching the U.S. bomber force; it was the United States that first proceeded with multiple warheads. Counterforce, because of the defense of Western Europe, was a vital element of the United States' strategic doctrine, before the Soviets acquired comparable means (and it was MIRVing that later allowed the Soviets to exceed, for a while, America's capabilities). The Soviet naval build-up aimed at providing Moscow with the same means of projecting power far beyond the nation's borders, a power that air and naval superiority had given to the United States. Fictitious gaps—the bomber gap, the missile gap, the "window of vulnerability" of the late 1970s—have spurred U.S. military efforts. And these, in turn, have often spurred Soviet ones.

7. A last issue concerns power versus ideology. On balance, I am struck by the role of traditional Russian factors (such as the passion for secrecy) and the logic of bipolar competition in the determination of Soviet goals, more than by the (undeniable) weight of ideology. A shared ideology has worsened, not dampened, the Sino-Soviet dispute in the 1960s. Opposite ideologies did not prevent pragmatic arrangements between the United States and the USSR. Where ideology matters is, first, in the long-term guidance it provides to Soviet external behavior—that is, in drawing attention to the weakness of Western positions in much of the so-called Third World, where the United States often blocks aspirations for social change and the USSR understands revolutionary phenomena far better than Washington; also, in ensuring final victory, because it is predicted by Marxist theory and promised by Lenin's praxis, and thus allowing Moscow to make tactical retreats and to wait for the adversary's blunders far more philosophically than if Marxism-Leninism had never existed. Second, ideology matters insofar as Moscow—in its own version of "credibility"—feels obliged to provide at least some help to regimes that take the USSR as a model and a diplomatic leader; and, especially in the 1970s, insofar as the Soviets deem it useful to "sell" to their clients the Soviet model of government. The "Brezhnev Doctrine," and its application in both Eastern Europe and Afghanistan, represents a blend of power and ideology: ideology as well as power require that "Socialist regimes" not be abandoned to deviationists or enemies; but power factors explain why no attempt was ever made to apply this notion to dissident China, and it is far from clear whether it would be applied to save Cuba from an American onslaught (it is rather clear that it would not cover a Communist Nicaragua).

IV

In conclusion, I will offer a preliminary evaluation of Mikhail Gorbachev's foreign policy and return to the three schools.

After a year in power, Gorbachev clearly appears to represent a new phase: for the time being, because of Soviet economic problems, foreign affairs are not the regime's priority—a major change indeed, for it *had* been a priority since Stalin's death. Domestic reform, or rather improvements without reform, is on top of the agenda.

No superpower can walk away from world politics, however. Gorbachev's first moves and speeches point toward restraint and show at least a rhetorical preference for reining in the arms race, though no drive toward retrenchment—something that the Reagan administration's own attempt at exploiting Soviet internal difficulties by raising the cost of Moscow's commitments in a variety of regional conflicts (the so-called Reagan Doctrine) would in any case make more difficult, by giving to retrenchment the appearance of retreat. These first moves and speeches suggest something rather similar to the domestic measures taken by the new leadership. On the one hand, there is a break with past rigidity, a willingness to correct some of the mistakes of the past—those of bluster as well as those of excessive stolidity. This has been particularly visible in the Soviet Union's relations with the United States. The various arms control proposals presented by the Soviets before and after the Geneva summit meeting of November 1985 have not only given Moscow an advantage on the propaganda front; they have also shown far greater flexibility and imagination than in the past, in the realm of deep cuts as well as on such matters as nuclear tests and inspection. Moscow has seized the initiative—in the direction of arms reductions, this time—and has shown the capacity to launch a long-term strategy, since the chances of a major breakthrough during the Reagan years are slim. Gorbachev's explicit condemnation of terrorism underlines the Soviet desire for respectability and may well be a hint of external restraint.

On the other hand, there has been no radical revision of Soviet foreign policy. Ideology has been neither demobilized nor demoted. The new tactical flexibility has not been matched by any willingness to make major concessions in the realm of Soviet security; the new foreign minister was unyielding about the Kurile Islands when he visited Japan, and the exploration of alternatives to the military quagmire in Afghanistan has so far not yielded any evidence that Moscow would accept risking a collapse of the pro-Soviet regime in case Soviet troops are withdrawn. The various arms control proposals are, at least initially, clearly aimed at putting the Soviet Union in a favorable position: the elimination of nuclear weapons would of course preserve Moscow's conventional advantages; reductions in offensive weapons would be made only if Washington gives up SDI; and the suggested removal of intermediate- and short-range nuclear systems from Europe is calculated to cause the greatest amount of turbulence in relations between the United States and its West European allies, since it revives traditional European fears of strategic "decoupling," would be carried out at the expense of British and French plans for the expansion of their own nuclear forces, and would leave Western Europe exposed both to Soviet conventional superiority and to long-range Soviet nuclear weapons. The disappearance of Gromyko from the Soviet diplomatic sky has so far meant neither a change in the Soviet foreign policy priority—that is, a dialogue with the United States (Dobrynin's appointment to a high party position confirms continuity on this point)—nor any new grand design with respect to U.S.-Soviet relations.

Finally, where does this analysis leave one with respect to the three interpretations of Soviet conduct? I disagree almost entirely with the first. The second one leaves out the offensive *methods* with which Soviet defensive goals are pursued and the offensive *effects* of the peculiar Soviet approach to security; it also leaves out the Soviet drive against the *status quo* (to explain it away as motivated by security considerations only shows that "defensive" is not the same thing as "conservative"). Am I, therefore, in the third camp? Yes and no: yes, insofar as the general approach is concerned; no, insofar as many of the members of that school are more impressed by the scope and successes of the "Soviet challenge" than I am. The growth of Soviet military might is indeed impressive. But the actual uses to which it can be put—for action or for intimidation—are limited. The acquisition of such allies as Cuba and Vietnam was more a windfall than a prowess; other allies are unreliable, or they represent liabilities. The break with China was a disaster that has not been redeemed. The Western alliance, for all its troubles and countless episodes of discord, remains strong. In much of the "South," the aspiration to independence frustrates both superpowers. The much desired accommodation with Washington has not been achieved. Opportunities certainly will continue to exist: in the Middle East, in Southern Africa, in places such as the Philippines or Central America, reliance on one's adversary's blind spots and blunders remains a sound guideline. But in almost all these cases, there are high risks of confrontation and risks of disproportion between costs and gains. For a multitude of reasons, the postwar world has been difficult for both superpowers. But a challenger whose regime, economic weaknesses, and limited role in all the arenas of economic interdependence constitute handicaps in the superpowers' contest is at a peculiar disadvantage.[10] Counting on and exploiting the other side's mistakes is not the surest way to success.

Notes

1. Mark Garrison, *The Roots of Soviet Insistence on Strategic Parity*, working paper for American specialists on the Soviet Union (November 1984), p. 6.

2. Seweryn Bialer, "Soviet-American Conflict: From the Past to the Future," in *U.S.-Soviet Relations* (Alternatives for the 1980s, No. 14) (Washington, D.C.: Center for National Policy), p. 13.

3. I have learned much from Stephen Meyer, "Soviet Perspectives on the Paths to Nuclear War," in Graham Allison, Albert Carnesale, and Joseph Nye, *Hawks, Doves and Owls* (New York: Norton, 1985), pp. 167–205.

4. I confess that I find far more similarity than difference between American behavior and Soviet behavior in these respects, even though the American emphasis on and definition of stability are distinctive. The biggest difference used to be in the concern for defense, a difference that remains in the realm of civil defense only.

5. Bialer, "Soviet-American Conflict"; Bialer, *The Soviet Paradox* (New York: Knopf, 1986).

6. Vojtech Mastny, "Stalin and the Militarization of the Cold War," *International Security* (Winter 1984-1985), p. 121.

7. Vojtech Mastry, *op. cit.*, p. 121.

8. See my chapter in Joseph Nye (ed.), *The Making of America's Soviet Policy* (New Haven, Conn.: Yale University Press, 1984).

9. Zbigniew Brzezinski, "The Future of Yalta," *Foreign Affairs* (Winter 1984-1985), pp. 279–302.

10. For similar conclusions, much more fully developed, see Régis Debray, *Les empires contre l'Europe*, Book 2 (Paris: Gallimard, 1985).

12

Cries and Whimpers: Thoughts on West European–American Relations in the 1980s

I

Can anything new or worthwhile be said about the relations between Western Europe and the United States? There have been so many diagnoses and prescriptions, so many warnings of crisis and sightings of turning points. And yet, something new is happening. To call it mutual estrangement would be too strong. But each side sees the other from a greater distance than before; each side seems to be moving away from the other. The reasons for this are partly revealed by the recriminations one hears in Western Europe, and we shall examine these complaints. But first, we must say a word about the West European situation; it is the background of the laments that are so frequently heard on the eastern side of the Atlantic Alliance, and also one of the causes of American grievances. Americans who take the time to think about their country's current relations with Western Europe know just enough about the latter's situation to be worried, annoyed, exasperated, or bored. West Europeans, on the whole, know much less about the situation in the United States, and do not appear to make much of an effort at understanding it. They select only those features that can be useful to them in their arguments against their domestic enemies (a classic French habit) or only those aspects that confirm their dislikes and strengthen their misgivings about America. After a look, then, at the West European situation and a discussion of the recriminations, I shall try to suggest what alternatives we face.

II

Western Europe has not yet resolved the identity crisis I wrote about twenty years ago.[1] Today it faces two distinct but related crises: the crisis of its attempt at unity, and the crisis of its industrial societies.

What used to be called "the building of Europe" is a field of paradoxes. Rarely have the foreign policies of the main West European states been so convergent: all of them have given firm support to the NATO decision of December 1979 to deploy American "Euromissiles" in several European countries; all would like to preserve economic talks and a political dialogue with the Soviet Union. Rarely have the economic policies of the members of the European Economic Community been so similar: all are trying to reduce inflation, to check the rise of wages and prices, to contain the costs of social security systems, to resist protectionist pressures, and to limit the size of budget deficits; all want to create conditions that will allow industry to modernize and stay or become competitive, even at the cost of very high unemployment. When one government tried—alone—to pursue a different policy of domestic expansion, the results quickly turned out to be so bad for the national currency, the balance of payments, and the country's competitiveness that it had to shift gears: Mitterrand had to move from Socialist reflation to Socialist austerity, from giving priority to employment and fairer distribution to giving it to the modernization of production and fiscal restraint. And yet, despite these similarities, the heavy vehicle of the EEC has gained neither power nor speed. Reality remains national, and (some would add: therefore) bleak.

To be sure, there have been some successful EEC attempts at coordinating social policies, some initiatives aimed either at reducing the burdens imposed by the decline of the steel industry or at launching joint research programs in advanced technologies. The Common Agricultural Policy has begun to reform by tackling the delicate problem of overproduction of milk. On the whole, however, two things stand out. One is that each nation wages its own battle against economic and social headaches—particularly unemployment—and looks at the EEC, at best, as a supplementary source of funds or as an occasionally welcome pretext for doing unpopular things (such as closing steel mills) by arguing that they were ordered by the bureaucrats in Brussels. More than ever, each country has its own way of coping with the common agenda, its own political necessities, rhetoric, and traditions, its own peculiar diversions that the neighbors find hard to understand (the school issue in France, the linguistic problem in Belgium, and so on), its own network of institutions and practices for industrial relations, its own constitutional setup and party system. There may be, in some respects, a Europe of businessmen: young people travel from one country to another as if borders did not exist, ministers from different nations but with comparable responsibilities meet or communicate incessantly. But the national systems simply refuse to merge.

Many reasons have been suggested: bureaucratic inertia; the fierceness with which governments defend what is left of their state's "sovereignty" when economic interdependence in fact deprives them of genuine autonomy; the multiplicity of electoral schedules and agendas; above all, the reluctance to give up national habits of decision-making and problem-solving (even when they only yield mistaken decisions and fail to resolve problems) in exchange for new institutional systems that nobody would know how to manipulate and that would become stakes in the battle for control. To this one could add the persistence of national suspicion or prejudices and the fact that in periods of rough weather—as in the past ten years—the citizens continue to turn, for benefits or blame, to their own governments.

The other obvious fact is the paralysis of the EEC machinery. Its financial resources, always limited because of the states' suspiciousness and needs, are now clearly insufficient, even for the tasks the members would like the Community to perform; but the states have not been able to agree on raising them. The EEC provides the spectacle of an organization that, more than ten years after the entry of a major member (England), still argued relentlessly about that member's financial contribution and, in effect, about the terms of its entry; of a political system in which the Parliament is both elected by universal suffrage and almost impotent (with the double result of frustration and occasional irresponsibility in the Assembly and of turning the election into a mere referendum on the domestic policies of each member state); of a set of institutions that spend far more of their members' energy on shuffling dossiers and deadlocks from one level to the other than on reaching decisions. The disproportion between the stakes—Western Europe's future—the means at the EEC's disposal, and the outcomes is overwhelming. And the fiasco of the machinery of the Treaty of Rome, only partly compensated by the survival of the common monetary system (which functions among some, not all, of the EEC's members), has now resulted in the decline of foreign policy coordination as well (the so-called political cooperation, which is juridically outside the provisions of the Treaty of Rome, appears comatose). Mitterrand's attempt at transcending inertia and bickering through a new treaty and a new agency for "political union" risks being more divisive than electrifying—what the French call a *fuite en avant* rather than a renewal.

The effects of these developments are clear. Much time is spent simply trying to pressure the formidable Mrs. Thatcher into conviviality. Since the handling of issues remains primarily national, the French misread the West German scene (during the long debate on Euromissiles) as if thirty years of cooperation had bred more ignorance than familiarity. The Italians, who in their speeches mention Europe more often than anyone else, continue not to pull their weight in the Community. Educational systems remain national, and the small European University Institute, stranded above Florence in its lovely renovated monastery, is still awaiting the day when higher education will be rescued from national bureaucrats, pressure groups, and routines. Above all, all economic experts lament that the continuing fragmentation of Western Europe breeds economic and social disasters: the "common" market is still riddled with barriers; the effort at scientific and applied research, while not lacking funds if one simply adds up the national programs, is partly vitiated by national "dispersion and barriers";[2] national governments, whose orders and purchases are vital for industrial development, continue to protect the "market" of public orders from one another, and private (national) enterprises often prefer to cooperate with extra-European ones than with other European companies. As Shirley Williams noted recently,[3] there are not enough European multinationals to compete with American and Japanese ones, and the EEC risks being "overwhelmed by the scale of operations required by some of the new technologies."

This brings us to the other crisis. One of the triumphs of the postwar recovery—this huge collaborative effort of Western Europe and the United States—had been the establishment of modern industrial societies in Western Europe, all of which, whatever their degree of egalitarianism, put their faith and energies into growth. They dreamed, more or less fantastically, of "pragmatic" politics, routinized industrial relations, and mass education. At worst, they seemed to move toward what Raymond Aron had called "querulous satisfaction," instead of ideological cleavages and class warfare. During the "thirty glorious years" (Jean Fourastié's term), the West German industrial machine was rebuilt and appeared more powerful than ever, while France and Italy finally underwent their industrial revolutions. Some of course remained skeptical about either the permanence of bliss or the triumph of economic rationality over all other forms of behavior. The eruption of 1968 (which remains even more baffling after the hundreds of volumes that tried to make it intelligible) showed that there were—now, or again—powerful, if confused and confusing, complaints about "modernity," "consumerism," "programmed living," and so on. But the real crisis turned out to be the post-1973 economic one, a combination of an almost classic recession (albeit in social and political systems very different from those of the 1930s) and of a technological revolution that challenged Western Europe's capacity to compete, just as its nations were being hit by the effects, first of the oil shocks, then of America's recession.

In a sense, this convergence of challenges has accelerated what the optimists of the sixties had predicted. The old working classes are disappearing (one reason the French Communist party, so much more *ouvriériste* than its Italian counterpart, is in trouble). They are being splintered: torn up by the evolution of the labor market; by the divergence in interests between the old, declining industries and the new ones; by the contrast between immigrant workers (who took the place of the old proletariat) and well-protected, almost unmovable workers; by the conflicting strategies of divided labor unions, some of which are trying to save every job, while others accept the logic of "industrial redeployment," and so on. To be sure, the welfare institutions of the West European states (so often sneered at by American conservatives and neo-conservatives) contributed to this dissolution by cushioning social distress and inventing a variety of ways of coping with unemployment, from retraining to all the tricks aimed at reducing the supply of labor—without either reducing private incomes or burdening enterprises or costing the state too much! It is difficult today for workers or unions to trigger proletarian solidarity. When the steelworkers of Lorraine, incensed by planned closures of factories, came to Paris to demonstrate, they marched alone. And none of the national political systems has collapsed this time under the weight and anger of the unemployed, even when the rates of unemployment reached 10 or 12 percent. This stability of the political institutions is a real achievement, one that refutes many of the arguments about "ungovernability."

And yet, the balance sheet is not positive. Socially, if class solidarity is down, piecemeal, querulous dissatisfaction is up: this succession or juxtaposition of group egoisms, professional demands, and fragmented greed, which either batters the state or tries to bargain with it—but in either case, squeezes it—is what political scientists rather ceremoniously call neo-corporatism. The workers of France's more advanced plants may not join the steelworkers or the automobile workers laid off all around Paris, but when the truckers closed down major roads, much of the public, thinking about its own sectoral interests, sympathized. Unions are often just strong enough to behave as nuisances in the eyes of employers or of users bothered by strikes, but they are neither united nor self-confident enough to be effective partners in social *concertation*. Moreover, economic hardships have created a new kind of grand (rather than "corporatist") cleavage between the immigrants and the natives—an issue eloquently described by Jane Kramer.[4] This adds to the tone of pettiness, of unideological anger and meanness (for it would be unfair to the old chiliastic ideologies to place them at the same level as present-day anti-immigrant racism).

Economically, many West Europeans are worried and dismayed by some obvious facts: unemployment there lasts longer than in America. This is partly because of greater labor mobility in the United States, which itself results, in part, from the existence of less extensive welfare systems and of unions that, unlike many of those in Europe, pay more attention to the creation of new jobs than to the defense of old ones. Another cause is insufficient capital for job creation in new technologies—in part, the result of heavier tax and social burdens on enterprises and of the state's need to spend so much on welfare.[5] Marina von N. Whitman mentions long-term demographic and social factors that could make structural unemployment pressures in Western Europe worse.[6] Another worrisome fact is Western Europe's lag in the new technological revolution: for every West European robot, there are two in the United States, three in Japan.[7] In the most advanced and promising sectors, few European companies are among the leaders—partly because their dimensions are too small. We are back at the vicious circle; the West European nation cannot compete because it does not have the proper resources and market, but the EEC, which has the right scale, has few resources and practically no policy. No wonder Mitterrand calls for a "European space for industry and research" (of which his project Eureka for space research would be a part);[8] but the very vagueness of the formulation shows that the solution, thus presented, is part of the problem.

The extent to which this lag results from deficiencies in West European educational systems is difficult to evaluate. It is true, however, that the proportion of young men and women who reach higher education is lower than in the United States and Japan, that European universities are often disconnected from economic life and produce both masses of dropouts and masses of people without adequate skills, and that contacts and exchanges between the national educational systems remain far too skimpy. One often gets the impression that European leaders and part of the elites are torn between a technological "discourse" that stresses the need to climb aboard the train of the new technologies, lest Europe become obsolete and irrelevant, and a cultural tradition that still despises the disenchanted world of profits, production, money, and merchandise, still dreams of art, prowess, the life of the mind for the mind's sake, and criticism of society rather than prosaic adjustment to and marginal reforms of it. This is, to be sure, one of Western Europe's glories. But reconciling its aesthetic-aristocratic inclinations with its modern economic and social logic has never been easy, and the tension once again acts as a brake. Nothing is more fascinating than seeing so typical a product of the cultural tradition as Mitterrand trying to become the champion of the new modernity: the emphasis on invention, creativity, and scientific innovation impresses as a skillful way of reconciling prowess and production, but by itself it can resolve neither the issue of unemployment nor the crisis of the French educational system.

III

The relevance of these considerations to the subject of European-American relations may not be obvious—yet it exists, because the West Europeans bring to their dealings with Americans a mix of feelings that the latter ought to understand better. The West Europeans know their weaknesses; they are masters of self-criticism, and they would like to be able to concentrate on these threats. Thus they resent calls to disperse their efforts further (just as, eleven years ago, they disliked Kissinger's call for a "new Atlantic Charter" at a time when they wanted to focus on building the European Community, after years of stalemate followed by Britain's troublesome entry). They resent even more American moves that in their eyes worsen Europe's diseases. And they know enough about, or console themselves enough with, their own successes—the survival of their political systems despite economic turmoil and social stress, the resistance of the EEC despite national divergences and overall heterogeneity, the brilliant performances of a number of European enterprises both in Europe and abroad—to be supremely incensed by American expressions of contempt. Rostand's Cyrano would have understood this: it is one thing for Europeans themselves to denounce and dissect their continent's decadence, but quite another for Americans— be it *Newsweek* or the former under-secretary of state, Mr. Eagleburger— to pick up the same tune. Moreover, the European situation creates one more factor of inequality between the two sides of the Atlantic. The Americans' specific grievances are merely aspects of a general diagnosis and denunciation of Europe's decline. A few years ago, some Europeans thought that they were witnessing a new "American disease,"[9] a shrinking of the virtues that had made the United States a model for postwar Europe. Political indecision, the pressure of short-term financial factors in industry, a "rising tide of mediocrity" in education, endless litigation, industrial decline, and so on—these were the new realities. Today, in Western Europe, whether or not one likes it, and whether or not one admires its effects, there is no doubt about America's new dynamism, competitiveness, and (so far) recovery. This gives to the Europeans' own recriminations either (usually) a certain defeatist quality, or else, in the milieus of virulent anti-Americanism, a quality of rage; in both instances, a note of hopelessness creeps in.

What do the West Europeans complain about? One can distinguish three categories of reproaches. The first, in the economic realm, consists of accusing the United States of harmful irresponsibility. In the days of Jimmy Carter, there was anger about American pressure for deficit spending in the Federal Republic, about the effects of Washington's "benign neglect" of a falling dollar and rising inflation. The United States, as the leading economic power in the world (not because of its position in world trade but because of the role of the dollar, of the American financial market and banking system) was guilty of not taking into account the external effects of its domestic economic policies. This is still—more than ever—the charge today. But now the villains are the strong dollar, the high American interest rates, and the U.S. budget deficit. Imports into Western Europe that have to be paid for in dollars—such as oil—have become more expensive, and while European exports are in principle helped by the high rate of the dollar, much of this advantage is wiped out by the drop in the capacity of developing countries to import goods from Europe: they "must engage in restrictive import policies because of their debt problem."[10] Moreover, America's interest rates drain Western Europe of capital and delay Europe's economic recovery by obliging governments to raise interest rates to slow down the outward drain of their nations' funds. The U.S. government's refusal to intervene to push the dollar down is seen as both an act of shortsighted selfishness and a contribution to domestic pressures for protectionism coming from American industries that do badly when faced by European, Japanese, and Asian competition. Finally, insofar as the budget deficit threatens the American boom, it reduces the chances for an export-led recovery by the European countries, and contributes to the drain of European capital. The American standard answer of the past four years—"in the long run, our victory over inflation and our subsequent recovery will benefit you all"—is seen as a mark of arrogance; but the West Europeans know they can only complain—and wait.

A second set of recriminations deals with the Reagan Administration's foreign policy. To be sure, there are more than nuances, not only between the views of European governments and those of opposition parties, as well as sizable parts of the public (the governments are less critical of Washington on the whole), but also among countries. The French political class and intelligentsia, for complex reasons that deserve a study of their own, have reached a broad enough consensus around the view of the Soviet Union as an evil empire, to coin a phrase; and a wave of pro-Americanism has risen as a result. This has been reenforced by a sudden revival of French anxiety about West Germany.[11] In the post-Adenauer period, the

French fear was about Bonn becoming too pro-American, that it would be America's second Trojan horse in Europe (after England), leaving no breathing space for France. In 1983 they feared that the Federal Republic was drifting away from Western Europe and the United States. They realized that France and the United States had a common interest in keeping the West German dachshund in the Atlantic kennel, away from the East German dachshund in the Eastern cage.

Nevertheless, the criticisms that follow are shared by most varieties of Europeans, the pro-Reagan as well as the anti-American ones. Even those who are worried by Soviet expansionism and military power have doubts about a view of the world that reduces it to the Soviet-American conflict and either treats all conflicts in terms of that contest or dismisses as irrelevant those in which Moscow and its clients play no role or cannot hope to gain. Even those who believe that the Soviet military buildup in Europe is not purely defensive, but is aimed, at a minimum, at political intimidation, and that insofar as relations with Moscow are concerned, containment, deterrence, resistance, and vigilance must never be relaxed (and who therefore found the first years of the Carter Administration baffling), believe also that the concern for the global and regional balance of power must be accompanied by serious efforts at a political dialogue with Moscow, at arms control negotiations, and at preserving economic links with the Soviet Union and Eastern Europe. (The grain deal signed by Washington after the lifting of the embargo by Reagan is seen in Western Europe as a shining example of U.S. double standards or contradiction between rhetoric and reality.) On all these points, Reagan's policies have been found disturbing. No West European leader, Mitterrand included, wants to endanger the limited but important results of the Soviet-West European détente. West Europeans realize that the Soviet-American détente is dead, and have often asserted that it was divisible; they know, however, that the European détente could not survive a considerable worsening of U.S.-Soviet tensions, and they are not reassured by the drift of superpower relations.

There are also more specific, if diffuse, criticisms of American policy in the Middle East and in Central America, along the same lines. In the Arab-Israeli conflict, a policy that minimizes or neglects the Palestinian issue and treats Syria as a foe one can only ignore or fight is seen as dangerous (and as ultimately good for Moscow), whether it is based on the notion of Israel as a bastion or on the myth of an anti-Soviet "strategic consensus." In the case of Central America, even those who share Washington's analysis of the Sandinistas and of the danger of Marxist-Leninist regimes worry about a policy that neglects the domestic causes of turmoil in El Salvador, hardens the Sandinistas through massive attempts at subversion, and locks itself into the dilemma of "covert and indirect military action or overt armed intervention"—as if these were the only conceivable alternatives to "bugging out." Many West Europeans—Socialists as well as Christian Democrats—know the scene well and have grave misgivings about either U.S. entrapment or American self-fulfilling prophecies.

Another political complaint embraces all the others, that concerned with American unilateralism. Many Europeans in the late seventies lamented Carter's indecisiveness and hoped for a more coherent foreign policy and a stronger America at home and abroad. They are shocked to discover that the champions of a stronger America, who are now in charge, have even fewer inhibitions about unilateral decisions, fewer inclinations toward a jointly decided strategy (which is not the same thing as consultations about enforcing an already set policy) than the leaders of the mighty America that dominated the postwar period. In order to explain this unwelcome surprise to themselves, West Europeans tend to argue that it is caused by the shift of demographic and economic gravity from East to West in the United States, the decline of a political class dominated by the WASP (and Jewish) Eastern establishment, and the ascendancy of the Sunbelt—but while these are all real, there is no evidence that the new unilateralism is the product of regional differentiation, sharper in one part of the country than elsewhere.

It would be even harder for many Europeans to face the fact that they are victims of a mental sea change rather than of a geographical shift. And yet the same "explanation" cannot hold for the third major American tendency that many in Europe deplore: the tendency away from the reassuring ambiguities of NATO's doctrine of "flexible response" (adopted in 1967 after years of U.S. persuasion and pressure). What many West Germans, for instance, accepted only reluctantly in 1967, because it seemed to them less reassuring for Europe than the discarded doctrine of "massive retaliation," is now desperately defended, especially in France, whose officials, in the early sixties, had found in America's change of dogma a proof of unreliability and an additional reason for the *force de frappe!* After all, NATO's post-1967 doctrine has been challenged first by perfect representatives of the old Establishment: the "gang of four" in 1982, George Ball and Irving Kristol in 1983, and Henry Kissinger for several years.

The realm of European security is by far the most confusing: not all Europeans charge the United States with the same sins, and they certainly do not propose the same remedies. It would not be wrong, however, to argue that many were able to rally around "flexible response," insofar as it did not seem to require too vast an effort at conventional defense *and* appeared to assure peace. The threat of an American first use of nuclear weapons was believed sufficient to deter the Soviets from either conventional or nuclear attack in a world in which the use of atomic weapons was likely to lead to "mutual assured destruction."

What West Europeans are still in the process of discovering is that the fools' paradise of peace through the threat of total destruction is being undermined by three developments. Technology provides each superpower with counterforce weapons that threaten the vulnerable nuclear forces of the other side: in a crisis, whereas invulnerable countercity weapons (or tactical weapons with limited counterforce capabilities) seemed to ensure "crisis stability," each side now has potent weapons it has reasons to want to use first, before it loses them to an enemy strike. Moreover, the precision of counterforce weapons—and their abundance—may encourage the military and statesmen alike to believe that nuclear wars can be fought and kept limited—for instance, in Europe. Conversely, the fear of crisis instability and doubts about the possibility of controlling a nuclear conflict create pressures for giving up nuclear threats altogether (especially since, in an age of parity, they appear like a bluff—who would really want to initiate a suicidal strike?) and for reserving nuclear weapons for the deterrence of nuclear attacks only, at most. Consequently, the superpowers ought to fight only conventional wars, if at all.

All three possibilities scare West Europeans, for all three spell doom for them. To many who have been demonstrating noisily, the introduction by the United States of rather vulnerable "Euromissiles," capable of either performing "decapitating" strikes or of hitting Soviet missile silos, was seen not as a reassuring way of buttressing nuclear deterrence nor as a way of proving to the Soviets that the defense of Western Europe is "coupled" to that of the United States, but as a reckless contribution to crisis instability—turning Western Europe into a target for nuclear preemptive attack. Some even thought, despite all reasonable arguments to the contrary, that these deployments might somehow allow the superpowers to keep a nuclear war limited to Europe. (Although if the United States wanted to spare the Soviet Union, it did not need to install missiles capable of hitting Russia; still, could one ever be sure that a Soviet nuclear attack on the "Euromissiles" only would be followed by a U.S. attack on the territory of the Soviet Union?) Others still—those who had asked for and supported the deployments—were deeply disturbed by American criticisms of the first-use strategy and by calls for giving up not only the use of nuclear weapons, but the threat of using them against a Soviet conventional attack as well. Had these Americans forgotten the merits of creating uncertainty for the potential aggressor? If Americans argued that the Soviets could anyhow never be sure that NATO would not resort to nuclear weapons rather than accept conventional defeat, and that this sufficed to preserve nuclear deterrence, why, then, repudiate the threat explicitly, and thereby either reduce the Soviets' margin of doubt or confuse them into taking high risks? Thus the missile deployments undertaken by the Americans brought home to many Europeans the ghastly possibility of nuclear war that technological developments on *both* sides had theoretically created—and led them to blame the Americans for it. Those Europeans who thought that these new deployments would, on the contrary, consolidate nuclear deterrence which Soviet deployments had, in their opinion, weakened, were aghast when Americans suggested that extended nuclear deterrence was no longer pausible and must be limited to the case of enemy nuclear attacks: Weren't Americans taking back with one hand what they had begun to give with the other?

Americans, it seems, were being accused both of being nuclear pyromaniacs and of getting cold feet about nuclear deterrence. It was hard for them to realize that these conflicting charges amounted to one common, central complaint: "*You* are undermining a reassuring notion of nuclear deterrence that has allowed us to live and do business in peace." But even if they had understood this more clearly, they would still have resented it. For in their eyes, of course, it was not America that was undermining the old strategy and killing the dream, but the evolution of technology, of the nuclear balance, and above all, of the Soviets, who had relentlessly striven first for parity and then for counterforce strategic and intermediate weapons that the United States itself did not have—and thus for some form (meaningful or not, but who could tell?) of superiority.

IV

Since the beginning of what has turned out to be their most lasting and entangling alliance, Americans have resented European complaints. They have pointed out that they were providing the main ingredients of Western Europe's security, after having provided for its economic recovery. The grand contest between Washington and Charles de Gaulle in the sixties produced profound bitterness among American officials exasperated by the General's casual charges about America's great power imperialism and unreliability. West European questioning of America's reliability in the realm of defense has always provoked angry answers. The United States, after all, still has almost three hundred thousand men in Europe thirty-five years after the installation there of divisions nobody thought permanently fixed, to say nothing of the several thousand American nuclear warheads there.

Today, however, American complaints are not just reactions to their allies' accusations of laments. There is a kind of global indictment of Western Europe's behavior, beliefs, and evolution. Here, also, one can distinguish three groups of recriminations. The first has to do with the shift in America's global priorities. From 1939 to not so long ago, Western Europe was the privileged continent—the highest foreign priority. Even though the Second World War began for the United States when Japan attacked in the Pacific, the European front received precedence. The Marshall Plan and the North Atlantic treaty demonstrated the importance Washington attached to Europe's economic recovery and security. The community of values was celebrated and defended. Today, many Americans believe that other parts of the world require greater attention than Western Europe. U.S. trade with countries of the Pacific now exceeds its trade with Europe; Japan has become the principal competitor—indeed, it has overtaken the United States in some important areas of technological innovation. In the realm of security, it is, paradoxically, Europe's very stability that drives attention away from it toward the multiple troubles of the Persian Gulf and the Middle East, and toward the new regional strategic system that has emerged in Northeast Asia. There, the Soviets have accumulated troops and SS20s; the Chinese are continuing their efforts at defense: the Japanese are increasing their own; and the United States is reenforcing its military presence—including sea-launched cruise missiles. Now, Central America has been declared a vital area, part of the U.S. "front yard."

The problem of priorities both affects and stems from American views of Europe in two respects, First, this shift is linked not only to a shift in perils and opportunities, but also to a judgment about Europe's decline. Some see it primarily in economic terms: the West German miracle is over, Western Europe in general has missed the train of the new technological revolution and has let it be driven off by Japanese and Americans, thus condemning itself to becoming an economic dependent. Western Europe represents the past, it will be a museum, not an engine. Others go further in their indictment and blame the West Europeans' social systems, the sterility of their higher education, the weight of their welfare institutions, the excessive and clumsy role of the state, and the rigidities of labor unions. Americans, it is well known, do not like losers, and today, Western Europe looks like one. The apparent inability to put the recession behind them, the sluggishness of their economies, and spectacular labor troubles in Britain and even in the Federal Republic contrast with Japan's dynamism—despite the oil shocks and the need to import every raw material—and with America's own classically brutal way of overcoming its economic troubles.

Second, Western Europe seems to be "turning inward" and refusing to behave as a set of countries with global interests or ambitions. It is their apparent refusal to support the United States in the other parts of the world that irritates Americans most. "We are protecting you; where are you when we need you?" The issue of NATO's role in areas beyond the geographical scope of the treaty was always a source of discord, but it mattered less when crises in those areas were discrete events. When most of the crises occur outside the Alliance's range, the debate cannot help but heat up. If West Europeans appear to hide between the lines of the treaty, why should they expect to be treated as anything but regional powers? Furthermore, if they leave the main burden of policing the world to the United States, why should they expect Washington to treat the size of American deployments in Europe as untouchable? To be sure, the Japanese have not shown much greater enthusiasm for helping the United States in the Middle East, but they are not really expected to: the Middle East is far from Japan, and that country's first duty as an ally of the United States is in the Pacific, whereas Western Europe is close to the Middle East and often reminds Washington of its experience in, and ties with, the countries of that area. And the Japanese usually refrain from criticizing Washington, whereas the West Europeans do not. This is particularly grating with respect to the Persian Gulf, where many Americans—including presidential candidates—believe that they are primarily defending their allies' vital interests, and with respect to Central America, a zone traditionally covered by the Monroe Doctrine as interpreted by Washington. Kissinger's remark[12] about the allies' "rush to condemn our actions in Grenada" is characteristic: "They could hardly have wanted us to fail . . . rather they must have assumed that their actions were irrelevant and costless," a way of gaining favor with "Third World radicals abroad." Of course, the allies did not want the United States to *fail*; they wanted the United States not to *try*. But in the eyes of Americans, not trying meant resignation to losing, another form of Europe's addiction to "elegant failure" or graceful retreats.[13]

Thus Americans look with some amusement at the recent discovery by their European allies of the growing importance of Japan and of the new industrializing countries of Asia—in France, the existence of a second ocean has suddenly burst upon the consciousness of the elites; and they look with some indignation at the West Europeans' way of preserving the right to criticize the driver while they refuse to share the driving.

The second category of recriminations brings us back to Western Europe's own security. Not everyone in America who thinks about Western Europe believes that the allies are engaged in "self-finlandization." Interestingly enough, the charge, or suspicion, can be found most frequently among Americans of European origin who have not quite recovered from the shocks of the 1930s—European appeasement, xenophobia, anti-Semitism, and occasional enthusiasms for totalitarian experiments. Nevertheless, the reluctance of practically all the allies to join the United States, since the watershed moment of the Soviet invasion of Afghanistan, in sanctions against Moscow, or against Jaruzelski's Poland, the way in which so many politicians seemed to want to preserve Europe's détente with Moscow from being contaminated by the superpowers' contest elsewhere, seemed to many Americans a mark of blindness and at least a predisposition to appeasement. The support provided by the key governments in London, Rome, and Bonn for the Euromissile deployments and, above all, the unexpected and spectacular endorsement of this policy by Mitterrand, have somewhat assuaged American fears. But in the smaller West European countries, divided governments have shown no comparable firmness; and some of the leaders, especially in Italy, have at times signaled that they would not mind compromises with Moscow that Washington would certainly find obnoxious. Moreover, many of the so-called pacifists or neutralists who have campaigned against deployment, particularly in West Germany, have both drafted a general, sweeping indictment of American society, culture, and political behavior (the charges being all too familiar to American ears, although they used to come more from France than from the Federal Republic: the harshness of capitalism; the treatment of blacks, Indians, and the poor; the commercialism of cultural life; the corruption of politics by money; the military-industrial complex; American imperialism in the Third World; the ravings of anticommunism, and so on) *and* developed a benign interpretation of the Soviet Union as a conservative, somewhat stolid, status-quo power whose arms buildup is a defensive reaction to Western might.[14] This current, whose importance may well have been exaggerated by the American media (but which has deeply shaken the French as well), has of course not helped Europe's image as a reliable ally.

Specific strategic disagreements have sharpened the perception of the West Europeans as demanding and whining free-riders. In the realm of nuclear weapons, both varieties of West European criticisms have provoked indignation. On the one hand, the apparent blindness of the "pacifists" to the threat of the SS20; their tendency to emote only about America's middle-range missiles but not about the Soviets'; their argument about the United States forcing the Pershing II and cruise missiles on Europe (whereas the process was initiated by Helmut Schmidt); their insulting charge about Washington planning a nuclear war limited to Europe—all of this has exasperated those in the United States who had decided to meet Schmidt's fear by sending the missiles, even though they themselves did not believe all of the arguments developed in West European strategic circles about the military importance of these weapons or about how much they were needed to "recouple" European and American security.[15] Many average Americans did not clearly perceive the fact that those Europeans who were noisily rejecting the missiles were not the same as those who had asked for them: the latter were officials; the former, members of the opposition or ordinary citizens. This (generally mistaken) view of European fickleness was reenforced by the spectacle of the German SPD's slide from Schmidt to the left.

On the other hand, those West Europeans who continued to support the deployments, particularly the French, and who shared American annoyance with the "pacifists," predominantly seemed to cling to the idea that only the threat of a first use of American nuclear weapons by NATO stood between the quasi-certainty of peace and a high risk of war.[16] And the number of informed Americans who now believe in repudiating a first-use policy—openly or de facto—has grown spectacularly. There is a continuum, from Robert McNamara's precise demonstration of the intolerable likely effects of a first use, to Kissinger's statement that "the growth of Soviet strategic forces deprived general nuclear war of much of its credibility" (and while he still argues for trying to find some "rational military objective" to nuclear strategy, he has not indicated which), to Irving Kristol's merciless warning to the Europeans not to expect Americans to commit suicide for them, or to George Ball's equally blunt statement that no American president would actually order a first use.[17] The West European fetishistic reliance on such a threat strikes many Americans as either an ostrichlike stance, based on a refusal to look at the evolution of the nuclear balance and of nuclear technology, or else an implicit questioning of the deterrent effect of American conventional and nuclear forces on the Continent. Moreover, they note that the only nation that is being asked to risk suicide for others is the United States: the French, who are so upset about no first use, have never offered to use their nuclear weapons first in case of a Soviet attack on West Germany.

If the threat of mutual suicide is no longer credible, the time has come to adopt a more sensible strategy. But, here again, a dialogue of the deaf has unfolded. Some American strategists believe that such a strategy could have a nuclear component, in the form of accurate discriminating counterforce weapons. But most Europeans (and many Americans as well) doubt that such a war could be controlled.[18] Many Europeans in particular still tend to believe that a threat of mutual destruction is a far more credible deterrent than a threat of counterforce nuclear war limited in scope: if this threat fails to deter, the strategy would ensure the destruction of Europe. Most Americans, however, seem to be turning away from any nuclear strategy toward a reenforcement of conventional armies in Europe. They ask their allies whether they do not understand that, should war come, a conventional one would be, for all its horror, preferable to a nuclear holocaust—and they are incensed at the Europeans' negative answer. What the Europeans know is that a conventional war would destroy them and leave America intact; and what they believe from history is that conventional forces are not a very reliable deterrent. Americans think that the combination of a conventional effort and the unavoidable risk of nuclear escalation would provide a sufficient deterrent against aggression. The West Europeans doubt it. Their interlocutors, who doubt that the *Soviets* could doubt it, therefore translate West European objections into a pure and simple refusal to do and pay more for a sensible strategy and a modern defense. West Europeans argue that NATO could never match Soviet conventional forces. Americans reply that you do not have to match in order to deter, or even to prevent the foe from winning (indeed, he will not attack unless he is reasonably certain he can win quickly). Again, the allies' refusal to accept this cheerful view is seen as a pretext for sticking to a strategy that saves them from further efforts and leaves the most fateful decisions to Washington.

There are, of course, Europeans who either sympathize with American arguments or understand that they signal an irreversible shift; and they recognize, therefore, the need for strengthening conventional defense. But they add that, precisely because its deterrent power is dubious, and Europe's objective is not to win if war comes, but to maintain peace, such an effort must be accompanied by attempts to improve relations with Moscow. Many Americans see in this plea another escape into wishful thinking. Altogether, the West Europeans' reluctance to think through what should be done if deterrence fails, their way of clinging to various methods—all dubious—for ensuring the permanent success of deterrence, strike many Americans as another proof of abdication from responsibility. And to some, there is only a difference in degree, not in kind, between the pacifists who dream of an all-European security system, or of neutrality à la Sweden or Switzerland, and governments that seem to believe in perpetual cheap peace, that fall behind NATO's schedule of conventional improvements, and that often fail to "meet head-on the disturbing trends toward pacifism and neutralism in their countries."[19] The Nunn Amendment of June 1984, which ties the size of American forces in Europe to that of the allies' efforts in conventional defense, is an important warning shot.

A third group of complaints concerns Western Europe's apparent inability to meet the challenges of the last years of the century. It used to be the subject of an experiment that Americans passionately favored almost to the point of embarrassing their allies: the experiment in transcending the nation-state, in building a community with a single market, central institutions, and a common determination to bury past quarrels. The very pragmatism of Jean Monnet's *démarche*, his art of applying to Europe the lessons he had derived from his American experiences, delighted his many friends in Washington. To some, the Europeans' capacity to create a United States of Europe based on a functional-federalist model became a test of the allies' vitality and vision. American enthusiasm provoked de Gaulle's distrust ("If they want it so badly, can it be good for France and Europe?"). His own *démarche*, in turn, provoked American hostility. But there was still hope that the march toward unity would resume after his departure.

His exit and his death have only made more obvious the deeper reasons for the failure of the dream. Already when Nixon and Kissinger came to power, skepticism in official Washington replaced earlier proselytizing. The new leaders believed neither in the chances for West European unity nor in the necessary convergence of interests between the EEC and the United States, especially in economic and monetary affairs or in the Third World. Skepticism has been gradually followed by a mix of indifference and contempt. In universities, for instance, interest in the complexities of European economic integration, legal harmonization, and institutional development has declined drastically. And those who watch closely the policy spectacle have been dismayed by the mix of acrimony and cowardice displayed by the EEC's members at the time of the oil embargo; by the Community's squabbling over the price of milk and Mrs. Thatcher's money; by its protracted reluctance to allow Spain and Portugal to join because of the determined opposition of small but powerful farming interests; by the paralysis of the EEC's institutions and the splits engendered by attempts at overcoming it; by the foreign ministers' habit of joint deploration and of giving advice without committing means. This brings us back to the issue of Europe's priority: Why grant it to a group of people who remain, of course, most important as a stake in the global contest, but who have failed to behave as if they wanted to become major actors again?

V

Writers who study European-American relations face a predicament of their own. They tend to highlight the disagreements and misunderstandings, and in recent years, they have often presented a diagnosis of very serious, if not terminal, illness—after which they offer either grand schemes devoid of any chance of success, precisely because the disease is not sufficiently advanced to induce the patients to try a drastic new treatment (and, indeed, also because the patient often fears that the cure might kill him off), or else placebos that, given the seriousness of the disease, appear inadequate.

I share the suspicion of grand designs; nostalgia for the postwar days of political creativity and community-building will not help us out this time. Two designs are currently being proposed. The first is a revamped version of the call for a "new Atlantic Charter" made by Kissinger in his "year of Europe" speech. Recently, both he and his old friend Helmut Schmidt have called for "a new grand strategy."[20] But there are interesting nuances. The former chancellor wants it, so to speak, on European terms. It must include economics—and when he speaks of "the global economic conduct" of the partners, it is rather clear that the curbs on inevitable "self-serving interests" would affect the United States above all. He also asks for an overall approach to the Soviet Union, one that would aim strictly at equilibrium in the realm of arms and, "above all," entail a diplomacy of arms limitation to serve the balance. He makes it clear that the Soviets in other parts of the globe would remain primarily America's problem. None of this quite fits the mood of the Reagan Administration or indeed of the American people. Moreover, he acknowledges the profound differences among the West European countries; he criticizes the Americans for tending "to overlook the controversy and antagonism, as well as the numerous speech barriers, that have persisted for more than a thousand years," and the "differences in political status" among European powers. It is therefore not too surprising to find Kissinger presenting his suggestion of a global strategy, with an agreed-upon "optimum division of responsibilities," as the *least* likely outcome of any reexamination of the Alliance. To be candid, the Americans want helpers rather than partners, and are more reluctant than ever to commit themselves to a set of imperatives and restraints that would have to be managed jointly. They want the Europeans to share the driving, but not to share in the decision about the car's direction. And the Europeans, both because they know or suspect this, and because they have no great desire for global responsibilities anyhow—fearing that even in an honest attempt at defining them jointly, the United States would prevail—ultimately prefer the combination of freedom of (in)action plus recriminations about U.S. behavior.

The other grand design is more limited: it is an answer to West European fears in the realm of security and takes the form of suggestions about a common West European defense. This has become fashionable again; the French want to reactivate the one organization in Western Europe that has jurisdiction over defense questions, the West European Union. But the more one looks into the issues, the fuzzier the talk appears, for excellent reasons. No West European official—Mitterrand has been especially clear on this point: an important precision, coming from the most independent-minded member state—wants a West European defense entity to be a substitute for the Atlantic Alliance. Thus it can only be either within NATO, or next to America's forces in Europe. The United States would therefore retain its role as the "pacifier" of Europe.[21] But the functional scope of the West European defense entity remains difficult to imagine. If it deals with conventional defense only, the heart of the disagreements with the United States would remain untouched, since they concern the place of nuclear weapons in the Alliance's strategy. Even in the conventional domain, two obstacles exist. One is the permanent American preference for an alliance that buys its weapons primarily in the United States—it is as if a deal had been struck in which the Europeans are allowed to be "inherently free riders when it comes to" the public good of defense,[22] in exchange for an American advantage when it comes to providing war material. The other obstacle is persistent French reluctance toward conventional defense. France's national defense stresses—still—nuclear deterrence of an attack on France. The French realize that a Soviet victory in Germany would put them in a dreadfully difficult position—for could a suicidal nuclear threat aimed at deterring Soviet conventional invasion beyond the Rhine be credible? (The majority of the French opt for negotiating with Moscow rather than carrying out the threat!)[23] Thus they understand that they have an interest in joining, in case of need, in the conventional defense of the West German *glacis* that protects France. But there is a double tension, between the emphasis on autonomy of decision and the need to plan participation in an "integrated" military structure, as well as between the financial priority given to nuclear weapons and the costs of a conventional contribution.[24] To be sure, the West Europeans could nevertheless better coordinate their armaments plans, build more weapons in common, and divide weapons production more intelligently among themselves, but this would hardly be very spectacular.

The domain of a common nuclear defense for Europe is even more troubled. It is not only because the British force is assigned to NATO whereas France's is not, or because even the MIRVing of these forces will not be sufficient to turn them into deterrents for Europe: they will, in fact, remain national deterrents (hence, opposition in London and Paris to having them counted in arms control deals between the superpowers). It is, even more, because of the problem of giving West Germany a "finger on the trigger": the right not just to veto a resort to nuclear weapons through a double-key agreement, but to take part in a decision to use them—and remember, it is the threat of such a use that many West Europeans deem indispensable for deterrence. Even if this could be resolved, can such decisions be made collectively? Above all, would the U.S. Congress and the president ever allow a West European entity to risk initiating global nuclear war by taking decisions that could force the United States to resort to its own nuclear weapons in Europe or lead the Soviets to attack U.S. nuclear installations in Europe? Of course, American decisions can drag Western Europe into nuclear war; and the Europeans who depend on the U.S. presence for their security cannot do more than fret. Americans have another option: pull out—or threaten to do so, in order to avoid such a situation.[25]

Some people on both sides of the Atlantic have suggested that the threat to pull out a sizable part of U.S. conventional forces in Europe, or their actual removal, could shock the West Europeans into establishing a defense entity of their own.[26] But this does not address itself to the nuclear conundrum, nor is it certain to have the desired effect: it would probably sharpen existing differences between the West Europeans—and in this case, the "pacifier" function would be affected. There are today three groups: those who agree, more or less reluctantly, that more has to be done in the conventional domain; those (the French) who cling to a nuclear Maginot Line despite rising misgivings; and those who would actually stress defense altogether less and seek security in "dialogue" with the East or in unilateral disarmament or "alternative" designs. As long as this division persists, European defense will be the contrary of Alsace-Lorraine in French affairs after 1871—always talk of it, never think of it. Thinking of it only shows how trapped Western Europe is in its dependence. A complete, self-sufficient conventional and nuclear defense is out of reach; a purely conventional one, without the Americans, would leave France and Britain largely out and doom the rest to either instability or to a very minor role in world affairs; greater efforts within NATO will leave the keys in America's hands.

Must we, then, come to the placebos? The problem is that even minor or fragmentary measures may prove as controversial as grand institutional schemes. For instance, making the Supreme Commander in Europe a European, and the Secretary-General of NATO an American, is unlikely to reassure the West Europeans, as long as these switches would be subordinated to a European acceptance of a "full conventional defense" and leave the United Sates more in charge of political strategies than ever.[27] A few things can probably be achieved, and they are not insignificant. The United States could preserve deliberate ambiguity about first use; one can hardly expect American officials to brandish the threat, but one can ask them to understand the benefits of uncertainty. In exchange, the Alliance should take measures that would make it possible, if nuclear deterrence fails, to postpone the use of nuclear weapons as long as possible against a Soviet conventional attack (this entails a relocation and reduction of the stock of tactical nuclear weapons).

As soon as one goes further, trouble begins. Of course the West Europeans should "assume the major responsibility for conventional ground defense." But even if their economic recovery proceeds faster and is more evenly spread than at present, one cannot expect them to change the balance between welfare and defense expenditures as drastically as the United States has done. This was easier to accomplish because the United States had never really become a welfare state. Of course, if state revenues should increase through economic growth, more money could go for defense in Europe. But the problems of structural unemployment, the cost entailed by supporting part-time work, the imperative of helping finance the new technologies, and the burdens imposed by heavy public debts will not leave very much for increased defense efforts. Conversely, none of the strategies Americans are offering for conventional deterrence and defense are likely to delight their allies. If greater mobility and maneuver means retreat first, after being attacked, and resupplying and reconquering later, the West Germans cannot be expected to be pleased. But if it means a quick counteroffensive in Eastern Europe, they will not be pleased either, since they want to avoid anything that might disturb their conversations with the East Germans or seem threatening to the Warsaw Pact (and would sending West German forces deep into Central or Eastern Europe be the best way to lure the satellites away from Moscow?). As for the miracle cure of precision-guided weapons, they may, of course, be helpful, but technology is no panacea—especially when one faces an enemy who is determined not to fall behind.

Many Europeans believe that the Alliance's troubles would be eased by a less confrontational American policy toward Moscow, and by less half-hearted American efforts at arms control. Much of this is true. But even a less militant U.S. administration would face two obstacles. First, it is not easy to define a policy toward Moscow that avoids both the perils of confrontation and the illusions of the détente of the 1970s. Détente without illusions, or the search for a modus vivendi, or regulated competition, which writers such as Marshall Shulman, Joseph Nye, Jr., Seweryn Bialer, Robert Legvold, myself, and others have advocated,[28] is easier to suggest than to spell out, easier to evoke by describing what it should not be than to substantiate it. When one rejects condominium, acknowledges the obstacles to more extensive economic links, and takes into account domestic difficulties on both sides, how much is left? Arms control, of course. But, on the one hand, it cannot be the only component of Soviet-American cooperative relations (for when this happens, it succumbs under the weight of the antagonistic ones), and, on the other, the speedy development of new offensive and defensive systems is likely to make agreements technically even more difficult and ever more complex.

Are Americans and West Europeans thus doomed to drift and divorce? What I would recommend, given the realities, is resignation to the inevitable— a loosening of ties, in order to preserve the indispensable—the alliance for the defense of Western Europe. For I do not believe that the realities described here can be easily reversed. To be sure, Western Europe could emerge from its protracted economic and social mutation and prove that it is not condemned to obsolescence, left behind by Silicon Valley and MITI, dragged down, so to speak, by the Pacific and by pacifism. *Le pire n'est pas toujours sûr.* Even the EEC could pull itself together. But I am afraid that even the best will not be quite good enough, that Western Europe is like a racer in a marathon who cannot quite get rid of a variety of chains and heavy equipment that weigh him down. Whatever domain one examines, one comes to the same conclusion: national efforts, however brilliant (few people believed Italy would manage its affairs so well) are not enough; and a collective will just is not there. It would require, among other things, the combination of these two: a complicity among the major West European leaders comparable to the relation between Adenauer, de Gasperi, and Robert Schuman (the Pompidou-Heath-Brandt trio was weaker because the first of these never quite understood or trusted the third), and, in the various countries, enough of the right sense of distress to allow these leaders to try and invent "Europe." Distress, today, is of a different kind: it has to do with specific interests, or else it looks for scapegoats or makes (mainly young) people want to drop out—it is fragmented or anarchistic (or unsocial), and therefore unproductive. As for the leaders who are likely to take over in the near future, they all appear rather intensely national. Thus, we must expect, for instance, Europe's elites, in foreign affairs, to remain oscillating between the kind of impotent, bombastic (yet sincere) antitotalitarian posturing that now prevails in the French intelligentsia, the temptation of turning inward denounced by Eagleburger, and a semisomnambulistic quest for normalcy on the world scene—not exactly what even Europe's best American friends wish to see.

As for America, one can, of course, hope that a second Reagan Administration decides to choose a "centrist" course in world affairs. It may no longer feel, however, that it has to give to domestic considerations (including, most specifically, the public's reluctance to fight protracted ground wars) the same priority as in the president's first term. That priority, which General Haig resented, underlined the contradiction between a domestic project entirely devoted to restoring private initiative and to curbing the state, and a view of the world as a struggle between good and evil, which requires a very strong and active American state. The factors that explained the priority of internal concerns were the need for reelection and for economic recovery. One is no longer there, and the second might be less demanding. A militant second term would exacerbate European-American tensions. But even a "centrist" one would not eliminate them.

Two American features strike me, if not as permanent from now on, at least as likely to endure. One is the advent of leaders (in politics but also in the business world) and of elites that will not accord to Europe the importance it had been given in the postwar period. This is the famous problem of the successor generation, and one ought not add much to the platitudes it has already provoked. It is not that the new elites are more attracted to the Pacific, as many Europeans currently believe. It is that they are both more turned inward themselves, more concerned with, or excited by, America's response to new technological challenges than their predecessors, *and* insofar as they worry about or act in the world, more "global" in their outlook. This is also what one finds among the students in college and universities today. The first business of America is America (and, to many Americans in high places, it is American business). The second is a world safe for America—and Europe, to use Paul Valéry's famous phrase, now looks, more than before, like a "small cape off Asia."

The second, and related, feature could be called selective unilateralism. It is definitely not isolationism (which the French still fear and somehow expect): very few people, among the educated and informed, want the United States to stop being a world power. Most, indeed, still believe that an attack on Western Europe should be resisted by American force. but three factors push toward a rather new way of exerting world power. One, bluntly put, is battle fatigue with internationalism, that is, with a way of handling world affairs through alliance cooperation, international organization, doing good for ungrateful "Third World" leaders, and apologizing for one's own power or values. There is a new assertiveness; one could already sense it in the early philosophy of the Nixon Administration. It was later reversed by Carter's emphasis on global issues and omnidirectional bargaining; but his fiasco brought unilateralism back with a vengeance. A second factor is the very transformation of the international system: the United States is no longer as dominant a power as in the late 1940s and 1950s, and cannot hope to control trends simply by committing itself all over the world through pacts and bases; and the world has become more turbulent. What is therefore required now is greater freedom of maneuver, more leeway in selecting where and when to intervene or fight, and with what means (it is not a coincidence that this also happens to be a time of grand naval rearmament: it is a sea power's strategy). Interestingly, even those worried Americans who are more disturbed by the perils abroad than by the opportunities, more concerned about moderating turbulence than about American mastery of it, more anxious about nuclear war than about Moscow, spontaneously act out their own unilateralism, as when they call for a nuclear freeze that many West Europeans deem oblivious of nuclear imbalance in Europe, or for a no-first-use stand.

The third factor is precisely the domestic mood and system. The mood is one of profound ambivalence: patriotism is up, reluctance toward "new Vietnams" is not down. (It is wrong to talk about the Vietnam syndrome: the Korean War was not any more popular. It is endless, inconclusive, "limited" wars that are hard to "sell.") Distrust of Soviet expansionism is very high; the fear of nuclear war is more explicit than anywhere else. Again, the only synthesis for these contradictions is selective engagement, preferably quick and decisive action, and definitely not nuclear or capable of provoking a nuclear response. This is not made to please the West Europeans, with their dogged concern for American ground forces *and* willingness to use nuclear weapons. As for the incoherence of the American foreign policy process, so eloquently denounced by George Kennan, it leaves room for only two alternatives: either the kind of strategy he has always advocated, based on a limited but stable definition of the national interest, and also relying a great deal on the self-interested efforts of those whom the United States protects; or selective unilateralism, which is more capricious (*vide* Grenada!) but more in conformity with the discontinuities of the political system, more adapted to the recurrent bouts of self-fascination or self-absorption, more pessimistic (or realistic) about the capacities or reliability of others, more in harmony with the current mood, with the desire for both globalism (every apparent Soviet gain anywhere being chalked up as a defeat) and freedom of action.

"Things being what they are," as de Gaulle used to say, there is no need to fear a collapse of the Alliance, but no way of concealing its devaluation. It remains necessary to both the United States and Western Europe—indeed, "pacifism" on either side and U.S. exasperation do not seem to challenge the legitimacy of NATO. Even West Germans who dream of denuclearized zones, defensive areas, and a Europe emancipated from both superpowers recognize that this is *Zukunftsmusik*, and that the music of today remains NATO's somewhat cacophonic military march. Even Americans who dislike Western Europe's "greedy" economic deals with Moscow, as well as moans and groans about American rashness, recognize that the

United States has a vital interest in Europe's security, and that a Western Europe that is not prosperous will contribute even less to the common defense.

But note the narrowing of concerns. Many say they are willing to protect Europe, not because it is Europe that is being threatened, but because it is threatened by the Soviet Union.[29] Many Europeans say they need NATO, but only for their continent's protection, not in order to defend "Western" values and interests all over the world. It is not easy for Americans to accept the idea of a limited partnership in an "interdependent world," where many areas may be far more explosive than Europe. But they will have to. Many Europeans, in turn, will not find it easy to accept American unilateralism in these areas, or America's increasing unwillingness to listen to its allies before defining its policy toward Moscow (except when *not* listening could have self-destructive effects, as in the squabble over the gas pipeline). But they will have to. Both sides will find it difficult to manage a military alliance whose strategy will be a compromise between conflicting fears, rather than a clear and decisive choice, one that will probably entail large, shadowy areas of ambiguity. But they will have to. And the reason is simple: anything else will not be any better for either side. As one French prime minister once put it to his contentious and divided majority, "We are condemned to living together."

No such uneasy conglomeration is entirely safe from the effects of massive irrationality: nations, as we saw in the 1930s, sometimes fail to defend their interests—or rather, define them in a delusive way. But—paradoxically— Europe is too fragmented to succumb to such a wave. And while one can concoct scenarios of American "abandonment" of Europe, it is more difficult to imagine the circumstances in which they would be played out than those in which a bungling America might drag Europe into a global war. One external force could strain the Alliance to the breaking point: the Soviet Union, should it revolutionize its foreign policy and suddenly offer to let its East European protectorates be "finlandized," in exchange for a West European reduction of dependency on NATO and the United States. But, until now, Soviet stolidity, brutality, fear of sacrificing well-established gains for uncertain possibilities, and unwillingness to run the risk of German reunification have carried the day.

As long as the Soviets, both through the pursuit of this durable policy and through the clumsiness of their attempts at driving wedges between the United States and its allies, contribute in their way to the preservation of the Alliance, there is no reason for anguish. But there is none for cheer either. The old bottle is only half full, and the wine is a bit sour. For the combination of Europe's mix of parochialism and impotence with America's mix of parochialism and arrogance is not a very pleasant brew.

Notes

1. "Europe's Identity Crisis," *Daedalus* 93, no. 1 (Winter 1964). See also "Fragments Floating in the Here and Now," *Daedalus* 108, no. 1 (Winter 1979).

2. Commissariat General du Plan, *Quelle stratégie européenne pour la France dans les années 80?* (Paris: Documentation française, 1983), p. 143.

3. In *Unemployment and Growth in the Western Economies*, edited by Andrew J. Pierre (New York: Council on Foreign Relations, 1984), p. 122.

4. *Unsettling Europe* (New York: Random House, 1980).

5. State expenditures represented 21 to 30 percent of the gross domestic product in Western Europe in 1980 (see *Eurostat*, June 1982).

6. *Unemployment and Growth in the Western Economies*, pp. 45–46.

7. This figure is mentioned in a French unpublished report, *La crise mondiale et l'avenir de la France*, prepared by a team from the Commissariat Général du Plan.

8. In his speech in The Hague, February 7, 1984. See also Laurent Fabius, "Le défi technologique," *Politique étrangère*, January 1984, pp. 49–56.

9. Cf. Michel Crozier, *Le mal américain* (Paris: Fayard, 1980), published in 1984 by the University of California Press under the milder title *The Trouble with America*.

10. Raymond Barre, in *Unemployment and Growth in the Western Economies*, p. 71.

11. In addition, the French Right admires Presisdent Reagan's domestic policies (as Jacques Chirac has put it, "*le truc de Reagan, ça marche, le truc de Mitterrand ça ne marche pas*").

12. In "A Plan to Reshape NATO," *Time*, March 5, 1984, p. 21.

13. Mentioned in a study of U.S. opinions about Western Europe, "Etats-Unis: solitude impériale," *L'Express*, June 1-7, 1984. By Dinah Louda, from which I have borrowed many points.

14. See, for instance, the May 7th memorandum to the French "Left" prepared by a number of West German Socialist personalities, and published in *Le Monde*, May 20-21, 1984, p. 5.

15. Many French political figures and authors appear to believe that "decoupling" was the result of John F. Kennedy's "deal" removing Jupiter and Thor missiles from Europe in exchange for the removal of Soviet missiles from Cuba. This new myth is now a companion of the older French myth about the deliberate division of Europe at Yalta by the superpowers.

16. See Josef Joffe, "Nuclear Weapons, No First Use, and European Order," *Ethics* 95, no. 3 (April 1985):606-618.

17. For Kissinger, see *Time*, p. 23; Kristol in *New York Times Magainze*, September 25, 1983, and in the debate "Should the U.S. Defend Europe?" *Harper's*, April 1984; Ball in "The Cosmic Bluff," *New York Review of Books*, July 21, 1983.

18. See the debate over Albert Wohlstetter's views, in *Commentaire* 25 (Spring 1984):43-65.

19. Kissinger, *Time*, p. 24.

20. See Helmut Schmidt, "Saving the Western Alliance," *New York Review of Books*, May 31, 1984, p. 27.

21. Josef Joffe, "Europe's American Pacifier," *Foreign Policy* 54 (Spring 1984): 64-82.

22. Ibid., p. 81.

23. See "Sondage Figaro-Sofres," in *Le Figaro*, December 1, 1983: in case of a Soviet invasion, only 6 percent would support the use of nuclear weapons; 58 percent would negotiate.

24. The plan for a French *Force d'Action Rapide* does not resolve these tensions. See Pierre Lellouche, "L'après Pershing," *Politique étrangère*, April 1983, pp. 859-878.

25. For further details, see my essay, "L'avenir de la défense européenne," *Intervention* 8 (February–April 1984):80–84.

26. Kissinger's idea of removing half of America's troops unless Europe agrees to "build a full conventional defense" (*Time*, p. 24) would leave one with the worst of all worlds: the strategy would still be based on a noncredible threat of nuclear war—the very thing he wants NATO to move away from—and there would be even fewer ground forces than now to ensure defense if the threat fails to deter!

27. Ibid., p. 22.

28. For several of these authors, see Joseph Nye, Jr. (ed.), *The Making of America's Soviet Policy* (New Haven: Yale University Pres, 1984).

29. A point I owe to Dinah Louda's study (fn. 13).

13

Domestic Politics and Interdependence

I

The study of international relations tends to follow the agenda of statesmen. In the sixties, both were dominated by strategic issues. In the past fifteen years, scholars and officials have devoted much of their attention to the problems raised by the interpenetration of societies and the interconnection of state policies in the world economy—the problems to which the term interdependence has been applied. On the one hand, students of world politics have tried to evaluate the extent to which interdependence changes the traditional, distinctive features of interstate relations, what Raymond Aron has called the logic of behavior of states competing in a "state of nature." More specifically, the question to which scholars have addressed themselves is whether the particular imperatives or constraints of interdependence merely provide new opportunities and some new detours for the age-old contest of sovereign units trying to reach their goals in a world without either substantive consensus or central power, or whether the new characteristics transform the game of nations so deeply that it begins to resemble what we are familiar with in domestic politics. Are we still in "the state of war," or already in "global politics"? On the other hand, conferences of statesmen, and meetings of members of national "establishments," have tried to find solutions to a vast number of highly complex problems, in the relations between OECD countries, in North-South relations, and in East-West relations. Reports of think tanks and of groups like the Trilateral Commission and the Brandt Commission have laid out alternatives for the monetary system, for East-West trade, for energy and commodities, for the law of the seas, for food or technology transfers, for aid to and trade with the developing countries, etc.

What has been strangely lacking in many of these efforts is a consideration of the domestic realities that determine which of these alternatives is most likely to be adopted, and indeed dictate the goals of the players. Nicholas Wahl, writing about American-West European relations, has stated that their "professional analysis . . . has left little role for a separate, autonomous weight to the internal dimension."[1] There are two different but convergent reasons for this neglect. The traditional model of world politics is the "realist" paradigm, which looks at the state as a rational actor whose ends are shaped by its geo-political position on the map: the National Interest is supposed to have a quasi-objective reality, and indeed the concept itself entails, as one of its functions, insulating foreign policy from the vagaries of domestic politics. The primacy of foreign policy is one of the dogmas of the "realist" model. To be sure, some allowance is made for fundamental variations among regimes: it would not be realistic to discard the difference between the way in which a totalitarian state like Nazi Germany sets and seeks its goals, and the way in which democracies behave. Yet even there the emphasis is on continuity, and the scrutiny of domestic factors does not go very deep. As for what might be called the "modernist" model, which looks at the interdependent world from the perspective of global politics, it tends to suffer from a double bias. Analytically, its focus is on the factors, inherent in economic development, which weave the different state strands into a single tapestry; normatively, its preference goes to "one world" solutions, to collective methods for the management of common problems. As a result, the literature of political science still falls into two different compartments. Books on domestic political systems say rather little about foreign policy. Books on the foreign policy of a nation, or on international issues, say rather little about domestic factors.

The purpose of this essay is obviously not to bridge the gap. It is to raise a few questions about the interactions between domestic politics and interdependence, in the light of our experience since the days of the Marshall Plan, and given the problems which the industrial nations face in the coming years. I will begin with some remarks about the meaning of interdependence for domestic politics; then, I will look at some typical state responses to interdependence, determined by domestic factors; I will present what I consider to be the key issues raised by those interactions; and I will end with some considerations about the future.

II

Interdependence can be described as a *condition*. It refers to a situation of mutual sensitivity and vulnerability which affects all states, because of the inability of each of them to reach its national objectives in autarky. Either they cannot be achieved unless other states or societies provide the goods and services that are missing at home; or else the costs that would have to be paid for liberating oneself from such dependencies and insulating the nation from such disruptions would be so prohibitive as to entail important sacrifices of national goals and values. It is because of this condition that one often hears about "all of us in the same boat," or about "spaceship earth." But this is not an adequate way of looking at world politics. For the common condition tells us nothing about the individual situations. In particular, it tells us nothing about the two central questions of politics: who commands and who benefits? It is clear that the balance of gains and losses from interdependence varies from country to country, that some are less vulnerable than others, and that the universal condition covers both states which are able, so to speak, to spread dependencies all around and to export more disruptions than they import, and states that are in a plight of one-sided dependence on a dominant master or partner. Moreover, there are also vast variations in the distribution of the gains from interdependence across the population of a given state, or in the location of the losses incurred within a society, depending on the domestic and external strategies adopted by the governments.

It therefore makes more sense to analyze interdependence as a *process*, or as a set of processes. From the viewpoint of this paper, this is doubly relevant—positively and negatively.

1. Interdependence is a process which enhances the importance of domestic factors in international politics. The agenda of world politics is no longer filled by traditional strategic-diplomatic issues (although these remain essential). It tends to be occupied by the very issues that are central to domestic politics, i.e., issues of economic growth and social welfare. Foreign policy becomes the external projection of domestic needs and drives, international politics the confrontation and conciliation of domestic *projets*. As a result, the constituencies of foreign policy have broadened: to the traditional and specialized "establishments" of foreign policy experts and "military-industrial complexes," one must now add all the groups whose interests are affected by what happens abroad. The scope of these groups depends, of course, on the issues, on the nature of the regime (is it one that allows for the expression of separate interests?), and on the degree of participation of the nation in the world economy. If we look at the OECD countries, that scope is pretty broad. It is true that in the past, and particularly in the pre-1914 world economy, citizens of these countries were already deeply affected by external economic events. But the connection was much less sharply perceived, both because fewer of the issues were the subject-matter of state politics, i.e. the responsibility of the governments and the concern of interstate politics, and because "the integration of the pre-1914 world economy was something of an illusion,"[2] due to the barriers imposed by nature (communications). Some groups, directly affected by free trade or by protectionism, were always part of the foreign policy constituency.

What is new is the susceptibility of all citizens, as producers or consumers, to becoming members of that constituency. This, in turn, corresponds to the end of the specialization of the foreign policy actors (decision-makers and enforcers). To the soldier and the diplomat, characteristic of the strategic-diplomatic chessboard, we now must add the functional departments and agencies (agriculture, industry, space, Treasury, etc.) which tend to have foreign policies of their own—not to mention the heads of multinational corporations, within their sphere of autonomous decision.

When we talk about domestic players in matters of interdependence, we must be careful to distinguish between constituencies and decision-makers. For while economic interdependence tends to enlarge both spheres, the broadening of the constituencies is tied to the nature of the political regime, that of the decision-makers' sphere to the degree of bureaucratic development (a key aspect of what is sometimes called modernization). A totalitarian regime which muzzles or shapes interest groups or ideological forces is, however revolutionary its goals, most able to stay close to the old model of the separation between domestic politics and foreign policy. A barely constituted state is unlikely to have a highly specialized foreign policy personnel. And yet, even when the constituencies are tightly controlled by the state, or when that personnel remains very small, the nature of the issues raised by interdependence will oblige leaders to pay close attention to domestic factors in their definition of the state's foreign policy.

2. To say that interdependence is a process, or a set of processes, is a way of saying that it is not a goal, or a set of goals. We should not speak of the "imperatives" of interdependence, and contrast them with the "obstacles" raised by domestic politics. For a given state, the imperatives consist in the goals which it has set, and which, in large part, emerge from domestic realities. Concerning these goals, two remarks are essential. First, for every government, they form a whole; while one can analytically distinguish domestic and foreign objectives, the two sets are intertwined. Every government, even (or especially) in authoritarian or totalitarian regimes, must legitimize its domestic power—in order to get reelected, or not to lose its bases of support; thus, the social groups that provide its lifeblood must be kept reasonably satisfied materially as well as ideologically—and this often entails the setting of *foreign* policy objectives (as in the case of French agricultural policy, or of West German industrial policy, or in the form of measures aimed at preventing inflation from being imported from abroad, or worsened by external commitments; if we switch from the material to the ideological realm, we can mention the British Labour party's rejection of European unity schemes, after World War II, or on the contrary the ardent embrace of such schemes by the Italian Christian Democrats). Conversely, even governments which seem to attach a much higher priority to foreign than to domestic affairs (say, the Nixon Administration) cannot help shaping their foreign policy in the light of their domestic problems (as in 1971). Governments look at the issues created by interdependence through the lenses shaped by their domestic experience (cf. America's and West Germany's preference for free market solutions to North-South problems). Foreign policy tends to be the extension of this experience.

Secondly, insofar as the foreign policy objectives are concerned, while it is impossible to put much order into the bewildering variety displayed by an ever growing number of states, one may, analytically, want to distinguish two ideal-types (if only in order to see to which one any given nation is closer). There is the ideal-type of the nation whose primary concern is its own internal development, or transformation, or conservation. Since it lives in an interdepedent world, since it is likely to need some external goods or services (material or psychological), it will, of course, pursue a foreign policy, but of a primarily instrumental nature. Then, there is the ideal-type of the nation whose primary concern is its figure, influence, and role on the world stage, and which tends to tailor its internal make-up to the needs of that role. One may well ask why such a distinction is relevant, since interdependence can be either an obstacle or a springboard for states in either category. Nevertheless, from the viewpoint of world order, it is the second group that is the most awesome. The states closest to the first ideal-type, even when their actions appear disruptive (through protectionism, or the expropriation of foreign capital, or claims on offshore resources, for instance), are above all interested in scoring absolute gains. The states in the second category, even when their policies are cooperative and seem to stress the possibility of joint gains, are mostly eager for relative advantages over rivals; and even when this drive does not make them overtly more aggressive or disruptive, it is likely to elicit their desire for a bigger share of the joint gain, and to provoke the resistance of others to such uneven solutions: this is the contagion of competitiveness, so well analyzed by Jean-Jacques Rousseau.

In the history of the OECD countries, the smaller nations (such as Belgium, Holland, or Norway) are close to the first ideal-type; the United States and Gaullist France to the second. Among the middle powers, Italy has chosen the first alternative; its foreign policy has aimed above all at buttressing the internal balance of political forces (i.e., the "hegemonic bloc" around the Christian Democrats), and at serving its economic and social post-war transformation. France since 1969, and Britain gradually, have moved from the second category toward the first. In the cases of West Germany and Japan, the very success achieved, in the fifties and sixties, by concentrating on absolute gains and on the economic dimensions of foreign policy, *and* the high degree of dependence on outside markets and sources of energy or raw materials, have combined in recent years at least to raise the question of a possible shift from the first to the second category; both nations seem to hesitate around the dividing line—with Japan still on the threshold, but Bonn perhaps already on the other side.

The process of interdependence affects each state both as a set of *restraints* on, and as a set of *opportunities* for, its domestic objectives and interests. These is no need to repeat Richard Cooper's classic analysis of the way in which interdependence constrains domestic autonomy. He and others have shown how such classical tools of statecraft as macroeconomic monetary, credit, and taxation policies have been impaired in a world of rapid capital movements and "quick responsiveness to differential earning opportunities."[3] A state trying to control inflation by raising the interest rate, and thus attracting foreign capital; a state strying to reduce demand by cutting imports, and producing not a return to balance or surplus, but a recession, because of the effect of such cuts on the clients of its exports; a state whose attempt to orient foreign investments results in their emigration to other, more liberal countries; a state eager to fight a recession through expansionary policies but obtaining instead higher inflation, a decline of the currency, and a balance-of-payments debacle; a state whose economic future is jeopardized by another power's (or group of powers') decision to change the rules of the monetary or energy games—these are all examples from the recent past. Decisions made in one country, by the government or by private economic agents, affect that country's partners immediately.

The ability of governments to limit the loss of autonomy varies greatly, of course. The critique of the monetary system of the 1960s by France was based on the indictment of America's privileged capacity to get other nations to finance its balance-of-payments deficits—and to buy foreign enterprises with its overvalued dollars. And yet the United States did not escape all restraints: insofar as "the privileged dollar was a subsidy to European economic expansion,"[4] and the overvalued dollar favored the European and Japanese export industries over those of the United States, various domestic American interests were hurt. The United States could appease them by changing the rules, in 1971—but OPEC, in turn, changed the rules of the world market of oil in 1973 and thus deepened the very recession that the need to check the American inflation of the 1960s had finally produced. The Reagan administration's decision to put its domestic economic goals first resulted again in a dollar so strong that it hurt America's exports and increased protectionist pressures, while raising the nation's current account deficit—thus making the financing of an ever-rising debt more difficult. Americans react with dismay at their vulnerability to outside trends and decisions, because, unlike the Europeans and the Japanese, the experience of dependence is new to them. Still, in the balance of constraints, Western Europe and Japan do more poorly than the United States, because of a higher ratio of trade to GNP, because of their greater dependence on energy imports, and because the dollar remains the world's currency. And Western Europe has done more poorly than Japan, to the extent that the fragmentation of Western Europe, and also, often, an obsession with the size of firms rather than with their efficiency, has played havoc with various important European industries.

The opportunities provided by interdependence, on the other hand, range from the formidable development of industries geared to export, especially in Japan and West Germany, to the high profits and world-wide expansion of multinational corporations, which are actually national enterprises operating abroad, to the skillful promotion of domestic interests by governments eager to take advantage either of a privileged position (let us think of French agriculture within the Common Market, of American sales of wheat, or of Iran's oil policy) or of an asset desired by others (such as Brazilian uranium, in the West German-Brazilian nuclear deal of 1977). The opportunities provided by external markets may lead to the expansion of an industry far beyond the domestic needs that fostered its creation, as in the case of the French aircraft or the West German nuclear industries. And governments often find that the best way of exploiting an opportunity is to withhold their support on an issue of importance to others, until the interest they want to promote is satisfied: a tactic used by France in the EEC's agricultural policy, and later by Britain, both in order to obtain subsidies for its consumers of EEC farm products and in order to get regional development aid from its partners. Sometimes, a government can find in interdependence an opportunity for desirable domestic changes, as in the case of the Carter administration's reversal, in November 1978, of its domestic expansionary policies, which had chaotic effects on foreign exchange markets and inflationary ones at home, or in the case of France's opening of its borders to its European partners in the 1950's and 1960's, thus transforming the outlook of a previously "Malthusian" business community, and finding in open competition across borders a powerful leverage for further industrialization and growth.

Sometimes, paradoxically, it is the restraint which is the opportunity. Whereas the loss of domestic autonomy provoked by interdependence usually compounds the restrictions on governmental freedom of maneuver already created by the necessities of domestic politics—the narrowness or composition of the electoral base, ideological and class tensions, bureaucratic inefficiency, etc.—there are cases when the external constraints actually result in a lifting of domestic obstacles, and may be deliberately sought by a government eager to remove these without direct internal collision. In the 1970's, negotiations between the IMF and the British and Italian governments resulted, after much bargaining, in the former "imposing" on the latter, in exchange for the money loaned, conditions of budgetary and social policy which partly liberated these governments from the grip of leftwing socialist ideologues in one case, and a host of pressure groups in the other. Inversely, it is often the external opportunity created by interdependence which makes it possible for a government either to obtain or to impose domestic restraints. It was the need for France to make full use of the industrial opportunities provided by the Common Market, i.e. to be competitive, which justified the restrictive policies followed, in the 1960's, with respect to wage increases; later, the argument used by the Japanese government to obtain the cooperation of the labor unions in the fight against inflation was the preservation of Japan's huge exporting capabilities.

So far, we have only mentioned the opportunities provided by interdependence for domestic interests within the nation that is acting on the world scene. But we must add the possibility for the nation to affect domestic forces elsewhere, thanks to interdependence. For its processes facilitate access to political and economic élites in the "target country," and thus extend the sphere of manipulation abroad—in two ways at least: more foreign groups can be affected, given the nature of the issues; and, within the acting nation, more groups can try to affect the foreign target. Sometimes, these machinations take rather scandalous forms: businessmen bribing foreign intermediaries or prospective clients, or trying to contribute to the overthrow of a hostile regime. But there are many other transnational links—between parties, or professional associations, or intellectuals—which can be used for the manipulation of a foreign society. As in the case of the restraints, such opportunities are unevenly distributed—along lines of might *and* skill: both are needed, neither can entirely substitute for the other. Insofar as so much of international politics today is the manipulation of interdependence—to minimize its restraints or to maximize its opportunities—without resort to the use of force, the most successful are likely to be those who know best how to affect, not only the governments with whom they have to deal, but the political and social forces to whose opinions and interests these governments must pay attention.

III

How have states reacted to the restraints and exploited the opportunities provided by interdependence? Let use examine two questions: the kinds of policies followed in response to domestic factors, and the kinds of domestic forces that have influenced these policies.

Minimizing constraints on domestic forces and policy instruments, and maximizing opportunities for such forces and interests, have come in two forms. One has been the setting up of procedures of cooperation that are meant to allow states to pursue their goals without endangering, and even by tightening, the network of economic interdependence. There have been three main groupings. The "Atlantic" one (which includes Japan and corresponds to OECD, but also to the management of the monetary system) was set up largely along the lines laid out by the one power for whom the balance of restraints and opportunities was most clearly positive—the United States. Washington's privileged position allowed it, throughout the sixties, to put off the domestic constraints which balance-of-payments deficits entail for "ordinary" states. Indeed, the move from fixed rates to floating rates, imposed by Washington, meant an overt repudiation of such externally imposed domestic discipline, and a recovery of dwindling opportunities. Other nations accepted the Atlantic bargain both because of the extraordinary possibilities it offered for economic growth (including liquidity to finance it) as well as military security, and because the United States allowed, in diverse ways, both Western Europe and Japan to protect their domestic markets from an unlimited invasion of American goods (and also, in the case of Japan, from the implantation of American multinationals behind the tariff barrier). The West European network was built by states, all of which, for different reasons, had come to the conclusion that national autonomy provided fewer opportunities for domestic development and external influence than the establishment of a common market and some common policies; as for the constraints that would result from these, they were seen either as bearable because of countervailing economic or foreign policy gains, or as actually desirable for domestic reasons, or as susceptible to renegotation or alleviation. The third network is the quasi-global one, which covers "First World–Third World" relations. It is the one that has suffered the most, precisely because of Third World complaints about the unfairness of the balance of restraints and opportunities, shaped by the advanced nations: insufficient opportunities to fashion their own development plans because of heavy debts, or the paucity of aid, or the prevalence of multinationals; insufficient opportunities to ship their agricultural or industrial goods to the developed countries; excessive restraints imposed by price fluctuations affecting both their imports and their main export products, etc. It is important to note that the challenge to this network has mainly come, not from those domestic forces that have least benefited from postwar economic development in the Third World—the peasants, the workers uprooted from the land and moved to urban slums—but from the very élites of the new states.

More interesting for the purposes of this essay is the other kind of behavior: policies that, deliberately or not, loosen or rift interdependence on behalf of domestic goals—either because they aim at increasing or restoring domestic autonomy or at shoring up domestic forces threatened by interdependence, or else because the manipulation of ties of mutual interest to make them more advantageous to the nation results in the weakening or destruction of these bonds. Recent years have presented us with a multitude of examples, which fall into three categories.

1. State *actions* of self-enhancement, or state actions taken for domestic reasons, but detrimental to interdependence. Most prominent in the former case are the OPEC decisions of 1973 and after, with their enormous effects on the world economy; the decisions of states to enlarge their sphere of control beyond the territorial seas; and the establishment by many states of vast arms industries that depend for their profitability or survival on exports of conventional, often highly sophisticated, weaponry abroad—at the risk of multiplying opportunities for turning conflicts into wars, whose effects on economic interdependence are likely to be disastrous. The drive to export nuclear technologies that could be used for the production of nuclear weapons may be even more dangerous. It is interesting to note that the nuclear energy industries of Europe, which have developed simultaneously with the institutions of the Community, have always proceeded on a national basis (except for limited cooperative ventures); there has been no real attempt to devise a common nuclear policy, despite the shadowy existence of Euratom. Among policies taken for domestic reasons that result in a disruption of interdependence, one can list the new American food policy of 1972, which shifted to reliance on the market mechanism, and resulted in a depletion of grain reserves.

2. State *reactions* against the constraints of interdependence. We have already mentioned the "international coup d'état" constituted by the August, 1971 decisions of Nixon and Connally and by subsequent demands presented to the West Europeans and the Japanese, aimed at turning the American payments deficit into a surplus. The generalization of floating rates represents a weakening of the disciplining of domestic economies through the balance of payments; and while it can be presented as a way of saving interdependence from a breakdown into competitive devaluations or monetary blocs comparable to the disasters of the 1930's, it is nevertheless a factor of uncertainty for the world economy. It has led to a growing discrepancy between weak and strong currencies, which in turn has contributed to the relative anemia

of the EEC. The recession of the mid-1970's, and either the balance-of-payments difficulties of some countries (such as Italy) or the plight of specific industries hit by foreign competition (in the United States or in Western Europe), led to a resurgence of protectionist pressures, in the United States against both Japanese and West European imports, in Western Europe against imports from Japan and from developing countries, as well as to import control measures taken by Italy. It becomes more difficult to ward off such pressures, or to avoid such measures, when the opportunities for compensatory gains, or for temporary domestic austerity measures—comparable to those adopted in France in 1958-1959 and again in the autumn of 1968—are wiped out or reduced by the state of the world economy. Another reaction to the mid-1970's crisis, apparently less destructive of the network of free trade, has been the adoption by the major industrial powers of policies of export-led growth; but, as many observers have pointed out, this is tantamount to a zero-sum game: not all countries can increase their exports simultaneously. Among the reactions against the costs of interdependence, one must also mention moves by developing nations to gain greater control over the activities of foreign enterprises. The most recent, and vigorous, challenge to the constraints of interdependence represented by international cooperation has been mounted by the Reagan administration: determined to provoke a convergence of economic policies by unilateral action rather than by bargaining, it has shown deliberate indifference to the external effects of its fiscal and monetary policies (draining the world's capital, slowing down recovery abroad because of high interest rates, worsening the burden of the debt for developing countries, etc.).[5]

3. State *inaction* due to domestic factors, yet dangerous for economic interdependence. The most striking example may well be the utter failure of the EEC in the realm of common industrial policy (even in the case of coal and steel). Neither earlier arguments about the technology gap, nor the failure of "national champion" policies, nor the growing preponderance of American computers, weapons, and civilian aircraft has led the separate members of EEC to give up often fleeting national control: the gains from common policies that would go beyond à la carte arrangements have not seemed big or probable enough to offset the loss of control. The fiasco of the EEC's common energy policy has been particularly remarkable, both before 1973 and after: in this connection, national interests and practices have been too diverse, and the exploitation of the North Sea oil by Britain has obviously given London little incentive for a common strategy that could constrain its moves or limit its gains. The slowness of the United States Congress in adopting a national energy policy that would aim, not at impossible energy independence, but at making inevitable interdependence with OPEC less uneven, was caused by the combined resistance of consumers and special interest groups. Protracted French inaction about inflation, due to the priority given to full employment, accelerated industrialization, and higher exports, in the period from 1969 to 1973, first kept France from joining the common float of European currencies proposed by Bonn in 1971, and later, twice, led to France's having to quit the West European

experiment in monetary cooperation. Earlier, U.S. policy-makers' "benign-neglect" of the growing world monetary crisis, and their reliance on other nations' willingness to absorb dollars rather than on domestic measures to eliminate the payments deficits, had led to the breakdown of the Bretton Woods system. And in the Reagan years, American inaction concerning the movements of exchange rates often strained relations with Western European countries.

We have been talking about state moves. It is necessary to be more precise in defining the domestic factors that play a role in the attempts to curtail or to reshape interdependence. Here again, there are three components.

1. In the first place, there is the *government* itself, as the force in charge of protecting and promoting what it considers to be the national interest. It is the government that integrates external and domestic concerns. As a result, even when several governments agree on the need to preserve economic interdependence, or on the imperative of avoiding a return to the conditions of the 1930's, there will, in all likelihood, be a contest about the specific institutional shape and about the scope which cooperation ought to have—a contest in which domestic and foreign policy considerations are inextricably mixed. *All* French governments have, since the late 1940's, "tilted" in favor of European as against more Atlantic structures (the biggest difference among these governments has been over the respective scope of supranational or intergovernmental European versus *national* control). The reasons for this have to do not only with considerations of power-in-the-world (i.e., minimizing dependence on the United States), but also with the fear of the economic consequences, for French industry and agriculture, of an Atlantic design that would lead to a huge free trade area without any buffer between American goods and the French market. Again for a mixture of domestic and external reasons, Britain and West Germany have leaned more in the Atlantic direction, and this was precisely the reason for France's long opposition to British entry into the EEC except on French terms (the story begins in 1950, not in 1958). The Franco-American battle over the monetary system, in the 1960's, can be seen as a contest between one government eager and able to exploit the rules of the game so as to export much of its inflation (and to preserve its external freedom of maneuver despite payments deficits), and another government eager to keep out inflation, hard pressed to control it (as Bonn was doing) by primarily domestic means, and hostile to much of what Washington was doing around the world; each one was keen to preserve internal as well as external autonomy, each one was accusing the other of undermining interdependence. The same struggle about institutional shape and scope goes on today in North-South relations.

2. It is necessary to look at the importance and the role of *bureaucratic* structures and bureaucratic processes of decision in different countries; for they have a major, often very specific influence in shaping the state's policy on issues of interdependence. One can document, for instance, the existence of an American "Treasury view" of considerable effectiveness, both in the

monetary turmoil of 1971-3, and in resisting Kissinger's attempts at moving away from the free market ideology toward some concessions to Third World demands in 1975-6. In the case of France, a long tradition of *colbertisme*, and the development of state institutions and procedures for post-war economic and social change, have resulted in an energy policy aimed at insuring maximum autonomy from foreign companies and from Middle Eastern oil, even at high prices—something which partly explains the resistance opposed by France to Kissinger's International Energy Agency, with its supranational features.[6] France also has a much more regulatory attitude toward monetary transactions and foreign investments than many of her partners. On the contrary, the Japanese bureaucracy has interpreted its role as one of supporting the formidable export drive of industry, hence of preserving an open world economy (while slowing down the dismantling of Japan's own protective mechanisms). As for bureaucratic processes, only agencies in charge of domestic interests were involved in the American monetary and trade decisions of the summer of 1971, and later in the soybean embargo; this explains why the bad effects on other countries were, in one case, deliberately accepted, and in the second case, neglected.[7]

3. Finally, specific interests, parties, and ideologies do influence the decisions of the statesmen. The switch of the American labor movement to protectionism cannot fail to affect the international trade policies of any Democratic administration, however strong its commitment to free trade: compromises will have to be found between the principles in which it believes (and which it also believes to be beneficial to the U.S. economy as a whole in the long run) and the demands presented by politically important groups. It was a combination of disparate interests—coastal water fishermen, petroleum and hard mineral industries, marine researchers—that contributed to the United States' change of position regarding the 200-mile economic zone in the oceans, following the initial "internationalist" proposal of 1970[8] favored by the Defense Department; and various industrial interests have clearly been in favor of a breakdown of the Law of the Seas Conference, as opposed to an International Authority for the seabeds of the high seas that could seriously curtail the advantages enjoyed by United States technology in the exploitation of seabed resources.

Radical ideologies that prevail among the elites of various Third World countries have not facilitated accommodation at UNCTAD, CIED, the United Nations, or the Law of the Seas Conference. In France, the Gaullists have resisted over the years the institutionalization of interdependence and, insofar as it appeared necessary, preferred formulas that would give France a possibility of leadership—for instance, European as against Atlantic intergovernmental cooperation, and "Euro-Arab" arrangements for energy rather than the U.S.-dominated International Energy Agency. Many observers were concerned about what the consequences for European and Atlantic cooperation would be if, in France, a left-wing coalition came to power and collided with economic interdependence. There were two reasons for this fear. One was the ideological hostility of the Parti Communiste Français and of a fraction of the Parti Socialiste to international structures dominated by "capitalist" states and principles, and their belief that the constraints of interdependence (especially where capital movements are concerned) could seriously hamper domestic social reform but should not be allowed to do so—a belief expressed previously by the British Labour party in the days of the Coal and Steel Community. The other reason was the possible resort by the Left to make protectionist moves or to safeguard provisions of international agreements such as the Treaty of Rome, as a result of economic and financial mismanagement. But when the collision with interdependence occurred in 1982, the latter prevailed—partly because of Mitterrand's foreign policy priorities (pro-West) and desire not to be tied to a process of radicalization. Paradoxically, one finds more evidence of the role of ideology if one moves across the Atlantic. Whatever one may think about who, in the long run, is likely to gain more from East-West trade, such commerce is an attempt at creating a network of mutual opportunities and restraints where none existed before. The Jackson amendment, voted by the United States Congress in 1973 at the request of a combination of "cold warriors" and Jewish organizations, brought the attempt, if not to a halt, at least down to very modest proportions. In 1981-1985, the Reagan administration's free-market ideology dictated both its hostility to coordinated interdependence in the realm of exchange rates and its resistance to the protectionist demands created by the huge trade deficit the United States owed to its strong dollar and comparatively stronger recovery.

IV

The problem of the interactions between domestic imperatives and the process of interdependence can be examined at two levels. At the highest level of generality, one can argue that there is an inherent contradiction between a global world economy, between the existence of problems which cry out for global solutions, on the one hand, and the fragmentation of the world into sovereign states on the other. As long as a small number of advanced nations seemed capable of playing a kind of collective steering role, the disadvantages of this tension could be reduced or disregarded. But the challenge from the Third World has put in question the legitimacy of this steering role. On key issues: energy, oceans, investments, trade, arms restraint, no solutions are conceivable without Third World participation. On some of these and on other major issues: food, arms, oil, trade, the participation of the Communist countries will also become increasingly necessary. Moreover, as the power discrepancies among the members of the steering group have fluctuated or sharpened, agreement among them along the lines of American policy has become less likely. Hence the need for a kind of leap "beyond the nation-state," either toward a world government or toward a considerable strengthening and broadening of collective institutions, endowed with substantial powers of management and decision.[9]

The problem with this analysis lies in the clash between diagnosis and prescription. If the diagnosis is correct (as indeed it is), how will the actors be led to the wholesale *auto-da-fé* of their residual powers of control—especially in a world in which many of them are new states whose first concern is to *create* domestic authority, and no consensus exists on the nature of the global solutions? Governments continue to derive their legitimacy from their home turf, however much their grip over it may have weakened. Most of the world is in the hands of governments which consider their first duty to be either the preservation of their control from external, ideologically hostile or economically exploitative intrusions, or else the establishment of their control over populations and resources still recently under the rule of colonial powers. This makes a leap or a sudden mutation perfectly implausible.

Let us therefore climb down to a more modest and realistic level. We can note that the contradiction between global issues and state fragmentation has so far been managed, by trial and error, partly because of the very restraints which interdependence imposes and which states observe in their own self-interest (cf. the Reagan administration's turnaround on the role of international financial institutions, in order to prevent the bankruptcy of several Latin American countries), and partly because of the opportunities for absolute, joint, or even relative gains which its exploitation provides. But there are three reasons for concern—which have become evident in the past seven or eight years.

1. The relatively successful management of the past was related to two conditions, both of which have changed. The first was regular economic growth—insufficient to close or even narrow the gap between the rich and the poor, but sufficient to provide absolute gains to most nations. The promise of constant growth is flickering, less because of the "limits to growth" or the population explosion than because of its inflationary consequences. For most states have neither the internal means to curb inflation (cf. below), nor the possibility of preventing its import from abroad without cutting themselves off thereby from the benefits of interdependence, nor the desire to establish a stringent monetary system that would oblige them not to live above their means, because of internal resistances and of fear that such a system would not provide enough liquidity for growth. And yet, the need to act against inflation, once it begins endangering either the fabric of domestic society or the competitivity of the nation, leads to recurrent recessions which reduce the ability of states to cooperate, and shifts the governments' attention to domestic priorities and pressures. The second condition was the preponderance of the United States, Washington's role as the leader of the steering group.

2. The willingness of states to bear the intrusive costs of interdependence is being severely strained by two phenomena inherent in interdependence. One is the permanent manipulation of all by all; for it means an enlarged capacity of foreign states to affect, accidentally (through their own domestic policies) or intentionally (through their foreign economic policies), the domestic affairs of others, and a similar capacity for foreign, private holders of capital. This in turn means that the state is at the mercy of foreign-

induced crises, which require emergency "solutions" that fully satisfy no one, and in fact prepare further crises. Moreover, this manipulation entails the ability of states (or non-state actors), if they are in a position of power, to harm others either by refusing or by unilaterally changing the rules of the game.

Secondly, such manipulation, and indeed the very existence of constraining ties, puts into stark relief the unevenness of power. The closer the bonds, the more troublesome is inequality: for there will be a permanent temptation to exploit or to reverse it. Interdependence among unequals is likely to be recurrently unbearable both to the very strong and to the very weak. It will be unacceptable to the very strong, if they are constantly summoned to make sacrifices on behalf of the weak and, so to speak, to subsidize them in order to prevent the system's unraveling, especially if such help would either save the weak from having to shape up, or allow them to challenge their benefactor—an experience which many Americans resented in the 60's, and which led to the reassertion of national power in 1971; an experience many West Germans resent now, in dealing with their EEC partners or in North-South relations. And the terms of interdependence will be unacceptable to the weak, if they have means of redress, either through the exploitation of an oligopoly (OPEC), or through coalition-building. In the 1970's, the growing discrepancy between Bonn and its partners within the EEC resulted, if not in a breakdown of a Community that continues to serve the interests of all its members (Bonn has to keep its weaker partners from imposing unilateral trade restrictions or from undergoing drastic political upheavals through economic disruption), at least in a virtual stoppage of attempts at common policies.

The two factors converge in the following way: the international economy, manipulated by its members, operates as a constant but unpredictable system of double redistribution—of incomes, jobs, status within nations, and wealth and power among nations. But the domestic victims of this redistribution do not acknowledge the legitimacy of a haphazard or shifty mechanism that is external to the nation, and competes or conflicts with the internal redistributive schemes that have been legitimately, authoritatively, or imperatively set up within the confines of the nation.

3. Conversely, the capacity of states to withstand domestic pressures that amount to a rebellion against the constraints of interdependence and a withering away of its opportunities, is also in doubt. Here again, there are two factors. One is the radical increase in the functions of states (not only in advanced societies): they have undertaken the roles of "creators—as well as redistributors—of the common wealth;"[10] they have the responsibility for welfare, full employment, cultural identity, the promotion of national technology or elites, etc.: tasks that often squeeze them between their obvious interest in increasing wealth thanks to the benefits from trade and foreign investment (or from investment abroad), and the threats which free trade and free capital movements create for national autonomy or for specific

sectors. The other factor is the growing self-assertion of domestic groups, either hostile to foreign control or competition, or unwilling to limit the growth of their incomes to whatever may be compatible with the monetary discipline or the external competitivity of national goods, which participation in an open world economy requires. In the developing countries, the pressure on governments frequently comes from élites that complain about the lopsided development which openness to foreign capital induces; they argue for a "basic needs" strategy that would entail greater efforts at self-reliance and less resort to trade with the advanced nations or to foreign investments in exportable commodities or modern industry.

The two factors converge in overloading the agendas of governments, in obliging them to spend more time on domestic coalition-building and negotiating than on international bargaining, and in making societies live above their means. Of course, here again, some nations are better off than others: the famed crisis of ungovernability affected Japan or West Germany less than Britain, France, Italy, or the pre-Reagan United States. But what has been called "the dilemma of rising demands and insufficient resources"[11] is a widespread phenomenon—it seems to affect even some of the newly oil-rich nations. And the consequences are likely to be either a retreat from interdependence, if its constraints are deemed unbearable, or the kind of hazardous manipulation aimed at improving the balance of restraints and opportunities which submits the world economy to dangerous shocks.

Thus, we are left with two paradoxes. One is the contradiction between the universal desire for development and growth, which leaves room for huge disagreements about the best strategy (capitalist versus Communist, "basic needs" versus the benefits of rapid industrialization, liberalism versus planning, international bargaining versus "domesticism,"[12] etc.), yet rules out autarky in most cases, and the revolt against the costs, inequities and strains of interdependence which has just been described: a revolt which results both from widespread trends in the domestic make-up of nations, and from increasing power discrepancies which play havoc with interdependence. The other is the contradiction between the fact that most governments, especially in complex societies, find it difficult to move in ways other than marginal or incremental, given the weight and delicate balance of domestic obligations, and the fact that, nevertheless, international compacts, especially in the economic realm, are likely to be subjected to rapid erosion or disruption. In the absence of a central executive, legislator, or judge capable of enforcing them despite changes in the respective positions of the partners, and given the unlikeliness of a resort to force to impose enforcement over most of these issues, such compacts are at the mercy of the more daring—the least encumbered by domestic burdens, or on the contrary, the most hard-pressed by domestic demands, or simply the most ambitious. Crises thus appear as altogether inevitable, useful insofar as they force governments to cope with essential issues left unattended by incrementalism—and dangerous because of the strain they put on the international system.

V

What can be done to prevent domestic priorities and concerns from destroying interdependence? Let us return to an earlier point. There is little to be gained by exhorting statesmen not to kill the golden goose, or the golden calf, even if it threatens to move from the backyard into the living room. Their primary responsibility is to their nation, and they will "respect interdependence" only as long as it serves the national interest. Nor are they likely to sacrifice an economic policy, geared to their assessment of national needs and moods, to outside demands for a different policy more profitable to other nations at least in the short run (cf. West German resistance in 1977–8 to pleas for a more expansionist policy that would accelerate its partners' recovery). The problem of world order, in this realm as in others, is to insure the compatibility of *national* objectives. For what, to an outside observer, looks like a clash between national and global considerations, appears to the statesman like a contest between different national interests.

One among many debates about future prospects has offered contrasting views.[13] Marina von N. Whitman has suggested that the best way to deal with "the darker side," the "vulnerability aspect" of interdependence—given the need to avoid a "widespread retreat into protectionism" and the fact that flexible exchange rates have not provided much "insulation from external disturbances"—is to match "the increase in integration at the market level with some increase in coordination at the policy level"; and she suggests both positive coordination of macroeconomic policies among the advanced countries, and negative coordination (primarily in trade) between advanced and developing nations. Thierry de Montbrial has expressed skepticism about the prospects of positive coordination: nation-states are not ready to accept limits on their "freedom about domestic economic policy in the name of global interdependence." The logical conclusion, he says, is that "interdependence should be somewhat reduced," or contained. In particular, there must be limitations to the free trade principle (and many exist already, in agriculture or commodity agreements). In fact, there is far less of a contradiction between these views than a superficial reading suggests. Both are concerned with saving the global world economy, and eager to provide states and individuals with a modicum of order and predictability. Both realize that it is necessary to "preserve the scope for countries to pursue legitimately different objectives with respect to their domestic economies." Mrs. Whitman acknowledges the need to "cushion the shocks of change" (in trade patterns, which create formidable adjustment problems) in the short run. Mr. de Montbrial would, I am sure, be willing to recognize that even a state that refuses, for example, to "bring deflation at home, in the name of international interdependence," would be well advised, in setting its domestic economic policies, to take into account likely effects on others that could boomerang (as when the American soybean embargo led to a loss of subsequent soybean exports), or other nations' policies that could vitiate the effectiveness of its own. And he might also recognize that the orderly limitation of the free trade principle would require a great deal of bargaining and coordination (he himself mentions the Lomé Stabex formula, and agriculture).

The fact is that few nations want to retreat from interdependence altogether, and face the losses of wealth or the foregoing of gains which would result. The real choice is not between decoupling the domestic polity from the world economy, and ever increasing interdependence. It is between a disorderly and crisis-ridden approach, and an orderly one which reconciles different domestic imperatives in an interdependent world. Such reconciliation cannot occur if one state—say, the United States in the 1980s—tries to impose its own conceptions and policies on others: for the guinea pigs will object, and the attempt will boomerang.[14] It can occur only through bargaining and cooperation. But these, in turn, will be successful only if ways are found both to reduce the costs and to increase the benefits of interdependence for the nations. Some of these ways will have to be explored jointly, as the goals and outcomes of cooperation. But some will have to be found through individual, domestic action, that would make the nation capable of orderly international cooperation. In other, clearer words, the problem discussed here can be solved only if states follow two, apparently divergent yet complementary directions. One is a self-imposed national reduction of vulnerability, aimed at reducing, so to speak, the pressure from the outside— at limiting the risks of interdependence (which is, however, one way of *improving* the balance of costs and opportunities). It may well entail, as Montbrial suggests, a curtailing, or a slowing down, or a cushioning of interdependence; for the nations as well as for individuals, constant and total manipulation from the outside is simply not tolerable. The other direction is the search for common solutions to global problems, by states eager both to prevent those external disruptions that starkly expose their loss of domestic autonomy (and thus bring about revolts against interdependence), and to maximize joint gains.

The reduction of vulnerability, at the cost of some sacrifice of interdependence, yet as the only way to avoid a far worse retreat from it, can take many forms. Three should be mentioned here.

1. Improved domestic management of the national economy is the best prerequisite for orderly cooperation, the best method for minimizing the impact of external shocks. This means, essentially, for the advanced countries, a sound anti-inflationary policy at home; endemic inflation, at inevitably uneven rates, disturbs trade patterns among advanced countries, provokes reactions which disrupt them even more (for in periods of recession and high unemployment, the loss of domestic jobs to foreign competition is particularly resented), and incites developing nations to try to raise in turn the prices of their own commodities, so as to protect their export earnings. To be sure, the international monetary system is often accused of contributing to inflation (the only debate seems to be about whether floating rates are less inflationary than the system of the sixties). However, certain countries

such as West Germany have shown skill in controlling inflation nevertheless, even before the drastic international recession of 1981-2. What seems necessary is either a domestic system that opposes no insurmountable obstacles to the occasional decline of real wages, as in the United States, or one that allows for an incomes policy agreed upon between the government and the labor unions (which does not imply that domestic inflation is due only to the push of wages; but that has been a major factor in past years).[15] For the developing countries, improved management that reduces vulnerability could take the form of a partial switch to a "basic needs" strategy, which would both reduce the need to gain massive access for industrial products on the markets of the advanced nations, and the need to let foreign enterprises shape the development of the national economy.

2. A second necessary action is the deliberate effort to thwart external blackmailing possibilities, or to reduce dependence on outside suppliers capable of extracting an exorbitant economic or political price for their supplies. I am referring to the need, in the advanced countries, for domestic energy conservation and development measures, and for the creation of stockpiles of fuel and other essential materials; to the need for reserves of food in countries threatened with shortages; to the need, for many developing countries, to regulate and orient the activities of foreign enterprises, especially when these control vital national resources.

3. Limiting vulnerability through national action must also take the form of more effective and farsighted domestic policies of adjustment to losses from trade and from the changes in the international division of labor that trade brings about. Adjustment assistance schemes are obviously inadequate in periods of mass unemployment. But, on the one hand, they can never be a substitute for the combination of domestic management and international cooperation that alone could perhaps avoid the disaster of huge lay-offs; and on the other hand, the choice governments face is between a policy of internal "concertation" with representatives of potentially threatened sectors, aimed at orderly adjustment and reconversion, and a policy of resistance to external competition (or to the elimination of obstacles to third world exports toward industrial countries) with dangerous consequences either for economic efficiency or for world order.

However, such domestic measures will be of no avail if the onslaught of interdependence is such as to make internal disruptions inevitable. Hence the need for cooperative solutions, aimed at making interdependence both generally bearable and mutually profitable. It would take several volumes to sketch out such schemes, issue by issue. Again, here, three points will suffice.

1. There must be cooperative attempts at mutual damage limitation. It is not in the interest of exporting countries to threaten simultaneously, in a given country (say, the United States), a number of industries that employ large quantities of workers, for such a threat would provoke irresistible demands for protection. It may not be in the interest of developing nations to press demands for preferential access to the markets of developed countries,

if the granting of preferences is compensated by an escalating resort to escape clauses and safeguards.[16] Agreements which would entail, not permanent voluntary restraints on competition but a *spacing* of it (over time and place), or assurances of equal access to the markets of industrial states without the latter's resort to escape provisions, would be preferable. Similarly, especially in periods of recession, agreements against beggar-thy-neighbor policies, or policy coordination aimed at avoiding the simultaneous resort to deflationary measures in the leading economies, or more effective attempts at "managing" floating rates so as to avoid major or manipulative fluctuations, according to common guidelines, would belong in this category. So would case-by-case agreements on the debts of Third World countries, to avoid the damage that would result, either from the total cancellation of all debts (a heavy blow to their own prospects for further credit, and to further profitable "Northern" involvement), or from the bankruptcy of the poorer and needier of these nations.

2. The major task will be the search for areas of mutual or joint gain. Among the industrial powers, the most productive area may well be that of trade—the gradual reducation of non-tariff barriers, given the demonstrated mutual benefits, for economic growth, from the huge expansion of international trade since the Second World War. Between advanced and developing countries, there do exist, within the limits discussed above, profitable mutual prospects in trade: advanced nations will be able to sell more goods and services to the developing countries, if they provide these with the means to pays for such imports, either through direct aid or through the granting of access to their markets for the goods produced, thanks to the technology and capital equipment provided by the industrial states. But even in the realm of commodity agreements, there may be room for broad (rather than strict) mutuality: one side accepting to pay for measures aimed at stabilizing prices, in exchange for guarantees of access to supply; and in the exploitation of the world's commons, there is ample room for joint gains. It is only if these occur that the populations of the industrial nations will be willing to make the quite considerable sacrifices entailed, for them, by the so-called new international economic order, or rather by a new international division of labor.

3. I have mentioned above the fragility of such compacts in a world of competing calculations, where the reciprocity of interests is never complete, and each side fears gaining less, or keeps trying to gain more, than the other. The bargains that have proved most durable are those which are founded either on a common concern for military security (and the preponderance of one provider of this public good), or on a common political will that both promotes and transcends the economic calculations. It is difficult to see new "common wills" comparable to that which animated, whatever their ambiguities, ambivalences, and animosities, all the champions of the European enterprise; and as for American military predominance, it is made less effective as an integrating force both by the many disagreements among the allies concerning diplomacy and strategy, and by the limited or

nonexistent role of force in the economic arenas of world affairs. In the mid-1970's, some saw in growing Arab interdependence a kind of replica of the European movement—but the latter was based on a will to reconciliation (especially between France and Germany); the former was based on a will to revenge, and fell apart.

We may well be doomed to imperfect deals between brittle bargaining structures, regional or ideological alignments of states with limited common interests. But even these would be imperiled if, on the strategic-diplomatic chessboard of world politics, states used their resources for, and tried to achieve mutual gains through, the development of vast weapons arsenals and industries. Ultimately, economic interdependence itself depends on moderation on, and successful management of, that chessboard. It is here, above all, that damage limitation is essential. For it is the precondition to all the cooperative enterprises necessary for damage limitation and joint gains in the economic realm. And while, as we have seen, domestic goals and pressures often submit interdependence to excessive stresses, economic interdependence does ultimately place on state power restraints that do not exist in any comparable way in the strategic-diplomatic realm. It is there that the model of world politics as a zero-sum game remains most valid; and it is therefore there that the conflict between domestic ambitions and world order risks, as in the past, being the most inexpiable. The resources devoted to traditional security concerns weigh heavily on governments and sharply reduce the gains from economic interdependence; these concerns often make the loss of domestic autonomy appear intolerable. In the short run, the extension of interdependence to the trade in arms may seem like an idyllic way of reconciling national objectives, of making interdependence compatible with domestic politics; but in the long run this may turn out to be the most self-destructive of delusions—and the area where there is both the greatest need and the greatest difficulty for cooperation in removing regional or global time bombs.

Notes

1. In James Chace and Earl Ravenal, eds, *Atlantis Lost* (New York: New York University Press, 1976), p. 230.

2. Richard Cooper, *The Economics of Interdependence* (New York: McGraw-Hill, 1968), p. 152.

3. Richard Cooper, *The Economics of Interdependence* (New York: McGraw-Hill, 1968), p. 152.

4. David S. Landes (ed.), in *Western Europe: Trails of Partnership* (Lexington, Mass.: Heath, 1977), p. 8.

5. See the chapters by Benjamin J. Cohen and Richard Feinberg in Kenneth A. Oye, Robert J. Lieber, and Donald Rothchild, *Eagle Defiant* (Boston: Little, Brown, 1983); and Henry Nau, "Where Reaganomics Works," *Foreign Policy*, no. 57 (Winter 1984-5), pp. 14–37.

6. Cf. Peter J. Katzenstein, "International Relations and Domestic Structures: Foreign Economic Policies of Advanced Industrial States," *International Organization* 30, no. 1 (Winter 1976).

7. Cf. Graham Allison and Peter Szantos, *Remaking Foreign Policy* (New York: Basic Books, 1976); and Commission on the Organization of the Government for the Conduct of Foreign Policy, *Appendices*, vol. 3 (June 1975).

8. Cf. Ann. L. Hollick, "Seabeds Make Strange Politics," *Foreign Policy* 9 (Winter 1972-3).

9. This is the position of the participants in the World Order Models Project; cf. Richard Falk, *A Study of Future Worlds* (New York: Free Press, 1975).

10. Edward L. Morse, *Modernization and the Transformation of International Relations* (New York: Free Press, 1976), p. 98.

11. Harold and Margaret Sprout, quoted in Morse, *op. cit.*, p. 98.

12. See the debate between C. Fred Bergsten and Henry R. Nau on "Reaganomics," in *Foreign Policy*, no. 59 (Summer 1985), pp. 132-153.

13. *Trialogue* (published by the Trilateral Commission), no. 13 (Winter 1976-7), pp. 2-7.

14. On cooperation as an alternative to and substitute for hegemony, see Robert O. Keohane, *After Hegemony* (Princeton, N.J.: Princeton University Press, 1984).

15. See the reflections of Raymond Aron in *Plaidoyer pour l'Europe décadente* (Paris: Robert Laffont, 1977), Ch. VII.

16. Cf. Richard Cooper, "A New International Economic Order for Mutual Gain," *Foreign Policy* 26 (Spring 1977), pp. 100, 118.

PART FOUR

Sermons and Suggestions

14

International Organization and the International System

Specialists in the field of international organization have noted with some alarm a decline of interest among students and foundations in the study of the United Nations system. There has been a shift first toward the study of regionalism and the theory of integration; later, toward that of international regimes. The interest in integration and regimes reflects both the persistence and the transformation of the kind of idealism that originally pervaded, guided, and at times distorted the study of international organization. The former shift resulted primarily in a displacement of interest toward those geographically more restricted institutions (such as the European Communities) whose main task seemed to be to promote integration. This reflects one reality of postwar world politics—the division of a huge and heterogeneous international system into subsystems in which patterns of cooperation and ways of controlling conflicts are either more intense or less elusive than those in the global system. We have now come to understand that integration, in the sense of a process that devalues sovereignty, gradually brings about the demise of the nation-state and leads to the emergence of new foci of loyalty and authority is only one, and by no means the most important, of the many functions performed by regional organizations. At first, this understanding led only in part to a more sober and searching assessment of these functions.

Those who remained concerned with the UN system have also gradually shifted their efforts; the study of the nature, preconditions, and effects of international regimes has focused attention both on the "functional" (i.e., primarily economic) agencies of the UN system and on patterns that are not necessarily institutionalized. The emphasis on the bargains struck by the actors is greater than that on the organizations. A different emphasis, advocated some years before, on a comparative study of the institutions still expressed a willingness to detach or abstract international organization from the international system. But it has become clear that international institutions, in their political processes and in their functions, reflect and to some extent magnify or modify the dominant features of the international system. Therefore, instead of concentrating on these institutions as if they were a closed universe, one ought to study them as patterns of cooperation and of muted conflict whose nature, evolution, effectiveness, and outcomes cannot be studied apart from the global system or from the relevant subsystem. In this respect the discussion of international organization by political scientists would follow the same curve as the study of international law or of war.

Since international organizations provide procedures for cooperation or for the temperate pursuit of conflict, it is obvious that their effectiveness depends on the degree of moderation of the international system. A revolutionary system wracked by inexpiable power rivalries and ideological conflicts is one in which international organization is reduced to impotence as a force of its own and to the condition of a helpless stake in the competition of states. This was the fate of the League of Nations in its second decade. On the other hand, not every moderate international system need be one in which global international organization plays a major role. This is not due to any built-in conflict between the balance of power, the traditional moderating mechanism in international politics, and international organization: Such a conflict exists only with respect to one function of international organization, collective security. Rather it is due to two other facts. A moderate international system will be one in which global international organization plays a major role in the muting of conflict and the spread of cooperation only if, in the first place, there exists a broad procedural consensus among states which makes of multinational institutions the legitimate channels for the management of conflict and cooperation and if, in the second place, there exists a preference for universal channels over regional ones. In other words, a moderate international system, or one in which there exist compelling reasons why even deep and lasting ideological and power conflicts must be kept under control, creates opportunities for international organization, but these opportunities may be meager and difficult to exploit (cf. the nineteenth-century international system).

It is impossible here to provide a thorough analysis of the international system or of the United Nations. I would like only to sketch briefly first the relations between the United Nations and the international system in recent years and second some of the possible relations in the future.

A Sketch of the Past

The image of the United Nations which guided the founding fathers of Dumbarton Oaks and San Francisco suffered from the huge discrepancy between the international system it postulated and the international system that emerged from World War II. The Charter assumed and required a pluralistic yet controlled world that never came into being. First, it was supposed to be managed and regulated by the concert of the Great Powers, a modern version of the European Concert. Secondly, it was supposed to be a moderate international system partly because that concert would keep it so, partly because of an optimistic evaluation about regimes (they would be "democratic"), economic conditions, and international legitimacy. Hence the primary responsibility for peace and security placed on the Big Five in the United Nations. Hence the famous provision of article 2, paragraph 7, about the respect for domestic jurisdiction—a precondition for moderation in past international systems—and the procedures of chapter VI which are traditional procedures of mediation and conciliation suitable for moderate conflicts. Hence, finally, the vague provisions about international economic affairs, inspired by "the free enterprise vision of the international economy,"[1] by the hope that there would be no fundamental imbalance between rich and poor countries, and by the expectation that, as in the past, economic development would be promoted essentially by private means.

The bipolar world of the late 1940's did not resemble this idyll any more than the Greek world before the Peloponnesian War resembled the international system after 1815. The Charter had created an international organization that was irrelevant to the revolutionary world in which two fierce ideological conflicts—East versus West and colonial versus anticolonial—seemed to destroy both the chances of any great-power consensus and the chances for moderation.

Facing a choice between permanent paralysis and transformation, a majority of the members of the United Nations opted for the latter even though it meant a drastic de facto revision of the Charter. Despite the legal primacy of the Security Council the UN, confronted with the breakdown of the great-power consensus, overhauled the system of the Charter through General Assembly Resolution 377A (V) of November 3, 1950 (the "Uniting for Peace Resolution"), which provided the General Assembly with some of the paralyzed Security Council's responsibilities in matters concerning force and thus appeared to reopen the road to collective security. Faced with life and death disputes, many of which originated within what the colonial powers claimed to be their domestic jurisdiction, the organs of the United Nations disregarded article 2, paragraph 7, tried to blur the differences between colonies and trusteeships, and innovated far beyond traditional diplomatic procedures by methods of collective intervention and the establishment of UN presences. When economic development emerged as a major problem in world politics, the United Nations multiplied agencies for technical assistance and development.

This de facto transformation of the United Nations was based on an image of the world that was at least as far removed from reality as had been the image of the original UN. It was the image of a fictitious world community able and willing to make of the UN a force that would represent and expand the common interest of mankind. It could be useful as a kind of Sorelian myth thanks to which one of the superpowers would rally a majority against its rival and enlist the UN behind its own policies, but it was once again bound to create illusions and disillusionment. For at the basis of these changes one finds two postulates. One was majority rule—a neat reversal from the days of the great-power unanimity principle and from the sober but paralyzing realism of those who had deemed international organization incapable of imposing the will of a majority, especially against a Great Power or its allies, in matters such as collective security or race relations. (And yet powers that were explicitly charged with aggression by UN organs turned out to be the Democratic People's Republic of Korea, the ally of the Union of Soviet Socialist Republics; then the People's Republic of China after its intervention in Korea; later the Soviet Union after its invasion of Hungary; and Vietnam because of its invasion of Cambodia). The second postulate was the capacity of the secretary-general to play a kind of executive role, carrying out mandates given to him by the General Assembly but also filling gaps, interpreting ambiguities in these delegations, taking political initiatives, enlarging, so to speak, the bridgehead toward one world, and defending the common interest of mankind.

Illusions have their virtue when they inspire action. The fiction of a world community has made it possible for the organs of the United Nations to concern themselves with most of the important political and economic issues that agitate the international system and to promote that equalization of concern which is a rudimentary, first factor of homogenization in a highly diverse and uneven world. Yet, as a result, a gap between attempts and achievements, resolutions and resolution, motions and motion appeared— a gap no smaller nor less frustrating than the original Charter's gap between legal possibilities and political aspirations. The majoritarian illusion has been short-lived. An obvious discrepancy between votes and compliance developed almost as soon as the Uniting for Peace Resolution was adopted. Thus the resolution was never to be fully put into effect insofar as collective security was concerned. Moreover, after the increase in UN membership since 1955 the art of obtaining sufficient majorities became subtle, arduous, and uncertain, and the hazards of such consensus building revealed all too often that numerical majorities in organs without weighted voting may breed as many disadvantages as the paralyzing vetoes of the Security Council. The hope for a largely autonomous secretary-general, executor or even shaper of the majority, was crushed twice: once when Trygve Lie had to resign because of Soviet obstruction, once when Dag Hammarskjöld, who after a cautious beginning in office and behind the misty screen of deliberately fuzzy language had become a bold manager and theorist of the "new United Nations," died in the midst of the most serious constitutional crisis of the organization.

And yet the demise of fictions has not meant a verdict of complete impotence and paralysis. The UN has been able to play a limited role as "universal actor" in the system because of certain favorable features that reintroduced a modicum of moderation into the international system. These features were quite different from those the founding fathers had expected. They have not obliterated either the revolutionary characteristics of the elements of the system (bipolar distribution of power; heterogeneity of the basic unit, of regimes, ideologies, and levels of development) or the revolutionary aspects of relations between units in the system (immoderate ends and means). But they have imposed certain limits on those means, thereby contained the inflation of ends within practical (if not verbal) limits, and restored some flexibility. It is the existence of these features which explains why in the UN in the 1950's even the minority went along (despite protests and filibusters) with the de facto revision of the Charter. The reason why the search for more elastic procedures of discussion and intervention, despite its excessive ambition, has allowed the United Nations to develop is the evolution of the international system. It is still an interstate system of competing units, but it is no longer the bipolar system of the late 1940's and early 1950's—neither "tight" nor "loose"; new features have emerged.

I have analyzed elsewhere[2] the nature of the present system in terms of three different layers; the fundamental, latent bipolar stratum; the manifest layer of polycentrism; and an emergent layer of multipolarity. Insofar as the relations between states which develop in this system are still revolutionary, the impact of the UN on world affairs continues to be severely limited. Thus, on the one hand, the bipolar contest has constantly reduced UN effectiveness: The UN has been timid or ineffective whenever one of the Big Two was determined to act freely with force or threats of force in its sphere of domination (the Soviet Union in Hungary, Czechoslovakia, and Afghanistan; and the United States in the Caribbean). Also, serious rifts between the superpowers have continued to result in UN impotence both during the "first" cold war and after the collapse of detente. There have been no attempts at organizing collective security in a world in which the mobilization of one camp against the other could all too easily mean world war III and in which those minor conflicts that find both superpowers determined not only to remain uninvolved but even to restore peace can be handled in less ponderous ways—ways which also do a better job of concealing the collusion of the otehrwise hostile superpowers. When serious disputes have broken out between the United States and its allies on one side and members of the now-splintered Communist world on the other, the role of the United Nations has been either nil (as during the second Berlin crisis of 1958–1962, the Vietnam War, and the Quemoy and Matsu incidents of 1955) or minimal (as during the Berlin blockade of 1948, the war in Laos, and the Cuban missile crisis of 1962). When moderation was observed or restored, it was not through the UN that this occurred. Whenever the great powers were at odds over a conflict that, even though it did not involve them directly, nevertheless greatly affected their interests, the effectiveness of UN peacekeeping operations suffered an eclipse, as in the Congo in the fall of 1960, or even collapsed, as in the Middle East in May 1967 and again in June 1982; or else the possibility of UN forces of interposition vanished (e.g., between Egypt and Israel, after the end of the second United Nations Emergency Force in 1981, and again in Beirut in the summer of 1982). The financial crisis that has affected UN peacekeeping ever since 1961 and has never been resolved is the direct result of a continuing constitutional conflict between the superpowers.

On the other hand, quite apart from cold-war situations, the prevalence of life and death conflicts between states or within states and the formidable challenge of the poor nations in the economic and social realms have left the UN incapable of finding remedies in the absence either of any substantive consensus of the superpowers or of any joint determination on their part to enforce such a consensus and in the presence of all the obstacles raised by state sovereignty. In major political crises the United Nations has sometimes been absent when it was obvious that intervention would meet with fierce resistance from one party (as in the Algerian War) or else when an attempt at intervening risked escalating, rather than resolving, a local conflict (as in Biafra). More often, the General Assembly or the Security Council have adopted resolutions that have not been effective (cf. the Indonesian attack on East Timor, the Moroccan move into the Western Sahara, the Falklands War, and Cambodia's occupation by Vietnam). A considerable difference has emerged between attempts at peacekeeping (or peace restoration)—which are often successful for the reasons to be discussed below—and attempts at solving the disputes that had led to violence—which are unsuccessful because of the resistance of some or all parties in matters that seemed to them to affect their essential interests; hence the long record of UN disappointments in Kashmir, Palestine, Cyprus, the Falklands, Namibia, Southern Rhodesia and South African apartheid, and in the war between Iran and Iraq. In economic affairs there has been no massive transfer of funds from the rich to the poor through UN channels. The story of efforts at creating agencies for capital development has been depressing, and the results of the UN Conference on Trade and Development (UNCTAD) have been disappointing. The bulk of aid to the underdeveloped countries continues to be handled by bilateral agreements. However huge the majority behind a resolution, if those who are asked to make a sacrifice, a gamble, or a move remain deaf, the majority will remain frustrated and the crises will stay unresolved in a world of states where the superpowers are often among the deaf and, even when they are not, distrust each other too much to establish a condominium.

There has, however, been some dampening of the superpowers' contest and a reintroduction not only of restraints but even of cooperation in multiple forms in the international system. I have stressed two factors as the main causes for these developments: the new legitimacy of the nation-state and the new conditions of the use of force in a nuclear world. A third factor deserves equal recognition: the heterogeneity of the system, which has made it impossible for the superpowers to engulf the whole planet into their rivalry (whereas Athens and Sparta had absorbed all of the Greek world into theirs). It has also made it possible for the lesser powers, protected by the legitimacy of nationalism and by the superpowers' fear of collision, to impose various restrictions on the Big Two duel. It has given to this duel and to the other contests in the system a variety of configurations depending on local and regional circumstances, and it has reintroduced—in what is the first worldwide international system in history—broad opportunities for balancing within and between regions. The second and third layers of the system—polycentrism and multipolarity—have thus appeared as a consequence of the muting of the bipolar conflict and as a reaction against the astringency of bipolarity. It is the combination of these three factors and of these changes in the international hierarchy which has given to the United Nations its chances and its role in postwar political and economic affairs.

The United Nations has reflected those features but also contributed to, exploited, and magnified them. Thus, the change in the balance of forces within the UN organs and the increasing need for bargaining and compromise in order to get resolutions passed reflects the shift from a bipolar world to the new, more complex system. In the bipolar one there could perhaps be thumping majorities piled up by one camp against another, but at the cost of effectiveness and with a purely symbolic meaning. In the present world, within the limits set by latent bipolarity (i.e., the exclusion of those issues over which an irreconcilable rift between the superpowers still condemns the United Nations to impotence) the lesser powers can play a conspicuous role on the world stage largely because of another kind of impotence: that of the superpowers which owe their dominant position to a kind of material might which they cannot freely use (i.e., weaponry). The relative deference with which the United Nations, even in colonial affairs, has treated France and the United Kingdom, its prudence toward Communist China, and the importance of India reflect the tendency toward multipolarity, i.e., the rise of secondary or potential nuclear powers. But the United Nations has also contributed to polycentrism because of the role which the voting procedures give to small states, each one of which counts as much as any large power and must be courted and coaxed for the requisite majority to be attained. Thus, the new balance of forces that emerged in the 1960's (both in a much larger General Assembly where no single bloc has any more the control of the requisite two-thirds majority and, more recently, in the broadened Security Council) has allowed the UN to mitigate somewhat the importance of bipolarity. What matters is not the positive agreement of the Big Five but the absence of deep disagreement of the Big Two. The enlargement of the membership gives an opportunity to third parties, whose votes are indispensable to the Big Two, to appeal to the common or convergent interests of the superpowers and thus to coax through their initiatives the kind of consensus which the original Charter had seemed to leave almost exclusively to the initiative of the superpowers themselves. In some instances it is the prodding of the smaller powers, dissatisfied with the gap between them and the superpowers, which produces a kind of defensive rapprochement of the Big Two qua superpowers, determined both to protect their superiority and to disarm the lesser powers' drive by occasional concessions that do not threaten their own position as top dogs (cf. the Treaty on the Nonproliferation of Nuclear Weapons, various votes on economic development; cf. also the attempt in the late 1960s to return to the Security Council its primary role).

Similarly, the United Nations reflects—indeed is based on—the principle of state sovereignty. But it has made quite a contribution to the legitimacy and sanctification of the nation-state. The increase in the importance of the General Assembly has heightened the attraction of statehood, and the ease with which the United Nations has, after 1955, given its blessing and opened its doors to new nations has been largely responsible for the huge rise in the number of new states: The United Nations, and especially its General Assembly, has been the matrix and target of new nation-states. Moreover, in the ex-colonial area as well as in economic affairs the organs of the United Nations have given a solemn endorsement to the nation-state (even to the mini-state) and have wrapped the rights and privileges of the Charter around the frail and shivering new nations, thus promoting a kind of pluralist and equalitarian legitimacy which inhibits considerably the more blatant moves the superpowers could be tempted to make in their relations with weaker states.

No one will doubt that the organs of the United Nations reflect the heterogeneity of the international system: In every major crisis submitted to the organization, such as the Congo or the Middle East, the diversity of regimes, ideologies, levels of development, regional concerns, allegiances, etc., engenders a drama of conflicting purposes and a process of painful negotiation. It is the combination of national legitimacy and fragmentation which accounts for the failure to establish an international police force and for the glaring weaknesses of past peacekeeping forces, for they have been crippled both by the nations' jealous defense of the principle of consent, as applied to the stationing and financing of those troops, and by the bloc conflicts that have shaped the composition of the forces and that led in May 1967 to the disintegration of the United Nations Emergency Force (UNEF). The more fragmented the international system, the less likely the establishment of a permanent army based on universally applicable principles and the more likely the reliance on ad hoc procedures and local balances. But the United Nations has also contributed to this fragmentation. The Sisyphean approach of its major organs, with their tendency to sacrifice precedents and legalism to flexibility and political expediency, has meant that each issue would be considered on its merits with due respect for the configuration of political forces at the moment and in the area. The attempt by Hammarskjöld and, more quietly, by his successor U Thant to engage in what the former had called "preventive diplomacy" so as to avoid the spread of the Cold War to all parts of the globe strengthened heterogeneity by reinforcing all those specific, sometimes parochial, forces that resist the absorption of local conflicts into the cold-war mäelstrom. The frequent reliance on, or deference to, regional organization has had the same effect.

Finally, the United Nations has of course reflected the new conditions of the use of force. Had the fear of nuclear war and the desire to prevent an escalation of major head-on collisions between the superpowers not dominated their policy and strategy, the United Nations would not have had the chance to become a test of coexistence. Had conquest and the subjugation of determined, well-organized peoples in revolt not become prohibitively costly, the United Nations would not have had the opportunity to intervene so often in wars of national liberation. The United Nations has been effective when there has been a sufficient consensus (explicit or tacit) between the superpowers to curtail third-party violence. If one examines the cases in which the Security Council or the General Assembly have been able to adopt resolutions which were put into effect by the organization or its members, one finds that they fall into three groups, all of which entailed such a consensus. First, there are the cases in which a concert of the superpowers developed for the restoration of peace in a troubled area in which they were not directly involved (Indonesia, Middle East crises of 1948 and 1956, Kashmir, Yemen). Secondly, there are the instances of resolutions adopted after a balancing process in which groups of states other than the two camps of "cold warriors" played a major role but succeeded in formulating an effective text only because of the explicit or tacit consent of the superpowers (Congo crisis in the summer of 1960 and after Hammerskjöld's death, Middle East crisis of 1958, Cyprus, Middle East crisis during the first week of June 1967 and later in November 1967; however, the superpowers' disagreement about the meaning of the Security Council resolution of November 22, 1967, deprived the initial concert in the latter case of its effectiveness—(again, Middle East crisis of October 1973, when UNEF II was created, and Lebanon crisis of June 1978, when UNIFIL was set up). Thirdly, there is a case involving both a concert and a balancing process: that of the nonproliferation treaty.

But the United Nations has, once again, gone beyond this: It has skillfully exploited what I have called the upper and the lower limits of the usefulness of applying force. It has buttressed the lower limit not by simply condemning the resort to force against peoples in revolt for their independence but by actually giving its blessing to the use of force toward the acquisition of statehood—much to the indignation of the colonial powers and despite the creation thereby of an apparent double standard toward violence (cf. India's attack on Goa): Wars of national liberation are legitimate, other resorts to force or threats of force are not (unless in case of self-defense). Also, the United Nations has done its best to strengthen the one barrier that is decisive for world peace—the upper limit on the use of force—through its practices of international neutralization in those military conflicts that it can handle. Its record of cease-fires, military observers, and peacekeeping forces expressed both the determination of the superpowers not to let world peace be upset by moves of (or conflicts within) the lesser powers and the determination of the small states to maximize the restraints on great-power intervention in such disturbances. The United Nations has thus provided indispensable devices for all-round face saving, making it possible, not only for belligerents to put an end to hostilities without humiliation, but also to install some impartial, if fragile, checks on peace once the fighting has ended. The result is original: Even though the stopping of armed conflicts through international pressure (including the tacit or explicit consensus of the superpowers) is an old practice of balance-of-power systems, the fact that UN peacekeeping mechanisms have kept aside the Great Powers contributes to the atrophy of the latter's coercive power.

A final judgment on the *role* of the United Nations in the system and on the *impact* of the UN on the system must, once again, be balanced.

Concerning its role, the change in legal practices and the emergence of new voting groups in the United Nations have increased the flexibility, maneuverability, and scope of interests of UN organs without drastically transforming the limits imposed by the international system. The record is complex. First, as an instrument of international cooperation and conflict resolution the United Nations appears as a kind of residual category. It is effective in the sense of having both authority and legitimacy in cases which prove to be neither too divisive (as are the cold-war conflicts, substantive disagreements in the Middle East or Asia, racial issues in southern Africa, etc.), nor too huge to be handled by the limited means of the organization (as was Algeria), nor capable of being treated primarily by or shunted to a regional organization (cf. the Organization of American States [OAS] for Guatemala and the Dominican Republic, the Organization of African Unity [OAU] for Biafra). The only exception to this has been the Korean war, which turned out to be neither a precedent nor a model.

Second, as a residual instrument the United Nations has been extraordinarily resilient. As an arena and a stake it has been useful to each of the competing groups eager to get not only a forum for their views but also diplomatic reinforcement for their policies in the Cold War as well as in the wars for decolonization. As an institution able to discharge various executive responsibilities in peacekeeping, technical assistance, or economic development, the United Nations has proven to be necessary almost to all. It has been necessary to those states that were the beneficiaries of efforts whose absence would have exposed them to greater poverty, more debilitating defeats, or more overt great-power pressure. It has also been necessary to major states that, had the United Nations not existed, would have had a difficult choice between direct, undisguised, and trouble-making involvement on behalf of their national interests and possibly damaging abstention. What has kept the United Nations afloat in a stormy world has been, and remains, the need for all states to find some form of deterrence against the most formidable of these storms (large-scale wars, major economic disasters) and the impossibility for even the superpowers to count exclusively on their own individual efforts or on direct agreements (ruled out by their context) for such protection.

Third, however, the UN, in the 1970s and 1980s, has become the victim of its own accomplishments: some of these have boomeranged. When the superpowers switched from Cold War to detente, their need for the UN as a dampener of their quarrels in gray areas diminished (and Henry Kissinger was no friend of the UN): in the Middle East crisis of 1973, the essential deals were struck either by the two major rivals or by the U.S. shuttle diplomacy, with the UN playing a minor role only. As for its contribution to polycentrism, the multiplication and emancipation of small actors led to a rash of violent conflicts that have often highlighted UN impotence (India-Pakistan over Bangladesh, Cyprus in 1974, Somalia versus Ethiopia, South Africa–Angola, Vietnam-Cambodia, Iran-Iraq, etc.): the UN, in this respect, has played sorcerer's apprentice and has had to resign itself to what Ernst Haas calls "toleration of low levels of conflict."[3]

Concerning the impact of the UN on the system, the United Nations has both contributed to defusing it by restoring elements of moderation and management and helped to subvert the international hierarchy. There are other, powerful reasons for this subversion, for the relative "impotence of power" of the great powers and the greater freedom of maneuver of the small states. But the United Nations, by its procedural practices as well as by the way in which it has exercised its legitimizing function, has reinforced the importance of the lesser powers. In this respect its contribution to world order is mixed, for although there remains the necessity to curtail the predominance of the superpowers in a world in which force is too blunt a tool and most of the tasks have to be performed through consent, too radical a reversal of the hierarchy can be pretty unhealthy. The UN propels on the world scene states or statesmen whose performance rests more on showmanship than on realities and thus divorces posture from responsibility. It has also thereby led both to the explosions and brushfires of violence among the smaller powers and to the partial collusion of the great powers, which are determined to restore or protect their supremacy. The role played by the United nations in legitimizing the nation-state helps safeguard national independence and integrity, but it also perpetuates all the obstacles that the traditional state of nature has accumulated on the road to peace and cooperation. The United Nations' contribution to heterogeneity has moderated and fragmented the relation of major tension between the United States and the Soviet Union, but it has also made calculations of deterrence and control more difficult and complicated the search for world-wide solutions to major problems. The UN approach to the use of force has added to the superpowers' inhibitions on conventional and nuclear war, but, combined with repeated UN failures in solving disputes and with the encouragement to wars of liberation, it has also helped the generalization of violence at lower levels, favored the "internationalization" of war, and encouraged further trends toward balkanization. Success in extinguishing fires has not prevented, indeed it has facilitated, the freezing of underlying conflicts and the incitation of troublemakers to resort to subversion, infiltration, psychological warfare, etc.

Thus, one can conclude that while the United Nations has been a significant factor in establishing a world order based on the nation-state and possessing a distorted, rather equalitarian hierarchy, considerable flexibility, and severe taboos on the traditional ways of using force, it has also perpetuated the drawbacks of sovereignty and bought overall moderation at the cost of making the resort to limited or subliminal violence endemic and the recurrent explosion of unsolved disputes inevitable.[4] Only utopians will find this mixed balance sheet distressing. Historians will recognize in this picture many (but not all) of the features of balance-of-power systems, in which the code of legitimacy was far less equalitarian and resort to force less inhibited but in which large conflicts used to be avoided or moderated at the cost of multiplying lesser ones.

A Query for the Future

The future relations between the United Nations and the international system and the role the United Nations could play in it depend essentially on what this system will be and this, in turn, depends much less on UN actions (given their limited effectiveness and the fact that they reflect state policies more than they affect them) than on other factors to be mentioned below.

The Evolution of the International System

We are living in what might be called the world political system, an international system which differs from past ones not only through its scope but also through features that deserve a theoretical and empirical study. The nature of this system is original, its future unclear.

It is marked, in the first place, by increasing interpenetration between domestic politics and international politics. The conceptualization of the latter as a "state of war," in contrast with the ideal type of the former as a community with central power, remains valid at the level of ideal types. There are however two new and important qualifications. On the one hand, there is a *rapprochement* in practice between the two kinds of politics. In many nations (new and old) there is little consensus, central power is more a stake than a force, and there is a potential and even endemic state of war. At the same time international politics has become more moderate. This is partly due to the new conditions of the use of force. There is another cause; for a variety of reasons (including those new conditions as well as economic enmeshment in an age dominated by the expansion of science and technology) the competition between states takes place on several chessboards in addition to the traditional military and diplomatic ones: for instance, the chessboards of world trade, of world finance, of aid and technical asistance, of space research and exploration, of military technology, and the chessboard of what has been called "informal penetration." These chessboards do not entail the resort to force. On most of them competition is based, not on the traditional kind of strategic-diplomatic interaction in which each player remains a separate unit following the logic of diversity, but on an interdependence which, to be sure, often covers relations of domination and dependence yet creates a logic of integration which restricts considerably the theoretical freedom of choice of each actor. Thus, "winning" presupposes the acceptance and mastery of considerable constraints. These constraints result either from the player's own entanglement in the web or (as, for instance, in the case of attempts at "playing domestic politics" abroad by manipulating foreign political movements or interest groups) from the hazardous nature of the game on this chessboard over which the actor rarely has adequate control. International politics thus becomes much more complex. Not only does each chessboard have rules of its own, but there are complicated and subtle relations between chessboards: For instance, depending on the national situation a state may be able to offset its weakness on one chessboard thanks to its strength on another or else be prevented from exploiting its strength on one because of its weakness on another.

On the other hand, there is a tight *interconnection* between the two kinds of political systems: While international politics still consists largely of interstate moves, a fourfold "internalization" of world politics is going on. Foreign policy entails increasingly attempts at influencing domestic affairs, i.e., at operating within rather than across borders. Major changes in the system result from revolutions rather than wars: Internal upheavals and crises short of all-out war (i.e., breakdowns which reflect the greater moderation of international politics) are now the two chief agents of change. Major shifts in rank in the international system result from domestic achievements or failures rather than from interstate contests. Finally, the international system of today is not one of cool, somewhat interchangeable, cabinet diplomats but one of "socially mobilized" polities which project on the world scene their domestic conceptions, experiences, and fantasies instead of following some external and objective national interest. Thus international politics becomes a kind of confrontation of domestic political systems in action (with an alternation of periods in which international politics is a frenzied clash of national designs or phobias and quieter periods in which the national systems "turn inward" and give priority to domestic demands, with a corresponding shift in priorities on and among the chessboards).

In the second place there is also a growing interpenetration between transnational society and world politics (defined as interstate politics). The *logic* of the "game" of world politics, so well analyzed by Raymond Aron, is shaped by the nature of the international milieu. But the *scope* and the specific *rules* of the game at any given time are determined, on the one hand, by the type of international system in existence (characterized mainly by the number of major powers, the presence or absence of major ideological cleavages, and the technology of conflicts) and, on the other hand, by the nature of the relations between state and society in the main competing units. Today, there is a world political system but no worldwide transnational society: There is still only partial contact between Communist China and much of the rest of the world at the level of society (whereas Communist China is definitely part of the international political system), and great discontinuities persist between the non-Communist transnational society and the Eastern world. Especially, but not only, in the latter there is—by comparison with the world of economic liberalism—a considerable politization of transnational society: The states control, directly or indirectly, the international economy and communications, international monetary relations, and the development of technology. The large so-called multinational corporations, due to their control, size, and wealth, cannot be considered either purely private or genuinely cosmopolitan. Their activities do affect the chips with which states play on several of the chessboards of international politics (hence the frequent resistance of states to their penetration by "private" foreign companies). Many of the transnational forces—such as the powerful anti-Western sweep of Islamic fundamentalism—aim at getting control of the state (as happened in Iran in 1979).

But, conversely, despite such politicization there is in much of the world a semi-autonomous transnational society in the sense that it too has rules of its own, determined by its functions, which the state players must respect or can disregard only at prohibitive costs given the degree of interdependence. One can speak of additional chessboards such as that of industrial technology, on which the actors are both states (either as clients or as initiators) and private groups (corporations, banks), or that of scientific research, on which the actors are states, universities (public or private), foundations, industries, etc. Thus the interstate competition of today, while it has reached an unprecedented scope geographically and functionally, must observe a variety of restraints which contribute to making the world political system look more like domestic polities (a term which refers both to the narrow political sector, i.e., the state, and to the state's relations to society).

In what direction is this world political system going? The two interpenetrations will persist. But, far from limiting the number of possibilities, this prediction actually increases them. If one examines the international system of today, one can state that some of its features are irrevocable. Nuclear weapons will not be disinvented, "social mobilization" (or the decline of apathy, or the growth of communications) will continue, and technological innovation will probably be accelerated. Other features are likely to persist but not with the same degree of certainty: the nuclear stalemate between the superpowers (yet who can be sure that there will be neither breakdown nor unilateral breakthrough?), the military gap between the superpowers and other states, the relative fragmentation of the system and its basic heterogeneity. All the rest—including the present balance between its three layers and its ad hoc restraints on force—is dubious. Moreover, the irrevocable or likely features are all ambiguous in their effects from the viewpoint of world order, i.e., cooperation and the moderation of conflict. Nuclear weapons have so far had a stabilizing and restraining impact. But in the long run the very fear of nuclear war may increasingly force the superpowers to do battle through proxies and thus to play Russian roulette with their interests: This could be destabilizing, as one observes in the Middle East. The other powers are caught between the unsettling attraction of nuclear diffusion and the recurrent crises which the freeze on the large-scale use of force engenders. Social mobilization has also had a stabilizing impact by making foreign penetration into internal political systems more difficult and total domestic concentration on foreign policy less likely; but it can be disruptive by making foreign policy too rigidly bureaucratic or on the contrary by exposing it to internal instability and passions. The fragmentation of the international system makes it possible to isolate local conflicts and limits the scope and significance of superpower gains or losses. But it also makes for more uncertainty in the mechanism of escalation and complicates the superpowers' dilemmas in maintaining world order.

Thus there is a broad range of choices for the future. One can only say that international relations in the world political system will be the manipulation of interdependence by the separate, competing units. This formula suggests the growing awareness by states of the limits of their freedom of action and of its risks on the military as well as on the other chessboards: i.e., it suggests the new dimensions of prudence, the triple safety net of nuclear deterrence, economic solidarity, and domestic priorities under the tightrope of competition. But it also suggests that world order remains precarious, since the name of the game is still manipulation and contest: The desire to preserve *a* world system is not synonymous with a desire to preserve *any* existing system or exclusive of the desire to establish a radically different one on the ruins of the present one. There will therefore remain a tension between, on the one hand, the states' tendency to manipulate interdependence for their own benefit, as well as the explosive consequences of big internal disruptions, and, on the other hand, the need to turn the world political system into more of a society, i.e., to tame the independence of its members, to provide for more cooperation and to keep violence within limits.

In a world which knows no political and psychological mutations (and short of the kind of mutation that might take place if there were a holocaust large enough to convert those not directly affected, yet not so huge as to annihilate us all) the establishment of world order means the achievement of a moderate international system. This rules out a return to an intense bipolar conflict. It does not rule out either a bipolarity of condominium (or collusion) or the prolongation of the present international system; yet I do not believe (for reasons described elsewhere) that either formula is either likely or capable of assuring moderation.[5] A moderate system will have to be a "multihierarchical" one. It is not possible to predict whether such a system will be moderate or not. The answer depends essentially on three factors. First, there is the behavior of the superpowers, their degree of competition and cooperation and their degree of involvement in other parts of the world (on those factors depend, in turn, the degree of autonomy of subsystems and the degree of superpower resignation to domestic changes abroad). Second, there is the behavior of the smaller and present and potential middle powers, with its impact on the relations between the superpowers as well as on the degree of moderation, coherence, and autonomy of the subsystems. Third, there is the scope, rate, and location of nuclear diffusion (and, perhaps, nuclear control). It is obvious that there are countless configurations, and it would be depressing to try to list them all or to give degrees of probability to each.[6] Let us therefore abandon empirical forecasting for normative political analysis and see what role international organization *ought* to play if a moderate international system is to prevail, i.e., if the present world political system were to become a true society.

The Role of International Organization in a Moderate International System

My assumption—which will not be accepted by all—is that there will be no institutional mutation; i.e., sovereignty, anything but absolute and probably emptied of much of its erstwhile meaning and sting, will remain a claim and a foundation for the states' foreign policies. Even though there may be a considerable development of international and regional institutions, including a successful pursuit of integrative policies in some parts of the world, there will be no "superseding of the nation-state" (whatever its devaluation) at the global level. Such a mutation is unlikely; moreover, a world political system based on the nation-state can procure world order as long as (and as soon as), on the one hand, its most important members adopt certain kinds of attitudes and policies and, on the other hand, the traditional state insistence on total freedom of decision and from outside interference is curbed on behalf of international institutions and procedures. In other words, a moderate world political system will require an expansion and strengthening of international organization, but it does not require the kind of centralization of power that world federalists have envisaged. It requires that international organizations, while continuing to be arenas and stakes, be allowed to develop greater autonomy, not in the sense of ceasing to be "expressions of the interests of particular states or other international actors,"[7] but in the sense of also expressing what might be called systemic interests, those long and short-term interests of states which aim, if not at maintaining the system (for it is futile to hope for a world of status quo powers), at least at maintaining moderation.

It is necessary to examine separately the conditions for the establishment of a moderate international system and the conditions of its maintenance. In each instance I will try to list the tasks which international organization ought to perform as well as its limits.

The establishment of a moderate international system requires three broad sets of conditions. First, such a system will emerge (or, if one prefers, continue to develop out of the original bipolar Cold War) only *if certain kinds of crises are avoided.* There ought to be no resort to nuclear weapons. The taboo that has prevailed since Nagasaki has become psychologically and politically essential (even though tactical nuclear weapons might conceivably be used without political and military disaster, the psychological effects could well prove deeply disruptive). In this respect the role of international organization will probably remain modest yet useful in a variety of ways: by providing what one might call a code of illegitimacy through resolutions and treaties; by establishing a legal framework for measures to restrict or slow down nuclear proliferation (which, if it became too widespread and especially if it reached certain countries with pressing grievances or fears, would strain the present taboo intolerably); by giving an international sanction to superpower agreements on arms control in the field of nuclear weapons and missiles; by lending the appearance of an international mandate to what might otherwise look like superpower collusion with respect to guarantees to third powers; by creating, in areas where surveillance by satellites does not suffice, sufficiently objective or depoliticized mechanisms of inspection as soon as the refusal of one superpower has vanished (for internal as well as external reasons) and thus has ceased to justify the reticence of other states. To be sure, one can argue that a small nuclear war between lesser powers could take place without destabilizing the whole system; only a nuclear war involving a superpower or middle state would disrupt it. However, any violation of the nuclear taboo, even if it is restricted and contained when it first occurs, could have repercussions in the subterranean world of attitudes and expectations. The same considerations apply to biological and chemical warfare.

For similar reasons there ought to be no large-scale conventional war. The imperative of limitation—in geographical area (the number of states participating in a conflict) and in intensity—must be maintained, both because of the danger of escalation if a superpower is or becomes involved and because of the fact that the control of violence requires a kind of progressive "ritualization" or routinization of strictly limited wars. Here the United Nations will have to play an important role. It will have to continue to practice "preventive diplomacy" and preventive peace restoration so as to keep local conflicts between nations (other than those between superpowers and their allies) from becoming superpower confrontations; the United Nations may well be aided here by the superpowers' unwillingness to be dragged into such confrontations by third parties. Also, in the future the United Nations will have to find more effective ways than it has found in the past of limiting conflicts in which a superpower or a middle power (such as Communist China) is or becomes involved. Even though—as before—the capacity to resolve such a dispute may be lacking, the willingness to apply some of the techniques of peace restoration and peacekeeping to these kinds of conflicts will have to develop; for whereas there can be no world order that fails to recognize the special position and responsibilities of the superpowers, there can also be no world political society if these states, while playing an important role in defining political legitimacy and the rules of the game, nevertheless insist on being above the latter and outside the former. To be more precise and blunt, in the long run there can be no moderate international system with a United Nations and a United States behaving as they have done during the war in Vietnam.

However, it will be impossible to curtail violence if its causes and opportunities remain unchecked. Despite past failures the United Nations (and regional organizations) have no alternative to trying even more persistently to solve or attenuate those disputes between states which the restraints on force have perpetuated and brought to periodic bloodshed. What is needed is a permanent engagement of all these organizations in diplomacy. This is the area in which the greatest efforts of imagination on the part of these agencies' secretariats will be needed and the most constant amount of gentle pressure by their bodies on states engaged in potentially destructive conflicts will have to be maintained. It would be wrong to say that past fiascoes are due to the sporadic, sputtering quality of the efforts made: The reasons go much deeper. It would also be wrong to believe that more persistent efforts could ever succeed if the member states, particularly the major powers, fail to provide support and pressure on behalf of such attempts. But moderation will require, here again, ritualization: Such disputes should be under constant mediation, not merely under a mixture of occasional mediation and preventive yet superficial or belated injunctions against force; international agencies often appear better centers for such mediation than specific groups of states. In a world in which, for many reasons, there may not be a permanent police force the development of diplomatic techniques may be the best hope and greatest challenge. (In this respect, as in a few others, one mght look back at the practices of the League of Nations.)

Since explosions remain nevertheless likely, a last contribution of international organization in this area should be helping to make the costs of military operations prohibitive, although the greatest obstacle to successful wars will undoubtedly remain the solidity and resistance of each party to a conflict. To the extent to which international agencies can participate in what has been called "nation building" (an ugly expression for a muddy concept) they will strengthen the two current limits to the usefulness of the resort to force.

This brings me to the last kind of crisis that will have to be avoided: large-scale economic disruptions, either in the relations between the rich and the poor or, more generally, in international financial mechanisms and through balance-of-payments problems. This is an area in which the chances for order and the development of international organization—as the framework of interstate cooperation, as a center for executive action on behalf of the states, and as the place in which a code of conduct for multinational corporations can be defined—are synonymous. There have been remarkable beginnings among the industrial nations (primarily in the non-Communist world). But enormous progress remains to be made both with respect to the regulation of transnational activity there and in relations between advanced and underdeveloped countries, particularly in order to protect the latter from balance-of-payments and commodity price fluctuations.

Such progress requires a change of attitude among the industrial nations. Here we come to a second set of conditions for the establishment of a moderate international system: *superpower restraint*. This is not the place to describe in detail the perils of superpower activism; the experiences of Nikita Khrushchev and Lyndon Johnson, of early Kissinger and late Brezhnev, are eloquent enough. The more active and involved the superpowers, the greater the perils of imbalance—through confrontation or disequilibrium between the superpowers and their protégés or tension between their external commitments and their internal troubles. Now, restraint will be incompatible with the pursuit of their policies and interests and therefore acceptable to the superpowers only under certain circumstances; here again, international and regional agencies will have a role to play. There will have to be a restraint on arms races that could lead to superpower confrontations. This means, of course, first of all, a limitation of their own arms race. What should contribute to their sense of urgency is the superpowers' fear of arms race contagion to middle powers, a contagion inspired by the superpowers' example and by their determination not to be immediately outdistanced by the Big Two. If the superpowers want to stop their challengers, they will have to make concessions to them: Reciprocity operates here, as the long negotiations over the nuclear nonproliferation treaty have shown. The United Nations and regional organizations provide the best framework (and face-saving façade) for such bargaining and balancing. Restraint also means curbing arms races among third parties whose conflicts might engulf the superpowers in their role as providers of weapons and supporters of clients. Here again, international and regional organizations can serve as arenas for negotiation, sources of inspection, and concealers of superpower collusion.

Restraint will also mean adopting a kind of residual, or reserve, position with respect to peacekeeping: The enforcement of peace by the superpowers in every conflict between third parties could either exacerbate their differences or lead to a breakdown due either to third-party resistance or to opposition within the superpowers' own political systems. And yet, the Great Powers will continue to want local armistices and settlements to reflect their own views and to satisfy their own ambitions. Again, in a world in which traditional military alliances have lost much of their advantage, both for the superpowers, scared of being too deeply entangled, and for their allies, afraid of being either abandoned or subjugated, only international and regional organizations can perform at the same time three important functions. They can provide the procedural battlefield in which the Great Powers' views and ambitions can be expressed and pressed; they can offer the channels of bargaining in which the lesser powers (without whose participation there can be no world order other than the dangerously activist one of superpower imperialism) can both amend the designs of the superpowers and be courted by them; and they can be the source of legitimacy once a solution has been adopted. In other words, insofar as crises break out in various parts of the world (whether they involve a superpower or not), the large states, in order to establish a moderate international system, will have to resort to international and regional agencies, first so as to end hostilities and restore peace, second so as to supervise and execute settlements (whether those settlements will have been negotiated directly by the parties, achieved through the efforts of the international or regional agencies themselves, or obtained through other procedures of mediation).

Finally, restraint by superpowers will mean a considerable change in their attitudes toward underdeveloped countries—both a willingness to separate economic aid from expectations of political advantage in the Great Powers' contest and (in the case of the United States) a resignation to inevitable manifestations of economic nationalism at the expense of American private interests deemed nefarious for the development of a national economy. Once more, recourse to international and regional agencies will be essential. The shift from bilateral to multilateral aid and the settlement of disputes arising out of expropriations through the efforts of such agencies and according to guidelines laid down by them (instead of a vicious cycle of mutual reprisals) should allow for the kind of superpower restraint that would not amount to neglect of the needs of the poorer nations, and for the sort of superpower retreats that would not amount to a dangerous humiliation of the rich.

This brings us to the conditions for maintaining a moderate international system. Some of these conditions concern the elements that make up the system, others concern relations among the actors. A moderate system will have to be endowed with a fairly complex hierarchy of superpowers, middle powers, and small states or rather with a number of functional hierarchies that will overlap but be much more diversified than the traditional hierarchy based essentially on military might. It will also, given the complexity and continuing heterogeneity of the world, require considerable regional decentralization. Despite (or because of) the multiplicity of regimes it will need an attitude of competitive coexistence on their part instead of one of mutual exclusiveness. And it will require strong transnational links, i.e., a broad transnational society that will provide the states with new areas of cooperative goals or with goals that cannot be reached through violent conflict. Thus, the elements of the system will by themselves require, and allow for, a multiplicity of regional as well as universal organizations (the latter consisting largely of functional agencies). Each one will have its own bargaining process and its own balancing mechanism, based on the specific hierarchy of power that corresponds to its region or to its function. Each one will contribute therefore to decentralization and functional specialization in the system and to the diversification of power; each one will come close to what Ernst Haas has called a self-contained negotiating universe.

The relations within the world political society, or the rules of the game, will consist both of the imperatives for the establishment of a moderate system, which will continue to be indispensable, and of further developments in two directions. First, a new international legitimacy will have to emerge, as in every past moderate system. The world political society of the future, if it wants to avoid becoming a jungle, will have to meet two requirements. On the one hand, even though at first sight the interpenetration of domestic and world politics, as well as that of transnational society and international politics, seems to rule out any gradual extinction of foreign policy efforts at manipulating domestic politics in other countries, such a withdrawal from manipulation will have to take place. It would be facilitated by the increasing impermeability of consolidated societies to foreign intervention in a world in which the overt use of force becomes the exception and by statesmen becoming increasingly aware of the risks and uncertainties of such attempts at controlling others. This does not mean that the old principle of nonintervention will become more sacred than in the past. It means that the scale and scope of interventions must shrink and that attempts at influencing the behavior of a state must aim primarily at its *external* behavior on the various old and new chessboards of international affairs instead of being aimed at *internal* control. This will require on the part of international and regional agencies both continuity and change. They would continue to defend their members' sovereignty against outside intrusion and to be prudently ready to intervene through "preventive diplomacy" or for humanitarian reasons in large-scale civil wars so as to deter more interested and selfish interventions by cunning or greedy powers. But they would change, insofar as it would become more difficult for certain states to utilize regional or international agencies as a cloak behind which they resort to the manipulation of domestic affairs, under the pretext provided by collective statements condemning certain kinds of regimes or endorsing certain kinds of domestic practices. Such a change will occur only if the elements of the system meet the requirements listed, i.e., if the international hierarchy and the panoply of power available to any given state are sufficiently complex and diversified to allow for the types of balancing and bargaining that would curtail such instrumental uses of regional or international bodies by a handful of dominant actors.

On the other hand, the nature of the new chessboards and the need to dampen conflict on the old ones will require in a shrinking world, if not an increasing transfer of sovereignty to international organization (which would gradually receive some of the attributes of statehood), at least an increasing pooling of sovereignties for the exercise of cooperation in the various economic, monetary, and technical fields; in communications; in scientific research and exploration, etc.; and even in peacekeeping. Thus, progressively, overt conflict and all-out competition would be replaced, not by harmony, but by competition in a framework of cooperation and by muted conflict, i.e., by bargaining (which is not at all, as labor negotiators know, necessarily a mild, easy, and brotherly activity). It is obvious that only regional and universal institutions can provide the framework, incentives, expertise, and rules of security and predictability required.

Second, along with the new legitimacy of nonmanipulation and competitive cooperation, the procedures for the maintenance of order will have to be fortified in two areas discussed in connection with the emergence of a moderate system. On the one hand, insofar as peacekeeping is concerned, there is obviously in the long run no substitute for international measures of arms control with a growing network of supervision, inspection, and enforcement. This network should cover both existing nuclear powers, as well as the prevention of further proliferation, through tighter controls over nuclear supplies and sanctions against delinquents. Even if no permanent world police force emerges, ad hoc forces in readiness for the policing of violent conflicts other than those involving major powers will be needed (even if the deterrence of nuclear war or of conventional aggression by secondary nuclear powers remains the preserve of the superpowers themselves). On the other hand, beyond the strengthening of the techniques of diplomacy for the settlement of disputes, international and regional bodies will have to develop regular procedures of peaceful change if the avoidance or limitation of the resort to force is to become a ritual; for there will always be tensions and pressures for change, and the more one insists on keeping them under control, the more one will need to develop mechanisms of review and nonviolent adjustment. This is the realm in which the outlines of the future are dimmest and in which the role of international organization may be greatest, especially by comparison with its past failures and present pallor.

A moderate world society will have to be based on two principles. One is the universalization of concern. This does not mean that (as in the theory of collective security) every conflict should be escalated to the world level rather than localized. Universal concern does not require universal involvement: Actual participation in the management of troubles ought often to remain within the boundaries of subsystems, and the need for superpower restraint has been stressed before. But in a worldwide political system the real alternative to universal concern is unilateral action, especially by a superpower within or even outside its self-proclaimed sphere of vital interests. If this recipe for immoderation is to be discarded, and although (or because) there can be no ironclad guarantees of security and there neither is nor should be any possibility for constant, worldwide policing by the superpowers, there will have to be collective intervention for peacekeeping and settlement so as to increase the disutility of the resort to force. Superpowers at the world level and middle powers in their regions will themselves find it necessary to obtain collective sanction for their interventions in interstate disputes or collective participation in the enforcement of peace or of settlements. The other principle is the need for safety valves for change, the more the uses of force are repressed. Hence the requirement that states both stop manipulating internal affairs and accept broad, even violent, domestic change and regimes hostile to their own conceptions or to private foreign interests, as long as the external behavior of these regimes or revolutionary forces is nonviolent and nondisruptive; hence also the necessary development of collective procedures of peaceful change for interstate relations.

At this stage in world affairs it is difficult to foresee whether a world society built on those principles will emerge. The listing of conditions and requirements provides a better critique of the present than a prophecy of the future. Whether such a society emerges depends only for a very modest part on what international organization initiates, even though, as we have seen, international organization will have many important roles to play if states allow this society to emerge. What can be stated is that such a society would afford the greatest opportunities and the widest need for international and regional organizations without which it would be crippled. We noted earlier that not every moderate system has a procedural consensus that makes of such agencies the legitimate channels for controlling conflict and for promoting cooperation; but it is obvious that a worldwide international system with a complex hierarchy of power and a formidable range of tasks and chessboards can have no other legitimate channels: The scope and intensity of interstate and transnational relations leave no alternative. It can also be stated, in turn, that such organizations—which today remain epiphenomena rather than prime movers—will not develop fully as long as the international system has not found more organic forms of moderation than the rather mechanical or tactical ones which have appeared in recent years. And it is perfectly possible to conceive of a diversified world society with a network of such agencies even though a (much tamer) nation-state would still, in theory and practice, be the highest form of social organization and center of allegiance.

Notes

1. Ernst B. Haas, *Tangle of Hopes: American Commitments and World Order* (Englewood Cliffs, N.J.: Prentice-Hall, 1969), p. 120.
2. Stanley Hoffmann, *Gulliver's Troubles, or the Setting of American Foreign Policy* (Atlantic Policy Studies) (New York: McGraw-Hill [for the Council on Foreign Relations], 1968), chapter 2.
3. "Regime Decay: Conflict Management and International Organizations, 1945–1981," *International Organization* 37, no. 2 (Spring 1983), pp. 189–256.
4. For an excellent balance sheet, see Thomas M. Franck, *Nation Against Nation* (New York: Oxford University Press, 1985).
5. Hoffmann, *op. cit.*, chapter 10; and *Primacy or World Order*, part 2 (New York: McGraw-Hill, 1978).
6. For a sobering example of what happens when one tries, see Herman Kahn and Anthony J. Wiener, *The Year 2000: A Framework for Speculation on the Next Thirty-Three Years* (New York: Macmillan Co., 1967), chapters 5, 7, and 9.
7. See Robert Keohane, "Institutionalization in the United Nations General Assembly," *International Organization*, Autumn 1969 (Vol. 23, No. 4), p. 862.

15

Taming the Eagle: U.S. Foreign Policy and National Security

This essay argues for a redefinition of U.S. foreign policy objectives and a corresponding revision of the requirements of U.S. national security. In the past, the debate about these goals and the means needed to reach them has often been a debate between isolationists, or neo-isolationists, alarmed by the costs and risks of outside commitments, and internationalists, who stress the United States' responsibility as a world power and as the champion of democratic values. This is a somewhat artificial clash: the scope of the United States' presence abroad, the size and needs of the U.S. economy, the contest with the Soviet Union make a return to isolationism impossible, but the assertion of global responsibilities leaves a great deal of leeway for disagreement about their nature, their magnitude, and the suitable American response. What I advocate is not a flight from these responsibilities but a retrenchment and a reorientation. My reaction is against dangerous trends that could lead to global disaster as well as to a variety of regional ones. Hence my objective is to examine what a sensible alternative might be and to discuss some of the military implications of this alternative.

I

There have been, in recent years, three disturbing developments in the realm of U.S. foreign policy and in the study of U.S. national security, by which I mean the United States' vital interests in the world and the various means (including force) assigned to the protection and promotion of these interests.

1. There has been a trend toward an indefinite extension of the scope of U.S. interests. "National security" is considered to be everywhere and constantly at stake. John L. Gaddis has distinguished between "symmetrical" and "asymmetrical" containment of the Soviet Union.[1] In the former case, the United States acts as if every Soviet move or gain constitutes a threat that has to be met; in the latter, the United States chooses only to respond to moves and gains that actually constitute threats to its interests. I would

propose a revision of this distinction, aimed at providing a better explanation of what actually happened.

In the first place, the United States' tendency, ever since the late 1940s, has been to treat every noncooperative move by Moscow as a threat and to define U.S. interests not objectively, according to the importance of a given area or issue, but in terms of Soviet moves and possible benefits. This trend has not been uninterrupted. For a while, it seemed to be the intention of the Carter administration to apply more discriminating criteria and to allow the Soviets to score points—for instance, in some parts of Africa—precisely because it did not consider important U.S. interests to be at stake. But this attitude provoked divisions within the administration and a storm among those Republicans and conservative or neoconservative Democrats who gathered in the Committee on the Present Danger; by 1980 Carter had completely reversed himself. The most articulate defense of a relatively narrow and objective definition of U.S. external interests and national security has been provided by George Kennan. But, with the temporary exception just mentioned, no administration has ever really adopted it. The cases of "asymmetrical" containment mentioned by John Gaddis turn out to pertain not to the *scope* of the vital interests but to the *means* of response to the "threat"; both Eisenhower-Dulles and Nixon-Kissinger, partly for domestic budgetary reasons, partly because of the unpopularity of the wars in Korea and Vietnam, decided that the United States did not have the resources to meet every Soviet probe or challenge with means (especially conventional forces) comparable to those committed by or available to Moscow and/or its allies. The Eisenhower administration tried to deter such probes by the threat of massive retaliation; the Nixon administration tried to enlist an increased support by allies and clients of the United States (see the Nixon, or Guam, doctrine). But in both instances, the United States continued to see itself as engaged in a global struggle in which every Soviet gain, in the noncooperative dimensions of world politics, was deemed an American loss and therefore had to be prevented, challenged, or reversed. Indeed, Kissinger argues at great length in his memoirs that even apparently insignificant challenges have to be met head-on, decisively and early, lest they lead to far more dangerous and unmanageable crises later. Brzezinski presents a very similar point of view in his memoirs. And the Reagan administration has adopted an equally extensive definition of U.S. foreign policy and national security requirements.

Not only has every noncooperative Soviet move been treated as if it automatically created an American interest, but "national security" has been inflated by two other sets of considerations. One could be called preventive containment: almost every U.S. administration has considered it in the national interest either to prevent developments that the Soviets could exploit to their advantage (say, the consolidation of a left-wing regime in Guatemala or Chile or Zaire) or to support forces and leaders deemed to constitute the best barrier against Soviet influence. Presidents have differed over what the best barrier consists of; some have only or primarily supported staunch anti-Communists; others have looked for "third forces" or "progressive" nationalists. But measures as diverse as the establishment of the Diem regime in South Vietnam following France's withdrawal, the overthrow of Arbenz in Guatemala, the U.S. landing in Lebanon in 1958, the Alliance for Progress, the intervention in the Dominican Republic in 1965, the Nixon-Kissinger opposition to Allende, unwavering support for the shah of Iran and almost to the end for President Marcos in the Philippines, Kissinger's hostility to Euro-communism, military assistance to the government of El Salvador and the contras in Nicaragua, and reluctance in applying sanctions to South Africa have resulted from this approach.

A second set of considerations relates to the U.S. economy. The United States tends to see its national security as entailing the maintenance of conditions abroad that will allow the economy to function adequately—i.e., to obtain the energy, raw materials, and markets necessary to its prosperity. Access to these has therefore been included in the definition of vital U.S. interests. Moreover, given the role of the dollar as the international currency for transactions and monetary reserves (a role the United States has wanted to preserve), the importance of American lending institutions in the world's financial system, and the need to increase or safeguard the buying capacity of clients, the United States has also made the defense of the open international economy and the avoidance of monetary blocs a major foreign policy interest. This interest underlies foreign aid programs, U.S. policies in GATT, the World Bank, and the IMF, American opposition to various Third World demands aimed at a redistribution of resources and at a sharing of power in international institutions, and so on.

That a power as enormous as the United States should define its interests widely is evident. This, after all, is how any great power defines itself; it is not only size or geographical situation that makes it great; it is the sum of its resources and the importance of its economy and armed forces. Means, especially expanding ones, tend to look for—and to find—ends. But both the scope that has been given to "national security" and the way in which it is being defined are dangerous. What is dangerous about the scope is that it is, quite simply, beyond reach. Universal direct involvement is more than the United States' material and psychological resources can afford, and more than other nations will allow—especially in a world which is no longer that of 1950, when the gap in military and economic power between the United States and the rest of the non-Communist world was huge. Particularly in periods of recession or slow growth, the competing claims of American society limit the material resources available for defense and for action abroad; in a democratic polity, domestic needs and demands can be compressed only so far. The attempt by President Johnson to wage war in Vietnam without curtailing the programs of the Great Society resulted in inflation, balance-of-payments deficits for the United States, and a deterioration of the world monetary system. As for psychological resources, the United States' experiences in Vietnam, in Iran, earlier in China, and currently in the Middle East and Central America leave one skeptical about the national ability to control, shape, or even understand political developments in deeply foreign cultures and countries. We looked for third forces in places where polarization had become so intense that democratic middle-of-the-roaders had been eliminated or forced to choose their camp; our ties with "friendly" leaders precluded timely contacts with the opposition; our emphasis on free elections as a panacea often made us blind to the complex preconditions that have to be created before elections can be really free and meaningful, especially in societies without a tradition of democratic procedures. Even when there are shared experiences and mutual understanding, the capacity to influence can be very limited: the United States' relationship with Israel proves this. Obtaining from others the resources we do not have ourselves has always meant demanding of allies and clients that they play the parts assigned by us in a symphony written by us. Again, recent events—Kissinger's Year of Europe, the difficulties encountered by every U.S. plan in the Middle East, the Falklands War, the difficulties over Namibia and in Central America, the pipeline fiasco with our European allies in 1982, their reluctance to join "Star Wars"—all prove that even those who depend on us (such as Mexico, at present) insist on writing their own music and defining their interests according to their own priorities.

The *way* in which we have defined our interests has been nefarious in two respects. It has been indiscriminate: at times, areas of secondary importance (such as Vietnam) have absorbed vastly more resources and received more attention than they should have obtained, and policy in areas of primary importance (such as the Middle East) has suffered. It is of course true that neglecting apparently trivial areas may have very bad effects, if such neglect offends important allies whose own interests are deeply affected in these areas (cf. Saudi and Egyptian annoyance over Carter's apparent passivity in the case of Horn of Africa and concerning South Yemen), or if neglect allows the Soviets to score cumulative gains. But it is often better to provide one's allies with the means to protect their interests than to do a (for us relatively unimportant and costly) job by oneself just in order to please them.

The "Soviet gains" argument brings me to my second charge. Although there is, indeed, a global Soviet challenge, it is a serious mistake—for several reasons—to superimpose on world affairs a grid that includes only or almost exclusively the U.S.-Soviet contest. It is a misreading of world politics: the world is full of important issues that simply do not let themselves be reduced to this contest and that, indeed, neither the Americans nor the Soviets have succeeded in absorbing into their cold war. The vital problems that affect the world economy and often determine the fate or the priorities of governments are problems in whose creation or solution Moscow plays only a very small role, if any: this is the case of the crucial issue of Third World debt today. Also, many factions and states resort to one or the other superpower, but for their own purposes: the superpowers are the ones that are being used, and thus become, in a sense, the victims of the dynamics of their own competition. Moreover, responding to every Soviet move, or engaging systematicaly in preventive containment, risks both letting the Soviets dictate the agenda of world politics and actually helping the Soviets expand their reach, if, as has often happened, our obsession with preventing the spread of Soviet influence makes us back the wrong horse, or chase after shadows, or engage in self-fulfilling prophecies (pushing those whom we suspect of being "leftists" or Marxists into the arms of the Soviets). It deprives us of a dimension they are much better at exploiting—namely, time—for it gives to U.S. diplomacy a breathless air, the appearance of a rush after emergencies, and the self-defeating necessity of producing fast results, lest domestic opinion feel defeated, or pushed around, and take revenge on failed leaders. Finally, while the superpowers' rivalry will undoubtedly go on, given the clash of power, interests, and ideologies, there exist common interests—particularly in survival (i.e., the avoidance of nuclear war and proliferation)—as well as opportunities for moderating the contest and thus for liberating the mental and material resources needed to cope with all the other essential issues of world affairs.

The scope and the way in which American interests have been defined have resulted in a policy of recurrent interventionism (interrupted only briefly under Carter in 1977-1979). The concern for worldwide stability and the fear of enemy gains make one look at victories of potentially or actually anti-U.S. forces as unacceptable disasters; intervention becomes the only alternative. But it too can result in a calamity, not only for the hapless people whom we see ourselves as protecting and who, in the process of being thus protected, lose either their autonomy or their lives, but also for us—either because, when we succeed (as in Guatelmala in 1954 or in the Dominican Republic in 1965), it is at the expense of our own values and leaves a bitter legacy, or else because, as in Vietnam and now in El Salvador and Nicaragua, we get dragged, step by step, into a quagmire of escalating military involvement, where the only alternatives are endless war or victory at a cost that far exceeds the significance of the stakes. Interventionism also makes our clients abdicate their fate into our hands while resenting their impotence (when his throne shook, the shah wanted us to tell him what to do); it breeds a mutually debilitating dependence; and it often turns into our enemies men and women who revolted in the name of values we profess to stand for.

2. There has been, simultaneously, an enormous expansion of *defense programs*. Here, the trend has oscillated to an even greater extent, what with the sharp reductions in expenditures after the Korean War, and again in the early and middle 1970s after the Vietnam War. Nevertheless, the present situation is alarming, for two reasons.

The first is a direct consequence of the vast extension of the scope of U.S. interests and of the expansion of the Soviet capabilities for military action abroad. The Reagan administration has dropped the admittedly artificial criterion that used to serve essentially as a lid on the demand for conventional armed forces: the notion of being ready to fight two and a half, or two, or one and a half wars. The risk created by an artificial lid is that of being caught unprepared, but the risk of removing any ceiling is that the sky may become the limit. Indeed, even a cursory look at the defense secretary's report to Congress for fiscal years 1983 and 1984 shows a profusion of shopping lists without any apparent priorities or rationales: tanks, helicopters, fighting and support vehicles, various types of fighter planes, and above all an ambitious program of naval rearmament that includes nuclear-powered aircraft carriers, amphibious forces, battleships, destroyers, attack submarines, and sea-launched cruise missiles.

The second reason concerns the evolution of nuclear strategy. Even though, in fiscal year 1983, the strategic forces represented only 9 percent of the defense budget ($23.1 billion dollars out of $258 billion—but one should add the bulk of the $18 billion earmarked for intelligence and communications, and much of the $20.1 billion assigned to research and development), the nuclear issue deserves the vast amount of attention it has received in recent times. Much of the literature and, indeed, many of the arguments of the current antinuclear movement focus on the evolution from "deterrence" to "war-fighting," and seem to attribute it either to the malevolence (or stupidity) of specific leaders or to intellectual confusion. But the situation is, unfortunately, neither so simple nor so reparable. "Mutual assured destruction (MAD)—i.e., the capability of destroying the adversary's cities without (as in the past) having to destroy its forces first in order to defeat it—still deters a Soviet nuclear attack on American cities or on Western Europe: it is a capability that both sides will keep. But MAD never was the strategic doctrine of either the Soviet Union or the United States: it describes a condition (termed "existential deterrence" by McGeorge Bundy),[2] an inescapable situation created by the existence and properties of thermonuclear weapons, a reminder of the horrible tragedy any resort to these weapons could ultimately provoke; and it served, under McNamara, as a budgetary safeguard against the demands of the armed services. But even in the days (of the 1960s) when the United States' *declaratory* policy was assured destruction, the U.S. nuclear *targeting* policy aimed at Soviet military objectives—as if nuclear weapons were no different from past ones.

This trend toward "war-fighting"—i.e., toward the development of accurate nuclear weapons capable, as were previous weapons in history, of hitting enemy *forces*—has been fed by two basic factors. One is technology, which in the 1970s, has produced three revolutions: multiple warheads, almost perfect accuracy, and the kind of miniaturization that marks both cruise missiles and the neutron bomb. The other is the geopolitical predicament of the United States: the need to provide allies or friends with "extended deterrence"—i.e., to try to protect them from attack by the threat of nuclear retaliation or even of the first use of nuclear weapons.

By the late 1970s, it became obvious that there existed a major disagreement in the United States—*not* over deterrence versus war-fighting, but over what deters. In the view of some, what deters either a nuclear or a conventional Soviet attack on a major U.S. interest is the risk of uncontrollable escalation to "mutual assured destruction." It is the *uncertainty* of war's dynamics, the impossibility of ever being certain that one will be able, so to speak, to escape from the condition of MAD and to return to the "safer," traditional universe of counterforce warfare. In this view, the acquisition of a vast first-strike, counterforce ability by the United States is unnecessary (for *we* would be deterred from being the first to resort to nuclear weapons, by that very risk of escalation); and dangerous (insofar as it feeds the illusion of limited nuclear war): a counterforce ability, if necessary at all, is useful only in very limited amounts, as a means of reinforcing the credibility of extended deterrence (since protecting allies by threatening Soviet cities, in an era of mutual assured destruction, is, in and of itself, not very credible)—in other words, as a means of warning the Soviets that a conventional attack on our vital allies could lead to a nuclear war that might result in mutual assured destruction.

According to others, however, precisely because a threat to blow up cities (and to commit suicide thereby) simply was not credible anymore at all, only an ample capacity to wage nuclear war would be a credible deterrent. Only the *certainty* of being matched or defeated at any stage could deter a potential aggressor. If the United States did not have the ability to prevent a Soviet victory at any level of escalation chosen by Moscow, it might encourage dangerous risk-taking by Soviet leaders; indeed, if the United States was *perceived* by others as not having this ability (however theoretical the notion of nuclear war-fighting may be), Moscow's capacity to exert *political* coercion might increase.[3] Therefore, Secretary of Defense Schlesinger, in 1974, sought to introduce into U.S. strategic doctrine the notion of "limited nuclear options"—at a time when the MIRV-ing of U.S. missiles was creating a plethora of warheads in search of targets. A few years later, the acquisition by the Soviets of the capacity to destroy part of the United States' nuclear forces was seen as requiring both the acquisition by the United States of a similar capability and renewed efforts at keeping the United States' counterforce weapons invulnerable. This threat led to the long quest for a new, mobile, and therefore invulnerable missile, the MX, capable of hitting Soviet silos; to the development of new, more accurate warheads on existing missiles, of the new D5 (or Trident II) missile for U.S. nuclear submarines, of the middle-range Pershing II missile for deployment in Western Europe, of a variety of cruise missiles; and, finally, to "Star Wars."

Secretary of Defense Harold Brown endorsed this second view. Its triumph was marked by Carter's 1980 directive, PD-59, which set up the so-called countervailing strategy and requires "not merely a capacity for destroying the full set of Soviet military, political and industrial targets, but also a sufficiently flexible and enduring force capable of carrying out smaller attacks."[4] The second view was confirmed by Secretary Weinberger's plan for "prevailing" in a protracted nuclear war, a plan that aims, not at waging such a war, but at giving the United States the means of waging it in order to reinforce deterrence, given the fear that anything less—any void in the continuum of weaponry, any lapse from "essential equivalence" with the Soviet arsenal—might induce the Soviets, especially in grave crises, "to take risks that would be unthinkable in more normal times."[5] The strategic programs of the Reagan administration, with their allocations of funds for the B1 and Stealth bombers, and for nuclear cruise missiles, reflect this belief.

The supporters of each of the two conceptions of deterrence make very sharp and convincing criticisms of each other. Those, like Paul Nitze or Colin Gray, who believe in deterrence through the threat of war-fighting, reject the opposite view as dangerous, because it allows for gaps and inferiorities that could tempt the opponent to challenge vital U.S. interests (Would we use nuclear weapons first to defend these interests if we knew that we could be overwhelmed by Soviet nuclear forces?) and also because it would leave us, in the event of a Soviet conventional or limited nuclear attack, with no choice other than to accept defeat or escalate to the suicidal level of mutual destruction. (The fundamental flaws of this position are its assumptions that the Soviets can be deterred only by our matching their counterforce potential, that a Soviet strike on our land-based missiles would leave us without counterforce means of retaliation, and that, whereas mutual assured destruction is implausible, limited nuclear war, or a nuclear war aimed only at military targets, is a rational prospect). It is exactly the opposite assumption that is made by those who, like McGeorge Bundy, stick to the notion that "existential" deterrence, resting on "uncertainty about what could happen,"[6] is sufficient. They criticize the opposite view for engaging in fancifully scary scenarios, for leading to an astronomical arms race, and for undermining the very deterrence it purports to buttress, by treating nuclear weapons as if they were like other weapons and by creating on each side incentives to strike first, before the opponent has been able to hurl its weapons at one's own.

The victory of the Nitze view results partly from the fact that military planning is driven, almost inevitably, by worst-case analyses and by the need to plan for what must be done should deterrence fail—i.e., by the need to "think through" a war-fighting strategy even in a nuclear war. In a country where military planning is far less autonomous, far more subordinated to civilian control than in the Soviet Union, the reasons for which the civilian leadership has endorsed this approach are many.

One reason is the influence of two groups of people: a vast corps of civilian strategists who have played the game of "scenarios" and developed the many possibilities of nuclear strategy with even more enthusiasm than the military planners, and a combination of bureaucrats and defense contractors whose careers and fortunes depend on the uninterrupted production of ever more sophisticated weapons systems. But the primary reasons for the triumph of the Nitze view are two sets of political considerations: at home, the fear of the price leaders would have to pay if the less demanding notion, the Bundy view, actually encouraged the Soviets to take risks in vital places; and abroad, the very extension of the scope of U.S. interests.

Their protection seems to require an ever expanding war-fighting arsenal, since any attempt to deter Soviet probes in areas that are not obviously of vital importance to the United States, by threatening possible mutual destruction, would be incredible. In fact, such an attempt would be a bluff, which the opponent would be tempted to call. Having to choose between a more relaxed view that, however, failed to be reassuring and appeared to rely on bluff, and a far more demanding view, which, however, "reassures" one only if one believes in the myth of a controllable, rationally wageable nuclear war, statesmen—on both sides—have preferred the second option.

This preference represents an extraordinarily dangerous development, for the following reasons. In the first place, it undermines crisis stability, which requires invulnerable weapons. ICBMs are becoming "use them or lose them" weapons. Soon, the United States' land-based missiles (the most reliable part of the U.S. arsenal) will at least theoretically be vulnerable to a Soviet first strike; they represent only one-fourth of our arsenal, but this percentage will increase if the Reagan administration succeeds in building the MX (with ten warheads each) and puts them in existing silos. Despite their theoretical mobility, the cruise missiles and Pershing IIs that are being deployed in Western Europe tempt preemption, because they are concentrated in a few well-known areas. In a few years, three-fourths of the Soviet arsenal, which consists primarily of land-based missiles, will be vulnerable to U.S. bombers, to the MX, to the new, more accurate warheads on the Minuteman missiles, and to the Trident II submarines. The combination of these weapons, plus the European-based Pershing II and cruise missiles, will provide the United States with the potential not for a "disarming" first strike—this is impossible—but for a crippling one against what is, today, the main part of the Soviet nuclear force. Furthermore, crisis stability requires that each side's command and communication centers be able to function safely. But they have become vulnerable to a "decapitation" attempt by the other side's missiles (some Soviet missiles are particularly threatened by the deployment of Pershing II missiles in West Germany—eight minutes away). A country that is afraid of losing its most potent weapons in a crisis (unless it uses them fast) and of not being able to mount a coordinated response to an attack, will, even if it is not tempted to use its weapons first, be far more jittery in the management of the crisis: the parallel with the summer of 1914 is ominous.

In the second place, arms control agreements are likely to become much more difficult to negotiate if both sides, in their drive toward war-fighting capabilities, acquire new weapons that will be difficult to verify. This is the case with ground- and sea-launched cruise missiles, weapons that can be equipped either with conventional or with nuclear warheads and can be easily concealed. It is also the case with mobile land-based missiles, such as the Soviet SS-20s and the planned U.S. Midgetman.

In the third place, the rationale for war-fighting capabilities, even when it is presented in moderate tones (as it was by Harold Brown,[7] who described a need to be able to "destroy" but not to "wipe out" every class of Soviet targets) consists of two very questionable postulates. One is the idea that Soviet superiority at any level in the process of escalation could incite Moscow to take dangerous risks. But both the possibility that this process might lead to mutual destruction and the implausibility of a controlled nuclear war are likely to inhibit such risk-taking. The other postulate is the danger of political coercion by the Soviets, if they should be superior at any level. But one cannot coerce a foe who has nuclear weapons or a nuclear protector, and a strong will of his own, with weapons that are militarily unusable (because of their suicidal potential) except as deterrent threats. This rationale also leads to an ever-increasing list of military objectives and nuclear delivery systems. Moreover, the line between the quest for "countervailing" and the quest for "prevailing," between "escalation control" and "escalation dominance"—i.e., between matching abilities and a drive for superiority—is very thin.

Fourth, all groups of advocates of war-fighting abilities present these as necessary not only to deter but also to terminate a nuclear war as quickly as possible, should it break out—long before "mutual destruction." But this stance assumes the possibility of controlling nuclear war, so as to keep it limited. Unfortunately, as Bundy has pointed out, "most 'scenarios' for nuclear warfare . . . reflect nothing more than the state of mind of their authors. . . . Moreover, they are estimates of interacting behavior under conditions of unprecedented stress and danger. . . . No one can have any certainty that credible communication would be possible between adversaries even hours after such a conflict began. . . . Yet without such communication, who knows how to stop the horror?"[8]

The actual waging of a nuclear war—the ability to keep it controlled, to bring it to rapid termination, and to prevent it from escalating to the destruction of cities—is a highly implausible as well as unsavory prospect. What Clausewitz called the "fog of war" is even more likely to blind those who would attempt to fight a completely unprecedented kind of war. A "limited nuclear option" is unlikely to lead to quick victory—the enemy would still keep the bulk of its nuclear forces (indeed, it could lose most of its ICBMs and still have enough forces left to devastate American cities). It is more likely to lead to retaliation; if it is retaliation in kind, an indecisive "exchange," in the heat of battle, might lead to further escalation; if it is massive retaliation, total destruction will not be far away. It is theoretically possible to conceive of the use of small and relatively discriminating nuclear weapons, such as neutron bombs. But history reminds us that states tend to throw in more weapons, rather than the sponge, if a "first-use" was not enough to win. It is the crossing of the threshold that separates non-nuclear from nuclear war that risks being fatal.

3. The third disturbing development is an *intellectual* one. Faced with the apparently inexorable evolution of the arms contest, and with the expansion of the scope of national security, specialists of international affairs and "concerned citizens" seem to have found varying ways of abandoning critical judgment and of escaping. One form is escapism into utopia. I am

not indulging here in a blanket indictment of the U.S. or Western European peace movement, whose members have expressed their awareness of and drawn attention to the very perils I have just presented. But I am referring to some of its leaders. They are intensely critical of the present state of affairs insofar as they (usually quite correctly) denounce the prevalence of "pre-nuclear thinking" and the lack of imagination of those who believe that societies could wage nuclear war, suffer enormous casualties, and yet cope with the disruption, recover, or else control escalation in the midst of a totally unprecedented and catastrophic kind of warfare. But sound judgment disappears at the point where some of these prophets of doom or Cassandras talk or write as if the problem consisted only of bringing *American* leaders back to their senses, as if the cold war were a purely *American* invention or a malevolent fiction, as if there existed no profound differences between Western socieites and the USSR (where such a peace movement is inconceivable). Moreover, there are some utopians who would wish states away, or would call for the "reinvention of politics" or for the establishment of a world government, in a world where the aspiration to a state of one's own is almost irresistible, and whose inexpiable conflicts, hatreds, and heterogeneities would require a world government to be all powerful or would doom it to impotence. What is needed is not a reinvention but a reorientation of politics, an intellectual effort at preventing current reality from turning into tragedy through "business as usual"—at restraining and at reversing the trends toward catastrophe.

Another form of escapism is often found among civilian strategists and policy analysts. It consists of accepting the basic hypotheses and assumptions that guide policy-makers and of spinning and spelling out implications, alternatives, and requirements without even stopping to ask whether any of it makes sense. It is a loss of perspective, a giving up of critical distance, which results in part from the American tendency, in the social sciences, by which they are turned into policy sciences out of a desire to be useful and out of a fear of lapsing into pure theory or abstraction. The effect, however, is increasing specialization, a cult of expertise at the expense of the ability to stand back, to take a general view, and to suggest an alternative not to the specific measure or set of measures that result from the prevalent conception but to that conception itself. It is just as dangerous to enter into the logic of those in power, if it is a faulty logic, and to partake of their momentum, if it is a mad momentum, as it is to repudiate the logic of international politics altogether. The first attitude implicitly assumes that the margin of choice is extremely narrow—technical and tactical only; the other one assumes that there is a choice, but only one between the (current) logic of disaster and a leap into an unknown that one paints in rosy colors. But utopia is not an option: there will be no world government in this century, nor will there be complete disarmament; and, in any case, within the world of competing states, the range of choices is far broader than is usually realized. What is distressing about the public debate today is that it isn't a debate at all: it is a dialogue of the deaf, in which each side excommunicates the other, and in which one group essentially upholds the status quo while the other one preaches not politics but transcendence.

What follows is primarily an argument against the first group—which, after all, has been in power for many years. Its members believe that there simply is no alternative to the course we have followed—that the political and military trends described above are inevitable and that the only problem is to find the resources to meet our worldwide interests. But I believe (1) that the trends are potentially catastrophic, because they point toward political confrontations as well as toward an escalation of the arms race that risks turning these confrontations into disasters and provides its own independent opportunities for confrontations (for instance, over the location of new weapons deployments); (2) that they are also nefarious domestically, because their costs put enormous strains on the internal consensus, pitting the administration in power against most of the elites, or splitting the elites, or else creating a gap between a more "internationalist" elite and a more inward-looking public (and inciting many citizens to dissent and protest); also, because domestic sacrifices—in terms of social programs cut or neglected, of resources drained by war industries that are often profitable but ultimately less productive and less socially beneficial than civilian enterprises—are not even likely to be compensated by successes abroad; and (3) that an analysis of contemporary world affairs, even one that tries to drive out illusions and complacency, reveals the possibility of a different political strategy.

II

I will attempt, briefly, to define an alternative foreign policy that might avoid the costs entailed by the trends I have described. I will deal here primarily with those aspects of foreign policy that can properly be said to concern national security—i.e., the survival of the nation, and the protection of vital interests either from threats of violence or from threats aimed at the economic life of the nation.

1. I will therefore mention only briefly a host of economic issues that involve U.S. interests, such as concern for the protection of what might be called a livable international milieu against such threats as the proliferation of nuclear weapons, and the promotion of American values and basic human rights. A world of twenty or thirty nuclear powers; a world of nothing but totalitarian and authoritarian regimes producing masses of refugees; a world of bankrupt developing countries, whose insolvency would bring about the collapse of international financial institutions and of major American banks, as well as a race war in Southern Africa—all of these prospects could obviously affect U.S. national security and values most adversely; hence the importance of "global politics" of the kind the Carter administration tried to pursue. "Benign neglect" of these issues (or not so benign subordination of such concerns to domestic economic priorities, ideological preconceptions, or the primacy of the cold war) could lead to disaster. What seems imperative is the following set of guidelines:

First, a far greater coordination of economic and monetary policies with the other major advanced industrial powers of the non-Communist world is called for. We must learn to avoid the global effects of an inflation or of a recession caused by deliberate U.S. policies and to soften the impact on our partners, and on world trade, of America's fluctuating interest and exchange rates. The study of the economic summits held since 1975 shows that good results can be obtained—usually in the form of mutual concessions across several issues—when there is a willingness on the part of Washington to take the interests of others into account, rather than a disposition to believe that whatever is deemed suitable for Americans cannot help but be ultimately beneficial to others as well.[9]

Second, what is needed in North-South relations is a similar American willingness to accept the suggestions recently made by the Brandt Commission in its new report.[10] These suggestions are aimed at expanding assistance to the developing countries by the international financial institutions (in which the United States plays a decisive role) and at making more flexible the usually strict, often socially regressive and economically deflationary conditions imposed by the IMF on countries in debt. These recommendations also propose both an increase in the amount of aid to the poorer countries and a new, diversified, and pragmatic process of negotiations on North-South issues. These measures have no chance of being adopted as long as the United States and its industrial partners have not fully recovered from recession; but recovery, by itself, is no panacea for the rest of the world. It is merely a pre-condition. The resources that the Brandt report would like to see assigned to the developing countries will not become available, if they go instead, as in the past, to the defense budget and military assistance.

Third, the United States ought to develop and strengthen the currently weak and fragmented international regime of human rights. This objective would require the reinforcement of the various private and public agencies that monitor, investigate, and report on the condition of human rights in various parts of the world. It would also entail the promotion of a joint policy with the other major donors of economic aid in order both to subordinate the granting of aid to the respect by the recipient governments of the most basic civil and political as well as economic and social rights and to ensure that such aid will reach the poorest people in the recipient countries. Finally, the United States, without neglecting its other interests— and in its relations with countries that depend on it or that need something from it—ought always to make sure that the defense of human rights is never sacrificed to these other concerns; when they are sacrificed, the effects on these other concerns (such as U.S. bases, or business interests) are often catastrophic, when murderous regimes protected by us collapse and are replaced by strongly anti-American ones. The promotion of human rights may at times have to be blended with other factors, or be pursued in a quiet and discreet way only when such discretion promises good results; but it should never be missing from U.S. policy toward any country or reduced to mere rhetoric. Such a guideline should be applied particularly when decisions on arms sales to friends and clients abroad are made.

Fourth, the United States must continue to try to slow down the rate of nuclear proliferation, by cooperating with other suppliers of nuclear materials in order to restrict the sale of dangerous technologies. Exceptions (such as those granted in recent years to Japan and India) ought to be made only when there is a justifiable economic need and when there are adequate controls—not on the basis of a distinction between allies and others. It is sensible to provide political reassurance to countries that are tempted to become nuclear powers for reasons of insecurity; but such reassurance ought to take the form of efforts to help settle regional quarrels, rather than that of conventional arms sales.

2. Turning now to the part of foreign policy that can properly be called national security policy, we find that the necessary reorientation should begin with a definition of vital U.S. interests, not with a list of threats posed by hostile forces, nor with a list of threats capable of being exploited by hostile forces: hostility may well be temporary, or else the list of interests created by these threats may become unmanageable, or some of these threats may turn out not to matter. We must therefore return, not to the list drawn many years ago by George Kennan, but to the same underlying question: What are the lasting national security concerns that, on the whole, would remain important even in a miraculous world without major enmities? I would list the following:

a. Protection from direct attack.

b. Preservation of the links (military, economic, and cultural) with the major *allies in Western Europe and Japan*, both because their own protection from attack is in the United States' interest (i.e., their occupation or subjugation by any hostile state would gravely affect the balance of power) and because they constitute, with the United States, the pillars of the world economy.

c. In the *Middle East*, preservation of Israel's survival, for reasons that have much more to do with our values and with history (and not a little to do with domestic politics) than with strategic considerations; but also the establishment of peace between Israel and the Arabs (because of the host of dangers any prolongation of the state of war—or of a situation of neither-war-nor-peace—engenders, in a part of the world that contains important resources as well as a most explosive potential for fanaticism and radicalization, and in which the superpowers are both deeply involved); and continuing access to the energy resources of the area for us and for our main allies.

d. In *Central America and the Caribbean*, it is important to distinguish national security concerns from other interests. The United States certainly has an interest in seeing to it that a series of hostile regimes is not established in the countries of its traditional sphere of influence. But what *means* we choose to protect this interest depends to a large extent on the degree to which the hostility of governments would affect national security. It seems clear that the latter would be challenged *only* by the establishment of Soviet military bases (and secondarily by that of Cuban bases) in this part of the world—an unlikely event, given Soviet aversion to high risks.

e. In *East Asia*, the preservation of a peaceful balance of power between the USSR and China is a major U.S. interest. A war would force us into a very difficult dilemma—supporting the weaker side (China) or else risking a Chinese defeat that would immensely improve Moscow's position; a full reconciliation between Moscow and Peking at Washington's expense would have the same effect. It is definitely not in the United States' interest to turn East Asia, and the Northern Pacific area, into a zone of armed confrontation comparable to Europe. The danger is real: the Soviets are deploying large numbers of SS-20s in the Far East, in order to cope with the growing Chinese nuclear force (just as they seem to have built their European SS-20s as a response to the United States' Forward Based Systems) and perhaps to deter Japan from further rearmament efforts as well. They may deploy more SS-20s aimed at the Northwest part of the United States if NATO continues to carry out the December 1979 decision to install 572 missiles in Western Europe. Not only is a four-power balance far more delicate than a two-bloc one of the sort that exists in Europe, but the inclusion of China in nuclear discussions would be even more difficult than the already thorny issue of the French and British nuclear forces; and a further militarization of that part of the world might someday lead, not to a conventionally rearmed Japan, but to a nuclear Japan.

f. Two commitments exist on the periphery of the Soviet Union: one to the security of *Pakistan*, and one to that of *South Korea*. Both of these commitments are important, and both are troublesome and should be managed with prudence (they should not exclude other considerations, such as regional balance and human rights). Pakistan has been in a difficult position since the invasion of Afghanistan. If it continues to support the Afghan rebels, its integrity could be directly threatened or subverted by the Soviets, but abandoning the rebels would mean appeasing a powerful and dangerous neighbor. However, the U.S. commitment to a strategically important country happens to tie Washington to a far from popular and narrowly based military regime, to handicap the United States' policy against nuclear proliferation, and to complicate relations with India (against which this regime keeps wanting the United States to guarantee it also). In the case of South Korea, the presence of U.S. forces may well be required not just as a deterrent against a North Korean attack but also as a deterrent against a South Korean one and as a guarantee against a nuclear South Korea.

Three important remarks must now be made. First, a list of vital interests does not tell us by what means they should be protected: in some cases, a U.S. military presence would be neither welcome nor helpful. Second, the range of vital concerns varies from area to area: for instance, the preservation of links with Western Europe and Japan obviously entails more than a protection from aggression. Third, the preservation of vital areas from aggression must entail not only measures of deterrence, or defense, against the crossing of borders by hostile armies but also means of preventing or thwarting what could be called subversive aggression—the setting up, by a coup, of a "friendly" but obviously unrepresentative puppet regime, which then calls in Big Brother's forces (I would distinguish sharply between the Babrak regime in Afghanistan, which fits this description, and the pro-Soviet governments in Ethiopia and Angola, and even the 1978 Communist regime in Afghanistan, which took power by a coup but did not call in the Soviets).

While it might appear logical to go directly from a list of vital interests to a discussion of the means with which they should be ensured, it actually makes more sense to address first three major issues raised by the list. All the items in it raise the fundamental problem of U.S.-Soviet relations; the Middle East and Central America, and to some extent Pakistan and South Korea, raise the problem of revolution; and, finally, Western Europe, Japan, the Middle East and East Asia raise that of diplomacy.

3. The means to be used on behalf of national security depend to a large extent on one's view of the "Soviet challenge" and of the range of possibilities in *U.S.-Soviet relations*. I see the USSR as being relentlessly opportunistic—i.e., ready to seize opportunities for influence and for expanding control, but without either a master plan or any desire to take high risks. Its armed forces are designed not only for defense but also so as to make possible the projection of conventional power abroad, when circumstances allow for it, and so as to deter the United States from using its own power in order to prevent or combat the use of Soviet forces outside the limits of the Soviet imperial domain. Soviet ideology provides a kind of Ariadne's thread for interventions abroad; it upholds the idea of supporting either "progressive" (Marxist-Leninist) or "objectively progressive" (anti-Western) factions on behalf of "national liberation," when these factions are in power or have a fair chance of seizing power. Soviet national security aims toward another goal as well: breaking "encirclement," loosening the noose, by trying to estrange Western Europe from the United States (but not in such a way that NATO would be replaced by a West European armed bloc under German leadership), by maintaining some influence in the Arab world, and by attempting to improve relations with China.

The Reagan administration began with the (linked) convictions that most troubles in the world were either caused or aggravated by Moscow, and that a "revitalization of containment"[11] was the answer to the Soviet threat. Both the diagnosis and the cure are flawed, however. One of the reasons this threat is manageable without hysteria and over time is the existence of a natural barrier to Soviet expansion. This barrier is constituted in part by the intractable autonomy of many issues that Moscow finds difficult to exploit (cf. the Iran-Iraq War, and indeed the whole Arab-Israeli conflict, given the limits observed in Soviet efforts to supply clients) and in part by the suspicious nationalism of many new states that want assistance but not subservience. There is another barrier: except for weaponry, the Soviet Union has little to offer, and in many parts of the world the road to any settlement of extant issues still passes through Washington, not Moscow. This is the case in Central America, in Southern Africa, and to a large extent in the Middle East.

It follows that a sensible U.S. strategy would look at containment, in areas other than Europe—where two vast armies confront one another—not as an immediate goal but as a by-product of desirable policies, as in Kennan's original but misunderstood position. It is the local situation that ought to constitute the barrier. Each one ought to be dealt with in its own terms, and on its merits, in such a way as either to deprive the Soviets of any opportunities to exploit (cf. the Zimbabwe settlement) or to limit the gains made by them (cf. Vance's tactics in the Horn of Africa, protecting Somalia from an Ethiopian attack). To try to build a barrier on unreceptive, unsuitable, or unsavory ground is to court failure or to risk war. Thus, a massive presence of U.S. ground forces in friendly parts of Southwest Asia could either destabilize a volatile area, in which anti-U.S. forces abound; or precipitate a military confrontation with a Soviet Union that would consider such a presence a threat. Trying to enlist reluctant friends in a "strategic consensus," as the United States did several times in the Middle East, never works. The very notion of containment—as Kennan found out, to this distress—suggests military pacts and bases. Yet the Soviets have shown a certain ability to leap over artificial barriers and to assert their presence by exploiting domestic or regional conflicts in favorable circumstances. Given the worldwide competition for arms, and our allies' desire for markets, the Soviets have found some ways of expanding their influence despite all dams. The notion of containment concentrates the mind on the most costly and least likely form of Soviet action, which is forcible expansion.

I can only summarize here what I have developed elsewhere.[12] U.S. policy toward Moscow ought to have three components. One, to which I shall return, is military containment—required by several of the vital interests listed above. The second one is preventive diplomacy—helping create conditions that by themselves, will make opportunities for Soviet influence scarce and poor (see below). The third one is what might be called a détente without illusions. The great error of Kissinger's détente was its unrealistic ambition: it was a scheme aimed at getting Moscow to ratify *the United States'* notion of stability through a mix of containment and incentives to self-containment. It was not the idea of the mix that was bad but, rather, the policy of linkage (sensible as a notion, but very hard to apply) as well as the goal. Arms control is too important an issue, and one too much in the interest of both superpowers, to be used as an instrument for obtaining Soviet "restraint" and to be linked to specific requests of Soviet "good behavior." Trade, which was supposed to create a Soviet interest in moderate political behavior, rapidly created a Western constituency for credits, grain and industrial exports, and energy imports, which proved difficult to turn off whenever Soviet conduct did not live up to Washington's expectations. In any case, Moscow proved unwilling either to forgo attractive political gains or to tolerate insecurity in its empire or on its borders, in order to protect its stake in economic benefits or its concern for arms control. Nor was Moscow ever willing to stop competing with the United States in the Third World; indeed, even in the days of détente, neither side was ready to abandon the search for unilateral advantages at the expense of the other: Kissinger pushed the Soviets to the fringes of Middle Eastern affairs, the Soviets exploited windfalls in Angola, South Yemen, and the Horn of Africa, and they tried (but failed) to do the same in Portugal.

We must, in the future, set our sights a bit lower. We must also give up the attempt, pursued at first—and often clumsily—by the Reagan administration, to return to a position of primacy (through multiple interventions, a huge arms build-up, and the denial of Soviet interests, say, in the Middle East): such a quest only guarantees enormous costs, risks, and frustrations. Instead, we must try to regulate the intensity, the means, and the location of the contest, without expecting the Soviets to give up all attempts at changing the "correlation of forces." Intensity refers above all to the rhetorical level of the competition, and also to all moves that tend to make of the Soviet Union a "pariah" state: especially if one believes that so militarily powerful and politically ambitious a state is dangerous, one must avoid pushing it against a wall or into corners, trying to humiliate its leaders, and feeding its own nighmare of encirclement and penetration. Concerning the means, I have in mind the need to exclude the use of force against the independence and territorial integrity of any state, to exclude the use of force at the request of a puppet government, to reduce the level of force employed on behalf of a "friendly" (but not puppet) regime, and to curtail the methods of subversion and espionage used with great gusto by both superpowers. Concerning the location, I believe that either side will continue to want particular restraint from the other in zones of vital interests; prudence is particularly to be sought in areas such as Europe and in "grey areas" of great importance where each side risks being dragged into a confrontation with the other by a client it cannot afford to leave unprotected.

We should not feed the Soviet illusion of, or hope for, condominium; it would be intolerable to the American people, unacceptable to third parties, and far too one-sidedly beneficial to Moscow, which would gain a right to settle affairs in areas where Soviet interests are few or involvement minimal. But this leaves a wide range of realistic goals and of convergent or common interests. There is a joint interest—not in signing grandiloquent though meaningless generalities, such as the declarations of principles that resulted from the 1972 and 1973 summit meetings, and from the Helsinki Conference in 1975—but in crisis management. Crisis prevention, a far more difficult objective in a world of multiple conflicts, presupposes the development of a network of mutual relationships. For only if the superpowers have developed links that will benefit both will the inevitable quest for unilateral gains, which breeds crises, or the desire to avoid a unilateral loss at all costs, at last come under control. These relationships should be sought in three areas: arms (see below), economic ties, and diplomacy. Neither the idea that economic links necessarily benefit Moscow more than its clients, and only help keep the Soviet war machine going, nor the idea that all such links are desirable is valid. The use of trade and credits as weapons in anti-Soviet warfare—to change Soviet policies or even the Soviet system—has turned out to be very unsatisfactory; the Soviets keep their war machine going anyway, and our allies simply will not accept a policy of economic denial. There are mutual benefits here, as long as direct contributions to the Soviet arms industry and military technology are avoided, and as long as credit terms do not amount to subsidizing the creaky Soviet economy.

As for diplomacy, I have in mind two sets of moves. The first is a permanent dialogue and review of the policies that could lead to confrontations, through either direct collision, creeping escalation, or misunderstandings. Such preventive exchanges may not produce any convergence of policies or decisive changes of course, but they will bring about greater transparency, calculability, and incentives for restraint and bargaining. The second set is the inclusion of the Soviets, at an appropriate state, in the settlement of conflicts in areas where they obviously have important interests and where no adequate solution can be found without them. This remains the case in the Arab-Israeli conflict, given Soviet links with Syria and the PLO; it is also clearly the case in Afghanistan.

One of the many reasons for suggesting such a "menu" for U.S.-Soviet relations is, of course, the danger of war resulting from an endless series of confrontations, or even merely from a strategy of hostile containment. One of the many lessons of the pre-1914 Europe that have not been made completely obsolete by the invention of nuclear weapons is the strain put on peace by the recurrence of crises—even crises "managed" by compromises. Another reason is that only such a policy has a chance of minimizing strains in U.S.-allied relations and, therefore, of helping safeguard the links between the United States and its chief partners.

What this policy would require in the near future, given the current state of U.S.-Soviet relations and the main contentious issues, are the following:

1. a rhetorical de-escalation, which would put an end both to the wholesale indictment of the "evil empire" (rather than to specific criticisms of Soviet practices and behavior) and to statements about the possibility of waging or winning a nuclear war;
2. a new series of arms control initiatives;
3. a resumption of economic relations (not only in the realm of grain) within the limits indicated above, as well as of cultural and scientific exchanges;
4. U.S. support for the negotiations that have been undertaken, under UN auspices, for a settlement of the problem of Afghanistan that

would entail the gradual withdrawal of Soviet forces, a neutralization of the country, and the establishment of a government acceptable to the forces of resistance as well as to the USSR;
5. conversations between the United States and the Soviet Union aimed at reviewing the possibility of a joint U.S.-Soviet approach to the solution of the Palestinian problem and of the problems of Israel's borders and security guarantees: a crucial case of crisis prevention and preventive diplomacy.

The issue of preventive diplomacy brings us to the second major issue: *revolution*. Countless are the factors that make violent change possible or probable in most parts of the world: the social disruptions of economic modernization in societies with traditional or authoritarian regimes, social injustice and oppression in many countries, ethnic or religious factionalism, unsatisfied aspirations for national self-determination, racial discrimination, and so on. Both superpowers have tried to suppress revolution in their spheres of influence: the Soviets, systematically and ruthlessly, in Eastern Europe; the United States, more fitfully and obliquely, in Central America. This is not the place to address the Soviet dilemma, which is real (any lifting of the lid risks leading to uncontrollable explosions, yet permanent repression severely limits Soviet influence in Western Europe). The American dilemma is, in a sense, more serious because it is worldwide. We have close ties with a number of countries that are candidates for violent upheavals; these include countries in which we have military bases (the Philippines) or important economic and strategic interests (Zaïre, or South Africa), countries that have resources vital for our economy and the economies of our allies (Saudi Arabia) or alliance treaties with us (Pakistan, South Korea). The Palestinian movement, which is doubly revolutionary (for self-determination and against traditional Arab regimes), looks at the United States with a mix of hostility and despair. Central America is a powder keg.

The diversity of situations makes it impossible to suggest any single or simple recipe. Some things, however, are clear. One is the impossibility of maintaining the status quo forever and everywhere; we have discovered this in Manila, most painfully in Vietnam and in Iran, and now in Central America; soon, perhaps, we will discover it in Pakistan and in Chile. Another is the moral cost, in terms of American values and influence abroad, of keeping in power murderous governments whose violations of human rights cannot be concealed by artificial distinctions between "totalitarian" and "authoritarian" regimes (see Chapter 17). Third, American attempts at shoring up repressive regimes, or too close an identification with a regime that is incapable of reforming itself in time, or American hostility to the revolutionary regimes, provide the Soviets with splendid opportunities to extend their influence and to appear as champions of good causes (as in Southern Africa). Fourth, not every U.S. "defeat" (through the fall of a "friendly" regime) is necessarily a Soviet gain; so far, the fall of the shah has not directly benefited Moscow: the fundamentalist regime of Khomeini has been as anti-Communist and anti-Soviet as it has been anti-American. Nor was it inevitable that the Sandinista regime would move as far in the direction of Cuba and Russia as it apparently now has. Its evolution was caused not only by the internal dynamics of the Nicaraguan revolution but also by U.S. actions—namely, the suspension of economic aid despite the Sandinistas' agreement to stop aiding the rebels in El Salvador, and the support and training of the *contras*, based in Honduras, by the United States. Fifth, even regimes established or maintained with the help of the Soviets, such as those of Angola and Mozambique, may be eager to preserve and develop economic relations with the West. Sixth, most revolutions have indigenous sources; it is dangerous to let situations develop where a rebellion against tyranny and injustice can turn only to Moscow for support, and absurd to act as if such support had actually caused the upheaval. Seventh, it is in countries devastated by repressive regimes, in societies marked by the combination of injustice and state terror, that the chances of Marxist-Leninist forces are often greatest: so, while it is true, as Mrs. Kirkpatrick and others have argued, that postrevolutionary regimes may be equally or even more oppressive than the fallen ones, it is the destruction by the latter of any democratic alternative that is to blame.

The policy I would suggest, and one that would have to be adapted to each case, would consist of five imperatives. First, we must not allow ourselves to be blackmailed into supporting the status quo when it is clearly unraveling, or is dangerously precarious, or violates our essential values. In our relations with Marcos's Philippines and with South Korea, we have time and again suppressed our doubts because of strategic considerations—the two large U.S. military bases in the first case, the threat from North Korea in the second. In El Salvador, we have provided military assistance without insisting that the military and parliamentary "death squads" stop murdering opponents or innocent civilians and that the wrongdoers protected by the army and by the Right be punished. Blackmail by the weak is obnoxious; so is that by the strong(er): I refer to Israel's remarkable ability to deflect or ignore U.S. pressures and preferences. Second, we must insist on reforms while there is still time and make clear that good relations with and help from the United States depend in some part on such reforms being undertaken. Third, should the regime resist our pressure or reject our advice, we must dissociate ourselves as much as possible from it, in order not to turn its opponents into our enemies, in order to keep the internal or regional conflict from becoming one between us and one party or even a conflict between the superpowers. Fourth, whenever possible, we must maintain correct relations with the revolutionary regime, should it come to power. Fifth, we must protect the national security interest of preventing Soviet (or Cuban) bases in areas of strategic importance, not by fighting Soviet or Cuban-supported revolutionaries but by raising the issue directly with Moscow or Havana—i.e., by "going to the source."

If these recommendations are read as an invitation to a partial disengagement from exposed positions, that interpretation is correct. Such disengagement may well be the only alternative to either bottomless or indecisive engagement, or else to drowning on a sinking ship. We were lucky in the Philippines: While we disengaged from Marcos only at the last minute, there was a democratic and pro-American alternative. But this may be an exception. We should not be caught once more (as we were in Iran) in the trap of responsibility without control (full control of a foreign country being, as indicated before, neither desirable nor achievable). The application of these precepts to the cases involving vital U.S. interests suggests the following policies. In the Middle East, we must stop resisting Palestinian self-determination (see below). Although we may want to protect the Saudi regime against a factional coup, we ought to encourage it to open up political life; moreover, we should not envisage military interventions against a revolutionary regime that might come to power there, or in Kuwait, or in the Emirates, unless such a regime decides not merely to reduce but to cut off the flow of oil. The need of the leaders in South Korea, and Pakistan for U.S. protection should give us some leverage for reform. In Central America, we should enlist the support of concerned Latin American countries in the quest for peaceful solutions in the countries now torn by civil wars; our support of the existing regimes should depend on their curtailing effectively the suppression of human rights and on their willingness to seek such solutions. In El Salvador, a settlement through free elections presupposes both a sharing of power to prepare such elections and some inter-American force that would ensure that the extremists on both sides do not sabotage the process and keep their powder dry. In Nicaragua, we should put an end to our intervention, which destabilizes not only the Sandinistas but their neighbors as well, and obtain the Sandinistas' agreement to the Salvadoran settlement.

In Southern Africa, which does not figure in the list of "national security" areas but in which the United States has other important interests, "constructive engagement" is a moral and political fiasco. The United States' leverage is limited. However, we should stop supporting the present regime by approving its token reforms, by encouraging further private investments, and by insisting on linkage (or "reciprocity") between a settlement in Namibia and a departure of the Cubans from Angola. Dissociation from the regime in Pretoria, if it does not give up the essentials of apartheid, should lead to a policy of strong sanctions—especially if it is endorsed as well by the nations and private economic actors with which South Africa does most of its business. Indifference on their part would contribute to the radicalization of Black African resistance there—a process that, as the events since 1985 have shown, has already begun.

5. Coping with the prospect of revolution entails great *diplomatic skills*—before and after. Such skills are also needed in many other areas. As I have indicated, three of these areas involve national security: our relations with Western Europe and Japan, a settlement of the Arab-Israeli conflict, and our policy toward China. The preservation of our links with our main allies requires not only that of extended deterrence (see below) but also a strategy toward Moscow that is acceptable to them and an American

willingness to take their own priorities seriously. This means understanding the reluctance they may feel, especially in periods of economic crisis, toward raising military expenditures (our pressure on the Japanese may actually produce more disadvantages—worrying former victims of Japan and provoking Soviet countermeasures—than strategic gains). Nor should we take domestic economic measures that hurt their economies.

In the Arab-Israeli conflict, diplomacy means willingness to put pressure on Israel in order to obtain from its government those measures—above all, a clearcut end to the colonization of the West Bank—that would make it possible for Jordan to negotiate, an end of the exclusion of Syria (a state with a powerful capacity to act as a "spoiler") from the peace process, endorsement of the principle of Palestinian self-determination, and a willingness to let the issue of the *form* of Palestinian self-determination be settled by the Arabs themselves: what ultimately matters are the security provisions and guarantees needed by Israel, whether the Palestinians have a state of their own or are closely linked with Jordan. In Lebanon we must support the aim of national reconciliation, but we must also realize that a restoration of full independence presupposes a settlement of the Arab-Israeli conflict. Such a settlement would not break up the wave of revulsion against Western "modernity" that has swept over Iran and spread in the Arab world, but it would slow it down and make it less fiercely aimed at the United States. In the Far East we should act in such a way that if there is a growing détente between Moscow and Beijing (a move that is in both sides' interest), it should not appear to be the result of a divorce between Beijing and Washington.

III

What military policies are entailed by such a foreign policy? I will distinguish the nuclear from the conventional aspects.

In the nuclear realm, it is important to reverse gears. We must stop the march toward the catastrophe described in the first part of this essay. In other words, we must adopt a course aimed at restoring crisis stability, at promoting arms control and reductions, and at decreasing reliance on nuclear weapons.

1. A sensible nuclear policy should be based on the following considerations. The United States will continue to need nuclear weapons to deter, not only a nuclear attack on itself, but also a nuclear attack by the Soviets on a vital U.S. stake. But the ability to do so is not in doubt. A nuclear attack on Western Europe, even if its primary aim is the military installations and nuclear weapons of NATO, is likely to be hard to distinguish from a "countercity" strike; in such a case, no Soviet planner could count on the U.S. president's refusal to resort to nuclear retaliation, either against remaining vulnerable Soviet missiles, against other Soviet military objectives, or against Soviet cities. This is precisely why the Soviets seem to envisage the possibility, in an acute crisis in which a nuclear "exchange" would look inevitable, of

a preemptive attack not against Western Europe only but against vulnerable forces and other strategic targets on American soil as well. In such a case, again, the very scope of the attack, as well as the likely casualty level, seems to guarantee U.S. retaliation; what is clear—and has been confirmed by the Scowcroft Commission Report—is that even if the Soviets succeeded in destroying the bulk of our ICBMs and a portion of the bombers on the ground, and even if remaining Soviet ICBMs did not wait in their silos for the United States' counterblow, we would have more than enough weapons left to hit the Soviet Union and more than enough military objectives if we wanted to spare the cities (a somewhat artificial distinction, since most of these targets—and many of the ICBM silos—are close to or in cities). For direct deterrence of a nuclear attack on itself, and for extended deterrence of a nuclear attack on its chief allies, the ideal capability of "assured destruction" needed by the United States is one that requires invulnerable weapons, no great accuracy, and limited numbers of warheads.

The real conundrum, for extended deterrence, is nuclear deterrence of a conventional attack on Europe or in the Middle East: How plausible is the U.S. threat of a possible first use of nuclear weapons? Some believe that, in an age of nuclear parity, it is not credible at all. The arguments of the 1982 "gang of four" (Bundy, Kennan, McNamara, Smith) and of George Ball are very powerful: a Soviet threat to retaliate, either against the United States or against European cities, after any NATO first use, would subject the president of the United States, in Ball's words, to "a shrill crescendo of domestic outcries demanding a prompt end to the European war"; moreover, an actual first use might result in the "Western alliance breaking apart like a melon"[13]—as well as in global destruction, since nobody knows how to keep nuclear war limited. In addition, it is difficult to imagine the conditions in which the Soviets would launch a general conventional attack on Western Europe—not only because of the risk of nuclear escalation in a continent full of nuclear weapons and vital to the United States but also because of the quite formidable conventional defenses of NATO: there is no certainty of Soviet victory, and this in itself may suffice as a deterrent. (Against a limited Soviet conventional thrust, a threat of nuclear war would be even more incredible).

And yet, reliance on conventional forces alone for deterrence runs into two formidable problems. Geographically, the Soviets have an advantage in the areas around their borders, and for the United States to renounce openly the possible use of nuclear weapons means accepting a possibility of defeat in vital areas. Moreover, in Europe's prenuclear experience, conventional armies have not been a very effective deterrent: this, far more than the high cost of raising such armies, explains not only the attachment of many Western Europeans, especially the West Germans and the French elites, to the first use doctrine but also their extreme reluctance to have all of NATO's eggs in the conventional basket; many of them, especially among the leaders, cling to nuclear deterrence as the only salvation: in their view, which can be debated but not disproved, the only effective deterrent is fear of nuclear death. A renunciation of first use is seen by them as likely to make war more, not less likely; in other words, such a switch could only be interpreted by Moscow as a form of American disengagement. A U.S. threat of first use might, they believe, appear implausible to overly rational Americans; but is it incredible for the Soviets, who would have to take the possibly fatal risk of initiating war?

Reliance on nuclear weapons for the deterrence of conventional attacks in Europe and the Middle East nevertheless entails two dangers. The first is that, in a crisis, as Ball puts it, "although the Soviets can never be absolutely certain whether a president would authorize the use of nuclear weapons to repel a conventional assault, they might become sufficiently skeptical to test the issue, influenced in that decision by the mood in America as they perceive it."[14] In other words, extended nuclear deterrence *may* fail to deter. The second danger is that of the actual use of nuclear weapons, by both sides, after such a failure. In all likelihood, such use would destroy Europe and be uncontrollable. Now, the use of nuclear weapons after the beginning of conventional war would be particularly likely if (1) the war went disastrously for NATO, which would have no other way to try to avoid defeat than the resort to nuclear arms, and (2) if one side had, in or near the battlefield, nuclear weapons that were particularly vulnerable.

What this suggests is the following military posture: a stronger conventional capability (see below), which would make the need to rely not only on the threat but also on the actual use of nuclear forces far less pressing; and neither *explicit* reassertion nor *explicit* renunciation of "first use" at present. A renunciation *now* would provoke an alliance crisis—not only with the full members of NATO but also with France—and in any case would not be credible in the first place, as long as Europe is stuffed with nuclear weapons: Why tempt the Soviets to take higher risks if, in the end, rather than accept defeat, the NATO powers may *still* decide to use nuclear weapons?

A renunciation would become useful after the conventional capability has been strengthened; after the allies have become convinced that no-first- use does not mean an increased risk of war, destruction, and defeat; and after an improvement in U.S.-Soviet relations that would dispel the fear of any war in Europe. An explicit reassertion should also be avoided for all the reasons indicated above.

McGeorge Bundy has often asserted that, in Europe, the Soviets were deterred from exploiting their conventional superiority by the fact that they could *not be sure* that the United States would not resort to nuclear warfare. This seems to be an adequate statement. It is even more valid in the case of the Middle East than for Europe. In the Gulf area, it is even harder to imagine what would trigger a general Soviet conventional attack than in Europe (where the greatest part of the Soviets' conventional forces are stationed); and there are no countries that would allow the United States to deploy nuclear weapons. It is, therefore, the *risk* that any large-scale war *could* lead to nuclear war, should vital U.S. intersts be threatened, that serves as the ultimate deterrent. When the stake is vital and one's commitment is manifest, extended nuclear deterrence is likely to have sufficient residual plausibility to be effective against the danger of massive conventional attack— as a fact of life, a condition, a by-product of "existential deterrence," rather than a doctrine. What deters the would-be aggressor is not his opponent's nuclear superiority; it is the risk of escalation to the nuclear level.

But this kind of deterrence is amply ensured by the combination of the United States' strategic forces (including the portion that is assigned to NATO) and of pre-1983 U.S. nuclear weapons in Western Europe (those of the Forward Based Systems and some of the battlefield weapons). The latter's existence makes more certain the Soviet conviction that a conventional assault would create a risk of uncontrollable escalation. But this counterforce ability should be limited in two ways. First, it should not consist of countersilo or "decapitation" weapons that would be provocative in a crisis; second, it should not consist of vulnerable weapons.

The two limits proposed here indicate that whatever counterforce ability is needed is provided by U.S. Forward Based Systems (FBS) and by U.S. strategic bombers and air-launched cruise missiles. These limits suggest, in the first place, the need for changing the number and deployment of U.S. battlefield nuclear weapons: they are far too numerous and placed too close to the Iron Curtain, where they are vulnerable to a Soviet attack—and are therefore both a tempting target and an incentive to preempt. Second, these limits rule out precisely the two types of nuclear weapons NATO is deploying in Western Europe: land-based cruise missiles have a countersilo, Pershing IIs have a "decapitation" capability, and both are vulnerable.

The NATO decision of 1979 illustrates the enormous difficulty of trying to obtain perfect ironclad nuclear deterrence of war in Europe. For complex political and strategic reasons, a European deterrent—which might indeed be quite credible, whatever its size—is not easily achievable. But extended deterrence on the part of the United States can never fully satisfy the European protegés, since they oscillate (or divide) between the fear of being dragged into war over purely U.S. interests or through U.S. blunders and the fear of American "decoupling"—that is, of the United States actually not resorting to the threat of nuclear weapons for the protection of Europe, in order to keep its own territory as a "sanctuary."

The issue of the intermediate nuclear forces is but the latest illustration of this problem. Militarily, the SS-20 and Backfire bombers were seen by many West Europeans as creating a new threat, not because the targets they can hit could not have been reached before by older intermediate forces, or could not be struck by Soviet ICBMs, nor because of the new weapons' precision (as I have already mentioned, the difference between counterforce and countercity in Europe is small), but because the SS-20s are invulnerable (mobile) weapons, unlike their predecessors, and because there was no middle-range NATO weapon capable of hitting the whole Western part of the Soviet Union. Hence the widespread European worry that the new Soviet arsenal would lead to the feared "decoupling," and Helmut Schmidt's 1977 call for a remedy. The European view is one that focuses not on the global strategic balance but on the regional, "Eurostrategic" balance (or rather imbalance). The 108 Pershing IIs and 464 ground-launched cruise missiles were selected for deployment by NATO because, given their placement *in* Western Europe, they would be proofs of coupling. In other words, as the Soviets could not be sure that these missiles would not be fired in case of a conventional attack, the only "sensible" alternatives for Moscow would be either no move at all or the initiation of nuclear war (in which case it would make no sense to spare American territory).

Why, then, did a decision so obviously aimed at reinforcing deterrence provoke such unexpected opposition? In Europe, there were two reasons: (1) Since the new missiles are under U.S. control, as are the older Forward Based Systems, there is still no way for the protégés to be sure that the protector will react with a nuclear "inflexible response": the Soviets could still gamble on a purely conventional war and either miscalculate, in which case all lose, or win, in which case the West Europeans alone lose. And (2), since the new missiles are concentrated in a few areas, and since they have countersilo and "decapitation" properties, they provide the Soviets with an incentive to preempt—i.e., they undermine crisis stability. In the United States, some have objected for an additional reason: if the security of Western Europe is inseparable from that of the United States—and that *is* the meaning of the U.S. guarantee—then the new missiles are militarily unnecessary. If the Soviets choose to have redundant weapons, that is *their* problem. But what deters the use of these weapons, or a conventional attack on Western Europe, is not the presence of any given weapon system *in* Western Europe but the ability of the United States to carry out a first nuclear strike on Soviet forces and targets in case of a conventional attack, or to retaliate against a nuclear one. In other words, it is the risk of any Soviet general attack leading to all-out nuclear war. And the long-range strategic U.S. arsenal—including Polaris submarines assigned to NATO—can hit every one of the targets that the Pershing IIs and GLCMs would aim at.

Since we are in the realm of psychology now, not military technique, one must ask whether the intended coupling effect on NATO and the deterrent effect on the Soviets have not been offset by the destabilizing nature of this particular coupling, and by the opposition and doubts that have mounted in Western Europe. After all, one of the two purposes (the other being a buttressing of deterrence) was to reassure the allies. And if half of the concerned Western Europeans are more scared than comforted because of the nature of the weapons and the prospects of becoming targets of nuclear war should deterrence fail, while the other half still worries whether the United States' increasing talk of better conventional defense does not indicate a drift toward "decoupling" (i.e., a willingness to fight a purely conventional war in Europe after all), then there may be more losses than gains. From the viewpoint of crisis stability, the assignment of more submarine-launched missiles would have been preferable—but some West European negotiators worried, in 1979, that the Soviets might have deemed these missiles less "coupling" than GLCMs and Pershing IIs on European soil.

2. The way of trying to cope both with the threat of the SS-20 and with the bad effects of the NATO decision to deploy 572 new missiles on land, as well as the way to prevent the drift toward crisis instability, unverifiable new weapons, and huge war-fighting capabilities, is to devise an arms control strategy that would allow not merely for a freeze in the superpowers' arsenals but for deep reductions as well, particularly where destabilizing systems are concerned—systems that threaten or are threatened by the other side's weapons, or are difficult to verify.

The most destabilizing trend has been the threat to the survivability of land-based missiles. The Soviets' theoretical ability to destroy our Minutemen has incited us to provide ourselves with a matching ability to destroy their far more important silo-based missiles: the MX (which, as currently planned, will be a highly tempting target for as well as a threat to the Soviet heavy missiles) and the D5 missiles on Trident II submarines. But we do not need the means to destroy Soviet land-based missiles. In a crisis over Europe or the Middle East, Soviet ICBMs would be on the alert in any case: our ability to destroy them before they are launched would be small. As long as we have vulnerable ICBMs, the Soviet incentive to destroy these first is high; even after we obtain an invulnerable countersilo capability (provided by the D5 and by cruise missiles), the Soviets would still have the strongest incentive to hurl their ICBMs at "soft" U.S. targets rather than see their silos destroyed.

Given the danger posed by countersilo weapons, I have recommended, first, that we give up the MX[15] since we cannot find an invulnerable basing mode on land, that we should not try to threaten Soviet land-based missiles (for the sake of crisis stability), and that we do not need it as a bargaining chip (for we do have the threat of the D5). My second recommendation is that we gradually eliminate our ICBM force. I do not favor a switch from Minuteman to Midgetman (i.e., the development of a single-warhead land-based missile), as mobile Midgetman would have the same problem of basing modes as the unfortunate MX and would open the way to a race of mobile, unverifiable land-based missiles. In addition, Midgetman, insofar as it could threaten Soviet silos, would be either redundant (if the Trident II is deployed and the number of mobile Midgetmen is limited by agreement), destabilizing (if no such agreement is reached and we build large amounts of them, and especially if we put them in vulnerable silos), or unnecessary (if the Soviets move toward mobile missiles). Should we want Midgetman in order to hit military objectives other than silos, with greater reliability than that provided by bombers and submarines, we might end up with a prohibitively expensive large number of single-warhead missiles, requiring a vast amount of land since they could not survive unless they were mobile. Land-based missiles are increasingly questionable as instruments of deterrence:

if they are fixed, hence vulnerable, they undermine crisis stability; if they are mobile, they make sense only when (as in the Soviet case) one has no adequate and equally accurate submarine or bomber force.

Third, although the phasing out of our ICBM force and its ultimate elimination could be accomplished unilaterally, we should also negotiate the kinds of agreements described in Chapter 16. Fourth, there is no need to build a B1 bomber to fill the gap between the present, increasingly unreliable bomber fleet and the stealth aircraft. In this conception, the United States would not deploy cruise missiles pending the outcome of negotiations. The nuclear deterrence of a Soviet attack on Western Europe or the Gulf area would be ensured not by vulnerable or provocative missiles but by the invulnerable submarine-launched missiles assigned to NATO or to the U.S. forces in the Gulf, as well as by U.S. bombers and air-launched cruise missiles.

3. The problem of conventional forces cannot be treated in detail here—nor am I qualified to do so. But a number of points can be made to illuminate the current debate on the Reagan program.

a. One of the biggest innovations carried over from the second half of the Carter period was the creation of the Rapid Deployment Force (RDF): potentially made up of 200,000 men and backed by increased sea and airlift capabilities aimed at the Gulf area. Quick airlift capabilities appear to be essential in any case—a capacity to react without delay to limited operations or probes is a better deterrent than a weightier but slower capacity, effective only against massive operations that are far less likely given the risks of escalation. What should be questioned is the need for a vast combat force in readiness. It isn't only that there are few available facilities for it in the area itself, and that the introduction of large U.S. ground forces there is likely to be counterproductive politically. The main reason for doubt is the nature of the more likely threats. The RDF planned by the Pentagon would make sense against the least probable contingency: a massive Soviet invasion. Against domestic subversion or turbulence, it would be either impotent or excessive. Against a Soviet "friendly" move into Iran, at the request of a puppet Iranian government, what would be needed is a small U.S. force capable of seizing the oil fields, backed by planes attempting to slow down the march of Soviet forces; matching what the Soviets would throw into a conventional battle is a hopeless enterprise. What is necessary is not a mere tripwire but the availability of a force just considerable enough to oblige the Soviets to face the dilemma: military confrontation (avoided since 1945, and in an area of vital U.S. interests—hence where escalation to the nuclear level cannot be ruled out) or bargaining.

b. Sealift capabilities and the need to maintain communications with allies, as well as access to threatened areas, require a powerful navy capable of repulsing efforts by the Soviet fleet to impede such communications. But there is an important area of controversy and choice. "Sea control is essential . . . for any viable conventional strategy."[16] But what kind of conventional strategy do we want for this navy? Is it to maintain sealines so as to allow for reinforcements to be sent and for trade to continue? Is it for offensive force projection against Soviet land targets and to permit countervailing operations where the Soviets are most vulnerable? The difference concerns the number of big aircraft carriers required and the size of the formidable fleets needed for their protection. The problem with offensive sea control is twofold: the carriers are vulnerable (especially if they operate close to heavily defended areas) and such a fleet is inadequate for more limited operations that require smaller and swifter ships. Indeed, the contingency for which it is being assembled—a major military conflict with the Soviet Union—is one that a strong navy could not win by itself, since the Soviets could still do such things as "overrunning Europe and the Middle East oil fields, emasculating or cowing China, or mounting a land-based missile and air threat to nearby Japan."[17] Attacking more vulnerable positions from the sea, presumably not Soviet but pro-Soviet positions (as in Cuba, Vietnam, etc.), would do little to protect the United States' vital interests from such a Soviet sweep. The $50 billion to be spent on the three new carrier groups and the increase in U.S. amphibious assault forces constitute a huge and dubious investment.

c. It is still Europe that remains the most likely area for conventional war because of the concentration of forces there, the importance of the stakes, and the inherent instability of much of Eastern Europe. Here, two issues are of great importance. One concerns the U.S. troops. Objections to the presence of approximately 250,000 men in Western Europe come from two main groups: those who believe that the allies do not carry a fair share of the collective burden and those who think that the main American task now is the protection of the Gulf area. The first argument is unconvincing—the demonstration of the scope of the allies' contribution to NATO has been made often. The second one is based on an erroneous view of the hierarchy of threats in the Middle East (which is not to say that some of our forces in Europe should not be sent elsewhere in an emergency, by agreement with our allies). Above all, there is a contradiction between the widespread notion that more efforts should be made toward conventional deterrence and a reduction of the U.S. force.

The second issue concerns NATO's state of readiness. The main goal ought to be to prevent a quick Warsaw Pact victory. Speed of reinforcement is essential. According to Harold Brown, "the great bulk of NATO resources should be directed toward improving immediate combat capabilities."[18] The Warsaw Pact's superiority in tanks is worrisome. We could propose to the Soviets at the stalled MBFR talks a reduction in the stock of NATO battlefield nuclear weapons (for which a precise use has never been found) in exchange for a reduction in the number of Warsaw Pact tanks. We have had a tendency to try to respond to Soviet conventional advances by developing technologically ever more complex and sophisticated weapons. James Fallows has made a powerful critique of this policy.[19] Serious doubts have also been expressed about the agility and reliability of the huge M-1 tank: "An aircraft carrier, an M-1 tank and MX missiles in dense pack all have one fundamental characteristic: they are high-value targets."[20] Simpler, less expensive, and more easily usable weapons may be far more cost-effective. This does not mean that advanced technologies should be avoided, as the example of Israeli success with remotely piloted vehicles has shown. But technological complexity can be a genuine liability.

IV

All the remarks and proposals made here aim at a foreign policy and strategy that would put the U.S.-Soviet contest—important, unavoidable, and geographically unlimited as it is—into perspective. This contest is not all of world politics; it is not doomed to lead to military confrontation; in a nuclear world, the most likely clashes between two equally prudent opponents (both of whom believe that time is on their side) are not of the cataclysmic variety, except through grievous miscalculations or self-fulfilling prophecies; and the relationship is not necessarily one of unmitigated hostility.

We must give up our obsession with "stability," which so often makes us try to prop up a collapsing or criminal status quo; we should be concerned with influencing change, or accommodating it.

We must give up our conviction that we know what is good for others; we should allow for a wide diversity of interests and learn how to manage differences, yet without hesitating to use our influence to prevent violations of human rights by governments that depend on us.

We must give up the notion, left over from the pre-nuclear age and from the days of imperialism, that only might "works"; we should concentrate on more subtle and reciprocal as well as on sharable and collective forms of power, because military power is increasingly dangerous and incapable of resolving economic and social issues.

We must give up the appealingly simple but misleading idea of automatic opposition to every move of the Soviets or of their allies; we should realize that this idea often traps us into quagmires and distracts us from the more important attempt to cope with the problems that provide our opponents with opportunities.

We must give up the dream of climbing out of the nuclear age by means of a technological miracle—Star Wars—and the temptation of matching every Soviet weapon system with one of our own; we should understand that the efforts made by each giant to match and to neutralize the nuclear forces of the other have undermined deterrence, by making the requirements of deterrence indistinguishable from those of nuclear war-fighting.

We must give up the notion that a clear distinction can be restored—through greater accuracy in warheads, or enhanced radiation weapons—between counterforce and countercity warfare; we should see that this attempt at reversing the nuclear revolution and at diminishing the moral horror of nuclear war drives the arms race toward ever more provocative and destabilizing weapons, without any guarantee that mutual destruction could be avoided anyhow.

We must give up, in our minds and in our planning, the idea that a nuclear war could be rationally initiated, waged, controlled, and satisfactorily ended; we should accept the fact that "existential deterrence" remains the best protection against nuclear attack, and that it may sufficiently extend its shadow over vital areas to provide some assurance against major conventional assaults there but cannot fully substitute either for conventional forces or for the patient diplomatic attempt to prevent armed conflicts between the superpowers from breaking out at all.

An approach to national security that would reexamine many of the current taboos and entail a drastic reduction of the nuclear arsenals—partly through negotiation but partly through unilateral measures as well—would free American energies and resources both for pressing internal issues and for the pursuit of important interests abroad, interests that would come into the national security category only if their mismanagement led to disasters. The main task is to persuade the American public and its representatives that there are fewer risks and more opportunities in this course than in the current one.

The public may not be the principal obstacle. Opinion studies show the depth of its concern about the nuclear arms race, its support of a freeze, its worry about the prospects of armed intervention in Central America.[21] And while the public remains suspicious of the Soviets, the enthusiasm for a bigger defense effort has declined. The main problems exist at two other levels. One is Congress, which hesitates to challenge the Executive in matters that the latter calls vital to the security of the United States and threatens to use against recalcitrant representatives. Members of Congress seem to fear getting claught between the president and his well-organized supporters in their constituencies, even on issues in which the public at large—often much less well organized—is very far indeed from the president (Central America, the MX, the freeze). The complexity of some of these issues, the dispersion of authority in Congress, the fear of being charged with responsibility for "weakness" or "defeats," have made the members of Congress eager for compromises that often yield the substance in exchange for the appearance of participation. They are unwilling to assert themselves against a president protected by his bonhomie from charges of imperial excesses or wrongheadedness, and skillful at exploiting the deep latent anti-Soviet feelings of many Americans whenever Soviet actions provide a good opportunity.

The other level is that of the U.S. foreign policy establishment (including the media concerned with foreign affairs), which suffers from two ills. One is a brand of utopianism that differs greatly from the brand I ascribed to some of the members of the peace movement: it is the kind of Americanism that has often been called "exceptionalist," a belief in the United States' sacred mission either as a world policeman or as a world benefactor. It results in extreme self-centeredness, in an inability to understand how burdensome other nations often find either form of American benevolence, and in an unwillingness to envisage the kind of sharing of decisions and devolution of power that will be increasingly necessary with friends and even with rivals. The other flaw is the establishment's mental timidity—a fondness for past formulas even if their time is gone, a ritualistic attachment to what worked so well in the brief period of American primacy, a concern for "tough-mindedness" or incrementalism that masks the scope of the changes in this threatened world and the need to discard old assumptions—in sum, a mix of unhelpful nostalgia and "business as usual." It contrasts with the discontinuity of the U.S. political system, but the paradoxical joint result is a kind of immobility, a lack of adaptation to the new conditions that call for the retrenchment and reorientation recommended here. To bring about such a course is no easy task. But it is worth trying.

Notes

1. John L. Gaddis, *Strategies of Containment* (New York: Oxford University Press, 1982).
2. *New York Review* (June 16, 1983).
3. See Steven Kull's critique of "perception theory" in "Nuclear Nonsense," *Foreign Policy*, no. 58 (Spring 1985), pp. 28–52.
4. Walter B. Slocombe, in Barry M. Blechman (ed.), *Rethinking the U.S. Strategic Posture* (Cambridge, Mass.: Ballinger, 1982), p. 34.
5. Ibid., p. 38.
6. *New York Review* (June 16, 1983), p. 4. Other critiques of counterforce can be found in Robert Jervis, *The Illogic of American Nuclear Strategy* (New York: Cornell University Press, 1984); and Robert J. Art, "Between Assured Destruction and Nuclear Victory," *Ethics* 95, no. 3 (April 1985), pp. 427–516.
7. Harold Brown, *Thinking About National Security* (Boulder, Colo.: Westview Press, 1983), Chapter 5.
8. *New York Review* (June 16, 1983), p. 4.
9. See Robert Putnam and Nicholas Bayne, *Hanging Together* (Cambridge, Mass.: Harvard University Press, 1984).
10. Brandt Commission, *Common Crisis* (Cambridge, Mass.: MIT Press, 1983).
11. Robert E. Osgood, "The Revitalization of Containment," *Foreign Affairs, American and the World in 1981* 63, no. 3 (1981).
12. Stanley Hoffmann, *Dead Ends* (Cambridge, Mass.: Ballinger, 1983); and "Detente," in Joseph Nye, Jr. (ed.), *The Making of America's Soviet Policy* (New Haven, Conn.: Yale University Press, 1984).
13. George Ball, "Cosmic Bluff," *New York Review* (July 21, 1983), pp. 37–38.
14. Ibid., p. 37.
15. See Chapter 16.
16. Robert W. Komer, "Maritime Strategy vs. Coalition Defense," *Foreign Affairs* (Summer 1982), p. 1132.
17. Ibid., p. 1133.
18. Brown, *Thinking About National Security*, p. 102.
19. James Fallows, *National Defense* (New York: Vintage, 1982).
20. Sheila Tobias et al., *What Kinds of Guns Are They Buying for Your Butter?* (New York: William Morrow & Co., 1982), p. 373.
21. John E. Reilly (ed.), *American Public Opinion and U.S. Foreign Policy Since 1983* (Chicago: Chicago Council on Foreign Relations, 1983).

16

Beyond Terror?

On the Concept of Common Security

In the traditional and still very widespread view of international relations as a "state of war" (actual war, preparation for war, or simply constant conflict for power, prestige, and primacy), there can be no such thing as common security. The causes of insecurity are the actions of other states (in addition to those of domestic enemies of the established regime or social order). Security can be achieved (or, rather, approximated) only through either unilateral moves (such as those that diminish one's own vulnerability) or deals and compromises that reduce the threats from the outside yet fall far short of replacing the permanent competition with anything like a common code of abstention from force. The best example is the European balance of power: it was essentially aimed at curbing the ambitions and abilities of troublemakers—if necessary, by threatening the use of force or by resorting to force against them. The flexibility of alignments necessary for the functioning of this balance reflected both the principle of sovereignty and the right of every state to use war as an instrument of policy. In a sense, the Concert of Europe in the nineteenth century tried to preserve the security of the status quo powers by making a potential revisionist or revolutionary power more insecure.

It is necessary to distinguish the concept of common security from that of collective security. The latter entails a commitment by all states to coalesce against an aggressor. The aim is similar to that of common security: protecting one's state and nationals from violent external threats, through collective action that requires (by contrast with the Concert) a sacrifice of sovereignty and an abdication both of the right to resort to war for purely national reasons and of the right to remain neutral. But the method is very different, inasmuch as it aims at deterring aggression through the threat of collective sanctions. In this scheme (as in Hans Kelsen's legal system), the use of force is either a delict or a sanction. The concept of common security, as defined by the Independent Commission on Disarmament and Security (Palme Commission), tries, on the other hand, to move away from the use of force altogether.[1]

In today's world, leaving aside threats to security that originate within a given state (a very vast category), outside threats need to be analytically distinguished in the following way. A first basic distinction is that between threats of force and threats to the economic well-being of a state that result either from nonmilitary moves of other states or from trends in the international economy. The latter trends can originate in the moves of nongovernmental actors (private capitalists, multinational corporations, etc.) or appear to be beyond the control of any state or transnational body. The competition for scarce resources, the dependence of advanced countries on raw materials, sources of energy and markets in the developing countries, and the desire of the latter for a drastic redistribution of power and income in the international system often tempt states to treat the world economic arena as a zero-sum game in the short run. But the amount of interdependence, however uneven and manipulated, is such—even between command economies and market or mixed ones—that an awareness of the need for common security has spread, often quite spectacularly. There may not be any consensus on redistribution—i.e., on many of the issues raised by the Brandt Commission. But there is a broad consensus regarding the need for common protection against shocks that would spread economic insecurities in an uncontrollable way. During the recent economic crisis, the resistance against a return to the sort of protectionism that destroyed the world economy in the 1930s and the emergency measures taken in order to cope with the debts of developing countries can be mentioned as evidence. There is still considerable disagreement about the best methods for reducing economic insecurity (cf. the reluctance of the dominant economy, that of the United States to curb its freedom of domestic maneuver by undertaking commitments to reduce the range of fluctuations of the dollar or of the rate of interest). But few dispute the concept of common security in this realm, because of the obvious way in which each nation's power is hostage to that of other states.

The use and threat of force, however, remain widespread despite the ban of the UN Charter. States continue to act as if the threat of force or the resort to war were effective ways of achieving gains or, at least, protections against outcomes deemed worse than the costs and sacrifices (of resources and values) entailed by military or subversive action. Many factors contribute to this situation: the intensity of ideological conflicts, between or within "blocs"; the murderous ambiguities of self-determination; the artificiality of so many borders; the heterogeneities of so many states; the weakness and corruption of so many regimes—to sum up, the interplay of civil strife and external meddling. In this realm, "commonality" remains largely an aspiration: there is no concept of community, and there are very few "international regimes" comparable to those that exist in the world economy. In the world economy, unilateral action is widely seen to boomerang, and collective action is seen as often beneficial. In the realm of force, the conflict of interests and designs makes collective action exceptional, and unilateral action is seen as preferable to inaction.

A second distinction, concerning the realm of force, must be introduced, however. It is the distinction between the superpowers' nuclear arsenals and all the other aspects and forms of the threat and use of force. A notion of common security is beginning to emerge with respect to the superpowers' nuclear capabilities, because of an awareness of the impossibility of their actually using these weapons for political gains, the meaninglessness of nuclear superiority, and the likelihood that any resort to nuclear weapons will become uncontrollable. The evolution of nuclear technology and the decisions made by both superpowers with respect to new weapons systems seem to be driving these powers—and the rest of the world—toward the possibility of total destruction: as the paradoxical dream of mutual security through the threat of mutual assured destruction recedes, as deterrence through the threat of nuclear war fighting takes over, it becomes clear that there is a stark choice between total insecurity (leading easily to total war) and moves toward common security. I describe below some suggestions about how to try to achieve the latter through drastic arms control. Improved political relations would also be indispensable.

We have not reached a similar stage with respect either to nuclear proliferation or to conventional armaments. In the case of proliferation, many states are tempted by a false analogy with the superpowers—that is, by the belief that the acquisition of a nuclear capability would provide them with the same deterrent against external aggression (i.e., with the same remedy against insecurity) as that provided by the superpowers' nuclear deterrents. In the cases of nuclear proliferation *and* conventional weapons, states continue to act on the belief that the acquisition, threat, or use of weapons can be decisive for political gains—i.e., that force still has a considerable positive productivity (in addition to its value for deterrence or defense). These gains can be sought abroad—through the control of coveted resources, the neutralization of enemies, and (increasingly) the shaping of a friendly milieu by means of the establishment of client regimes—and they can be sought at home—through the consolidation of a weak government, the marshalling of domestic unity, and the imposition of a simple and single criterion and priority ("national security").

It is for this reason that I disagree with one of the principles of common security listed in the report of the Palme Commission. Linkages between arms negotiations and political events should be avoided in the realm of the superpowers' arms race, because the introduction of such linkages can only make nuclear arms control more difficult, and also because their nuclear arsenals are disconnected from any specific geopolitical concern (by which I mean that the needs of extended deterrence, usually invoked to justify certain types of weapons, can actually be met in a wide variety of ways, given the high level of "existential deterrence": whether or not extended nuclear deterrence exists or works is much more a matter of will, a question of the importance of the stakes involved, and the result of a gamble on credibility than a question of specific weapons). But in all the other areas of the realm of force, there is a strong connection between policy decisions about weapons and political fears, ambitions, or objectives. To ignore this link is to court frustration. For many of the measures that are usually advocated—suppliers' agreements to curb the export of arms, the strengthening of international peace forces, the creation of regional zones of peace, and so on—will not be taken unless the political interests of the parties (the states and their regimes) are addressed.

The establishment of common security in the realm of nuclear proliferation and of conventional armaments is therefore a formidable task that far exceeds the difficult and limited issue of coping with the weapons themselves. It is a political enterprise that must operate at two apparently conflicting levels. One is that of the state itself: not so paradoxically, common security requires that the insecurity and vulnerabilities of states and regimes be reduced, and while the task of "nation-building" that is involved is primarily a national effort, much of this attempt at strengthening existing structures and at creating national self-confidence will have to take the forms of international assistance and redistribution discussed in the Brandt report—i.e., the forms of international economic cooperation. The other level is that of regional and international organizations. Common security requires a variety of regional and global "regimes," both in order to provide mechanisms of peaceful change (for in the absence of such procedures, force will remain the *ultima ratio*) and in order to provide collective, neutral, yet effective mechanisms of peace-keeping, reporting, inspecting, and sometimes enforcing joint decisions. Common security may not require a world federation or government—i.e. a mutation of international politics. But it certainly entails a colossal departure from the traditional politics of national sovereignty.

One may well ask under what conditions states are most likely to accept the creation and reinforcement of regional and global security regimes. The recent work done on economic regimes suggests, as a prerequisite, precisely what has been missing in the realm of force: an awareness of the fruitlessness, or of the relative unprofitability, of unilateral action, and of the advantage of collective procedures and restraints. Three political conditions are to be sought. One is a rapprochement between the superpowers—not in order to reach a condominium, which would be neither achievable nor desirable, but because in this realm their discord dooms the establishment of any meaningful antiproliferation regime or any effective regional arms control regime. A second condition is the enlisting, in each region, of those states that, for whatever reason, have come to the conclusion that the unilateral threat of or resort to force does not ensure their security and that their best protection from threats rests in a collective regime, armed with real powers. The third condition—one that would allow more states to reach that conclusion—is the spread of democratic institutions, as foreseen by Kant. Although there is little that can be done through external action, both the efforts at international economic assistance mentioned above and a vigorous human rights policy would be helpful and necessary. Thus, the task of moving toward common security is inseparable from the other essential tasks of world order.

The rest of the chapter will concentrate on the issue of the superpowers' nuclear arms contest. What can be done to tame it by political means?

What moral imperatives could affect it, even if they cannot agree on drastic curbs?

On Nuclear Arms Control

Everybody realizes that the nuclear arms race between the superpowers will escalate in extraordinarily dangerous ways unless means are found to reverse the trend. Whatever reasons may have existed for complacency in the past have disappeared. Thus:

1. It has become much more difficult to believe that deterrence—i.e., the avoidance of a war between the superpowers because of the certainty of devastating retaliation in case of an attack—will continue to ensure peace. There was a time when theorists as well as statesmen could believe that the prospect of unavoidable destruction of cities and industries would suffice to deter any aggressor. Having a "survivable" retaliatory force, leaving one's population exposed, and letting one's enemy also build a survivable force—these were the (partly counterintuitive) recipes for nuclear stability, a condition in which neither side would have an incentive to strike first. But the bizarre reassurance offered by "mutual assured destruction" is gone. Once both sides possessed the ability to ravage each other's territory and people, the likelihood of retaliating against the aggressor's cities in case of a conventional attack by that aggressor on important allies decreased, since such retaliation would have been suicidal. Far from resulting in a reduced reliance on nuclear weapons in the superpowers' strategies, the fact that both sides had obtained the capability for mutual assured destruction only led to a more intense nuclear arms race.

What has happened is simple: each side has acquired weapons capable of destroying part of the enemy's nuclear forces and command systems, and has given itself arms way beyond the minimum required by the pure theory of deterrence. Why? In abstract terms, we can be seen as living in two ages. One age we can call post-Clausewitzian: nuclear war is a disaster, and in the absence of disarmament the only rational behavior is a combination of stable deterrence and arms control. Here, we live with the paradox of peace through terror, since the emphasis is on the certainty of the retaliatory second strike, aimed at cities. But we also continue to live in a Clausewitzian age, for the contest of states still goes on. Deterrence could fail; and if it did, one would need something less suicidal than "mutual assured destruction"—a different rationality for deterrence and for the possibility of its failure. One would also need a means of "damage limitation"—i.e., not discontinuity between traditional war and deterrence but a continuum that would entail the construction of defenses for one's population, nuclear weapons, and command systems—and (especially if passive defenses are only of limited use and active ones of dubious efficacy) means to destroy part of the enemy's forces before one is hit by them.

In concrete terms, we live in two universes. There is that of, literally, the United States versus the USSR: each one can deter an attack on the other—which can only be from a distance, since these are not contiguous polities—by a threat of mutual destruction. But far more "real" is the universe in which an armed confrontation of the two giants would be triggered by hostilities in a third area of vital importance to both: Europe, the Middle East, China. To prevent a Soviet nuclear attack there, the best deterrent is not a suicidal countercity threat but the possibility of attacking those of Moscow's nuclear weapons that would not have been used in a first strike on one of these stakes, in addition to other Soviet military targets. In order to prevent a Soviet conventional attack, the best deterrent is not a conventional build-up (which is neither always possible—think of the Middle East—nor, in history, always compelling), but, again, a credible counterforce capability. The problem is that if I give myself such means, the enemy will have an incentive to do the same—to give himself the capacity to destroy my counterforce capabilities, for two reasons: "intimidate the intimidator" (i.e., neutralize mine); and, if it should seem almost certain that I am on the verge of using them first, or of escalating from short-range to strategic nuclear weapons, in order to protect an ally, preempt, and thus limit damage to himself. Thus, in this "real" world, there is a depressing continuity between deterrence and war—for the most plausible deterrent is deemed the one that relies not on the threat of total destruction (plausible only against the least likely hypothesis: a massive attack on one's territory, out of the blue, so to speak) but on the threat of a counterforce attack (postdeterrence rationality thus creeping back into the rationality of deterrence itself). There is a profound disconnection between the "reassuring" theory of MAD, which requires a finite number of not particularly accurate weapons and allows for crisis stability, arms control, and no incentive to war, and the counterforce theory, which entails crisis instability, an endless arms race, and a risk of nuclear war-fighting.

Counterforce for the protection of an ally has been the United States' "formula" for deterring a Soviet conventional attack on Western Europe—i.e., for neutralizing the Warsaw Pact's conventional superiority—ever since the late 1950s. NATO's deterring strategy relies on the threat of a first use of the nuclear weapons at its disposal: tactical ones, but also those of the United States' "forward-based systems" and, later, those of the nuclear submarines assigned to NATO and of the Pershing II and cruise missiles deployed after 1983 on European soil. The Soviet Union, applying traditional concepts of war, also developed a missile (the SS-20) aimed at European military targets, and decided that the best way of deterring the United States from ever resorting to nuclear weapons in order to prevent a Soviet conventional victory—as well as the best way of limiting damage to the Soviet Union, should the United States resort to nuclear weapons in retaliation against a Soviet conventional or nuclear attack—was to provide itself with the means of wiping out a substantial part of the United States' nuclear force; hence the development of heavy missiles that, once equipped with multiple warheads of great accuracy, are theoretically capable of destroying the United States' land-based missiles. The United States has sought the means of attacking Soviet military targets with nuclear weapons in the hope both of keeping such a counterforce war limited should it come and of making deterrence more plausible than the old deterrent threat of mutual assured destruction; hence the Johnson and Nixon administrations' decision to proceed with MIRVs and the development of cruise missiles. The Soviet ability to hit U.S. missile silos later gave the United States an incentive to expand its counterforce into countersilo warfare capabilities; hence the development of a more accurate warhead for existing ballistic missiles and the plans for the land-based MX and the sea-launched Trident II or D-5 missile.

Accordingly, the choice today (unless a breakthrough toward disarmament occurs) is *not*, as some suggest, between deterrence and "war-fighting": today, both superpowers proclaim that actual nuclear war risks being neither controllable nor winnable, but both act as if the only valid form of deterrence was one that tells the adversary that, should it commit aggression, it would be militarily defeated, whatever else may also happen to its cities and noncombatants. This marks a return to the classical conception of war: deterrence by the ability to destroy the enemy's forces. All of history shows that the record of this kind of deterrence is poor. To be sure, the risk of mutual destruction—i.e., of uncontrollable escalation beyond "traditional war-fighting"—still injects prudence into statesmen: MAD as a *condition* (existential deterrence) reinforces, stands behind, and neutralizes the dangerous potential of counterforce deterrence. But is this a safe combination?

2. It has become difficult to believe that negotiated arms control could provide a cap to the arms race and ensure stability. The only successful arms control negotiations have been the limited test ban of 1963, the nonproliferation treaty (NPT) of 1968, and the SALT I agreements of 1972. The limited test ban did not affect underground explosions; the NPT failed to prevent attempts by nonsignatories to develop their own military capabilities; and, although SALT I succeeded in banning ABM systems, neither the interim agreement on offensive weapons nor the SALT II negotiations that followed constrained the development of new offensive nuclear weapon systems by both superpowers. Today, of the three forms of stability deemed desirable—deterrence or strategic stability (the assurance that one's forces can inflict unacceptable damage on the other side even after suffering a nuclear blow), arms race stability (a condition in which neither side needs to worry about its opponent's attempt to build dangerous new weapon systems), and crisis stability (a condition in which neither side has an incentive to strike first in a crisis)—only the first one exists. The announcement, by President Reagan, of an all-out U.S. effort at building a defense against ballistic missiles in space is a further nail in the coffin of arms race stability and crisis stability (since a nation moving toward such a system could be seen by its lagging rival as planning an aggression on it, and could thus tempt the anxious opponent to preempt). It could also lead to a collapse of the ABM treaty.

3. It has become difficult to believe that improved political relations and communications between the superpowers would constrain the arms race

and diminish the risk of an actual military clash between them. The deterioration of U.S.-Soviet relations after 1979 has been dramatic, and it has affected the prospects of success of the current arms control negotiations.

All this means that the trend noted above, toward a recognition by the superpowers of a choice between mutual insecurity and common security, is neither smooth nor in any way guaranteed to lead to joint measures of nuclear arms control and reduction. Insecurity takes the form of uncertainty about the rival's possible resort to these weapons and about risks of escalation. So far, this uncertainty has had positive effects, injecting prudence in ends and means. Thus insecurity is seen as ambivalent: it makes *me* live in Kafka's burrow, but it also delays the enemy's knock on its walls. Conversely, common security is also potentially ambivalent. Since nuclear prudence does not put an end to the game of states—to the quest for advantages, since this quest is still tied, albeit in more oblique or complex ways, to the uses or possibility of uses of force—the possession of a nuclear arsenal may both shield a diplomacy of expansion and appear indispensable for the protection of important interests. Joint measures that would severely curb the unilateral efforts of each rival to look after its security and other goals are both unlikely, insofar as they would threaten opportunities for gains at the expense of rivals or complicate the safeguard of allies, and difficult to devise, insofar as the geopolitical situation of the two foes is different (cf. the frequent Soviet emphasis on "equal security," a way of demanding that the USSR be allowed to match the forces of all its potential enemies [the United States, Britain and France, China], something that would give Moscow a right to superiority over the US alone; cf. also the different scope of "extended deterrence" needs for the two superpowers).

What can nevertheless be done to diminish the tension between their desire to retain maximum freedom of movement (i.e., the traditional approach to "national security") and their need to reduce the more ominous and increasingly negative aspects of insecurity that result from this freedom?

Clearly, in a climate of cold war, initiatives aimed at reversing the trend of the arms race run into formidable obstacles. If they emanate from private citizens, they are not too likely to be picked up by the government—or if they are, it may turn out that they are not of a kind that leads to a breakthrough. As for the superpowers' own initiatives, they are often no more than moves in a protracted political-military chess game. A review of past initiatives suggests why there have been so many more fiascoes than successes.

On the American side, several initiatives were taken that were not primarily *aimed* at putting the Soviets in a bad light if they rejected the proposal, and at a lasting disadvantage if they accepted it. But they were *seen* by the Soviets as distinctly disadvantageous for them, and were therefore rejected. The Baruch Plan of 1946, setting up an International Authority in charge of nuclear energy, could have functioned despite Soviet opposition, by taking decisions (including sanctions) that could have been determined by a Western majority and would have severely constrained Soviet sovereignty.

The USSR was determined to catch up and to preserve its freedom of movement in order to do so. Eisenhower's open skies proposal of 1955 was seen by Moscow as legitimizing espionage, at a time when it was not yet possible for both sides to obtain information by satellite technology. The U.S. proposal of 1955 for a verified cut-off of fissionable materials for use in weapons production was rejected because, at the time, the U.S. stockpile of nuclear weapons was much higher than that of the Soviets. When the suggestion was made again, in 1970 and 1971, the Soviets did not respond: the SALT I negotiation, in process at the time, had taken a very different track, and there was an obvious contradiction between this proposal and both sides' intention to MIRV missiles as rapidly as possible.

The "deep cuts" proposal taken by Secretary Vance to Moscow in March 1977 was rejected both because of the way in which it was presented (a drastic departure from the previously accepted SALT II principles, it had been made public before it was communicated to the Russians) and because it demanded deep Soviet cuts in the area of greatest Soviet advantage—the SS-9s and -18s—in exchange for the nondeployment of U.S. weapons that were not yet operational, such as strategic cruise missiles and the MX. President Reagan's zero option for the European theater—calling for the dismantling of all SS-20s. SS-4s, and SS-5s, in exchange for the nondeployment of the 108 Pershing II and 464 ground-launched cruise missiles called for by NATO's decision of December 1979—was also rejected because, in the eyes of Soviet officials, the SS-20s are a mere measure of "modernization" of the Soviet arsenal as well as a response to those nuclear systems that have been deployed in Europe by the United States, Great Britain, and France and are capable of reaching the Soviet territory.

There have been more Soviet initiatives that have been rejected by the West. Some were seen as propaganda diversions from ongoing negotiations—for instance, the Soviet proposal of 1975 for the prohibition of new weapons of mass destruction; the Soviet proposal, also in 1975, for a treaty prohibiting all nuclear weapons tests (but without provisions for on-site inspection); also, Brezhnev's call of November 1977 for a halt to the production of all nuclear weapons and a ban on all nuclear tests. The latter proposal stated: "The pace at which agreements on limiting the arms race are being achieved is slower than that at which the arms race itself is developing. Moreover, in some highly dangerous aspects of the arms race, a point may be reached beyond which it will no longer be possible to conclude arms limitations agreements based on mutual verification. Weapons systems are already being developed which do not lend themselves to such verification at all in terms of limiting their quantity and their qualitative characteristics." This was an accurate assessment. But both sides were actually engaged in the complex negotiation of SALT II, and then as now, there was a conflict between the sweeping approach of a comprehensive freeze (or ban) and the delicate compromises—and deliberate omissions—of the strategic negotiations.

Other Soviet proposals were rejected because they were seen as one-sided efforts aimed at constraining the United States or NATO. Thus,

Brezhnev's February 1981 mention of a proposal limiting deployment of new submarines and banning modernization of existing ones was clearly addressed to the problem created for the USSR by the planned development of the Trident II submarine. The United States and its NATO allies have, over the years, rejected Soviet or Warsaw Pact proposals for the establishment of nuclear free zones in Europe, or calls for an agreement on no first use of nuclear weapons, because NATO strategy, before and after the adoption of the notion of flexible response in 1967, has relied on the threat of a first use of nuclear weapons in case of a Soviet conventional attack. Pledging no first use—unilaterally or through agreement—has been seen as doubly dangerous: in reassuring the Soviets that a conventional attack (in which the Warsaw Pact forces would have many advantages) would not escalate (i.e., weakening deterrence) and in upsetting the United States' allies, whose survival depends, as they see it, on avoiding *any* war—nuclear or conventional—and on the 100 percent success of nuclear deterrence. A nuclear free zone has been dismissed as introducing into NATO strategy—wedded to the concept of forward defense—the grave handicap of distinguishing between zones in which defense (in peacetime at least) would have to be entirely conventional and zones in which conventional and nuclear weapons could be integrated, and of creating thereby two categories of allies. The December 1977 Soviet proposal for a mutual renunciation of the production of neutron bombs—at a time when the NATO allies were engaged in difficult discussions over the production of this weapon by the United States and its deployment in Western Europe—was rejected as an attempt to prevent the United States from exploiting an area of technological advantage and to intervene in and circumvent a NATO decision.

More recent initiatives have been part of the gamesmanship of arms control. In the INF negotiations, the United States, supported by its allies, rejected the Soviet proposal of reducing the number of SS-20s aimed at Western Europe to the number of British and French strategic missiles (162) if the NATO powers agreed not to deploy Pershing II and ground-launched cruise missiles; the Soviets rejected President Reagan's March 1982 proposal, which called for reductions in the deployments planned by NATO in exchange for a reduction in the number of warheads on longer-range Soviet INF missiles "to an equal level on a global basis." In the START talks, the original U.S. proposal would have obliged the Soviet Union to restructure its nuclear forces—away from land-based missiles—without constraining the United States' own new programs (MX, Trident II, BI and Stealth, cruise missiles); the Soviet proposal would have banned cruise missiles with a range of more than 600 km. and freeze the deployments of new, large submarines. At this point, the gap between the two sides remains very wide on strategic weapons and defenses.

Given this deadlock, a number of Americans have recently offered initiatives of their own. They fall into several categories.

The most discussed have been the various proposals for a nuclear freeze. It is around the idea of a mutual freeze on testing, production, and deployment of nuclear weapons that the greatest number of people have been mobilized. As a form of symbolic politics—as a protest against the dangers of the arms race—it deserves the support of all those who are worried. But there are serious difficulties. First, while there is a rough parity between the superpowers at the global level, many of the political leaders of the European countries consider that there exists a "Eurostrategic imbalance" created by the SS-20 (and other Soviet nuclear deployments aimed at Western Europe), which a freeze would perpetuate. In their opinion, unless these deployments are dismantled or unless NATO is allowed to carry out its decision of December 1979, there could be a serious risk of "decoupling" between the security of Europe and that of the United States (without adequate nuclear forces in Europe capable of hitting the Soviet territory, NATO could be subjected to a Soviet conventional attack, and the U.S. president would then be faced with the choice of keeping the war conventional, even if NATO loses, and initiating strategic nuclear war; with the new weapons in place in Western Europe, the Soviets would be deterred, since the risk of a conventional attack escalating to the nuclear level would be much higher—indeed, a Soviet assault would have to begin by attacking NATO's nuclear forces: a terribly risky move). This "decoupling" could, many Europeans fear, lead to Soviet political blackmail of Western Europe, even if it does not result in any war. Second, the most serious danger to peace comes not from the quantitative arms race but from a qualitative threat; the undermining of crisis stability by specific systems, such as the SS-18, or the new U.S. warheads, which the freeze would not eliminate, or the undermining of deterrence stability by countermeasures, such as antisubmarine warfare, which the freeze would not affect. Third, negotiating a verifiable freeze (especially on the production of nuclear weapons) would be extremely time-consuming. During this period, more destabilizing systems would probably be developed and deployed. Would not the time be better used to negotiate reductions in particularly dangerous areas?

These difficulties have given rise to a second category of proposals: initiatives for reductions or "build-downs." They have proliferated during the past year. Two broad classes of proposals can be mentioned. The first class contains sweeping suggestions: those of George Kennan (May 1981) for a 50 percent cut in the nuclear arsenals and delivery systems of the superpowers, and those of Admiral Noel Gayler, calling on each side to "turn in an equal number of explosive nuclear devices," with each weapon counting the same. The Gayler plan assumes that "self-interest will make each side turn in its more vulnerable weapons"; but this is far from certain: each side might turn in merely its more obsolete weapons and prefer to keep even vulnerable ones, if these are weapons that threaten the other side's, as long as the other side hasn't agreed to turn in those of its own which threaten its opponent's weapons. In other words, we might want to deploy and keep an MX (even in existing silos), and the Soviets may want to keep their SS-18 and -20. The Kennan plan could also have destabilizing effects if, for instance, the reductions are made in the single warhead rather than in the MIRVed missiles (thus producing a higher ratio of warheads to targeted silos), thus leaving only a small number of submarines at sea that could then be more easily tracked by the other side.

The second class of proposals for reduction all have to do with "de-MIRVing." There have been several such plans. All of them, as well as the 1983 Scowcroft Commission report, favor smaller, single-warhead ICBMs over larger MIRVed ones, because the former would not constitute either as tempting a set of targets or as threatening a set of weapons for the land-based missiles of the other side. Thus, a step would be taken toward crisis stability. However, here again, there are some serious problems. Small ICBMs placed in fixed silos would still be highly vulnerable, and the incentive to "use them or lose them" in a crisis would remain. If there is no agreement with the Soviets on de-MIRVing, Kissinger's suggestion of gearing the size of the new ICBM force to the number of Soviet warheads could lead to a force both vulnerable and quite threatening to the Soviets. As for a mobile force, it would encounter the same basing mode problems as those which have plagued the MX, and make verification more difficult. Finally, the nebulous SDI program has made agreement on reducing offensive strategic weapons more difficult.

* * *

A new approach is needed, which would be based on the following principles. First, insofar as part of the "mad momentum" of the arms race has been caused by technology, it is necessary to try to constrain further dangerous technological developments. It can be done: witness the ABM treaty.

Second, while one can imagine uses of nuclear weapons that would be morally acceptable (by meeting traditional criteria of *jus in bello*, such as discrimination and proportionality) and technically limited enough to appear containable, the cost of crossing the threshold that separates conventional from nuclear weapons could be very high: an inconclusive resort to these weapons is just as likely to lead to escalation as to "war-termination" or "intra-war deterrence," to use the strategists' jargon; and nobody knows whether a nuclear war could be controlled. Indeed, even measures aimed at insuring that leaders and commanders be able to exert control over their nuclear forces in case of war and to communicate with the enemy, "may give our leaders the illusion that they can limit or control a nuclear war, and they may therefore be less frightened of fighting one," in Emma Rothschild's words. It is therefore necessary to step back from war-fighting scenarios, or from notions of "escalation control" or "escalation matching": for these assume either that there is a meaningful notion of victory in a protracted nuclear war, or else that the only thing that deters a Soviet attack in Europe or the Middle East is the specific prospect of being "matched" or "prevailed upon" at some distant rung on the ladder of escalation, rather than the general risk of provoking a nuclear war that would in all likelihood be uncontrollable. As McGeorge Bundy has often observed, it is that fear (what the strategic thinker Thomas Schelling called the threat that leaves something to chance) that deters, not the certainty of being stalemated or defeated in a nuclear war. Consequently, what is essential is the preservation, or restoration, of crisis stability: the establishment of conditions that will not, in a crisis, incite either side to preempt out of fear of having its forces destroyed if it waits, or to launch on warning.

Third, while nuclear weapons have probably been useful—until now!—for preventing war, they are not useful as instruments of political coercion against other nuclear powers or against states covered by a nuclear umbrella. The use of nuclear threats by the Soviets since the 1950s has been singularly unrewarding: Soviet political gains have resulted from the exploitation of windfalls (Cuba) or from Western miscalculations (Angola) or from opportunities provided by regional conflicts (the Middle East, the Horn of Africa). Soviet military gains abroad have resulted from conventional operations by the Red Army or Hanoi's army. The use of nuclear threats by the U.S. has been effective only for very limited purposes (a Korean armistice, deterrence of attacks on Quemoy and Matsu), at the expense of non-nuclear powers, in a period of overwhelming superiority. It is difficult to see what advantage the Soviets have derived from their missile-modernization program in Europe, or can derive from it as long as the United States considers, and conveys to its European allies the fact that it considers, the security of Western Europe inseparable from that of the United States. It was not American nuclear superiority that deterred a Soviet conventional attack, or thwarted Soviet blackmail attempts in Western Europe in the 50s and 60s: it was the risk of starting a nuclear war; and this risk is just as strong at a time of nuclear theater inferiority for NATO, but nuclear parity at the global level. What risks "decoupling" Western Europe from the United States is not the absence in Western Europe of nuclear systems capable of hitting the USSR (an absence which is far from complete, given not only the British and French forces, but the American planes and nuclear submarines assigned to NATO); it is the danger that any American first use of nuclear weapons (whether these weapons reach Moscow from West Germany or from the high seas) could escalate to a full nuclear war. Yet what has preserved deterrence in Europe so far is the risk an aggressor would take of provoking an American nuclear response, despite this danger, because of the magnitude of the stake. Therefore, the problem of extended deterrence is not one of matching every Soviet deployment: here too, crisis stability is essential. The problem is one of having *just enough* of a counterforce ability to keep the threat of a first use of nuclear weapons in case of Soviet conventional attack credible—while trying to improve conventional defense in such a way as to make an early first use unnecessary.

Fourth, just as crisis stability is an essential concern, so is verifiability. Without the former, the management of crises would become much more hazardous—in a world in which, as in the past, the threat of war will continue to be, not that of "attacks out of the blue," but that of confrontations over concrete issues leading to military moves and countermoves. Without adequate verifiability, agreements limiting the arms race will only make the superpowers more distrustful of one another, more afraid of the danger of a sudden "break-out" or violation, or more determined to exploit every non-verified or non-verifiable latitude for arms build-up left to them by the accord. And if nonverifiable weapons begin to proliferate, the chances for agreements will diminish even further.

The following initiative is based on these principles:

1. The United States should announce a suspension of underground tests for a period of a year, during which it will both expect a similar moratorium on the part of the Soviet Union and negotiate the conclusion of a comprehensive test ban treaty (see below).

2. A second unilateral move would be a decision not to deploy the MX, both because of the impossibility of finding an invulnerable basing mode and because of the danger for crisis stability created by countersilo weapons.

3. A third unilateral decision would be the gradual phasing out of land-based missiles, the length of execution depending on (a) the speed with which communications with nuclear submarines can be improved and made to reach the same degree of reliability as communications with land-based missiles, and (b) the speed with which a comprehensive arms reduction agreement with the Soviet Union is reached. The main arguments produced in defense of land-based missiles have concerned the complexity of calculations imposed on the Soviets by the existence of the triad, the greater accuracy of the missiles, and the reliability of communications. While it is true that the phasing out of ICBMs by the United States would allow the Soviets to concentrate their countermeasures on antisubmarine warfare and anti-aircraft defense, the fact is that such a move would deprive the Soviet heavy missiles of their targets and turn the huge Soviet investment in them into waste; Soviet land-based missiles would become either gradually vulnerable to the United States' Trident II and cruise missiles, should these be developed and deployed (for they will have the same accuracy as the ICBMs), or unnecessary in the absence of their targets, the U.S. fixed land-based missiles, even if the United States, in an arms control deal, gives up the Trident II and cruise missiles. Far from being a boon for Moscow, the American move, if not accompanied by a comprehensive arms agreement, could thus become a disaster for the Soviets.

4. A fourth unilateral decision would be to suspend further deployments of Pershing II and ground-launched cruise missiles in Western Europe for a period of two years, during which an arms control agreement along the lines suggested below would be negotiated, and on the condition that the Soviets stop deploying more SS-20s. Similar restraints would be observed concerning the testing of antisatellite weapons and of Star Wars components.

5. The initiative would also entail proposals for a new comprehensive arms reduction agreement that would combine the currently distinct INF and START negotiations. This separation is doubly absurd—both because it suggests a possibility of decoupling that is politically nefarious, and because the nuclear threat to Western Europe is constituted by middle-range Soviet missiles aimed at Europe as well as by whatever fraction of their strategic

force the Soviets may want to assign to targets in Western Europe, just as the threat to the Soviet Union is constituted by missiles deployed in Western Europe and capable of reaching the territory of the USSR as well as by the U.S. strategic arsenal. A merging of the two negotiations would also make it clear that the nuclear protection of Western Europe can, as in the past, be ensured by the assignment of long-range U.S. nuclear weapons to NATO.

The arms reduction initiative would aim at eliminating countersilo and so-called decapitation weapons—weapons capable of hitting the enemy's fixed missiles and of attacking its command and communication centers in a matter of minutes. It would also aim at curbing unverifiable weapons, such as sea- and ground-launched missiles and mobile ballistic missiles. The elements of this initiative would be as follows:

- A comprehensive test ban, along the lines agreed upon in the days of the Carter administration, which included the possibility of on-site inspections. A limited number of flight tests might be allowed in order to prevent the deterioration of the superpowers' deterrent forces.
- A ban on the development of antisatellite warfare and on the development and testing of all other kinds of space warfare. The contributions such systems might theoretically make to defense are far outweighed by the opportunities they would appear to provide for aggressive action (by disrupting the adversary's means of surveillance) and for an endless race between offensive and defensive systems; the ABM treaty of 1972 would also be confirmed. The phasing out of our ICBMs would eliminate the "need" to defend them.
- An agreement to ban sea- and ground-launched cruise missiles with ranges of over 600 km. Their proliferation would breed massive insecurity, and their capacity to hit ballistic missile silos—even if only after several hours of flight—could incite the targeted country to launch its land-based missiles before they are hit.
- An agreement to reduce the number of long-range bombers and of bombers carrying long-range cruise missiles.
- An agreement by the Soviets to reduce drastically, over a period of ten years, the number of warheads on their land-based missiles (long- and medium-range) and on their sea-launched ballistic missiles, in exchange for a reduction in the number of warheads on U.S. sea-launched ballistic missiles and the elimination of U.S. land-based missiles (the current total is around 7,000 on the American side and around 7,500—not including the 1,000 or so warheads on the SS-20—on the Soviet side).
- An agreement by both sides not to build any new land-based missile systems, fixed or mobile, nor to deploy any new medium-range ballistic missiles capable of hitting either the Soviet Union (i.e., no Pershing IIs) or Western Europe (no additional SS-20s).
- An agreement by both sides not to deploy submarines capable of destroying silos (i.e., the United States would not deploy the D-5; in

the absence of an agreement, however, should the Soviets move towards mobile ICBMs, our investment in the D-5 would be wasted in any case).

If this proposal were adopted, the Soviets would have to engage in *some* restructuring of their forces, but, in exchange, they would obtain the curtailment of U.S. ground- and sea-launched cruise missiles, the nondeployment of the D-5 (as well as of the MX), and the limitation of the U.S. bomber and air-launched cruise missile force. Their silos would remain vulnerable to U.S. bombers and air-launched cruise missiles, but they could either reduce this threat by multiplying targets (i.e., by de-MIRVing their land-based missiles) or eliminate it by "moving to sea"—a move that goes against Russian traditions but that the disappearance of U.S. missile silos (which the Soviets' submarines do not have the means to destroy) might make more attractive.

On the Western side, it is true that the Soviets could still concentrate a large number of accurate warheads on military targets in Western Europe; but the distinction between counterforce and countercity warfare in Europe makes no sense: any nuclear war against Western Europe would kill millions of people and would thus carry a strong risk of U.S. nuclear retaliation.

This initiative does not amount to ridding the world of nuclear weapons. It does not deal with the problem of other nuclear powers by whom the Soviets feel threatened. But the United States might commit itself to inviting its two nuclear European allies to join, later, in the negotiations and to accept limits or reductions if the superpowers agree on the proposal outlined here. Nor does it deal with the battlefield or tactical nuclear weapons of NATO, for which it has never been easy to find a role acceptable both to the Americans and to the West Europeans; the fate of these weapons ought to be linked to that of the conventional forces (with which they are supposedly integrated) that are the object of the MBFR talks. But it would go far toward reversing the evolution of deterrence, toward restoring the original difference between deterrence through the threat of retaliation and deterrence through war-fighting, toward making extended deterrence (which is necessarily a threat of war-fighting, insofar as it is aimed at preventing a conventional attack) less risky and ominous for the defenders without, however, removing the mantle of the United States' nuclear protection from its key allies, and toward restoring the three kinds of stability defined above. It could also be a decisive element in an effort to create, in U.S.-Soviet relations, a new détente without illusions. The agreements envisaged by the superpowers in 1986 would not reach all these goals.

On Nuclear Morality

The proposals presented in the previous pages may well be utopian; moveover, we could be faced either with no such drastic combination of unilateral and negotiated restraints, or with an agreement that merely slows down the "qualitative" race or softens its most disturbing edges (such as the deployment of space-based defenses). However, even in the traditional universe of "national security," restraints are often a major part of wisdom—both those dictated by prudence and those dictated by ethical considerations. I will not deal here with the former, which several of my Harvard colleagues have ably addressed;[2] I will make some remarks only about nuclear ethics.

Discussions about nuclear morality have been plagued by a variety of factors. One is the "dialogue of the deaf" phenomenon: philosophers and theologians seem transfixed by the horrors of total nuclear war, whereas strategists are attracted by the chances technology itself may provide of limiting nuclear war and of ending it rapidly if it breaks out; theologians and philosophers concentrate on the terrible consequences a failure of nuclear deterrence would have, whereas strategists emphasize the benefits that successful deterrence has brought in the last forty years. Another factor is the discomfort associated with both of the major ethical positions found in the literature of the past thirty years. One, nuclear pacifism, often confuses a decision to accept a risk of nuclear war in order to protect an important interest with a decision that makes nuclear war certain; it is also debatable in that it expresses the conviction that the risk of nuclear war entailed by the possession of nuclear weapons is less tolerable than the sacrifices of values and risks entailed by unilateral disarmament. In addition, it is politically most unlikely to be accepted by any government of a country that has a nuclear arsenal.

The other position is the attempt to apply the concepts and categories of traditional Christian just-war theory to nuclear realities. The problems associated with this position I have indicated elsewhere.[3] In other words, concerning the *jus ad bellum*, there are the difficulties having to do with the elasticity of the "cause" of self-defense—especially collective self-defense—and the problem of deciding whether leaders have the "right intention." Concerning the *jus in bello*, although one can try to apply the criterion of "discrimination" as a way of sorting out good from evil nuclear weapons, the concept of "proportionality" is slippery (if one deems the cause grandiose enough—for instance, in the words of one self-styled theologian from the Arms Control and Disarmament Agency, saving souls from Communism, everything becomes proportional, even, I suppose, if it means destroying the bodies in order to save the souls); and the famous "rule of double effect" (about no deliberate killing of the innocent) only engenders a formidable casuistry of double talk. Concerning nuclear deterrence, the theory is obliged to innovate: judgments vary depending either on one's assessment of the consequences of deterrence (or of its solidity) or on one's assessment of the intention. (Is it peace, or a monstrous execution of the threat? The casuistry, on that point, is even more depressing.)

A third difficulty lies in the limitations of the two usual forms of moral reasoning. The deontological approach, which relies on categorical precepts, can never be *the* ethics of politics, a domain in which consequences matter. Nuclear pacifism, as already indicated, could lead to Soviet expansion and domination, or to a proliferation of conventional wars. The "absolutist" moral advocacy of Star Wars—it would replace the ethical crime of nuclear retaliation with the clean surgery of destroying only missiles—is fraudulent insofar as it leaves out all the destabilizing effects of the program and assumes technical perfection. But the consequentialist approach is plagued by our uncertain knowledge of consequences. There are antinuclear consequentialists, whose position rests on their conviction that a failure of deterrence would bring nuclear winter. But how certain can one be about that eventual failure, and must every failure lead to Armageddon? On the other side, can those who defend the morality of nuclear deterrence because it has helped keep the peace and safeguard various nations from blackmail and subjugation (cf. the position of the French Bishops) be sure that deterrence will never fail catastrophically? Can those who defend the morality of some kinds of nuclear war-fighting be sure that preparing for those kinds will not incite statesmen to take bigger risks, and thus weaken deterrence, or that such fighting will not get out of control?

Indeed, the fourth difficulty lies in all the uncertainties about nuclear deterrence and warfare that have already been mentioned (see Chapter 9). The subject is like a labyrinth of questionable trade-offs. Is nuclear deterrence morally acceptable (as the American Bishops have said) only against a threat or risk of nuclear attack, but not in order to protect an ally from conventional aggression? It depends on whether one believes that the threat of a first use of nuclear weapons in the latter case is either an incredible bluff or a decision to commit a crime, or whether, on the contrary, one is convinced that such a threat is likely to deter war because (in Josef Joffe's words) deterrence is the mathematical product of the size of the threat (to the potential aggressor) and the probability of its execution: "a very low probability multiplied by potentially infinite damage still yields a deterrence product of potentially infinite value."[4] Is it morally right to try to enhance deterrence by adopting a "strategy of decapitation" or of launch-on-warning, even though it might make war termination impossible if deterrence fails, or to plan retaliation, even after one's centers of command and control have been destroyed, because of the "rationality or irrationality"—i.e., because of the higher deterrent effect of such a design? Is it morally proper to substitute as widely as possible conventional weapons for nuclear ones in planning counterforce attacks because the former cannot perform the countersilo missions of the latter and are therefore less destabilizing for deterrence, or would such a scheme weaken deterrence by encouraging the opponent to believe that it signals one's unwillingness ever to use nuclear weapons?[5]

One might begin to look for a way out of the maze by asking where the moral originality of nuclear deterrence lies; after all, deterrence is as old as international politics. Clearly, it lies in the possible effects of an execution of the threat: not, or not merely, in the destruction of the opponent's forces but in that of his population. Hence what might be called the quantitative temptation—trying to remove this gruesome originality by finding ways of reducing the devastation, by planning strikes against military objectives, or by using weapons that will do little "collateral damage." But there is no way out of moral ambiguity: as long as nuclear weapons exist, there is a risk of escalation, there is also the danger that counterforce planning will weaken nuclear deterrence, either by undermining its stability or by making nuclear war more acceptable.

Another, more stringent attempt at a way out was made by the American Catholic Bishops. They gave a conditional endorsement to nuclear deterrence (against nuclear threats); they showed grave concern for crisis stability if deterrence came to rest increasingly on countersilo weapons; and they expressed, with respect to the actual uses of the weapons, total opposition to countercity warfare as well as skepticism about the chances of limiting counterforce warfare. They have been attacked from two directions: on one side by those who, like Susan Okin,[6] believe that the "centimeter of ambiguity" they left about limited counterforce war was dangerous, and that the present weaponry of deterrence violates the very criteria that the just war theory and the bishops themselves set up; on the "realist" side, by those who criticize their no-first-use stand for its consequences on the United States' alliances and, like Robert W. Tucker,[7] fear that the combination of their approval of nuclear deterrence and their condemnation of most conceivable uses puts a heavy a burden on "existential deterrence"—deterrence through mere possession—and weakens the credibility of the deterrent.

My own position is close to that of Joseph Nye, Jr.[8] Insofar as deterrence is concerned, the primordial concern for crisis stability is both prudential and ethical. In other words, not every nuclear weapon can be justified by the magic word *deterrence*. The need for the credibility of deterrence to rely not on bluff or chance but on actual plans for execution if deterrence fails means that deterrence can neither consist exclusively in possession (although the mere fact of possession contributes to it) nor entail countercity targeting, which would be suicidal *and* violate all moral requirements (although the mere possibility of escalation to that level also contributes to deterrence). It ought therefore to mean what Nye calls countercombatant counterforce targeting. Since deterrence is weakened when nuclear weapons are treated as ordinary arms, war plans should avoid complete integration of nuclear weapons into military forces and, in the case of NATO, incorporate the principle of no early first use.

What if deterrence fails? In the abstract, there are two legitimate concerns: use and termination. As described above, "ethical" targeting would mean countercombatant uses. But, on the one hand, combatants often move through heavily populated areas, and targets vital for military operations are close to or even in cities: the line that separates countercity from any counterforce is thus very thin—even if one thinks of increasingly more accurate and discriminating weapons, as long as they are used on populated areas. On the other hand, can one be sure that our controlled uses will not provoke—through misinterpretation or actual intent—an indiscriminate reply? Limitation takes two, not one, and it almost assumes a tacit agreement.

Regarding hopes for termination, quite apart from the debatable or optimistic wager on sober recoil prevailing, the morning after, over the combination of murderous passion and friction that characterizes war, those who believe such termination possible skip over the contradiction between the aim of a quick and merciful ending and the escalatory nature of the very decision to use (even in limited ways) nuclear weapons—to cross the decisive threshold—in the first place.

I thus find myself boxed in by the following dilemmas. Like the Bishops, I remain skeptical about the possibilities of "moral use" in most plausible scenarios (war on sea being the main exception). Hence my conviction that we need a *jus contra* (or *ante*) *bellum*—a way of saving nuclear deterrence; for if it fails, the moral consequences are more likely to be horrendous than tolerable. On the other hand, I recognize that either the moral condemnation of most probable uses, or the planning of very limited uses only, may weaken deterrence, either by affecting its moral legitimacy, as Tucker believes,[9] or by making its failure seem less catastrophic. A moral position that supports stable deterrence yet condemns most uses is torn between two logics that point in opposite directions. If one emphasizes the benefits of deterrence, then the uncertainties that surround it, the impossibility of relying on possession alone—both because of the needs of allies and because of the importance of not leaving what happens if deterrence breaks down to improvisation and fate—can easily lead to a quest for a full panoply of weapons, for a "prudential" accumulation of arms deemed necessary to make every kind of deterrence plausible. If one emphasizes the perils of most uses, then the logic points in the direction of disarmament.

Thus, while the moral risks and dilemmas of use can be avoided only by avoiding nuclear war altogether, the moral risks and dilemmas of deterrence can be alleviated only if one steps out and goes far beyond the traditional universe of self-help and competitive definitions of security. One comes back to the same three paths to which political analysis led us earlier. First, there is the path of radical unilateral prudence—no piling up of weaponry just because the other side gives itself redundant means; the self-denying ordinance of eschewing decapitation and countersilo means or first-strike capabilities in general; the refusal either to use nuclear weapons for political "signalling" or blackmail, or to proceed with the deployment of defenses or antisatellite weapons; the strengthening of one's own system of decision and control and one's own chain of command so as not to be at the mercy of technological "imperatives" or of military pleas for delegated authority, and so on. Second, there is the path of arms control, along the lines laid out above. Third, there is the political path that points not merely toward "denuclearizing international politics"[10] but toward reducing the role of force altogether. For in a world with nuclear weapons, which "present us with a danger from which there is at present no apparently feasible way out,"[11] a focus on denuclearization alone could make the scene riper for conventional violence, and if it breaks out between the superpowers, the risk of escalation to the nuclear level would still be there. Thus, one needs altogether the limitations on nuclear deployments that would make any major gains from nuclear war-fighting unlikely and the replacements of nuclear with conventional means that would make a resort to nuclear weapons appear less necessary. But one also needs a political context in which both conventional confrontations (which can turn nuclear) and "controlled" nuclear war-fighting appear untempting. How to make nuclear deterrence (existential and planned) continue to humble the ends and constrain the means of states, without either undermining deterrence through technological "progress" or, on the contrary, being so successful at pushing the nuclear nightmare out of the daily lives of statesmen that they might be tempted to take excessive risks again? It is a delicate balancing act, requiring rare political and moral acrobatic skills. But only if it is well conceived and performed will we be able to give substance to "common security" for the superpowers.

Notes

1. See the Commission's report entitled *Common Security* (New York: Simon & Schuster, 1982).
2. Graham Allison, Albert Carnesale, and Joseph Nye, *Hawks, Doves and Owls* (New York: Norton, 1985).
3. Stanley Hoffmann, *Duties Beyond Borders* (New York: Syracuse University Press, 1982), Ch. 2.
4. Josef Joffe, "Nuclear Weapons, No First Use and European Order," *Ethics* 95 no. 3 (April 1985), p. 613.
5. Cf. George Quester, "Substituting Conventional for Nuclear Weapons," *Ethics* 95, no. 3 (April 1985), pp. 610–640.
6. Susan Okin, "Taking the Bishops Seriously," *World Politics* 36, no. 4 (July 1984), pp. 527–554.
7. Robert W. Tucker, "Morality and Deterrence," *Ethics* 95, no. 3 (April 1985), pp. 461–478.
8. Joseph Nye, *Nuclear Ethics* (New York: Free Press, 1986).
9. Cf. Robert W. Tucker, "The Nuclear Debate," *Foreign Affairs* (Fall 1984), pp. 1–32.
10. See the article with this title by Richard Ullmann, *Ethics* 95, no. 3 (April 1985), pp. 567–588.
11. Tucker, "Morality and Deterrence," p. 468.

17
Reaching for the Most Difficult: Human Rights as a Foreign Policy Goal

As a problem of policy, the promotion of human rights can be envisaged at two different levels. One is that of the domestic political system. The defense of these rights remains above all a matter of internal arrangements. It was through domestic battles between, on one side, individuals and groups determined to obtain legal recognition and effective protection of their claims, and, on the other, a hostile state and other groups resisting such demands, that progress was achieved in Western democracies. This was the case of the civil and political rights that have their roots in eighteenth-century liberalism, and of the economic and social rights defined in the nineteenth and twentieth centuries by a variety of intellectual currents, socialist and Christian in particular. But the protection of human rights also became a matter of international relations after the Second World War, when various codes were drafted and the components of an international regime, and of various regional regimes as well, for safeguarding these rights were set up.

In an essay, John Ruggie asks whether the acceptance by most states of the principle that human rights are a legitimate international issue has amounted to a shift in the principles of legitimacy, mechanisms of governance, and social framework of the international community or society.[1] His answer is negative, and I agree with his analysis. My concern here differs from his in three ways. His approach is essentially empirical; mine is primarily normative. He tells us how things are (or what they are not); I present a plea for change toward the goals we have not reached, and I make a case for trying to reach them against enormous odds. He focuses on the international milieu; I look at the actors in this milieu and at human rights as a morally and politically necessary subject for the foreign policy of states. He shows the elements of continuity in world affairs—before and after the "reemergence of the individual in international relations"; I try to argue that there is a great deal of discontinuity—not between a world of competing sovereign states and a (still distant) world in which the rights of individuals are recognized by, and protected from, their states, but between the international systems of the past, in which those rights did not enjoy international recognition, and the current international system, in which their official "legitimacy" coexists and conflicts with colossal violations.

The Predicament

The distinction between the traditional Machiavellian ethics of statecraft and a more cosmopolitan ethic is an important one for our discussion.[2] The former is a codification of sacred egoism: the statesman should concern himself only with the common good of his community. The latter asserts that his moral duties do not stop at the borders of his polity. The former, insofar as it sees the wisdom of introducing some order into the jungle of states, nevertheless recognizes only the mutual rights of states: it is an ethics of reciprocity among sovereign entities. The latter includes obligations toward individuals in foreign countries; humanity, not the (partial) society of states, is its constituency.

The promotion of human rights to the agenda of international politics is part of an effort at moving beyond Machiavellian statecraft. The United Nations Declaration on Human Rights, the two UN Covenants, and the various regional instruments reflect a sense of moral obligation after the crimes and horrors of the Second World War. In this area, the creation of a legal network was particularly important. The relations between moral and legal rights and duties are complex. In international affairs, there can be moral obligations despite the silence of the law. The various imperatives recently proclaimed by the American Bishops' pastoral letter[3] concerning the use of nuclear weapons go far beyond the prescriptions and proscriptions of either the UN Charter or the conventions that regulate the *jus in bello*. The latter do not deal explicitly with nuclear weapons; the former certainly does not rule out a resort to these weapons in retaliation against nuclear or conventional aggression. It often happens that the human conscience, including that of statesmen, is ahead of laws or treaties and customs, and expresses itself, not through legislation, but through unilateral policy decisions or diplomatic understandings.

In the field of human rights, however, legalization is indispensable. It is the prerequisite to the empirical efficacy of moral obligations; it makes it possible for this sense of moral duty to have political effects. If I, as a statesman, sign a treaty in which I accept the legal obligation to respect certain human rights, it means that I acknowledge not only a domestic responsibility, but a "cosmopolitan" one as well: I recognize that you, too, have a right to see to it that I respect these rights. This is a major breakthrough in a world in which previously you were entitled only to ensure that I treated fairly your nationals settled in or visiting my country. If *you* sign such a treaty and don't carry out your legal obligations to your people, I can, as a cosignatory, raise the issue of your neglect or violation. Thus the significance of a legal code here is double. First, the treatment of individuals (including nationals) is now a legitimate concern of the members of the international society; the notion of sovereignty, the very cornerstone of the "Westphalian order"—which essentially reduced international affairs to arrangements and conflicts about and among states, and left almost everything happening *within* a sovereign state to its jurisdiction—has been breached. Second, international law now grants not merely states, but individuals as well, a set of rights: they are recognized as being both the citizens of their states and entitled to certain rights, whatever their states' practices.

Without such a legal code, the so-called conscience of mankind, often aroused in the past by mass atrocities in distant lands, would lack a handle. This does not mean that there is necessarily perfect correspondence between moral and legal obligations. A statesman, or indeed a citizen, of a country that has signed any of the legal codes may well believe that the legal provisions exceed what can be morally required of his state (a fortiori, of a foreign state). For instance, can one morally require the government of a poor country to provide for the "periodic holidays with pay, as well as remuneration for public holidays" prescribed by Article 7d of the Covenant on Economic, Social and Cultural Rights? Conversely, one may believe that one's moral duty exceeds the limits of a somewhat niggardly code. Tom Farer points out that the American Convention on Human Rights has only one, very broad and vague, article on "progressive development" of economic, social, and cultural rights.[4] But whereas, in the realm of distributive justice, a rich state can carry out a moral duty to the poor abroad by embarking on a policy of economic assistance, or by opening its borders to the products of poor nations, and can even try to see to it, by various strictures, that the aid it grants does indeed reach the destitute in that country, in the realm of human rights, the barrier can only be crossed if the state that wants to help foreign victims of violations can use an international legal document as a crutch or a club or a ladder.

Nevertheless, the revolutionary significance of the international legal network has failed to transform either the basic realities of international politics or the conditions in most countries. This is so because of a triple predicament: the legal framework is shaky; the distance between the normative order and the political one is huge; and the opportunities for internal improvement of the latter are limited.

The network *is* a very weak one, and it suffers from many characteristic flaws of contemporary international law. Several of the rights that are to be protected are defined so vaguely as to make violations easy. We are all familiar with the difficulties of self-determination: *What* is the "self" that is entitled to it? *Who* determines either what it is or under what conditions self-determination will occur? Does it necessarily mean statehood?—and so on. And yet, both UN Covenants merely recognize a "people's right to self-determination." Similarly, the Covenant on Civil and Political Rights guarantees "equal protection of the law" and outlaws discrimination: these are anything but self-evident notions.

Also, and more important, many of the rights are granted in a way that makes excessive restriction or even elimination legally possible. Some rights are only provided within the limits set by national legislation; others are saddled with exceptions through which whole police forces may pass (there is a right to freedom of expression, but propaganda for war, or advocacy of national, racial, or religious hatred that "constitutes incitement to discrimination, hostility or war" shall be prohibited by law). Various rights can be restricted for reasons of national security, public safety, or public order. The Helsinki agreements acknowledge the principle of noninterference in internal or external affairs of the signatories.

Above all, there are all the weaknesses of the mechanisms of enforcement that John Ruggie reviews: the economic and social Covenant, given the nature of the rights it recognizes, is largely left to the signatories for implementation; the procedure of complaints remains predominantly in the hands of states, not individuals; the various international bodies lack powers of enforcement, and so on.

The fact that only fourteen states have adhered to the interstate complaints procedure set up by Article 41 of the Covenant on Civil and Political Rights points to a second predicament: the abyss between the legal network and the states' political practices. "At least there is now an international law to be violated."[5] But the scope of the violations tells us much more than the obvious fact that we still live—in terms of power—in a world of states that defend their sovereignty, use human rights primarily as a tool of warfare against each other, and severely restrict the capacity of individuals to escape from their national cage or to call in relief from outside.

Tension between the international normative and political orders is neither surprising nor new. There is always tension between the legal codes and the moral rules that prescribe how people *ought* to behave and the way they *actually* do. This gap usually reflects the subjects' fallibility. Sometimes it results from their desire to change the norms if these have become obsolete or harmful, or if they no longer correspond to the prevailing new sense of what is right. The tension also serves as a goad to orderly progress, when the rules embody new ways of arranging social affairs or recognize new claims and responsibilities that meet the resistance of entrenched interests. But when the gap between moral and legal norms and practice is so great that it can be described as an abyss, it has then become pathological. It happens in two typical cases: when power is lawless, and when there is anomie. In the first instance, state power recognizes no limits; it installs the rule of arbitrariness, either in disregard of existing law or behind the cloak of a pseudo-law that provides it with all the authorizations it needs, and removes from its victims all the protections they need—something like the famous, interminable Article 58 of the Soviet criminal code under Stalin. It can also be the case of a hegemonial power mighty enough to disregard moral and legal restraints in its conduct of foreign affairs, and to deal with weaker states the way Athens treated Mytilene and Melos during the Peloponnesian War. The second instance—anomie—

is that of a civil war in which, as Thucydides remarked, "words change their ordinary meaning," and moderation becomes "the cloak of unmanliness . . . [and] frantic violence the attribute of manliness."[6] It is also that of the present international system.

How, the reader might ask, does it differ from systems of the past? After all, we have had no general war for almost forty years; the actors—five of whom have nuclear weapons, many of whom are new, poor, inexperienced, and unsteady—have managed, on the whole, to keep their conflicts limited, and to find in the fear of physical destruction and the intimacies of economic interdependence both a basis of cooperation (however grudging or competitive) and a reason for developing various kinds of international law. Is the gap between the latter and the behavior of states any wider today? My answer is "yes," partly because international law itself, in reaction to the excesses of their behavior—as a magical reassurance against the evils of practice (or the practice of evil)—has become so much more demanding and so much less accommodating of national sovereignty than it had been in the nineteenth century. This is particularly true in the two areas that are at the core of sovereignty. One is the right to wage war, intact in nineteenth century law, restricted after the bloodbath of the First World War, and severely curbed in the UN Charter, which recognizes its legitimacy only in self-defense or in collective resistance to aggression. The other is the state's right to treat its subjects as it sees fit.

In both these domains, the gap between the new international law and the practice of states is enormous. In the realm of force, at least, the abusive resort to the excuse of self-defense, the imaginative ways of disguising or diluting outright aggression, or of using the ambiguities that surround such concepts as "territorial integrity" and "political independence" when applied to states with unsettled borders and with shaky or puppet regimes—in other words, all the attempts to get around the ban on the use or threat of force—have not yet led to a global war or even to an unlimited war in the Middle East. The leaky dam of the Charter is buttressed by the fear of a nuclear holocaust. But in the realm of human rights, there is no comparable, if bitter, consolation. Here, the differences with the past certainly do not lie in the novelty of human rights violations. In the nineteenth century, the massacres of Armenians in the Ottoman Empire may have provoked high emotions, but the behavior of colonial powers (or colonial sovereigns like Belgium's King Leopold) in Africa or Asia was often brutal and racist (indeed, the protection of the Indians of America colonized by the Spaniards had already been Vitoria's concern in the sixteenth century). Many of the "civilized" countries of the nineteenth century had repressive governments. The differences lie elsewhere, not merely in the absence of an international network of recognized human rights before 1945, but also in the end of the colonial era (which means that standards of humanity— i.e., of public morality—that even Liberals often tended to reserve to the governments of "civilized" peoples are now assumed to be valid for the regimes of all mankind); and in the sad fact that, unlike the trend of *aspirations*, which went up, the trend of *expectations* is going down. In the nineteenth century, the way in which the Turkish sovereign treated his subjects and the pogroms that occurred in Tsarist Russia were seen not only as deplorable, but as a mark of decadence as well. In the present international system, comparable behavior is often considered morally and legally reprehensible, but empirically normal (we all know the phrase: moderately repressive). In the nineteenth century, slavery was being abolished, and revolutionary movements demanding national self-determination and the rights associated with self-government were strong, won many victories, and expected to prevail over the forces of prejudice, absolutism, and authoritarianism. Today, it has become clear that self-determination does not necessarily breed either satisfaction or self-government; and the number of countries that can be called democratic, even if one adopts a rather modest or Schumpeterian definition of democracy (one that focuses on the free competition of political candidates for election), is extremely small. The number of countries that respect all the rights defined in the UN Covenants is smaller still, and the prospects for improvements are dim. We may now aspire to a kind of legal and moral perfectionism; but the expectation of progress is gone.

Thus the incorporation of human rights into the international moral and legal order coincides with the dismal reality of human rights violations, just as, after 1918, the fall of the legitimacy of war from the international normative order, and the advent of collective security principles in it, coincided with the age of aggression and appeasement. When the tension becomes an abyss, what disappears is the pressure that the normative order usually puts on the behavior that this order excommunicates, behavior that may previously have been either not recognized as bad by that order or deemed perfectible only by a different normative order altogether. (In the case of human rights, insofar as they were acknowledged at all, it used to be only in liberal domestic systems.) And the normative order itself, when practice contradicts it blatantly and repeatedly, usually ends up collapsing—which means that the law ceases to be taken seriously. A violation is no longer perceived as such, nor are the provisions of the law any longer seen as conferring genuine rights and duties: we are merely in the realm of rhetoric, not of norms. The commands that the law expresses are recognized no longer as moral imperatives, but as hypocritical disguises or superstitious incantations aimed at keeping the evil eye away. For any normative order to deserve being called by that name, it must partake both of the realm of "oughts" and of the empirical one: it must be *at least in part* a set of rules *of* actual behavior; it must not only ask for, but actually inspire, some practice. Otherwise, it withers away.

To be sure, as evidence of that "germ of universal consciousness" mentioned some time ago by Raymond Aron, there is a new official sensitivity to the charge of violating human rights. As Patricia Derian, President Carter's Assistant Secretary of State for Human Rights, put it, "All countries say that they are great defenders of and believers in human rights. . . . No country really admits it is a human rights violator."[7] This is the usual tribute of vice to virtue, of immoral or amoral practice to moral obligation. On the other hand, there are structural elements in the present society of states that make massive violations inevitable. Once more—as in the realm of force after 1918—the legalization of concern reflects both a moral revulsion against reality and the desire to exorcise it *faute de mieux*, that is, in the absence of any political possibility of removing the fundamental causes of evil (the "international regime" of collective security put in place by the League, and later by the UN, turned out to be no stronger than the human rights regimes discussed by John Ruggie).

These structural elements are of two kinds. One could be called the exacerbation of traditional violations. Three categories stand out. First, tribal or ethnic conflicts within countries have multiplied, in a world in which the quite exceptional legitimacy granted by all states, whatever their ideology, to the principle of self-determination only emboldens groups that feel oppressed by their current masters to seek autonomy, and encourages those masters to get rid of irredentist or unassimilable minorities. Thus we have witnessed, recently, massacres of Tamils by Sinhalese in Sri Lanka, Moslems by Hindus in Assam, Hutus by Tutsis in Burundi, a political conflict with tribal overtones between Mugabe and Nkomo in Zimbabwe, the expulsion of ethnic Chinese from Vietnam, the murderous fragmentation of Lebanon. Such violations are always worse when the ethnic tensions are stirred up by psychopathic rulers such as a Bokassa and an Idi Amin.

A second traditional category consists of the traumas of self-determination itself—of the massive violations that accompany the struggle of nations to achieve or preserve independence, or the clash of intensely nationalist groups that claim the same territory. The litany is familiar: the civil war in Biafra, the massacres leading to the independence of Bangladesh, the bloody, interminable contest between Indonesian militant (and military) nationalism and the independence movement in East Timor, the South African raids into neighboring countries in the battle against Namibian nationalism, the fight of the Eritreans against the Ethiopians and of the Afghans against the Soviet Union, above all, the Palestinian issue and its human rights ramifications—terrorism on one side; on the other, the denial of various human rights in the occupied territories; and on both the Israeli and Arab sides, the massacres in Palestinian camps.

A third traditional category comprises the dismal effects of revolutions (or failed revolutions): the massacres of Communists and alleged Communists in Indonesia in 1965 (a mix of ideological and ethnic barbarism, since many of the victims were Chinese), the violations of human rights that accompanied and followed the fall of the Shah of Iran and those that accompanied the fall of Somoza. Ethnic conflicts, wars of national independence, and revolutionary brutalities are not new; but the global extension of the principle of self-determination and of ideological conflicts—the diffusion of Western ideas (such as Marxism-Leninism) and the reaction of anti-Western movements (such as Islamic fundamentalism) to the diffusion of Western culture and practices—has widened the battlefield.

The second structural element is more original; it is the institutionalization of cruelty. World moral anomie, which undermines the new international normative order, results not only from the chaos bred by the traditional conflicts I have just described, but also from the existence of regimes that have turned the domestic legal order into tools of power at the expense of human rights. This is the more serious and intractable source of violations and of the ineffectiveness of the various international and regional regimes. One can imagine that many of the battles of tribes and ethnic groups, that most of the conflicts over self-determination, will be resolved, and even that—as has usually happened in history—ideological hatreds will lead to cynicism and the armistice of exhaustion. It is more difficult to imagine the destruction of the domestic fortresses of inequity—or to believe that it will be achievable without further colossal violence.

Three kinds of regimes constitute such fortresses. One can be called institutionalized inequality; it is the apartheid system of South Africa. Not only are more than four fifths of the land reserved for the whites, not only are the resources available for health and education of the black majority pitiful, but the blacks are deprived of both the economic and social and the civil and political rights defined in the UN Covenants. They have no political possibilities of self-expression and participation, no free trade unions, no right to racially mixed marriages; above all, they are submitted to the demeaning system of passes described so well by Athol Fugard in his play *Sizwe Bansi is Dead*. The government can detain indefinitely anyone suspected of terrorism, and impose restrictions on the freedom of expression and movement of political suspects; acts against apartheid are criminal offenses. The number of deaths occurring in prison has been considerable. Here, clearly, the law has no higher function than preserving the separation of the races, reducing the blacks to their manpower role, and covering violations of human rights with the mantle of apartheid "legality."

The second case is one of institutionalized political oppression. I am referring to regimes based on the Leninist-Stalinist model. This model has been enforced ununiformly; even in the Soviet Union, where the apparatus of terror has been partly dismantled, it is no longer applied fully. But this model entails depriving the people of their civil and political rights in exchange for some economic and social achievements. In particular, there are no rights of political expression and free association; sharp restrictions are imposed on the independence of the judiciary, on the fairness of criminal procedures (cf. the use of psychiatric hospitals against some dissidents in the Soviet Union and the harsh penalties inflicted on others), as well as on freedom of movement. While lip service is sometimes paid to the concept of human rights, the system is usually rationalized as one that puts an end to the "bourgeois" conflict between the individual and the state. (Hence, Soviet abstention on the vote of the UN General Assembly adopting the Universal Declaration of Human Rights in December 1948. The Russian delegate argued that "in a society where there are no rival classes, there cannot be any contradiction between the government and the individual since the government is in fact the collective individual."[8] In such a conception, it is clear that a dissident or deviant can only be seen as either an enemy of society or insane.) Civil and political rights are treated as purely formalistic—empty, unless a material base of economic and social services is provided. But these are indeed only *services*: they are granted and organized by the state and can therefore be taken away by it. They are not rights that individuals or groups can claim. Those who—correctly—point to the achievements of communist regimes in matters of health, social security, education, or housing sometimes fail to note the difference between a right that can thus be fought for (even if it is a right to a service that only the state can provide) and a mere grant of benefits by an all-powerful state. The two categories of rights recognized by the UN are interdependent: civil and political rights are often meaningless to people living below the subsistence level or in traditional structures of dependence and social oppression, but economic and social rights cannot be made effective unless individuals and groups can express themselves, mobilize and agitate for their realization, act in courts, and seek redress.

The Leninist-Stalinist model has led to the most extensive violations of human rights whenever the national circumstances approximated those of a civil war. In China and in Vietnam, when the communist regimes came to power after a protracted struggle, whole classes of people were submitted to "reeducation," forced labor, and humiliation; the horrors of the Pol Pot regime in Kampuchea are well documented. Indeed, such regimes sometimes create a kind of deliberate civil war to carry out their ideological program or to preserve their ideological vigor. This is what Stalin did in the 1930s when he destroyed the Kulaks through repression and famines, and purged the party and army; this is what the Chinese Cultural Revolution of the mid-1960s amounted to.

The third type is institutionalized state terrorism. As in the previous one, ideology is at the root of the disease, but in a different way: here, the militant ideologues are in the opposition (often in clandestine opposition). It is the threat created by insurgents or by (usually) leftist movements that serves as the pretext for a state response which, under the cloak of national security, entails brutal repression, extensive control of social organizations, and the suspension of many civil and political rights. The plea of necessity or supreme emergency is thus moved from its usual domain—foreign affairs—to the domestic scene. In Brazil after the 1964 coup, in Chile after the fall and murder of Allende, in Argentina after 1976, in the Philippines under Marcos's rule, in Turkey during the years of military government, in the Shah's Iran, one witnessed neither *exceptional* measures nor *limited* restrictions to rights, but a pattern: arbitrary arrests, disappearances, the widespread resort to torture (admirably described by Jacobo Timerman), the taming of institutions that could have harbored or fostered opposition. In many of these cases, the violations of human rights have been accompanied by an often savage economic policy of laissez faire, perpetrated under military rule, with the officers wrapping themselves in the mantle of nationalism and quite naturally practicing their expertise against their enemies.

As in the case of the Leninist-Stalinist regimes, these violations are most brutal when the opposition has been able to organize an insurgency and conditions of quasi-civil war exist, as, for instance, despite a facade of elections, in El Salvador, and also in Guatemala. There, according to Amnesty International, twelve thousand unarmed civilians have been massacred since 1978; under the previous military ruler, whole villages have been destroyed by ground and air raids, and large numbers of people have been removed from their homes.

These political realities point to the third predicament. Not only are the legal nets full of holes and the gap between law and practice enormous, but the possibility of narrowing it through political action at the international level is extremely small. This is so for two sets of reasons: the nature of the international system and the moral-ideological significance of human rights.

We find a good way of measuring the obstacle constituted by the international system in Kant. In both his *Idea for a Universal History* and the essay *Eternal Peace*, we find that he believed there could be no peace without a league of republican, that is, constitutional, states—states that provide their citizens precisely with the kind of autonomy and chances for self-fulfillment that the legal provisions on human rights in national constitutions and international documents try to promote. He considered the creation of such regimes to be "the most difficult problem and at the same time the one which mankind solves last." But their establishment "depends upon the problem of a lawful external relationship of the states and cannot be solved without the latter." In other words, there can be no peace without constitutional regimes, but no such regimes without peace. In a world of intense interstate conflicts, the fate of regimes respecting human rights cannot be good: the "state of war," which inflicts on the polity "the very same evils which oppress individual human beings and which compelled them to enter into a lawful civic state," would soon disturb or destroy the harmonious polity. On the other hand, a league of states for the abolition of war requires a "republican" civil constitution in these states: "Under a constitution where the subject is not a citizen and which is therefore not republican, it is the easiest thing in the world to start a war. The head of state is not a fellow citizen but owner of the state."[9]

Thus the domestic and the external problems—let us call them a political regime of human rights and peace—must be solved simultaneously. Kant's intriguing philosophy of history tells us that "the excessive and never-ending preparation for wars, and the want which every state even in the midst of peace must feel," will force governments to do what reason suggests: enter into a union of states for peace. But he also told us that such a union will last only if the states have the right constitution. We are therefore left in a very uncomfortable position. This (necessary) union will make it *possible* for states to become enlightened (since their resources will no longer be wasted on expansion and defense): what Kant also calls "a pathologically enforced coordination of society" will thus finally *be able* to "transform it into a moral whole." Both the union and the enlightened commonwealth appear as moral duties *as well as* objectives of "a hidden plan of nature" to produce concord through conflict. But this union will remain fragile *unless* its members have the right regimes, and those regimes can't get rooted, or survive, unless there is peace. A first reading of Kant suggests that (thanks to nature's plan) a perfect constitution ("the only state in which nature can develop all faculties of mankind") and "a perfect civic association of mankind" will both be achieved: all good things coming together. A second reading, alas, suggests a vicious circle.[10]

Let us transpose this conundrum into the present world scene. The absence of peace serves to justify, and in some cases engenders, regimes that violate human rights; they can blame the troubles that "require" repression on external agitators or explain that the conditions of "encirclement" in which they operate allow no relaxation of state power and control. Interstate tensions require soldiers, and soldiers often take over their own countries. The very strength and spread of such regimes, many of which feel profoundly insecure and act accordingly on a world stage marked by a profusion of interventions, make a peaceful international order difficult to establish, and a successful international regime of human rights hard to conceive, as well. As Michael Doyle has pointed out, only liberal states have succeeded in creating a zone of peace: they have not been at war with one another, and have achieved both of Kant's (and nature's) goals.[11] Kant was right in this respect; but while he stressed the interdependence of the solutions to the two problems of human rights and peace, he was also right in stressing the decisive character of the *domestic* system. Whether a country observes human rights or not depends, ultimately, not only on whether external peace allows for domestic civility or on favorable internal circumstances, on the whims of passing rulers, but also on the nature of the economic system, of the social structure and values, and of the political regime: the state of human rights is the mirror of the polity. Enforcement of the international normative order requires certain internal changes. Can we really expect these changes to come through the processes and mechanisms of international politics? Indeed, would even a world at peace (either because of the fear of nuclear war—the hidden plan of nature—and/or because of respect for the normative order curtailing the use of force) be capable of transforming its members? The dilemma is obvious: the effectiveness of the international normative order of human rights requires both a genuine (not just a rhetorical) consensus on the values that inspire this order and a world enforcement system—in other words, an end of international relations as we know them. The transformation of international relations and of domestic regimes that the world recognition of human rights should logically engender presupposes a revolution in the structure of the international milieu. Not even the kind of halfway house between a system of sovereign states and a world federation, suggested by Kant, would suffice (his League had no powers of execution, and its "cosmopolitan law" was reduced to hospitality).

Not only would an effective international order of human rights require, as a precondition, a decline in the role of states and the emergence of powerful collective mechanisms or regimes, but it would also, in the long run, amount to a revolution in the nature of most political regimes. The idea of human rights is dangerously subversive of many existing polities, for two reasons. The first is that it pretends, and appears at first sight, *not* to be so revolutionary. Political regimes are not being asked, by international law, to cease being communist, or socialist, or single party, or economically laissez faire; they are "merely" being asked to observe or to set up rights to which they have themselves, in various treaties or even in their constitutions, subscribed. What could be more reasonable? But the fact is that if these rights were effectively granted, the nature of the regime would be drastically transformed. It is a mistake to look at them as a mere set of guarantees given to individuals and groups, which they should and could enjoy in *any* state. Even when they aim at creating a sphere in which no state can intrude, *they are all political rights*, they concern individuals as citizens, and groups as actors, in the polity. As Claude Lefort has suggested,[12] if they were only "private" rights, a state could always justify a transgression by arguing that the necessities of power or revolution (or, I would add, those of the "state of war") require a temporary displacement of the private by public needs. But if they are seen as political rights, then they become the basis for a polity that has very little in common with many of the political regimes of today. The notion of the sacred sphere of civil rights, like that of a state which fulfills economic and social needs by erecting them into rights, is a political notion that defines a certain kind of polity and excludes others.

Indeed, human rights are subversive, in the second place, because, under the cloak of a demand for basic guarantees, they constitute a program for a politically liberal, economically social-democratic (or welfare-liberal) commonwealth. This, of course, explains the hostility of all kinds of tyrannies, and the reticence, in the United States, of the more conservative, antiwelfare-state liberals. It is true, as Ruggie indicates, that the international documents are a compromise, not the expression of any one "hegemon's" values, and also, as he puts it, that "different clusters of rights enjoy differential normative status in the international community." Nevertheless, as a whole, these documents are a kind of war machine for a slightly left-of-center liberalism. And this brings us back to our predicament: In a decentralized and cacophonic world society, how can one expect antiliberal regimes to yield to such a vision and to allow the entry of Trojan horses?—for the history of human rights shows that granting some of these rights always leads to demands for more, to that very questioning of existing laws and practices, to that very search for new forms and meanings of self-mastery and self-fulfillment, that is both the glory and occasionally the doom of liberal polities.

There is a fundamental ambiguity about the international normative order of human rights. On the one hand, it pretends to represent a consensus, to offer a kind of common floor on which very different regimes can stand—

both because conceptual trade-offs and verbal agreements made these documents possible, and because the only chance this order has of becoming more than a display of collective hypocrisy is the establishment of some kind of common denominator, some form of "peaceful coexistence" and minimal convergence of all the ideologies in competition. On the other hand, it is also, however much concealed, the ram of one particular ideological faction against all others. Being both an offer of an armistice and a tool of warfare—the continuation of ideological competition by other, potentially more dangerous means (action at the international level)—the politics of human rights ends up suffering from both the clash of *arrière-pensées* behind the (verbal) armistice, and from the heightened resistance this new form of warfare cannot help but provoke.

The Imperatives

Despite all these obstacles, I consider it imperative for the United States and other democracies to take the international dimension of human rights seriously and to make the promotion of these rights a major goal of their foreign policies. This is so for two sets of reasons—the very same kinds of reasons that made up the political predicament.

In the first place, it is a moral imperative. To be sure, this argument will not convince those who believe that the only command a state must heed is its national interest, or that its lodestar should be prudence and expediency. But, as has often been argued, there are different ways of conceiving the national interest, and it is only when international relations are a hell of inexpiable hatreds and life-and-death situations, when physical survival is immediately at stake, that a case can be made for eliminating moral consideration *extra muros*. When the system is less like a jungle, and indeed when there are different ways of ensuring survival, chances for a not purely Machiavellian ethics exist. What is prudent or expedient is itself partly determined by what the statesman considers right.

Why is it right to act for the promotion of human rights abroad? It is not only, or primarily, because the American public requires idealism. The publics of many democracies do not expect their governments to fight for causes other than the purely national ones—that is, they seem to accept the distinction between (to use Kantian terms) moral politics at home and amoral politics abroad. As for American idealism, it has often found itself satisfied with what Kant would have called political moralism, concealing purely selfish objectives behind moral rationalizations. It is because the values of the international normative order of human rights—the moral and political ideology of human rights, if you prefer—are the values and ideology of liberal democracies and have an inherently universal thrust, whatever the philosophical basis for endorsing these values (a philosophy of rights or "rule utilitarianism") may be. If statesmen believe in these values, and even if they also believe that the diversity of situations, dogmas, and cultural traditions does not allow for their successful promotion everywhere at once, they would be both timid and inconsistent if they did not try to promote this ideal (unless they accept the counterarguments that I shall try to refute later). Deciding to promote it does not tell us what the best tools are, how far it is wise to prod other regimes into reform, whether discretion or publicity are the best approaches, and so on. Here, we are in the domain of practice and skill, of balancing and trade-offs. But such a decision means rejecting relativism and neutrality; relativism, because if one believes that—to quote from Tom Farer—"the value of liberty defined as control over one's life" is a value worth living and dying for, one should not hesitate to try to make it prevail—peacefully—over inferior values; neutrality, because other moral-ideological codes are most unlikely to show comparable restraint, and also because the form that the international rhetorical consensus of clashing value systems has happened to take is that of the liberal credo. This is an invitation to press those who have chosen to salute it, for whatever reason, to adjust their conduct to their words.

For reasons of necessity, of prudence, and of philosophy, a Liberal (or a liberal polity) must take as a starting point the coexistence and free contest of different value systems; tolerance, respect for diversity, and resignation to dissent are basic liberal values. But the version of liberalism that reduces it to an open flea market, where all merchants come and peddle wares of equivalent worth, is unacceptable. The values I have just described define the nature of the contest; they do not rule out an attempt at propagating one's faith and at consolidating the rights that embody the liberal creed. My plea is against the brand of liberalism (so powerful in the nineteenth century) that was unreservedly anti-interventionist abroad—for instance, for the antipaternalistic reasons given by John Stuart Mill. Wholesale noninterventionism abandons the victims of illiberal regimes to their masters. Is this, then, a plea for intervention? Yes, within very strict limits: the purpose and effects must be to increase the autonomy of such victims (many American interventions abroad, despite fine intentions, have actually deprived those whom we wanted to help of responsibility for their fate), with the means carefully tailored to these ends. Existing legal mechanisms must therefore be used as fully as possible, and in order to guard against the temptation of self-serving action or selfish benevolence, the policy should be carried out by a "front," of several countries.

One powerful moral reason for such a policy is that it would aim not only at spreading the benefits of liberal democracies, but also at overcoming the antinomy between what has been called "the morality of states" (based on the principle of state autonomy[13] and on the mutual recognition of a range of states' rights) and a cosmopolitan morality that subordinates these rights to the human rights of individuals and groups. Staying strictly within the former means either denying the primacy of human rights or subordinating their protection to the consent of states, even when those states are repressive shells within which there is no "fit" between the government and the people, no recognition either of the principle of self-determination or of the ideal of self-government. The present international order has actually gone beyond this morality, insofar as it grants legitimacy only to states that respect the principle of *self-determination*. But despite the legal network of human rights treaties and declarations, states behave as if the disregard of the ideal of *self-government* were no bar to the legitimacy of regimes, no ground for external action on its behalf. A consistent liberal world order would erect both values as criteria of governmental legitimacy; in this way, the conflict between states' rights and human rights would be resolved, and states (or rather their agents, the governments) would be recognized as entitled to a full panoply of rights only if they were at the service of their citizens' human rights.

The second imperative for such a policy lies in the realm not of ethics, but of politics. It is in the long-run interest of liberal democracies to transform the nature of the "game" of international politics. In a world armed with nuclear weapons and marked by "complex interdependence," politics-as-usual, the clash of security calculations, and the manipulation of all by everyone guarantee physical destruction and economic chaos. Development, social progress, a modicum of psychological, economic, and physical security, and a reduction of violence all require, not a "reinvention of politics" or the abolition of the sovereign state (for if this were the prerequisite, we might as well resign ourselves to our doom), but a reorientation of politics and a redefinition of the national interest—so that it incorporates more of the international interest as well—a pooling of sovereignties, and the spread and strengthening of international regimes. These provide the member states with benefits unilateral action cannot obtain; they give states a stake in preserving such procedures and institutions even if the momentary balance of gains and losses for a given member shows a deficit; they enforce mutual restraints. Such a transformist, or reformist, strategy clearly aims at narrowing the gap between the international normative order and the practice of world politics.

The promotion of an international human rights policy is an important part of such a strategy of change. On the one hand, at the global level, strengthening the machinery set up for the protection of these rights, while certainly not ensuring individual happiness and stability among states (promoting rights is inherently contentious), would at least help remove some of the most basic causes of violence in world society; it would enlarge the sphere of transparency and increase chances for redress. On the other hand, going back once more to Kantian wisdom, we have good reasons to believe that the global preconditions for individual self-fulfillment—peace and an effective international system of distributive justice—are most likely to exist when the main actors are states that respect human rights; such a strategy would tend precisely to protect the states that already do and to nudge the others in a similar direction. The political objective, distant as it may appear, would be the same as the moral one: a world in which the conditions of legitimacy of regimes would be both self-determination and the observance of the other human rights recognized by the international normative order. It would be a world in which what Ruggie finds still missing badly, a more integrated global society (more consensus) with a collective machinery of enforcement (more centralization), would emerge gradually.

The case that has often been made for international regimes in such realms as the oceans, trade, world finance, communications, nuclear proliferation, and so on, can be argued just as powerfully with respect to human rights, even though most of the former concern transnational flows that no single government can control (or where attempts at national control boomerang), whereas the field of human rights seems to consist mainly of national struggles between individuals or groups and their governments. But the massive violations that occur today are likely to provoke flows, or floods, of refugees seeking asylum abroad; the alternative to collective regulation is generalized misery or the backlash that inevitably results when certain countries, having opened their borders more than others, come to resent the selfishness of the latter and to experience domestic friction. Conversely, national attempts to regulate the flow of migrant workers are likely to result in violations of human rights, and if these rules are too restrictive, in violent explosions in countries whose surplus active population could no longer use "exit" instead of "voice." Without international norms and regimes, the conflict between "cosmopolitan" moral duties and a national government's primary responsibility for the welfare of its own citizens would become unmanageable.

Against this moral and political plea are aligned a number of counterarguments that can be divided into two groups: "You *should not* try," and "It *cannot* be done." The first group consists of a variety of positions, all of which amount to saying that while as human beings we should all be concerned with the fate of human rights anywhere, a foreign policy of human rights will only make things morally and politically worse. Three types of arguments can be distinguished.

The first one puts the greatest emphasis on the moral harm such a strategy could cause. It deplores it as a form of moral imperialism, as the arrogant attempt by one nation or group of nations to impose their peculiar values and practices on other cultures and on countries with different political experiences and traditions. What right does any one nation have to be righteous and to set itself up as a model? Isn't such pretension a form of cultural and political expansion? Doesn't it in fact violate the basic norms of the international milieu, since the principle of noninterference in the domestic affairs of states is designed precisely to protect each national group's right to have its own practices (however obnoxious they may appear to others) and to stop foreign governments from trying to reshape other states? Replying to critics who had accused him of ruling out as immoral external intervention by force to help victims of a tyrannical regime win their revolutionary attempt at achieving self-government, Michael Walzer wrote of a people's right to have its rights violated by its own state.[14] This point, often made by Reinhold Niebuhr, is reinforced by George Kennan's observation about another moral flaw, the arbitrary selectivity with which the concern "for other people's liberties" is usually expressed.[15]

A second argument presents a mixed case—partly moral, partly political: the strategy I have recommended would aggravate the predicament discussed above, and make both international relations and the condition of human rights abroad even more difficult. Doesn't, in practice, a diplomacy of human rights amount to political warfare, not on behalf of certain values, but against specific countries? Hasn't the cause of human rights been used as a weapon in America's cold war against the Soviet Union (or Cuba or, today, Nicaragua)? What about the anti-Zionist resolution pushed by Arab states and their patrons in the General Assembly and other UN bodies? Violations of human rights abroad can become pretexts for cutting off foreign aid, and thus for hurting the poor in developing countries; that is, they can fuel a hypocritical desire to turn one's back on the outside world and provide a moralistic disguise for sheer selfishness. Thus the universalistic language of human rights, this alleged common discourse or conversation shared by all ideological systems, would actually be abused for particularistic and harmful purposes.

The third argument is the most heavily political. Paradoxically, it derives from a kind of moral Manichaeism. It suggests that not all states that appear to violate human rights (or actually do so) should be put in the same basket: there are, so to speak, good violations (or tolerable ones) and bad ones. Two such cases have been made; they are mutually exclusive in their effects, despite a similar structure of arguments. One is derived from Marxism; it asserts that the array of civil and political rights cannot be provided by a government unless the basic economic and social needs of the population, and the possibility of economic development, are provided first. Since these conditions cannot be met in poor countries under the capitalist system, as the theorists of *dependencia* argue, the only true violator of human rights is capitalism.

The other case is derived from a certain interpretation of liberalism. It proclaims the primacy of the "negative" rights of the individual, that is, of civil and political rights, and focuses on the antagonistic relation between society (whose autonomy is seen as a major value, and which is conceived as a sum of individuals) and the state (whose powers are to be curtailed). In this scheme, there is one categorical villain: totalitarian regimes, which deny these rights, destroy all limits to state power, and throttle society. To be sure, authoritarian regimes restrict political rights also, but they do not remove all restraints on governmental power. They may try to control political institutions and limit the flow of ideas, but they allow for (non-political) independent organizations in society, do not try to absorb all social institutions into the state, and often, as Jeane Kirkpatrick has argued, "leave in place . . . habitual rhythms of work and leisure, . . . habitual patterns of family and personal relations."[16] She recognizes that they also leave in place "existing allocations of wealth, power, status (that) maintain masses in poverty." Remember, however, that economic and social rights other than the right to free enterprise and property are not, in this conception, recognized as "real" rights. A Kissinger variant is that authoritarian regimes are distorted versions of traditional regimes, which observe customary restraints, but totalitarian ones are perversions of absolute populist or nonliberal democracies, in which the people's will is supposed to be unconstrained by checks and balances, and unfiltered by representative government.[17]

All these arguments strike me as morally defective and politically unconvincing. The last one is doubly embarrassing, and for this reason, I will discuss it first. Morally, the suggestion that there are bad violations, and, if not good, at least tolerable ones, provides no consolation for the victims of the latter, and evaluates the ills they suffer, not according to the harm inflicted on them nor on the basis of the nature or importance of the rights violated, but on the basis of the essence or nature of the regime. Empirically, the case is extraordinarily weak. The Marxist variant assumes that economic development and social progress are best assured by certain restrictions on civil and political rights ("luxuries" that poor societies still riddled with injustice cannot afford) and by revolutionary violence. It postulates that such development and progress are more likely in leftist authoritarian (or totalitarian) regimes than in liberal democratic ones. The record is far more murky. Leftist regimes that limit civil and political rights have a better record in social issues, particularly in the redistribution of income, in Latin America and in Africa. If we define rights as control over one's life, we must remember that even in the realm of economic and social affairs, this progress consists of services provided, not of rights granted. Moreover, the economic record of progress is far less impressive than that of social change: many of the economies of Marxist countries have stagnated or reached levels of growth below those of comparable capitalist or partly socialized economies, and there is considerable evidence of waste, a lack of incentives or innovation, and a stifling price of bureaucratic regulation. Finally, as Warren Weinstein shows,[18] violations of civil and political rights are damaging for economic development—many resources are spent on repression, and many talents squashed by it—and also for social justice, because of corruption and favoritism at the top.

As for the famous distinction between totalitarian and authoritarian governments, it rests, as has often been pointed out, on a confusion between the world of ideal-types—which provide criteria for identifying, "placing," and comparing existing regimes—and the world of political realities. As a result, it tends to ascribe to actual totalitarian governments attributes of the pure ideal-type, and to credit (or debit) them with a capacity of mass mobilization and an ability to control all sectors of society that far exceed their resources. Such a view distorts a reality that is often marked, not by idealistic zeal, but by cynicism and apathy, not by the politization of all groups and social institutions, but by intense privatization, the ultimate form of social and individual defense. Also, the distinction beautifies unduly many authoritarian regimes. Today, such regimes are often anything but "traditional"; they are either sophisticated modern versions of fascism, with its emphasis on controlling the corporate groups it pretends to resuscitate or to create; or they are systems of uncontrolled bureaucratic and technocratic rule. They are not satisfied with banning political parties (or creating fake ones) and limiting freedom of political expression, but insist on preventing society from organizing itself in a way that could challenge the arbitrary power of the state—hence the purging of unions and universities.

The distinction neglects the fact that not every authoritarian regime is easily replaceable by a liberal one. Such a change has happened only in places that had a pre-authoritarian democratic experience. Some authoritarian governments have been remarkably self-perpetuating, or, when shaken, succeeded only by another variety of authoritarianism. Conversely, some totalitarian regimes have been quite adept at undermining themselves: in Hungary, Czechoslovakia, and Poland, they have survived, not because of the formidable power of the state (which in Poland in 1982 had largely withered away), but because of the military—the Red Army and the Polish army; in Yugoslavia, "totalitarianism" has evolved into a rather original and complex brand of authoritarianism. From the essence or ideal-type of a system, one cannot derive valid conclusions about the possibilities of democratic conversion of real states.

Above all, the distinction ignores one point of crucial importance. Whatever the two ideal-types may tell us about the relations between the state and society, they (as well as the regimes that correspond to them) share what Montesquieu called a principle, which he defined as the government's spring, "what makes it act," whereas its nature is "what makes it so." Nature is structure; principle is the set of "human passions that makes it move."[19] The principle of all despotic governments is fear; neither honor nor virtue constitute adequate barriers to its power. This matters particularly for the subjects of human rights: individuals and social groups. Montesquieu understood that politics is a matter of psychology (shaping and shaped by laws and institutions): the fundamental differences between regimes are the differences in psychological springs, in the passions that governments manipulate, in the character of the subjects thus molded.[20] Fear can be a complex and subtle tool, one that a despotic government can manipulate and modulate according to circumstances. Mass terror is the most spectacular and scary example, and we have all been darkly fascinated by what we have learned about death camps and Gulags. But fear can operate more quietly without losing its effectiveness: the notion of the economy of force applies also to terror. Several disappearances, some executions, strategic purges, a sudden display of arbitrariness, can have the same cowing effect and succeed just as well in "beating down anyone's courage." If we consider human rights, as I suggested, as political rights, the distinction between the two types of illiberal regimes vanishes.

Both the dichotomy derived from Marxism and that of the neoconservatives, derived from C.J. Friedrich and Hannah Arendt, tell us: Do not try to pursue a policy that aims at defending human rights everywhere, because the primary moral and political duty of a leader is to win in the struggle of "us" (the forces of good) against "them." The contest between rival powers is, of course, a reality that the "moral politician" described by Kant must take into account. But it cannot be morally determining: it is a constraint, not an ethical imperative; and it should not be disguised as virtuous if it leads, for instance, the champions of the good to ally themselves with perpetrators of evil who happen to be on their side against the common enemy. If our government has to do so (which is questionable), we might as well recognize candidly that we are forced into it by the contest and led to it by the pro-American sympathies of these dubious allies, rather than pretend that they deserve our protection because the failings of the adversary are so much worse.

The second counterargument, about the bad effects of a serious concern for human rights on international relations, is based on some good evidence. In a world of competing interests and self-help, the risk of contributing to the "state of war" without helping the cause of human rights at all is real (the Jackson-Vanik Amendment did nothing for Jewish emigration from the Soviet Union; Carter's public concern for prominent Soviet dissidents served neither their cause nor that of arms control). Collective sanctions against South Africa's apartheid policy might well render hopeless the situation of those South African politicians and elites who understand the need for gradual evolution. But this counterargument should be taken only as a warning against a human rights policy that would ignore the criterion of effectiveness, sacrifice it to spectacle, or be motivated by considerations of political warfare. The case of Timerman, that of many other prisoners liberated under American pressure during the Carter years, and that of the elections of 1978 in the Dominican Republic show that a policy can be effective without aggravating international relations. What the counterargument suggests is prudence and skill in means, and vigilance against a slide in ends; it should not lead us to give up trying to reach just ends.

As for the first, the condemnation of moral imperialism, again the risk exists; but abandoning the attempt because nobody is good enough to try, or capable of giving, in Kennan's words, a "very fair and principled devotion to the cause" consistently, evenly, and universally, is an argument of despair. It would amount to avoiding moral imperialism by moral cowardice. Let us generalize it; there are, some people tell us, "macho" cultures in which rape is tolerated, where women who are raped are presumed to have "asked for it." Why should I impose my condemnation of rape—a violation of the victim's right to physical integrity—on such a culture? And since I clearly cannot pursue a Quixotic attempt at getting rapists caught and punished everywhere, why should I get so indignant about a crime that happens to have occurred within my reach? In other words, despite the noble concern that this argument shows for humility, and for the distinctive features of other societies, it can all too easily become an alibi for bad governments and for abandoning the victims. The argument about specific mores and institutions that are incompatible with American or Western liberal expectations is all too often used as a shield behind which harm safely continues to be inflicted on the innocent and even the most basic human rights are trampled. Once again, we need to be cautioned against both ignoring those particularities of customs and rituals whose character and pervasiveness may prevent the achievement of the full range of human rights recognized in the international normative order, and against imposing our own structures and strictures on polities that they don't fit. But the realities that these legal norms aim at creating happen to meet the aspirations and needs of most individuals and groups—except when they have been repressed so long that they don't even realize that chances for self-fulfillment exist. It is usually governments and their defenders that argue about the obstacles, even though they signed these documents or even acknowledged these aspirations in their constitutions. Whether a human rights policy is morally imperialist or not is a matter of practice; it is not of the essence.

Thus, none of the "thou shall not" exhortations is fully convincing. But Kant also taught that there is no moral duty to pursue the impossible. We must therefore turn to the second set of admonitions: Don't try, because it can't be done. Again, we find three principal arguments. The first concerns the information on which a human rights policy must be based: it is impossible, we are told, to know exactly what goes on abroad, because some countries are very good at concealing mischief (we still don't know what happened, for example, some years ago in Sverdlovsk). Even when we know the facts (such as massacres in a Central American country), we can't always find out who committed the crime or under what circumstances. Even when this can be figured out, we have to try to make sense of the whole context, which is very difficult to grasp from the outside, and often fiercely controversial.

A second argument deals with the perennial issue of consistency. The inevitable trade-offs will make a coherent policy impossible. We must, after all (or before anything else) protect our strategic interests: the "relation of major tension" cannot be ignored, and we have to avoid weakening our allies, however deplorable some of them may be, in order not to strengthen our adversary or throw our disgruntled clients into his arms. We must also protect other legitimate "world order" concerns—the international normative order does not consist of human rights alone. For instance, in the realm of force, we have a major political and moral interest in slowing down nuclear proliferation; diverting a country from becoming a nuclear power often involves providing it with guarantees, or tightening links between it and our own: this could be incompatible with an assault on its human rights violations. Last but not least, our own moral sense, our long-term political and economic interests, the pressures from developing countries, and recommendations of groups like the Brandt Commission argue for our helping these nations to meet the basic human needs of their people— even by providing assistance to governments that trample the civil and political rights of their subjects as they try to raise the level of wealth and improve social conditions.

The third argument goes back to the political predicament I dealt with earlier. Improving human rights abroad means persuading and forcing a foreign government to change its ways. This cannot be achieved without massive intervention: armed, perhaps, when we try to stop genocide (cf. the Indian move into Bangladesh, the Tanzanian against Idi Amin), or more peaceful yet highly intrusive—for instance, if we attached to our economic and military assistance to El Salvador strict conditions about the behavior of the army and paramilitary groups there. Now, such intrusions, in addition to being potentially catastrophic for world peace (they could lead to local bloodshed and to counterinterventions), are most unlikely to reach their goal. If they are brief or scattered, their effects will vanish; lasting improvements will require lasting involvement; and this is most unlikely to be acceptable at home, in addition to creating deep resentments abroad. For there is a fundamental contradiction between trying to increase the dose of "control over one's life" in a foreign country and, so to speak, taking it over.

These points are not fully convincing either. To be sure, information is often spotty or imperfect. But there are, by now, so many ways, public or private, of obtaining a good overall picture and of finding out not only about specifics, but about trends (often a more important consideration), that it is, in fact, more a feat to ignore what crimes and inequities are being committed than to know. As for the second and third arguments, they are perfectionist: they suggest that only total consistency or complete effectiveness would be acceptable, a demand rarely presented in the more usual realms of foreign policy. It is obvious that in the real world, the complex calculation of trade-offs will make perfect consistency impossible. But so long as the concern for human rights does not disappear, so long as the need to protect other interests does not result in the elimination of our effort, a certain degree of unevenness is perfectly acceptable. Indeed, it may even be desirable.[21] For a crucial objective of a human rights policy must be effectiveness, and we cannot either be effective everywhere with the same methods or, whatever methods we use, be equally effective in the results we achieve all over the world. From the viewpoint of effectiveness, a case can be made for concentrating our efforts, not on adversaries who are largely beyond our reach, or on "friendly violators" too difficult to handle because our ties with them are too few (such as China), but on clients who are largely dependent on us, for whose governments, or for whose governments' actions, we cannot escape a big share of responsibility, and whose reform is both our moral duty and in our political interest. For the violations perpetrated by these governments are likely to undermine them, to weaken our own position, and to plunge us into the dreadful, familiar dilemma of either trying to save them by giving them whatever assistance they need (on their own terms, since it is, by then, too late for reform) or else risking a double disaster: the collapse of our own power position, and the coming to power of forces that will be both hostile to us and, from the viewpoint of human rights, not necessarily any better than our suicidal client.

Changing regimes from the outside is obviously difficult. But it is not a matter of all or nothing. It is a matter of using and expanding the leverage one has in order to obtain significant results without becoming trapped in self-defeating intrusions. What this requires, as I have argued elsewhere, is a triple strategy. First, we ought to aim at achieving a common floor (i.e., require of all states the respect of the most basic human rights, those of physical integrity—freedom from torture and arbitrary deprivation of life as well as from famine and disease) and a movable ceiling (since the range of what can be expected will vary from place to place). Second, the policy must entail acts both by governments and by international institutions, including international financial ones. Human rights considerations are perhaps "political," but there are many other political considerations these institutions, sometimes clandestinely, take routinely into account. Moreover, economic or financial measures are only means to goals; the promotion of human rights ought to be one of the goals sought, in accordance with the dictates of various international legal documents. The policy must also entail acts both by public bodies and by private individuals and organizations. A public policy that tries to use available leverage against a violator can be defeated by bankers, traders, and investors who keep pouring far more money into the country in question than the government that takes human rights seriously ever gave or lent to it. What is needed here is both a greater "cosmopolitan" moral sense among private, especially corporate, groups and the use, on behalf of a human rights policy, of the kind of legislation that curtails business activities with adversaries and that even many champions of free enterprise, or of the notion that profitability should be the only business of business, find quite tolerable on behalf of national security. Third, it must be a multinational policy, to guard against the diversions or temptations of one nation's moral imperialism and to increase the chances of effectiveness.

Samuel Huntington has suggested that democratic governments have spread abroad when America has been powerful, and receded when its power declined.[22] Quite apart from the fact that he focuses only on civil and political rights, he ignores all the cases in which American power has been used to strengthen or to preserve regimes whose attitudes toward human rights were anything but compatible with democratic values. The promotion of human rights abroad is not synonymous with "the expansion of American power." Neither the pluralism of our institutions nor our own liberal-democratic values have guaranteed us against the misuse or corruption of American power abroad. These institutions have functioned either badly or too late, and our leaders have either confused the expansion of our power with that of our ideals or tacitly put aside the latter to ensure the former. What the promotion of human rights abroad requires is a coalition of liberal-democratic states willing to heed, in their foreign policy, the dictates of their values, and to recognize the congruence between these values and their long-term interest in a transformed international system composed of states that respect human rights.

Notes

1. "Human Rights and the Future International Community," *Daedalus* (Fall 1983), pp. 93-110.
2. I discuss this at length in *Duties Beyond Borders* (Syracuse, N.Y.: Syracuse University Press, 1981).
3. "The Challenge of Peace: God's Promise and Our Response," *Origins* 13 (1) NC Documentary Service, May 19, 1983).
4. "Human Rights and Human Welfare in Latin America," *Daedalus* (Fall 1983), pp. 139-171.
5. Peter Meyer, in *The International Bill of Human Rights*, edited by Paul Williams (Entwhistle Books, 1981), p. xli.
6. *The Peloponnesian War* (New York: Modern Library, 1934), p. 189.
7. *Human Rights and Basic Needs in the Americas*, edited by Margaret E. Graham (Washington, D.C.: Georgetown University Press, 1982), p. 316.
8. Quoted in Meyer, *The International Bill of Human Rights*, p. xxxi.
9. *The Philosophy of Kant*, edited by C. J. Friedrich (New York: Modern Library, 1949), pp. 122, 123, 124, 438.
10. Ibid., pp. 126-27, 120, 127.
11. "Kant, Liberal Legacies, and Foreign Affairs," in *Philosophy and Public Affairs*, June 1983 and October 1983.
12. *L'invention démocratique* (Paris: Fayard, 1981), pp. 50ff.
13. Cf. Charles Beitz, *Political Theory and International Relations* (Princeton: Princeton University Press, 1979), pp. 63ff.
14. "The Moral Standing of States," *Philosophy and Public Affairs*, Spring 1980, p. 226.
15. *The Cloud of Danger* (New York: Atlantic, 1982), p. 44.
16. "Dictatorship and Double Standards," *Commentary*, November 1979.
17. *Years of Upheaval* (Little, Brown, 1982), pp. 312-13.
18. "Human Rights and Development in Africa," *Daedalus* (Fall 1983), 171-96.
19. *The Spirit of the Laws*, part 1, book 3, chapter 1.
20. See Judith Shklar's book, *Ordinary Vices* (Harvard University Press, 1984).
21. See Alan Tonelson, "Human Rights: The Bias We Need," *Foreign Policy*, no. 4, (Winter 1982-83): 52-74.
22. *American Politics: The Promise of Disharmony* (Harvard University Press, 1981), pp. 246-59.

18

Liberalism and International Affairs

I

Thirty-three years ago, when I came to this country as a student, I discovered not only an academic effort to turn the study of international affairs into a discipline, detached from the traditional approaches of international law and diplomatic history, but also a noisy battle between "realists" and "idealists." At first glance, it seemed to be a joust between, on the one hand, utopian liberals keen on taming the international state of nature through the establishment of those norms and institutions that had apparently succeeded in limiting the functions of the state and the powers of government in liberal polities, and, on the other hand, hard-headed analysts of the logic of world politics, keen on explaining why such restraints and agencies could not succeed in the international milieu and why unrestrained power was bound to remain both the currency of interstate transactions and the "name of the game" played by states.

This debate seems very far away, and a bit quaint. Yet the points scored by each side against the other remain valid. The realists were right to put their fingers on the two distinguishing characteristics of the international milieu that rule out the pure and simple transposition of hallowed domestic recipes: an-archy (the lack of central power above the actors) and dissensus (the absence or paucity of common values, substantive or procedural). The idealists were right to say that the realists' analysis favored the conflictual over the cooperative dimensions of world affairs and led to a conclusion that was morally and politically hard to accept: the intractability of the game, apparently condemned (and condemning us all) to reproduce its deadly moves forever. But what is striking today is, first, retrospectively, that many of the "realists"—especially Hans Morgenthau, George Kennan, and Raymond Aron—either smuggled in or openly injected liberal values and goals whenever they went, beyond empirical analysis, into their own attempt at showing how the jungle could be made livable, how the "right" understanding of the game could make its inevitable perpetuation tolerable.

Second, on the international as well as domestic fronts, liberalism is in disarray. Liberals appear to be divided into three groups. Some analyze the world as the scene of a grand contest bewteen the free and the totalitarians; these liberals have become the champions of a crusade against the latter—at the cost, often, of arguing "right or wrong, my country, insofar as it is free and leader of the free." Some have not given up the quest for utopia and keep imagining schemes in which the logic of international politics would be finally abolished and replaced—through the disarmament of the states and the proliferation of communitarian practices, norms, and institutions; but they still have no answer to the questions: How are you going to achieve such a mutation? And how shall we go from here to there? A third group, to which I belong, seems to have taken Sisyphus as its inspiration, although, unlike Camus, it can't imagine either him or its own members happy. They try to find ways of instilling as many liberal concerns and ideas as possible into a game that, they know, cannot be wished away but that, if played as in the past, risks leading us all to destruction and chaos. Of course, each of these groups is usually bitterly critical of the other two—much to the enjoyment of nonliberals.

The reasons for the liberals' disarray in foreign affairs are quite different from the causes of the shortcomings of the liberal model in the politics of modern industrial and bureaucratic nations.[1] I will try to analyze them, from the viewpoint of a student of international relations. I will then turn around, so to speak, try to suggest why the rather colossal fiasco of liberalism in world affairs is, nevertheless, no excuse for giving up, and summarize what, as a liberal, I deem both desirable and—perhaps—possible.

II

Like all ideologies, liberalism has always been far from coherent or unified. Not being a political philosopher, I shall circumvent the learned and passionate debates about negative versus positive liberty, a rights-based versus a utilitarian liberalism, or laissez-faire versus social democratic liberalism. For the purposes of this lecture, I shall—*ex cathedra*—define liberalism as the doctrine whose central concern is the liberty of the individual: both his or her freedom from restraints and contraints imposed by other human beings ("political liberty in this sense is simply the area within which a man can do what he wants")[2] and his or her freedom to participate in a self-governing polity. The establishment and preservation of the state are necessary in order to prevent my liberty from being arbitrarily destroyed or harmed by the exercise of yours, and in order to deal with the problems of common concern. But the state is only the servant of society: its role is to remove the obstacles to freedom, and its function extends only to the issues that the members of society, acting as citizens, have freely decided to treat as common issues—beyond those protected from even majoritarian infringements. Self-government is necessary both as the safest precaution against arbitrary intrusions of the rulers into the sphere of individual liberty (or, if you prefer, as the form of government most likely to make the individual capable of ethical undertaking) and as a powerful human aspiration. While it is true that "the desire to be governed by myself" is not the same thing as the wish of "a free area for action,"³ ultimately "freedom from" means making "freedom to" possible, and "it is a great discouragement to an individual . . . to be reduced to pleas from outside the door to the arbiters of [his] destiny."⁴ Finally, the need to prevent any government, even a democratic one, and any social group, from exceeding the limits I have mentioned requires a whole pattern of institutional restraints—the familiar liberal arsenal of checks and balances as well as all the varieties of pluralism.

Now, it is easy to see why international affairs have been the nemesis of liberalism. The essence of liberalism is self-restraint, moderation, compromise, and peace. The state must be kept within its sphere; government can use its powers only in the ways set by law; groups and individuals must avoid trespassing and curtailing each other's freedom. Conflicts, the stuff of social life, have to be settled by reason—through negotiated deals or by resort to freely established authorities—not by violence. The essence of international politics is exactly the opposite: troubled peace, at best, or the state of war. The ever-present risk of war makes of military power, traditionally, the most important yardstick in the measurement of power; restraint, when it occurs, usually results from deterrence, from the fear or the crush of greater force. Compromises happen and cooperation develops, but both have a way of collapsing when the parties' interests change and when power shifts.

On the domestic scene, liberal institutions aim at compensating for, or at discounting, the considerable inequalities of power and wealth among individuals and groups, and at preventing the most powerful and wealthy force itself—the state—from crushing all the others. These institutions do not exist on the world scene, where full play is given—as, indeed, in the jungle—to the inequalities and inequities of power and wealth; there is nothing liberal about the Melian dialogue. If the logic of liberalism is that of the average or the weak individual against the mighty, that of international affairs remains the logic of might and the story of the rise, fall, and succession of the powerful.

What keeps liberal norms and agencies effective in liberal polities is more than the fundamental consent of the citizens; it is, as Tocqueville had so well understood, *les moeurs*—mores shaped by the procedures and institutions of liberalism but indispensable to their survival, for what would otherwise prevent each faction (especially those that are armed, privately or publicly) from smashing the intricate mechanisms of the liberal clock, or, to change the metaphor, from blowing off the dense cobweb of liberal rites, and of turning once again the moderate, regulated society into a jungle? There are no comparable *moeurs* among states on the world scene, except, it seems, among the small number of liberal states, which, as Michael Doyle has recently shown,⁵ have practically never been at war with one another. The *moeurs* of international affairs have remained those of the vigilante—or of Machiavelli's Prince. For a liberal polity to survive and prosper, it must gradually include (i.e., both take in and tame) the groups that have been originally, or feel, left out. On the world scene, the very division of humankind into competing units amounts to the triumph of a principle of exclusion.

In the liberal conception, the enemy is "them": the liberal epic is that of the individual threatened by concentrations of privilege, prejudice, and power, and liberated from these by the creation of a sacred sphere of noninterference as well as by that of a state so conceived and constructed as not to be capable of becoming an enemy again. But on the world stage, this very state, far from being the solution, becomes the problem, given the international state of war ("force, or a declared design of force, upon the person of another, where there is no common superior on earth to appeal to for relief, is the state of war").[6] Locke himself explains that the Federative power—the state's capacity to act on the world stage—"is much less capable to be directed by antecedent, standing, positive laws than the executive; and so must necessarily be left to the prudence and wisdom of those whose hands it is in to be managed for the public good":[7] in other words, institutionalized domestic restraints are out.

Two fateful results follow—fateful, that is, for the liberal vision. First, as long as the state of war exists abroad, the dream of individual liberty will be imperiled at home, for such liberty risks being trampled both by foreign oppressors and by the individuals' own states, which "will use all their resources for their vain and violent designs for expansion and thus will continually hinder the slow effort toward the inner shaping of the minds of their citizens"[8] or, indeed, violate the citizens' freedoms in the name of national defense or honor. Second, foreign affairs do not merely drive us back to that unequal battle between us and state power that liberalism had wanted to terminate in a way favorable to us: on the world stage, as history has shown in the nineteenth and twentieth centuries, the enemy of individual liberty is often not just that abstract entity, or artificial construct, or elitist preserve, the state, it is us—the people; or the nation-state to which liberalism grants rights because it is supposed to rest on the people's consent. In the liberal drama, the people want peace, and their victory will bring it about (it is in this way that the domestic solution to the problem of reconciling liberty and authority is *also* supposed to resolve the problem of war). But in our post-Enlightenment experience, we have seen liberal polities, in their relations with the nonliberal or with the less developed world, launch, or join, those very wars of passion or of "ambition, or insolence, or rapine" that Jeremy Bentham had deemed on the decline. No liberal polity has ever behaved, in international affairs, entirely as a liberal polity: for the very nature of the game, that of many of its players, and the opportunities provided by inequality, license the instincts or atavisms of racism, brutality, and intolerance that liberalism tries to keep in check at home. Indeed, in such a jungle, behaving as if the liberal principles could be applied might even be disastrous.

In the liberal philosophy that starts from natural rights, the problem is how to protect them from encroachments; in history, however, it was the other way around: it was, so to speak, encroachment or rather concentrated power that came first, and it had to be chipped away so that freedoms could be established. In domestic affairs, liberalism could (sometimes) win becasue concentrated power found itself blocked or even overthrown from below—by the individuals who wanted to climb out from under. In international affairs, we actually start with freedom, with the age-old game of independent players, who spend their energy and resources on preserving their independence. They perpetuate their play, not only because there is no one above them to put an end to it but also because those below, whose freedoms are indeed threatened by the play, nevertheless still tend to see in their respective states a protection against foreigners and the highest form of community available.

In domestic affairs, the protection of freedom, once it has been excavated from under the crushing mass of power, requires new arrangements of power so that my freedom and yours can coexist peacefully. In world affairs, all actors resist comparable arrangements—the weak, because they fear becoming its victims, since the strong would run the show, and the strong, because they reject all external restraints. Anarchy, in one case, is carefully avoided; it is fiercely preserved in the other. In one case, what the individuals are asked to "give up"—self-help, in sum—is something most have never enjoyed, and whose exercise would indeed make life, liberty, and the enjoyment of possessions impossible. In the other case, states, if the same reasoning were applied to them, would have to give up what they enjoy most, what constitutes their essence, and what they think they can keep at less cost or with fewer risks than if they gave it up.

* * *

This conflict between the liberal perspective and the logic of world politics explains the incompatibility between the game of states and each particular brand or branch of liberalism. In terms of its philosophical foundations, neither the liberalism of natural rights, of Lockian origin, nor the utilitarian liberalism of a Bentham or a J. S. Mill can find the world scene congenial. They share an assumption of universality. But, quite apart from the fact that so many governments deny or destroy their subjects' rights (something that liberalism fully expects, and fights against, but which is made possible, and is indeed shielded by national sovereignty—i.e., the state's right to treat its people as it sees fit, a right liberals have usually endorsed, especially if the state is based on self-determination), different cultures disagree on the existence, nature, and content of rights, and particularly on whether it is the individual, or the social group to which he or she belongs, or the state, which is the primary unit. As for the greatest good of the greatest number, the calculus, artificial and difficult already for citizens with common values within a community, becomes absurd on a world scale; for the previous question is whether there is any global community at all; and if there is not, then we are faced, at best, with a coexistence and at worst with a clash of common goods, whose addition is an intellectual exercise of little consequence: the greatest good of "humankind" is what a detached observer decrees, not what "the people" want—or rather, they may well want it (peace, for instance) but each people wants it on its own terms.

Similarly, the two classical conceptions of liberty do not fit the conditions of world politics. Take freedom as noninterference, as a sphere established and protected by law: if we talk about the individual's freedom, it will often be abridged by the requirements of the federative power; if we talk about the state's sovereignty, it constantly challenges, twists, and overturns the very peculiar law that is called the law of nations. Freedom as autonomy, or self-mastery, or the triumph of the higher self conceived as the "civic" part of one's personality either requires some leap into universality, so that man the citizen of a fragment of mankind becomes a cosmopolitan, a citizen of the world; or else, as long as the political communities confront one another, it is nothing but a recipe for unhappy consciousness, since the general wills of clashing polities lead men and women not to the realization of the categorical imperative but to rationalized murder. Indeed, as long as there is neither a sense of nor a political structure for a community of humankind, the famous difference between the lower self of our desires and the higher self of our duty degenerates all too easily into a distinction between "us" natives and "them" foreigners; each separate community defines its commonality in terms of what distinguishes it from—and makes it, in its own eyes, better than—the others.

The incompatibility between the liberal script for the good polity and the harsh choreography of the states' contest has posed two series of dilemmas for liberalism. First, liberals have been notoriously divided over the best way to cope with the "real world" of international relations. Should a liberal polity intervene in the affairs of other states in order to promote either self-determination or self-government? Interventions to liberate oppressed peoples were approved, or called for, by William Godwin, by Giuseppe Mazzini, by J. S. Mill, who carefully distinguished this case from interventions on behalf of self-government. For them, self-determination as the precondition for self-government (itself both the political expression of and the precondition for individual liberty) was sufficiently important to overcome the liberals' distaste for the nondefensive uses of force. But it was that very distaste (often disguised as, or reinforced by, skepticism about the liberating effects of military interventions) that led Thomas Paine and Richard Cobden to plead, in essence, for liberal isolationism. Kant's stern demand for nonintervention "in the constitution and government of another state"[9] excludes outside help to what we would, today, call fighters for national liberation, with the same argument Mill would later use only against help to people fighting for self-government.

Should, indeed, liberals—whether or not they favor intervention from abroad—encourage national self-determination at all (i.e. the "nationality principle" as the constitutive principle of the state system)? Mazzini and Mill were, respectively, the lyrical and the rational advocates of nationality.

Free institutions, wrote Mill, were "next to impossible in a country made up of different nationalities": there, "public opinion, necessary to the working of representative government, cannot exist."[10] Mazzini, like Michelet, defined the nation as "a community of free and equal men bound together in a concord of labor toward a single end."[11] But Charles Renouvier and Lord John Acton warned against the un-liberal potential of nationality, the risk of individual liberty being sacrificed "to the higher claim of nationality," of the legitimate diversity of interests (Acton) or the universal imperative of justice (Renouvier) being pushed aside by the "fictitious unity" of the national state.

Should liberals approve of colonial expansion? Mill argued that the rules applicable to relations between civilized states did not apply to the relations between civilized people and barbarians, even though colonialism should ultimately lead to independence. For different reasons, Bentham, Spencer, and Hobson condemned colonialism as evil. (What Hobson endorsed was internationally sponsored trusteeship in certain cases.) Should liberals approve of, or resign themselves to, the balance of power, scathingly mocked by Rousseau? Hume thought that the "maxim of preserving the balance of power is founded . . . on common sense and obvious reasoning":[12] it was both a guarantee of freedom for the peoples threatened by the strong and a force for moderation. Bentham endorsed the balance because it stabilizes the international system—and thus leaves room for and directs energy toward internal reform. On the other side, Godwin, Cobden, and later Woodrow Wilson, condemned the balance as a permanent goad to the lust for conquest and a permanent fuel of militarization.

In the second place, not only were liberal theorists divided, but students of the logic of world affairs often told their audiences that the domestic institutions of liberalism, for all the freedom and prosperity they may have brought to individuals, actually put liberal nations at a disadvantage in the tough contest of states. If the federative and executive powers, "distinct in themselves," are nevertheless "always almost united," won't all the restraints built into the domestic political system in order to keep the government from stepping on the liberties of the citizens, along with the checks and balances of the separation of powers and of judicial review, make it impossible for the government to define and to carry out a coherent policy abroad? Won't pluralism, the exercise of the individuals' freedom to form either parties, for political participation, or pressure groups, for the pursuit of their interests, submit the nation's foreign policy to the divergent pulls, selfish pushes, or ideological passions of forces unconcerned with the national interest—so that the latter will tend to be defined merely as the sum of special interests, or as the satisfaction of domestic demands at the expense of external power, prestige, or necessities?

At a deeper level, isn't there an incompatibility between the virtues required of liberal rulers and those needed by statesmen engaged in the pitiless drama of interstate politics? Max Weber's fascinated and gloomy view of this drama, almost as much as his disenchantment with modern bureaucratic rule, explains his interest in charismatic leadership, his search for a ruler who could somehow respect liberal values at home (unlike Bismarck), yet heroically defend his nation's distinctive culture and interests on the battlefield of the world. Today, nonliberals such as Henry Kissinger in the United States and Régis Debray in France tell us that the successful statesman must be free of domestic shackles, whether they be the entanglements of bureaucracy, the thick ropes of party politics, ideologies, and legislative pretensions, or the handcuffs of public opinion.[13] A profound, unabashed liberal thinker, Judith Shklar, points out the contrast between the sober virtues needed by liberal leaders and "the politics of the great gesture,"[14] which appealed to Weber and which he borrowed from Machiavelli. She is right to say that, at home, politicians rarely make "stark choices and great decisions" and that "to forget the mundane, the quotidian, is to forget liberal politics, which are the practices of peace and compromise, not of war and revolution." However, this reminder only highlights the plight of liberalism, torn between a domestic "mundane" to which it is best suited and, on the world stage, the nightmare of wars, the challenge of revolutions, the all-to-frequent need for "stark choices and great decisions"— indeed, the reality of military threats or economic calamities that submit domestic politics to their own agenda and make even the internal "mundane" often both intensely tragic and quite unmanageable.

* * *

That international realities could foster both tyranny and chaos is a truth that thinkers such as Hume and Kant expressed. Liberals, after all, had read and pondered the works of those we consider to be the founding fathers of "realism": Thucydides, Machiavelli, Hobbes. The realist orthodoxy was clear and coherent. Ordinary morality had little or nothing to do with the practice of foreign policy (because of the role and effects of force, or of the statesman's duty not to be good on behalf of the state's survival and security). However, the international state of nature can be accepted—either because, despite all its horrors, it leaves room for wisdom and moderation or because (for the reasons Hobbes gives) wars among states are less destructive of individual life than wars among men in the state of nature, and because the very inequality of states that distinguishes the international from the hypothetical state of nature puts some "sword" behind the covenants passed by sovereigns, thus providing a minimal order based on reciprocity. But liberalism was dissatisfied with this message: partly because of the centrality of war in the realists' vision of international affairs and the centrality of revulsion against war in that of the liberals; partly because of the implications of a "state of war" abroad for domestic society (civil war, or the Prince's tyranny justified by the primacy of foreign policy); partly because of the liberals' concern for individual self-fulfillment, and their sense that this could only be made possible through some breach in the citadel of the state, some measure of cosmopolitanism.

Thus liberals devised, so to speak, reformist strategies aimed both at refuting realist orthodoxy and at changing the world state of nature. Three strategies were followed. Two of them described international relations as being actually more benign than in the realists' books, and therefore morally less disastrous for individuals and less totally constraining for statesmen. One version, the more philosophical one, rejected the realists' view of human nature; Locke and Hume represent the two forms of that rejection. The second version, a more historical one, stressed the prospects of progress. The third strategy was that of Kant, who accepted the somber image drawn by the realists but concluded that it made man's moral duty to change it even more compelling; he also tried to show that the success of such an effort was not ruled out, that indeed conditions for its success were being created by "nature's mechanical course."

The first approach left one with a less than totally reassuring view of an international scene in which actors would be restrained either by the moral dictates of the law of nature or by a balancing of power that could mitigate the frequent violations of the "fundamental rules of justice" and the excesses of self-help. The second and third approaches went much farther; but as either programs or prophecies, they have, to a large extent, failed. Once more, we find a sharp division. The champions of progress predicted a sort of rollback of war by reason and a victory of commerce over conquest. They foresaw a world in which state power would have been shrunk and rendered largely harmless by the growth of the sphere of individual transactions across borders. Kant, on the other hand, seems to have believed that war would more likely be vanquished by its increasing destructiveness than by the effects and contagion of constitutional governments. Above all, in his scheme for perpetual peace, the role of the individual is much smaller, that of the (right) state much greater, the idea of a fundamental contest between individuals and government much less present than in the writings of English or French liberals—and, as a result, his notion of cosmopolitanism is both different (here, it consists above all of republican states behaving peacefully and openly) and narrower (the transnational opportunities for individuals are reduced to "universal hospitality").

Moreover, each of these versions had its own pitfalls. Kant's ingenious "plan of nature" might have aimed "at a perfect civic association of mankind," but Kant's own speculation only established that nature forced men to create *a* state "in order to be prepared as a power against its enemy" (the same idea is found in Hume). He could not "prove" that nature "wanted," and that men *would* want, this state to be constitutional: only that men, as they are and as nature had, so to speak, pushed them around, *could*, if they wanted to, organize such a state. And, although he thought that constitutional regimes could not be preserved if the state of war persisted, he also wrote that peace depended on the existence, association, and contagion of such states: a chicken and egg problem that could be resolved only if one assumed that the "plan of nature" would, through war and trade, first create the conditions for peace and thus make constitutional regimes, and a league thereof, possible. But still—and especially if it is a peace of fear and deterrence rather than a peace by conscious choice of the moral will—what could assure us that the states would be republican? And if they are not, how durable would be the peace? What could assure us that the ever-growing horrors of war would instill wisdom and peace, rather than—if the traditional "state of war" persisted—miscalculation, folly, and total destruction?

As for the prophets of progress, they have not been vindicated by the history to which they turned for hope. The spread of democracy has remained radically incomplete, and the twentieth century has seen the rise of the most formidable and crushing concentrations of power: those of totalitarian systems. Even in constitutional states, central power has gained in scope and intensity. The ability of individuals to operate across borders has been anything but irreversible: it has fluctuated depending on both the domestic political regime and the evolution of the international economic system; above all, it has often been the victim of war's triumphant survival.

Finally, both versions have shared grave illusions, which can be summed up as the faith in harmony and the belief in tamed anarchy. The paradoxical harmony through terror and avarice described by Kant; the conviction that the publics of enlightened nations would form a benevolent world opinion, rather than a cacophony of national prejudices and passions; the mystique of free commerce promoting at the same time the wealth of nations, the happiness of individuals, and the greatest good of the greatest number through the invisible hand that guides the interplay of selfish interests; the confidence about the compatibility between individual liberty and the nation-state as well as about the close connection between self-determination and self-government; the neglect of all the ambiguities of self-determination in practice; the certainty with which a Mazzini, a Jaurès, or a Wilson asserted that self-determined nations would live in peace, under law, and provide, in Michelet's words, the "necessary initiation to the universal fatherland"—all this reflected a faith in reason that went way beyond reason. It ignored the lengths to which states might go to thwart a harmony that could prevail only at their expense; and it assumed a sort of psychological abundance thanks to which the separate "missions" of nations would somehow be compatible. Under ideal circumstances—liberal national democracies everywhere—maybe the dream of harmony might have become a reality. But what if the forces of light were not strong enough to overcome the forces of darkness all over the world?

Above all, the liberal vision of the good international order remained the hybrid concept of the "legal community of mankind." Almost no liberal, before the First World War, thought in terms of a world state, assuring the freedoms of its members, limiting their excesses, and providing for their paticipation in the same way as liberal states deal with free individuals. Like Hobbes, many liberal authors drew their view of men without or before civil government from the spectacle of the world state of nature; then they turned around, and explained that the differences between men and states ruled out a world government. Kant, who thought that a republican constitution did not require that all citizens be good, but only that there be a mutual balancing of selfish, private concerns—so that even "a people of devils" could devise it—did not ask of even republican states that they submit to a similar solution of the problem of war: nature did not want it, states with internally legal constitutions would not accept it, and a world state would be either tyrannical or ineffectual. A Belgian jurist, Francois Laurent, explained that whereas individuals had to be kept in check by the state, states are "fictitious beings whose agents are generally the most intelligent and most ethical men of their time."[15] Liberals intent above all on reducing the power of the state, repelled above all by its "monopoly of force," were unwilling to conceive of a superstate with its own coercive power. Hence the profusion of schemes for *disarmament*, for world courts (but *not* a world executive), for a league of members bound only by a common law (Kant); hence the reluctance to entrust the power of enforcing that common law to anything higher than the states themselves or more potent than world public opinion.

This was another form of wishful thinking: the state as naked power was wished away; the notion of the state's entitlement to the rights of sovereignty *as if* its effective expression—the government—had always actually derived its power from the individuals' consent and respected their rights was matched by the myth of a world community functioning without central power *as if* such power existed (this became, in legal theory, the ingenious notion of *dédoublement fonctionnel* of the state, agent of the world community as well as of its own country's drives). This myth was carried beyond Kant's simple league, into post-1918 international organization. In the covenant of the League of Nations, obligations were defined; but enforcement was left, once more, to the states. In the Charter of the UN, collective enforcement was stressed but left to the good will of the great powers, with well-known results. Both the UN and the League have demonstrated that Walter Schiffer said of the League: "as far as the prevention of war was concerned [its] successful functioning depended on conditions which, if they had existed, would have made the organization unnecessary."[16]

Precisely this fiasco of the fictitious or impotent world community in the realm of war has led liberals who remain dubious about a world government's virtues or about its possibility to search anew for methods to reduce the Leviathan's powers obliquely. The old hopes placed in commerce and public opinion have been transmuted into functionalist theories of "peace by pieces," through specialized agencies quietly eating away morsels of state sovereignty, while the sovereigns doze. Those theorists who, like Charles Beitz,[17] want to go far beyond the "legalist paradigm" of an international law and morality of states that leave, on the whole, the fate of individuals at the states' mercy, yet who resist the logical but unpracticable idea of a liberal world state, try to square the circle in a familiar way: by applying, *contra* Rawls, his principles of justice to the whole world *as if* it were a community—enforcement against unjust states being left, it seems, either to moral consciousness or to just states. But if old quandaries are approached in new ways, old divisions have persisted: liberal writers today are still torn over the legitimacy of military intervention by liberal states, and controversies over distributive justice reflect both the more than a century old split between economic liberals and social democratic ones, as well as the traditional split between universalists and isolationists.

Some years ago, Kenneth Waltz saw a parallel between the liberals' acceptance of the necessity of the state, plus their determination to circumscribe it (by making it liberal), and the liberals' acceptance of war, plus their determination to minimize it (by limiting it to self-defense and, at most, collective security).[18] But if the states could not all become liberal, war would not be minimized. Insofar as the spread of liberal domestic institutions is concerned, the cunning of history has ultimately, in a backhanded way, partly benefited liberalism. Liberals had been sharply divided over the right of revolution, and yet it is through revolutions (and wars) that many liberal regimes were born. They had wanted nations to understand the rational superiority of free commerce over conquest, and yet it is through bloody revolts against colonial conquerors that many colonies became free (although not always liberal). In international affairs, however, neither revolutions nor wars have brought about the tamed world of Kant's league, or of Bentham's global legal society; the proliferation of states is not the fulfillment of the dream of nationality (since so many of the states are not true nation-states), and it is certainly not the triumph of liberal self-government.

III

Is the conflict between the liberal vision and the logic of interstate politics, and the failure of the former in that realm, so total that one has to give up any hope for the promotion of liberal values on the world scene? Must one return to that combination of tart analysis of the tricks of power and of the twists of moral dead ends, *cum* pious mutterings about the lessons of experience and the need for prudence, which are realism's trademarks? I do not think so. And I shall try to suggest the possibilities and directions of a liberalism without illusions. I know that such an attempt always risks colliding either with the Scylla of lofty generalities or with the Charybdis of policy-oriented laundry lists; what I do not know is how one can avoid coming perilously close to one or the other.

One point is certainly not in doubt, if one agrees with what precedes. The international milieu is, by nature, inhospitable to liberalism. What liberalism tries to achieve founders on the mix of sovereignty and inequality characteristic of international anarchy, and also falls in the trap of its own confusions. For it is concerned, here, altogether with (1) the freedom of the individual from oppressive restraints imposed by the state or society because of the interstate contest as well as because of the state's illiberal regime or the society's repressive mores; (2) the freedom of the state itself from outside aggression and domination, against which it shields its citizens; and (3) the freedom of both states and individuals, particularly in poor countries, to do what they would have to do for their own development—beginning with equality of opportunity in a world political and economic system that does not provide it. Not only do the rule of self-help and that other concomitant of sovereignty, the principle of nonintervention, represent formidable obstacles to such a program, but a liberal action from abroad, backed by power, aimed at achieving these goals, would always risk degenerating into one more selfish exercise of imperialism. Moreover and above all, there are clearly sharp contradictions between the various parts of the program. Equality of opportunity for states often does not help the individuals in it, any more than preserving the independence of a state necessarily helps liberate its subjects from internal restraints or ensures a fair treatment of aliens within its borders.

Indeed, the *present* global scene seems particularly inhospitable. If one looks at the domestic political systems in general, one finds a small number of democracies that have, on the whole—albeit with lapses—succeeded in protecting liberties from the pressures of a fierce international contest, but whose liberalism has often turned restrictive and pinched because of those of the world economy (I am thinking of the treatment of refugees or immigrant workers). All the rest is made up of authoritarian regimes (many of which preside over countries in which nationhood remains to be created and in which freedoms are restricted either in order to forge it or simply in order to stay in power) and totalitarian systems. On the international scene the combination of nationalism, revolutionary conditions, and bipolar conflict, which I have discussed elsewhere,[19] all taking place amidst nuclear arsenals, seems to provide unlimited opportunities for domestic cruelty, exernal interventions that aggravate violence, bloody wars, and terrorism.

What opportunities are there, then, for liberals? None, of course (but it is a point often forgotten in the literature despite its obviousness), unless liberals with a sense of strategy are in power in a sufficiently large number of sufficiently important countries. For since we have not yet "reinvented politics," in Jonathan Schell's phrase, our pleas and our impeccable arguments shall not blast away the walls of Jericho, behind which, if I may mix my metaphors, the minotaur of state power remains intact. The first duty of liberals concerned with world affairs is to protect the achievements—never definitive, always reversible—of liberalism in their own countries. One of these achievements, incidentally, concerns the foreign policy of a liberal nation, which must be conducted, as Kant insisted, on the basis of maxims that can be made public and indeed "require publicity in order not to miss their purpose."[20]

But assuming that such a liberal base, or bridgehead, exists, what are the opportunities for expanding it, or for injecting as much of liberalism as possible into the darker scene? Kant also taught us that "ought" must imply "can": there is no duty to achieve the impossible. Fortunately, there are cracks in the walls of Jericho. They are not parts of a "plan of nature"—

i.e., a philosophical hypothesis about history's march. They are realities of the present world—and, as such, are often ambiguous and fragile. I have often listed three such realities.

The first is a purely empirical fact: the heterogeneity and complexity of the international system, both of which temper the extent to which the U.S.-Soviet conflict can absorb into its vortex all other issues (and thus make it possible to deal with those primarily on their own merits); in addition, they are reinforced by what might be called nuclear prudence (the effect of which is a fragmentation of conflict).

The second is an empirical fact that suggests not only a possibility but an imperative: nuclear inter-action among the possessors of the "absolute weapon" has so far injected restraints into the international system and made the great powers behave according to an unwritten code of *jus* that is neither *ad bellum* nor *in bello* but *contra bellum*—at least among themselves. The survival of humankind must be the first goal of liberals. Even those who "put their country first" because it is a liberal country must realize that its survival is not distinguishable or separable from that of the rest of humankind. And, therefore, the paradoxical restraints entailed by (so far) successful nuclear deterrence must be reinforced and expanded.

The third is also an empirical fact that suggests a duty. Economic interdependence is neither a myth nor simply a contemporary form of the old liberal illusion about the benefits and irreversibility of free trade. (Indeed, it is as much an international interdependence of states with vastly expanded jurisdiction over economic affairs as it is a transnational interdependence of individuals at the expense of states.) Like the nuclear reality, this is both an opportunity and a threat. We live in world economy made of boomerangs, in which states are tied both by their mutual needs (or fears) and by the unforeseen effects of their own domestic decisions or external entanglements. In the early 1980s the debt problem of the developing countries, resulting from credits granted by American institutions (and by those of other advanced countries) was made worse by the United States' domestic economic policies (the high interest rates) and in turn threatened the U.S. financial system. OPEC's blitzkrieg of the 1970s contributed to a world recession and provoked countermeasures that led to an oil glut disastrous for its members. This too points to the need for restraints. For while the theorists of interdependence may have underestimated both the state's capacity to act as if economic affairs were a zero-sum game and the strength of mercantilist and protectionist appeals, they are right in pointing out the long-term solidarity of factors and actors, the cost of such measures to all, and indeed, often, the impossibility of purely national solutions.

Does this mean that we can trust historical forces to provide liberal opportunities? Clearly we can't: this is not a "self-regulating system" (whatever that phrase means, in the social sciences). In the realm of force, three formidable problems confront us: the generalization of "limited" wars (limited in scope only) and of violent interventions; the dangerous destabilizing evolution of the nuclear arms race between the superpowers (the undermining of what the experts call crisis stability and arms race stability); and the problem of nuclear proliferation. In the realm of economic interdependence, the unevenness of economic and social conditions, and of the constraints imposed by existing international rules, leads some states to the temptation of withdrawal and disconnection in order to reduce vulnerability or responsibility and some to the temptations of short-term gains at the expense of others—in other words, to the perils of manipulating mutual vulnerabilities. Economic wounds are also inflicted on others by the domestic decisions of major economic actors. A protracted recession in advanced countries always strengthens protectionist impulses, which hurt all the countries that can neither grow nor repay their debts without exporting. Interdependence is thus a condition, like "existential deterrence," but it is neither an irreversible policy of states nor even a global affair: a mercantilist set of economic practices, fiercely protected against loss of control, continues to prevail in Communist countries (and consequently, East-West trade remains an element of the contest of states). Finally, there are all the bad connections between the realms of force and of wealth—namely, the economic difficulties leading to domestic turmoil that breeds violent external intrusions and the costs of military build-ups that drain resources away from the world economy.

* * *

What is needed is a conscious liberal strategy. And what I suggest is the paradox of a minimalist strategy designed to introduce the maximum of liberal values and politics into the hostile environment of international relations. It can *only* be minimalist, because of the resilience of the states as the main actors and because of the moral importance so much of humankind attaches to the existence of independent states as a bulwark against foreign oppression. And yet, it is still the states that are the problem, both because of the reckless effects of their behavior on the world strategic and economic scene and because the domestic practices of so many of them destroy or prevent liberty for their subjects. A state of affairs that allows each government to treat its people exactly as it pleases would be both politically disastrous and morally intolerable—politically disastrous because the victims, out of despair, could turn to totalitarian promises and because such governments both provoke and court external intervention; morally intolerable because no self-respecting liberal can pretend to be unconcerned by the injuries and pain inflicted on human beings just because they suffer and die beyond the borders of his own nation. In this realm, and in that of international distributive justice, *international* action to protect and promote liberty and fairness is made necessary by the very bleakness of the domestic scene in most of the world: a grim world stage must be the court of appeals against domestic horror shows. Hence the need to introduce as much liberalism as possible on that stage for progress both in domestic and in international affairs.

This duty puts an enormous burden on the few states that respect human rights, understand that the prosperity or development of other nations is necessary to their own, and prefer methods other than force for the settlement of disputes. The very difficulty of the task is an incentive to modesty. What we need on the world scene is a liberalism with three general characteristics. In the first place, it must concentrate on essentials: making more room for peace and compromise at the expense of interstate and civil violence; making more room for the international version of pluralism, which is multilateral action, at the expense of unilateral moves; and focusing on the most essential human rights rather than on the whole Western panoply.

In the second place, the top priority in these essential areas is merely to avert certain disastrous outcomes of the "game of states," the worst effects of self-help: a nuclear war, large-scale conventional wars, a collapse of the world financial system and of the economies of bankrupt countries, massive disruptions, leading to chauvinistic self-protection, caused by the huge flows of population that misery could send from the poorer to the richer countries, an increase in repression and oppression brought about either by civil wars (which, today, almost always have external connections) or by the pretext that the tension between Washington and Moscow, or the state of war between local enemies, provide—even sometimes to liberal polities.

Third, and something certain liberals always find unpalatable, such a limited strategy, waged by liberal nations, can succeed only if it uses these nations' power. This does not mean that hortatory or declaratory policies are necessarily ineffective: if they are enunciated by major actors, they might be interpreted as a prelude to action, and other states may well want to please or need to comply. But a liberal policy can only be, on the whole, a set of decisions about how power is to be used; and power remains a complex set of rewards and punishments—not always available, and not always used or effective.

The obvious implication is that total disarmament remains an unachievable goal, that deterrence (at, however, a much lower level of arms) will remain the condition of security, that drastic equalitarian and communitarian schemes for the global redistribution of resources and income will remain actually quite debatable academic musings, that many violations of rights will continue in this world of often unsavory regimes. None of these constraints will satisfy those who see no other satisfactory solution that an abolition of the "war system" and, indeed, of the state system. But arguments about its obsolescence, its deadly logic of destruction and domination, still leave us with no other program of action than a romantic call for cleansing revolution and destruction, or less apocalyptic calls for people to transcend states, or paper schemes for disarmament.

Nor will any of these constraints satisfy those who believe that the only duty of liberals is to defend themselves against, and to push back, the totalitarian monster. I do not deny the importance of the Soviet challenge to liberal democracy, but hyperbolic concentration on it does, in many instances, become a self-defeating, self-fulfilling prophecy—and one that always tempts liberals into adopting the enemy's methods (nothing bolsters more the patriotic fervor that is the Soviet regime's main brand of residual legitimacy than liberal policies that seem to vindicate Moscow's myth of encirclement and fear of external hostility;[21] and it is our indifference to human rights crushed by some of our authoritarian "friends," such as Pinochet's Chile, or in South Africa, that may ensure the victory of the Communists over the democratic opposition). In other cases, this concentration misses the few opportunities that exist for a less warlike and ultimately less repressive world. Liberals must, of course, accept the reality of ideological warfare, but within two sets of limits: those of political and military prudence, and those set by the imperative of consistency: we can wage this war effectively (both in a moral and in a strategic sense) only if we actually practice what we preach. Ultimately, defeating the *Soviet* challenge requires knowing where to work against, where to work with, and where to work around the Soviet Union. As for the challenge of totalitarianism, it suffers from handicaps liberals can exploit—namely, its own divisions and failures.

Utopians and cold warriors share one traditional *démarche* of liberalism that we must discard—or at least modify—in international affairs: "us" against "them," with liberalism representing the triumph of the forces of good over those of evil. In the utopian version, "us" refers to the people of all countries, "them" to the governments along with the beneficiaries of the war system and of economic exploitation; in the cold warriors' version, geographic segregation has replaced the hierarchical one: it is the free world against the totalitarians. Alas, no transnational populist coalition or revolution shall destroy the warmongers and exploiters the way laser beams destroy evil beings in star wars movies; and a world more hospitable to liberal values will have to be built with all countries, including that great majority of them which are in no way liberal.

* * *

What ought such a world look like? Let us move from the general characteristics to the substance. For all its limitations, a nonutopian liberal strategy nevertheless must be ambitious in one sense: it must be transformist, not incremental. Incrementalism is morally questionable. The best it has to offer is a kind of moderate Machiavellianism, which still relies excessively on force and on the manipulation of the weak by the strong. It shows little concern for what happens, within sovereign states, to victimized human beings. It is politically dangerous, because it is based entirely on the logic of self-help (with fateful consequences in areas such as the choice of weapon systems, or military interventions), and—even when it seeks restraints on the abuses of state power—it rarely goes beyond short-range measures, stopgap improvisation, or "*ad hocery.*"

Transformism means finding a way between the insufficient and the impossible. It means using the (traditional) logic of world politics in order to change it. It means exploiting those realities that seem to vindicate Kant's perceptiveness when he postulated his "plan of nature": the fear of violent death, and the desire for prosperity and development—the desire for survival in a world of weapons of mass destruction, and the fear of economic collapse. It means consolidating and enlarging the contemporary transformations of power, which provoke so much controversy among specialists of international relations, between those who celebrate and sometimes exaggerate these changes and those who deny their existence or their importance. For power, like sovereignty, is profoundly affected by the inadequacy of military might for important state goals (in economic affairs, or against national liberation movements) as well as by the domestic and external constraints (nuclear prudence being the most obvious one) under which force must operate. In the realm of economic interdependence, power is affected by the way in which the strong are themselves at the mercy either of the weak or of their own blunders, and by the sharp limits to what each state, even a rich and mighty one, can achieve by itself.

A transformist liberal strategy—going way beyond Kant's gradually expanding but (functionally) minimal union of republican states—would aim, on the one hand, at improving the hold of liberal values and institutions in as many polities as possible. This means not only the kind of human rights policy I have described elsewhere (see Chapter 17). But also a deliberate strategy, by the liberal nations, to help democratic forces in repressive countries—if only by publicizing their plight, protesting their persecution, and providing them with nonviolent means of survival and consolidation (the training of potential leaders, for instance)—and to give preferential treatment, in matters of trade, economic, and financial assistance, cultural exchanges and diplomatic cooperation, to democratic polities, especially to fledgling democracies recently liberated from the grip of tyrannical regimes. This is a strategy in which a careful division of labor between the government and the organized citizenry of liberal countries is essential.

On the other hand, a transformist liberal strategy would aim at turning the international *system* into a global *regime*, in the sense given by contemporary students of world affairs. They define a regime as a set of norms, procedures, practices, and (usually) institutions that provide the "rules of the game" in a given area (money, trade, the oceans, oil, civil aviation, etc.), for the solution of problems that states either cannot resolve through separate efforts or else attempt to handle separately only at the cost of obtaining unwelcome or less than optimal results.[22] Such a regime, based on the calculations and cooperation of the states, would be an alternative both to "politics as usual" and to a world state, against which Kant's objections still hold. It would try to bring to its members and to individuals most of the benefits the enthusiasts of a world government have always expected from such a state. It would be based on recognition of the fact that the state, and especially the nation-state, is still endowed with value and enormous staying power (indeed, that a liberal's first duty is to protect, and if possible to promote, the "formula" of republican government, rather than to fight for abolishing the state). But it would also be based on recognition of the fact that the state is neither capable, by itself, of providing the citizens with the public goods they crave, nor likely to survive *unless* encased in a global regime, nor morally immune from outside concerns about domestic violations of rights. Finally, it would express awareness of the fact that we are in the midst of a major evolution—involving the shrinkage of the planet, if you will, through technology and ever-multiplying connections among people whose number is growing explosively—but that this evolution is indeterminate. It could lead either to Kant's state of peace or to destruction and chaos, and therefore requires conscious guidance.

A liberal transformist strategy would try to enforce the following principles:

1. *Transparency.* Despite the deliberate opacity of the Soviet system, we must attempt to broaden the opportunities for openness and increase the flow of free information. This would require the multiplication of functional international regimes (including, in the realm of human rights, one much stronger than the deplorably flawed current UN regime, whose aim would be to publicize both the plight and the progress of political and economic rights in every country, and which may well be set up initially by the liberal nations only; also, in the realm of security, one for observing, reporting, and devising what are called "confidence-building measures"). The expansion of transnational contacts and exchanges would be another instrument.

2. *Accountability.* This principle results from the notion that the polity is not an extension of the ruler and that the ruler is only a trustee. In a world where tyrannies flourish, making leaders accountable for their acts is a formidable task; it requires a strategy for human rights and, again, more international regimes restricting the sphere of arbitrary actions and penalizing cheaters. Strengthening an organization such as the International Atomic Energy Agency, creating a World Security Organization with powers of inspection, getting liberal polities to elect their delegates to the General Assembly of the UN, so as to begin changing its nature and giving it a more powerful, new kind of legitimacy—these are the types of measures one could imagine.

3. *Responsibility.* Making leaders pay for grievous errors and crimes could become possible if strong regimes and provisions were set up for collective assistance to victims of aggression, for joint action against terrorism (and sanctions against states that sponsor or protect terrorists), and for multinational humanitarian interventions against genocide.

4. *Solidarity.* However much argument there can be about the scope and foundations of our obligations to human beings outside our own country, we have both interests and duties beyond its boundaries. Solidarity requires considerable strengthening of the system of international distributive justice: collective measures and agencies against mass poverty, with controls designed to ensure that the individuals, not the aided governments, are the true beneficiaries; increasing possibilities for development assistance, conditional upon satisfactory performance; and a better global organization for industrial policy (which is what world trade now mainly means).

5. *Nonviolence.* This principle dictates the avoidance of force for purely national goals, the legitimate uses being reserved for agreed upon common

goals. The realm of the use of force, of course, has witnessed some of the greatest fiascoes in the past, and it remains the most difficult, given the proliferation of life-and-death situations as well as the intensity of the global cold war. What is imperative, therefore, if the journey toward nonviolence has any chance of leading anywhere at all, is the control of the arms race and of nuclear proliferation, and the gradual development of international police forces.

These principles thus require specific *policies*. I do not have the space to spell them out here (and, in any case, I have tried to do so in excessive detail elsewhere).[23] I will therefore only touch on a few points—in shorthand. First, another one of Kant's insights needs to preserved and reinterpreted. His hopes for perpetual peace depended on the establishment of a sufficient number of "right" polities. Today, hopes for a global regime hinge not only on their existence but also on the rightness of their domestic policies. Their own internal decisions about what weapons to build or to forgo, or about their economic and fiscal policies, will affect the possibilities for freedom *from* and freedom *to* elsewhere.

Second, the fight against the most perilous aspects of war requires a complex and continuous set of moves. In the nuclear realm, stopping the undermining of crisis stability by ever more accurate and unverifiable offensive weapons and by a race between offensive and defensive ones is the first imperative. On paper, one can try to distinguish wars that result from rational calculations, from wars of misperception or accident; in real life, it is always a mix. We need to integrate the lessons of both 1914 and the 1930s, the two biggest disasters for liberals: neither appeasement of aggression nor drift into situations in which one side comes to believe that preemption or war is likely to be less devastating for it than delay or diplomatic defeat. Preventing such drift requires a combination of political measures—essentially a return to a serious political dialogue with Moscow. It also requires a mix of unilateral and negotiated military measures—essentially to stop adding nuclear weapons far beyond the needs of the few missions that can sensibly be designed for them, to eliminate powerful but vulnerable nuclear systems, to keep the number of accurate, "war-fighting" ones as small as possible, and to do the same for the unverifiable ones that are being developed. Above all, it means preventing a new race that is utterly mindless from expanding into space, and subordinating the development of defensive systems to the prior reduction of offensive ones. It means moving away from the folly of provocative strategies of "decapitation" and from the chimera of perfectly controlled, limited nuclear wars; for if leaders have been irrational enough to launch such a war, can one expect the sudden wisdom of frightened recoil to prevail over the traditional logic of escalating the means in order to win the wager? Arms control is a crucial liberal cause, not because it will solve the world's political problems but because, without it, the inevitable crises they will provoke will become far more difficult to manage.

However, as George Kennan has pointed out, along with the Catholic Bishops of this country, one ought not to make the world safe for conventional wars (especially not between the superpowers). They are often abominable, accompanied by the kinds of savage civil conflicts Thucydides had so powerfully denounced, and they are capable of escalating, even beyond the nuclear threshold. This is why a liberal strategy would require, here also, action both on the diplomatic fronts—for the peaceful settlement of disputes, not only through patient but often ineffectual mediation but also through rewards and sanctions—and on the military ones, through the control of conventional arms (and, most important, of arms sales).

A nuclear powers' arms control "regime," other regimes for regional conventional arms, a stronger global antiproliferation regime, would form the elements of a world security regime. In the past, as Robert Jervis has shown, such a regime could never have been established because of the high degree of competitiveness in the strategic realm of security, the importance of the stakes, and the dreadful effects of relaxing vigilance, despite the obviously high costs of "the individualistic pursuit of security."[24] The future has a chance of being different only because these costs now risk reaching infinity, and insofar as cooperation could be so constructed as to reduce the advantages of cheating or the cost of temporarily falling behind.

Third, the other issue that liberals have always had to confront—revolution—will continue to pose enormous problems to them. Revolutions only rarely lead to liberal institutions, and they often bring wars. But they result mostly from the violation of essential human rights by governments. This is one more reason for a collective, coherent human rights policy by liberal polities (consisting of their governments but also of their citizens), aimed at establishing what I have elsewhere called a floor—i.e., the minimal requirements—for the treatment of human beings, and at enforcing these limited but stringent standards primarily in those parts of the world where liberal polities have responsibilities and influence. Taking rights seriously on the world scene is often just as urgent, and ultimately as important politically and morally, as taking peace seriously. Even so, many revolutions will occur, and they will replace tyrants with new, perhaps even worse ones. Forcible interventions to suppress unwelcome revolutions should remain anathema to liberals, except when really genocidal conditions prevail and the intervenors meet the necessary tests of impartiality, strictly limiting the scope and duration of their intervention. Nonmilitary interventions on the side of the status quo are justified only when they aim, not just at preventing revolutions, but also at inducing the governments in place to correct the evils that have created revolutionary conditions.

A liberal perspective that seems to offer little more than a maze of "regimes" is bound to appear not only pale or bloodless but also merely as a revamped version of the liberal illusions excoriated above—about harmony, and about a world jungle considered fictitiously *as if* it were a community. The first charge can be disposed of, if we ask in response: Compared to what? Is there anything better *and* possible to suggest? Against the charge, indeed, of impossibility, and illusion, it is not easy to be convincing. Even in the areas where world or regional regimes exist already and where both the irrelevance of force and the solidarity of economic variables weaken the case for unilateral action, the obstacles are huge. There has to be a positive balance of benefits and constraints for each member; the constraints accepted in return for predictability and rewards must appear evenly distributed among the members; the disadvantaged within each country must not consist of groups capable of forcing withdrawal or sabotage; the lure of gains itself must not be so great as to incite members to try to change the rules in their favor; the common institutions must have enough authority and autonomy so that even dissatisfied members have a stake in their preservation; and so on. Moreover, even the best bargains do not always serve justice; even the best regimes do not always survive the disastrous policies followed by their leading participants. In short, the other liberal patron saint, next to Sisyphus, is Penelope. But a constantly-to-be-rewoven tapestry is still better than a military or economic battlefield.

IV

In conclusion, one must return to a constant theme of this essay: liberalism in international affairs requires liberals with authority, power, and awareness. Today, the trouble with statesmen in liberal polities is not that they play Corneille on the world stage and Molière on the domestic one; it is that they don't know what to play, and don't remember their lines. They act as if what they are elected for—taking care of the domestic rights and prosperity of their citizens—could be accomplished without much account of outside winds, or of the drafts their own acts can cause abroad. And abroad, they behave either as if victory in the struggle in which their countries are engaged was their only responsibility, or as if short-term calculations were the most that could be expected of them. We must, of course, beware of Corneillian heroes, except in Corneillian times; but we must, above all, avoid leaders who deal in deviousness or fear, who ignore the constraints and complexities of domestic and international pluralism, who fail to see that liberal government must do more than making the tribe feel good, keeping it strong, and hoping that national prosperity and strength will *ipso facto* benefit humankind.

As for the citizens of liberal polities, they too have a role to play. At home they must act together, so as to help their country avoid doing wrong or contributing to evil, and so as to resist, nonviolently, when their country does so, fully accepting the penalties for such resistance, and with the goal not merely of resisting but of transforming as well. They must also, themselves, reject the appeals of chauvinism and show the imagination and empathy that cosmopolitanism entails. Abroad, they should form networks of transnational cooperation and concern. Private groups such as Amnesty International, and semipublic organizations such as, for all their failings, the Brandt and Palme Commissions of recent years, are good examples.

If there can be no Sisyphean or Penelopean international liberal policy without liberal polities, there can be no concerted strategy by them without an active and thoughtful participation of the most powerful liberal country, the United States. This is so for two reasons. The end of the brief period of U.S. hegemony makes it necessary for Americans to think again about their role, and to give up the pipe dream of America the rule-maker for the world. And yet the resources of this country, its importance in the world economy, its technological advantages, the role of the dollar, the existence of a greater welter of groups and movements than anywhere else concerned about world issues, continue to make of the United States the potential liberal lever of opportunities and responsibilities. That its leaders are liberals cannot be denied. But it is a liberalism which, at home, has recently been singularly indifferent to equality of opportunity and to some of the rights painfully wrested by the disadvantaged; and it is, abroad, a liberalism with extremely nationalistic overtones, hostility to international agencies not under U.S. control, little worry about long-term calamities, and ideological indifference to the plight of victims of repression or misery. Moreover, the public itself is going through a curious phase of self-congratulation and denial. Except in the so-called peace movement, which is both divided and often very American in its own self-righteousness and utopianism, there is little awareness of the pace-setting role played by the United States in the matter of arms and of the United States' responsibilities in the propping up of a host of petty tyrants. There is even less of a sense of responsibility of the richest nation on earth for the fate of those, advanced or backward, whose economies are either intertwined with or subordinated to its own.

An internationalism that does not appeal to American salvatory hubris (as had Woodrow Wilson's, with disastrous backlash effects) will always be less glamorous than the archetypes of the sheriff of High Noon or the Samaritan-missionary, and less electrifying than the nationalistic simplicities of social Darwinism. But in international affairs, missionary angels turn into beasts, and social Darwinists into bullies. Therefore, let liberals not be discouraged, and remember that one of the merits of liberalism is precisely that it "imposes extraordinary ethical difficulties on us: to live with contradictions, unresolvable conflicts, and a balancing between public and private imperatives which are neither opposed nor at one with each other."[25] In world affairs, even if we no longer share Kant's belief that the liberals' task is one that "gradually solved, steadily approaches its end," we must act not *as if* the world already were what we want it to be but *as if* "the eternal peace which will take the place of" mere "truces" were "no empty idea" but an achievable goal. It is, in any case, a duty.

Notes

1. See Stanley Hoffmann, "Some Notes on Democratic Theory and Practice," *Tocqueville Review* 2, no. 1 (Winter 1980), pp. 59–75.
2. Isaiah Berlin, *Two Concepts of Liberty* (Oxford: Clarendon Press, 1958), p. 7.
3. Berlin, *Two Concepts of Liberty*, p. 15.

4. James Stuart Mill, *Representative Government* (New York and London: Dutton, 1944), p. 216.
5. Michael Doyle, "Kant, liberal legacies, and foreign affairs," *Philosophy and Public Affairs* 12, no. 3 (Summer 1983), pp. 205–235; *Philosophy and Public Affairs*, 12, no. 4 (Fall 1983), pp. 323–353.
6. John Locke, *The Second Treatise of Civil Government* (Oxford: Blackwell, 1948), p. 11.
7. Ibid., p. 73.
8. Immanuel Kant, *The Philosophy of Kant* (New York: Modern Library), 1949, p. 126.
9. Ibid., p. 434. The exception Kant seems to allow—outside assistance to a group that, during a civil war, has set up a state in part of the country while laying "claim to the whole," so that this country, in effect, no longer has a constitution, a situation that resembles that of Spain during its civil war of 1936–1939—he actually revokes at the end of the paragraph: such interference would "be a trespass on the rights of an independent people struggling only with its own inner weakness"—indeed "an offense which would . . . tend to render the autonomy of all states insecure."
10. Mill, *Representative Government*, p. 361.
11. Giuseppe Mazzini, *The Duties of Man* (London: Henry S. King & Co., 1875), p. 315.
12. Hume, as quoted in Arnold Wolfers and Laurence Martin, *The Anglo-American Tradition in Foreign Affairs* (New Haven, Conn.: Yale University Press, 1956), p. 72.
13. See Régis Debray's *La puissance et les rêves* (Paris: Gallimard, 1984).
14. Judith Shklar, *Ordinary Vices* (Cambridge, Mass.: Harvard University Press, 1984), p. 243.
15. Laurent, as quoted in Walter Schiffer, *The Legal Community of Mankind* (New York: Columbia University Press, 1954), p. 160.
16. Ibid., p. 199.
17. Charles Beitz, *Political Theory and International Relations* (Princeton, N.J.: Princeton University Press, 1979).
18. Kenneth Waltz, *Man, the State and War* (New York: Columbia University Press, 1959), p. 103.
19. Stanley Hoffmann, *Dead Ends* (Cambridge, Ballinger, 1983).
20. Kant, *The Philosophy of Kant*, p. 476.
21. Conversely, a relaxation of East-West tensions is no short-term guarantee of a relaxation of repression within the USSR; there are enough domestic reasons for preserving the apparatus of repression. But in the long run, a détente that would deprive the Soviet system of its arguments about the external threat could lead to domestic changes, especially if it reinforces internal factors pushing in the same direction.
22. See Stephen Krasner (ed.), "International Regimes," *International Organization* 36, no. 2 (Spring 1982).
23. See Stanley Hoffmann, *Primay or World Order* (New York: McGraw Hill, 1978) and *Duties Beyond Borders* (New York: Syracuse University Press, 1982).
24. Robert Jervis, in Krasner, "International Regimes," p. 362.
25. Shklar, *Ordinary Vices*, p. 249.

19

On the Political Psychology of Peace and War: A Critique and an Agenda

What brings us together here is the conviction that politics—the task of defining the goals of a community, of choosing and pursuing the means to reach them, and of selecting the leaders—cannot be understood except by reference to the intentions of the actors, and to the perceptions that shape their acts.[1] The term *political psychology* is a pleonasm: not all psychology is about politics, thank goodness, but politics is wholly psychological. Even those of my colleagues who study political behavior through quantitative techniques or formal theory operate from assumptions (far too often implicit only) about the motives and goals of human behavior.

My subject is one particular branch of politics: the study of international relations—and, within that branch, the study of strategic and diplomatic affairs. It is a fascinating and frustrating subject, for two reasons at least. First, there seems to be something implacably constant about the logic of behavior of sovereign actors in the international state of nature. The differences in size, complexity, economic and social structure, and relations between the public and the private, which exist between, say, the Greek *polis* and a contemporary nation-state, are enormous (and they make nostalgic laments about past communal life quite irrelevant). But the student of present-day world politics who turns to Thucydides finds in his masterpiece, certainly not relief, but enlightment and shock: the empires and nations of today seem to be playing the same ballet; the music may be different, but the choreography hasn't changed. Second, our fate depends on the future of interestate relations. In the nuclear age, some states have the capacity to put an end to the show, and to much of civilization, for the first time in history.

The fact that the show has been playing for so long, through so many upheavals and holocausts from which mankind as a whole as always recovered, and above all the fact that the world remains organized in separate communities whose internal needs and passions are the dominant concerns of most citizens, explains why, so often, those citizens fail to worry enough about the implications and perils of the game of states, about the threats to peace and the risk of war. This is why they tend to leave these worries to experts, or to leaders elected or selected on quite other grounds than wisdom or skill in foreign affairs. On the other hand, the awareness of danger that cannot fail to come either with expertise or from reflections about the drift of the world explains why, in many countries, a large portion of the educated public, especially among intellectuals and professionals, and a smaller fraction of the citizenry have been sounding the alarm.

It is about that part of the alarmed public which consists of students of world politics that I want to talk—not about that segment of the public that reacts either with blind faith in the leadership's policy or with a ritualistic ethnocentric self-righteousness that justifies Erik Erikson's remarks about pseudo-speciation; nor about that unfortunately large body of experts that consists of policy scientists who serve, write for, or rationalize the decisions of the nations' leaders, because they share the goals and outlook of these leaders, see themselves as mere technicians, or—as in so many countries—are simply not allowed to question the leaders' assumptions. These two populations are part of our problem. But there is another part: a deep split among those of us who are professionally concerned with world politics, and are disturbed or anguished by politics-as-usual.

In a recent issue of *Political Psychology*,[2] Richard Smoke described two "universes of discourse" for the same topic—survival in the nuclear age and the era of U.S.-Soviet confrontation. He was talking about the antinuclear movement on one side and the "mainstream national security analysts" on the other. I am referring to the same division, but one even among those of us who are neither in charge nor advisers of official policy. Smoke labeled these two viewpoints the deterrence model and the abolitionist model, thus focusing on nuclear weapons. The focus is right, although perhaps too narrow. The labels are more questionable, for in the camp of what Smoke calls the deterrence model there are many critics of deterrence, aware of its past failures and multiple ambiguities, and in the other camp there are people who believe that nuclear weapons cannot be wiped out.

The split exists. It is not about values: the concern for survival, the anxiety about black-and-white thinking, cognitive closure, and deadly miscalculations, are the same in both groups. Nor is it necessarily about what each camp expects if politics continues as usual: those who appear shortsighted to the other group are often far from reassured about the outcome of the current contests of states. It is, above all, a split about *what is possible*, which is tied to a different reading of reality.

In order to simplify, I will use my own labels. I am aware of their limitations, but I wanted them to be as neutral as possible. I will refer to *traditionalists* and *radicals*. The two groups agree on the obvious: the existence of international anarchy, of a state of nature in which the actors pursue their separate goals without a common superior and without any broad consensus of values. In such a state, the resort to force is an ever-present possibility, and the actors spend much of their time preparing for, or against, this use, calculating the forces of potential or actual rivals; the common norms or procedures are weak and premanently imperiled. Thus, both groups begin with what Rousseau deplored: the absence of a "general unity of mankind," the division of mankind into separate units.

This is all, I think, that the two groups agree on. The traditionalists' reading of reality is often denounced, by the radicals, as complacent, or as a denial of reality, or even as resulting from an identification with those who cause the present dangers. I will not deny that some of the less sophisticated champions of what, in my branch of politial science, is called the realist school of international affairs often sound as if they believed that what is is fine and that this state of affairs could be well managed as long as the actors are rational and pursue moderate goals. But many traditionalists, even among those who accept the label of realism, have no illusions about rationality or the "rational actor" model of decision-making. They know that the very fragmentation of mankind breeds both the emotional distortions that students of prejudices, ideologies, national images, and national styles describe, and the cognitive distortions that the parochialism of perceptions, the uncertainty about the motives of other players or about the costs and benefits of alternative courses, the policy-maker's own need for consistency, the organizational pressures for continuity or loyalty, and the weight of past commitments or current domestic constraints inevitably entail. They know that the many contests among states, the states' desire to dominate or their determination not to be dominated, inject into their concerns considerations both about image and about power that twist their definition of needs, their selection of ends, their choice of means, in strange ways. They know that deterrence has often failed in the past, and that such fiascoes also are of the essence in a world of fragmented units and perceptions in conflict; for what is defensive to one power is offensive to the other, and each actor constantly has to choose between a move that could fail to deter because the rival will interpret it as a provocation and a policy that could fail to deter because the rival will interpret it as a sign of weakness and appeasement. And yet states, yesterday and today, still aim at deterring each other, not because, by necessity, any evidence of inferiority, any deficiency of power *must* lead to blackmail or attack—as several writers have pointed out, there are many factors of self-deterrence at work[3]—but because there is always a *risk* that weakness might tempt a rival or foe. To be prepared for the worst in a situation in which Gresham's law operates is a basic, unavoidable rule of thumb.

The traditionalists' approach to reality is thus neither uncritical nor Panglossian. Indeed, it could be called doubly tragic, because—like their Founding Father, Thucydides—they are fully aware of the errors and horrors that the actors unceasingly commit, *and* because they do not believe that the essence of world politics is susceptible to drastic and early change, barring disasters. In their eyes, easy, quick transcendence, a sudden mutation, is not at all possible. They do not usually rule out the emergence of identities wider than the current nation-states; but they note that, in the past, the widening of identity has been both slow and violent, and that, at present, the creation of a nation-state out of far narrower identities is still unfinished business in much of the world; today, in the states, there are more demands for narrower identities than for wider ones. Traditionalists do not deny that states might learn new modes or cooperation to cope with common needs and fears, and gradually tame violence in their relations; they are aware of the forces and processes that operate across borders, reduce the autonomy of the states, and sometimes create actors other than the states. But they are not convinced that transnational agents, be they multinational corporations or religious movements, always contribute to peace, or that transnational forces are more integrative than disruptive. They remain skeptical about the states' willingness to give up fully either sovereignty, however leaky, or arms, however suicidal, and they remain aware of the enormous potential for interstate violence that lies in the countless powder kegs of domestic strife.

Above all, they look at international politics as a field with rules of its own, derived from the very nature of the international milieu. Any reasoning by analogy—for instance, from the domestic politics of well-integrated nations—is thus seen by them as a mistake (they are, on the whole, very dubious about driving "lessons" for state behavior from labor mediation). They realize that violence, which it is the function of the state to curb within its borders, is both a result and a perpetuator of international anarchy; but they also realize that neither of the two techniques that have produced wider identities (but never an end to war) in history—conquest and voluntary association—is likely to eliminate anarchy and violence in the near future. Consequently, what is on their agenda is, on the one hand, a better, deeper, broader theoretical understanding of the logic of interstate relations, of the different political, sociological, psychological factors that affect it in practice, of the specialized grammars of diplomacy, war, trade, etc.; and, on the other hand, a (modest, by necessity) agenda of reforms, aimed at introducing as much moderation, as many opportunities for cooperation and the pooling of sovereignties, as much taming of the beast, as the structure and the logic allow.

When the traditionalists look at the world, they see nuclear weapons, of course. Their failure to march for abolition results neither from love of the bomb (what a silly idea!), nor from the conviction that nuclear deterrence will always be successful, nor from a denial of the peril. It comes from their conviction that the very nature of international reality rules it out. When they look at the world, they see the contest between Washington and Moscow, of course; and they do not usually agree among themselves either about Soviet intentions, behavior, and achievements, or about U.S. actions and effects, or about the best way of dealing with the contest. But they believe that this contest, too, cannot be transcended, both because it is of the very essence of international politics that the two biggest actors must be rivals, that the growth of the power of one must cause fear in the other, that each one shall see the other as malignant, itself as benign;

and also because *these* two actors have (objectively, as *Pravda* would say) widely conflicting interests and worldviews.

It seems to me (I am a traditionalist, in case you didn't know it) that the radicals' approach differs from what precedes in three ways. I will try—knowing that many, perhaps most of you, are not traditionalists—to be as fair as possible, but it is clearly a traditionalist's view of the radicals that I will offer, along with an explanation of why my group takes issue with their approach. Let me make one thing perfectly clear, as someone used to say: not all radicals are psychologists, social psychologists, psychoanalysts, or psychiatrists. Some of these are to be found wandering or toiling among the traditionalists, and there are a number of political scientists and jurists among the radicals. What I will say about them may be more true of some than of others, but I am concerned here with ideal-types rather than with a complete coverage of all the nuances.

First, the radicals' impulse is *therapeutic*, whereas that of the traditionalists is *analytic*. Insofar as the latter are concerned with "cures," interested in suggesting norms for behavior that would make the international "state of war" less lethal, they derive these prescriptions from their sense of the limits of the possible; they insist that the steps to be taken remain, so to speak, within the boundaries of the stage on which the ballet is performed. The radicals—even when they agree with the description of the stage offered by the traditionalists—begin with a critique and rejection of the whole show. The members of one side take the show as a given, even as they deplore its flaws and wish for revisions. The members of the other side is so sensitive to cacophony, so worried about the potential for disaster, that they denounce not only the players but also those who seem—to them—largely satisfied with analysis and resigned to the fundamental status quo.

This is why I talked about a different reading of reality. One group, looking at the show, concludes that it is utopian to wish it away, or to suggest cures whose adoption cannot be imagined unless it were already fundamentally different from what it is now and has been for ages. The other group, looking at the new weapons on the stage and remembering the show's past breakdowns, argues that the only way of preventing the fire next time is to move to a totally new stage, and to change the play and the actors.

As I said already, not all the traditionalists promise world peace, nor do all the radicals believe in the mathematical certainty of nuclear war and winter. But they are convinced that even a small risk of global calamity requires a drastic transformation, whereas the others are convinced that the very impossibility of a mutation *before* disaster limits the scope and indeed the types of measures that can realistically be taken to avoid it. Radical impatience with what is (wrongly) often interpreted as a professional commitment of traditional analysts to the perpetuation of the current state of their field—as a failure on their part, as well as on the part of statesmen, to be shaken, like Ionesco's characters, by the sudden irruption of rhinoceroses in our midst—is matched by traditionalist annoyance at what is often perceived as mere rhetoric of indignation, denunciation, and exorcism, fist-shaking at unwelcome facts and unfair name-calling addressed to actors who, caught in a game they did not invent, do, at best, what they can to keep it from blowing up and, more usually, at least what they have been selected for.

This brings us to a second difference. The radicals, who tend (often correctly) to perceive the policy scientists' stance as a *trahison des clercs*, write and behave as if they were above the fray, seeing through the rationalizations statesmen endlessly provide and the sterotypes in which citizens cloak their fears, frustrations, and aggressions. At the same time, they can't help but belong to different communities: while calling for a global identity, they remain, say, Americans or British, or Indians, or Israelis. Their recommendations are usually addressed to, or hurled at, their own governments, or (in the case of many intellectuals from less powerful countries who deal with the global cold war) at the superpowers. The underlying assumption, once again, is that the seriousness of the peril should push their own national government, or, in the latter case, the great powers' leaders, into adopting the drastic measures needed for salvation. The traditionalists, even when, in their own work, they try scrupulously to transcend national prejudices and to seek scientific truth, believe that it is unrealistic to expect *statesmen* to stand above the fray: by definition, the statesmen are there to worry not only about planetary survival but—first of all—about national survival and safety. To be sure, they ought to be able to see how certain policies, aimed at enhancing security, actually increase insecurity all around. But there are sharp limits to how far they can go in their mutual empathy or in their acts (unlike intellectuals in their advice), as long as the states' antagonisms persist, as long as uncertainty about each other's intentions prevails, and as long as there is reason to fear that one side's wise restraint or unilateral moves toward "sanity" will be met, not by the rival's similar restraint or moves, but either by swift or skillful political or military exploitation of the opportunity created for unilateral gain, or by a formidable domestic backlash if national self-restraint appears to result in external losses, humiliations, or perceptions of weakness.

There is little point in saying that the state of affairs that imposes such limits is "anachronistic" or "unrational." To traditionalists, the radicals' stance—condemnation from the top of Mount Olympus—can only impede one's understanding of the limits and possibilities of reform. To be sure, the fragmentation of mankind is a formidable obstacle to the solution of many problems that cannot be handled well in a national framework, and a deadly peril insofar as the use of force, the very distinctive feature of world politics, now entails the risk of nuclear war. But one can hardly describe as anachronistic a phenomenon—the assertion of national identity—that, to the bulk of mankind, appears not only as a necessity but as a positive good, since humanity's fragmentation results from the very aspiration to self-determination. Many people have only recently emerged from foreign mastery, and have reason to fear that the alternative to national self-mastery is not a world government of assured fairness and efficiency but one of alien domination.

As for "unrationality," the drama lies in the contrast between the rationality of the whole, which scholars are concerned about—the greatest good of the greatest number, in utilitarian terms—and the rationality or greatest good of the part, which is what statesmen worry about and are responsible for. What the radicals denounce as irrational and irresponsible from the viewpoint of mankind is what Weber called the statesman's ethic of responsibility. What keeps ordinary "competitive conflict processes"[4]—the very stuff of society—from becoming "unrational" or destructive is precisely what the nature of world politics excludes: the restraint of the partners either because of the ties of affection or responsibility that mitigate the conflict, or because of the existence of an outsider—marriage counselor, arbitrator, judge, police officer, or legislator—capable of inducing or imposing restraints.

Here we come to a third point of difference. The very absence of such safeguards of rationality, the obvious discrepancy between what each part intends, and what it (and the whole world) ends with, the crudeness of some of the psychological mechanisms at work in international affairs—as one can see from the statements of leaders, or from the media, or from inflamed publics—have led many radicals, especially among those whose training or profession is in psychoanalysis or mental health, to treat the age-old contests of states in terms not of the psychology of politics but of individual psychology and pathology. There are two manifestations of this. One is the tendency to look at nations or states as individuals writ large, stuck at an early stage of development (similarly, John Mack in a recent paper talked of political ideologies as carrying "forward the dichotomized structures of childhood").[5] One of my predecessors has written about "the correspondence between development of the individual self and that of the group or nation" and concluded "that intergroup or international conflict contains the basic elements of the conflict each individual experiences psychologically."[6] Robert Holt, from the viewpoint of cognitive psychology, found "the largest part of the American public" to be immature, in a "phase of development below the Conscientious."[7] The second related aspect is the tendency to look at the notions that statesmen or publics have of "the enemy," not only as residues of childhood or adolescent phases of development but as images that express "disavowed aspects of the self,"[8] reveal truths about our own fears and hatreds, and amount to masks *we* put on the "enemy" because of our own psychological needs.

Here is where the clash between traditionalists and radicals is strongest. Traditionalists do not accept a view of group life derived from the study of individual development or family relations, or a view of modern society derived from the simplistic Freudian model of regressed followers identifying with a leader. They don't see in ideologies just irrational constructs but often rationally selected maps allowing individuals to cope with reality. They don't see national identification as pathological, as an appeal to the people's baser instincts, more aggressive impulses, or unsophisticated mental defenses; it is, as Jean-Jacques Rousseau so well understood, the competiton of sovereign states that frequently pushes people from "sane" patriotism to "insane" nationalism (Rousseau's way of preventing the former from veering into the latter was, to say the least, impractical: to remain poor in isolation). Nor do they see anything "primitive" in the nation's concern for survival: it is a moral and structural requirement.

Traditionalists also believe that the "intrapsychic" approach distorts reality. Enemies are not mere projections of negative identities; they are often quite real. To be sure, the Nazis' view of the Jews fit the metaphor of the mask put on the enemy for one's own needs. But were, in return, those Jews who understood what enemies they had in the Nazis doing the same? Is the Soviet domination of Eastern Europe, is the Soviet regime's treatment of dissidents, was the Gulag merely a convenient projection of our intrapsychic battles? Clichés such as the one about how our enemy "understands only force" may tell us a great deal about ourselves; but sometimes they contain half-truths about the enemy and not just revelations about us. Our fears flow not only from our private fantasies but also from concrete realities and from the fantasies generated by the international state of nature.

In other words, the psychology of politics that traditionalists deem adequate is derived not from theories of psychic development and health but from the logic of the international milieu, which breeds the kind of vocabulary found in the historians and theorists of the state of nature: fear and power, pride and honor, survival and security, self-interest and reputation, distrust and misunderstanding, commitment and credibility. It is also derived from the social psychology of small or large groups, which resorts to the standard psychological vocabulary that describes mental mechanisms or maneuvers and cognitive processes: denial, projection, guilt, repression, closure, rigidity, and so on. But the use of this vocabulary does not imply that a group whose style of politics is paranoid is therefore composed of people who, as private individuals, are paranoid. Nor does it relieve us of the duty to look at the objective reasons and functions of these mental moves, and of the duty to make explicit our assumptions about what constitutes a "healthy," wise, or proper social process.

Altogether, traditionalists find the mental health approach to world affairs unhelpful. Decisions about war and peace are usually taken by small groups of people; the temptation of analyzing their behavior either, literally, in terms of their personalities or, metaphorically, in terms borrowed from the study of human development, rather than in terms of group dynamics or principles of international politics, is understandable. But it is misleading. What is pathological in couples, or in a well-ordered community, is, alas, frequent, indeed normal, among states, or in a troubled state. What is malignant or crazy is usually not the actors or the social process in which they are engaged; it is the possible results. The grammar of motives that the mental health approach brands as primitive or immature is actually rational *for the actors*. Traditionalists fear that this particular approach leads to the substitution of labels for explanations, to bad analysis and fanciful prescriptions. Bad analysis: the tendency to see in group coherence a regressive response to a threat, whereas it is often a rational response to the "existential" threats entailed by the very nature of the international milieu; or the tendency to see in the effacement or minimization of individual differences in a group a release of unconscious instincts rather than a phenomenon that can either be perfectly adaptive—in response to stress or threats—or can result from governmental manipulation or originate in the code of conduct inculcated by the educational system, and so forth; or the habit of comparing the state, or modern society, with the Church or the army, and to analyze human relations in these institutions in ways that stress the libidinal more than the cognitive and superego factors, or equate libidinal bonds and the desire for a leader; or the view that enemies are above all products of mental fantasies rather than concomitants of social strife at every level; or the view that the contest with the rival fulfills internal needs, which may be true, but requires careful examination of the nature of these needs (psychological? bureaucratic? economic?), obscures the objective reasons of the contest, and risks confusing cause and function.

Indeed, such analysis is particularly misleading in dealing with the present scene. The radicals are so (justifiably) concerned with the nuclear peril that the traditional ways in which statesmen and publics behave seem to vindiciate the pathological approach. But this obsession, in turn, incites radicals to overlook the fundamental ambiguity of contemporary world politics. On the one hand, there is a nuclear revolution—the capacity for total destruction. On the other hand, many states, without nuclear weapons, find that the use of force remains rational (in terms of a rationality of means) and beneficial at home or abroad—ask the Vietnamese, or the Egyptians after October 1973, or Mrs. Thatcher after the Falklands, or Ronald Reagan after Grenada. The superpowers themselves, whose contest has not been abolished by the nuclear revolution (it is the stakes, the costs of failure that have, of course, been transformed), find that much of their rivalry can be conducted in traditional ways—including limited uses of force—below the level of nuclear alarm. They also find that nuclear weapons, while unusable rationally perhaps, can usefully strengthen the very process that has been so faulty in the pre-nuclear ages: deterrence (this is one of the reasons for nuclear proliferation). The pathological approach interprets deterrence as expressing the deterrer's belief that his country is good and the enemy's is bad. This interpretation is often correct, but it need not be; deterrence can also reflect the conviction that one's country has interests that are not mere figments of the imagination, interests that need to be protected both because of the material costs of losing them and because of the values embedded in them. As for war planning, it is not a case of "psychological denial of unwelcome reality"[9] but a—perhaps futile, perhaps dangerous—necessity in a world where deterrence may once more fail.

The prescriptions that result from the radicals' psychological approach also run into traditionalist objections. Even if one accepts the metaphors of collective disease or pathology, one must understand that the "cure" can be provided only by politics. All too often, the radicals' cures consist of perfectly sensible recommendations for lowering tensions, but they fail to tell us how to carry out those recommendations: they tell us only how much better the world would be if only "such rules could be established."[10] Sometimes, they express generous aspirations—for common or mutual security—without much awareness of the obstacles that conflicting interests, fears about allies or clients, and the nature of the weapons themselves continue to erect. Sometimes, they, too, neglect the ambiguity of life in a nuclear world: the much-lamented redundancy of weapons, a calamity if nuclear deterrence fails, can also be a cushion against failure.

Finally, many of the remedies offered are based on an admirable liberal model of personality and politics: the ideal of the mature, well-adjusted, open-minded person (produced by liberal education and healthy family relations) transposed on the political level and thus accompanied by the triumph of democracy in the community as well as by the elimination of militarism and the spread of functional cooperation abroad. But three obstacles remain unconquered. First, a major part of the world rejects this ideal and keeps itself closed to it (many of the radicals seem to deny it, or to ignore it, or to believe that it doesn't matter). Second, the record shows that real democracies, in their behavior toward nondemocratic or less "advanced" societies, do not conform to the happy model (think of the United States in Central America). Third, the task of reform, both of the publics and of the statesmen, through consciousness raising and education is hopelessly huge, incapable of being pursued equally in all the important states, and, indeed, too slow if one accepts the idea of a mortal nuclear peril.

These, then, are the dimensions of a split that should not be minimized or denied.

II

Dialogues of the deaf risk becoming battles of the equally self-righteous. The exasperation of each group with the other has already contributed to the divisions and confusions of the peace movement in this country. What is at stake in this quarrel is more than a "narcissism of small differences" or a rivalry of scientific imperialisms: this is precisely why I have spent so much time on it. But there is a danger: that of forgetting what the two groups have in common, and what separates them from all those who consider the structure and logic of world politics to be not only hard to transcend but reasonably safe and desirable as well. On two conditions, the groups I have described could cooperate fruitfully and extensively. What I shall do now is to outline, sketchily, an agenda for cooperation.

The first of the two conditions is that those traditionalists who, in their work, have stressed what one could call "hard" factors, such as power and interests (and who therefore tend to be more impressed by the monotonous recurrence of the same steps on the stage, because they concentrate on the logic of behavior of competing units), show themselves more willing to move into the jungle of perceptions, images, and distortions that provide both for the many variations on the constant themes and for the multiple quirks of a "logic" that forces the actors to engage in apparently rational calculations yet rarely saves them from huge errors and disastrous surprises. Second, the radicals should accept the validity of some of the criticisms I have presented—especially the idea that one must enter into that very logic (however much one disapproves its effects)—and understand both its rules and the hold it has on statesmen and on citizens. Indeed, one must accept, in Raymond Aron's terms, the notion that "institutional tensions show in individual tensions, but we cannot diagnose and define the former by studying the latter."[11] One must even accept the notion that what would be considered pathological in an individual is often perfectly normal in society and politics. Let us turn to the common agenda.

There is nothing original about it. Some of it has already been undertaken, both by political scientists interested in what actually goes on in the minds of decision-makers and by social psychologists concerned either with small groups that make political decisions or with the collective beliefs, attitudes, and behavior of political communities—scholars such as Alex George, Robert Jervis, Ned Lebow, Irving Janis, and Herbert Kelman. It is an agenda both for research and for prescriptions, and it is based on three major assumptions.

The first is the need for a more sophisticated model of political community. There is an almost infinite number of ways in which leaders and followers relate to each other, and in which what Montesquieu called *corps intermédiaires* (organized groups) complicate the picture. The rather crude model Freud derived from Gustave Le Bon may approximate reality in some cases of extreme anomie and distress, but it accounts neither for the modern bureaucratized polity (as Philip Rieff has pointed out), nor for the ego functions often served by the state, nor for the way in which the state can strengthen rather than undermine the citizens' superegos, nor for the criss-crossing of loyalties whenever groups are allowed to form and to promote their interests freely. How much the leaders can twist and shape the minds of the followers depends on the regime, the laws, the mores, and the moments. Even societies in distress do not all behave in the same way; the outcome depends on national patterns of ideas and behavior, and also on what kind of "heroic leadership" is available for guidance—or for surrender: an F.D.R. or a Hitler, a de Gaulle or a Mao.

Next, despite the inevitably competitive character of international politics, despite the failure of the liberal and social-democratic dream of a harmonious coexistence of nation-states under law and through trade, conflict, the stuff of social life, need not be as violent and destructive as it often is when it breaks out in a structure of anarchy, where autonomous actors are able to resort to force. This suggests both a warning and a goal. On the one hand, we cannot ask *now* that statesmen and publics behave *as if* that structure had been discarded, *as if* a global society comparable to a well-functioning polity had already been established; nor should we think that such a society will necessarily be built on the model of the state as we know it. "World government," should it ever come, would be very different, more differentiated, diffuse, and decentralized, than the governments of nations. On the other hand, we ought to study the possibility of acts and policies that, from within the present anarchic system, nevertheless depart from "politics as usual" and move toward a different kind of international system. It would still be fragmented and conflictual, no doubt, but with far stricter limits on the use of force and far greater opportunities for cooperative arrangements in all the realms (security included) in which unilateral action is insufficient or actually self-defeating. I have in mind a system in which the priority that so many states, old or new, want to give to their internal economic and social development would be rewarded, and in which quests for aggrandizement or diversion through violent conflict beyond one's borders would be firmly and collectively resisted.

Finally, when it comes to the central issues of today, even though the U.S.-Soviet conflict has extraordinarily deep roots and is unlikely to melt away, even though existential deterrence is a fact of life that no amount of denunciation will wipe out, we must see to it that the cold war between Washington and Moscow continues to stay cold. This is unlikely, however—unless areas of cooperation are found and the nuclear arms race is controlled. Moreover, we must never forget that deterrence is not a Procrustean (albeit hard) bed. Its stability is constantly challenged by technology; its ability to prevent war thanks to the nuclear revolution is constantly put in doubt by the attempts both superpowers make to find ways of actually using nuclear weapons should deterrence fail; its credibility is shaken by the theological disputes about what kinds of capabilities deter most, and about what kinds of threats deterrence can effectively protect one from. (Nuclear threats only? Against oneself only or also against allies?)

What sort of research on peace and war in the past (distant and present) do these assumptions suggest? I will make five recommendations. First, insofar as one of the causes of war in the modern world (since the French Revolution) has been the bursting of the reservoir of *collective emotions and passions*, we need to do more work to find out to what extent and when such feelings and images constitute mere restraints on the freedom of action of governments; to what extent and when they actually push statesmen in directions states might otherwise not have taken; to what extent and when certain beliefs and attitudes (I am thinking of the attitudes of so many people in the United States toward Communism and toward the peoples of Central America) give a green light, if not a *carte blanche*, to the government; and to what extent and when they are little more than a stagnant, often stinking pool that can be stirred up either by the media or by interest groups or by political parties or by the governments for their own purposes. There are vast amounts of data, for all the wars and major crises leading to wars of the last hundred fifty years. My own research, both about the 1930s and about contemporary world politics, suggests that the public at large, and sometimes the decision-makers themselves, are often extraordinarily susceptible to sudden crystallizations of fears, prejudices, and interpretations produced by small but influential groups whose members come together from many circles: politics, business, the media, the intelligentsia, and so on. And these crystallizations then guide, or misguide, both the public and the government, because they seem to offer a convincing explanation of a bewildering world as well as a convenient road map.

This research also shows that the more the public is torn between conflicting fears, the more it tries to ignore and deny the lesser fear, in order to conjure the bigger one and thus achieve a fragile, fallacious cognitive and emotional consistency. Indeed, insofar as collective images and prejudices are concerned, or episodes in which large numbers of people display those symptoms of regression, of scapegoating, or of massive denial of reality (which can be catastrophic in their effects) we need more understanding—from social psychologists—of the mental mechanisms at work. (Do we really know how individuals who are dispersed, who live in different places and groups, produce a sort of collective mind, mood, and pattern of conduct that may be quite independent of, and often contrary to, their character and behavior as individuals?) We also need, from other social scientists, to find out more about the economic and social factors, the cultural traditions, the historical marks, that explain when and why such phenomena occur, and why certain ideological choices appear, to those who make these choices, to be answers not only to the needs of their personality but to their experience in society as well. Again, Europe in the 1930s but also the Arab-Israeli conflict, or the first cold war, provide endless material.

Second, the work that has already been undertaken about the behavior of small *groups of decision-makers* faced with issues of war and peace needs to be expanded. Thanks to the research of several of the authors I have named, we begin to have a sort of repertory of the mental and organizational mistakes most commonly found—information processed according to misleading postulates, overvaluation of past successes, excessive investments in established policies, exaggeration of the costs of alternatives, inability to empathize with foreign decision-making groups or to understand their concerns, a stake in beliefs that justify the existence or importance of one's agency, and so forth. But the many case studies we now have, most of which focus on disasters, often reach contradictory conclusions. For instance, we find cases in which "groupthink"[12]—a form of concurrence and closure under stress in which loyalty to the leader or to the organization plays a major role (but so does the desire for effectiveness)—seemed to be an important factor of failure. However, we also find cases in which fiasco resulted from the divisions of the decision-making groups, from the outside pressures that weighed on them, or from their inability to control or discipline "deviants" or dissidents.[13] Clearly, we need to know more about the circumstances in which it is unanimity that is dangerous, and those in which it is discord; and we have to be more precise and discriminating in our concept of decision-making "groups": the structures and the degrees of intensity and of openness vary considerably. We have to be more systematic about the effects of failure; sometimes, they force statesmen into a corrective relaxation of the tensions that had produced the crisis (Richard N. Lebow discusses Fashoda and the Cuban missile crisis); sometimes, however, they have exactly the opposite result—a determination to be tougher the next time. Inded, the gradual erosion of restraints through repeated crises that, while "managed," leave one or even both sides feeling cheated is one of the major causes of ultimate disasters.

We should not neglect the importance of the "map of the world"— derived from past experiences, education, expectations, images of the collective self and of others—that is often common to decision-makers of very different backgrounds and personalities (and hence helps provide "groupthink"), as in the United States' Vietnam drama, or even common to actors otherwise divided over tactical and bureaucratic issues (as in the Reagan administration, or among the German leadership in July 1914). Moreover, we need to go beyond the small circle of decision-makers and look at the way in which their decisions are either institutionalized and turned into policies that bureaucratic momentum preserves long after any justification, or else subtly undermined or neutralized by bureaucratic independence or resistance. Here, organizational strategies, group dynamics, and the impact of personality come together.

Third, some shoddy books have given "psychohistory" a bad reputation. However, insofar as decisions on peace and war are made by leaders who experience and interpret the logic of world politics in different ways, we need more studies on the *psychology of leadership*—as long as they do not conform too slavishly to the Lasswellian psychopathological approach. At least they should understand that even in cases of displacement of private frustrations on public objects, what matters is what the leader does with what may be pathological in him, and especially with his aggression, as well as the ways in which, in his public performance, his character fits, filters, and is reshaped by the demands of the role—how it is, so to speak, harnessed, constrained, or, on the contrary, let loose by the nature of the country's institutional system. In particular, how do all these factors interact in foreign policy crises? Also needed, of course, is an understanding of the many variables that intervene between character and policy decisions on war and peace. Many wars have occurred because the leaders were far too ordinary or mediocre (1914), others because one dangerously charismatic leader managed to provoke a conflagration (1939). Average leaders caught in the logic of their role, or subjected to too many pressures, can make fatal mistakes (as the appeasers); partly psychopathic leaders can be extremely cautious abroad (Stalin) or use their talents, for a while, in brilliantly instrumental ways (Hitler 1933–1939).

Fourth, after this rather grim series of invitations to look at wreckage, let us turn to the historical record in more encouraging directions. We need to examine more systematically not only the way in which crises have been managed or mismanaged in the past but, on the one hand, the whole art of *crisis avoidance and prevention*: why and how some tensions never burst into crises and some conflicts were defused or remained moderate despite (or perhaps, because of) expectations of trouble and without leaving deep scars on the international system. To what extent were such successes due to military deterrence, and to what extent were other factors—calculations of interests, or moral restraints—decisive? On the other hand, we also need to study all the cases of successful *conflict resolution* in order to evaluate both the contributions, positive and negative, made by negotiated or imposed settlements and the role played by other factors, psychological and political.

Fifth, what can we learn from the record of past and contemporary cooperation? We need to study what Karl Deutsch and his associates once called "*security communities*,"[14] the oases of peace and cooperation in the desert of conflict and competition: What has made such zones possible, under what conditions have they lasted, what has it taken for former enemies to overcome their hostility and become associates? (Has it always been the combination of exhaustion and emergence of a greater threat that lies behind Franco-German reconciliation?) In a comparable vein, the research launched in recent years by teams of political scientists and political economists about what Robert Keohane and Joseph Nye have called *international regimes*; the conditions in which such regimes can be established, surmount crises, or collapse; and the reasons why some last and others don't—all of these issues are of considerable importance to political psychology. For we find in this context leaders and (frequently transnational) groups at work, often—for once!—in highly creative ways. In some cases, we also find here the expectations, calculations, and demands of larger groups—farmers, bankers, businessmen people, fishermen, sailors, and aviators—focussing on the benefits (or costs) of such regimes. Thus, they provide a learning experience in new forms and frameworks of political behavior.

All of these suggestions aim at using the tools, theories, and insights of a variety of disciplines in order to dredge the huge pond that lies in between the very simple, stark landscape described by the theory of interstate behavior—the logic of strategic-diplomatic conduct—and the jungle of past and present international and national events. This logic, as I have stated above, tells us that conflicting units in search of "rational" policies will make mistakes because of misperceptions, miscalculations, and the mischief of uncertainty. It does not tell us how each unit will, at any moment, interpret what is "rational" for it, nor what those distortions and gropings in the dark will be. Is there anything the two groups of political psychologists could also do in order to ensure that the steps of the actors will, in the future, be more enlightened, keep the world safe from destruction, and move toward the kind of world society with minimal interstate violence that I have alluded to?

As intellectuals and as citizens, we all can, of course, push for the causes that we hold essential and warn, protest, petition, pressure against those we deem evil. Since we are undoubtedly divided, politically as well as methodologically, there might seem little point in offering a program for action: it could add one more split to the Society [ISPP]! But I have been talking about those students of world affairs who *are* alarmed by current trends; and I think it is possible for an association of scholars and professionals to engage, in their daily work, in activities—writings, lectures, all the forms of public education—that could help preserve peace, go beyond that fragile and ominous accumulation of deadly weapons called deterrent (which, as the American Catholic Bishops have said, is only conditionally acceptable as a lesser evil), and inch us toward a safer world. Let me suggest, again, five directions.

One is a matter of action and research. At a time of growing ethnocentrism and parochialism in this country, when the public and much of the political class oscillates between the conviction that we know what is good for others and the desire to be left alone by them, it is essential for us to broaden our membership abroad and to multiply *scientific contacts and cooperative projects* with colleagues from other countries. We need candor, of course; too often, for instance, meetings of American independent scholars or professionals with their not-so-independent Soviet counterparts turn either into ritualized, generalized proclamations of common interests and denunciations of obstacles to peace and friendship or into traps or encounters between masochists and sadists—when only moves or mistakes of Western governments are described as dangerous, and nobody mentions the massive contribution Moscow has often made to international tensions or Western distrust. Only candor, indeed, will make such exchanges useful: for the exchanges will then provide Soviet experts who are, I repeat, not purely private citizens, with valuable insights into our ways of looking at common problems. And we need these contacts in order to understand, and then to spread our understanding of, the images, prejudices, perceptions, hopes, and fears of representatives of foreign cultures. Whenever we can foster a project that would entail the cooperation of people from nations in conflict, Americans and Russians, Israelis and Palestinians, South Africans and Africans from the frontline states, we have a chance, however small, of being useful.

My second and third suggestions are also for research and action. They take us back to this country. My second suggestion concerns our contest with Moscow. Despite all the tons of literature already produced (I have contributed to it myself) there is no adequate and convincing study of the sum of obstacles: mental as well as institutional, economic and political (and so on), that reduce the ability of any U.S. administration to go as far in the direction of unilateral restraint, or tacit understandings for arms control, as the nature of the U.S.-Soviet contest and the need to preserve essential American interests abroad would actually permit, to settle on and stick to a narrower definition of these interests (or to a more sensible interpretation of the "Soviet threat"), and to pursue toward Moscow the mix of competition and cooperation that seems prudent and desirable. Recent studies on the failure of détente in the 70s are a useful beginning, but no more; here, one needs the concerted efforts of political scientists, social psychologists, economists, sociologists, and historians of *mentalités* capable of helping us understand the formation of American beliefs and attitudes toward the use of force, or toward radical social revolutions.

We ought to pursue in particular the task that has been brilliantly undertaken by a number of scholars—political scientists such as Seweryn Bialer, Marshal Shulman, Robert Legvold, and Alexander Dallin, and psychologists such as Ralph White—about *American perceptions and misperceptions of the Soviet Union*, in order to understand the origins of these beliefs and attitudes, to evaluate the extent to which they are rational reactions to Soviet conduct, and to ascertain the degree to which they are distortions—i.e., expressions of American prejudices and insecurities. It would be important to report on and to combat our misperceptions, while remembering that comparable work about Soviet misperceptions of the United States is unlikely to be undertaken in the USSR. Indeed, it would be important for the American public and decision-makers to know more about those Soviet views, in order for us, as a nation, to avoid feeding and reinforcing the Soviets' own anxieties and their own tendencies toward black-and-white thinking. Of course, a better understanding of mutual feelings is not likely to eliminate conflict: many of the respective perceptions are based on fact or spring from strongly held values. But few things are more striking, in the U.S.-Soviet relationship, than the failure of each side to evaluate and to take into account the psychological effect of its moves, or statements, on the other. What I suggest here might help our statesmen at least become more aware both of the impact of their own behavior and of some of the reasons for that of the Soviets.

My third suggestion concerns *nuclear weapons*, again. Changes in technology and the tense U.S.-Soviet rivalry in recent years are rapidly making the prospects for significant arms control more hopeless. We need to do what the Bishops did—acquire, if we don't have it already, the technical and military expertise necessary to make informed suggestions about and generate public pressure for the kinds of measures (unilateral acts, tacit deals, and explicit agreements) that would make the inevitably nuclear world more livable. They ought altogether to shore up crisis stability, reduce the number of conflict situations in which a bad turn of events might incite a party to initiate the use of nuclear weapons in the hope that escalation will be prevented or controllable, keep the nuclear arsenals verifiable, and gradually and drastically reduce them, starting with the elimination of the most destabilizing systems. Although many of my radical, or abolitionist, colleagues will find such measures insufficient or flawed, I recommend the comprehensive list of do's and don'ts recently compiled by my Harvard colleagues in *Hawks, Doves and Owls*. Their "agenda for avoiding nuclear war," insofar as it stresses the most likely peril: war coming out of miscalculations, of mismanaged crises, of "loss of control and nonrational factors,"[15] exactly fits my concern, whatever minor disagreements I may have on certain points.

Fourth, an item for creative reflection: What kinds of *international or regional regimes* are conceivable *in the realm of security*—a domain in which past mechanisms of restraint (such as the balance of power) are either not relevant to or not sufficiently effective for our needs, and never fully amounted to what we now call regimes? Under what political conditions could they be set up? What favorable balance of advantages and restrictions would be likely to attract states, especially states in conflict, to such innovations? How far could one go in separating the establishment of mutual controls and limitations on arms from the solution of underlying disputes? How much expansion and development of international institutions and safeguards would be required? Needless to say, such research would have to be done area by area (preferably, again, with the participation of experts from each area); indeed, measures such as demilitarized or denuclearized zones that make sense in one part of the world make much less sense in others.

Finally, another item—for reflection, above all, but also, ultimately, for action: What are the qualities that citizens of free countries would want in their *leaders*, who will have to deal with international conflicts in a nuclear world? George Ball's lament[16] about resistance to complexity suggests one major missing element in U.S. leadership. The public's desire for both strength and peace sets the outer limits within which U.S. leaders can move. But inside those limits, there are many possibilities; and recent experiences have mainly shown us what ought to be avoided. Heroism and crookedness are equally dangerous, albeit for different reasons; so is ignorance of the outside world, which risks breeding delusions about the righteousness of our course and a simplistic projection of our past achievements. Mere managerial skills, or the gift for public relations and spectacle, are clearly not enough. In the United States and elsewhere, our schools of public service train their students for expertise and for administrative cleverness. What they should be more concerned with is character and insight—a sense of the needs of people more than a mastery of the techniques of public policy; a grasp of the traditions, ambitions, and dreams of foreign leaders; a mix of responsibility, imagination, and honesty; a balance between the ability to compromise and a steadfast defense of essential principles. What can be done—in complex mobile and acquisitive societies where the notion and lure of a career prevail over old values of service—to identify, nurture, encourage, and reward those who have the necessary qualities? We have tended to let established patterns of selection produce whatever they can, however faulty these structures and procedures may have become. They certainly have become so in the United States, where, as a result, we are all too often left at the mercy of money, blind ambition, or chance. Neither for the solution of our domestic problems nor for the sake of peace can we afford to be so indifferent, or so resigned, to what ultimately determines our fate.

Notes

1. This essay constitutes the text of a presidential address given at the International Society of Political Psychology (Washington, June 20, 1985).

2. Richard Smoke, "The 'Peace' of Deterrence and the 'Peace' of the Antinuclear War Movement," *Political Psychology* 5, no. 4 (December 1984), pp. 741–748.

3. See, most recently, Richard Ned Lebow, "Windows of Opportunity: Do States Jump Through Them?" *International Security* 9, no. 1 (Summer 1984), pp. 147–186.

4. See Morton Deutsch, "The Prevention of World War III: A psychological perspective," *Political Psychology* 4, no. 1 (March 1983), p. 6.

5. John Mack, "Toward a Collective Psychopathology of the Nuclear Arms Competition," *Political Psychology* 6, no. 2 (June 1985), p. 307.

6. Vamil D. Volkan, "The Need to Have Enemies and Allies: A Developmental Approach," *Political Psychology* 6, no. 2 (June 1985), p. 221.

7. Robert Holt, "Can Psychology Meet Einstein's Challenge?" *Political Psychology* 5, no. 2 (June 1984), p. 222.

8. Howard F. Stein, "Psychological Complementarity in Soviet-American relations," *Political Psychology* 6, no. 2 (June 1985), p. 257.

9. Joseph V. Montville, "Introduction," *Political Psychology* 6, no. 2 (June 1985), p. 211.

10. Deutsch, "The Prevention of World War III," p. 26.

11. Raymond Aron, as quoted in International Sociological Association, *The Nature of Conflict* (New York: UNESCO, 1957), p. 178.

12. See Irving L. Janis, *Groupthink* (Boston: Houghton Mifflin, 1982).

13. Cf. Richard Ned Lebow, *Between Peace and War* (Baltimore: Johns Hopkins University Press, 1981).

14. Karl Deutsch, *Political Community and the North Atlantic Area* (Princeton, N.J.: Princeton University Press, 1957).

15. Graham Allison, Albert Carnesale, and Joseph Nye, *Hawks, Doves and Owls* (New York: Norton, 1985), p. 210.

16. In a speech prepared for delivery at the June 1985 International Studies of Political Science (ISPP) convention.

PART FIVE

Conclusion

20

The Sound and the Fury: The Social Scientist Versus War in History

I

Revolutions may not be "among the most recent of all major political data," but wars are indeed "among the oldest phenomena of the recorded past."[1] Crucial as revolutions have been in the life of most nations, they appear nevertheless like exceptional developments, avalanches that suddenly bury the road on which the travelers are moving. Wars, on the other hand, have blasted open many roads, and they have been constant companions to the travelers. Revolutions interrupt and transform the domestic polity; wars transform but also define the international milieu. Revolutions tear up the fabric of domestic law and order and inflict occasional wounds on the body politic. Wars are the seamless web and ceaseless wound in international relations.

Whoever studies the causes of war—as seen by political thinkers or revealed by history—and the place of war in international systems and foreign policy comes to contradictory conclusions, none of which is comforting. On the one hand, men's thoughts and actions prove that war is (or has been) a fire that almost anything (or any combination of things) can ignite and feed. Countless biological, psychological, material, and political factors can provoke war; countless elements of the international system, countless choices of foreign-policy goals and technological means can shape its contours. In all societies, conflicts break out because of scarcity— material often, psychological always. The world is not a world of plenty, it never appeases all fears, meets all needs, fulfills all desires. Even if goods became suddenly abundant and well distributed, power would remain a rare commodity, and mutual understanding would still be as unevenly distributed as common sense, Descartes notwithstanding. Among nations, conflict turns into war almost inevitably. For the contest between groups that feel themselves intensely different from one another and whose highest loyalty is to themselves prepares the ground for violence, and war is there to serve as an available method of action and outlet of passion, as an instrument in the calculation of gains, a carrier of the dreams and delusions of the great, the fears and faiths of the many. Scarcity and inequities in a fragmented world make war appear obvious. How many goals could never have been even sought if leaders and nations had not been able to use force? The game of power—part bluff, part blows—has always presupposed that the player could at some point use his power coercively.

On the other hand, if such is the fundamental cause of *war*, it is too general to serve as the explanation of *wars*. War has this air of fatality, but the study of the concrete causes of specific *wars* shows that this or that war was hardly inevitable, that it broke out only because someone behaved in a way that could have been different or prevented, or that it could have happened at another time, or with different effects. In a sense, every war could be called a miscarriage of diplomacy, as Aron called World War I, or an unnecessary war, as Churchill called World War II.

This contradiction has led students of war and history to ask three different but related questions. One is the question of freedom versus necessity: what margin of choice, what impact on events do men have in history? Are they merely the pawns of forces beyond their control? If so, are those forces compelling laws comparable to the laws of physics—*necessitá*—or are they the random manifestation of *fortuna*? Secondly, is there to be found in the historical record of wars what the French call a *sens*—a direction or pattern, and a meaning,—a way of making a particularly frequent, destructive, and cataclysmic form of human behavior intelligible, not merely by accounting for its causes, but also by finding in its unfolding and in its effects a logic, a convincing or compelling force that saves it from being mere sound and fury? (Were we to conclude that men are the tools of *necessitá*, we could perhaps find, not the ultimate *why* for those laws of destiny, but some principle of order comparable to that which governs the movements of planets; were we to conclude either that men are the victims of *fortuna* or that they are free agents, we might well find neither pattern nor meaning in their behavior.) Finally, what do the social scientist's methods contribute to the discussion of these problems? Are his tools helpful in coping with largely philosophical issues? The social scientist's daily work—the empirical study of social events—cannot but provoke such questions, unless social science dwindles to a mere compilation of small investigations, a mere sniffing of the ground with never as much as a glance at the sky. But does the social scientist have anything to contribute to the discussion of these problems? To be sure, any abstract answer to questions of philosophy runs the risk of being illusory, but perhaps the social scientist is condemned by the very nature of his work to stick to the ground, to see the distant sky but never to explore it, to raise questions but never to be able to answer them. What is at issue here is not only the famous gap between *is* and *ought*, but another gap between two kinds of *is*—one that can be empirically examined, and one that may well not.

II

One man has tried to answer these three questions—Tolstoy, in *War and Peace*. His starting point was, not the contradiction at the level of whole societies—between inevitable war and contingent wars—but the contradiction in the experience of the individual, between the evidence of necessity and the evidence of freedom. The evidence of necessity he demonstrates throughout the novel—when he shows the insignificance of the acts of minor individuals caught in the war, and in his frequent charges that the will and power of statesmen and generals are self-delusions, that the leaders' impact on events is remote and minute, that neither great men nor ideas nor rationally determined goals have the force to move peoples and shape history. Yet, there is also the indestructible consciousness of freedom, experienced by all men, and the notion of good and evil—moral responsibility—which comes from this awareness. Like Rousseau and Kant, Tolstoy has chosen to show in war the annihilation of man's freedom by history; but, where Rousseau insures the triumph of man's freedom by abolishing history, where Kant resorts to a philosophy of history in which Nature's hidden plan leads man to the realization of freedom and to peace, Tolstoy remains torn by the contradiction and incapable of finding a satisfactory resolution.

There are two attempts, not at resolution, but at accommodation. The first[2] is the opposition between individual life and gregarious "swarm-life"—between inner freedom, the freedom of will and action insofar as the actor alone is concerned, on the one hand, and the diminishment of freedom whenever our acts are tied to others, a diminishment tantamount to disappearance when the tie is that of great historical cataclysms such as wars, on the other. Here, Tolstoy proposes a kind of objective criterion: the magnitude of our connections with others. His second attempt[3] deals exclusively with the latter mode of being—man's life in history, man's behavior with others. Our study of history shows that both freedom and necessity operate, that every act *appears* partly free and partly determined. The key word here is "appears." The proportion of freedom or determinism depends *on the point of view*: the act appears more free if its link with the outside world appears not very close, if its distance in time is not very great, if its causes seem obscure; the act appears more determined if the ties in space, time, and causality appear clearly to us. Man's actions in history cannot be seen as totally free, for we cannot imagine man out of space, time, and causality. But man's actions cannot appear entirely determined, because we do not *know* the infinite number of conditions in space, the infinite period of historical duration, the infinite series of causes. The criterion here becomes much more subjective: acts *appear* free because we do not know the laws that govern men. Freedom is a vital force that we experience in our consciousness—a force comparable to weight or chemical affinity; but man acting in history is subject to laws, just as planets are, and his freedom cannot suspend those laws any more than celestial bodies can. The more distant man's actions are from the observer, the more visible are the laws.

Tolstoy's second answer thus seems to be: if we only knew the laws of history, we would recognize that freedom of action in history is an illusion—

comparable to the illusion that the earth is immobile. But he does not mean to say that empirical knowledge will provide the answer. Indeed, his novel is a long and telling attack on the methods of the social sciences insofar as they are concerned with causes. In terms comparable to Bergson's, as Sir Isaiah Berlin has said,[4] he shows the vanity of causal analysis: there are too many facts for it to be able to grasp them all; history is a flow that such analysis interrupts arbitrarily, and the causes thus discovered are always either tautological or ridiculously unequal to the events they supposedly explain. What the historian (or social scientist) should try to discover instead is laws comparable to those of physics; laws that tell us *how*, and give up *why*. Tolstoy's final answer to our three questions is: man's freedom-in-history is an illusion despite what our conscience says; there is a still undiscovered order in history, which is the order of necessity and whose meaning cannot be sought in causal terms (any more than it would make sense to ask, what is the meaning of the planets' movements); social sciences are useless unless they turn from the search for causes to the search for laws.

Berlin's analysis notwithstanding, there is fatalism and mysticism in such a vision. We are told that there is a pattern in history that we will discover only if we cease asking why. This assertion that man's actions in society are ruled by laws of necessity that are knowable yet not understandable is a philosophy. Its merit is to make us realize that every so-called scientific approach to the study of man and history is based on *a priori* assumptions. An approach that treats men as if they were planets, and societies as constellations, and that tries to define the peculiar laws of motion of the social universe is certainly plausible. Indeed, it has been followed by many contemporary social scientists. Tolstoy's advantage over them is that he was explicit about the underlying assumption of this approach—that these laws do not describe how man behaves in consequence of his own drives, interests, or ideas, but how man is moved by forces beyond his comprehension; they are not laws of manmade history, but laws of man's rape by history.

The approach I have advocated in these essays is of a different kind. It refuses to prejudge the issue of freedom *vs.* necessity; finding evidence of both, like Tolstoy, it avoids declaring in advance that the former is an illusion. Moreover, it believes that in human affairs necessity itself is of man's own *making*, although history may well be governed by forces beyond man's *control*. For there is a difference between a necessity imposed from without—by God, Providence, Destiny, or Nature—capable of being recognized but destined to be revered (or detested) without comprehension, and a necessity due to man's moves without mastery, a necessity that results from statistical regularities of human behavior, or from the capricious interplay of human intentions, or from the contrasts between intentions and results, or from the clash between wills and empirical (not mystical) forces, or from the irresistible effects of processes launched by men who are unaware of the ultimate consequences of their sorcery. Such contradictions, contests, and recurrences may well have been planned by God or

Nature, but the working out of the plan can be accounted for in nonmystical terms—or at least we must try.

Precisely because of this conviction about man's part in the design, such an approach refuses to divorce the "why" from the "how" of human affairs. The laws of motion or behavior that we may seek or find are grounded in, and grow from, the realities and complexities of human nature as it unfolds in history. Any approach that focuses on the "how" exclusively, forgetting that men are political beings—i.e., beings in quest of ends— literally turns them into objects and drains all that is man's own contribution to history from the study of man in history. Thus, the final postulate beneath this approach is that "sociological determinism" is not of the same order as that which rules inanimate objects; its laws are more conditional and limited; their nature is altogether descriptive (like laws of physics), explanatory (in the sense of causal analysis), and comprehensive (in the Weberian sense of psychological understanding). Tolstoy starts with the assumption of a pattern. We begin with a concept that may well reveal there is no pattern.

III

Let us look first at the problems of *direction* and *meaning*. Without deciding whether men are free, or how free they are, do we find that the record of wars forms any pattern? Does any sense emerge from it?

Historians and social scientists have tried hard to discover patterns. When one looks for curves and lines, for recurrences and cycles, one tends to find them! And yet, the findings have not been impressive.[5] First, the various workers have not labored in the same vineyard: some have looked at civilizations, others at nations; some have dealt with large-scale violence, others with crises of all kinds and sizes. Moreover, not a single one of their terms of reference is beyond dispute: in Toynbee's case, the concept of civilization obscures the fact that some of the worst violence in the record of mankind has erupted between rival or hostile units within the same civilization; even if it be true that every time of troubles is followed by the rise of a universal empire, it makes a difference whether the time is long or short, and whether the empire emerges from within or has been imposed from without. It may well be, as Kant prophesied, that men are being dragged to peace through ever-worsening wars, but the record of the wars shows neither a straight line from primitive warfare to modern total war (if our means of annihilation have become more sophisticated, it is also true that the number of civilizations or units annihilated by our cruder forebears is not exactly unimpressive) nor recurrent cycles of limited and unlimited wars. There may be *partial* orders—certain types of international configurations that can be shown to result in certain types of wars—but there is no discernible over-all order that dictates the succession of the partial ones. The search for a *sens*, meaning a direction, leads to a blind alley if applied to the whole of history. This does not mean that directions cannot be found in parts of the record—especially since the advent of industrial society, but here we do not yet know to what kind of a turning or terminal point the road leads.

So we must turn to the difficult problem of meaning. The obvious question is: meaning for whom? There is a primary distinction between the social scientist who observes and reflects on the record, but is, so to speak, *outside*, detached from it, and the historical actor caught *in* it. Also, there are different perspectives for different kinds of actors. One is the perspective of the private individual—the cog in the machine Tolstoy described. One is that of the society as a whole—the agglomeration of men living a common history, shaken by war's tempest. One is that of the leader who supposedly makes the decisions. The social scientist confronted with the problem of the meaning of war must ask his questions at all three levels, and each time he must distinguish between the meaning of war for the actor and the meaning for himself, when (retrospectively) he reflects upon the record from the angle the actor had occupied. It might be asked whether the social scientist can do all this. The answer is that he must. A comprehensive social science cannot avoid taking into account the meaning the action had for the actors. A social scientist who seeks to understand cannot but be a humanist concerned with man's fate, a historian concerned with the evolution of societies, and a specialist of international relations studying the behavior of competing units.

From the angle of the individual, the social scientist can hardly fail to see history as a graveyard of men, buried after having killed and been killed for an incredible number of causes. Retrospectively, it is hard to find a meaning here—and easy to lament with so many poets the absurdity of the whole story. Has there been a single cause for which men died that did not collapse despite their sacrifices or that did not oppress men despite their aspirations? Was there a single cause that was worthy of the sufferings it inflicted? It is easy, on the grand scale, to sympathize with the pacifist's sermon or to acquiesce in Brechtian cynicism. If one is a philosopher of progress who sees in the gradual mastery of man over his environment and in the unfolding of his freedom the true meaning of history, he must admit that this meaning was not easily revealed to the individuals who made that history; the disproportion between the brief span of man's life and the rewards in freedom's progress is obvious, and so are the countless tours and detours on a road that was anything but straight, anything but continually ascending. Consequently, Camus' precept—do not sacrifice man today to an uncertain tomorrow—has a certain force. Even if the end of the adventure were peace and freedom for all, the story would have been long and bloody enough to make of this final meaning a rather belated consolation. For the individual who died in dubious battle in, say, 413 B.C., the ultimate meaning of man's sufferings will be revealed too late—especially since we do not know what the end of the adventure will be, and since we do know that it might be annihilation.

On the other hand, while the social scientist *qua* humanist finds the meaning of the record both clouded and grim, the men whose acts and deaths composed this record did not, on the whole, find their conduct meaningless. It is our retrospective knowledge of the sequence of events that makes their behavior appear absurd; but the actors—perhaps misled, perhaps for foolish reasons—did not behave as if they were pawns of fate or hostages of a blind and bloodthirsty destiny. The pacifist (and the Brechtian) are "lucid" because they stand outside. But the meaning men have given to what seems senseless to the outsider is precisely what the outsider cannot grasp: it is the assertion of solidarity with one's fellow men, of one's own community, and the conviction, which is acted on, that there is no such solidarity without sacrifice. In this light, as Philip Rieff has seen,[6] war is not only the sudden outlet of barbaric impulses repressed by society and state in ordinary times, but the outcome of man's identification with his society and state; what is denounced as regression or repression by the psychologist (standing outside) is experienced by the citizen as the price to be paid for the moral and psychological gains he owes to society, for the preservation of a community in which alone he feels able to fulfill himself. The state may well be the pied piper of death, but pied pipers succeed only because of the bonds of affection and loyalty that tie their followers to them. Therefore, whoever stands outside and denounces is in an ambiguous position: he places an absolute moral standard—respect for life, for instance— above his own group. With the benefit of hindsight, we always tend to celebrate Antigone; only her purity, it seems, can redeem the crimes committed on behalf of communities or factions that come and go. And yet we should be careful, for if we praise her too highly, we condemn not only Creon but all those who thought that Creon's cause was worthy of support. A certain moral blindness accompanies the assertion of solidarity that carries men to wars, but denial of solidarity on behalf of peace or life has a certain moral arrogance.

Thus, at the level of the individual, two conclusions emerge. The meaning of his acts is *ambiguous*, because of the contrast between the sense he had intended them to have and the results, which so often deride the hopes and debunk the faith that animated him. Also, the meaning of his acts is *tragic*, because they show that once the feeling of community reaches a certain degree of intensity—the degree of heat that sets off the explosion, war—this feeling demands two kinds of atrocities: it expresses itself at the expense of other communities (solidarity with one's group is affirmed at the expense of mankind), and it requires the sacrifice of its champions.

The dose of tragedy has considerably increased in this century. Modern total war, which distinguishes itself from past general wars both in the material means at the disposal of the combatants and in the involvement of whole populations not merely as potential *victims* (as often before in history) but as emotionally and actively mobilized *participants*, assures that the rival assertions of solidarity will inflict on mankind sufferings far more hideous than in many past centuries, and that the loyalty of the citizen to his community will be inseparable from a heavy load of guilt. In modern total war, where murder without risks, slaughter in anonymity, and the denial of the humanity of the foe prevail, the sacrifices of conscience which national loyalty demands have reached a new high. The range of crimes that the notion of just war is supposed to cover and legitimize is such that the justification itself stands exposed. Should total war be succeeded by nuclear war on a large scale, tragedy would be accompanied not merely by ambiguity, but by *absurdity* pure and simple. The meaning war had for the individual in the days when annihilation was only one possible outcome of the hazards of battle would disappear if total destruction were certain; and the meaning war had even when the annihilation of the community through battle was certain—a meaning found in the hope that the future would somehow redress and vindicate the horrors of the present—would disappear if the future itself became uncertain. War would have meaning only for those who saw in the joys and sorrows of this life a mere prelude to immortality after death—i.e., for those who find in this earth no autonomous meaning at all. The prospect of nuclear war throws light on Hobbes' philosophy. The meaning of war, and death in war, for generations of individuals, was found in the principle of community. If communities act so as to condemn themselves to certain obliteration, what except the force of habit and the constraints of force keeps the individual tied to his polity? The solidarity in nuclear death of men from conflicting communities would *ipso facto* dissolve national solidarity.

Let us move on to the next level: that of societies. Here, ambiguity marks both the judgment of the detached historian who surveys the record, and the experiences of the various societies that have come and gone through history. The historian sees war as a capricious but unextinguished fire whose flames both consume and weld. On the one hand, the record of chaos is almost overwhelming: whole civilizations have been annihilated by conquest. (Here again, there is contrast between intentions and behavior, or between behavior and results. The most pacific societies, whose social philosophies and organization shun war, are not always the most moderate when war comes; they are capable of fighting with utmost ruthlessness in order, so they think, to wipe war from history. Military societies, such as Sparta, are not always the more destructive ones.) And yet, chaos is not the final word: there is meaning in the madness. If history shows any (partial) directions at all, it is war that burns open a way. The meaning of war is to be found in its *historical* functions. Through war, the basic types of polities have appeared and disappeared, regimes have been established and destroyed, techniques and ideas have spread, the balance of power has been maintained and has broken down within the international system, world politics has moved from one system to the other. In other words, war has often brought the answers to the fundamental problems of politics. In carrying out those tasks, war has acted as the twin of revolution and as both the client and foe of commerce or technology; war has developed new tools for peacetime industry and trade, and technology has in turn provided war with new means.

The ambiguity experienced by societies that have gone through the trials of war are of a different kind. It results not from a contradiction between meaningless chaos and meaningful historical functions, but from the equivocal way in which the *social* functions of war—that is, the functions societies expect war to perform for them—are actually carried out, from the possible discrepancy between hope and outcome.[7] Sometimes wars stabilize and integrate a society; sometimes they disrupt it, paving the way either for upheavals at the center or for secessions or mergers. Sometimes, wars bring gains—through the defeat of the enemy—or help to avoid losses; sometimes wars bring gains to the enemy and losses or frustrations to oneself. Sometimes, the social function of war is to bring about the extermination of a hated foe; sometimes, hatred leads to one's own extermination. Also, the social and the historical functions of war often operate in contradiction: a war that stabilizes a society may also delay a necessary diffusion of ideas or techniques; a war that performs the latter may do so only by inflicting grievous losses on or by disintegrating a society.

Once more, tragedy is inseparable from ambiguity. In the past, it lay in the fact that the benefits of change—the spread of civilization, the destruction of frozen or obsolete patterns of culture—had to come through violence and the splintering of civilization. It lay also in the contrasts between expectations and results. Today, the tragedy lies first of all in the autonomous growth of the means of war. The total wars of this century have already taught us three sinister lessons: the prevalence of dislocation over integration; the predominance of the function of extermination over the functions of agonistic and instrumental wars; the militarization of peacetime life in preparation for war. That is, they have brought us the reversal of the situation Hegel deemed usual—a relaxation of social ties in peacetime and a return to integration in war. If we cross the line from total war to nuclear war, tragedy will triumph and meaning collapse. War, the great force of change, would then transform change into end. Tragedy today lies also in the contrast between the fact that those new means have deprived large-scale war of much of its historical function, and the fact that the social functions of war have not disappeared. The great historical changes listed above take place presently either without violence, through the domestic acts and efforts of the units, or through revolutionary violence, in which war is an adjunct. In other words, domestic processes of change have largely displaced inter-state war. But agonistic war, whose function is the integration of a unit, has rarely been felt to be more functional than in a world full of inchoate nations; if wars for profit have largely ceased to pay, there remain many other goals for which war may be thought instrumental; even a war of extermination can be deemed functional if one can hope, by striking first, to get rid of a hated and threatening foe while avoiding punishment. Thus, we live in a world in which only total nuclear war appears clearly dysfunctional to the observer as well as to societies but in which other kinds of wars are still perceived as functional by various societies. Moreover, war is being "internalized" through the permanent preparation of deterrence as well as through the substitution of revolutionary wars for classical war. In the final analysis, a limited war deemed socially functional, and war "internalized" by contemporary history can always become precisely the kind of war that has no other function but the destruction of meaning: nuclear war.

Let us reach the third and last level: the behavior of the competing units. Here, the problem is posed in terms the reverse of those we saw at the level of the individual. For the social scientist, there seems to be clear meaning. He studies the contests of units in a state of nature, but it is a state of nature profoundly different in one respect from that of the philosophers. In the latter, violence was either absent (Rousseau) or, more usually, the result of the absence of civil society (Hobbes, Locke, Montesquieu, Kant); i.e., violence was asocial. In the international state of nature (as in Rousseau's *de facto* society), violence is the direct consequence of civil society. It is both asocial in that it marks the absence of a general society of mankind, and social insofar as it is one of the instruments available to the units, one of the elements of their calculations and policies. For the specialist in international relations, the meaning of war is inseparable from that of the international competition itself. War has meaning because the competition itself has one—it has its own logic (which, as Clausewitz recognized, is also the logic of war), that of a clash of ambitions expressed in antagonistic policies. Thus, war derives its meaning both from the nature of the Policy that entailed it—the kinds of *visions* pursued by the statesmen, the types of *objectives* set by them in accordance with their visions, the kinds of courses of action (or *policies*) selected in order to reach the objectives, the elements of *power* available—and from the nature of the international system.

For the leaders of the units in an international system, the experience is much more ambiguous. On the one hand, they find war an available and useful tool in a game that has its rules and its institutions. Literally, they have never had the choice that detached observers (philosophers or moralists, psychologists or plain men of good will) sometimes assume they enjoyed— the choice between conflict and joint subordination to a common higher goal. The choice they experience is between satisfaction of their respective goals and frustration; between self-assertion and subservience. Thus, the ultimate frame of reference for action and justification remains the separate polity, and war becomes a meaningful "option"—especially since there are procedures and mechanisms of restraint or moderation that can make what is useful to one actor bearable to all. But, on the other hand, the very indeterminacy of the international competition makes this regulated and patterned state of nature not so different after all from the state of nature described by the philosophers: each participant lives in insecurity, makes his decisions on the basis of judgments that are gambles rather than predictions, and perpetuates through his own actions the vicious circle of risks and uncertainty. To the participant, the system is at the same time a "given," a challenge, and a mystery; the shaping of his own policy is an alchemical procedure that tries to take into account not only the system outside, but the capabilities, the political and social pattern of power, and the political culture within—not in order to "balance" them all but in order to reach goals. It thus resembles a shot in the dark, more than a keeping of accounts. The meaning will become clear only after the participant is through playing the game; whether he was right to play the way he did, whether he did well by exercising or renouncing the option of war, whether he improved his nation's lot or not, or even whether the long-term effects of a temporary improvement were good or bad is rarely clear at once. Thus, meaning for the actor remains doubly ambiguous—in part because of the gap between expectations and achievements in the leader's own time span, in part because the game is not over.

Tragedy, once more, goes hand in hand with ambiguity. In the past, the rules and institutions of the international competition served only to perpetuate the divisions of mankind from which the competition sprang—as if Sisyphus had found a way of introducing the maximum of variety and suspense into his athletic activity, while carefully preserving its harrowing nature. In this century, social scientists and participants alike have noticed that the costs of the game have risen, that efforts to make it more tolerable have failed, and that the new means of war have loaded the actor's balance of calculability and uncertainty toward the latter. Total war has carried tragedy to its highest historical peak. What is this total war, if not "absolute war" that represents both the essence of war (according to Clausewitz) and the spectacular denial of his assertion that war has its own grammar but not its own logic? What is total war, if not the self-destruction of the rules and institutions of the game, a technological Frankenstein that subordinates political calculations to military necessities, a vampire that injects public passions into the body politic until political calculations disappear altogether, a minotaur that obliges leaders to make choices that exceed the possibilities of ethical calculations? Today, political leaders live and act on the brink of the kind of total war that would compound tragedy with absurdity. Political and moral calculations would be flushed out completely once a certain level of intensity is reached. Statesmanship would lose its meaning in large-scale nuclear war: no political goals could be achieved; nor would moral action, which supposes not only restraints on the ends but also restraints on the means of action, remain possible. The statesman's life at the brink of nuclear war is life in tragedy and on the verge of absurdity; his continuing reliance on force, justified by the need to survive, makes sense only if deterrence works and would destroy the actor as well as the game if the gamble should fail. If war becomes the master of those who once saw it as a tool, the meaning of the game is lost. For the first time, the basic postulate of the game—that there will be a victor or a survivor to go on playing—is threatened. Either the leader will make of the state of nature a thoroughly asocial scene of total carnage, or else war will have to be tamed, and the scene will become far more social than before.

Thus, our conclusion is the same at all levels: the meaning of war is both ambiguous and tragic, and mankind has entered a phase where tragedy may blot out meaning. There will be meaning only if the tragic element in war is somehow reduced, if war is limited far below the scope it has already reached in this century. The question to which this assertion leads is as obvious as the assertion itself: are individuals, societies, leaders really able to master their fate? What are man's powers to act? We are back at the problem of freedom versus necessity.

IV

We are concerned here with man's freedom in his relations with others, with his capacity to act on others. Two different aspects of this freedom are of interest. One is a negative element: the degree of *indeterminacy*. A man is free if the different pressures that weigh on him, coming either from within his own personality or from the environment, are not so powerful as to annihilate his margin of choice, to dictate his behavior, to permit him the plea "I had no alternative." Indeterminacy is only a prerequisite of freedom; it is not to be mistaken for the exercise of freedom. However, not any such exercise can be seen as evidence of man's ability to shape events. For a second element, of positive character, must be taken into account: the *capacity to act effectively*, i.e., to choose among alternatives in such a way as to influence others. Indeterminacy requires that the causal network not be compelling for us; the capacity to act effectively requires that we be sufficiently in control of that network to be able to affect others. Man-in-history cannot be called free if the necessity that closes off his choice is a determinism of any kind, or if fortune (the interplay of forces beyond his control) deprives his acts of effects. The citizen of *The Social Contract* is free, both because he finds his law in himself alone and because this law of his (higher) self is the operative law of the community; in a corrupt state, the citizen who would follow the same law would have no real impact on public events and cannot be called a free citizen. (Indeed, his conscience will be torn between his inner law and the law of the corrupt polity.) He will be free only insofar as he restricts the circle of his acts and involvements to the area in which he can be effective; this is what *Emile* demonstrates.

If one accepts this distinction, then the problem of freedom in history becomes a matter not of point of view but of degree. And the detailed investigation of the degree of freedom becomes one of the chief, if not the chief, functions of the social sciences. Consequently, any generalization is bound to be misleading, even if it is limited to one sector of reality. Here, we are concerned with man's freedom in the realm of war. Two generalizations can be presented, with due awareness of their flaws.

The first one concerns the difference in the margin of freedom enjoyed by effective units in international relations—i.e., the political leaders—on the one hand, and that enjoyed by the individuals within those units on the other. On the whole, the margin is greater for the former. The exact amount of freedom at the leaders' disposal varies enormously, of course, depending on a broad range of concrete circumstances such as the geographical position of the unit in the system, the nature of the constellation of outside forces, the level and quality of consensus and support within, the amount of power available, etc. Sometimes, those data conspire to produce a situation that is almost entirely determined, in which all the vital decisions are made elsewhere; thus, Poland at the time of the partitions, or Denmark or Belgium in 1940. And yet, complete determinism is rare: the Poles, the Danes, or the Belgians could do nothing about avoiding invasion, but they could still choose between giving in without a fight and fighting the invader despite the outcome. Even within a narrow margin of indeterminacy, there remain possibilities for choice.

Here we must look at the second element. Is this choice capable of influencing events at all? In a situation of almost complete determinism, there may still be a significant capacity to act effectively, precisely because the game is played over long periods of time. Poland, closed in, has no freedom to prevent partition. But the choice between submission and resistance, while not affecting the immediate outcome, may affect a more distant future: submission may spare the inhabitants, resistance may facilitate revenge and compensations if fortune changes. When the margin of indeterminacy shrinks, the statesman's duty to find a way of affecting the future—and his definition of the way—become primordial.

Conversely, there may be situations of considerable indeterminacy, in which the forces outside and inside are complex enough to leave the statesman a great number of possibilities of maneuver; yet whatever course he chooses, he may find himself unable to leave a deep mark on events, to make events conform to his desires, or to make others follow his directions. This may happen either because of accidents, because others are even more skillful in using the same underlying forces so as to thwart his designs, or because trends that were not compelling enough *at the time to* rule out a certain choice are nevertheless *in the long run* irresistible enough to deprive this choice of any efficiency. Thus, Metternich was free to take measures to repress various nationalisms, but ultimately nationalism annihilated a good part of his work. Precisely because of the fundamental indeterminacy of the game, the statesman's most frequent problem is not so much the constraint that precedes and commands his decision, but the caprices of the contest that deprive him of control of the consequences of his decision. The very indeterminacy that leaves him with his options may deprive his choice of success.

The leader's freedom of action is to a large extent a function of his skill. The skillful leader is one who exploits the uncertainties that remain after all the constraints defining his situation have been measured, and either imposes on the uncertainties the consequences of his own choice, or at least exploits in his favor those probabilities that emerge amidst them. The bad leader is one who unleashes events beyond all reasonable hopes of control or who loses control over events that were within reasonable possibilities of control—i.e., a Mussolini or a Daladier—and thus needlessly sacrifices the capacity to act effectively. The drama of a Napoleon or a Hitler is not that their heady assertions of will and power were mere delusions, as Tolstoy stated, but that after a period of real and considerable freedom in which they manipulated constraints and dominated events, their *hubris* made them lose their mastery over the scene, thus creating constraints that reduced to nothing both their final margin of indeterminacy and their capacity to affect others.

If we look at the case of individuals, we find that both elements of freedom are reduced even more, although, of course, the degree varies. Even in a modern democratic state, the range of indeterminacy for the citizen is narrow. The state is organized so that only occasionally is the citizen called on to express himself—i.e., to act on matters of public concern. Society is organized so that it lets its members make choices much more easily along the lines of their professional specialization—*qua* workers, farmers, lawyers, teachers, etc.—than as citizens; paradoxically, it is when the state is in crisis that they tend to regain some freedom of choice as citizens and that politics regains its primacy.

If the constraints of society and the compelling apparatus of the state manage almost everywhere and always to reduce the freedom of choice of the citizen almost to naught, the capacity to act effectively is also limited. The citizens of various states are not primary actors on the international stage; they can influence interstate events only insofar as they can control events within their own societies, insofar as they have an impact on their own leaders. Freedom for the citizens depends ultimately on the degree of democracy of their state. But democracy, a necessary condition, is not a sufficient one; one can influence events only if one has some mastery over them, and the trouble is that the public's expertise in international affairs is small. As a result, either its wishes will be disregarded by leaders who want to remain in control, or it will leave full responsibility to the leaders, more or less enthusiastically, or else, when the leaders let themselves be guided, the result will likely be the nation's loss of control, with disastrous results for all. For even when the desiderata of one's public govern one's own actions, they are without impact on, and all too easily exploitable by, other players in the game.

Another generalization would distinguish between time of peace and time of war. For both the state and the individual, the circle of freedom narrows during war. The state's area of indeterminacy shrinks because the resort to war entails a fully coercive use of power—the one use that requires the mobilization of most of the state's material assets. A war thus introduces both an almost tangible limit to what the state can hope to accomplish (although, of course, a skillful leadership can find ways of stretching the limits) and an almost categorical imperative (the subordination of most, if not all, of its other objectives to the one goal or set of goals for which the war is fought). Thus in wartime, the area of indeterminacy tends to be defined by the state's power. But the capacity to act effectively, while heavily dependent on such power, remains separate; what reduces it here is the hazard of battles. The paradox of war is that states often resort to arms because they see in it the only effective way of shaping events according to their ambitions or needs, and yet this very resort submits them to uncertainties far greater than those of the peacetime contest of wills. They are like men anxious for gain, tired of the slow, fluctuating ways of making an honest living, who decide to gamble in order to get rich fast. It is not surprising both that statesmen should find more advantages in brinkmanship—in wielding the threat of war after having put themselves in advantageous positions—than in the actual execution of the threat, unless the advantages are so clear as to reduce the uncertainties to the utmost.

For the individual, the difference between peace and war is not just the difference between more and less liberty, but the contrast between some and none. The mobilized citizen is under a constraint that few are strong enough to resist; those who do are barely capable of influencing events. The soldier's capacity to affect events reveals another paradox: whereas he loses practically all freedom to shape his own fate *qua* individual, he retains a certain capacity to affect his nation-state—not *qua* individual, but as a spare part in the machine of the state, as an instrument of the nation's policy. The advent of war means a divorce between one's private personality, temporarily repressed or suppressed, and one's vicarious public personality as the servant of a community on behalf of which one commits acts that one would never conceive of as a private man.

If these statements are correct as generalizations, then certain lessons emerge, which bring together what we have said about freedom and about meaning. For the state, the temporary decline of freedom brought on by war appears tolerable either when a gain is expected thereby or when the alternatives appear worse—i.e., in a situation of acute constraints or one in which influencing the immediate course of events appears impossible but in which war has at least the symbolic merit of indicating one's commitment to certain values or possessions. For the individual, the temporary loss of freedom is accepted not merely because there is usually no alternative, but also because of solidarity with the community, because of the process of identification with the nation that war sets in motion. The decline or loss of freedom are justified by the meaning—however ambiguous—that war possesses.

But this raises again the problem of total nuclear war. Along with meaning, nuclear war would annihilate what is left of freedom; it is clear that past a certain threshold, no state could in any way control events. The total wars of this century extended to all individuals the deprivation of freedom once reserved to those who were actually mobilized, and they curtailed the capacity of effective action not only for the vanquished but for most of the victors too. The victors of World War II could still justify this submission to the hazards and horrors of "hyperbolic war" in the terms mentioned above—the gains made by the Soviet Union, the losses avoided by the Western Allies that chose to fight Hitler. But those arguments collapse when gains are no longer to be expected, or when the alternative to such losses is annihilation. As for the individual, the price of group solidarity now means not merely the loss of freedom and the possibility of death, but the possibility of death for all.[8] It is not surprising if statesmen and strategists, unsure of the self-atrophy of war in a world that is seething with conflicts, desperately try to find ways of preserving a modicum of control, so as to assure both a margin of freedom at least to the statesmen, and a minimum of meaning to the rulers and the ruled. Far from deserving the scathing invectives of perfectionists and utopians, always prompt to assume that nations (and nationals) have far more control over the game than is actually the case, such efforts deserve the highest praise. And yet, the very uncertainty that makes war still possible also decreases the chances of control once it comes. Those exercises in abstract limitation which assume that moderation, flexibility, rational calculation will still be conceivable below a very high threshold of violence have simply ignored the lessons of past total wars. The preservation of meaning and (some) freedom requires efforts to control war, if war comes; but the very difficulties of control in a world such as this require that those efforts aim (in addition to deterrence) at keeping the level of violence much lower than it has been in the recent past.

V

The uses and the limits of social science in helping us to understand issues such as the meaning of war and the freedom of the actors are familiar and obvious. In many ways, Tolstoy's attack was justified. Social science, however hard it tries to appear not to do so, does rely on causal analysis: even a "systems" science entirely expressed in a few mathematical formulas describing interactions would still be based on causal postulates, not necessarily sounder for being implicit. The dilemma remains the same: single-cause analysis is invalid, multiple causation is valid but too complex for scientific treatment, since it is not possible to follow in all their meanderings the interrelations among a large number of factors. Consequently, the best social science can do, in dealing with a problem such as war, is to accomplish a double, and doubly modest, task. On the one hand, it can show (and certainly it should never conceal) the limits of our knowledge. On the other hand, it can provide tools for the analysis of concrete situations. For instance, it can provide concepts for the study of both international systems and foreign policy; but, before any generalization can be made about the interaction of these two—one of the key problems in international relations—there must be many more case-by-case analyses. In the meantime, our generalizations can be no more than still untested hypotheses.

Even after such analyses have multiplied, and our concepts and schemes have been sharpened, we should not expect to be able to answer definitely why a certain war, why certain types of wars, happened when they did. As A. J. P. Taylor has shown in a brilliant passage of his most perverse book,[9] the social scientist's definition of the hierarchy of causes cannot but be largely subjective, precisely because there are so many causes at work and because one's ranking depends in part on the framework of one's study (is it of the immediate origins, does it go far back in time?), in part on the specific questions one tries to answer. Consequently, many different readings of the same reality are possible. Even if all historians agreed on the facts, they would still disagree on the respective weight of these facts; in the act of "imaginative reconstruction" that any causal analysis performs, assessments of motivation and causal efficiency vary considerably. What social science can do is show how the logic of human drives, ideas, impersonal forces, state calculations and reactions, leaders' personalities in a certain milieu—how all these made the resort to war as instrument, outlet, or outcome likely. More it cannot do, because reality itself does not lend itself to greater certainty. Social reality, to use Aron's distinction,[10] contains a part of necessity (such as, to borrow his own example, the development of industrialization), and this explains why reality is not so thoroughly unstructured that any reading of the record has surface plausibility. It also contains a part of human action, which can give to those irresistible processes any number of delays or accelerations, distortions or embellishments. The part of necessity gives us a minimum of certainty and predictability—but only a minimum, because its certainties are of a very general long-term order and the predictions we need most are those that are concerned with the field of human action, i.e., with the realm of uncertainty. The field of human action will always contain a heavy dose of mystery: both because interactions (especially in crises) have a chemistry of their own that would remain elusive even if we knew much more about the decisions made by the various players, and because those decisions themselves (especially under pressure, and especially when they are collective) always preserve a margin of contingency. The task of social science cannot be to dispel entirely a mystery that is part of human thought and life; it can surround the mystery, but it must stop when the story it tells is probable or plausible.

Those who are disappointed with such modest accomplishments are often philosophers of history, avowed—like Tolstoy—or in disguise, like many contemporary heirs of a Comtean *scientisme* that tries to reduce the sum total of human activity to a set of laws. The trouble with social reality is that it obstinately refuses to support any such philosophy or science. There are trends, to be sure, but any interpretation of reality that retains only those trends, and decrees that they constitute *the* meaning of history is an arbitrary one that gives a privileged position to one portion of the truth on the basis of philosophical predilections. But if the record frustrates the philosophers of history, it need not discourage the philosophers. Although social science invariably shows that utopias cannot be achieved, that attempts to bring the city of heaven to earth lead to the strangest aberrations, that courses of action advocated in *abstracto* entail in reality risks, costs, and bad (or unintended) results inseparable from their benefits, it shows something else too: the very uncertainties of social reality that so often thwart our ambitions indicate also that there *is* room for action; the very ambiguities that mark the meaning of our conduct also signify that we can try to give it meaning, and even the basic forces that belong to the realm of necessity—

industrialization, nuclear weapons—provide mankind with opportunities, not merely with risks and losses.

Moreover, although the gap between "is" and "ought" remains as obvious as ever, we seem to have reached a point in history where the "is" does dictate, if not an "ought," at least an "ought not." The conclusion we reach from a study of the record is that there will be no more record unless total nuclear war is avoided. The "counsels of wisdom" that follow from social science are twins of the philosophers' imperatives: peace, or at least the avoidance of all-out war, is the prerequisite for freedom and the prerequisite for a continuation of history; it is the condition without which men will have no chance to give their history any meaning at all. Social science tells us no more than that; it does not tell us with any degree of certainty what the safest way of avoiding nuclear war is, or what the chances for peace are if other forms of war persist and proliferate, or whether all-out nuclear war could still be prevented once a "controlled" nuclear war started. Nor does it tell us that the imperative of peace will be heeded.

And so, the tension between ambiguous history and the dictates of conscience, between facts that show the costs and clashes of values in society, and values that clamor for fulfillment in history, goes on. In the nuclear age, Sisyphus is caught between the threat of annihilation, which would retrospectively make his long contest with the gods meaningless, and the uncertainty that continues to mark his attempts to prevent the rock from crushing him at last. Mankind is caught between awareness of the meaninglessness of all-out nuclear war, the tragic ambiguities that would continue if politics-as-usual led to war-as-usual, and hope in the germ of a conviction that the avoidance of large-scale war is an imperative for each and all. International law, which bans the use of force as an instrument of policy, is obviously well ahead of the facts. But if the conviction grows, it may not be foolish to hope that the facts may slowly (no doubt deviously) move in the direction of the law; that is also the direction of the philosophers' most pressing imperative. It is certainly not foolish to work toward this end.

Politics has been the ambiguous art of conflict as well as of cooperation. Domestic politics has subordinated the former to the latter, and although the deprecators of violence forget too easily that many of mankind's achievements have been obtained through violence, it becomes impossible to justify or sanctify violence when the balance of gains and losses clearly leans to disaster. A world without large-scale violence may well not be a world of justice; as long as rival units with a common history but no common cause remain the highest possessors of power, even a world without major wars will still, for all its advances in the direction of society, be one of conflict, profoundly different from most domestic polities. But given our state of suspense between the probability of continuing injustice and hostility in a world without major war, given the difficulty of even reaching such a stage—when the proliferation of nuclear weapons continues and there is no sure way of limiting their spread—given the quasi-certainty of annihilation, if the future resembles the not so distant past, our duty is to use whatever freedom we have so as to avoid that annihilation, overcome the clear and present peril, and reach at last a world without major war. Prometheus will be rid of the vultures only if he returns the fire to the gods.

Notes

1. Hannah Arendt, *On Revolution* (New York, 1963), p. 1.
2. *War and Peace*, tr. by Louise and Aylmer Maude (London, 1922-23), Book IX, chap. 1.
3. *Ibid.*, second epilogue.
4. *The Hedgehog and the Fox* (New York, 1963).
5. See Raymond Aron, *Peace and War*, chap. 11.
6. *Freud: The Mind of the Moralist* (New York, 1961), p. 273.
7. See Hans Speier, *The Social Order and the Risks of War* (Cambridge, Mass., 1964).
8. See Hans Morgenthau, "Death in the Nuclear Age," *Commentary* (September, 1961), pp. 231-34.
9. *The Origins of the Second World War* (Greenwich, Conn., 1963), p. 102.
10. *The Dawn of Universal History* (New York, 1961).